The Correspondence of
Sigmund Freud and Sándor Ferenczi
Volume 3, 1920–1933

The Correspondence of
SIGMUND FREUD
and
SÁNDOR FERENCZI
Volume 3, 1920–1933

Edited by
Ernst Falzeder and Eva Brabant
with the collaboration of
Patrizia Giampieri-Deutsch
under the supervision of
André Haynal

Transcribed by
Ingeborg Meyer-Palmedo

Translated by
Peter T. Hoffer

Introduction by
Judith Dupont

The Belknap Press of Harvard University Press
Cambridge, Massachusetts
London, England
2000

Freud material copyright © 2000 by A. W. Freud et al.
Ferenczi material copyright © 2000 by the Estate of Sándor Ferenczi
Editorial matter copyright © 2000 by Ernst Falzeder and Eva Brabant
By arrangement with Mark Paterson and Judith Dupont
Translation and Introduction copyright © 2000 by the President and Fellows
of Harvard College

All rights reserved
Printed in the United States of America

The introduction by Judith Dupont was originally published in French
by Editions Calmann-Lévy, Paris, © Calmann-Lévy, 2000.

Library of Congress Cataloging-in-Publication Data
Freud, Sigmund, 1856–1939.
[Correspondence. English. Selections]
The correspondence of Sigmund Freud and Sándor Ferenczi/edited by Eva
Brabant, Ernst Falzeder, and Patrizia Giampieri-Deutsch, under the
supervision of André Haynal; transcribed by Ingeborg Meyer-Palmedo;
translated by Peter T. Hoffer; introduction by André Haynal.
p. cm.
Includes bibliographical references and index.
Contents: v. 1. 1908–1914—
ISBN 0-674-17418-6 (v. 1: alk. paper)
ISBN 0-674-17419-4 (v. 2: alk. paper)
ISBN 0-674-00297-0 (v. 3: alk. paper)
1. Freud, Sigmund, 1856–1939—Correspondence. 2. Ferenczi, Sándor,
1873–1933—Correspondence. 3. Psychoanalysts—Correspondence.
4. Psychoanalysis. I. Ferenczi, Sándor, 1873–1933. II. Brabant, Eva.
III. Falzeder, Ernst. IV. Giampieri-Deutsch, Patrizia. V. Title.
BF109.F74A4 1993b
150. 19'52'0922—dc20
[B] 93-17479

Contents

Translator's Note	vii
Note on Transcription of the Original Correspondence	ix
Abbreviations of Works Cited	xiii
Introduction by Judith Dupont	xvii
Correspondence	1
Works by Freud and Ferenczi Cited in the Text	453
Index	457

Translator's Note

ALL TRANSLATIONS REQUIRE a compromise between a desire to retain the literal meaning and stylistic peculiarities of the original and the need to render it in acceptable, idiomatic English. Translations that are too literal are often cumbersome or stilted, whereas those that attempt to follow the norms of colloquial English run the risk of losing or distorting some essential meaning. In translating the letters of Freud and Ferenczi, an attempt has been made to retain, to the fullest extent possible, the style and meaning of the original. This entailed having to render many of Freud's idiosyncratic and imaginative metaphorical constructions in forms that have no exact English equivalent while retaining the otherwise precise yet uniquely intimate conversational tone of his epistolary prose style. In the case of Ferenczi, whose native tongue was Hungarian and whose German was flawed, obvious grammatical and stylistic errors have been silently corrected. But at the same time an effort has been made to translate certain peculiarities of Ferenczi's formal yet flowery, enthusiastic, and occasionally redundant prose into English. Correctness of style has thus, in some instances, been sacrificed for the sake of authenticity.

Certain conventions of translation have been adhered to throughout the volume. Salutations and closings have for the most part been standardized, except in a few instances where certain personal remarks were included. Abbreviations of names and terms regularly used by both writers have been silently spelled out, with the exception of the commonly used ΨA (ψα) for psychoanalysis and cs., pcs., and ucs. for conscious, preconscious, and unconscious, respectively. Original spellings of names and places have, for the most part, been retained.

Recent criticisms by Bruno Bettelheim, Darius Ornston, and others of James Strachey's translation in *The Standard Edition of the Complete Psychological Works of Sigmund Freud* have been taken into account in translating the correspondence. In instances where certain technical terms that have been called into question appear in the letters, I have chosen what I consider to be more appropriate alternative translations and have provided brief explanatory notes where the new translation is at variance with specific passages cited in the *Standard Edition*. In a few others I have elected to retain terms such as "libidinal cathexis" and "parapraxis" where the scientific context would make alternatives seem strange to the ear of a public which has grown accustomed to Strachey's terminology over the years. This would appear to be a prudent course to take until such time as a completely new translation of the *Standard Edition* is undertaken.

I gratefully acknowledge the support and assistance of Axel Hoffer, the late Otto Hoffer, and Ernst Falzeder in the preparation of the translation.

Peter T. Hoffer

Note on Transcription
of the Original Correspondence

THE TRANSCRIPTION of this correspondence was accomplished in several stages. Initially I worked with enlargements of microfilms of the manuscripts (typewritten versions). These reproductions were, however, so full of errors that it proved necessary to verify the texts systematically by referring to the originals preserved in the National Library of Austria, in Vienna. In addition, all the letters have been compared with the rough transcription prepared by Michael Balint in the 1960s. These various documents are discussed in the annotation, at the appropriate points. Passages that remain obscure or fragmentary, despite efforts to clarify them, are likewise pointed out in the notes.

The letters, postcards, telegrams, and notes have been numbered in chronological order. (The corresponding references from the catalogue of the National Library of Austria have been omitted in this edition.) The annotation discusses the physical characteristics of the letters, material that appears in the headings, missing elements, the conjectural dating of undated items, and passages that proved difficult to decipher. Corrections in the originals themselves have been noted only if they were made in a different hand, or could not be clearly deciphered, or are explicitly referred to in the text by the writer of the letter.

In his correspondence Freud almost always used one of two kinds of large-format letterhead which he would reorder from the stationer-engraver according to his needs, keeping the layout and typography essentially constant. It was his habit to write out the date by hand, just above the address. To avoid overscrupulous repetition of the same comment in item after item, the preprinted line is transcribed without comment. Only the rare instances in which Freud departed from this general model are noted. Ferenczi used letterheads of many different sizes and formats: often paper without any preprinted heading, sometimes large sheets which he himself folded into smaller formats, and so on. For this reason, the notes appended to his letters contain a remark on each preprinted heading.

In general, anything that has been added to the original text to facilitate understanding appears in brackets. Inadvertent omissions, as well as errors in writing that may possibly have some sort of value as failed acts, have been either completed in brackets in the text or signaled in a note. Numbers that appear as numerals in the manuscript are, as a general rule, spelled out in the text. This is not the case for fractions, ordinal numbers, sums of money, weights and measures, days, months, and years, page numbers, hours of the day, tabular material, and groups of numbers, unless these were spelled out in the original.

At various points in the manuscript, proper names, place names, and other geographic designations were imprecise, illegible, or badly written. These have been verified and silently corrected in cases where no uncertainty existed; wherever the meaning was open to doubt, a note has been appended. Abbreviated proper names have been silently written out. An exception is "Frau G." (Mrs. G.)—for Gizella Pálos, who became Ferenczi's wife—since this abbreviation was used by the authors consistently throughout their correspondence. (But wherever the name was spelled out in the original, the complete spelling has of course been preserved.) Some characteristic abbreviations used by both Freud and Ferenczi have also been preserved.

Titles of books, journals, and contributions to books and journals, wherever these appear in the text of the letters, are in every case reproduced as in the original.

Postscripts always appear at the ends of letters, even if in the originals they were written in the margin.

Telegrams have been rendered throughout with a minimum of added punctuation.

Words underlined either once or twice have been reproduced in italics. Other forms of emphasis have in each case been explained in a note.

The transcription of a correspondence as vast as this could not have been accomplished by one person. Many individuals have contributed to the realization of this project. Their efforts must be acknowledged here, since only the cooperation of all of them—whatever their field—could have made possible the completion of this transcription. To all these people I extend my personal thanks. They have earned the gratitude of this volume's readers.

First and foremost is Ilse Grubrich-Simitis, who, beginning with her collaboration with Michael Balint in the 1960s, made a major contribution to the project of publishing these letters. Not only did she apply her energies unstintingly and in numerous ways to the preparation of the transcription, but she also succeeded in raising funds for the project and in convincing other people of its importance. Throughout the lengthy task of transcription, she worked with me closely and sustained me with her advice and knowledge.

Those who donated funds played an essential role; without their support this project could never have been realized. They include Helga Breuninger and Horst Kächele of the Breuninger Foundation (S.A.R.L.) for Research in Psychoanalysis, in Essen, which financed the largest part of the work; Lotte Köhler of the René A. Spitz Society, Association for the Promotion of Psychoanalysis, in Munich, which helped make it possible to consult the original letters in Vienna; and Clemens de Boor of the Sigmund Freud Foundation in Frankfurt, which aided with part of the financing.

Also among these benefactors is Monika Schoeller, who at the outset generously placed at my disposition the technical, physical, and other facilities of Fischer Verlag in Frankfurt, including support for a substantial period of research at the National Library of Austria, in Vienna.

At the library itself, Eva Irblich and her colleagues in the Collection of Manuscripts and Incunabula extended an exceptionally gracious welcome. Owing to their cooperation, their specialized training, and the opportunity they gave me to devote sustained, intensive scrutiny to the originals, a great many baffling problems were resolved. Gerhard Fichtner gave readily and generously of his time, helping me at numerous points to decipher particularly difficult passages in the manuscripts. In the reading and translation of passages in Hungarian, Katarina Haeger and Inspector General István Nemeth of Vienna provided invaluable assistance. By helping me in a thousand ways, rendering those frequently underestimated services that may appear ancillary but are always indispensable, Barbara Mohr contributed enormously to the project.

A great many other people, too numerous to be mentioned here, provided me with encouragement, information, guidance, and suggestions.

For any errors remaining in the transcription, I of course assume sole responsibility.

Ingeborg Meyer-Palmedo

Abbreviations of Works Cited

Freud's works in the text are cited in conformity with the method used in the *Freud-Bibliographie mit Werkkonkordanz* compiled by Ingeborg Meyer-Palmedo and Gerhard Fichtner (Frankfurt, 1989). The number following the date at the beginning of each citation of Ferenczi's works conforms to the numbering system of the bibliography in volume two of the *Schriften zur Psychoanalyse*.

Bausteine	Sándor Ferenczi. *Bausteine zur Psychoanalyse*. 4 vols. Bern: Verlag Hans Huber, 1984.
Brome, *Jones*	Brome, Vincent. *Ernest Jones: Freud's Alter Ego*. New York: Norton, 1983.
C.	Sándor Ferenczi. *First Contributions to Psychoanalysis*. Trans. Ernest Jones. London: Hogarth Press, 1952. American ed. *Sex in Psychoanalysis*. New York: Basic Books, 1950.
Diary	*The Diary of Sigmund Freud, 1929–1939: A Chronicle of Events in the Last Decade*. Ed. Michael Molnar. London: Hogarth Press, 1992.
F. C.	Sándor Ferenczi. *Further Contributions to Psychoanalysis*. Compiled by John Rickman. Trans. Jane Suttie et al. London: Hogarth Press, 1926 (2d ed., 1950).
Ferenczi, *Clinical Diary*	*The Clinical Diary of Sándor Ferenczi*. Ed. Judith Dupont. Trans. Michael Balint and Nicola Zarday Jackson. Cambridge, Mass.: Harvard University Press, 1988.
Ferenczi/Groddeck, *Briefwechsel*	*Sándor Ferenczi / Georg Groddeck Briefwechsel, 1921–1933*. Frankfurt: S. Fischer, 1986.
Fin.	Sándor Ferenczi. *Final Contributions to the Problems and Methods of Psychoanalysis*. Ed. Michael Balint.

	Trans. Eric Mosbacher et al. New York: Basic Books, 1955.
Freud/Abraham	*A Psycho-Analytic Dialogue: The Letters of Sigmund Freud and Karl Abraham.* Ed. Hilda Abraham and Ernst L. Freud. Trans. Bernard Marsh and Hilda C. Abraham. New York: Basic Books, 1965.
Freud/Groddeck	Georg Groddeck. *The Meaning of Illness: Selected Psychoanalytic Writings by Georg Groddeck, Including His Correspondence with Sigmund Freud.* Selected and with Intro. by Lore Schacht. Trans. Gertrude Mander. New York: International Universities Press, 1977.
Freud/Jones	*The Complete Correspondence of Sigmund Freud and Ernest Jones, 1908–1939.* Ed. R. Andrew Paskauskas. Intro. Riccardo Steiner. Cambridge, Mass: Harvard University Press, 1993.
Freud/Jung	*The Freud/Jung Letters: The Correspondence between Sigmund Freud and C. G. Jung.* Ed. William McGuire. Trans. Ralph Manheim and R. F. C. Hull. Princeton: Bollingen, 1974.
Freud, Letters	*Letters of Sigmund Freud, 1873–1939.* Ed. Ernst L. Freud. Trans. Tania Stern and James Stern. New York: Basic Books, 1960.
Freud/Weiss	Edoardo Weiss. *Sigmund Freud as a Consultant: Recollections of a Pioneer in Psychoanalysis.* Intro. Martin Grotjahn. New York: Intercontinental Medical Book Corp., 1970.
Harmat, *Freud, Ferenczi*	Paul Harmat. *Freud, Ferenczi und die Ungarische Psychoanalyse.* Tübingen: Edition Diskord, 1988.
Imago	*Imago: Zeitschrift für Anwendung der Psychoanalyse auf die Geisteswissenschaften.* Ed. Otto Rank and Hanns Sachs.
Jones, I, II, III	Ernest Jones. *Sigmund Freud: Life and Work.* 3 vols. New York: Basic Books, 1954–1957.
Journal	*The International Journal of Psycho-Analysis.* Ed. E. Jones. Directed by Sigmund Freud. London, 1920–1939.
Korrespondenzblatt	*Korrespondenzblatt der internationalen psychoanalytischen Vereinigung.* Ed. C. G. Jung and F. Riklin. Zurich, 1910–1911. 6 nos.; thereafter published as a section in occasional issues of the *Zentralblatt* and *Zeitschrift*.

Minutes	*Minutes of the Vienna Psychoanalytic Society.* 4 vols. Ed. Herman Nunberg and Ernst Federn. Trans. M. Nunberg. New York: International Universities Press, 1962–1975.
Mühlleitner, *Lexikon*	*Biographisches Lexikon der Psychoanalyse, Die Mitglieder der Psychologischen Mittwoch-Gesellschaft und der Wiener Psychoanalytischen Vereinigung 1902–1938.* Ed. Elke Mühlleitner in Collaboration with Johannes Reichmayr. Tübingen: Edition Diskord, 1992.
Roudinesco & Plon, *Dictionnaire*	*Dictionnaire de la Psychanalyse.* Ed. Elisabeth Roudinesco and Michel Plon. Paris: Editions Fayard, 1997.
Schriften	Sándor Ferenczi. *Schriften zur Psychoanalyse.* 2 vols. Ed. M. Balint. Frankfurt: Fischer, 1970.
Schur, *Freud*	Max Schur. *Freud: Living and Dying.* New York: International Universities Press, 1972.
S.E.	*The Standard Edition of the Complete Psychological Works of Sigmund Freud.* 24 vols. Trans. James Strachey and Anna Freud, with Alix Strachey and Alan Tyson. London: Hogarth Press, 1953–1974.
Studienausgabe	*Sigmund Freud Studienausgabe.* 11 vols. Ed. A. Mitscherlich, A. Richards, and J. Strachey; supplementary vol. ed. Ilse Grubrich-Simitis. Frankfurt: Fischer, 1969–1975.
Young-Bruehl, *Anna Freud*	Elisabeth Young-Bruehl. *Anna Freud: A Biography.* New York: Summit Books, 1988.
Zeitschrift	*Internationale Zeitschrift für ärztliche Psychoanalyse.* Vienna, 1913– .
Zentralblatt	*Zentralblatt für Psychoanalyse; Medizinische Monatsschrift für Seelenkunde.* Wiesbaden, 1911–1913.

Introduction
by Judith Dupont

THIS THIRD AND FINAL VOLUME of the Freud-Ferenczi letters covers the period from 1920 to 1933. It includes some of the richest, most intense, and most poignant moments of the relationship between the two correspondents.

The personal, professional, and public events chronicled in these pages are so closely interwoven that I found it impossible to analyze their various aspects separately. So I will reserve detailed discussion for a few major episodes, and for the rest limit myself, at the end of this introduction, to recalling a few milestones that struck me as particularly interesting or important.

My aim is to shed light on five chief events of the period: the first appearance of Groddeck and his meeting with Ferenczi; Freud's illness; the discord between Freud, Ferenczi, and Rank, which was both a theoretical and a personal misunderstanding complicated by organizational conflicts (1924–25); Ferenczi's trip to the United States (1926–27); and finally the emotional upheaval between Freud and Ferenczi beginning in 1929–30.

During these years, Freud, who had been ill since 1923 and was increasingly weary and disillusioned, took part only halfheartedly in the internal polemics of the movement, even when his positions were clear and well argued; nevertheless, he weighed in forcefully on the question of lay analysis (1926–27). Ferenczi was more combative; his development and research occupy a major part of the correspondence of this period.

This volume opens shortly after the end of the First World War, the effects of which were still being strongly felt. On August 8, 1919, Ferenczi was dismissed from his university professorship in psychoanalysis and excluded from the Hungarian Medical Society. His public career ended, he devoted himself thereafter exclusively to psychoanalysis.

Nineteen hundred and twenty was a year of mourning for the entire psychoanalytic movement, and more particularly for Freud. The death on January 20 of Anton von Freund, a wealthy businessman, doctor of philosophy, and patron of the psychoanalytic movement, affected both Freud and Ferenczi deeply. With the aid of lawyers, and through laborious negotiations with the Hungarian authorities, they sought to protect the funds bequeathed by von Freund to the psychoanalytic movement from being seized by Hungarian officials. The rescue attempt was only partly successful.

Only days after von Freund's death, Freud's daughter Sophie fell victim to the epidemic of Spanish flu then sweeping the globe. Freud was profoundly shaken by her death. A letter dated January 29 (letter 832) shows the extreme restraint he tended to display in times of strong emotion: "Wafted away! Nothing to say.... I think: La séance continue. But it was a bit much for one week."

Nor had Freud seen the end of his woes. Two years later, on June 19, 1923 (see letters 932 and 933), his favorite grandson, Heinele, died of miliary tuberculosis. The loss of Heinele proved to be the most difficult of his life.

In Hungary as well as in Austria, the postwar period was very trying financially. Patients had no money to pay with, and for Freud as well as Ferenczi, income was meager. There was no heat in winter, and food was scarce. Freud's family survived mainly on resources sent by friends in the West. Yet although the analysts were doing badly, the analytic movement was doing well.

Freud, like Ferenczi, complained frequently of health problems. What at first appeared to be hypochondriasis eventually developed for both into real frailty, and then serious illness.

During this time Ferenczi was analyzing a Polish patient and student, Eugénie Sokolnicka, described as fragile and exceptionally talented but very difficult. First Jung's student, then Freud's analysand in 1913, she resumed analysis with Ferenczi in Budapest at the beginning of 1920, after practicing for some time in Poland. This perceptive woman succeeded in diagnosing in her analyst an issue he was trying to ignore, which was that he was still not entirely happy with the choice he had made in marriage. Freud declined to get involved in this personal discussion. Moreover, he could not stand Sokolnicka: "She has always been repugnant to me.... I ... consider her ... a basically disgusting person" (848, June 17, 1920). Nevertheless, he recommended her to his contacts in the world of publishing when she moved to Paris in early 1921, though he did not send her as his representative, as was claimed for a long time (Duhamel 1998). In Paris she would play the founding role for which she is remembered in the French psychoanalytic movement.

The next years were a good period for psychoanalysis in Hungary as in

Berlin, and unlike the situation in Vienna. The Hungarian school was developing its specialty, producing a generation of distinguished analysts such as Géza Róheim, Alice and Michael Balint, Imre Hermann, István Hollós, Vilma Kovács, Joseph Eisler, and others, inventing its own method of training, and establishing a psychoanalytic polyclinic. For a time, Freud even considered moving the central organs of the psychoanalytic movement to Budapest.

On May 6, 1921, Freud's birthday, Róheim received an award for his work in the area of psychoanalytic anthropology, a discipline he created. Reunited for the occasion, the fourteen members of the Hungarian association extended their collective congratulations to Freud. He had just turned sixty-five and was feeling very old. The problem of aging had always worried him. Now he had the impression that "seven organs are vying with one another for the honor of being allowed to make an end to my life" (870, May 8, 1921). And on July 19, 1921 (876): "I am still inclined to regard every year and every month as the last of my existence."

From this period onward, a kind of rivalry existed between the two men over the question of illness. Freud expressed it very clearly in his letter of July 29, 1921 (879): "I think you are engaging in 'unfair competition.' Because I write to you in every letter about the prospect of death... you take the cue and think you have to do it simultaneously with me—or ahead of time." Of course it was Ferenczi, the younger, who would win this sad race.

Ferenczi felt tired that year, but he applied himself all the same. On October 6, 1921 (893) he wrote: "The hours are still fun for me, in part; to be sure, I now seem to be less focused on finding new things than I am on achieving better results with improvement in technique." This is the first clear reference to what would be his main topic of research for the rest of his life. His interest in therapy impelled him to undertake the experiments that would precipitate his disagreement with Freud and evoke the hostility of a good portion of the psychoanalytic community. It is also on account of this interest that he would be accused of *furor sanandi (a rage to heal—Trans.)* Of course the debate between analysts for whom a cure is an extra benefit and those for whom therapy is what matters (theory being the extra benefit) is still unresolved. Freud would doubtless side with the former group, Ferenczi most certainly with the latter.

Meeting Groddeck

On June 3, 1917, Freud declared to Ferenczi that he had just read "the most interesting letter from a German physician that I have ever received." The person in question was Georg Groddeck (see letter 678, Volume 2). Afterward, as Freud's enthusiasm for Groddeck lessened, Ferenczi, critical at the outset, was increasingly drawn to his research in the area now known as psychosomatics. On August 17, 1921, Ferenczi wrote to Groddeck; he hoped to visit Groddeck's clinic in Baden-Baden, with the goal of improving his mind and getting some rest at the same time. Groddeck promptly invited him. It would be a significant meeting in Ferenczi's life: although he went with the goal of studying the ideas and methods of his host, he also hoped to get some personal help. An almost instantaneous friendship sprang up between the two men that would last the rest of their lives. A long letter from Ferenczi to Groddeck, dated Christmas Day 1921, a few months after their first encounter, bears this out. Ferenczi described his childhood, his overly stern, prudish mother, his efforts to confide as openly to Freud: "[He] was too big for me, too much of a father," he wrote. One gets the impression that Groddeck, a little older than Ferenczi but younger than Freud, took on the role of older brother to Ferenczi; it is with Groddeck that he seems to have developed the relationship of analytic candor and total reciprocity that he tried in vain to establish with Freud. Ferenczi bridled at Freud's attitude toward Groddeck, an attitude of indifference tinged with gentle mockery, and he lobbied endlessly on behalf of his friend. Criticisms notwithstanding, in *The Ego and the Id* (1923b), Freud borrowed and developed in his own way Groddeck's concept of the "It." For, as he later noted in his letter of December 1, 1925, Groddeck was "not the right man for working out an idea."

Following their first encounter, Ferenczi spent several weeks each year at Groddeck's sanatorium at Baden-Baden. Ferenczi was intrigued by Groddeck's investigations into the monist conception of the human being, which denied any separation between body and mind, as well as his therapeutic application of his work. In the 1930s, aware of the precariousness of his health, Ferenczi would pour all his own last hopes into this research.

At the beginning of 1922, Ferenczi regained his energy and his pleasure in clinical and theoretical work; he published an article on stuttering. In a letter dated May 15, 1922 (902), he wrote that he was establishing independence from Freud: his discoveries no longer represented simply a way of pleasing the master but reflected his interest in science for its own sake. "The stage in which I now seem to find myself is . . . [one of] weaning."

In a letter of July 16, 1922 (907), Ferenczi indicated that he had at last resumed work on his theory of genitality, which would be published as *Thalassa*. He had been thinking about and working on this theme since 1910, and especially since 1915, during the war. Abandoned many times, the work finally appeared in 1924.

In his reply of July 21, 1922 (908), Freud complained of persistent hoarseness. The hoarseness may have been the second sign of the cancer that would appear the following year. Freud himself had noticed the first sign of it during the war, writing in a letter dated November 6, 1917 (713), of "the painful swelling of my gums (carcinoma? etc.) which has been noticeable since the meager days. Then a patient brought me fifty cigars, I lit one . . . and the gum irritation rapidly abated! . . . Totally Groddeck."

This period was marked by a reconciliation between Ferenczi and Rank. Together they were preparing a project titled *The Development of Psycho-Analysis*.

At the Berlin Congress, in September 1922, the friction between Ferenczi and Rank on the one hand, and Jones, Abraham, and the Berliners on the other, became obvious. Although it crystallized around theoretical and practical problems, it was essentially a result of their very different approaches to psychoanalysis. Abraham, Jones, and the Berliners as a group were concrete, scientific thinkers in the narrowest sense. Ferenczi and Rank were more imaginative, more creative.

Rank reacted bluntly; Ferenczi sought to mitigate the dispute. And in a letter of November 23, 1922 (913), Freud had some harsh words for Jones's attitude in the debate: "Here there are real defects in character and behavior." It was to Jones, however, that Ferenczi, elected president of the IPA at the Budapest Congress in 1918, was obliged to give up his seat, owing to the isolation of Hungary, which prevented him from effectively carrying out his mandate.

An undercurrent of irritation thus put Vienna and Budapest at odds with Berlin and London, Freud and Ferenczi at odds with Jones, and Ferenczi and Rank at odds with Abraham. Moreover, Freud and Jones were privately feuding, as we learn from Freud's correspondence with Jones (361, Jones to Freud). The crux was the rivalry between Ernest Jones and Joan Riviere over the editorship of the English version of the *Collected Papers*. Riviere's analysis with Jones (359, Jones to Freud) had left certain countertransferential problems unresolved, and she pursued her analysis with Freud. Freud would have liked to entrust her with the responsibility for the publication, but Jones was incensed at the idea. Freud reacted (364, Freud to Jones) by criticizing the way Jones had analyzed Riviere, treated his colleagues, and directed the *International Journal*. The effects of all these tensions burst out into the open when the controversy arose over the work of Rank and Ferenczi in 1924–25, which is discussed further on.

Freud's Illness and Its Consequences

In April 1923, Freud was diagnosed with cancer of the jaw. From then on his life would be punctuated by a series of operations, prosthetic corrections, and painful treatments. In *Freud: Living and Dying*, Max Schur, one of the last physicians to treat Freud, describes step by step the development of Freud's illness and its consequences, from beginning to end.

In the face of his illness, Freud oscillated among hope, pessimism, and resignation. His prosthesis was a torment. Periods of adapting kept him in various clinics for weeks, even months. His hearing grew weaker, he had great difficulty speaking, and he stopped going to the congresses. Patients exhausted him, but he had a large family to maintain and could not afford to stop working. His weariness and impatience led him sometimes to express himself very harshly with regard to his analysands. Speaking to Ferenczi about certain patients, he used terms such as "dishonest," "full of himself," and other not very flattering adjectives. In his *Clinical Diary*, Ferenczi wrote of Freud: "Shared with only a trusted few, that neurotics are a rabble, good only to support us financially and to allow us to learn from their cases: psychoanalysis as a therapy may be worthless" (p. 187). The more critical Freud was toward his patients, the more Ferenczi stressed the need to love them, to be indulgent and flexible with them, and, above all, to be totally candid with them. We must not forget that Ferenczi himself was an analysand of Freud. Freud's attitude, even taken as a consequence of his illness, could only wound Ferenczi; everything that Freud expressed with regard to his patients Ferenczi took very personally. For Freud, Ferenczi's analysis was a closed chapter, even though he never considered it truly over; but for Ferenczi, it was simply unfinished. And in the end, Freud realized this; in his letter to Jones (612) dated May 29, 1933, just after Ferenczi died, he wrote: "[Ferenczi was convinced] that I did not love him enough, did not want to acknowledge his work, and also that I had analyzed him badly. His technical innovations were connected with this, as he wanted to show me how lovingly one has to treat one's patients in order to help them."

THE QUARREL AMONG FREUD, RANK, AND FERENCZI

The quarrel among Freud, Rank, and Ferenczi—the major episode of the period covered by this volume—heralded the traumatic effect that the Freud-Ferenczi controversy would have on the psychoanalytic movement.

In May–June 1923, Rank wrote *The Trauma of Birth*. Freud and Ferenczi were very interested in the work, although they did not like the tone. Ferenczi (940) enthusiastically began testing Rank's ideas in his practice. Freud agreed to let the book be dedicated to him. For his part, Ferenczi had just finished drafting *Thalassa: A Theory of Genitality*. Even as these two books were in preparation, Ferenczi and Rank had begun editing their collaborative project, *The Development of Psycho-Analysis*, which would cause a scandal within the psychoanalytical world.

Freud was at first very favorably disposed to the ideas put forth in *The Development of Psycho-Analysis*. But during a visit Ferenczi made to Vienna at New Year's in 1924, Freud revealed that he didn't agree at all with the conclusions of the two authors (944, January 20). For Ferenczi, this disagreement came as a complete surprise (946, January 30).

The main ideas raised in *The Development of Psycho-Analysis* can be summarized as follows:

> Repetition is a factor in therapy. Although this might appear to contradict Freud's emphasis on remembering, repetition of an unconscious experience can aid remembering.
> A termination date for psychoanalytic treatment.
> Acting out allows affect to come into play, but it must be connected with earlier experiencing to have a psychic effect.
> It is useless to offer theoretical explanations to analysands, even in a didactic analysis.
> A negative transference is no more a resistance than an intensely positive transference, and is therefore worth analyzing.
> Analyst countertransference, especially when it is of a narcissistic nature, is a problem the analyst must always keep a self-critical eye out for. In addition, the narcissism of the patient is not only analyzable but also a permanent and unavoidable feature of treatment.

An important chapter in the work deals with the interaction of theory and practice—the idea that motivated the book in the first place. Ferenczi and Rank stated the question in the following way: "If one sees the analytic technique as a means for finding out new psychological facts and connections, that is, for the investigation of mental life, one will be able to say that its therapeutic value is purely accidental; or, on the contrary, looked at from the standpoint of therapy, the scientific findings would be a welcome by-product" (Ferenczi 1924, 264, p. 46).

Ferenczi and Rank warned that although it is tempting to justify theory by clinical practice, on the contrary, theory must be constantly corrected by clinical data.

In concluding, Ferenczi and Rank argue for reintroducing a little hypnosis and suggestion into analytic therapy; they recommended simplifying technique to some extent, hoping in this way to speed up treatment.

Freud was reluctant to follow them in either their approach or their conclusions. As early as September 8, 1922, he had already written to Rank: "The fresh daredevil initiative of your joint draft is really gratifying. I have always been afraid that I might be keeping those closest to me from taking up independent positions, and I am pleased to see proofs to the contrary." But he remained unconvinced. He especially criticized the way the authors settled the problem of the Oedipus and castration complexes.

Ferenczi, who had not been aware of these objections, was utterly taken aback by them (946, January 30, 1924). Freud (947, February 4, 1924) was apologetic and somewhat perplexed by his friend's extreme reaction. But he repeated that he didn't like the joint work. He feared that it would become a "path for traveling salesmen," and would veer away from psychoanalysis. He was also wary of attempts to hasten the course of psychoanalysis: an intervention of any depth had to follow the natural rhythm of the psyche, and required time.

In his letter of February 14, 1924 (948), Ferenczi argued that there was nothing in the book that could be construed as veering away from the solid ground of psychoanalysis. In a letter of remarkable clarity, Freud detailed his objections: he distrusted repetition, which had brought him failures; although the authors were performing a service by calling into question certain routine analytic procedures, they did not adequately discuss the techniques implied by their changes. Moreover, Freud thought that the technical innovations were not without danger. Returning to *The Trauma of Birth*, he noted that birth trauma might constitute the biological substructure of the Oedipus complex. But Rank wanted to replace the Oedipus complex with the birth trauma. What implications did that have for the incest taboo, or anxiety, or paternal prohibition, or authority, or reality? Freud did not see how a premature interpretation of transference as a link to the *mother* could hasten treatment.

Ferenczi stuck to his guns. His intent was not to hasten the course of treatment at all costs; he only objected to prolonging it for purposes of research, at the patient's expense.

Freud's article "The Dissolution of the Oedipus Complex" (Freud 1924d), published that same year, contained the response to Rank's doctrine: the Oedipus complex disappears because children's hopes are disappointed, or because it is written in our genes that, at the appropriate time, the Oedipus complex will give way to the latency period. The infant has a choice of two kinds of satisfaction: it can take the place of its father beside its mother or the place of its mother beside its father. The realization that girls have no penis precipitates the castration complex and thwarts the two kinds of satisfaction. Both events imply loss of the penis, either by punishment or by renunciation. The investment of the object is thus replaced by identification, which gives rise to the superego. If the Oedipus complex is repressed, the result is a neurotic; normal development implies the dissolution of the Oedipus complex at the appropriate time. Freud thought that, in the theoretical and practical doctrine of *The Trauma of Birth*, Rank was seeking to bypass this entire phase of development.

The Development of Psycho-Analysis represented a thinly disguised attack on the therapeutic methods of the Berliners. It is also not surprising that Berlin (Abraham, Eitingon, Sachs) and London (Jones) reacted very strongly to the two publications. Consequently, Rank and Ferenczi were violently attacked by the other members of the Secret Committee, which henceforth was riven by the hostility that prevailed among its members. Any future friendly collaboration seemed to be out of the question.

Freud sought to champion his two closest colleagues (950, March 20, 1924): "My trust in you and Rank is unqualified," he wrote to Ferenczi.

Rank's contributions "were inestimable; his person would be irreplaceable." Freud feared that Rank would leave for America, a move that had been talked about for some time. Moreover, he was exceedingly annoyed by the growing confusion of personal, administrative, and scientific problems.

Indeed, the administrative flap roused no small amount of passion. A new president was to be named during the Salzburg Congress in April 1924. The presidency had been promised to Abraham. Given Abraham's hostility to *The Trauma of Birth* and *The Development of Psycho-Analysis*, however, Ferenczi would have preferred Eitingon, who was more impartial and a better diplomat. For his part, Rank was expected to be made secretary. But now a collaboration between Abraham and Rank seemed unthinkable. Freud refrained from going to the Salzburg Congress, partly because his health would not allow it, and partly because he had no desire to participate in the wrangling.

Ferenczi longed to reestablish peace, if not harmony, within the analytic community, and especially to reduce the tension between Freud and Rank. Rank, however, was becoming increasingly uncompromising. The scientific discord that pitted Rank against Freud and against his colleagues was difficult to explain, since he would not reveal the details of his technique.

Doubtless Rank, even more than Ferenczi, felt the need to establish a certain independence from Freud, who since their meeting had played an almost fatherly role toward him.

In 1925 Rank left for the United States to give lectures, train analysts, and treat patients following his own method. Given the catastrophic economic situation that prevailed in central Europe, Ferenczi was thinking about emigrating too. As early as May 1924, the suggestion was made to bring him to Vienna to succeed Hitschmann as director of the polyclinic. There was talk of his going to the United States as well, for the opening of a psychoanalytic polyclinic. Rank invited Ferenczi to join him there, to relieve him of a heavy workload. Financially at least, the project seemed worthwhile.

Then, in a letter to Ferenczi in August, Rank withdrew his invitation, on the pretext that there was no longer enough work. The letter had megalomaniacal overtones: Rank believed he had saved psychoanalysis, even the entire international movement, by his activity in the United States; the American analysts were complaining that their analysis with Freud had done them more harm than good.

As a matter of fact, things were not going well between Freud and his American patients. The case of Horace W. Frink represented his most egregious mistake and did him as well as psychoanalysis the greatest harm. Probably impelled by his obsessive aversion to America and Americans, among other reasons, Freud compounded his "diplomatic" errors after beginning with a diagnostic error. Frink plunged into psychosis and died in a psychiatric hospital. Thus Rank had some grounds for his claims to be correcting Freud's failures; but he probably overestimated his abilities in promising his American colleagues a better result in a tenth as many hours.

Meanwhile, Ferenczi's ideas were evolving. On August 14, 1924 (971), he spoke of reconsidering his "active" technique, at the same time expressing increasing doubt concerning Rank's discoveries.

On August 27 (972), Freud mentioned a letter of virtual rupture sent by Rank that affected Freud deeply. Ferenczi, however, had not entirely left off defending Rank's ideas. He indicated his interest (974, September 1, 1924) in the role of the mother, which his practice seemed to confirm. But he admitted that it is indeed the role of the father that is the major pathogenic factor.

Freud attributed Rank's attitude to an increasingly evident neurosis (976), which he described in his next letter as "discoverer paranoia." "It grieves me greatly that Jones may be right after all" (977), he wrote. Jones (435, September 29, 1924, to Freud) added that Rank's neurosis of 1913 (a period during which Rank was considering undergoing analysis with Jones, plans that were preempted by the war) had returned. As for Ferenczi, Jones could not "refrain from the diagnosis of narcissism combined with poor judgement."

On December 15, 1924 (994), in a letter addressed to all his colleagues, Ferenczi accepted the enlargement of the Secret Committee proposed by the Berliners and hoped to welcome Anna Freud into it. This time he publicly set himself apart from Rank.

One week later (995, December 21, 1924), Freud announced that he had received reassuring news from Rank, who said he was "awakening from a condition that one [could] summarize hardly any other way than psychiatrically" to become as before, even "better." Ferenczi remained suspicious, for Rank had still not provided any details at all about his technique.

No effort to resolve the ongoing conflicts seemed to work.

In a letter of April 18, 1925 (1009), Ferenczi mentioned an American analysand of Rank's—most likely Elizabeth Severn, who would later be a patient and student of Ferenczi's and would play a major role in his final research, reported in his *Clinical Diary* for 1932.

Rank was deeply shaken by the hostility of his colleagues and by Freud's rejection; he oscillated between aggressiveness—even arrogance—and apologies to Freud and to his opponents. Torn between his attachment to Freud and his need for intellectual and emotional independence, he teetered on the edge of depression. Finally, a rupture did occur: Rank, who was back in Europe and staying for a time in Paris, emigrated to the United States for good and severed all ties with Freud and the analytic movement.

It was Ferenczi's criticism of Rank's book *The Technique of Psycho-Analysis* that put an end to the debate (Ferenczi 1927, 277). Ferenczi found the work disappointing and its title misleading: the technique Rank proposed would no longer have anything to do with psychoanalysis. Ferenczi especially reproached Rank for pushing to the absurd intrinsically interesting ideas such as the importance of transference and the maternal role of the analyst. He also criticized the traumatic effects of interpretations that aimed at practically forcing patients to repeat the birth experience in treatment.

Ferenczi's Trip to the United States and the Question of Lay Analysis

Ferenczi set out for America on September 22, 1926, to teach, train analysts, give lectures, and treat patients. He passed through Paris, where he met Rank. The meeting was a cold one, and confirmed their breakup.

At the time, the psychoanalytic community was engaged in heated debate over whether non-physicians—"laypeople"—had the right to practice analysis. The discussions were passionate, and sometimes violent. Arrayed on one side were almost all the American analysts, along with Jones and a significant number of Europeans, who thought that medical training was essential for anyone who wanted to treat patients. On the other side were Freud, Ferenczi, and the entire Hungarian group, as well as a small number of other analysts. This controversy would cast a pall over Ferenczi's stay in America.

Freud opposed the trip in no uncertain terms. The attitude of the American analysts with regard to lay analysis only increased his contempt for America and Americans. To defend his point of view, Freud had just written a pamphlet titled "The Question of Lay Analysis" (1926).

Ferenczi stayed six months in the United States. Gizella went with him. It was a difficult and exhausting trip. He endeavored to counter Rank's influence and to put right the image Rank was promulgating of psychoanalysis; he trained non-physician analysts and encouraged them to form a group, angering his American colleagues.

As Ferenczi wrote in his letter of November 30, 1926 (1084), he was "fighting on three fronts (Rank, Brill, public opinion)."

Concerning his impressions of America, Ferenczi wrote on January 8, 1927, to Vilma Kovács (unpublished letter): "I did not seek to disarm my psychoanalytic colleagues; I was firm with them. But on a few occasions I simply countered with knowledge—they are weaker than I am in this area. The result is that they have in large part, or at least in significant part, ceased their hostilities toward me. As for the business of lay analysis, I have of course won only a tactical advantage (a simple postponement)."

On June 2, 1927, Sándor and Gizella embarked for London, where Ferenczi gave a lecture titled "Gulliver Phantasies." The reception in London was impressive and cheering. During his stay, Ferenczi remarked the prominent influence of Melanie Klein on Jones and the London group. Afterward, the Ferenczis spent four days in Paris, where Ferenczi met and liked Laforgue, but they were unable to meet Princess Marie Bonaparte, who was out of town. Finally, on June 30, Ferenczi was back in the peaceful haven of Baden-Baden, with Groddeck.

Ferenczi's trip to America and the hostility he attracted there exacerbated Freud's anti-American sentiments. Only the influx of psychoanalytic trainees and patients seeking analysis in Europe and leaving their dollars behind excused what he called the "crime of Columbus."

Yet the trip turned out to be financially profitable for Ferenczi: he earned three times what he would have made in Budapest. He was not unhappy with his activity, despite the hostility it brought him. After all, the ill feeling might have resulted in part from the tendency of European analysts to see themselves—the founders of the psychoanalytic movement—as its sole owners and only truly competent representatives, a view the Americans did not tolerate gracefully. The American analysts refused to accept the role of permanent—and not very talented—students. The Europeans and Freud himself no doubt behaved tactlessly toward them.

In the end, the entire psychoanalytic community was consulted on the subject of lay analysis, and their responses were published in an issue of the *International Journal* in 1927. If, at the time, an overwhelming majority of analysts were opposed to analysis by non-physicians, doubtless owing to a lust for power but also out of economic concerns, future developments ultimately would prove them wrong. Still, the American stronghold resisted for a long time before finally being obliged to adapt to what was happening in the rest of the world, following a memorable lawsuit.

The correspondence from 1927 to 1929 contains many remarks that foreshadow the deepening rift between Freud and Ferenczi. Freud felt abandoned by Ferenczi; he feared that Ferenczi would end up moving to America permanently. He wrote above all of his failing health and his weariness. He seemed depressed and disillusioned. The two men had trouble accepting the disagreement between them, and sought to ward it off.

On October 25, 1927 (1110), Freud wrote to Ferenczi: "Since 1909 we have covered a nice piece of trail with each other, always hand in hand, and it won't be any different for the short stretch that still remains to be trod."

Ferenczi's letters became scarcer. He, too, complained increasingly of his health. His symptoms could well have been early signs of the pernicious anemia that would kill him.

At the same time, he professed to be very satisfied with the therapeutic results he was getting from his new experimental techniques.

Freud (1115, January 4, 1928) congratulated Ferenczi on his article "The Elasticity of Psycho-Analytic Technique," which complemented his own "Recommendations to Physicians" perfectly. He feared, however, that the famous Ferenczian idea of "tact" would encourage some analysts simply to act at their own discretion. In his reply, Ferenczi stressed that if analysts were properly analyzed, they would be able to resist such influences.

In autumn 1928, Ferenczi left for a vacation in Spain, where he was extremely well received. He devoted himself to the pleasures of sightseeing, and gave a lecture before a very select audience of "Marquesas and Contessas." But he returned home immediately at the end of his holiday because he wasn't feeling well. Like Ferenczi, Freud too was in declining health. Yet neither of the two men wished to acknowledge the other's condition.

In 1929, prior to the Oxford Congress, the problem of the presidency came up again. Ferenczi did not want to be a nominee unless the question of lay analysis was satisfactorily resolved. Freud insisted that he seek the office.

In his letters, Ferenczi constantly referred to the success of his new technique, but gave no detailed description of it. Nevertheless, he promised to say something about it at the next Congress. Then there was a long silence: no letters were exchanged between June 19 and September 9, 1929. Meanwhile, at the Oxford Congress, Ferenczi failed to be elected president. After the Congress, Ferenczi, who was still feeling unwell, went to visit Groddeck to rest.

The Falling Out between Freud and Ferenczi

On November 6, 1929 (1170), Ferenczi broke another two-month silence, which he tried to explain as a "temporary calling upon of even highly significant libidinal relations for the purpose of some kind of inner process." Psychoanalytic politics interested him less than scientific problems. Impelled by a desire to develop and deepen ideas of long standing, he was working with fervor on all sorts of problems. But fearing to come into contention with Freud, he wanted to see how his ideas turned out before he divulged them. It took Freud more than a month to respond. He had the impression that Ferenczi had distanced himself from him in the last years; was it out of pique at not being made head of the IPA?

Ferenczi was at pains to express himself. He feared that Freud would disapprove of him, or worse, misunderstand him. He admitted that not getting the presidency had hurt him. But having relinquished all hope of it, he was turning increasingly to research; and he summarized in a few lines the four basic elements of his position:

1. In *all* cases where he had penetrated deeply enough, he found the traumatic-hysterical basis for neurosis.
2. Where he had succeeded in this, the therapeutic effect was much more significant.
3. He thought that psychoanalysis was much too one-sidedly concerned with obsessional neurosis and character analysis (ego psychology), neglecting the organic-hysterical basis of analysis, owing to the overestimation of fantasy and the underestimation of the traumatic reality in pathogenesis.
4. Newly acquired experiences implied a return to Freud's old theories on trauma but, considered in a new light, would have an effect on details of the technique; harsh measures should be relaxed.

But Ferenczi was adamant that his approach was not oppositional to psychoanalysis. Rather, it tried to even out the discipline's one-sidedness.

This was the beginning of the difficult and painful period between Freud and Ferenczi. Their correspondence, as well as the gaps in it, bears ample witness to this. Resolutely oriented toward therapeutic issues, Ferenczi sought to determine the origin and structure of disturbances in the seriously ill patients who for a few years now had been coming to him from all over the world. He was increasingly interested in the repercussions that psychic trauma had at the somatic level—namely, how hard it was for subjects to survive certain traumatic psychic events. The question is not one of somatization. Ferenczi, who defined himself as an "agnostic monist," saw the human being as a whole, who lives, perceives, expresses himself, reacts, and suffers with the totality of his being, and who would prefer to cease to exist rather than lose his essential self, to protect himself from denaturation or intolerable suffering.

Doubtless, when Ferenczi spoke this way he was also thinking about himself: he had chosen to go his own way, had taken a path his master could not follow. He felt their estrangement keenly, but he could no longer live in a state of emotional dependence; at the same time, however, he needed it. He never managed to express openly his negative feelings toward Freud, and dreaded doing so, probably out of guilt as much as out of fear of rejection. Moreover, Freud was now too old and too sick to tangle with. And despite all his bitterness, Ferenczi loved Freud deeply and felt the extent to which Freud, in turn, was devoted to him. All these contradications, virtual deadlocks, caused him great anguish and sapped his strength—his "orpha," as he called it in his *Clinical Diary*, a private journal that provides many clues to understanding his emotional turmoil during this period.

Freud, for his part, toward the end of his life became more and more skeptical about the therapeutic potential of psychoanalysis. He still spoke with difficulty, had trouble hearing, and was obliged to undergo treatments that exhausted and irritated him. Research interested him infinitely more than improving the curative properties of analysis. Ferenczi, by contrast, was profoundly convinced of the therapeutic value of the method; faced with disappointments, he insisted that psychoanalysis had to devise techniques that suited different pathologies rather than select good psychoanalytic risks.

This approach was very alien to Freud at the stage at which he found himself. For this reason, he felt betrayed, abandoned by his most loyal friend. Lack of understanding became chronic between the two men, and attempts to explain no longer worked. Both were deeply saddened by these developments. Freud was distressed to see his dearest disciple wander down paths of research that seemed to him to promise little.

Moreover, Ferenczi was increasingly less interested in the IPA presidency, engrossed as he was in his research. Freud perceived this attitude as desertion—at the very moment when he felt so close to death, his "paladin and secret Grand Vizier" refused to assume leadership of the "cause," his life's work—for Freud was convinced that the psychoanalytic movement would be safe only in the hands of Ferenczi.

On January 11, 1930 (1177), Freud wrote Ferenczi one of the harshest letters of their correspondence, taking him to task for having detected in Freud's missives neither tenderness nor humor, only objectivity. He wanted to understand why. Was Ferenczi angry with Freud for not having supported him against Jones? Similarly, Freud reproached Ferenczi for not giving an account of the analysands Freud had sent him. Did he think he was a better analyst than Freud?

Ferenczi defended himself glumly. A few days later (January 17, 1930), he began a letter "Dear friend" (rather than his usual "Dear Professor"), and explained this "parapraxis" as the expression of his true feelings. In this important letter, he rebuked Freud for the second time for not having analyzed his negative transference in the past. But he also did not spare himself: he should have had the courage to communicate his ideas and criticisms to Freud, especially with regard to Freud's lack of interest in the therapeutic function of analysis. He acknowledged that Brill's and Jones's behavior had no doubt contributed to his own withdrawal. Nor did he wish to brush aside the political problems of the International Association.

Freud (January 20, 1930), mollified, denied having neglected the negative transference; he reiterated his argument on this subject four years after Ferenczi's death, in his article "Analysis Terminable and Interminable."

He interpreted Ferenczi's sensitivity in the conflict with Brill and Jones, and with regard to the presidency, as a reactivation of his past neurosis. Freud sought to minimize their disagreement: What could be more normal between "two different workers"? He had no intention of resuming the role of analyst of his "tried-and-true friend." Reading this exchange, one has the impression of two people groping toward each another. But they were talking at two different levels: Ferenczi was living an intense experience in the present, which Freud sought to analyze with respect to the past, failing to recognize the weight of the present. All the difference between their therapeutic attitudes is contained in this dialogue.

In his letter of February 14, 1930 (1182), Ferenczi acknowledged having been upset by Freud's use of the term "ill feeling." Moreover, he thought the question in his case was not one of reactivation of his neurosis, but rather one of progress—of a freer, less inhibited way of talking. He said that the reason he had reacted badly to Freud's jokes about his getting old was that he hadn't been feeling well. That was why he felt under pressure to publish his ideas. Rather than wanting to become Freud's analysand again, what he longed for was to reestablish a climate of mutual openness.

Ferenczi, who had just moved to a new house, pursued his research. On June 29 he reported that "the finer mechanism of 'psychic trauma' and its relation to psychosis [was] also shaping up into a very impressive picture."

On July 5 (1191), Freud urgently returned to the problem of the presidency. He insisted that Ferenczi declare his candidacy; if he refused to seek the office, Jones would be the only plausible choice left, an eventuality Freud deplored. He appealed to Ferenczi's emotions: when Freud died, which he thought would happen soon, he didn't want anyone other than Ferenczi to give the eulogy for him. On July 20, Ferenczi, whose health was increasingly fragile, echoed the theme of death. He felt ill; his bodily self-love had been sublimated into scientific interest; this experience allowed him to better understand what patients in a similar condition were going through, imagining themselves in lethal danger, real or supposed. In this way he was freshening up his temporarily abandoned trauma theory. To be sure, this was subjective research, but it wasn't without objective value. He was writing and taking notes constantly, and for this reason he had been neglecting his correspondence. As for the presidency, he would accept it if need be, but in close collaboration with Eitingon, whose mediation would be necessary to deal with Jones, whose "unreliability" he complained of and whose character he described as "despotic and hateful."

On September 12, 1930, Freud's mother died. Freud claimed to feel neither pain nor mourning, but a sense of liberation, of being set free. He did not feel he had the right to die so long as she lived. In the same letter (1195, September 16), he said he was interested by Ferenczi's "very ingenious" idea of traumatic fragmentation. But, he objected, one could hardly speak of trauma in the synthetic activity of the ego without treating the reactive scar formation along with it, since it "produces what we see."

Ferenczi (September 21, 1930) objected to the term "ingenious"; "correct . . . or even only plausible" would have pleased him better. For the question was one not just of speculation but of an approach originating in the clinic and useful in the clinic. He was in agreement with the synthetic tendency of the ego; but he rejected the expression "scar formation," for, to his mind, the pathological psychic reaction to trauma is less rigid than a scar. (This exchange opened the path that, later, would lead Balint to the notion of the "basic fault.") Here again we realize how far apart the two men were. Freud thinks Ferenczi is engaged in an intellectual process, but for Ferenczi it is emotionally charged therapeutic research. But like most of their meetings, Ferenczi's trip to Vienna in November 1930 brought new reassurance. Ferenczi noted with pleasure that, in the end, their differences were not all that great.

At the beginning of 1931, Ferenczi wrote that he was overworked and overloaded with cases that "can't be postponed," including a very serious one detailed in his *Clinical Diary*. From time to time, the letters become scarcer, less personal. In a letter to Freud dated March 22, 1931, Ferenczi claimed to be too busy with his daily meetings, too isolated, to keep up to date with the business of the movement. "Perhaps you will find time to write again occasionally!" he ended sadly, after recalling the pleasures of their trips together in the past.

In May–June 1931, after Ferenczi, it seems, made a visit to Vienna, an exchange of letters took place with regard to one of the two themes that Ferenczi wished to treat in his lecture to the Congress planned for autumn—to wit, "Does the Dream Have a Second Function?" The other theme was "A Possible Extension of Our Metapsychological World of Ideas"; it dealt with the importance of trauma in psychoses, as opposed to the mechanism at work in neuroses according to Freud, and the effect of the fragmentation caused by these traumas. Freud indicated that he himself had already discussed, in *Beyond the Pleasure Principle,* the second function of dreaming—that is, mastery—which characterizes the dreams of traumatics. Of course, questions of priority always matter a great deal in the scientific world in general, and they did for Freud in particular. Ferenczi replied immediately that he was not unaware of Freud's priority in this regard. But now he wanted to emphasize the point and to generalize it. In the end, in July the Congress was canceled—despite the wishes of Ferenczi, Eitingon, and Anna Freud—owing to currency problems in the divided Europe of the period. It was the will of Jones and Ophuijsen that prevailed.

There would be no more letters before Ferenczi's of September 15, 1931:

> I was and still am immersed in a very difficult inner and outer, certainly also scientific, "work of purification," which has not produced any final results as yet—and one can't come forward with anything that is half finished. The scientific is still grouping around technique, the working over of which, however, allows some theoretical things to appear in a somewhat altered light. In my usual fashion, I do not shy away from coming to conclusions, to the extent that this is at all possible—often up to a limit where I lead myself "ad absurdum"; but that doesn't discourage me. I try to move forward in other, often precisely opposite ways, and I still have the hope of finding the right path at one time or another.
>
> That all sounds very mystical—please don't be frightened by it. As far as I can judge myself, I am not (or only rarely) overstepping the bounds of normality. To be sure, I often make mistakes, but I am not rigid in my prejudices.
>
> Healthwise, I have been doing somewhat better very recently. Will that also become connected with the psychic? I don't know for sure.

Freud's reply (1211, September 18, 1931) was immediate and endeavored to be warm; but he was too disillusioned and disappointed to pull it off. He felt that Ferenczi was drawing away from him—which was not, he wrote, to say that they were becoming alienated from each other. In any event, he did not feel that he was personally to blame, for Ferenczi had always been, even in recent days, his dearest colleague. But, he added, "It is with regret that I term it an expression of inner dissatisfaction that you are trying to press forward in all kinds of directions which to me seem to lead to no desirable end. But I have—you, yourself, bear witness to this—always respected your independence. . . . With you it could be a new, third puberty, after the completion of which you will probably have reached maturity."

This remark hurt Ferenczi almost as much as the one about his getting old. It took him three months to respond. He defended his research, recalling the words of Schiller to the effect that "emboldening interest [should] also be brought to what is unaccustomed, even if it looks in part to be erroneous or fantastic." He did not want to publish anything before he had clearer results.

The exchange also touched on the problem of the presidency. Freud feared that the thinning of their correspondence would cut him off from the future president. Ferenczi, seeming to smell some kind of blackmail, considered withdrawing his candidacy. Freud repeated his imprudent words: he wanted Ferenczi to take on the position.

Yet another of Ferenczi's visits to Vienna, this one on the way to a delayed vacation (at end of October), allowed them to explain themselves. Then on December 5, 1931 (1215), Ferenczi came back to Freud's criticisms. Freud had reproached him for not publishing what he was doing (as both of them had reproached Rank in the past). But Ferenczi did not want to publish before he had adequate confirmation of his findings. Recall, he said, that Freud had also criticized Rank for publishing before taking the time to verify his results.

Freud's reply, on December 13, 1931 (1216), is well known; it is the "kissing technique" letter, cited many times, first by Jones in Volume 3 of his biography of Freud, in fairly shortened form. Freud seemed to perceive the chasm in their exchanges and sought a tone that Ferenczi would understand. To be sure, his criticisms concerning the excessive gratifications bestowed by Ferenczi on his patients, and especially female patients, were perfectly justified on both the technical and the theoretical level. For if Ferenczi indeed perceived the need to award certain gratifications to patients in profound regression, at the level Balint would later call the level of the basic fault, where adult language is useless, he was making no distinction at all between gratifications leading to benign, therapeutic regression and those that risked unleashing a malignant regression, ending in a spiral of endless demands and an impasse in the therapeutic process. There was no way Freud could follow him down this road. There were a good many reasons for this, in addition to the existence of generally accepted rules of practice. At the time, no specific technique had been developed to deal with patients stuck in a pregenital phase, whether the case was borderline or represented a regressive episode. Moreover, it seemed that Freud had always felt a certain aversion to physical contact. Any approach that implied such contact could only make him ill at ease and provoke his disapproval, especially when the available evidence seemed to prove him right. But the jovial, even ironic tone of the letter must surely have wounded Ferenczi, as well as the reminder of old mistakes involving patients (such as the case of Elma). No doubt that is what Freud meant by a "new puberty." In this letter, he put himself in the position of the father at precisely the moment when Ferenczi was trying to disentangle himself from the role of son. Freud accused Ferenczi of autoanalytic deafness, whereas Ferenczi was plunged into a deep and painful exploration of himself. Once again, the gap between them kept them from understanding each other. For his part, Freud was suffering; he must have been reliving Rank's defection, but probably also other abandonments and breaks, such as the separations from Fliess, Jung, and a few others. He recalled certain phrases from that time and used them almost verbatim: "It is most assuredly not my fault . . ."

It took Ferenczi two weeks to get over this blow (1217). He objected to Freud's injunction to publish his unconfirmed conclusions without delay. As for his "youthful sins," he thought he had sufficiently overcome and worked through them, and that they might even have made him wiser and more careful. He would keep Freud's warning in mind, but he could not bring himself to conclude his research. He closed with these words: "Since I overcame the sorrow about the tone of our correspondence, I can't help expressing the hope that the amicable personal and scientific harmony between us will not be disrupted by these developments, or: that it will soon be restored."

Then, gradually, Ferenczi appeared to calm down, although he went through periods of doubt regarding his work. Freud remained rather reserved.

On April 24, 1932 (1222), Freud tried to bring Ferenczi back to the realities of the present with a few forceful words. Eitingon, who had lost all his money, was depressed; he would have to be replaced as president: "I hope you will find in yourself the willingness to sacrifice the comforts of your isolation to date to the duties of a leader of the movement," Freud wrote. The criticism was not lost on Ferenczi (1223, May 1, 1932). He wrote: "[I am] immersing myself in a kind of scientific 'Poetry and Truth,' from which at some time or other, sometimes I think: definitely, something not worthless will come [here he was referring to his *Clinical Diary*]. . . . [Do] you want to have a president whose interest is in part manacled in this way? If so, then I will do my utmost to fulfill the tasks that are before me." Freud was worried about Ferenczi's isolation and thought this "drastic measure" might bring him out of it. But Ferenczi (May 19, 1932) did not feel himself to be suffering from any kind of psychic illness, and defended the utility of his work, which he intended to continue. Nevertheless, he wrote, if Freud still thought him suited for the presidency, he would consider it an honor. But then on August 21, 1932, Ferenczi announced to Freud that he had decided not to seek the presidency after all. He had "gotten into decidedly critical and self-critical waters," which seemed to him to necessitate in certain respects "not only extensions but also corrections" at the practical as well as the theoretical level. He felt this to be incommensurate with the dignity of a president, "whose main concern should be conserving and consolidating what already exists." Freud accepted reluctantly; he objected that so long as Ferenczi was not proposing a new variety of psychoanalysis, nothing obliged him to avoid the presidency. And indeed, Ferenczi denied any desire to found a new school. He intended to present his ideas and submit them for discussion during the Congress, and he hoped to be understood. (We know now that he was not.) But he still felt that his degree of critical spirit was more appropriate for an ordinary member than for a president.

Prior to the Wiesbaden Congress, in autumn 1932, Ferenczi read aloud to Freud his lecture titled "Confusion of Tongues between Adults and the Child: The Language of Tenderness and Passion" (Ferenczi 1933, 294). The meeting was a disaster. From the very start, the atmosphere was explosive. Freud violently rejected the work and advised Ferenczi not to present it, indeed, to refrain from publishing for another year, until he had come to his senses. In his biography of Freud, Jones gives a detailed description of the meeting, as if he had been there, but his account is based entirely on a very personal interpretation of Ferenczi's letters to Freud. Once the analytic community got wind of the news, it was thrown into turmoil. Nonetheless, Ferenczi presented his paper, then left on holiday. Jones was elected president. As early as September 9, Jones offered his sympathy to Freud (595, Jones to Freud) over the difficulty that had arisen with his dearest friend and comforted Freud by reassuring him of the affection of those such as Jones himself, whose acceptance of the unconscious was unshakable.

In Ferenczi's next letter (1237, September 27, 1932), he admits to having been deeply shocked by the discussion in Vienna. And his health showed it. He wished, however, to acknowledge his own errors: "More courage and more open talk on my part about practical and theoretical things would have been advantageous to me. But," he wrote, "unfortunately, there is usually a lack of such courage in those who are younger and weaker."

Ferenczi's illness was now full-blown. His holiday had been a "voyage de lit-à-lit" (trip from bed to bed). But he continued to think about his experiments and his research. In September, at Luchon, he noted: "Balint takes up things where I got stuck" (see letter 1050, n. 3), sensing that Balint was on the trail of a solution that had eluded Ferenczi. But Freud (1238, October 2, 1932) was still out of sorts and not inclined to patch things up. He reproached Ferenczi for having systematically turned away from him for several years, behavior as unjustified in Ferenczi's case as in Rank's, in the past. He was convinced that Ferenczi was no longer "accessible to any doubts" and concluded: "I don't any longer believe that you will rectify yourself, the way I rectified myself a generation earlier." Ferenczi must have been sufficiently staggered by this letter not to reply.

But Freud sent him a copy of *New Introductory Lectures on Psycho-Analysis* for which Ferenczi took care to thank him, on December 14, 1932, in a brief letter in which he also gave reassuring news of his health and expressed concern about Freud's.

On January 10, 1933, Ferenczi wrote a few lines of greetings for the New Year, seeking reconciliation. Freud replied warmly to the letter first thing the next day. He described their relationship as "an intimate community of life, feeling, and interest," but did not see in what way he had contributed to the change.

On March 29, 1933 (1243), seven weeks before his death, Ferenczi sent a handwritten letter to Freud, notable for its distorted penmanship and many errors. He explained his long silence as "childish sulking." This time he had two reasons for writing: to send news of his health, a nervous breakdown from which he was slowly recovering; and to express alarm over the rise of Nazism in Berlin. He was of the opinion that things would go no better in Vienna, or even in Budapest, and he advised Freud to emigrate to England while it was still possible. Lajos Lévy, Ferenczi's doctor, naturally thought this advice was evidence of pathological pessimism. But Ferenczi entreated Freud to take his warning seriously.

Freud replied immediately, on April 2. This letter, the last Ferenczi would receive from him, was very warm. Freud urged Ferenczi to rest and regain his health. The technical and theoretical innovations could wait. He refused to consider Ferenczi's warning. He did not believe that Nazism would overpower Austria, and if it did, it would in any event be less brutal than in Germany. The Jews would be uncomfortable, but they would not be in danger; and besides, to be knocked down by the Nazis was one kind of death, like any other. On April 9, Ferenczi had to dictate his reply: Freud's "kind and understanding letter" had made "a deep and beneficial impression" on him. Referring to his warning, he wondered whether he hadn't simply been a little panicked on account of his physical debility. "The feverish . . . concern with psychoanalytic problems" had also abated. He was prepared to postpone the discussion.

On May 4, Ferenczi, who realized the gravity of his condition, wrote to congratulate Freud on his birthday. It would be his last letter. Obviously he no longer believed that he would recover, nor did Gizella, who added a few sad, despairing lines to her husband's letter. Ferenczi died on May 22, 1933, of neurological complications of pernicious anemia.

Ferenczi's health during the last years of his life was the subject of endless speculation. According to Jones, he was suffering from paranoiac delirium, exacerbated in the final months. It was a diagnosis Ferenczi's students and those close to him rejected. Moreover, neither his work nor his correspondence reveals the least hint of paranoia. This fact was confirmed by Lajos Lévy, his physician, in a letter to Robert Waelder and another to Anna Freud, dated 1957, the year Jones published Volume 3 of his biography of Freud, which unleashed the storm of controversy over Ferenczi's mental health. But for anyone reading the letters today, it hardly matters. Whether he was mentally troubled or not, Sándor Ferenczi's work represents an invaluable contribution to psychoanalysis, one whose worth is now universally recognized.

After Ferenczi's death, the correspondence between Freud and Jones showed to what extent Freud himself detected a psychotic decompensation in Ferenczi's scientific approach. Those of us who understand the enormous influence that Ferenczi's final articles have today can appreciate how wrong Freud was at the time. Jones only accentuated Freud's judgment, motivated no doubt by his own convictions, but also perhaps by a little jealousy and the desire to assume the place of Freud's favorite. Indeed, just as Ferenczi had reproached Freud for not having analyzed his negative transference, Jones could have made the same reproach to Ferenczi, who had been his analyst. Freud died only six years after Ferenczi, but that gave him enough time to begin to change his mind about his friend's work. In 1939, in London, Balint had Freud read the last notes Ferenczi wrote, most likely the ones we know by the title "Notes and Fragments" (Ferenczi, Posthumous, 308); Freud's reaction was to say that there were after all a lot of interesting things there.

The coolness between Freud and Ferenczi had a genuinely traumatizing effect on the entire psychoanalytic movement, as Michael Balint shows in Chapter 23 of his book *The Basic Fault*, "The Disagreement between Freud and Ferenczi, and Its Repercussions." The analytic community had a classic reaction: repression, but also splitting. Many analysts used Ferenczi's ideas without citing him, probably forgetting he had invented them. For a good number of them, it was as though Ferenczi had never existed.

In fact, the correspondence of the final two years gives the impression of an enormous misunderstanding: each of the two men felt betrayed by the other. One would claim that all of Ferenczi's technical experiments were wrong. But it is important to remember that we are talking about research—trial and error—and not an established method. These were experiments in the true sense of the word. Every one of them was instructive. No one could defend mutual analysis as a technique. But it was an interesting and fruitful experiment. Besides, Ferenczi himself said that he could work only by pushing the limits, even to the absurd, and then to backtrack. Each of his experiments—activity, flexibility, indulgence, even mutual analysis—left a mark on the way we do analysis today, even if the innovation was simply adaptation of the method to the patient rather than that of the patient to the theory. This was the approach of a therapist who sought above all to treat. Freud's own approach was something else entirely. He wished to understand; it was fundamentally knowledge, science, that interested him. Once he detected the error, he no longer saw the need for research, with its inevitable trials and gropings. Nor could he accept that the companion he most needed to share ideas with, to discuss things with, to think with, would go off and take up a deep personal exploration that he could not be part of. Freud avoided communicating and discussing his ideas with Ferenczi until they were ready to be verbalized at the intellectual level. But Ferenczi's ideas from the last period of his life were still gestating at the moment of his death.

Ferenczi's filial dependence on Freud certainly played an important role in the sad evolution of their relationship. Freud even reproached Ferenczi for it. Ferenczi's efforts to disentangle himself entailed a difficult personal battle; no doubt Rank also went through something similar, but Ferenczi did not wage his battle for independence with the same rigidity. He never stopped arguing, trying to explain himself, despite his personal sorrow. At the time, almost nobody in the psychoanalytic community understood Ferenczi, except for most of the members of the Hungarian school. Nor could it be otherwise. Only those who, like Balint, were constantly in Ferenczi's company, working and talking with him, were capable of seeing the value of his research. This was the reason Balint was able to pursue Ferenczi's ideas, sidestepping some of the pitfalls Ferenczi encountered. Today, "The Confusion of Tongues" is considered a classic of the psychoanalytic literature. Analysts encounter new pathologies and, in Ferenczi's work, find ways of understanding them and confronting them; the techniques have become more numerous and, for this reason, more flexible. If in the past Ferenczi was considered by many of his colleagues as a deviationist, today his work and his research have become indisputably integrated into the analytic movement. These days, it is possible to be both Freudian and Ferenczian.

SELECTED MILESTONES FROM 1920–1933

1920

Creation of the *International Journal of Psycho-Analysis.*

Eitingon and Simmel found the Berlin Polyclinic and the Berlin Psychoanalytic Institute.

September 8–12: Sixth International Psychoanalytic Congress, at the Hague, Ernest Jones chairing.

Freud works on *Beyond the Pleasure Principle.*

December 11: Sándor Ferenczi's mother, Rosa, celebrates her eightieth birthday. Her son has not seen her in six years.

The members of the Secret Committee organized in 1912 at the instigation of Ernest Jones begin to communicate by regular circular letters.

1921

Ferenczi works on his article on tics; the article stimulates lively discussion among the members of the movement.

Founding in Moscow of the Psychoanalytic Association for Research on Artistic Creation.

Ferenczi's mother dies July 22, after great suffering, with Sándor by her side.

Freud finishes *Group Psychology and the Analysis of the Ego.*

1922

A psychoanalytical society is founded in Kazan, and later in Moscow.

The Indian Psychoanalytical Society is created in September.

September 25–27: Seventh International Psychoanalytic Congress, in Berlin, Ernest Jones chairing.

1923

Conflicts among analytic groups or members of the Secret Committee are becoming obvious; at the same time, a series of events punctuates the life of the analytic community; including the following.

On January 25 (917), Freud announces his separation from the Verlag and press, necessitated by the lack of money and by "the audacity and clumsiness of the English."

In a letter dated March 19 (922), Freud alludes to earlier problems with Reich, who once had been an active member of the Communist Party. This time, however, the problems are ironed out.

On April 10 (927, April 17, 1923) Oliver Freud marries, for the second time. Freud did not approve of his first marriage, in 1915 to Ella Haim, a medical student who was determined to have a career. Freud thought that a couple could not survive unless the wife devoted herself entirely to her husband, following him and sticking by him no matter what. And in fact, the marriage ended in divorce after only a few months. Curiously, Freud never mentions the name of Oliver's second wife in any of his letters. He always refers to her as "the young woman."

Heinele, son of Sophie and Freud's favorite grandson, dies in June.

In July, Ferenczi turns fifty. Freud presents him with a set of the *Encyclopaedia Britannica* as a birthday gift, which gives rise to a minor but very revealing incident in their relationship. Apparently, Ferenczi had requested the present; then, mortified by the expense to which he had put Freud, he offered to pay half himself. Freud refused the offer, but not without reminding him that he had directly expressed the wish for it.

Freud publishes *The Ego and the Id*.

Ferenczi works on a whole series of short clinical texts, a genre that is his specialty, among which is "The Dream of the Clever Baby."

1924

Easter: Eighth International Psychoanalytic Congress, at Salzburg.

In September, Hermine von Hug-Hellmuth is murdered by her nephew and analysand Rudolph Hug.

An institute of psychoanalysis is founded in London.

Ferenczi finally publishes *Thalassa: A Theory of Genitality*, the product of continuous reflection since the 1910s.

1925

On June 20, Joseph Breuer dies.

August 14: Freud announces that he has just finished *Inhibitions, Symptoms, and Anxiety*, written in part to challenge Rank on the question of anxiety. Ferenczi receives *Negation* to read.

Freud works on his autobiography.

Ferenczi publishes "Psycho-Analysis of Sexual Habits."

In August, Elizabeth Severn visits Freud at the Semmering. At the time, she is already in training analysis with Ferenczi.

September 2–5: Ninth International Psychoanalytic Congress, in Bad Homburg, Abraham chairing.

On October 18 (1031), Marie Bonaparte begins her analysis with Freud.

Abraham falls ill. He dies at the end of December, the result of a pulmonary ailment.

1926

In a circular letter from Ferenczi dated April 18 (1057), the idea of allowing general practitioners to practice is suggested. Michael Balint has finished his analysis with Ferenczi and has become his collaborator. Perhaps the idea was the product of a discussion between the two men. We know that in the end it was Balint who developed it into a renowned method.

The Paris Psychoanalytic Society is established.

Ferenczi works on "Contra-Indications to the Active Psycho-Analytical Technique," a critique of experiments in active technique; he also publishes another major article, "The Problem of the Acceptance of Unpleasant Ideas."

1927

In August, Freud writes his article on fetishism, and another on humor.

Creation of the *French Review of Psychoanalysis*.

Anna seems to take on a role of increasing importance, equally by Freud's side as in the life of the association.

In September, after the Innsbruck Congress (the Tenth), which Eitingon chairs, the Secret Committee becomes the Administrative Committee of the International Association.

Creation of the Brazilian Psychoanalytic Society.

1928

Creation of the Japanese Psychoanalytic Institute.

In September, Ferenczi makes a trip to Spain, where he gives two lectures: "On the Training of Psycho-Analysts" and "The Psychoanalytic Therapy of Character."

During the same year, he publishes two important papers: "The Adaptation of the Family to the Child" and "The Elasticity of Psycho-Analytical Technique."

1929

Eleventh International Psychoanalytic Congress, in Oxford, Eitingon chairing.

Creation of the Frankfurt Psychoanalytic Institute.

Freud drafts *Civilization and Its Discontents,* and asks Ferenczi to read it. For his part, Ferenczi works on "The Unwelcome Child and His Death Instinct."

1930

In March, Ferenczi visits Freud in Vienna; the meeting is reassuring to both of them.

On May 25, Ferenczi tells Freud that he has just bought a house on the right bank of the Danube at 11 Lisznyai utca. The purchase fulfills a long-standing dream. Freud is quick to congratulate him warmly on May 28.

On August 1, Freud writes to Ferenczi that the city of Frankfurt has awarded him the Goethe Prize. Anna will accept it for him on August 28 (Goethe's birthday).

Freud publishes *Civilization and Its Discontents.* Ferenczi publishes "The Principle of Relaxation and Neocatharsis."

During this period, the Hungarian Association is evolving and working assiduously. Vilma Kovács conducts a technical seminar, Imre Hermann teaches courses on theory; two free clinics for children and parents are in operation in Budapest.

1931

In March, Radó emigrates to America to supervise the organization of the New York Psychoanalytic Institute.

On May 6, Freud turns seventy-five.

H. G. Wells pays Freud a visit.

Ferenczi writes "Child Analysis in the Analysis of Adults."

In October, Martin Freud begins to work at the Verlag; he will take over from Storfer as director the following year.

Also in October, the city of Freiberg votes to hang a plaque on the house where Freud was born.

1932

Ferenczi begins to edit his *Clinical Diary*. At the same time, he continues editing his research on trauma, begun the previous year. The group of five articles written on this subject will be published in the *Zeitschrift* under the title "Some Thoughts on Trauma" one year following the death of their author.

September: Twelfth International Psychoanalytic Congress, in Wiesbaden.

1933

May 22: Ferenczi dies.

For their careful reading and invaluable suggestions I would like to thank Suzanne Achache-Wiznitzer, Eva Brabant, Ernst Falzeder, André Haynal, Axel Hoffer, Susanne Hommel, Pierre Sabourin, Françoise Samson, Isabelle Seguin, Bernard This, and my very first reader, my husband, Jacques Dupont.

WORKS CITED

References to works cited in the Introduction not listed below can be found in "Abbreviations of Works Cited" or "Works by Freud and Ferenczi Cited in the Text" elsewhere in this volume.

Balint, M. *The Basic Fault*. New York: Brunner/Mazel, 1968.
Duhamel, P. "Eugénie Sokolnicka." Psychiatric conference held at Bordeaux, October 12, 1988.
Rank, O. *The Trauma of Birth*. New York: Dover, 1993.

Translated by Giselle Weiss

The Correspondence of
Sigmund Freud and Sándor Ferenczi
Volume 3, 1920–1933

829

Vienna, January 1, 1920
IX., Berggasse 19

Dear friend,

Cheers to 1920, and may you, who are so much younger, still emerge from this sea of misery!

Your detailed letter, brought over by Lajos Lévy, makes no mention of my writing before the telegram (α, β, γ, δ); accordingly, I will repeat in more detail what I had indicated there. I greatly regret the impression that you didn't get further with Bódy;[1] I consider him a cowardly and false beast, and I think one must approach him differently, in a more peremptory fashion. You seem to place yourself before him like humble audience-seekers whose suggestions he has no time to address, whereas you could deal with him as a party with equal rights. Your idea to call upon a privy councillor (Moravcsik) to act as a witness also seems to me to have fundamentally missed the mark. It's a good thing the result was only a refusal.

You know what is at stake for us in the big fund. Aside from its actual purposes, we need it as backing, since we have received fifty thousand more than the amount of the endowment, and we need it to pay the eighty thousand if we can really take possession of the (up to now untouched) foreign securities. The Verlag, I believe, no longer has that much cash in its possession at all. Even the document that Toni wrote up here anticipates backing by the big fund.

So I suggest that you no longer beg for a gracious audience with Bódy, but rather have Béla Lévy[2] write him a formal letter in a resolute style with approximately the following content: you, as the authorized representative of the founder, do not delude yourself over the fact that the representatives of the city are assuming an inimically negative attitude toward the use of the fund intended by the founder and approved by the previous mayor.[3]

Bringing in a witness on the part of a person who is, to be sure, official, but protected by no knowledge whatsoever against the most common prejudices, is a certain indication of that. This attitude on the part of the city is very regrettable, for an institute for the treatment of indigent people with nervous illnesses would have been an eminently humanitarian and scientifically very valuable enterprise, through which Budapest would for once have gained an advantage over other centers of culture.

Since Budapest refuses this, you, in the name of the founder, would have to refuse to impress your conviction upon the city; in addition, you are also certain that the council's fulfilling its mission with alien elements who are ignorant of the matter and are striving in other directions would only be a source of continuing discord and would inevitably lead to paralysis of the enterprise.

On the other hand, you—again in the name of the founder—can assure that he will make absolutely no other use [of the fund] than that which was intended by him. In case of his demise he will see to it that his will will be represented just as unswervingly by his lawful successors. The consequence of this difference and bilateral inflexibility will only be that the fund would find no utilization, and the city would get just as little from it as would science. The representatives of the city should only make it clear to themselves that all efforts to make use of the fund at their own discretion are certainly, now as later, destined for failure.

In view of this unpleasant possibility, you—again in the name of the founder—suggest the following settlement, which can remove all difficulties. You are ready to leave $\frac{1}{2}$ million of the fund amounting to 1.75 million to the free disposal of the city, if in exchange the remainder is given to you, as representative of the founder, *unrestricted* and *without any further control, limitation, or influencing,* for the fulfillment of the scientific intentions of the founder. If the representatives of the city do not accept this division and clear separation, then you would have to burden them with the responsibility of thwarting the humanitarian intentions of the founder.—

So much for the letter; it can be even rougher, under no circumstances milder. Refuse flat out any dissipations and requests for compromise. Ultimatum! In negotiations one could (not gladly!) accept the division of one million and 750 thousand (for the city).

Your resoluteness will make an impression in the end. Further expert testimony [*Gutachterei*] superfluous. Prerequisite for such a procurement is your own refusal to carry out completely Toni's original intention. That won't go in Budapest now. Preservation through autotomy!

Rank returned late this evening and has gone home. I won't see him until tomorrow. Then I will give you a report.[4]

There is another snag in the matter of Toni. He has not yet designated his lawful successor. Lajos Lévy has promised to occupy himself with this matter. He thinks we still have a few weeks.[5] Rapid and energetic proceeding on your part seems to be called for.

Cordially,
Freud

1. The mayor of Budapest, with whom Ferenczi was negotiating about the von Freund endowment; see letter 789 and n. 3, and letter 828.
2. Doctor of Laws, brother of Lajos Lévy.
3. István Bárczy; see letter 769, n. 4.
4. "Rank returned from London yesterday . . . His trip was completely unsuccessful, insofar as his (or, more precisely, Freund's) dealings are concerned; apart from that, he organized and learned a great deal on our behalf" (Freud to Eitingon, January 4, 1920, Sigmund Freud Copyrights). A transcript of the Freud-Eitingon correspondence is available in the archives of Sigmund Freud Copyrights and the Freud Museum; publication by Michael Schröter is in preparation.
5. Until von Freund's imminent death.

830

Vienna, January 21, 1920
IX., Berggasse 19

Dear friend,

Yesterday, Tuesday, January 20, 5:30 P.M., our good friend Toni died.[1] I last saw him on Saturday; he was a painful sight. Lajos played the angel of death with him; the postmortem examination showed how much good was done to him with that. The immediate cause of death was a sepsis proceeding from the kidneys; the last symptoms were uremic,[2] couldn't be properly interpreted.

You know what we have lost in him. Now we have to protect his legacy, Vera[3] and the foundation.

Emil,[4] who looks after everything that was dear to Toni's heart, is now making a much softer impression than ever before. I think our interests are well preserved with him; he will follow through with what has to be achieved.

Incidentally, our Verlag is not yet in danger; it can last the year, and help could come by year's end. Our flawless unity and absolute community of interests will guarantee its sure continuation.

I didn't quite understand why you are so anxious in the matter of the securities. They lie untouched and will remain so until everything has been clarified. Only it is not in our interest voluntarily to turn down a big opportunity for profit (from the exchange according to the situation then). I will not give the Verlag a supplement of 11,000 crowns that I received from Toni some weeks ago; I will probably use it to support a Ψα lay society, which is supposed to be founded here at the urging of Bernfeld.[5]

Your Elma was with us a few days ago, beautiful and blossoming. Martha procured a hat for her. I was very pleased to hear that she has reconciled with her husband and is supposed to be fetched by him this summer. Frau Gizella should not consider holding her back. Elma spoke very sensibly.

From the newspapers you know the state of our money and commercial relations. Personally, we are doing well. "We are poor people, but we live well," Lajos quoted to us from the Hungarian this evening.

A medium-sized essay about a case of female homosexuality is finished.[6] What is happening with the paleobiology?[7]

I am looking forward to hearing soon from you both, and greet you cordially.

Yours,
Freud

1. January 20 was a Wednesday. "Freund was buried on January 22; the next morning the first telegram came, from Max. On January 25, they all went back to Budapest" (Freud to Ernst Freud, February 8, 1920, Library of Congress). See the obituary by Freud (1920c).

2. Pertaining to toxicity in the urinary tract.

3. His daughter; see letter 730, n. 4.

4. His brother.

5. Siegfried Bernfeld (1892–1953), Doctor of Philosophy, from 1915 on a guest, and from 1919 on a member of the Vienna Psychoanalytic Society. A practicing analyst from 1922 on; secretary and librarian of the Vienna Society, and Helene Deutsch's representative at the Training Institute. At the end of 1925 he moved to Berlin and underwent an analysis there with Hanns Sachs from 1930–1932. From 1926 to 1930 he was a *Dozent* at the Deutsche Hochschule für Politik in Berlin. In 1932 he returned to Vienna, and in 1934 he emigrated, first to France and then, in 1937, to London; in the same year he emigrated to San Francisco, where he assisted in building the Society there. Bernfeld was one of the most shimmering figures of early psychoanalysis; Marxistically oriented, he became involved in pedagogic and social issues, in the youth movement, and in Zionism. The "lay society" did not materialize. See Karl Fallend and Johannes Reichmayr, eds., *Siegfried Bernfeld oder die Grenzen der Psychoanalyse: Materialen zu Leben und Werk* [Siegfried Bernfeld or the Limits of Psychoanalysis: Materials for Life and Work] (Basel, 1992).

6. "The Psychogenesis of a Case of Homosexuality in a Woman" (Freud 1920a).

7. The work *Thalassa: A Theory of Genitality* (1924, 268), which had been delayed again and again by Ferenczi.

831

Budapest, January 27, 1920

Dear Professor,

By way of Lajos I received your letter of the 21st. From its mood, as well as from the communications of (happily arrived) Elma, I gather what, incidentally, I could imagine even without this, how gripped you are by the death of our friend Toni. From a distance such events take on more and more of a shadowy quality. I still can't imagine Toni any differently than seemingly healthy, intellectually alert, the way I last saw him in the sanatorium, and I have again and again forcibly to make myself aware that he is lost forever. Our friendship solidified more and more in the last few months—it was looking as though I had succeeded—(a rarity at my age)—in gaining a friend in the most beautiful sense of the word. Now, this hope also disappeared, just like all the beautiful dreams connected with his ability.—

January 30, 1920

Frau Kata[1] and Lajos did *not* inform me of the death of your dear Sophie.[2] You can imagine my consternation when the terrible news was read to me from the Neue Freie Presse. Two days have already passed since I know this, and I still seem to myself to be dumb and paralyzed when I am supposed to write down even a word of consolation or sympathy. I treasured and loved your Sophie, often had an almost paternal affection for her, and was pleased about the always similar-sounding news about her courage and ability. One can't bear to think that you must also be experiencing that.

Please, if you are at all able, at least reassure me about the fact that your strength of spirit is also a match for this misfortune.

Yours,
Ferenczi

1. Kata Lévy had been in Vienna since the end of 1919 and just prior to that had returned to Budapest (Freud to Kata Lévy, November 15, 1919; Freud to Kata and Lajos Lévy, February 4, 1920, Library of Congress).

2. Freud's daughter Sophie had died on January 25 at the age of twenty-six from the effects of the "Spanish influenza," which was rampant at the time, when she was pregnant with a third child. Over 20 million people died in this influenza pandemic of 1918–1919.

832

Vienna, January 29, 1920
IX., Berggasse 19

Dear friend,

Just received your telegram;[1] thought you had learned it from Kata Lévy before the newspaper. We were only worried for two days, Friday and Saturday. The news of death came on Sunday afternoon. The whole illness was over on the fifth day. Wafted away! Nothing to say. It was the typical septic pneumonia of influenza. The cremation was at noon on Wednesday. Ernst and Eitingon went from Berlin. Oli was already there. Max is said to be calm and to be behaving in a dignified fashion. Eitingon called from Berlin an hour ago and informed us that, for the time being, Max's widowed sister-in-law is moving in. (The wife of Dr. Rudolf Halberstadt, who was killed in the war.)[2]

My wife wanted to go there at the first disturbing news. Naturally, it was impossible, no train was running. Only today Mathilde and Robert are able to go to Hamburg, since a train, the nature of which we have to keep strictly secret, is taking them as far as Leipzig. They could stay away for two to three weeks.

And with us? My wife is very shaken. I think: La séance continue.[3] But it was a bit much for one week.

With kind regards and thanks to Frau Gizella and you.

Yours,
Freud

1. The telegram has not been found.
2. See letter 741 and n. 5.
3. French for "the performance continues." An allusion to the custom in the theater to continue the show without interruption upon the death of an actor.

833

Vienna, February 4, 1920
IX., Berggasse 19

Dear friend,

Don't worry about me. I am the same except for somewhat more fatigue. The death, as painful as it is, does not overturn any attitude toward life. For years I was prepared for the loss of my sons, now comes that of my daughter. Since I am profoundly unbelieving, I have no one to blame, and I know there is no place where one can lodge a complaint. The "eternally uniformly set clock of duty"[1] and the "sweet habit of being"[2] will do the rest, in order to let everything continue on an even keel. Very deep within I perceive the feeling of a deep, insurmountable narcissistic insult. My wife and Annerl are severely shaken in a more human sense.

This week we are expecting Oli, who, incidentally, seems to have found a position. He, Ernst, and Eitingon were present at the cremation. Yesterday we spoke to a guest from Hamburg who was also there. Mathilde and Robert have been there since Saturday. We know that Max will not separate from the children and that for the time being the widow of his fallen brother will live with them for a few weeks.

I press your hand in friendship and ask you to give heartfelt thanks to your dear wife for her tender words.

Yours,
Freud

P.S. On Friday I will talk with Varga.[3]

1. "Des Dienstes immer gleichgestellte Uhr" [the always uniformly set clock of duty] (Schiller, *Die Piccolomini*, I, 4).
2. "Keine Rettung!—Süsses Leben! schöne, freundliche Gewohnheit des Daseins und Wirkens! von dir soll ich scheiden! So gelassen scheiden!" [No Salvation!—Sweet life! beautiful, friendly habit of being and acting! I should part from you! Part so calmly] (Goethe, *Egmont*, V, 4).
3. Probably Jenö Varga (1879–1964), noted personality in the Hungarian and international labor movement, politician, economist, and university professor. In 1919 he was chair of the Supreme Council of the People's Economy of the Council Republic. In 1920 he emigrated to Vienna, later to the Soviet Union. In the 1930s and 1940s he was one of the leading managers of the Soviet economy and was responsible for setting up several five-year plans. Varga was for a short time (1918–19) a member of the Hungarian Psychoanalytic Society.

834

Budapest, February 10, 1920

Dear Professor,

Both of your letters (which reassured me) arrived here after a journey of six to eight days.

I will inform you briefly about the few things that will interest you.

1.) Béla Lévy told me that we can expect on the part of Emil von Freund the liquidation of a rather large sum, probably to the account of the big fund. I don't yet know any details; if I am not mistaken, it has to do with approximately 300 thousand. But it is uncertain as to whether the whole thing isn't based on a misunderstanding (on Béla's part). I will ask Emil for a talk.—

2.) Frau Rózsi[1] is terribly beside herself. For days she has been saying almost nothing. Yesterday she asked me for a conversation, from which I gathered how close she is to a psychotic illness. She wishes to continue the conversations, which I take as a good sign.

3.) As you know, Frau Margit Dubovitz[2] inherited from Tóni a number of stocks from the "St. Stephen's Corp." In the letter of gift, Tóni asks that, in the event the stocks are intended to be sold, they first be offered to Emil Freund, and, in fact, at a price indicated by Tóni, *which is much lower than the present value of the stock.* (Unless absolutely necessary, the stocks should, in my opinion, not be sold now.) But very soon new stock is going to be issued, to which the subscription right belongs first and foremost to the old shareholders. Hereby the value of the inheritance increases *by a significant amount*, since the stock is much more valuable than the sum of the subscription right. But now Dr. Dubovitz,[3] who has control over the stock until the divorce, has to get an explanation (a letter) from Margit, in which she declares herself in agreement with the exercise of the subscription right and also expresses herself about the sale of the stock. I ask you if you would be willing to see to it that Frau Margit writes this letter to Dr. Dubovitz, or at least expresses herself about it through your mediation. This matter is very urgent and extremely significant for Margit's future. Her inheritance could increase from 150 to 250–300 thousand. If she doesn't respond, Dubovitz lets the whole thing rest, and the subscription right becomes invalid.—

Incidentally, Dr. Dubovitz has become more understanding in the last few days; his cure is beginning to get more normal.—

4.) It will interest you to know that Frau Sokolnicka[4] has been in treatment with me for about six weeks. She is completing her analysis here. Please don't tell anyone about this matter for the time being.—

Yours,
Ferenczi

1. The widow of Von Freund; see letter 582 and n. 2.
2. Von Freund's former lover; Freud's analysand.
3. Margit's husband, in analysis with Ferenczi.
4. See letter 724, n. 4.

835

Vienna, March 12, 1920
IX., Berggasse, 19[1]

H[err] Dr. S. Ferenczi
Nagydiófa ut 3
   with a request for a response to both as quickly as possible.[2]

Fr[eud].[3]

1. Correspondence card.
2. The enclosure has not been found.
3. Following this are four lines in a different hand in Hungarian: "Dr. Lévyné is kapott egy példányt./ Sziveskedjék viszaküldés elott vele is telefon érintkezésbe / lépni. szivélyesen üdvösli / 1920.III.17.—[signature illegible]" [Frau Dr. Lévy also received a copy. Before you send it back, be so kind as to contact her by telephone. Kind regards . . .]. On the back of the card is a pencil drawing, above which are the words "Sublimest intelligence, receptivity, extreme tactfulness," likewise in pencil, in an unknown hand.

836

INTERNATIONALE ZEITSCHRIFT FÜR
ÄRZTLICHE PSYCHOANALYSE

Budapest, March 20, 1920[1]

Dear Professor,

This time—and in the last few months altogether—I am not in a position to excuse my long silence with the fact that nothing new has happened. On the contrary, hardly a day passes when nothing of vital importance does not take place. The fact that there is little that is gratifying to report may serve as more of an excuse.—You are certainly well informed about the political and social conditions. The material situation is almost unbearable.[2] Up to now I have borne the struggle with the price increases, but my strength is beginning to fail. I am working nine or ten hours a day, on top of that three office hours a week, get paid 100 crowns, and in spite of that (with *the greatest* austerity, without renouncing the necessities, to be sure), I can barely maintain the balance of income and expenditures. In addition to that there is the uncertainty about monetary conditions altogether, e.g., the threatened stamping of banknotes, which—I fear—will result in no corresponding increase in buying power.—But the worst thing is that I obviously don't possess that inexhaustible source of energy that I admire in you, so that in the evening I am completely exhausted and incapable of any intellectual work. I was *absolutely* unable to take care of the most pressing scientific tasks, to write the reviews, to conceive the paleobiological paper, to work out some good ideas, to realize two medium-sized plans of work (1. on the scholasticism of obsessional neurotics;[3] 2.) on the further development of active therapy[4]). *Not a word* has yet been brought to paper about all that. I can still talk about happiness, if my health stands up to the overwork.—The other malady, from which the rest of my colleagues are suffering, is not less regrettable; they certainly all have quite a lot of time—they lack money all the more. Lately I was able to send them only a few patients.—The idea of emigrating is taking on more and more concrete form with me. Hereabouts Ψα. has been so well introduced that from now on it can dispense with me without difficulty. America would come into consideration as a place to emigrate to. I would like to ask you, if you write to Brill or McCurdy,[5] to communicate my intention to them and to request that they take steps to enable me to secure entry and to set up a practice. Over there I would limit my work time and be able to dedicate myself much more to science. We would be terribly far apart from each other, but—haven't we for years been in the same predicament anyway?—and do we have hopes that this will change?—I don't think so.— If you believe that Switzerland or Holland should sooner come into consideration, then I would gladly alter my intention. I would like best to move to where you live. But Vienna doesn't come into consideration for the time being.

In the meantime, our small but active society is continuing to work. Recently Róheim gave a lecture on *Totemism in Australia*, a brief excerpt from a larger work of the same name. He is the first ethnologist who has placed himself completely on our standpoint, and is achieving true miracles with this magical potion. His new work is of *eminent* significance for ethnology, but also for Ψα. He wrote the work in *English*. Could it be published by our Verlag?[6]

I enclose with this letter a few small contributions,[7] among others, one from the sower of intrigue Eisler,[8] the only one who is trying to disturb the good harmony of our group (if only by means of stupid remarks about my person and my works, about which I have not up to now reacted, since I only received indirect knowledge of them).

Dr. Hollós is very eager; he gave us a number of very good psychiatric-analytic lectures.[9] I hope soon to receive a few papers for the Zeitschrift from him. Frau Dr. Sokolnicka is attending our sessions, which are being held in German for her sake. I had a small but quite pretty observation of hers noted down.[10] It is enclosed with this letter.

I can give a brief report about our personal relations. Elma is here; she complements our family circle quite well. The recent past of our relations is completely buried with her, as it is with me, and we retrieved the old, natural tone of friendship with each other.

Gizella is outdoing herself in love and true devotion for me and her family. She does, to be sure, exhaust herself too much with domestic torments. It often pains me very much that I don't compensate her with the tenderness that she would deserve.

From the family of our good Toni I see almost exclusively Rózsi, who now comes to analysis every day. Under the influence of Ψα, her morbid brooding, with which mourning expressed itself in her and which initially looked like a psychosis, is beginning to abate, and gradually we are connecting with her old analysis, in which she had already brought things far along. Little Vera stands under the good tutelage of Frau Vidor;[11] she is the proper, good-natured, motherly nurturer and caretaker of all three children.[12] Rózsi herself is, for the time being, not up to this task.

You have been instructed by Béla Lévy as to the state (that is to say, stagnation) of the fund matter.

Only one more request: At our departure I was unable, on account of packing difficulties, to take along the photograph which was given us as a gift. If somebody or other with an appropriate suitcase comes to Budapest, we ask you if you would send us the picture.

We are expecting a detailed report from you about everything that is happening with you. (In previous years, I, instead of this letter, would have come for Easter to have a look around; now I have to rely on this inadequate means of information . . . —From America I would be able to come to you for at least three months every year!

Most cordial and kind regards to you all from

Yours,
Ferenczi

1. See letter 358, n. 1. The letterhead has been crossed out. The "2" of "1920" is superimposed over the final, preprinted "1." The date has evidently been erroneously written (see Freud's reply in the letter of March 15, 1920); perhaps it should read March 12.
2. Galloping inflation was decreasing the value of the Hungarian crown to one six-thousandth of its prewar value.
3. No publication fitting this description has been found.
4. "The Further Development of an Active Therapy in Psycho-Analysis" (Ferenczi 1921, 234); presented in September of the same year as a lecture at the Sixth International Psychoanalytic Congress (September 8–13, 1920) in The Hague. Shortly after this letter was written, Ferenczi also spoke about active technique in the Hungarian Society (March 28, 1920); the debate about it was continued on April 11 and 24.
5. Spelling in the original. John Thompson MacCurdy (1886–1947), co-founder and first secretary of the American Psychoanalytic Association (the group from Ward's Island, to which Brill also belonged). From 1913–1922 he was a teacher at Cornell University, and from 1923 on a lecturer in psychopathology at Cambridge University. On April 22, 1914, he had been a guest at the Vienna Society (*Minutes* IV, p. 256).
6. A two-part lecture of February 15 and 29 (*Zeitschrift* 7 [1920]: 133); Róheim also gave a lecture on the same subject at the Hague Congress. The book, *Australian Totemism: A Psycho-Analytic Study in Anthropology* (London, 1925), was published not by the Verlag but by Allen & Unwin (London, 1925).
7. The contributions have not been found.
8. See letter 213 and n. 2.
9. Lectures of December 7, 1919 ("Kasuistische Mitteilungen" [Casuistic Communications]), of December 28, 1919 ("Über die Entwicklung der Wahnvorstellungsinhalte" [On the Development of the Content of Delusional Ideas]), and of January 18, 1920 ("Psychoanalytische Beziehungen in der vor-Freudschen Psychiatrie" [Psychoanalytic Relations in Pre-Freudian Psychiatry]); see *Zeitschrift* 7 (1921): 133.
10. Probably "Analyse einer infantilen Zwangsneurose" [The Analysis of an Infantile Obsessional Neurosis], lecture of March 4, published in *Zeitschrift* 6 (1920): 228–241.

11. Regina, married name Vidor, von Freund's sister.
12. Besides Vera, Antal and Erzsébet.

837

Vienna, March 15, 1920
IX., Berggasse 19

Dear friend,

Received today your long-awaited but in consequence content-rich letter and don't believe that my reply will reach you so quickly—with an early arrival of five days. The day before yesterday I sent you, by way of Partós,[1] a proof of my obituary for Toni, another one to the family.

I only need to echo what you say about the conditions of existence there to make it valid for my case. Just the same, even though I get 250 crowns an hour. To some extent the Anglo-Americans, of whom I now have two and expect a third after Easter, are helping out.[2] But what will happen if Jones can't send me any more?

You have surely been informed by telegram that Jones and Sachs have announced themselves for March 30 and how much we would like to have them here for a $\psi\alpha$ symposium around Eastertime. After we have truly shared everything in life with each other for ten years, the closing of the borders is now a severe deprivation. I hope you come whenever you can.[3]

[I] honor your plans to emigrate, which are certainly nourished by Elma,[4] but it is not convenient. Above all, you must wait until after the Congress, for correspondence with Brill is impossible for reasons unknown,[5] and about McCurdy we know only that he has left the American group. I now have two hours daily of practicing English, and I can assure you that treatment in a foreign language is a very hard thing. Analysis has certainly been well introduced in Hungary, but with your leaving, everything would fall apart. Of course, your life's plan doesn't have to take me much into consideration. I am already too old to resist the burdens of today's situation for long. Béla Lévy said we should not give up the big fund, and if it delays too long, he has promised that in the meantime the Verlag will be supported by the new Anton von Freund Foundation. With the unbelievable paper and printing costs, it could soon be in a position to require it.

I am extraordinarily pleased about what you write about Róheim. It goes without saying that I will exert influence on Jones to have his work accepted into the Verlag.[6] Your "sower of intrigue" Eisler is certainly very talented and can write; his forthcoming case study[7] which is now in galleys is excellent; you really should try to capture him; he is probably only suffering from neglect. The contributions bear fine witness to the work of your group. Here they are very lazy; nothing to be had from them.

I can report little to you about private things. The pressure since Sophie's death has not left us; my wife wants or wanted to go to Hamburg at the end of the month, which is being called into question by the latest events in Germany.⁸ Minna is back from Reichenhall, much recuperated. Oli is here, sees all his chances for work disappear, which doesn't sit well with him; Ernst has gone for convalescence in the Allgäu (Bavaria) after a case of the flu; Anna looks bad. Martin's marriage is going well.

I am suffering from headaches and dizziness as a result of a dreadful nasal suppuration and can't work at all, not even the new editions of Theory of Sexuality and Jokes.⁹ The Verlag is laboring on 10,000 external difficulties, and Rank, who is as well behaved as ever, does seem to me to be depressed and not properly capable of accomplishment. He is very probably a periodic [manic-depressive].

It is an amusement when, from time to time, alms come in from Holland and America. Loe¹⁰ is still supplying the greater part of our sustenance by means of her shipments from The Hague. We hope to see her there in the fall.

The most gratifying thing at this time—apart from new editions and translations—is the opening of the Berlin polyclinic, founded by Eitingon (February 14), at which Ernst, Mathilde, and Robert happened to be present.¹¹ Ernst had also looked after setting up and equipping it.

I greet you, Gisella,¹² and Elma cordially and do hope to see you with us at Easter. Don't postpone; in the summer we want to be with the orphaned children¹³ in North Germany.

Yours,
Freud

1. Possibly Dr. Zoltán Pártos, mentioned in letter 641, who translated *Totem and Taboo* into Hungarian.

2. Dr. Bieber, a dentist from New York, and Claude Daly. Major Claude D. Daly (1884–1950), former analysand of Jones's (ca. 1916) and Freud's (1920); shortly thereafter he underwent analysis with Ferenczi (see letters 1002ff.). Daly became a member of the Indian Psycho-Analytical Society. See letter of Jones to Freud, January 25, 1920 (*Freud/Jones*, pp. 364–365). Included in this group was John Rickman (1891–1951), later a prominent member of the British Society. After his analysis with Freud, he was also an analysand of Ferenczi's and Melanie Klein's, whose theories he espoused for a time, only to become finally an adherent of the "Middle Group." "John Rickman is known for his pioneering role in the organization of psychoanalysis in Great Britain . . . , for his militant pacifism, for his activity in the reform of psychiatry during the war, and . . . more generally, for his ideas about the psychology of small groups" (Roudinesco & Plon, *Dictionnaire*, p. 904).

3. At the beginning of April, Ferenczi, Jones, Rank, and Sachs met with Freud in Vienna; Abraham and Eitingon were unable to come on account of difficulties in gaining entry. "It is a virtual private Congress in my room for several hours a day, and Toni looks on so sadly from the wall" (Freud to Sándor Szabó, April 4, 1920, Library of Congress).

4. Elma had become an American citizen by virtue of her marriage.

5. There were differences between Freud and Brill, especially because of the English translation rights. Sometimes Brill didn't answer letters, sometimes letters got lost or arrived late; but Freud had assured him in January: "From our first acquaintance I put a complete confidence in you, not shaken to this day, such as a Jew can only put in another Jew . . . The only fault, for which I often took the liberty to upbraid you, was your excessive susceptibility, this too a peculiarity of our race" (letter of January 19, 1920, Library of Congress, in English in the original).

6. I.e., into the Press, the short-lived English division of the Verlag.

7. "Eine unbewusste Schwangerschaftsphantasie bei einem Mann unter dem Bilde einer traumatischen Hysterie" [An Unconscious Pregnancy Fantasy under the Picture of a Traumatic Hysteria], published in two parts in *Zeitschrift* 6 (1920): 50–63, 123–139.

8. The so-called Kapp Putsch of March 13–17, 1920, an attempted right-wing coup d'état named for its ringleader, Wolfgang Kapp (1858–1922). The coup temporarily forced the imperial government to flee, but collapsed after a few days as a result of a general strike.

9. Freud 1905d-(4th ed., 1920); 1905c (3d ed., 1921), both with Deuticke.

10. Loë Kann, wife of Herbert Jones. She was once Ernest Jones's lover and Freud's former analysand. She was visiting her Dutch homeland.

11. "A few weeks after his [von Freund's] death, thanks to the energy and liberality of Dr. Max Eitingon, the first psycho-analytical out-patients' clinic has been opened in Berlin. Thus von Freund's work is carried on" (Freud 1920c, p. 268). The institution, headed by Eitingon and Ernst Simmel, served to treat patients free of charge, that is to say, favorably, as well as to provide training, whose structure (training analysis, theoretical education, control analysis) was soon to be generally adopted. Hanns Sachs, who moved to Berlin not long afterward, took over the training analyses and Eitingon the controls. An entire generation of analysts was trained in Berlin (Franz Alexander, Alice and Michael Balint, in part, Suzanne and Siegfried Bernfeld, Felix Böhm, Erich Fromm, Edward and James Glover, Karen Horney, Melanie Klein, Hans Lampl, Rudolph Loewenstein, Barbara Low, Heinrich Meng, Josine Müller-Ebsen and Karl Müller-Braunschweig, Sacha Nacht, Sylvia Payne, Sándor Radó, Ella Freeman Sharpe, and Alix Strachey, among others). Mathilde and Robert Hollitscher had been in Berlin from February 10 to 15, 1920 (Eitingon to Freud, February 11, 1920, Sigmund Freud Copyrights).

12. Spelling in the original.

13. Ernst and Heinerle, Sophie's children.

838

Budapest, March 17, 1920

Dear Professor,

Just received the proofs from Emil. Am in complete agreement with both; you should approve of the two small changes.*[1]

Received Rank's telegram yesterday. I immediately took the necessary steps here, in order to be able to visit you at Easter, and asked Rank by telegram to help me in gaining entry and securing lodging. My patient

*I consider it *necessary* to leave out the political allusion.

Vásárhelyi² should come to Vienna tomorrow and pick up the entry documents; but the telegram to the Austrian embassy here will not be made superfluous thereby.

I³ regret that I must ask Rank for another favor in this matter, which I ask you to communicate to him *as soon as possible.* In consideration of the disruption in train traffic, I intend to come by Danube ship; but I have to see to the *return trip* in a timely fashion, otherwise I will get stuck in Vienna, which would be impermissible now, at a time when I am living from hand to mouth. He should be so kind as to reserve and pay for, *as soon as possible, with the Danube Steamship Company,* a sleeping berth (in a cabin) for the *first* ship after Easter, which to the best of my knowledge leaves Vienna on Wednesday. I will naturally be liable for the amount. If I should not be able to come, it should be easy to sell the ticket (hotel porters) in the worst case.

What I crossed out has become immaterial in consequence of a telephone conversation with Vásárhelyi. He promised me secure round-trip train reservations, by which I save time. Vásárhelyi is also taking this letter with him.

Kindest regards from me and my wife.

Ferenczi

1. The proofs of the obituary for Anton von Freund. Freud accepted Ferenczi's "correction... without reservation" (Freud to Kata Lévy, March 23, 1920, Library of Congress).
2. The patient has not been identified; in any case, he is not the painter of the same name [Vasarely].
3. The paragraph that follows has been crossed out.

839

March 28, 1920¹

arriving friday evening = ferenczi +

1. Telegram.

840

Dr. Ferenczi Sándor
idegorvos¹
Budapest, April 18, 1920

Dear Professor,

Already more than two weeks have again passed since I left Vienna without my having decided to write a letter. To be sure, nothing out of the ordinary has happened since then. For a few days I was still half-living in the memories of Vienna, but soon everything moved into the far distance; the everyday interests and the local difficulties absorb a great deal of interest. What is left is dedicated to Ψα (as science). The Society is very busy; we are working almost every Sunday. Today we heard an *outstanding* lecture by a henceforth accepted member by the name of Aurel *Kolnai* about "Psychoanalysis and Sociology."² One would never have ascribed *so* much ψα understanding to a man who has hitherto been so distant from us. Since I know your current interest in questions of group psychology,³ I am having the paper sent directly to your address. You will certainly find points of contact in his remarks. A little paper by *Hermann*⁴ is being sent along with it.

A brief train of thought about "Group Psychology": Should not *ambivalence,* the division of antagonistic strivings into two separate psychic acts, be brought into relation with the beginning formation of the ego ideal out of the common ego? The *hostile* impulse toward the father is an attempt to realize the ideal of becoming a father; the *subordinating, [the] impulse to obedience* (that of suggestibility in the tendency on which "paternal hypnosis"⁵ is based), would be the more primitive (group) mode of reaction.

Many members are registering for the Congress; most, however, are counting on support.

Our summer plans are unchanged for the time being (Aussee—The Hague).—

I am very eager to hear how the talk with Varga about the securities went and what else you have decided with Jones and Rank.

Kindest regards from the both of us and thanks to Frau Professor for the hospitality tendered under difficult circumstances.—The hotel director in the Regina also wanted to bill you for the room; I couldn't allow that, naturally.

Yours,
Ferenczi

1. See letter 783, n. 1.

2. Aurel Kolnai (1900–1973), journalist, writer, and philosopher. A member of the Galilei Society, he studied philosophy, history, and economics in Freiburg. He graduated from the University of Vienna in 1926. In 1937 he emigrated to Paris and in 1940 to the United States; in 1945 he became a professor of philosophy at Laval University in Quebec and in 1959 at Bedford College of the University of London. His book *Psychoanalyse und Soziologie: Zur Psychologie von Masse und Gesellschaft* [Psychoanalysis and Sociology: On the Psychology of Mass and Society] was published by the Verlag shortly thereafter, and occasioned heated controversies about the relationship between psychoanalysis and Marxism. In the early 1920s Kolnai published a few more papers in the *Zeitschrift,* but then distanced himself gradually from psychoanalysis. See Harmat, *Freud, Ferenczi,* pp. 109–112.

3. After Freud, in May 1919, had "with a simple-minded idea . . . attempted a ψα foun-

dation for group psychology" (letter 813), in February 1920 he began working on *Group Psychology and the Analysis of the Ego* (1921c). A draft was completed in August 1920, the final version in March 1921 (see *S.E.* 18:67).

4. Probably Imre Hermann, "Intelligenz und tiefer Gedanke" [Intelligence and Deep Thought], *Zeitschrift* 6 (1920): 193–201.

5. See letter 85 and n. 1.

841

Vienna, April 22, 1920
IX., Berggasse 19

Dear friend,

I, too, gladly give in to the need to write to you. Thanks for your announcements of works; I will be mindful of your theoretical stimulation. I have been incapable of work the whole time—beyond the nine hours of analysis. But my condition probably sprang from an intolerance toward the good cigars, which I had smoked in greater frequency on account of the diminution of the weak ones. A kind of abstinence is slowly improving it.

Varga is still slyly running around, but he intends to put the matter in order before he leaves on vacation.

The episode in the Hotel Regina was a new indication of the unreliability of the Viennese in every situation.

My wife went to Hamburg on the 19th of the month; she will have seen Ernst with his bride[1] in Berlin.

All kinds of little things are happening here. It will interest you to know that my brother-in-law Bernays in New York[2] donated a million crowns in his wife's name to the children's relief organization here. I have the honor of sitting on the steering committee of the endowment with Tandler,[3] Pirquet,[4] dean and mayor.[5]

I hope you are well with wife and daughter, and that in a week Kata Lévy brings me a letter from you.

Cordially,
Freud

Endowment letter from Toni's estate!!

1. At the beginning of April, during Ferenczi's stay in Vienna, Freud had learned of Ernst's engagement to Lucie ("Lux") Brasch (1896–1989). The wedding took place on May 18. The couple had three sons, Stephan Gabriel (Stephen), born 1921; Lucian Michael (Lucien), born 1922; and Clemens Raphael (Sir Clement), born 1924.

2. Eli Bernays (1860–1923), brother of Martha Freud and husband of Freud's sister Anna.

3. Julius Tandler (1869–1936), from Jihlava/Iglau in Moravia. He studied medicine in Vienna (graduated 1895), completed postdoctoral work in 1899, occupied a chair in anatomy, and was dean of the medical school from 1914 to 1917. As the Social Democratic

city councilman for health and welfare policy (1920), Tandler, along with Breitner, Glöckel, Seitz, Speiser, and others, stood for the far-reaching social reforms in "Red Vienna." Relieved of all duties after the failed revolt of February 1934, he finally took up residence in the United States, China, and the Soviet Union.

4. Clemens Pirquet (1874–1929) studied theology, philosophy, and medicine (graduated 1900). He completed postdoctoral work in 1908, taught at Johns Hopkins University (Baltimore) in 1909, in Breslau in 1910, and in 1911 became professor and chairman of the Univerity Children's Clinic in Vienna. The theory of allergies, the discovery of serum pathology, and the tuberculin skin reaction test (1907) originated with him. In addition, Pirquet is considered a pioneer of the modern theory of nutrition for children.

5. Jakob Reumann (1853–1925), a skilled lathe operator, in 1918 became the first vice mayor and in 1919 the first Social Democratic mayor of Vienna. In the postwar period Reumann carried out a number of significant social policy measures, among them a generous residential building program.

842

Dr. Ferenczi Sándor
idegorvos
Budapest, April 27, 1920

Dear Professor,

I was not a little annoyed about the incorrect address from the mailing from your brother-in-law in America; I would have been able to tell him a better address. Perhaps he will send another little sum, and this time *not* for children.

According to Frau Rózsi, [the] endowment letter is *not* to be found in the estate. I will have further research carried out. In the worst case we can get a replacement letter from B. Emil can bring that about whenever.—

I spoke with Lajos Lévy about our lack of money; he will consult with Emil about it sometime soon. Perhaps he will give us a freight car full of paper as an advance.

Frau Sarolta, my sister-in-law who lives in Rome, writes us that she attended a lecture by *Sante de Sanctis*[1] at the University. He spoke for the entire hour about your "Interpretation of Dreams," supposedly with expressions of the highest recognition. Frau Sarolta knows him personally; he also knows my works and asks me for offprints.

A professor of philosophy and pedagogy at the University of Bonn (Walter Frost)[2] demanded of me by letter the speedy publication of my "Gesammelte kleine Schriften"; he didn't write anything about where I am supposed to get the paper for it.

You should be somewhat sparing with the strong cigars. Forced abstinence will be good for you.

Kind regards from both of us and from Elma.

Yours,
Ferenczi

As already mentioned, you must be careful with Varga. He is basically very sly; a faux bonhomme.³

1. Sante de Sanctis (1862–1935), Italian psychiatrist and psychologist, professor of experimental psychology at the University of Rome (1920). In 1919 he became director of the psychiatric clinic and, in 1929, of the neuropsychiatric clinic in Rome. See the note in *Zeitschrift* 7 (1921): 108 about de Sanctis's treatment of psychoanalysis in his lectures. Freud had frequently cited de Sanctis's works about dreams (esp. *I sogni* [Turin, 1899]) in *Interpretation of Dreams* and met him in 1925 (Jones III, 110).
2. Walter Frost (1874–?) received his degree with a work about Kant (1905), and authored works about Bacon and Hegel.
3. French, roughly, "a false fellow."

843

INTERNATIONALE ZEITSCHRIFT
FÜR ÄRZTL. PSYCHOANALYSE¹

[Budapest,] April 27, 1920²

D[ear]. Pr[ofessor].!

Interesting *misprint* on *p. 74 in vol. IV Sammlung Kleiner Schriften zur Neurosenlehre;* third-to-last word of the *note: discredition* instead of discretion!³

It should be found out whether the error appears in the manuscript itself or whether it was only overlooked in the proof (also a parapraxis, by the way).

Greetings!
Ferenczi

Just discovered a *second* characteristic misprint, on p. 76 of the same volume, ninth line from the top:

"Jung himself, at the time of [*von*] (instead of *before* [*vor*]) his illumination."⁴

F[erenczi].

1. Postcard with sender's address preprinted.
2. Date at the end in the original (the postmark reads "920 APR 28 N 4".
3. "Since I cannot allow that a psycho-analytic technique has any right to claim the

protection of medical discretion"; in Freud's "On the History of the Psycho-Analytic Movement" (1914d, n. 2., p. 64), which had been accepted for the fourth volume of the *Kleine Schriften zur Neurosenlehre* (Vienna, 1918).

4. "In the days before his illumination, Jung himself . . . carried out and published an analysis of this kind with a child" (1914d, p. 65).

844

Vienna, May 14, 1920
IX., Berggasse 19

Dear friend,

After not writing to you for so long (thanks for the misprints!), I can give you good news today. The analytic fund received a big gift from America, approximately a million crowns, through the mediation of Eitingon and as just a little something for the sixth of the month.[1] To be sure, our books and periodicals demand so much that we are still not rich, but we are protected from threatened bankruptcy, and we can hold on again for a while. Up to now I have done nothing with it except give Rank 1000 crown and Reik 500 crown monthly raises,[2] which was urgently necessary and to which you will, I hope, be agreeable.

Incidentally, I am in favor of not letting the fact be known beyond our *most intimate* circle. Eitingon himself asks that his name not be mentioned, according to a "famous pattern," which also reveals itself in the fact that the collection is being continued in America. The main contributor could be a brother-in-law and nephew of Eitingon, whom he always presented to me as a personality of the same caliber as Toni; we will gladly accept *that* similarity.

If we still get something from the other quarters—we will energetically pursue the matter with Varga—then we still have to be concerned about paper, just as important as money. Rank is taking great pains over it. My "Lectures" are supposed to be being readied at Prochaska's,[3] I am just now proofreading "Everyday Life," and I am making the necessary changes in the "Theory of Sexuality."[4]

My condition has improved; Martha is still in Hamburg, Annerl is going to Berlin Monday morning to Ernst's wedding with Lucie Brasch, which has been set for Tuesday the 18th.

I spoke to Dr. Munro again before he went to Budapest. In London he had confirmed a rumor about you, which caused Jones much concern. I reassured Jones immediately.[5] In America it was once said during the war that I had committed suicide. Strongly exaggerated, as Mark Twain said.[6]

The things that were sent from your society are really good and attest to strong talent. The editors thank you very kindly.

I am eager also to hear personal things from you.
Kind regards to you with wife and daughter.

Yours,
Freud

1. Freud's birthday.
2. For their activity with the Verlag.
3. The printer in Teschen.
4. Freud 1916–17a, 3d rev. ed., and 1901b, 7th expanded ed., both in the new Verlag; 1905d, 4th ed., with Deuticke.
5. In 1913 Hector Munro, with Jessie Murray, had founded the Brunswick Square Clinic in London, which also trained lay analysts and for that reason was harshly criticized by Jones (see, e.g., Jones to the Committee, November 2, 1920, Butler Library). On the day before, Freud had written to Jones: "I saw Munro . . . and really got the impression he was not very reliable. . . . Dont [sic] believe in the Ferenczi rumour" (*Freud/Jones*, p. 380). Regarding the rumor, see letter 846.
6. See letter 364 and n. 3.

845

Vienna, May 25, 1920[1]

Dear friend,

In her book "Psychoanalysis 1919,"[2] Barbara Low quotes a sentence of yours: Our unknown repressions lead us ever further in the way of repression.[3]
Where is it? I need it for "Beyond," on which I am now working.

Cordially,
Freud

1. Postcard.
2. Barbara Low, *Psycho-Analysis: A Brief Account of the Freudian Theory* (London, 1920). Freud had received the book the day before (*Freud/Jones*, May 24, 1920, p. 383). Barbara Low (1877–1955) was a teacher who became interested in psychoanalysis through her brother-in-law David Eder. She was analyzed by Hanns Sachs in Berlin. As a founding member of the British Psychoanalytical Society, she was very active in the Association; she supported Anna Freud and Edward Glover in the Freud-Klein controversies.
3. Sentence in English in the original [Trans.]. Freud subsequently cited Low's "Nirvana principle" in *Beyond the Pleasure Principle* (1920g, p. 56) and a passage from Ferenczi's "Stages in the Development of the Sense of Reality" (1920g, n. 3, pp. 41–42), but not the sentence referred to here.

846

Budapest, May 30, 1920

D[ear] Prof[essor]!

A very unpleasant depression in the last week kept me from letter writing. Munro is certainly not correct with his communication, but he seems to have been well informed about something having been planned. I have known for about a week that the gentlemen in the Medical Society here will announce the termination of my membership. That happened yesterday with the greatest publicity.[1] I was, naturally, not there. The newspapers published the list of those expelled.—Naturally, I didn't allow myself to be disturbed in work, but I reacted organically, as usual, with a transitory heart condition. Animosity toward $\Psi\alpha$ was certainly the reason why this treatment was accorded only to me by the "professors." The basis for it was flimsy: acceptance of the professorship and the (untrue) assertion that I also gave lectures elsewhere.—

The news about the Eitingon fund has pleased me *uncommonly*. It was the only, certainly shining point of light; otherwise only thunderstorms and threatening clouds everywhere, whose description I would rather pass up.[2] Dr. Eisler will tell Rank everything.

In consequence of the new income, *Eisler's* offer to lend us 50 or 100 thousand at approximately 4% long term should be superfluous; at most to be gratefully put on account as a sign of working collaboration. And that I did, appropriately. Also, his last lecture here (the case that the Zeitschrift already printed) gave me an opportunity to grant Eisler the recognition he rightfully has coming to him. I hope from now on he will also come personally closer. Perhaps you will also write him a few lines in which you express yourself about his offer. He lives in V. Nádor utca 5.

I hear that you and Fräulein Minna have remained the sole inhabitants of the big apartment. It must seem strange to you. I have still been able to greet Ernst by telegram.

You ask about personal things from me. It is, briefly stated: ten hours a day socage, then fatigue—otherwise only the constantly alarming novelties. Healthwise (with the above exception), well, Frau G. remains true to me in good and ill. The presence of her daughter has a calming effect on her.

Summer plans not quite assured. Room reserved in *Altaussee* for July 15, but residency permit denied by Graz for the time being.—What have you decided? A rumor had you coming to Aussee. Would that be possible? I would be infinitely happy.

I definitely want to go to The Hague, would also like to take Frau G. along, *but I haven't received a reply from Ophuijsen.*

I am hesitating as to whether instead of the paper on "Further Development of Active Therapy" I shouldn't rather present a communication about the explanation of convulsive tics at the Congress.[3]—The quotation by Barbara Low seems very familiar to me; but I can *not* cite the source.

Kind regards from your eager to emigrate

F[erenczi].

1. In August 1919 the Physicians' Society of the Interior Ministry had received a request to determine which of its members had "compromised" themselves during the Council Republic. The investigation was completed on April 24, 1920; on May 28 a general meeting took place at which it was decided to expel twenty-two persons, including Ferenczi. Nevertheless, his expulsion had no direct legal or professional consequences. See Ferenc Erös et al., "Ferenczi Sándor és a budapesti egyetem 1918–19-ben" [Sándor Ferenczi and the University of Budapest, 1918–19], *Pszichologia* 7, no. 4 (1987): 584–592.
2. See letter 819, n. 1.
3. Ferenczi did talk about the active technique (see letter 836 and n. 3). "Psycho-Analytical Observations on Tic" (1921, 232) was published in the *Zeitschrift*.

847

Budapest, June 4, 1920

D[ear]. Pr[ofessor]!

I hope you [are] already in possession of my letter, which I had to get to you by means of Eisler's mediation, so that now—unrelated to your last, gratifying news (fund)—I can discuss purely personal matters, which are nonetheless not uninteresting scientifically (to me); therewith I also accede to your request to write "personal things" about myself.—

Point of departure is the analysis of Frau Dr. Sokolnicka, which I would now like to summarize in more detail. You recall that she—without producing any other nervous symptoms—was incapable of achieving full sexual satisfaction with a man, so that she always indulged in self-gratification. Rank's wedding[1] made her fall unhappily in love with him, after the fact, although, where she might still have had an opportunity to do so, she was unable to love him totally. She came with complaints against you. You had turned her down only because of money matters, you see, you are such that you don't like to accept money from poor people, and out of that personal motive you interrupted her almost finished analysis.—The divorce from her husband was well on its way on her arrival and seems now to be ended. It ended with a dispute over money between the marriage partners, in which she, in part, got the short end of the stick. Nonetheless, behind the exaggerated propriety in money matters, her original inclination toward getting justice and her sensitivity in questions of money came to the fore in this dispute. From time to time during the analysis a retrospective (albeit rapidly transitory) regret about the divorce was put into words.—

The analysis here went quite smoothly in the beginning. The patient acquainted me with her prehistory and her current difficulties, allowed herself also to be given instructions and enlightenment, but actually carried out the greatest part of the work herself. From time to time, especially in the reconstruction of certain early infantile occurrences (observation of parental coitus), she believed herself to be almost finished and talked about leaving in a few weeks. But soon thick clouds gathered between us.—

Connecting with my experiments with "activity," I advised her to give up masturbation.[2] She complied; the reaction was the transitory freshening up of a little infantile obsessional neurosis—at least a hint of it. She admitted certain stool ceremonials to me. But she seems to have been inwardly enraged by this intervention, for, although she still expressed agreement in principle at the lecture about the development of activity that I gave about two and a half months ago, her contradiction of the "new method" became more and more energetic; she began to analyze *me*, compared me to Adler and Jung, called me a sadist, like Federn, and from now on suspected everything, no matter what I did, whether I spoke, whether I remained silent, of being "activity."

In retrospect I must note that, although she at first made herself generally well liked in the boardinghouse where she lives, she gradually got herself into arguments with several ladies or withdrew from them, insulted. On such occasions she was thoroughly in control of herself; it was noticeable that she wants at all costs to keep the appearance of passionless propriety *to herself* and to others.

As new material there resulted from her dreams a *very strong* homosexual (sooner perhaps virile) component. It was not at all difficult to overcome her neurotic shyness about public appearances; on my suggestion she gave a lecture in our group (which for her sake has been functioning in German all semester), which succeeded admirably, to be sure.[3] She proved herself (which I also knew from her self-analysis) to be a sensitive, especially technically talented analyst; her lecture found general recognition. At my suggestion she also wrote a very pretty analysis of a novella by Lagerlöf.[4] In all these works she acted *as though* she allowed herself to be helped by me, but did everything on her own (although she ostentatiously claimed the opposite). [That way she also wants to salvage her self-gratification in sexual intercourse.][5]

In a word: she exaggerated her femininity in order to conceal her virility. The desire to please (and a kind of erotomanic conceit about her feminine seductiveness) expressed itself from the very beginning. She also claimed, e.g., *I* had been somewhat in love with her in Vienna; and she verified this claim with indications about *the way* in which I once asked her in a coffeehouse to tell me where else one could meet in Vienna (I meant, naturally: where one could also get to see psychoanalysts outside the session). I wasn't shy about reproaching her about this character trait, which surprised her very much; but she didn't close herself off totally to this insight.—

Her penis envy expressed itself most strikingly in a dream, in which she had a penis-like long growth in place of each nipple.

The first big "conflict" resulted when she declared herself to be insulted because Frau Rózsi, whom she knew from the Congress, came for her hour directly after her and was able to ascertain either that she is neurotic or that she comes to me to learn, which, of course (after she was already with you), would be nonsense. I hastened *not* to comply with her wish to change the hour, whereby I provoked an outburst of rage in her that lasted a few days. Finally, I accommodated her and wanted to analyze the entire event once and for all, i.e., interpret it as a *repetition* of earlier (at the time perhaps suppressed) rage fantasies. That also went on for a while.—But soon she began to find fault with my *indulgence*; in every hour she found fault with something else in my technique (which she praised earlier as especially fine); but this time I remained steadfast, i.e., continued to be indulgent, let her do everything herself (which she also did gladly, without being asked); but this indulgence increased her anger even more, finally there came words like "idiot," "ass," "washcloth," "characterless," but not as "associations" [*Einfälle*], but as her ironclad conviction. I did not yield (i.e., I continued to be indulgent), until finally, today, after some weeping, she hesitatingly resumed work (which she evidently wanted to interrupt).

Lately (since the feeling of her psychoanalytic superiority with respect to me has solidified), she turned the spear around, began to anlayze *me*, called me a severe neurotic, whom her keenness would have paralyzed, counted out my analytic sins to me, my inability to work out my ideas, etc. In spite of this I remained steadfast and hope that *in the meantime* we will be able to continue working.

Now, the striking thing was (and that is the scientifically interesting thing in the matter) that my supposition: *character traits are like paranoid symptoms because they belong to the ego* also found its confirmation in the fact that the analysis of her character also allowed (slight) paranoid traits to shine through; she often dreamed of spies, during the day [she] also occupies herself too much with what others think about her; her erotomanic impulses and her virility agree very well with this sub-diagnosis.

Naturally, the case does not appear easier because of this! Her suicide threats, which appear in a questionable light through an attempt at poisoning herself (in Poland, still) and through the infantile suicide attempt known to you (jumping into hot water), command me not to give up the case. She is a very valuable personality.—On the other hand, she made a plan *to follow me over the summer and to want to take analytic lessons during the vacation as well!* This prospect is certainly *very* unpleasant to me. It costs me no slight mastery to remain philosophical with her bickering; but I want to have peace and quiet in the summer. Unfortunately, I did not protest immediately, out of an excess of caution; she was just then at her unhappiest. I told her only that I can't give her any date, and admitted that the analysis can also continue in the fall. That is unbearable to her; she feels abandoned here, her means, as mentioned, have become smaller, she can't earn money here (as I told her) because of the language difficulties. So I got to talking about whether (if she has no trust in me) she doesn't want to go to you again; but she is (you will say: thank God) much too insulted by you. N.B. I later corrected this to the extent that I said this only on account of her material situation and offered myself in further assistance, as befits my tactic of being mild with her.—As a supplement to her characterization, this much: she recognizes only one single analyst; you are he. She feels herself to be superior to the others, without exception. Despite her *real* talent, I see herein a pronounced grandiose idea.—

That is how matters now stand. Now, where is *the personal* in all this, you will ask. The answer is that the patient has this time diagnosed something correct in the doctor. With her observation sharpened by the neurosis, she has guessed that my "laziness" in working cannot[6] be explained by the (justified, by the way) tiredness. There is something else neurotic behind it.—Naturally, I must report to you once more about my married life.—

You must recall the tragic circumstances under which I sealed my marriage.[7] The effect did not express itself acutely; I did not seem to take the coincidence of my wedding with that death at all tragically. Today I know that that happened at the expense of my ability to love. I found dissatisfaction in the whole first year of our marriage: the sexual performances were more duty than they were libidinous for me. For about two months (so, beginning exactly from the time of year of the wedding) the *unconscious year of mourning* seems to have run its course for me; my love for Frau G. is warming up again, although she has become neither younger nor more beautiful in the interim. *Elma's* arrival seems to have accelerated this process. I think I was still secretly waiting for her. But the comparison was dropped in favor of Frau G.

Perhaps I am partially indebted to my patient for the ripening of these insights. For the time being, I doubt whether she has also cured my "laziness" in the process.

Despite my analytic mildness, the patient seems to have guessed that scolding and bickering out of the mouth of a woman affects me as *extremely* unpleasant. That has to do with the most painful and effective traumas of my childhood, the relationship with my strict mother.[8]—

Now, I ask you, however, to express yourself with regard to the case of Frau Sokolnicka 1.) diagnostically, 2.) therapeutically-technically. If you also give me a good idea about the defense against her summer plans, my gratitude will increase significantly.

N.B. A dream, which I am not able completely to comprehend, goes somethign like this: I. An elderly gentleman lies on a divan, two spies stand in the room; the gentleman acts as if he were her (the patient's) friend, but at the same time he seems to be in league with the spies, who are hostile to the patient. II. The patient's liquor bottle (in the boarding house) is half empty (stolen by someone); there are many (odd) liquor glasses which don't belong to a set there. Frau *Karpinska*[9] lies on the divan and seems to know about the matter, but she smiles about it, as if someone had committed the theft as a joke. The patient remonstrates with her.

She analyzed the first part as follows: *I* am the old gentleman on the divan, because I am a neurotic, like her cousin's boyfriend, who is accustomed to lying on the divan in her home. (I.e., *she* is actually *my* analyst.) She wasn't able to say anything about the spies.

It occurs to me, however, that *Karpinska* is also lying on the divan (that will certainly be a different Pole, namely she, herself), and that she committed this one theft. She is also inwardly not quite sure whether it is she or I who is sick, that is to say, a criminal. The liquor business reminds the patient that she was invited to our table and that we probably expect revenge from her.—I didn't understand much more about the dream. Do you have any idea [*Einfall*] about it?

Right! The patient also tries to project her grandiosity onto me; she claims I want to outdo *her*; that's why I am so slavishly subservient to you. The idea is good, but not new to me. What do you think, is this complex still active in me?

Now I have written enough, at least in terms of quantity. But you have called the spirits![10]—Please, would you share with me your opinion about the questionable points, in not too long a time, if possible.—

Today I received a dear card from *Ernst* with a drawing of his young wife.

Fund, securities, Congress, English journal—and everything else—naturally interest me uncommonly.

Yours,
F[erenczi].

Postscript. (June 5).

Both the factual and the personal require a later supplement. As is shown by today's session, the patient is beginning to accept my method;

today she recognized the origin of her reactions from the prohibition of masturbation, accepted the interpretation of her dream, etc.

As a supplement to the personal I dreamed during the night according to this psychic balance sheet: "Elma kisses me; I find that sweet. She shows me (or I give her, in any case she holds in her hand) a handkerchief, in the middle of which the imprint of the lines of a piece of writing can be seen. I am ashamed." Interpretation: So, a remnant of transference to Elma, after all; I must also admit to her (and to you) that, since my marriage, a one-time (incomplete) indiscretion occurred (with a psychically insignificant girl, category: upstairs maid at my brother's). The improvement of my sexual relations with Frau G. is directly connected to this case.—The handkerchief played a role in this case (as it did in Sokolnicka's nasal secretion ceremonials).—I will spare you further details of the interpretation.—

Kind regards,
F[erenczi].

1. On November 7, 1918; see letter 774, n. 5.
2. Cf. "Technical Difficulties in the Analysis of a Case of Hysteria" (Ferenczi 1919, 210).
3. See letter 836 and n. 10.
4. "Selma Lagerlöfs Herrenhofsage" [Selma Lagerlöf's Manor House Tale], lecture of November 21 in the Hungarian Society; it was not published, to the best of our knowledge.
5. Brackets in the original.
6. After this word, the word "only" [nur] has been crossed out in the original.
7. The death of Géza Pálos on their wedding day.
8. Cf. Ferenczi's letter to Groddeck of December 25, 1921: "Was I demanding, or was my mother—the mother of eleven living children, of which I was the eighth—too strict: by my recollection it is certain that as a child I experienced too little love and too much strictness from her" (Ferenczi/Groddeck, p. 36).
9. Luise von Karpinska (1871–1936) was from Poland (Zakopane), as was Sokolnicka. Karpinska was a professor of psychology at the University of Lodz.
10. "Herr, die Not ist Gross! / Die ich rief, die Geister / werd' ich nun nicht los!" [Lord, the need is great! I will not rid myself of the spirits that I summoned], from Goethe's ballad "Der Zauberlehrling" [The Sorcerer's Apprentice] (1798).

848

Vienna, June 17, 1920
IX., Berggasse 19

Dear friend,

For a long time I haven't got to work any more before my epistolary duties,¹ and in these last two weeks I didn't get to writing letters either. Ernst was here with his wife, Lux, who won everyone's heart, and didn't leave until day before yesterday. Yesterday was the last Society session, discussion about Jaspers's well-known work,[2] international audience, Demol (Geneva),[3] v. Wyss (Zurich),[4] a young Dutchman, a doctor from Australia, Frau Dr. Kempner from Rheinau,[5] who deferred Sachs very well over the summer, etc. After a nine-hour torment I was still able to give a philosophic-critical lecture.

So I can only tell you today how much your communications interested me. First, I congratulate you on the public honor which has been done you, but which will, let us hope, not touch you very much.[6] Then, I am pleased about the favorable turn in your personal affairs and ask you to give your dear wife cordial greetings from me.

Unfortunately, I won't come to Aussee; Anna is going to Rie's for a few weeks. You will certainly still get to enter the country. On July 30 I am going to Gastein with Minna, and at the end of August with Anna to Holland by way of Berlin—Hamburg. It will cost a fortune.[7]

Don't let yourself resolve to take Sokolnicka along on vacation. She has always been repugnant to me, despite undeniable talent. Her ψ analysis seems quite excellent to me; the therapeutic prospects should be good, for you know that she always held onto her men, not out of love but rather out of unsatisfied anger, and you gave her the possibility of finally getting this affect out. But she also won't let go of you so soon. I don't consider her a paranoia but a basically disgusting person; she doesn't want to see now that she has already become an old woman. In that there is little to be done, and the development of quite crazy [*meschuggener*] traits can hardly be impeded.

We have a bright sky here at the moment. Verlag business, foreign interests, very good, the new fund in Eitingon's hands has excellent terms. Everything about this second Toni is so solidly reliable. There is so much to report here that I won't begin with that at all.

In June–July I want to finish the "Beyond," which has yielded some strange sequels, which I would like to tell you about. I am quite well and capable of accomplishment. You should verify your quotation, or else I won't be able to cite it, which would be too bad.

Next time, when I have my big letter paper again,[8] much more from

Yours truly,
Freud

1. In responding to the birthday congratulations on May 6.
2. Probably *Allgemeine Psychopathologie für Studierende, Ärzte und Psychologen* [General Psychology for Students, Physicians, and Psychologists] (Berlin, 1913, 1920). Karl Jaspers (1883–1969), German philosopher. In 1916 he became a professor of psychology at the University of Heidelberg, and of philosophy from 1921 on; he was prohibited

from teaching from 1937 to 1945. In 1948 he became a professor of philosophy in Basel. He was a leading representative of existentialism.

3. Possibly Victor Demole, credited by Grinstein with two works in the *Index of Psychoanalytic Writings*.

4. Possibly Walter Heinrich von Wyss (1884–?), author of works about affectivity and psychophysiological phenomena, among others.

5. Salomea Kempner (1880–194?), from Plock in Poland, assistant physician at the Cantonal Insane Asylum in Rheinau, Switzerland. In 1921 she moved to Vienna, and in 1923 to Berlin, where she participated in the work of the polyclinic. In 1925 she became a member of the Berlin Society, and in 1936 a training analyst. She disappeared in the Warsaw Ghetto. See Mühlleitner, *Lexikon*, pp. 181f.

6. "Ferenczi has now been excluded from the Budapest Medical Society as a penalty for his Bolshevik professorship. As a consequence of the still existing letter censorship I could only congratulate him on the honor" (Freud to Abraham, *Freud/Abraham*, June 21, 1920, p. 313).

7. On July 17 Anna drove to Aussee to visit the Rie family. After a surprise visit from Lajos Lévy and Ferenczi in Vienna, on July 30 Freud and his sister-in-law Minna went for recuperation to Gastein, where he finished writing *Group Psychology and the Analysis of the Ego* (1921c). His wife, Martha, went to Goisern in the Salzkammergut with the Hollitschers. After a month in Gastein, Freud and his daughter Anna traveled to Hamburg to visit his widowed son-in-law Max Halberstadt and his two grandchildren. Eitingon went also, and all three then traveled to the Congress in The Hague, arriving on the morning of September 7.

8. This letter is written on small sheets.

849

Dr. Ferenczi Sándor
idegorvos
Budapest, July 18, 1920

Dear Professor,

It was my intention, even in the event that we spend our vacation in Hungary, to go to Vienna for a few days in order to be together with you after such a long time. Unfortunately, I didn't succeed in getting the Hungarian passport. The exit prohibition is valid only for Austria; the journey to Holland by way of Czechoslovakia–Germany is permitted to me. In any case (namely, in case of a possible intervening hindrance), I asked *Jones* by letter if he would have an official letter written to the English High Commissioner in Budapest in the interest of my Congress trip. I will also send a similar letter to Ophuijsen, through whom I expect permission to enter Holland.—The exact discussion about our meeting in The Hague (date, place, etc.) must therefore be left out this time. Instead I must ask you to instruct me as precisely as possible about the plans you have made so that I can adjust myself accordingly.—

In consequence of the travel difficulties mentioned, I lengthened my stay in Budapest until August 1. *In all probability* at the end of July we are going to *Siófok* on the Plattensee, where I plan to write the Congress lecture and another paper. More exact address not necessary. Herr L. Stein, a relative of our new member *Kolnai*, is the director of Siófok.—

Whether we will surely ever again spend the summer at a beautiful point in the world, close to each other, calm and satisfied? Now it seems almost impossible to me! Even the trip to Holland, despite its closeness in time, is an improbability to me.—

I must complain about the unkindness of fate in general. Our correspondence, which is supposed to substitute for talking things out, is becoming more and more halting. In the end one has so much to say that one doesn't begin with it at all—all the more since what is essential can only be communicated orally. I feel morally and intellectually isolated, cut off from the psychoanalytic movement. At least in *this* connection I would like to restore contact in one way or another. Perhaps Rank will take the trouble to inform me about what has happened since our meeting (Easter). Young Schächter will take care of transmitting the letters. (From this end I have nothing new to communicate to him.)—

I am working less now, six to seven hours a day; enough for this terrible heat; bathe two to three times a day.

Nothing new to report about the family. My wife and Elma send you kind regards.

Kolnai, who will look you up before you leave Vienna, can report about everything to you in more detail.

Kind regards,
Ferenczi

850

Vienna, July 18, 1920
IX., Berggasse 19

Dear friend,

With the current limitation in traffic, I am writing you only about the one practically important matter which has to do with our Congress in The Hague.

A sum of 50,000 crowns has been designated to make it possible for members of the Berlin, Budapest, and Vienna groups to participate. Berlin finds that, because it is less distant, it can claim only half as much as both of the others. We calculate that we can offer each of six to seven members from Vienna and Budapest a travel expense allowance of 3,000 crowns. The Dutch will look after room and board for approximately twenty guests. When I depart for Bad Gastein on the 30th of the month, I will leave the money with Rank, who won't leave Vienna before the Congress.

So, I ask you to let him know who from your group is claiming the subsidy—functionaries and lecturers should be given first consideration—, and to deliberate with him about the best way to deliver the sums to the members.

I hope the distribution of passports to Holland will encounter no difficulties with you as well, on account of the scientific purpose. Your reply to Rank can go the same route as this letter, by way of Kata.—

Otherwise, I would have so much to tell you that it excludes communication by letter. The "Beyond" is finished; you didn't help me cite your statement. I have disgustingly much to do up to the last day, am also correspondingly taken to task, and the heat is awful. On top of that, I am posing for a young sculptor[1] whom Eitingon has sent, for a bust, which promises to be very good, however.

Annerl left for Aussee yesterday; Martha is going to Goisern with Mathilde and Robert. I have obscure information about your efforts regarding the stay in Aussee. Everything is again in the hands of Rank, of whom we can use a few more.

I hope still to see Lajos Lévy here.

Kindest regards to you, Frau Gisela, and Elma.

Yours,
Freud

1. David Paul Königsberger, from Vienna. Freud received the original on May 6, 1921, as a gift for his sixty-fifth birthday. A copy of the bust was presented to the University of Vienna by Jones and unveiled in the Arkadenhof on February 4, 1955 (Jones III, 25).

851

Dr. Ferenczi Sándor
idegorvos
Budapest, August 15, 1920

Dear Professor,

Now we can at least correspond with each other. Who knows when and what hindrances are yet to come; let us hope not before our meeting in The Hague, for which I and my wife are making all preparations.

Since August 2 we have been living in a small, not very luxurious, but quiet boardinghouse with ample cuisine in the immediate surroundings of Budapest (in the "Cool Valley").[1] I keep office hours once a week in the Nagydiófa utca. I was no longer able to withdraw from continuing the treatment with Sokolnicka.

Since I have been here I have been writing the Congress lecture and a paper about "tic." I didn't receive the invitation to the Congress course[2] from the Berlin group (dated June 21) until today. I replied in the affirmative.

The boardinghouse is near the insane asylum where Hollós is chief physician of the section.³ We see each other often and want to do a psychiatric work together.⁴ You see, I came upon the idea that the organic psychoses, which demonstrate so much similarity to the functional (narcissistic) psychoses, are actually *cerebral pathoneuroses,* which form *their* symptoms on a similarly regressive path as the functional ones. The cases speak in favor of the correctness of this assumption. So, almost all psychoses should be considered as belonging to the narcissistic group. If I remember correctly, that also corresponds to your expectations.

The weather was very nice. We took a few little hikes in the mountains. There are scarcely any mushrooms in this dry summer. We thought about you and Gastein often. We would be very happy if we could still receive news about your itinerary before your departure.

N.B. How do you want to participate in the Berlin course if you still want to go to England after Holland? Or is the Berlin week supposed to take place *before* the Congress? That seems improbable to me.—

Many kind regards from both of us to Fräulein Bernays and to you.

Yours,
Ferenczi

Address: Nagydiófa u. 3.

1. Hüvosvölgy, a residential section of Buda with many villas.
2. Abraham had planned, for the week after and, later, for the week before the Congress, a course of lectures in Berlin with contributions from Freud, himself, Ferenczi, Jones, Ophuijsen, Rank, and Sachs. The whole plan was dropped after Freud withdrew (*Freud/Abraham,* June 10, 1920; June 27, 1920; July 16, 1920, pp. 311–316).
3. The big municipal clinic for nervous diseases, called the "yellow house" by Hollós, where, as chief physician, he worked with analytically oriented therapy. In 1925 he was relieved of this post on account of his Jewish origins, and described his experiences in a 1927 book, *Hinter der gelben Mauer,* [Behind the Yellow Wall] (German ed., Stuttgart, 1928).
4. Hollós and Ferenczi, *Zur Psychoanalyse der paralytischen Geistesstörung* [Psycho-Analysis and the Psychic Disorders of General Paresis] (Ferenczi 1922, 239), published in the Verlag in 1922 as a fifth supplementary volume to the *Zeitschrift.*

852

[Bad Gastein,] V[illa] Wassing
August 20, 1920¹

Dear friend,

Happy from the bottom of my heart to have a letter from you! One learns modesty. Berlin course is off, supposedly because I didn't want to take part. But I have had enough torment, have utilized the recuperation here to write "Group Psychology." I am pleased that you are working again

(I differentiate between torment and work). I will let you know my itinerary as soon as I know it myself. Looking forward to seeing you and Frau G. in The Hague.[2]

Yours,
Freud

1. Postcard.
2. The Sixth International Psychoanalytic Congress took place from September 8 to 11 in The Hague under Ferenczi's chairmanship. Freud spoke on "Supplements to the Theory of Dreams" (1920f), Ferenczi on "The Further Development of the Active Therapy in Psycho-Analysis" (1921, 234). Ernest Jones, already acting president of the IPA, was elected its new president, and John Flügel was elected general secretary. The *International Journal of Psycho-Analysis* became the official organ of the English-speaking groups within the Association. See the report of the Congress in *Zeitschrift* 6 (1920): 376–402, with Ferenczi's detailed introductory paper and the presenters' abstracts of their own papers. After the Congress, Freud and Anna intended to go to England, but Anna did not receive a visa, so they took a trip through Holland with van Emden and van Ophuijsen. On September 28, Anna went to Hamburg to see her nephews, while Freud returned, via Berlin, to Vienna, where he arrived on September 30 (Jones III, 28).

853

Vienna, October 11, 1920
IX., Berggasse 19

Dear friend,

In the Dutch tumult it was altogether impossible to talk intimately with each other. I also have no intention whatsoever of letting our private correspondence dissipate in the circular writings of the Committee, no matter how purposeful the latter may prove to be.[1] So, I am writing to you today as a reopening, and I thank you, first of all, for the beautiful coffee machine which was sent by your sister-in-law from Rome, which will become functional as soon as the glass which was damaged in transit is replaced. Second, for your intention to present me with a ring, which I learned about by chance. I ask you to renounce it for the time being and perhaps to reserve it for my 80th birthday.—

Furthermore, I will share with you the fact that we seem to be on the brink of a very favorable turn in our business relations. The sale of the Verlag to Kola[2] could become possible, assure Rank's immediate future, give us back half a million in cash, and permit the greatest possible expansion of our activity, so that we can publish what we want and what seems worthwhile. Naturally, we haven't closed the deal yet. Rank still has to present a balance sheet, and the drink can still be spilled, 'twixt cup and lip.[3] There then remains the satisfaction that a big businessman like Kola has viewed the International Verlag as not a bad business, and we haven't lost anything.

Next Thursday I will have the pleasure all morning of functioning as an expert witness in the trial of the Commission for Military Violations of Duty against Wagner-Jauregg and others. It has to do with the war neuroses. I will naturally treat him with the most distinct benevolence. It also isn't his fault.[4]

Curiosity: I spoke with the London Rothschild, the real one,[5] for an hour. He has a not yet fixated paranoia and refused treatment accordingly.

It is strange with me. As if my scientific interest had gone to sleep since the Group Psychology. I am also limiting the number of my patients with the clear intent of tormenting myself less. Will it be feasible?

Just read your paper on tic. It seems very ingenious to me, quite correct and thoroughgoing, also forward-looking, but an actual high point or punch is missing.

Our household is very small, two persons, like at the beginning. Kind regards to you and Frau Gisela.

Yours,
Freud

1. It was decided at the Congress by the members of the Committee that they would also remain in contact by means of regular circular letters. The first such circular letter had been written by Ferenczi on September 20. Gerhard Wittenberger and Christfried Tögel, eds., *Die Rundbriefe des "Geheimen Komitees*, vol. 1, *1913–1920* (Tübingen, 1999); vols. 2–4 forthcoming.

2. Richard Kola (1872–1939), who was considered to be the richest man in Austria, had offered to buy the Verlag, to incorporate it as an independent division of his finance, newspaper, and publishing concern, and to appoint Rank to head this division. But the negotiations fell through, and in the circular letter of March 11, 1921 (Butler Library), Rank finally stated that the matter had "gone to sleep" (kind communication from Gerhard Wittenberger). Jones mentions the episode (III, 31), but erroneously attributes the collapse of the arrangement to Kola's death.

3. "Zwischen Lipp' und Kelchesrand / schwebt der finstern Mächte Hand" ['Twixt lip and cup / the hand of the dark powers hovers]; from a poem (1802) by Johann Friedrich Kind (1768–1843), which derives from an anecdote by Aristotle, according to which a legendary king was killed by a wild boar as he put his cup to his lips.

4. In reaction to incidents in which the so-called electrotherapy of war neurotics had been so gruesomely applied that deaths and suicides had ensued, in December 1918 the Commission for Military Violations of Duty, to which Freud's university friend Julius Wagner-Jauregg also belonged, had been founded. Among the charges there was also one against Wagner-Jauregg himself, who subsequently resigned from the commission. The hearings pertaining to his case took place on October 14 and 16, 1920. Freud, the principal expert witness on the first day, limited himself essentially to representing the differences between his and Wagner-Jauregg's theoretical and clininical views, and refrained from any criticism of "friend Wagner." Kurt R. Eissler, *Freud und Wagner Jauregg vor der Kommission zur Erhebung militärischer Pflichtverletzungen* (Vienna, 1979), p. 55. Wag-

ner-Jauregg was absolved of all guilt and fully reinstated. See Magda Whitrow, *Julius Wagner-Jauregg (1857–1940)* (London, 1993).

5. Possibly Lionel Walter Rothschild (1868–1937), son of Sir Nathan Meyer Rothschild (1840–1921). The author of zoological studies, he studied in Cambridge and Bonn, and in 1899 became co-administrator of the British Museum.

854

Dr. Ferenczi Sándor
idegorvos
Budapest, October 16, 1920

Dear Professor,

The private correspondence, freed of the ballast of official communications,[1] can only gain in intimacy and caliber. Here we can report to each other—next to personal communications—about germinating ideas (scientific ones), as in the good old times. To be sure, I can't be of service with such germs just today.—The tic paper was an attempt to think through to the end the idea of the sensory-narcissistic origin of tic. I am very curious to learn something new about this from you. I presume you already have a different, better solution to this question. My main "punch" was intended to be the identification of the motor expressions in tic and catatonia. I would be sorry if it didn't land.

How were you able to learn anything about the purchase of the ring? Who committed the treacherous faulty action [*Fehlhandlung*]?—Since I have had a pronounced heart palpitation for several days, I would not like to postpone carrying out the plan until your 80th birthday; I don't trust myself to make such far-reaching plans.

Apropos 80! My mother will be 80 years old on December 11; the whole family will visit her in Nyiregyháza, where she is living with her eldest daughter. I haven't seen her for six years. It seems that I found a complete substitute for her in marriage.

I am curious as to whether Dr. Radó, who is going to Vienna shortly with his wife, can arrange something with Rank (who will in the meantime, let us hope, already be directing in Kola's $\psi\alpha$ Verlag). If Vienna should really become a center of $\Psi\alpha$, then you would have to subject your decision regarding my person to a revision. Radó will report to you about Budapest and the decision.

I am curious as to how young Kolnai will establish himself with you in the Society. I am sorry that I had to lose him so soon after his discovery.

My hours are full. I was only able to send a few to others. The people cling to names.

Too bad the coffee machine arrived broken. We also have one, which functions very well. Unfortunately I must pass up my favorite alkaloid for the time being.

Kindest regards to you and Frau Professor.

Yours
Ferenczi

Enclosed *(for Rank)* a postscript to the annual report[2] and a few reviews[3] left lying, which I found hidden in my portfolio.

1. Which were being treated in the circular letters.
2. Ferenczi's review of "Allgemeine Neurosenlehre" [General Theory of the Neuroses] for the *Bericht über die Fortschritte der Psychoanalyse in den Jahren 1914–1919* (1921, 236).
3. The reviews have not been identified.

855

Vienna, October 31, 1920
IX., Berggasse 19

Dear friend,

The circular correspondence certainly gets the material away, but doesn't bring any time; so it happens that I can't reply to you until this Sunday. I am suffocating in practice during the week, business with Rank, emergency responses, etc., and I am being totally paralyzed by the five hours of English conversation with still inadequate means of hearing and speaking (the chaps all whisper or mumble, and I will never learn this foreign language properly anymore).

With all the foreign currencies, which, when recalculated, yield fantastic numbers, I am now earning about 2/3 from the peacetime situation.

With patients it is going with me the same as with you in Budapest. The locals make themselves hard to get rid of. No, Vienna has no qualification to become a center. The matter with the $\psi\alpha$ section is thoroughly questionable, and I would basically be done a favor if it never came into being.[1] It is not suitable for Vienna; a raven shouldn't wear a white shirt![2] You are also too optimistic in the Kola affair. I doubt whether he will pay Rank the salary that he may request. The business of the Verlag is going very well, incidentally. I am eagerly awaiting the first balance sheet, which is now being prepared.

Kolnai was generally well liked in the session the day before yesterday. Meanwhile, he didn't bring much more than a transcription of sociology in our $\psi\alpha$ dialect, and Radó, who spoke after him and in a very astute talk really undertook an application of analysis to elucidate sociological phenomena, outdid him by far. The impression of Radó was so favorable that we are looking forward to being obliged to keep him. The Dubovitz woman upbraided his character, the way he is supposed to have shown himself in the difficult times in Budapest.³ What is your opinion about this?

I intentionally refrained from going more deeply into your tic, because, as on earlier occasions, I am striving not to put anything in the way of your independence. Also, connections to the trains of thought of others don't usually set in with me until very late.

I consider your palpitations to be less tragic and am only in doubt as to which part I should ascribe to the Basedow and which to the motionless lifestyle. I also wasn't serious about the 80. I am hoping for earlier redemption. On the problem of the ring, however, the question is probably appropriate: Don't you have any other things to be concerned about?

I greet you and Frau Gizella cordially and hope for favorable development of this side correspondence.

Yours,
Freud

1. "The [psychoanalytical] society is at present trying to obtain a psycho-analytical department in an extension of the general hospital. This is very much against my wishes, because if we got it, it would have to be in my name, I could devote no time to it, and there is no-one in the society to whom I could entrust its management" (Freud to Abraham, *Freud/Abraham,* July 4, 1920, p. 315). The Vienna psychoanalytic "ambulatorium" would not be opened until May 22, 1922.

2. A simile used by the German dramatist Christian Dietrich Grabbe (1801–1836).

3. Radó had been a high-ranking functionary during the Council Republic (see, e.g., letters 802, 810, 812, 814). He was known for both his sharp mind and his sharp tongue.

856

INTERNATIONALE ZEITSCHRIFT
FÜR ÄRZTL. PSYCHOANALYSE¹

Budapest, November 20, 1920²

Dear Professor,

Indisposition, which has already been mostly overcome, hindered me in replying to you. Hope to find time and mood for it tomorrow (Sunday). By the way, you are—so I hear—also being informed by Dr. Lévy.—The weekly report³ also had to be let slip and is supposed to be sent tomorrow or the day after.

Meanwhile, kind regards.

Yours,
Ferenczi

1. Postcard with sender's address preprinted.
2. Date and place at the end in the original.
3. The circular letter, which was already being sent at weekly intervals.

857

Vienna, November 28, 1920
IX., Berggasse 19

Dear friend,

Lajos has informed me as much about the state of your health as has become clear to him, and in so doing has certainly reassured me. I see that it is the same as it was years ago, and I understand it just as little as I did then. No doubt you are working it out hypochondriacally, strong suspicion that you have some real nucleus or other.

Your work and the conditions in your city certainly play a part in the causation. It is in any event very sensible of you to limit yourself to seven hours. I wish I could do it, too.

My apparent lack of participation has to do with the fact that I now write no letters at all during the week. The six hours of English a day make me so tired that in the evening I am of no use for anything more. At the same time, nose and throat are still tormenting me, the "smoking cure," which I apply in a thoroughgoing manner, is of no use this time. My bladder is also reacting terribly to the prevailing cold. But otherwise I am healthy and am resisting the annoyances.

If you want to send me more precise data about place and time, give us also the possibility of participating in your mother's 80th birthday by means of a telegraphic greeting. My mother is between 85 and 86, which not infrequently causes me concern. It is incautious to get so old. To go over to the other side: in March Martin is expecting a son, the way it should be after wartime.[1]

If it amuses me, I can count myself as rich. In consequence of the worthlessness of the crown, I now possess 2.4 million. So, I am a millionaire, but I didn't come to the million, it came down to me. In reality, my worth amounts to about a quarter of what it was before the war. It happens that I work hard for a whole week in order at the end to be poorer than before, because in the meantime a decrease has taken place in the value of the foreign currencies. Others are doing much worse here.

Rank had the happy idea of suggesting to you that you should spend the days before Christmas here. Qu'en pensez-vous? It will, of course, not be as nice as it was that time in Brioni, but it would still be something.

I can well imagine your dear wife and guardian as a merciful sister. Is Elma still with you?

Kind regards,
Freud

1. Anton Walter Freud, born on April 3, 1921, later became a chemical engineer in London.

858

INTERNATIONALE ZEITSCHRIFT
FÜR ÄRZTL. PSYCHOANALYSE

Budapest, December 6, 1920[1]

Dear Professor,
My mother's birthday is on December 11. Address:
Ferenczi, Nyiregyháza

Kind regards,
Ferenczi

1. Postcard with sender's address preprinted; date and place at the end in the original.

859

Dr. Ferenczi Sándor[1]
Budapest, December 21, 1920

Dear Professor,
This magnificent letter paper is naturally a remnant of the luxurious prewar times. I found two full boxes of it in an old desk, where it was left lying as a disdained gift; today they are again being honored.

I want to relate to you the further course of my indisposition.—After long hesitation I decided to look up, in addition to Lajos Lévy, another colleague, who is equally reliable but not prejudiced by amicable relations, and who would certainly, and did, tell me the truth. His—in regard to the heart, which was most suspect, very reassuring—information laid the main basis on the hypochondriacal part of the condition; there followed momentary psychic relief, which then also had a favorable secondary influence on the real condition of heart weakness. The neurotic part of the malady can be traced back to intestinal disturbances, which should, for their part, be interpreted as autoerotic compensation for the not completely satisfied libido. I have seen a whole series of similar cases originate (under the same conditions).

Unfortunately, this process moved along with a really significant introversion of libido (which is characteristic for the inventor of the name "pathoneuroses"),[2] so that I am only gradually approaching the psychic condition before falling ill and have also not yet now regained complete desire for work. It surprises me that, in the time of the depression, I was also able to give analyses and to lead sessions of the Society without patients' and colleagues' noticing anything in me.

Two smaller works, one with the title "Something Unesthetic about Esthetics,"[3] the other a "Contribution to the Understanding of the Sense for Mathematics,"[4] the text of which has not yet been written, should be the first tests of my ability to achieve. If it works with these, then the "bioanalytic" essays will finally get their turn.

In Nyiregyháza I found my mother to be in an astonishing intellectual freshness, also quite well physically. It was a real "family day." All nine living children[5] were present, even brother Siegmund from Berlin with wife and child. Your telegram arrived punctually and made the jubilants especially happy.—

After our departure we learned that the celebratory mood was disturbed by a disagreeable event; my nephew Berti's father-in-law, a rich and respected landowner of 64 years of age!, has been attacked and beaten on account of a bagatelle.—The rest is silence.[6]

I am please to have heard favorable reports from Margit Dubovitz about the state of your health. The rejection of the American invitation[7] is very agreeable to me. America should continue to fulfill her duty by sending you dollar-patients, but your health shouldn't be put to the test, no matter how great my trust in your bodily vigor is.

Rank has invited me several times to Vienna for the days around Christmas. But since the little detour to Nyiregyháza together with the loss of honoraria has cost 10,000 crowns, I have to pass it up this time. I do hope to see the whole Committee at Easter; that way, to be sure, I will miss the opportunity once and for all to talk things out properly with you. If the Committee meeting is postponed until Whitsun, I will certainly come to Vienna for Easter, or to whichever place you are residing.

I think sadly about the times when I was able to be with you every few weeks and spend half of the summer with you.

Most cordial greetings, and extend the best New Year's wishes from me and my wife to all the members of your family.

Yours truly,
Ferenczi

1. Name preprinted in green.
2. "Disease- or Patho-Neuroses" (Ferenczi 1917, 195).
3. The work was either not written or lost.

4. Posthumously published notes ("Mathematics"; Posthumous, 301).

5. Zsigmond, Ilona, Maria, Jozsef, Gizella, Sándor, Károly, Lajos, and Zsofia. Those deceased were Vilma (1879), Miksa (ca. 1905), and Henrik (1912).

6. The words "disturbed," "disagreeable event," "father-in-law," "has been attacked and beaten," and "The rest is silence" are all written in English in the original [Trans.]. The last quotation is from *Hamlet*, V, 2. The fact that this incident is described in English is evidently owing to the censorship of the mails.

7. "The Professor received an offer for America from his nephew [Edward Bernays], which would obligate him to be there for half a year from the beginning of January, for the purpose of giving lectures and treating patients, with a guaranteed sum of 10,000 dollars. But the Professor disputed having to pay the costs of transportation and lodging out of this amount itself. These conditions seemed unsatisfactory to the Professor, and he wired his refusal" (circular letter from Rank, December 5, 1920, Butler Library).

860

Vienna, December 25, 1920
IX., Berggasse 19

Dear friend,

You give me the desired excuse for a Christmas letter by reminding me how different and how much more beautiful it was years ago. Intercourse also requires a certain continuity, and when one sees one another only at great intervals, it works like an intraurban telephone conversation, where one also never knows what to say. I find the passage in your last Rundbrief[1] excellent, where you say that we are all doing badly, but our cause is doing well. It really is such that the cause is consuming us and that we are being dissolved in it, as it were. And it is probably quite right that it is, only I would have wished for the younger, second analytic generation to be able to resist the solution for a while longer.[2]

I don't understand anything about your illnesses and satisfy myself with the constantly repeated confirmation that they don't mean anything serious or threatening.

I accept my own sicklinesses [*Kränklichkeiten*] as unavoidable phenomena of aging, but I am very set against secret intentions of celebrating my birthdays. I presume that something of the sort, which is masked as a Committee meeting, has been planned, and I strongly request that you abandon it, otherwise I would have to place all my hope on Jones, who has already explained that he can't travel at that time. At the beginning of May I am also immersed in work, and there is little to be got from a meeting in Vienna altogether. I am in favor of a trip over Whitsun or a Committee meeting in place of the Congress in the last days of September. I would probably not come to the Congress in Berlin, should it be set for 1921. Abraham is very stubborn, but for me, not convincing.[3]

Both of your announced works make me very curious. In the new year I will undertake the Group Psychology, the draft of which is now with Rank. I have spent these last three months in a kind of dull meditation, exhausted by the six hours of English a day.

The American offer has shown in its paltriness how hollow, indeed, all assertions of popularity, esteem, and the like are.

On March 10 I am expecting Dr. Frink,[4] who is said to be a capable person, for analysis. Dr. Stern,[5] who departed in the beginning of December, was uninteresting, nothing special. Holidays should always appear in twos, like the Carabinieri.[6] On the first, only the tiredness comes out. Such is the case this time, fortunately.

Anna is home again, and was allowed to set up the two boys' rooms, since the three boys have finally flown away. Young life sprouts here and there.

Kind regards to you and Frau G.

Yours,
Freud

Cheers, 1921!

1. Circular letter of December 21 (BL). The German designation, *Rundbrief*, will henceforth be used [Trans.].

2. Evidently a play on words, involving the similarity in German between "dissolved" *(aufgelöst)* and "solution" *(Lösung)* [Trans.].

3. The next Congress had been set for Berlin. Since everyone except Abraham wanted to postpone it until 1922, that is what happened. The seven members of the secret Committee met at the end of September 1921 in the Harz Mountains in Germany.

4. Horace Westlake Frink (1883–1936) was in analysis with Freud for three periods in 1921 and 1922. He was an instructor at Cornell Medical College, a founding member, and, favored by Freud, president (1923) of the New York Psychoanalytic Society. During Frink's analysis, Freud intervened in favor of divorce from his wife, Doris Best, and of marriage to a rich former patient, Angelika Bijur. This intervention and the later outbreak of a manic-depressive psychosis in Frink prompted severe criticism of Freud. See Lavinia Edmunds, "His Master's Choice," *Johns Hopkins Magazine* (April 1988): 40–49.

5. Adolph Stern (1879–1958), American neurologist and psychiatrist of Hungarian extraction, received his M.D. from Columbia in 1903. He had been a member of the American association since 1915 and was its president from 1927 to 1928. He was an analysand of Freud's and Frink's, and president of the New York Society, 1922–23, 1924–25, and 1940–1942. He was probably the first American analyst to go into analysis with Freud. Adolpdh Stern, "Some Personal Psychoanalytic Experiences with Prof. Freud," *New York State Journal of Medicine* 22 (1922): 21–25; Arnold Eisendorfer, "Adolph Stern, 1879–1958," *Psychoanalytic Quarterly* 37 (1959): 149f.

6. According to a humorous popular saying, Carabinieri (members of an Italian army corps, whose name was derived from the weapon known as a carbine) always appear in twos, because one can only read and the other can only write (kind communication from Patrizia Giampieri-Deutsch).

861

INTERNATIONALE ZEITSCHRIFT FÜR
ARZTLICHE PSYCHOANALYSE

Budapest, January 6, 1921

Dear Professor,

I couldn't imagine a more beautiful way of celebrating your birthday—if not with calendarlike punctuality—than by finding ourselves together in a small common Whitsun trip. We have completely abandoned the plan to offer some "surprises" or other, especially after such tendencies became known "by chance." I will propagandize for the idea of a Whitsun trip in the next Committee letter; let's hope Jones can also get away at that time. Let's also hope that in the meantime there won't be any passport difficulties for me. As a meeting place one should consider first and foremost Salzburg or Munich, or perhaps a place in the German or Austrian Alps; secondarily, one could also (for a short time!) decide on South Tirol, although the currency conditions should not be left totally out of consideration. If you should allow yourself a somewhat longer vacation for Whitsun, then I would gladly decide to spend this time with you; for that I would lop off something from the summer vacation. Naturally, I would also like to know something about your summer plans. You see: I don't want to give up the illusion that, despite the many changes—war—impoverishment—marital duties—it will still be possible to maintain our old summer meetings or trips.

There is little to report about myself that is new. My still wavering health did not stand up well to the increased demands of the holiday dinner parties. But I have almost completely overcome the acute gastrointestinal catarrh without the aid of a physician.

At the end of this month, Sokolnicka is supposed to move to Paris, where for the time being she will find lodging with her brother who lives there. Intellectually, she has developed well here. She was always very smart, but here she has developed into a capable force in the Society and through her own work, as well as by sloughing off a certain hardness in her character (in the analysis). Lately she also visited Hollos's section and proved herself to be a remarkably perceptive interpreter in psychiatry as well. Her earlier relations with Rank don't permit her to turn directly to him; she is also "bräuges"[1] with him. But I think we should show some goodwill toward her; therefore I offered to request the *Verlag Direction* to recommend her officially in Paris to the translator of the "Interpretation of Dreams" (Dr. Jankelevits)[2] and to the publisher Payot, and, if warranted, also place a notice in the next issue of the Zeitschrift about her move. As far as her neurosis is concerned, we have come many layers deeper, but the suicidal intent, which she still carries around with her, is still present. She also feels insulted by Rank's behavior at the Congress; I think that an amicable, semiofficial letter, signed by Rank himself (and by you?) and sent to the above Paris addresses, would take much of the danger out of her lethal intentions. Copies of the letters mentioned could be sent to me, so that I can show them to Sokolnicka. The last weeks of her analysis could be much enhanced by these letters. Perhaps the Verlag will also write to *Flournoy* on her behalf and ask him to use his connections in France to her advantage.

Many thanks from me and my wife for the pretty New Year's card.[3]

Yours truly,
Ferenczi

Please show this letter to Rank, or—if you prefer—share its content with him.

1. See letter 816, n. 8.
2. Serge Jankelevitch (1869–1951), translator of noted authors such as Semjon Dubnov, Georg W. F. Hegel, Robert Michels, and Friedrich von Schelling. He is the author of *Mishnah: le Shabbat* (Paris, 1947). He was one of the early principal translators of Freud into French, though not, however, of *The Interpretation of Dreams*.
3. The card has not been found.

862

Vienna, January 16, 1921
IX., Berggasse 19

Dear friend,

Our postal strike is supposedly over, and I am able to answer your dear letter of January 6. Let's take the non-personal matters first. I am ready to notify Jankelewitsch, to whom I am writing today anyway, about Sokolnicka's arrival, and to recommend her, which probably won't do much good, since the fellow has not yet up to now sent me any demonstration of his art and has not pardoned me for a reprimand about his earlier behavior. The Verlag will send off the recommendation to Payot as soon as she has arrived in Paris. Before that it doesn't seem quite sure. But we could also send this introduction direct to you. I will talk to Rank about it. Besides, we *both* don't like her, whereas you evidently have a weakness for the disagreeable person.

As regards my birthday, I am depressed by the fact that it is being treated as if it were my last instead of the 65th. If I had my druthers, it shouldn't take place at all, and the Committee meeting should be handled independently of that date. Its feasibility will depend first and foremost on Jones's mobility. A Whitsun trip would be quite all right by me, only I can't accommodate more than four days, one before and one after the two holidays, because I will have foreigners who lie in wait for every day, who can't extend themselves, and whom I have to exploit as irreplaceable as long as they are here.

My worth has, to be sure, increased by several million through the treatment of foreigners, but, in view of the worthlessness of our crown, this state of affairs is comparable to complete impoverishment. This becomes immediately evident as soon as one has to buy something. I possess approximately a quarter of what I possessed before the war. Certainly others are doing much worse, but I don't know how long I will still be able to earn, and providing for my wife, who even in the civil service would have a right to a full pension after thirty-five years, gives me the greatest difficulties. I also have to help constantly with Martin and Oli and Max; none of them can earn what he needs. Hence, I have to hold back with vacations during the work year. I still don't know anything about summer plans. Perhaps I will again go to Gastein from July 15 to August 15. With the intention of meeting, you should strive for Aussee at the proper time. If South Tirol is not easily accessible, we could also go there. One can't do anything for certain. Already this time we were expecting the flap about German-Austria; now it seems to be postponed again.

I am now making an effort to work out the Group Psychology, which is known to you.

In an American patient I was able to look unexpectedly deeply into the mechanism of jealousy paranoia and found something new, which seems to be of fundamental importance.[1] I always read your Rundbriefe with the greatest pleasure.

Kind regards to you and Frau Gisela.

Yours,
Freud

1. See "Some Neurotic Mechanisms in Jealousy, Paranoia, and Homosexuality" (1922b), probably written by Freud in January (Editorial Preface, *Studienausgabe* 7, p. 218) and presented at the Committee meeting in September.

863

Vienna, February 6, 1921
IX., Berggasse 19

Dear friend,

While Elma takes tea with the ladies, I want to write a cordial greeting to you and Frau Gizella. I don't have anything to give with it, for you receive my books through the Verlag, and I don't have anything else; I also never go shopping.

A few days ago I received a telegram from Philadelphia from a certain Harris, [asking] whether I can't send over an English-speaking analyst from somewhere or other under the guarantee of $5,000 for the first year of the practice (exact words in the next Rundbrief).[1] Martha doesn't give me any peace; that would also be an opportunity for you that one oughtn't to miss. But I am against it for many reasons:

1.) I think that you don't know enough English to analyze in the language, which, from my experiences this year, is beastly difficult;

2.) you can, if you want, also go to New York in your own name, without support;

3.) you evidently face a great improvement in Budapest;

4.) you would feel bad in America without pupils and friends, in an extremely unfree society, which really knows only the hunt for the dollar;

5.) we can't do without you here, without losing Hungary and all that is being accomplished there;

6.) I would never see you again and learn nothing from you, etc., etc.

If Frau Rozsi should be surprised that I haven't written her on the anniversary of Toni's death, tell her that I also didn't write to Hamburg on January 25. If she believes in personal continuity and reunion [after death], etc., then explain to her that I, probably the next in line for such reunion, am prepared to extend greetings and take over tasks.

I now have free afternoons, since I am expecting foreigners on March 1, but I am not working on anything, without reproach.

Cordially,
Freud

1. Harris was a well-to-do businessman who had had a psychoanalyst come to treat him personally for $5,000 and, upon the success of the treatment, wanted to pay a bonus of $10,000 (Rank's *Rundbriefe* of February 13 and March 1, 1921, Butler Library).

864

Budapest, February 7, 1921

Dear Professor,

The specific reason for my letter of today is as follows: Yesterday, a painter whom I know telephoned me with the news that some Englishmen would like to speak to me about matters of psychoanalysis, that is to say, to make my acquaintance. They are invited to tea with him, and might I also come. I found there the president of the Danube Commission, Admiral Troubridge,[1] with his son, and was already hoping for a lucrative analysis—but it turned out that the ones actually interested are two ladies,[2] 1.) an analysis begun by a pupil of Jung's, whose healthy human intellect was not able to deal with the Jungian conception of symbolism, and 2.) a Miss Skinner, a beginning student of philosophy, who is supposedly interested only from a scientific point of view. After a one-and-a-half-hour colloquium, in which she was the examiner and I the examined, she declared herself no. 1) very relieved and freed of many doubts, no. 2) that she would like to be analyzed by me, especially since, after a short stay in Vienna, she will come back to Budapest. She vehemently repulsed my objection that my English was insufficient for that.—Nevertheless, she asked me also to give her a recommendation to take along to Vienna to you, which I did. It would not be unpleasant for me if you could send this student back to me, since this would be the only chance to improve my finances. In any case, I ask you for a report as to whether you shouldn't rather keep her yourself—and, if not, a hint as to how high a fee *I* could charge her per hour.

When I get a chance I will tell you about the difficult and changeable vicissitudes of the character analysis with Sokolnicka (for it has to do with such). If one confronts unpleasant character traits from the same standpoint that is as affect-free as possible, as one does with neurotic symptoms, then the analysis of them can yield much that is of interest—one can learn very much about the psychology of the ego. My "weakness" for the patient is limited exclusively to the recognition of her unusual psychoanalytic talent.

The possibility of a Whitsun trip with you—if only for four days—sounds very promising to me; we have actually never had a proper talk for years. This Whitsun vacation could be very beautiful. Please do as you like regarding time and place. I am counting on it!

The Group Psychology on which you are now working is, unfortunately, known to me only by name and from the little information you gave me on a beautiful Sunday walk. I eagerly await its publication.

A short contribution on the subject of jealousy (not of jealousy paranoia): jealousy very often has the peculiarity of being based on both hetero- and homosexuality, i.e., the partly narcissistic wish *that other people don't love one another, but that each should give his love to him (the jealous one)*; jealous children want, e.g., to separate father and mother from each other, in order to keep both father's and mother's love for themselves. In the process, the propensity for separation is often more pronounced than the wanting-to-be-loved.—That is probably nothing new for you; but I was too caught up in the specific homosexuality theory of jealousy.

In the Rundbriefen, Rank ought to be somewhat more considerate of Abraham's sensitivity, perhaps rather in the tone than in the content of his admonitions. Abraham's intent to resign[3] shows that it is hard for him to

bear recriminations. His bona fides and his diligence certainly remain elevated over all doubt.
Many kind regards.

Yours,
Ferenczi

1. Ernest Charles Thomas Troubridge (1862–1926), English admiral, former commandant of the British Mediterranean fleet. From August 1919 on he was president of the International Danube Commission in Budapest.
2. Written in English in the original.
3. In the previous few months Abraham and Rank had got into various disputes with each other; one main issue was the inadequate management of the Berlin Society on the part of Liebermann. Abraham wanted to dismiss Liebermann; Eitingon and Sachs were opposed. Abraham conceded to the majority, but was of the opinion that, "should the occasion arise again," he would "resign the directorship" (*Rundbrief* of January 31, 1921, Butler Library).

865

Budapest, February 11, 1921

Dear Professor,

Excuse me for burdening you again with the case of Sokolnicka.

I can summarize her case briefly by saying that she is now about to move to Paris after an analysis of one year. Actually she has suffered and is suffering not from a typical neurosis but from pathological sensitivity, compulsion to masturbate, and inhibitions regarding the male sex. Her suppressed outbreaks of rage incline her to turn against her own person (1. suicide attempt, probably already in earliest childhood [she jumped into boiling water],[1] 2. failed attempt to poison herself, after she [as she says, because of inability to pay] was not further analyzed by you).—Last root of the whole thing: rage against her father, who presented her with a sister.

Her character has become significantly milder here; she has made good progress (despite countless strong protests against my analysis). The only thing that I was unable to get across to her is that she should give up the idea that *you* (i.e., interrupting the analysis) are to blame for the fact that she had to lose Rank.

Now, I believe that we should offer her the opportunity at least to restore normal polite relations with you, without which she also cannot exist as an analyst. She is, after all, only waiting for a sign from you, without which her pride forbids her to approach you. If you want to be especially friendly with her, then you will ask her sometime to let off a little steam toward you.

But *first*, it would suffice, in my opinion, if you would communicate to me in a few friendly lines, that you are prepared to discuss her professional and personal prospects in an interview with her, who is about to take on an important new position in the West.[2] (Give her to understand right away that you hold firm to your earlier view that she may on no account continue her analysis interminably [*ins Endlose*]; she finally has to get out into life.)

Next time, more about other, more important things (Philadelphia, etc.)!

Yours,
Ferenczi

P.S. I am writing in bed (have a terrible cold), hence the hard-to-read handwriting.

1. Brackets in the original, as below.
2. The following parentheses have been crossed out.

866

Budapest, March [6], 1921[1]

Dear Professor,

I probably don't need to write any more about the case of Sokolnicka. She has, I believe, made not insignificant progress in the development of her personality; one cannot call her cured. She was a very uncomfortable patient; I became practiced in patience and consideration in her analysis. I would still be interested to know how she behaved with you. She must certainly have scolded me thoroughly.—

I thank you for the willingness with which the Verlag decided to publish my works,[2] and I thank you in the name of the Budapest group for the honoring recognition that you expressed about their achievements. In today's session I was able to promulgate your praise in a festive manner.

Today Eisler gave a lecture on, acually a review of, your "Beyond."[3] Aside from a few misunderstandings, the work is quite good and—as is always the case with Eisler—also well written. The discussion was lively.

The American's offer sounds so good in the new version that I would like to ask you to find out about the man and his offer from Frink,[4] when he arrives, and also to ask Frink whether I—especially if I practice English somewhat—would be suited for this position. We have calculated that in one, at most two years there, I could save so much that, if necessary (e.g., in case of illness!), I could live modestly on it. I would *not* be able to save that much here, not even in ten to twelve years; it is altogether questionable whether there will ever come a time here when one can put something aside.

I am very sorry that things have come so far with Brill.[5] Don't you consider me the person best suited to deal with him? He has always been agreeable with me and only recently invited me to America. In his letter he alluded to a profound vexation—about which he could tell me only by word of mouth. Shouldn't I advise him to visit you in Vienna?

Margit Dubovitz is not doing well. She is having attacks more frequently than usual, and, lately, also depressive states, etc. Her husband's condition is also not improved. How will it all end!?

Frau Kata Lévy and Rózsi are diligently attending the sessions. The latter has recently been taking three hours a week with me. She has already calmed down a great deal.

Many kind regards from all of us.

Yours,
Ferenczi

1. The day is missing in the original and is inferred from the reference to Eisler's lecture.

2. *Populäre Vorträge über Psychoanalyse* [Popular Lectures on Psychoanalysis] (Leipzig, 1922) (Ferenczi, 1922, 240), according to Freud "the best 'Introduction to Psycho-Analysis' for those who are unfamiliar with it" (1923i, p. 268).

3. "Referat über Freuds 'Jenseits des Lustprinzips'" [Review of Freud's *Beyond the Pleasure Principle*], *Zeitschrift* 7 (1921): 346–356.

4. See letter 863 and n. 1. "In the last two years" the patient "had had Frink come once a week from New York to Philadelphia" (Rank's *Rundbrief* of March 1, 1921, Butler Library).

5. Since Brill had hardly reacted to queries for months (see letter 837 and n. 4), Freud finally gave him an "ultimatum" (Rank's *Rundbrief*, January 21, 1921, Butler Library): "I am terribly sorry that . . . I have received no answer to my last serious and, I hope also, friendly letter of October 21 of last year . . . Despite my feelings of friendship toward you, there remains nothing but to assume as a fact that nothing can be done with you: an outcome of our relations that I had actually not reckoned with" (Freud to Brill, January 21, 1921, Library of Congress). But Freud and Brill reconciled again in a conversation at the beginning of September 1921 (Freud and Brill to Rose Brill, September 2, 1921, Library of Congress; see letter 882). "Brill . . . understood his neurotic attack" (Freud to Eitingon, September 5, 1921, Sigmund Freud Copyrights).

867

INTERNATIONALE ZEITSCHRIFT FÜR
ÄRZTLICHE PSYCHOANALYSE

Budapest, March 28, 1921
Easter Monday

Dear Professor,

I understand completely your displeasure over my American inquiry; but if you consider all the circumstances you will perhaps find my idea less crazy. Naturally, if in your authoritative experience, so much knowledge of English is necessary for the analysis of an English-American, my application for this position will drop by itself. But you must find understandable my striving somehow to increase the—despite the large rise in honorarium (300 crowns)—still inadequate sources of income by means of foreign currencies. My total worth today amounts to about 3 to 400 thousand Hungarian crowns, thus, less than what we need in a single year. My American idea was based on the large difference in the exchange rate. If I had been able to save 5,000 $[1] in one to two years there, then I would—in contrast to my proletarian state of today—have become the pure capitalist; for it is out of the question that I would be able to save *here* in the foreseeable future. So, I didn't mean to retire with a pension after these two years, but rather at least bring along a reserve in the capital to be saved, while now I am living only from hand to mouth, and at the moment when I get sick—or, at the latest, after a year of work disability—will stand vis-à-vis du rien.[2] And since I had no hope of getting German-speaking Englishmen or Americans to Budapest for analysis (which would naturally be preferable to me, for countless reasons), I had to concern myself with this, as I see it, illusory prospect.

Perhaps you have been informed by Rank about our summer plans. I wrote to him today that we would like to spend the month of August in the neighborhood of Mödling[3]—perhaps in the Brühl—; we are considering spending the first weeks of September in Aussee, where we are being enticed by the prospect of meeting you there. I hope at least that your plan to stay in Aussee after Gastein is still in operation. I believe your summer plan is as follows:

July 15–August 15   Gastein
August 15–September 15   Aussee
September 15–October 1   Hamburg and Committee-Congress, in North
   Germany.

It is, by the way, not out of the question that, in order not to change domiciles so often, we will go to Aussee right away. *We don't know the particulars.*

Fräulein Anna was so kind as already to be helpful to us so often with her rich experience in matters of hotel, boardinghouse, and scenery—, to be sure, in the last few years we have not been at all in the fortunate situation of visiting the places that she has championed. Perhaps she has still not lost patience with us and will give us a few good addresses. We would like to go somewhere nicely situated in the mountains, where one can eat well and work peacefully. If you don't get to Aussee, then this place can be somewhere in *German-Austria* (in the only country where our money still counts for something).

I hope you are already in possession of my Groddeck review,[4] and am curious as to whether you can use it in this form.

The Rundbriefe are the main event in my isolation from the world at large. I can't imagine at all why we didn't introduce this institution already earlier. Aside, naturally, from the work of the peerless Rank, I find the fight that Jones is waging in England on behalf of $\Psi\alpha$ to be praiseworthy.[5]— An idea, which I would only like for the moment to express to you, is as follows: The lazy Dutch are mired in their good life and aren't participating properly. So I, for the moment personally, would like to get into closer contact with the only one among them who really amounts to anything: *Stärcke*. You see, I hope that in the foreseeable future he will be able to be accepted into our Committee. Before I bring this idea to the Committee, I wanted to communicate it to you in private.

Many kind regards.

Yours,
Ferenczi

P.S. I would like to ask you for Stärcke's exact address.

1. Position of dollar sign, written as a pound (weight) sign in the original.
2. French, "face to face with nothing."
3. Near Vienna.
4. A discussion of Groddeck's *Der Seelensucher* (*Imago* 7 [1921]: 356–359; Ferenczi 1921, 238). Ferenczi defended the crudely comical novel; the Swiss Society, for instance, had protested against its publication in the Verlag and wanted to prevent its introduction into Switzerland (Rank's *Rundbrief* of February 21, 1921, Butler Library).
5. Jones was fighting against an unauthorized English Freud edition and was embroiled in a trial which was supposed to be instituted against a purportedly "psychoanalytic" book for endangering morals (Jones's *Rundbrief* of March 21, 1921, Butler Library). Ferenczi "pursued with intense interest the courageous fight" that Jones was leading "against the legion of our enemies" (*Rundbrief*, April 1, 1921, Butler Library).

868

Vienna, April 17, 1921
IX., Berggasse 19

Dear friend,

The letter that I am answering here is the one of March 28. It contains nothing, to be sure, that would have required a speedy reaction, but you can draw a conclusion about my state of affairs from the time interval. With nine hours of work (four of which in listentins to English), correcting proofs, reading manuscripts, carrying out correspondences, there is really not much of me left.

Your motives about wishing different, foreign practice are certainly unassailable; your project will not become more feasible by dint of that. I have written to Jones to the effect that he should think about directing patients to Budapest: I am taken care of for a long time to come. Naturally, my security plunges when the crown increases. What brings foreigners to Vienna is purely and simply the currency.

I was certainly surprised that you could express the worries of a retiree. We had decided among ourselves that one doesn't worry too much about the future, lives and works as long as it goes, and doesn't feel responsible for anything else. What you fear, especially, is also not anything at all current.—

Our summer plans are also not firm. July 15 to August 15, Gastein with Minna, while Mama and Anna go to Aussee. A Berlin [lady] friend is supposed to bring little Ernst from Hamburg along to us there. (Both children are said to leave much to be desired, healthwise.) But what will happen afterward has not been determined. I would like for the four of us to go to Brioni, where we had three such beautiful days in 1914; then, from September 15, North Germany, Congress. The latter should be paid from the monies of the endowment.

Your project with Stärcke has greatly interested me. But one knows so little about him personally and has so little opportunity for contact. Such a requirement would probably have to be connected with an intervention which elevates him from his inferior financial position. It should be considered.

Two weeks ago today, on April 3, Martin welcomed his eldest child, a nice boy, who will be given the name Anton and will probabaly also answer to it.[1]

I am very satisfied that you have decided about the two books of collected papers.[2] You will find great approbation. Our Verlag is also maintaining itself very well materially.

I greet you and Frau Gisela kindly; I believe I recognize a working out of Elma's influence in your America fantasies.

Yours,
Freud

1. Named after Anton von Freund, according to Freud's wish (Freud to Kata Lévy, April 4, 1921). See letter 857 and n. 1.
2. Only a one-volume anthology was published (see letter 866, n. 2). In the case of the second volume, it seems to have been that "collection of his purely technical [psychoanalytic] medical writings" whose publication the Verlag would pursue "as soon as more favourable times make it possible" (Freud 1923i, p. 268).

869

Budapest[1], April 1921[2]

sending heartfelt congratulations[3] in old love and devotion = ferenczi family

1. Telegram.
2. The date is missing, or was illegibly stamped in the postmark.
3. On Freud's birthday.

870

Vienna, May 8, 1921
IX., Berggasse 19

Dear friend,

I thank you kindly and may certainly ask you also to give my thanks to the Society, which has no other address. Likewise to Frau Gisela and Frau Elma. One should not venture to draw any conclusions about the intimacy of our relations from the intensity of our intercourse.

Eitingon was here for a few days and unveiled the bust by Königsberger,[1] which now, as a ghostly threatening bronze doppelgänger, is awaiting definitive exhibition in some nook or cranny in the house. Its resemblance [to me] is being judged in various ways; there is no doubt about its artistic worth. Naturally, I was taken in; I really thought Eitingon wanted to have it for himself, otherwise I wouldn't have sat for it last year.

I am now terribly old, and notice that one generally also accepts this as such. People are pressing me to limit the hard work, and I feel how I am succumbing to suggestion, and how, despite the contradiction of the demands of reality, I am preparing myself for a leisurely workday of only six or seven hours. In any case, not until from fall on.

Nonetheless, I have already experienced the triumph of analysis and the perseverance of the best and truest friends. In that area, therefore, not much can happen to me. In the family there could be more happiness, or more opportunity for it. One must say, the earlier one dies, the more one remains spared having to experience necessary trouble firsthand.

On March 13 of this year I very suddenly took a step toward really getting old. Since then, the thought of death no longer leaves me at all, and sometimes I have the feeling that seven organs are vying with one another for the honor of being allowed to make an end to my life.[2] There was no real occasion for this except that Oli departed for Romania on that day. But I haven't succumbed to this hypochondria, but rather observe it in a coolly superior way, somewhat as I do the speculations in the "Beyond."

It was noticed the last few days that in early times you were much more mobile and made your way from Budapest to Vienna much more easily. I know that it was also much shorter. Goslar and Hildesheim[3] certainly also meet with your approval. Our summer is also very uncertain, except for Gastein.

Cordially,
Freud

1. See letter 850 and n. 1.
2. Perhaps a paraphrase of the Greek pentameter "Seven cities are vying with one another for the honor of being Homer's birthplace."
3. The localities in the Harz Mountains which had been suggested for the meeting of the Committee in the fall.

871

MAGYARORSZAGI
PSZICHOANALITIKAI EGYESÜLET
(Freud-Társaság)[1]

Budapest, Whitsun Monday,
May 16,] 1921

Dear Professor,

From the lines of both of your letters to which I have to reply, there resounds in my ears only the "warning" that you are supposed to have received on March 13. I presume a heart condition, to the production of which your use of nicotine may have made a prominent contribution. As an experienced hypochondriac, I can only tell you that also very unpleasant subjective symptoms—whether organically based or not—can be dissipated by a small lessening of your all too strict and strenuous lifestyle. I can immediatly give you a current example. Two days ago I awakened—to be sure, after a not completely hygienic sexual act—with distinct pains in the aorta; on the next day I was weak and almost incapable of work. After *one* good night I was able, yesterday—Whitsun—to climb a mountain in the heat of the sun without difficulty; on this vacation day I also felt a clear desire to work and pangs of conscience about the scientific activity postponed again and again; the ideas only pressed in that way.—So, I think: You should set aside a few hours already *before fall*, and begin to carry out the plan—"decided between us"—not to bother about the later future, with some lazing about. What you have been accomplishing for decades is really abnormal. Nine—ten—eleven hours of analysis a day, and only then the scientific work! And the many, many cigars on top of that!!—You told me once that you have to feel some bodily unpleasure in order to be stimulated to work.—Perhaps this was the method adapted to your—up until recently, undoubted—*youthfulness*. Try it for once with the more conventional mode that we others, who age early, always used to apply: rest, and wait until the accumulating, unoccupied libido seeks and finds material for work. But you must finally, once and for all, be considerate of your "poor Konrad."[2] At most, you, too, for once, will get to sense the feeling of boredom, which is evidently still unknown to you. That should be quite "healthy."—So I ask you once again not to wait until fall with your work limitation.

Naturally, I thought a great deal about whether I shouldn't visit you on your birthday. Hypochondriacal misgivings, which also—as you may have noticed—were accompanied by a certain anxiousness in matters of money, held sway over my unquestionably ardent wish to see you. The trip would have cost me, along with the lost earnings, approximately 10 to 12,000 crowns. Stupidly, one allows oneself to be intimidated by the magnitude of these sums, even though in real terms they don't mean more than 100 to 120 crowns before the war.

Our summer plan is approximately as follows: We will ask Rank to get us a good boardinghouse in Mödling or Hinterbrühl, in which we would like to spend the month of August and half of September. Perhaps I will utilize the peace and quiet of such a place for some scientific work. In the second half of September I would like to join you, so that I cannot again spend only the time close to you that is overfilled with business and scientific discussions. But you must tell me honestly whether I won't stand in your way, that is to say, in the way of your family matters. It would be sufficient for me if I can talk to you for one to two hours daily (and the long trips). I would kill the remainder of the time one way or another.—In that way we could again conjure up the illusion of the beautiful peace trips of olden days—if only in a more modest form.

Please forgive me for the bad ink; it's a holiday; I wasn't able to get any other.

Many kind regards from us all—and once again the request to take care of yourself.

Yours truly,
Ferenczi

1. Preprinted letterhead: Hungarian Psychoanalytic Association (Freud-Society).
2. See letter 131 and n. 2.

872

[Budapest,] June 6, 1921[1]

The members of the "Hungarian Psychoanalytic Association" (Freud-Society), who gathered for a banquet on the occasion of the bestowing of the literary prize to Dr. Róheim,[2] send Professor Freud their most devoted and cordial greetings.

S. Ferenczi

[Additional signatures:]

Dr. Hollós	Róheim
Rózsi Eisler	Olga Hollós
Dr. Eisler	Bébi Róheim
Sándor Radó	Felszegy Béla
Elisabeth R.	Révész Frau G.
Dr. Feldmann	Frau D. S. Pfeifer
Dr. Pfeifer	Dr. Imre Hermann

1. The date is at the end of the lines, which are written in Ferenczi's hand.
2. Róheim had received the prize (see letter 758, n. 1, and Freud 1919c) for applied psychoanalysis, given for the second time, for "Das Selbst" [The Self], *Imago* 7 (1921): 1–39, 142, 179, 310–348, 453–504; and as a book in the Verlag, and for his Congress lecture, "Über australischen Totemismus" [On Australian Totemism]. August Stärcke received the prize for medical psychoanalysis (see Freud 1921d).

873

[Budapest,] June 16, 1921[1]

Dear Professor,

In questions of symbolism I feel more secure when I also ask someone else. Should you approve this little postscript to "Bridge-Interpretation,"[2] then hand it over to *Rank* for the Zeitschrift.

Thanks and regards.

Ferenczi

1. The date appears at the end of this message, which was written on a piece of notepaper.
2. Probably "Die Brückensymbolik und die Don Juan-Legende" [The Symbolism of the Bridge and the Don Juan Legend] (Ferenczi 1922, 242); cf. "The Symbolism of the Bridge" (Ferenczi 1921, 233).

874

[to an unknown patient]

Vienna, July 8, 1921
IX., Berggasse 19

Dear Madam,

Please go to my friend Dr. S. Ferenczi, Nagydiófa utca 3, who is also especially knowlegeable about such conditions.

Sincerely,
Prof Freud

875

INTERNATIONALE ZEITSCHRIFT FÜR
ÄRZTLICHE PSYCHOANALYSE[1]

Budapest, July 11, 1921

Dear Professor,

This time I only want to wish you a happy, peaceful holiday. Perhaps you will have time and leisure in Gastein to write me a few lines about how you are. I am better, for the moment. In the beginning of August we hope to arrive in *Tegernsee* (Bavaria), Hotel Bayrischer Hof. What is your program for September?

Kind regards from both of us!

Postscript: The state of my health wobbly.

1. Postcard with sender's address preprinted.

876

B Gastein
July 19, 1921
V Wassing[1]

Dear friend,

I haven't written to you for a long time; I also, to be sure, waited for an intimate letter from you that didn't come. In its place came a letter from Lajos, which, in its matter-of-factness and assuredness, was able to calm me completely about the state of your health. He relates the recent wobbliness to Elma's departure; who knows if he isn't right. The endlessness of the demands of the libido!

Your work and that of your group has a very successful year behind you. You have heard this confirmed from many quarters. We can all be gratified by the progress of this work year. The propaganda has developed uncommonly, the Verlag has worked well, the journals are again at their peak. I didn't participate much personally, the Group Psychology was already in essence finished in September, and what was added is not well done. The work, nine hours a day, among them four to five in English, was rather too much for me. In the end it turns out that I don't bear it badly, and it had the advantage of making me at least nominally so rich that I don't need to deprive myself and my family of anything in the summer. The inflow of foreigners, especially of pupils, is so great that I hope next year to be able to make Rank and Reik secure as well. If it weren't for the language difficulties, we would have been able to divert a part of the increase to Budapest a long time ago. Perhaps a beginning can be made in the fall.

Although I am still inclined to regard every year and every month as the last of my existence, I still can't report about the beginning of a decision about the technical mechanism of the endgame. None of the seven organs is getting serious with its claim. I have also not gotten any stupider, only more indolent. In this vacation I am working on—nothing.

You ask about my September program. Seefeld in Tirol until about the 15th, then on to Hamburg—I don't know whether alone or with my wife—and then to the meeting, which still awaits further definition. Until then I still hope to hear from you often, so that room remains for all appointments.

I greet you and Frau G. cordially.

Yours,
Freud

1. The words "B Gastein" and "V Wassing" are written by hand above and below Freud's standard letterhead (IX., Berggasse 19).

877

Nyiregyháza, July 21, 1921[1]

Dear Professor,

They called me here on the 16th of the month to perform the last medical services for my 81-year-old mother, whose heart weakness can no longer be counteracted. Her decline is rapid. The house physician thinks that everything will be over in one to two days, and, unfortunately, I have to agree with him.

We are keeping her under the effects of morphine. In the interims she suffers greatly and is completely clear, intellectually. I, myself, am better, evidently because I have no time left over for myself.

Kind regards from my wife and from your

Ferenczi

Address: *Budapest*

1. Postcard.

878

MAGYARORSZAGI
PSZICHOANALITIKAI EGYESÜLET
(Freud-Társaság)

Budapest, July 24, 1921

Dear Professor,

Now I would like to write you the long-heralded "intimate" letter. Unfortunately, I have enough material for it. We buried our mother, who died on Thursday morning after an indescribable death struggle, in Miskolcz on Friday. I was opposed to the transfer, but the rest of my brothers and sisters wanted to respect fully my mother's presumed wishes in this regard. Immediately after her death I had (after a dose of Adalin) the hypnagogic hallucination that at the burial, the coffin would fall out of the hearse and the corpse would tumble out of the coffin. Psychoanalytically seen, certainly an ambivalent fantasy: revenge up to the grave and the wish for her resurrection.—On the way to the cemetery (which is situated on a mountain), the coffin (in reality) was loaded onto a smaller car, but, because the coffin was large and was threatening to fall off, it had to be loaded onto the big car again. As the coffin was being lowered into the grave, the latter proved to be too narrow: the foot sank to the ground, but the head didn't, so that the coffin stood vertically. They had to work for an hour until the difficulty was removed.—The rational explanation for all these disturbances is that the coffin—pursuant to the regulations for the transport of corpses—was a metal coffin, whereas the ritual burials in Miskolcz usually take place in wooden coffins.—In the above hallucination, I (who knew about these things) must have anticipated these disturbances.—

The last hours that I spent all alone with the dying woman were terribly exhausting and upsetting. I had to support the dying woman, who was sitting in an armchair, and in the process I was always in the conflict between the wish to lengthen her life and the one to spare her pain. Finally, I also assisted in laying the corpse on the bed, binding up its chin, etc.—

I awakened from the sleep, induced by Adalin, after about an hour with a strong heart seizure and breathing difficulty, and from then on I was unwell until last evening, when we arrived in Budapest. Today I feel—after a good night—better.—

Now, to my illness. I find that our friend Lajos—a former patient of mine!—is, all too tendentiously, putting the psychic in the forefront; he evidently wants to pay me back in his own coin. I concede that the psychic does come into consideration. On the one hand, the organic itself can owe its existence partly to the Groddeckian mechanisms, on the other hand, the psychic utilizes what the organic brings to it for its own purposes. There is no doubt that the libido plays a part in this; an indication of this is the following: a few days ago, after a severe heart seizure, I felt so touched and loving toward my wife, who takes care of me so indefatigably and lovingly, as in the most beautiful hours of our young love. So, if my illness is also being directed by a tendency, then this can be no other than to drive the love to its old heights by producing the situation of being nurtured (certainly an infantilism). Elma's departure (which was *consciously* a relief to me) could certainly ucs. have provoked an aggravation.

But now I believe that the internist should not occupy himself all too eagerly with these things, otherwise he runs a risk of missing something or overlooking something organic. Whether psychogenic or not: he must know above all what is happening in the organism, how I produce these attacks, in order, where possible, to take out of my hand the weapons with which I (ucs.) want to commit suicide.—Heart, aorta, kidney, and lung are not healthy.—On Wednesday I want to go to Vienna to consult Dozent Dr. Deutsch;[1] I will let my further summer plans be contingent on this consultation.

The successes of the Budapest group are for me only a weak consolation for my own sterility in the last few years.

I am very happy that you, that is to say, your organism, is so briskly resisting the lesser and greater difficulties that the years bring along. Your life is of significance, not only to you and your family. You still have much to do!

I will report to you soon what is supposed to happen with me. For now, I greet you cordially and wish you well for the remainder of your vacation.

Yours,
Ferenczi

Postscript. At today's visit for a checkup, Lajos Lévy was much more in favor of the organic than before. I won't go to Vienna to see Dr. Deutsch until Friday, am considering staying there until Monday (incl[usive].). The plan from there depends on Dr. Deutsch's vote.

1. Dr. Felix Deutsch (1884–1964), husband of Helene (née Rosenbach). *Privatdozent* for internal medicine at the University of Vienna and director of a clinic for organ neuroses; one of the pioneers of psychosomatic medicine. He was a member of the Vienna Society (1922–1938), in analysis with Siegfried Bernfeld and under supervision with Otto Rank. Deutsch was Freud's personal physician, who concealed the dignosis of Freud's cancer from him out of fear that he would commit suicide, whereupon Freud, enraged, replaced him with Max Schur. In 1935 he emigrated to Boston, where he served as a training analyst (from 1951 to 1954 he was president of the Society there), and he taught at Harvard University, among other things. See Mühlleitner, *Lexikon,* pp. 72f.; Roudinesco & Plon, *Dictionnaire,* pp. 72f.

879

Bad Gastein, July 29, 1921

Dear friend,

I can't say that your letters cause me concern, but they do vex me. I recognize the justification for your critique of Lajos's assertions, and for that reason I am very happy that you want to consult an inoffensive internist, but I also see how unassuming you are when you want to find a basis for your own diagnosis. In short, I don't believe in your organic illness, whereby it should be conceded that no organ enjoys the freshness of twenty years ago, which is supposed to be the fate of people in general.

I think you are engaging in "unfair competition." Because I write to you in every letter about the prospect of death—strangely, only to you; I don't even know why I do that—, you take the cue and think you have to do it simultaneously with me—or ahead of time. At the same time, with me it is also only a project, preparation, not even preparedness, for I am still so keenly interested in many outcomes, so curious, that I am in no hurry at all, provided that I maintain a bearable form of existence. If we contemplate it further, it could be some very dark cruelty or other on my part.

So, you buried your mother, She was, as far as I knew her, a very respectable woman; she had something superior. I presume that gives a strange feeling of being alone in the world. With me, conversely, there is the fear that my mother's life force will hold out so long that one would have to keep my death a secret from her, and I feel very unfree toward her. Science is now also beginning to become crazy, in that it is giving up its best prejudices. Jones sent in the little enclosure relating to the questions raised in "Beyond."[1] I hold fast to death in accordance with law; should that also be only a comforting illusion, like immortality?

Write to me as soon as you have consulted Deutsch, although the results of this examination won't surprise me. I call out to your hypochondria, for that is what it is: In multos annos.[2]

I could leave Gastein on the 13th and go to Seefeld in Tirol by way of Innsbruck.

Kindest regards to you and Frau G.

Yours,
Freud

1. Evidently the (unidentified) press clipping that Jones had sent to Freud on July 22 (Freud/Jones, p. 432).
2. Latin salutation, "for many years."

880

Garmisch-Partenkirchen,
August 7, 1921
Dr. Wigger's Kurheim

Dear Professor,

As you may have learned from the Rundbrief and from Rank's communications about my stay in Vienna, my doctors agree that I am still not healthy, so that I belong in this spa.[1] Here I was subjected to renewed highly embarrassing examinations, the results of which are approximately as follows: the kidney is not actually diseased to the extent that it is inflamed, it is only suffering from a peculiar difficulty in concentration, which could have somehow vascular[2] (vasomotor?) origins. Structural elements are harmless, albumin minimal.—The nocturnal states independent of the kidney, caused by the not completely eliminated disturbance in nasal breathing.—The fact is that, since I am seeing to it that the nasal passage is sufficiently widened, the nocturnal disturbances have almost ceased.—Let us hope this is the beginning of a "circulus benignus."

Do you know that Seefeld is only three stops away from Partenkirchen, that we will therefore certainly see and speak to each other after August 15?! Of course, to visit you I need a "red border certificate"; but I will bring everything to bear in order to get one. As an Austrian citizen, you will get one without difficulty.

I can't describe to you in how touchingly caring a fashion the Rank and Deutsch families have exerted themselves on my behalf. Dozent Dr. Deutsch, a clever man and physician—sacrificed almost the whole day for me. I am indebted to him for much enlightenment and reassurance.

Here I was already visited by a woman from Berlin (F. Sommerfeldt) and a physician from Munich, Dr. Ludwig. I learned many interesting things from them about the ψα conditions in Munich. I will talk about them personally with you.—You might know that Frau Lou Salomé is doing analyses at Marcinowsky's (in the neighborhood of Munich).—³

It is *very hot* here. One can go out only in the morning and evening. But for me, who is supposed to rest a great deal, that is very propitious. In the room it is mostly pretty cool.

Today I received from you the corrected proofs of my "Elements of Psychoanalysis" (are you in agreement with this title?)⁴. I was ashamed that you had to put up with my stylistic and syntactic howlers. Many thanks!

On the whole, I am—as mentioned—already better. If things stay that way, I will be able to participate in the Hildesheim meeting. Possibly I will also begin work on a paper.

Kindest regards from me and my wife to you and Fräulein Bernays.

Your old
Ferenczi

1. On August 2, Ferenczi had arrived in Garmisch, in the Bavarian Alps, after making a stop in Vienna (Ferenczi's *Rundbrief* of July 12, 1921; Rank's *Rundbrief* of August 1, 1921; both Butler Library).

2. Pertaining to the blood vessels.

3. See Andreas-Salomé to Ferenczi: "What a *colossal* pity it is that it is only here at home [Göttingen] that I find out about your presence in Partenkirchen! . . . It would have been an endless pleasure for me to see you and to speak with you" (August 31, 1921, Library of Congress).

4. See letter 866 and n. 2.

881

Excursion from Partenkirchen
(unter dem Wankenberg),
August 17, 1921¹

Dear Professor,

Confirm with thanks the receipt of your letter of condolence.² Yesterday, ignoring subjective complaints, disregarding the many doctors' orders, I decided to take longer walks. Hope soon to report favorable things about condition. Too bad we can't talk with each other. We must try!

Regards to all from both of us!

Ferenczi

[Written by hand on the lower edge of the picture side:] 1020 m. above sea level. Almost a mountain tour.

1. Picture postcard: "Gschwandtnerbauer bei Partenkirchen. (1020 m.)."
2. This probably relates to letter 879.

882

Seefeld Kurheim
August 18, 1921

[. . .][1]
[ex]isting border restrictions and the laziness which exists, here, at least, there is a question as to who should visit the other first. It is magnificently beautiful in Seefeld, the cuisine is doing my wife, who came from Aussee in a rather miserable state, much good; the little one (Ernstl) is thriving excellently,[2] and for that reason I would like to make large monetary sacrifices in order to be able to stay, if we can. The hostess, you see, is an exploitative, arid, anti-Semitic goose, who acts respectable and [conveys] the feeling of being tolerated only in Paradise. Also, daughter and niece (Maus)[3] have very poor accommodations. But there is no lodging to be had anywhere, and one is helplessly delivered to the enemies.

[. . .] [Con]gress [. . .][4] probably only a peak of depression. My occult review[5] is finished. Novelties: Jelliffe[6] visited me on the last day in Gastein, an imposing swindler; Brill is coming on board on August 23 to visit Jones and me, in order to make peace with us from August 30 to September 14. I still don't know where. The (first) French translation of the Five Lectures[7] has been published. The Verlag has not sent me any more of your proofs; it would be a pleasure for me to participate. You should also let your wish be known. The title "Elements of ΨA" is perhaps too systematic.

With kind regards to you and Frau Gisela, your

Still older
Freud

1. The first two lines are missing. The page was torn and has been glued together (upside down, however), though with part still missing. It could read something like: "Dear friend, [new paragraph] Because of the ex——"
2. See letter 868.
3. Cäcilie ("Maus"), born in 1899, the daughter of Freud's sister Regina ("Rosa") and Heinrich Graf (1852–1908). A year later she committed suicide when she discovered that she was pregnant (Jones III, 86; Lisa Appignanesi and John Forrester, *Freud's Women* [London, 1992], p. 21).
4. The bracketed passages indicate that, again, one or two lines are missing, this time on the reverse of the page.
5. "Psycho-Analysis and Telepathy," on which Freud lectured at the Committee

meeting in the Harz. The text was published posthumously in an abbreviated version (Freud 1941d).

6. Smith Ely Jelliffe (1866–1945), prominent American analyst, a pioneer in psychosomatic research. He and his friend William Alanson White were also key figures as editors of, e.g., *Journal of Nervous and Mental Disease, Medical News, New York Medical Journal, Nervous and Mental Disease Monograph Series,* and *Psychoanalytic Review.* Freud was skeptically disposed toward Jelliffe, above all because of his relations with C. G. Jung. About his visit, Rank reported: "He acted very sincere, tried to get chummy, but on the next day he was seen by the Professor in Stekel's company. The Professor considers him to be a dangerous, unscrupulous American" (*Rundbrief,* August 25, 1921, Butler Library). John C. Burnham and William McGuire, *Jelliffe: American Psychoanalyst and Physician, and His Correspondence with Sigmund Freud and C. G. Jung* (Chicago, 1986); see also letter 2, n. 4, and letter 480, n. 3.

7. Freud 1910a; translated by Y. Le Lay and published by Payot. A somewhat earlier translation had already been published in the *Revue de Genève* 6 (December 1920) and 7 (January 1921), and by Sonor, likewise in Geneva (1921).

883

Seefeld, August 24, 1921[1]

Dear friend,

I was angry enough about the inept evasion yesterday. Incautiously, a visit without announcement. Now I would like to know how long you are staying, and ask you to send a telegram in advance of your next visit. I could be out for a walk in the woods. It is much nicer if you come here, to the heights, but you or your wife shouldn't forget about the possibilities of the weather. Naturally, you should come in such a way that you can take a meal with us, so, as early as possible.

Cordially, to you and Frau G.

Yours,
Freud

1. Postcard.

884

INTERNATIONALE ZEITSCHRIFT FÜR
ÄRZTLICHE PSYCHOANALYSE[1]

Partenkirchen, August 26, 1921

Dear Professor,

Our last—unhappily concluded—visit was only a preliminary trial. It wasn't until about noon that we got possession of the "red border certificate" in Scharnitz, and tried to find out if we couldn't get to see each other right on the same day. We are staying here until September 2. As soon as the weather clears, we will telegraph you (one day before our visit to Seefeld).

Many kind regards.

Yours,
Ferenczi

1. Postcard with preprinted sender's address, which has been crossed out.

885

INTERNATIONALE ZEITSCHRIFT FÜR
ÄRZTLICHE PSYCHOANALYSE

Partenkirchen, August 29, 1921

Dear Professor,

My sister (Frau Fleissner from Budapest) just wrote to me that she has turned to you with the request that you might help her son, who has taken on the name Ferenczi,[1] matriculate in the Medical Faculty of the University of Vienna; at the same time, she asked me, for my part, also to influence you in that regard.—But, unfortunately, I can *not* do that, since I consider my nephew, who has got it into his head to be a psychoanalyst, unsuited for this profession in every respect, and in addition to that, also unreliable in some respects. Incidentally, I never made any bones about this view of mine. So that we can circumvent any unnecessary upset on the part of my sister, you should perhaps not respond at all regarding the merits of the case, but have it said directly, or through me, that you will not give the requested recommendation for formal reasons.

If the weather is halfway favorable, we will be in Seefeld tomorrow, Tuesday.

Cordially,

Yours,
Ferenczi

1. Son of Gizella (see letter 362, n. 9) and Zsigmond Fleiszner (see letter 70, n. 2).

886

Partenkirchen,
[August] 29, 1921[1]

arrive tuesday early train

Ferenczi

1. Telegram (handwritten in ink).

887

Badersee, August 31, 1921[1]

We didn't want to spoil the weather for you, so today we didn't go to Seefeld, but to Eibsee and Badersee, which is so well known to you, where I proved a failure as a rainmaker; it is dazzlingly beautiful weather. Despite all that—it was very beautiful with you in Seefeld. The meeting with you, Herr Professor, also seems to have enhanced my health.

Many regards to you, to Fräulein Anna, Fräulein Mausi, Master[2] Ernest from

Ferenczi
and wife.

[In Gizella Ferenczi's hand:]
Dear Annerl—your stockings[3] are here! Come get them! If not, I will give them to your Papa in Hildesheim.

G. Ferenczi

1. Picture postcard: "Badersee with Hotel."
2. The words "Master Ernest" are written in English in the original [Trans.].
3. Reading uncertain.

888

Partenkirchen,
September 2, 1921

Dear Professor,

I would like to share our itinerary with you. On September 6 we are traveling to Munich (probably Hotel Rheinischer Hof); we want to arrive at Groddeck's at 8 o'clock in the evening.[1]

I think I should send you the enclosed letter of Frau Lou Salomé, since it gives us information about the precarious position of our friend, into which she has gotten by virtue of her loyalty to principle; and also about the real value of the work and the activity of Marcinowsky (about which, incidentally, I was never in doubt).[2] Possibly I will visit Frau Lou on the trip from Baden-Baden to Berlin, i.e., Hildesheim.

The rest of the plan for September is approximately as follows: around the 15th to the 17th we want to go to Berlin, where we will be put up at my brother's (Sigmund Ferenczi, address: SW, Dessauerstrasse 2, editor's office of the newspaper). In the meantime I hope to find out the exact time and place of the Congress.

Kind regards from both of us.

Yours,
Ferenczi

1. The first of numerous visits by Ferenczi to Groddeck, at the same time a close friendship and also mutual analytic relationship (see Ferenczi/Groddeck, *Briefwechsel*).

2. Andreas-Salomé had written to Ferenczi that she "had broken completely" with Marcinowsky and had been "decried as a Freud-slave" in his sanatorium, "for: 'Prof. Freud is behind by fifteen years' and Stekel is ahead" (letter of August 31, 1921, Library of Congress).

889

Sanatorium Groddeck.
Villa Marienhöhe.
Baden-Baden, September 9, 1921
Werderstrasse 14[1]

Dear Professor,

The surprising communication just arrived from Rank that he is traveling to the location of the Congress alone—without his wife. That requires us to arrange our trip in such a way that my wife will go from here to Vienna alone, and I will come alone to the location of the Congress. If we had known that, we would have organized ourselves that way in the first place.—

I will write to you about the up to now very favorable impressions, or—since you will soon depart from Seefeld—I would rather tell you everything personally.[2]

Many kind regards.

Yours,
Ferenczi

1. Preprinted letterhead with a picture of Groddeck's villa in the upper left-hand corner of the letter paper: "Sanatorium Groddeck. Villa Marienhöhe."

2. The members of the Committee met on September 21 in Hildesheim. They visited,

among other things, the Egyptian museum there, as well as Goslar and Schierke at the foot of Brocken Mountain, which they climbed. Along with "Psychoanalysis and Telepathy," Freud also lectured on "Some Neurotic Mechanisms in Jealousy, Paranoia, and Homosexuality" (Freud 1922b). The "Congress" lasted until the end of September. See Phyllis Grosskurth, *The Secret Ring: Freud's Inner Circle and the Politics of Psychoanalysis* (Reading, Mass.: 1991); and Jones III, 80–82.

890

Internationale Zeitschrift für
Ärztliche Psychoanalyse[1]

Budapest, October 4, 1921

Dear Professor,

The purpose of this card is only to inform you that the mail and passenger traffic to Budapest is again functioning quite normally, and that we have arrived at home without any disruption. At the moment, five hours are occupied.

Kindest regards.

Yours,
Ferenczi

1. Postcard with preprinted sender's address crossed out.

891

Vienna, October 13, 1921
IX., Berggasse 19

Dear friend,

Only two weeks have really passed since we so unceremoniously took leave of each other. I didn't get to see your wife at all.

On September 30 in Vienna, I found all the newly announced and several of the former patients, and after failed attempts to shove one or the other off onto you or to Rank, I had to begin with ten people on October 3. In order not to touch Sunday, I had to limit each individual to five hours a week[1] and to manufacture a very artificial distribution of hours. None of them is actually very strenuous, but it comes to a total of nine hours a day without a break, and it is quite out of the question for me to get to anything else in the evening. The consequence is, to be sure, that I am swimming in crowns, but the wealth is essentially negative; it consists in the fact that I don't suffer like the others under the pressure of the tremedous price increases.

Yesterday was the first session of the Society,² forty-four persons in a room no bigger than our dining room. We have lost our beautiful meeting room and had to accept Reik's hospitality. The Verlag also has to move, can't find a place, and is, for that reason, almost incapable of work, very serious difficulties.

In the family, everything is in order. My cold³ is showing improvement today for the first time.

Schmideberg⁴ should have telegraphed you today about a shipment from The Hague which the accompanying physician of the children's train (Holland–Budapest), a Dr. Micske, was supposed to drop off in Vienna for me. But the train passed through Vienna four hours earlier than it was supposed to, according to the official arrival time, and so Schmiedeberg was not at the station. If you really get it, the question still arises as to how it will get to Vienna, but at least it will be safe with you.

Kind regards, prepared for news soon.

Yours,
Freud

1. The beginning of the psychoanalytic "five-day week."
2. With a guest lecture by "Dr. Prinzhorn, from the Heidelberg clinic . . . about 'art works of the mentally ill'" (Rank's *Rundbrief* of October 11, 1921, Butler Library).
3. The meeting in the Harz was "slightly marred by our all having severe colds. Freud's was particularly bad" (Jones III, 81).
4. During the war, Walter Schmideberg (1890–1954) had met Eitingon, who got him interested in psychoanalysis and acquainted him with Freud and Ferenczi. He studied medicine but did not complete his course of study. He was a member of the Vienna Society (1919–1922), and associate member (1923) and secretary of the Berlin Society. In 1924 he married Melanie Klein's daughter Melitta. In 1932 both emigrated to England, where they became members of the Society there. Following their divorce, Schmideberg went to Switzerland after the Second World War, and died there from the effects of alcoholism. See Mühlleitner, *Lexikon*, pp. 289f.

892

Vienna, November 6, 1921¹

Dear friend,

Traffic has been restored. We miss greatly your Rundbrief² and personal reports about how you are. Much activity here because of the foreigners. The members of the Society are giving courses for the Americans and are thus disrupting them in their enjoyment of the city of Vienna. We are awaiting Frau Lou, who has announced herself for the 8th of the month.³ The Verlag still has no accommodations, and is for that reason very inhibited.

How far behind us lies Hildesheim and Schierke.
Kind regards to you and Frau G.

Yours,
Freud

1. Postcard.
2. See Ferenczi's *Rundbrief* of November 3 (which Freud evidently had not yet received): "I didn't want to write until I could convince myself of the regularity of the mails outside the country . . . The Budapest letter of October 21 fell by the wayside" (Butler Library).
3. Andreas-Salomé came on November 9 (Freud to Eitingon, November 11, 1921, Sigmund Freud Copyrights) and stayed until December 20 (Freud to Ernst Freud, December 20, 1921, Library of Congress). "She was a charming guest as well as altogether an outstanding woman. Anna worked with her analytically, paid visits to many interesting personalities, and benefited a great deal from being in her company. Mama took very good care of her; with nine hours of work I didn't have much time for her, but she behaved discreetly and unpretentiously" (Freud to Ernst Freud, December 20, 1921).

893

Budapest, November 6, 1921

Dear Professor,

The "Groddeck-mood"[1] had disappeared again for the time being, and I wanted to wait with my reply until the hypochondriacal attack (which, incidentally, was not so strong) abated.—

Unfortunately, I can't say anything all too gratifying about myself: the day's work (eight to nine hours) tires me so that I don't get to anything else. Thus, the good work resolutions remain just that—resolutions. Incidentally, it is also a purely material question with me. In the past year (the coming December calculated along with it), I earned about 500,000 crowns—and we spent about the same amount this year. And that with strenuous work, at the expense of all literary ambition.

The hours are still fun for me, in part; to be sure, I now seem to be less focused on finding new things than I am on achieving better results with improvement in technique. My specialty is very long treatments with final success, which also extends to the radical change in the patient's character. Practical results, even with significant alleviation of symptoms, don't seem to satisfy me. It is rare that I send a patient away. Thus, I am then in a position to turn newcomers over to others.

The society is working well, as usual. Of course, there is no question about an increase in the work force. The $\psi\alpha$ youth are consuming the biological morsel that I threw them in bits and pieces rather than working it out properly; the whole group is already working biologically, whereby they naturally forget the source from which they drew. Such a "filius ante patrem"[2] by Pfeifer will appear shortly: the biological explanation of musicality.[3] Intelligently done, incidentally.

The case of Dick is causing me great concern. The uncertainty about rights seems to make it possible for that scoundrel to have your works translated without your assent. This and the commerce difficulties between Vienna and the remains of Hungary make me think that it might be more instrumental to make a compromise with Dick for the coming five years, under the full maintenance of all rights *after* this time has expired. The Verlag could negotiate a contract with him in which the right to sell certain works (explicitly) for five years would be spelled out in such a way that the Verlag would get 50% of the net proceeds, or thereabouts. So that Dick doesn't make illegitimate use of the production, the *Verlag* could have the books printed and give the copies to Dick on commission, the way I want to do it. I intend all this only in the event that I am unsuccessful in frightening Dick by the threat of taking *my* books away from him.

Yesterday I learned by chance that he has already handed over *Jokes* and *Everyday Life*[4] to a translator (a layman).

Tomorrow I will talk to Dr. Dukes about this, but I would like to get a report from you about whether the Verlag will empower me, or Dukes,[5] with the right to conclude a contract, if called for, along these or similar lines. Or does Rank want to negotiate with Dick directly? I could put them on track.

Today we buried Toni Freund next to his first wife.[6] Tomorrow the second one is coming to me again for treatment. Perhaps the separation will be more succesful now.

Many kind regards from your

old, faithful
Ferenczi

1. I.e., psychically determined somatic disturbances. Cf., e.g., letter 713: "Totally Groddeck."
2. Latin for "son before the father."
3. "Musikpsychologische Probleme" [Music-Psychological Problems], *Imago* 9 (1923): 453–462; based on two lectures in the Hungarian Society (October 22, 1921, and December 10, 1921).
4. A translation of *Everyday Life* (Freud 1901b) by Márta Takács and Ferenczi was published in 1923; the book about jokes (Freud 1905c) was not translated.
5. See letter 528 and n. 4.
6. Von Freund's body had been transferred from Vienna to Budapest (Ferenczi's *Rundbrief* of November 11, 1921, Butler Library).

894

Budapest, November 13, 1921

Dear Professor,

As a postscript to my last letter I must unfortunately correct a bad, albeit well-intended, slip of the pen. I wrote to you that Dick was paying me 50% of the gross. In reality he is paying me 50% of the *net proceeds* of my books, and in future, instead of this, he wants to pay *10% of the gross*, immediately upon publication of an edition.

So, he might also come out with these or similar numbers in the negotiations over the translation rights to your works, in the event that it comes to such negotiations at all. For the time being I will assume a totally negative position with regard to him and will strive, with Dr. Dukes's aid, to secure your rights of authorship.

In the event that you are not opposed *in principle* to an amicable agreement with him (but in any case only for a few years), and in the event that we don't dispense with him differently, we (Dr. Béla Lévy and I) will do what is necessary.

Many kind regards.

Yours,
Ferenczi

895

Vienna, December 15, 1921[1]

Dear friend,

Since you won't be in Vienna simultaneously with Abraham,[2] we can ask you to get accommodations nowhere other than with us. The drawing room has been set up as a guest room, and is currently inhabited by Frau Lou, who is leaving before Christmas.

Kind regards,
Freud

1. Postcard.
2. Abraham, Ferenczi, Róheim, and Sachs had been invited to lecture by English and American analysands in Vienna. Abraham had originally planned to arrive in Vienna on January 3, 1922, but—because of a railroad strike—he did not come until the twenty-second or twenty-third (Abraham to Freud, December 25, 1921, and January 18, 1922, Library of Congress; Abraham's *Rundbrief* of January 11, 1922, Butler Library; Rank's *Rundbriefe* of January 11, 1922, and January 22, 1922, Butler Library).

896

Budapest, December 26, 1921

Dear Professor,

As I already had you informed by way of Rank, I gratefully accept your kind invitation and will arrive there on January 5, probably toward evening. I will let you know more precisely about the hour by telegram.

The task which has been set for me (metapsychology)[1] is not easy; I will see how I do with it.

I will save up all communications for the personal talk, and greet you, also in the name of my wife, on the occasion of the New Year.

Yours,
Ferenczi

1. Ferenczi's lecture in Vienna on "Freud's Metapsychology" (see Rank's *Rundbrief* of December 11, 1921, Butler Library) was published in Hungarian in *Gyogyászat* 25 (1922): 360–363. Ferenczi also gave a second lecture on "pathoneuroses" (Ferenczi's *Rundbrief* of January 12, 1922, Butler Library; see Ferenczi 1917, 195) and returned to Budapest between January 8 and 11, 1922 (Freud and Ferenczi to Andreas-Salomé, January 8, 1922, Library of Congress; Rank's *Rundbrief* of January 11, 1922, Butler Library).

897

Magyarorszagi
Pszichoanalitikai Egyesület
(Freud-Társaság)

Budapest, January 25, 1922

Dear Professor,

The trip to Vienna seems to have had an extraordinarily refreshing effect on me. Most of the symptoms and symptomlets [*Symptömchen*], which also gave me no peace in Vienna and prevented me from being able to yield undisturbed to the rare opportunity to see you, have disappeared, at least for now. I am working at full steam, am also capable of work in the evening, now and then I get an idea; the hypochondriacal-melancholic ill humor has made room for a certain jollity. All kinds of juvenile libidinous fits betray a certain manic triumph over the "black gall"[1] that has tormented me for so long. For the moment I am unable to decide with certainty whether I should trace this change only to certain hygienic measures which I recently took, or also to the liberating effect of the conversation with you.

It would be nice if I could come to Vienna again in the present, improved edition, and erase the gloomy impression that I must have made on you.

Or shouldn't I negotiate with "Harmonia" about your coming here after all?!

Among the ideas which I am boasting about, I will mention an observation which seems to illuminate more deeply the essence of *stuttering*. If the case comes out halfway good, I will make the Congress lecture out of it.—A more difficult problem (about the mechanism of *compulsive thinking*) is occupying me with equal intensity. I find that compulsive thinking is a protective measure against affects in much the same way as compulsive action is against the compulsion to think. The strange logic of compulsive thinking also keeps me hopping.

The revision of the paper on paralysis[2] has flourished only to the extent that I looked over the "observational part" of the essay, expunged the theoretical, and put together the plan of the theoretical chapter. But it could still be around February 8 before the manuscript gets to Vienna. I am writing this because I have to fear that this way we won't accommodate any more in the first issue of the Zeitschrift. But on no account would I like to be the reason for the delayed publication of the Zeitschrift.

Now, enough of myself, and let us rather think back on the pleasure of being togther, where I was especially pleased about your health and energy. You should no longer reproach me for being all too much inclined to father transference with regard to you. Your and your family's boundless friendliness could also seduce to that one who is less "inclined."

Kindest regards from

Your, again somewhat rejuvenated,
Ferenczi

1. According to Hippocrates, the cause of melancholy (atrabiliousness).
2. Ferenczi and István Hollós, *Psycho-Analysis and the Psychic Disorder of General Paresis* (1922, 239); it was published not in the *Zeitschrift* but as a book in the Verlag.

898

Budapest, February 9 [1922][1]

paralysis paper finished sent off morning = ferenczi

1. Telegram.

899

Vienna, March 30, 1922
IX., Berggasse 19

Dear friend,

I will take my congratulations on the publication, at last, of your popular lectures[1] as an opportunity to write to you once again and to say that your last letter from the long past month of January has pleased me very much. The time since then has passed quickly, dreamlike, with the aftereffects of the flu, monotonous analytic work, business considerations, to which the Rundbriefe attest, and plans for the summer that can't come to fruition. The house is now empty, for Anna, who by nature dominates it more and more, has been in Hamburg for four weeks, and our niece Judith,[2] whom we are putting up as a "house American," cannot be a complete substitute, with all her goodness.

Of the summer, only the first four weeks, July 1 to August 1,[3] are firm, at the same time the only time I can write anything, since I am inhabiting one room alone, which will not be achieved anywhere else.

I am naturally glad to hear you rave about my youth and capability for achievement, as you do in your letter, but when I turn to the reality principle, I know that it isn't true, and I'm not surprised about it. My interest flags so easily, i.e., it likes so much to turn away from the present, wants to connect with something else, and something in me bridles against the compulsion still to earn much money, which can never be enough, and to perpetuate the same psychological skills that have maintained me for thirty years against contempt for mankind and disgust with the world. Strange secret longings rise up in me, perhaps from the legacy of my forebears, for the Orient and the Mediterranean, and for a life of a completely different kind, belated childish wishes, unfulfillable and maladapted to reality, as if to indicate a loosening of the relationship to it. Instead of this—we will probably see each other on the sober ground of Berlin in September.[4]

I am happy to think that we are all sharing practical interests by way of the Rundbriefe. To the more sensible, albeit just as difficult to fulfill, wishes belongs the one for a large sum of money, to realize our Toni's plan for Vienna, to develop the Verlag, to found a training institute for psychoanalysis here, to which the foreigners are supposed to make pilgrimages. All the popularity in America has not produced for analysis the goodwill of *one* of the dollar uncles there. I will leave behind quite a lot of worries for you all.

Farewell, and give in again to the impulse to write privately. Greet Frau Gisela cordially for me and tell her that I recently read several old books by

Groddeck (A Child of the Earth—Tragedy or Comedy—Over to God's Nature),[5] which are very German and bad.

Cordially,
Freud

1. See letter 866 and n. 2.
2. Judith ("Ditha") Bernays (1885–1977), eldest child of Eli Bernays and Freud's sister Anna in New York.
3. Which Freud spent in Badgastein.
4. For the Seventh International Psychoanalytic Congress (September 25–27).
5. *Ein Kind der Erde* [A Child of the Earth], 2 vols. (Leipzig, 1905); *Tragödie oder Komödie? Eine Frage an die Ibsenleser* [Tragedy or Comedy? A Question to Ibsen Readers] (Leipzig, 1910); *Hin zur Gottnatur* [Over to the Nature of God] (Leipzig, 1909).

900

Budapest, May 3, [1922][1]

kindest regards for birthday from your devoted ferenczis

1. Telegram.

901

[Postmark: Budapest,]
Wednesday, May 10, 1922[1]

Dear Prof[essor].!
Please inform Schmiedeberg that Dr. Micska's children's train will stop *next Monday* morning between 9 and 12 Vienna-Ostbahnhof.

Kind regards,
Ferenczi

1. Picture postcard: "Budapest. Halászbástya—Fisherman's Bastion."

902

Budapest, May 15, 1922

Dear Professor,
I must wonder myself about the fact that I don't give in more often to the impulse to write to you. When I think about how great a space your person and the thoughts about common interests take up in my psyche, I am

forced to seek more deep-seated reasons for this tardiness.—There is no doubt that I also was unable to resist the temptation, as a recompense for everything that I have from you, to "bestow on" you the entire extent of overtender and oversensitive impulses of feeling which are appropriate only in relation to one's own father. The stage in which I now seem to find myself is the—badly belated!—weaning and the attempt to submit to my fate. If I am not greatly mistaken, I am, the way I am now, a much more comfortable collaborator than at that time in Palermo; perhaps I am also free of the inhibitions that, for instance, might have been contributing factors in my being late for trains in Italy. In a word: I have—unfortunately—become older and more sensible. This, as they say, "self-possessed" constitution also permits me, totally devoid of self-interest, to be pleased that you were able to celebrate your birthday again in complete freshness and health. Devoid of self-interest, that is to say, undisturbed by the fact that I was not in the fortunate position to greet you personally. The fact that we now meet so seldom forces me, among other things, also to a kind of intellectual self-reliance. Earlier I was happy about an idea mostly as a favor to you. I could hardly wait for the moment when I could offer you the discovery. Gradually, I learned to renounce this pleasure and to occupy myself with science for its own sake, thus, in a more matter-of-fact way. This matter-of-factness comes to the advantage of the sobriety of my views. But I admit that I think not without sadness about the time when I was that much more stormy, happy-unhappier.

To get to speak about practical things: my intellectual constitution is not unfavorable for work. Now and then I have not bad ideas, but I feel more and more secure in $\psi\alpha$ technique; in general the tendency toward rounding off, enlarging old experiences and accomplishments, seems to predominate in me.

I must still spend the month of July—for financial reasons—at work, but I want to spend these four weeks in the "cool valley" (something like Dornbach in Vienna). Then come three to four weeks in beautiful Seefeld (together with the Ranks), finally, a few weeks of "body culture" in Groddeck's sanatorium, and the Berlin Congress.

My wife thanks you for the greetings and returns them.

Tell Fräulein Anna that I am quite delighted with the book by Varendonck.[1]

Many kind regards to you all.

Yours,
Ferenczi

---

[1]. Juliaan Varendonck, *The Psychology of Day-Dreams* (London, 1921), translated by Anna Freud as *Über das vorbewusste phantasierende Denken* [On Preconscious Fan-

tasizing Thinking], published in 1922 by the Verlag. With an introduction by Freud (1921b). Juliaan Varendonck (1879–1924), Ph.D., pioneer of psychoanalysis in Belgium, a member of the Dutch Society. See Roudinesco & Plon, *Dictionnaire*, p. 1081.

903

INTERNATIONALE ZEITSCHRIFT
FÜR ÄRZTL. PSYCHOANALYSE

[Postmark: Budapest,]
June 9, 1922

Dear Professor,

I just heard from Dick that negotiations are going back and forth between him and Deuticke about the translation rights to the Interpretation of Dreams. Should Deuticke turn to you in this matter (or if you made the effort to call Deuticke up in this matter), I ask to insist that the translation right (however this takes place when the time comes) be granted not to Dick alone, but to *both of us*. Only in that way could I successfully preserve my rights with regard to Dick.

Kind regards,
Ferenczi

904

Budapest[1] [June 11, 1922][2]

since letter reply missing, telegraph whether and extent compromise negotiation permitted regarding freud translations = ferenczi

1. Telegram.
2. The stamped date is indecipherable. Placement has been inferred from the previous postcard and Freud's reply of June 12, 1922.

905

Vienna, June 12, 1922[1]

Dear friend,

That goes without saying. Only the translation right can be obtained by the publisher. The author grants the authorization for the translation itself. I gave it to you a long time ago, and Dick couldn't publish any translation other than one that has been sanctioned by me, therefore by you. Show him this card.

Cordially,
Freud

1. Postcard.

906

INTERNATIONALE ZEITSCHRIFT
FÜR ÄRZTL. PSYCHOANALYSE[1]

Budapest, June 16, 1922

Dear Professor,

It will interest you to know that that distingushed erythrophobe, whom you treated at the time, has become the successor in office to that other distinguished one with whom you once became acquainted in the Alps. Perhaps a chance to rescue Toni's fund.

Kind regards,
F[erenczi]

1. Postcard with preprinted sender's address crossed out.

907

Budapest, July 16, 1922

Dear Professor,

Since the beginning of June I have set the work machine at half-steam. We are living in an (unfortunately, overfilled) boardinghouse in the "cool valley," where I work only six hours a day, and that in good air, as well, so that I can set out on the trip to Tirol in an already strengthened condition. In the evenings I read old manuscripts—I do intend, once and for all, to dispose of my "Theory of Genitality." It is now exactly nine years that it has been ripening; so I am literally following the rule of the ars poëtica.[1] After Seefeld we are also going to Baden-Baden, to Groddeck's. One of my wife's sisters (from Canada) and Elma (who is divorcing her husband, after all) will also be there. Only then comes the time of the Congress, where the Hungarians seem to want to unfold a very lively activity. I scarcely need to tell you this time how I look forward to seeing you and Fräulein Anna (this time already as a member!)[2] again. Let us hope that Gastein also does its due this year; and only after Berchtesgaden will you accompany my thoughts good and proper. The unforgettably beautiful days of Dietfeldhof[3] (for which at the time I had to thank my youthfully naive impudence) belong to the most beautiful recollections of my life.

What are you working on? And what will you lecture about in Berlin? Please, don't allow yourself to be intimidated by hoarseness; that would be incompatible with the modern "active" technique. Without your contribution there would be only half a Congress.

Next Sunday (on the 23rd), we will move back to the city apartment (Nagydiófa utca 3), but only for eight days, because on the 30th/31st we are already going to Innsbruck-Seefeld (Hotel Wetterstein) by way of Vienna.

If you get a chance to write me a card, I would be particularly pleased. Many kind regards, also from my wife.

Yours,
Ferenczi

1. On *ars poetica*, see letter 579 and n. 1. At the Congress in Berlin, Ferenczi spoke on the "Versuch einer Genitaltheorie" [Attempt at a Theory of Genitality] (Ferenczi 1922, 246; self-review in *Zeitschrift* 8 [1922]: 478f.).
2. Since 1918 Anna Freud had been participating as a guest in the meetings of the Vienna Society and had become a member on June 13 after a lecture, "Über Schlagephantasien und Tagträume" [On Beating Fantasies and Daydreams] (May 31, 1922; *Imago* 8:317–332). See Jones III, 85.
3. On the first vacation that they took together, in 1908.

908

Bad Gastein, July 21, 1922

Dear friend,

Our formerly so lively correspondence has gone to sleep in the course of the last few years. You write only rarely, and I reply even more rarely. But that is in the spirit of Schiller's words in Wallenstein: That's not necessary between us.[1] The practical needs are taken care of through the Rundbriefe, the emotional ones have come to rest in a safe harbor.

Today, on vacation and on a day when my head doesn't want to work, for a change, I gladly write to you again and am letting the letter be until it reaches you securely in your city apartment.

What I am doing here? Working more diligently than in Vienna, but in complete freedom. I am finally reacting to the billions of impressions that I have to take in from ten people, nine hours a day for nine months, naturally not appropriate, otherwise I would have to be able to produce volumes. So far they have become only two essays, which are already out of the house. One is called: Remarks on the Theory and Practice of Dream Interpretation,[2] and is a collection of what hasn't found a home in consequence of the unaltered printing of the book;[3] the second: Neurotic

Mechanisms in Jealousy, Paranoia, and Homosexuality, approximately that which you heard in the Harz. The latter is being published in the Congress number of the Zeitschrift.[4] Besides that, I am occupied with something speculative, which is a continuation of "Beyond," and will either become a small book or nothing. I won't reveal the title to you yet; all I have to say is that it has to do with Groddeck.[5]

I was only able to withdraw completely from the practice for these three weeks. From today on I have to give Dr. Frink's future wife,[6] who is here with him, an hour a day; another American woman is awaiting me in Berchtesgaden, and, if I want, so is her treatment.[7] On Sunday an Englishman is supposed to come, who will negotiate with me in vain about a series of lectures in Cambridge,[8] etc.

My poor wife is freezing miserably in the Harz with our little boy. The arid nest is called Hohegeiss. Anna is not far from there, in Göttingen,[9] and is very much enjoying the stay and company. Around the 4th we all intend to be together on the Salzberg, Oliver and Mathilde as well. My mother, who is very unsteady with her eighty-seven years, is said to be doing better in Ischl.

Your encouraging me to speak at the Congress does not penetrate easily. What is aggravating in the symptom of hoarseness is the fact that I am so very much in agreement with it. It is actually not a symptom, but a materialization of the resistance which I am very familiar with. The beginning was in Worcester, where everything went well when you told me what I should talk about.[10] Since then, the falling out has become complete, and I know that I simply don't want to. There also has to be a transition to the later Congresses without me.

I was very pleased about your various travel intentions. I still won't say: auf Wiedersehen, but greet you and Frau Gisela cordially.

Yours,
Freud

1. *Wallensteins Tod* I, 3.
2. Freud 1923c.
3. Freud 1900a; the sixth (1921) and seventh (1922) editions were unaltered reprints of the fifth.
4. Freud 1922b, published in *Zeitschrift* 8 (1922): 249–258; see letter 862 and n. 1.
5. *The Ego and the Id* (Freud 1923b). Freud took the expression "it" from Groddeck. Nietzsche, for example, had already talked about the "it" earlier. See J. Ph. Kerz in *Psyche* 39 (1985): esp. 131–132.
6. Angelika Bijur; see letter 860 and n. 4.
7. "Here on the Salzberg another American is fighting for treatment; she would certainly have paid $50 a day, since she was accustomed to giving Brill $20 in NY for *half* an hour ... But she won't accomplish anything; I won't sell the time here" (Freud to Rank, August 4, 1922, Judith Dupont Archive).

8. "Mr Sprott is a young man of excellent manners and good connection, a favourite of Lytton Strachey and friend of Maynard Keynes, a Cambridge student of Psychology, who came to invite me for a course of lectures to be given at Eastertime . . . I accepted for the case that I should feel so tired at Easter, that I had to give up work, and yet fresh enough for some other enterprise, which, as you see, is only a polite way of declining" (Freud to Jones, September 3, 1922, *Freud/Jones*, pp. 500f.)

9. At the home of Lou Andreas-Salomé.

10. "In the morning, before the time had come for my lecture to begin, we would walk together in front of the university building and I would ask [Ferenczi] to suggest what I should talk about that day. He thereupon gave me a sketch of what, half an hour later, I improvised in my lecture. In this way he had a share in the origin of the *Five Lectures*" (Freud 1933c, p. 227). Freud did give a Congress lecture, "Some Remarks on the Unconscious" (Freud 1922f).

909

Seefeld, August 17, 1922
B[oardinghouse]. Wetterstein

Dear Professor,

The previous part of the summer has taken shape as a chronic psychoanalytic Congress. Following in your footsteps, a whole flock of professional comrades (Hitschmann, [Helene] Deutsch, also Bernfeld, passing through, then the Ranks and we) made a pilgrimage this season to this wonderfully situated nest; in addition, Abraham visited us here, further, we saw in his entourage the two Glovers,[1] then Sachs and an Englishwoman (Dr. Cole),[2] who came here in order to learn "active technique" from me, but instead of that had to experience a piece of normal analysis on her own person. To my astonishment, it turned out that my English is, indeed, up to the task of moving forward with this patient.

The interesting symbiotic relationship between nourishing patients and teaching physicians seems to be generally settling in. I, for example, am taking mine along to Baden-Baden.

Our stay here will last another week. We are leaving on the 24th, and from the 25th on our address will be the Groddecks' (Baden-Baden, Werderstrasse 14).

You will find out the results of our discussions about the Congress from Rank's Rundbrief.[3] Nothing of my lecture[4] is finished yet. I hope to find the leisure time necessary for it in Baden-Baden.

One of my wife's sisters and her husband (from Canada) stayed at Groddeck's for a few days, but fled from the somewhat violent "psychic massage." On the other hand, Elma, who has been staying there for three weeks, seems to feel well with him.

Let's hope you recovered in Berchtesgaden from the stresses and strains of the Gastein cure. I anticipate with keen interest the communication of your ideas about Groddeck's organic animism. I am very afraid that no opportunity for that will offer itself in Berlin.

We are very much looking forward to seeing you soon, and ask you to give our regards to Frau Professor and all your loved ones.

Yours,
Ferenczi

Dr. Rie[5] was here until yesterday with his big family. Now they are gone, except for a few members of the family.

About two months ago you wrote in the Rundbrief that Dick acquired the Hungarian translation rights for the Interpretation of Dreams from Deuticke. But Dick claimed, already before my departure (beginning of August), that he had not yet concluded the deal with Deuticke. Please enlighten me about this in a postcard.

1. The brothers James and Edward Glover, both analysands of Abraham; members of the British Society (1922). James Glover (1882–1926), M.D., was one of the most brilliant figures of British psychoanalysis. "Glover had galvanized the British Psycho-Analytic Society with his personality" (Perry Meisel and Walter Kendrick, eds., *Bloomsbury/Freud: The Letters of James and Alix Strachey, 1924–1925* [New York, 1985], p. 307). In fragile health, he left the London climate and went to Brazil, from which he returned with dysentery and malaria, and died at the age of forty-four. Edward Glover (1888–1972), M.D., later played a decisive role in the British Society, above all in the Freud-Klein controversies of the 1940s, during which he sat on all the important committees of the Society and Institute and chaired many of the special meetings. Originally an adherent of Melanie Klein, he later became critical of her theories; the situation was aggravated by the fact that Klein's daughter, Melitta Schmideberg, who strongly attacked her mother, was his analysand. He was chair of the Training Committee until his resignation from the Society in 1944, after which he changed over to the Swiss Society.
2. Estelle Maude Cole, a member of the British Society. She originally wanted to do a six-week analysis with Freud, who declined, however (Freud to Jones, June 4, 1922, *Freud/Jones*, p. 487).
3. Rank's *Rundbrief* of August 16, 1922, from Seefeld, written in consultation with Ferenczi and Abraham (Butler Library).
4. See letter 907, n. 1.
5. See letter 110, n. 6.

910

Salzberg, August 24, 1922

Dear friend,

Although as a consequence of a severe misfortune in the family—Maus, whom you surely remember, poisoned herself with Veronal and died on the 18th;[1] we don't know how my sister, a virtuosa of despair, is—I am not very cheerful or eager to write, but I do want to send you a greeting at the Groddecks', whom I also ask you to greet for me.

I have been very happy about the intensification of your intimacy with Rank; it promises good things for the future. Lévy and Kata have been here since the day before yesterday, charming as ever. Deuticke has not notified me of any payment from Dick.

We are thinking of staying here as long as it goes.

Cordially, to you and Frau G.

Yours,
Freud

1. See letter 882 and n. 3.

911

Baden-Baden, Werderstrasse 14,
August 31, 1922

Dear Professor,

The sad news, which we received already in Seefeld, also shocked us very much. We very much liked the dear, pretty girl, as did all those who knew her; she made the impression on me of a cheerful, levelheaded being. But we already know that that doesn't mean much.

I can imagine how stunned you must be by this tragic event; I fear that the whole extent of rest and recuperation that we were hoping for you from the vacation has been put in question, but we still hope that your strength will win out in the end, and that you will be up to the exertions of the Congress and the coming work year.

The stay in Seefeld was, in fact, significant for me, since the unity between Rank and me, which was also never disrupted earlier, was sealed there, as it were. I hope we can find a little bit of time in Berlin when we can present our plan to you personally.

We feel very well here in Baden-Baden. I am, in addition to taking the physical cures (hot baths, massage), going through a piece of self-analysis, as it were, in Groddeck's presence, also with his help, to be sure. By the way, I find that Groddeck actually sets about things very circumspectly and cautiously, and is true to the teachings of psychoanalysis in all essentials. I hope that certain misunderstandings which make him appear in the light of Stekel's methodology will disappear.

My resistance toward writing down the bio-analytic thoughts which have not been worked up for so many years has made me postpone finishing the Congress lecture from one day to the next. But "tomorrow" I will begin in earnest.

Elma and the sister-in-law who lives in Rome are also here and are feeling well. They all send you kind regards. The Groddecks also thank you for your greeting and return it.

Perhaps I will still learn, directly or by way of Rank, how you are. And we will certainly see each other very soon in Berlin.[1]

Yours,
Ferenczi

1. The Seventh International Psychoanalytic Congress took place in Berlin from September 25 to 27. Jones was reelected president, and Abraham became central secretary. Ferenczi opened the scientific portion with his "Attempt at a Theory of Genitality"; Freud spoke on "Etwas vom Unbewussten" [Something of the Unconscious], prefiguring *The Ego and the Id*. At the Congress the question of a "certificate" for analysts was discussed for the first time. Freud set up a prize for the best work on the topic "The Relationship of Psychoanalytic Technique to Psychoanalytic Theory." The Indian Psychoanalytic Association was provisionally accepted. See the report of the Congress in *Zeitschrift* 8 (1922): 478–505. The famous photograph of the secret Committee also originated during the Congress (Abraham's *Rundbrief* of October 16, 1922, Butler Library).

912

Budapest, November 22, 1922

Dear Professor,

As an impartial observer of the events within the Committee, I hasten to share with you my views about them.

In the current question (the trifle about the secretary's report to the Korrespondenzblatt),[1] Rank is definitely right. It would have been nonsense to value formalities and agencies as more important than the interest of the cause itself. But on the whole I find that the (often quite unjustified) sensitivity of Abraham and Jones must be spared, precisely *in the interest of the cause*. We must do everything to forestall dissension within the Committee. Misunderstandings should be eliminated by amicable discussion, and even in scientific questions one shouldn't offend the most loyal adherents. I am convinced that both Abraham and Jones, if we make them aware of certain errors (while sparing their sensitivities, of course), will not be closed off to insight into certain of their own insufficiencies.

But I can't protest vehemently enough about the idea of Rank's, which was certainly only planted in the heat of the battle, that the constitution of the Committee, or even the form of the Zeitschrift should be tampered with. The Zeitschrift is and remains the soul of the whole movement; it must under all circumstances be saved and maintained.

It was, perhaps, unavoidable that little special alliances also formed within the Committee from time to time. But all our efforts must be aimed at making such alliances, which are permitted only for dealing with current questions, superfluous as soon as possible, by making the good that we aim at therewith into a general good, and, above all, win the Committee members over to it.

It is regrettable that we were also unable to maintain our unity without your help, and that *you* have to mediate again among the disciples. But in the next Rundbrief I will also direct a serious word to the Committee members; perhaps I am disinterested enough to get a hearing with all of them.

At the same time I also wrote to Rank, whom I warned of being overzealous.

Rank asks me if I won't come to Vienna for the Christmas holidays. I also had this idea, independently of him, but it is still questionable if I can bring my English hour in harmony with that. Naturally I would prefer it if I could come to you not for smoothing out personal conflicts but, in the good old style, for discussing scientific problems. Too bad that time and space keep us apart that way.

Personal things can be better talked about personally—especially when (something natural) the correspondence gradually dries up.

My wife and I myself greet you and all your dear ones most cordially.

Yours,
Ferenczi

1. There had been friction for several months between Rank, on the one hand, and Abraham and Jones, on the other, which for the most part revolved around organizational details (cf., e.g., letter 864, n. 3) but already pointed to the coming severe crisis within the secret Committee. In the cited instance it had to do with how, in what form, and to whom the reports of the individual branch societies should be sent for the *Korrespondenzblatt*. Rank (the editor of the *Zeitschrift*) had, with Freud's knowledge and support, chosen a form and sent it to the secretaries of the branch societies. It did not correspond to the recommendations of Jones (president of the IPA) and Abraham (who, as central secretary, was designated as responsible for the *Korrespondenzblatt*). They felt that they had been passed over and presented with a fait accompli. (Abraham's *Rundbrief* of November 12, 1922; Jones's *Rundbrief*, undated; both Butler Library).

913

Vienna, November 23, 1922
IX., Berggasse 19

Dear friend,

Your letter which arrived today crosses my intention to write to you and facilitates carrying it out. I think just as you do and grant that you are right on all points. The fact that Rank [is thinking of] changes in the Committee and the Zeitschrift was certainly new to me; he hasn't told me about it, and he probably gave these wishes up again. It should not be surprising if, under the accumulated attacks, he occasionally and temporarily succumbs to bitterness.

I really wanted to ask you to raise your warning and mediating voice in the next Rundbrief, and was also glad to read that you have made this decision spontaneously. Yesterday there was a long meeting with Rank, and he was also in agreement with the idea of my appearing independently in the next Rundbrief and trying to exercise my influence.[1] On the whole, I'm not taking it hard. In Abraham, who is fundamentally gracious and correct, there is operating only the jealousy which has been accumulated by Eitingon and which is exploding in Rank. Jones is more serious; here there are real defects in character and behavior with which one can't confront him quite honestly and which he must conceal by means of some arrangement or other. (To that extent, Adler is right).[2]

Perhaps it would be good for me to exclude myself from the next Committee meeting (1923) and give you an opportunity to adjust yourselves directly to one another.

Aside from these dark clouds, there are also all kinds of other difficulties. The crisis of the Verlag is quite serious; a piece of it is the absolute lack of money. But we won't let it get stuck, but rather, for the time being, help with our own money. The problem of the Press has suddenly been made clear by the events, and will have to be resolved shortly. Rickman[3] is expected tomorrow; Jones intends to come for Christmas; I hope, one more motive, to drive you to Vienna around the same time. Vienna is getting arid, nothing can be had from the natives, foreigners are no more to be seen. I am afraid of every visit by an analyst, in anticipation that he will apprise me of his imminent bankruptcy, because I have nothing to send him. I myself have only three reservations, two of which are due in March, but I am still overbooked. Frink, whose cure and—marriage is being delayed considerably, is still here. As long as I still have nine analyses a day, I can't do anything in the evening, also avoid every letter. Hence the fact that our correspondence has gone to sleep. When I get to eight cases because of attrition, I will work again. Naturally, I have become "rich" in the process, but everybody around me is poor and in need of support.

Today I distinctly have a very muddled head, for the preservation of which I will conclude this letter, which is not finished by a long shot. Not without appending the most cordial greetings to you and Frau G.

Yours,
Freud

1. Freud's *Rundbrief* of November 26, 1922 (Butler Library). Freud supported Rank and spoke of Abraham's "tendency . . . to bring affects which apply to me to the fore in Rank," and, concerning Jones, that he, Freud, was "the main recipient and that Rank comes into it rather innocently, as a screen, which has to gather up the negative portion

of an ambivalence distortion . . . If my criticism of Jones is justified, then something else should happen: Jones should allow the brief analysis that he had with Ferenczi back then to be completed."

2. An allusion to Adler's idea of neurotic "arrangement," *Über den nervösen Charakter* [The Neurotic Constitution] (Vienna, 1912), passim.

3. Rickman came "to study the situation [of the Verlag] and to gather the material on the basis of which Jones, along with his Englishmen in London, will make the decision [regarding the Press]" (Freud's *Rundbrief* of November 26, 1922, Butler Library).

914

INTERNATIONALE ZEITSCHRIFT
FÜR ÄRZTL. PSYCHOANALYSE

Budapest, December 17, 1922

Dear Professor,

I would like to go to Vienna on the afternoon of the 30th and spend the 31st and 1st there. Please inform *by telegram* if you won't be inconvenienced.

Yours,
Ferenczi

915

[Postmark: Vienna,]
Christmas, 1922[1]

Dear friend,

Come, you will be most welcomed by us! Rank has snatched away any concern about putting you up.

Best regards to Frau Gisela!

Yours,
Freud

1. Postcard.

916

Budapest, January 22, 1923

Dear Professor,

I feel gradually compelled to create a new kind of "Rundbriefe," into which only you and Rank can get insight. You see, I am not in agreement with the tone of the last letter from Berlin and, particularly, from London.[1]

In Jones I miss the energy that he should have developed if he really wanted to defuse the separatist tendencies of the London group. Every member of the Committee should strive, in his own sphere of work, so, above all, in his own group, to realize the idea of a central direction of all scientific and business affairs, which is the purpose of the Committee. But I find that Jones either doesn't do this, or does it insufficiently, which is attributable either to too slight an influence on his co-nationals, or to too weak (because it is not quite honest) a will.—Abraham still seems, after so many discussions, to want to play the sensitive one; he grouses about every formal triviality—but he is insulted when one calls his procedure "petty."—Sachs is all too easily inclined to bury the hatchet and to leave the Anglo-Americans to their own devices; that seems to me to be all the more dangerous, the deeper an insight I get into the need for leadership and the naïveté of the English, of all people. If you and Rank consider it appropriate, I am prepared to give unreserved expression of this opinion of mine in the next Rundbriefe and offer you, Herr Professor, occasion to make a statement.

The pleasant memory of the two holidays in Vienna is beginning to fade. The analyses are dropping off pretty much uneventfully. Unfortunately, our Frau Radó-Révész is doing quite poorly. She is evidently suffering from a severe pernicious anemia, which worsened immediately after the death of her father. The doctors here seem to be of the opinion that her pregnancy has to be interrupted, and, in fact—as they say—because of the additional dangers of bleeding and threatened exhaustion—by means of sectio caesarea! I visit her often, try to "treat" her analytically, but I have very little confidence in success.²—N. B.: in her dangerous situation it would not be possible to upset her with broaching the Feldmann question.³ So, the execution has to be postponed.

With kind regards from all of us to you and yours.

Yours,
Ferenczi

1. Jones's *Rundbrief* of January 11, 1923 (Butler Library) was concerned with the situation between the Press and the Verlag—a source of constant conflict between him and Rank. Abraham (letter of January 17, 1923, Butler Library) complained about the "copiously late decision" on Rank's part that he, Abraham, would now be responsible for the production of the *Korrespondenzblatt*, and about Rank's tardiness in communicating things.

2. On Erzsébet Révész, see letter 630, n. 19. Ferenczi doesn't mention her husband, Sándor Radó's, moving to Berlin.

3. See letter 789, n. 2, and letter 920.

917

Vienna, January 25, 1923
IX., Berggasse 19

Dear friend,

I am replying to you on the same day, after I have written for an hour on my "devil's neurosis,"[1] because it is only 12:30. I share your impressions; I, too, am not satisfied with our Western Committee members and, unfortunately, have heard as much about Jones—it is my fate to be informed from so many quarters—that I don't look to the future with confidence. But your intention for an "active therapy" leaves out of consideration an important factor, namely, that now we—Rank and I—intend, that is to say, have carried out the full separation from Press and Verlag, while Jones would much rather see the old gloomy condition perpetuated. So, now you don't have anything to demand, or you would demand it in opposition to us.

The separation has also not been easy for us; it was a painful autotomy. But our lack of money, on the one hand, and the audacity and clumsiness of the English, on the other, have necessitated it for us. Collaboration with them is not very possible. When they are alone, they will probably do it well, in any case better. Jones is in many respects a personality unsuited to be a leader.

I wrote to Radó today; I didn't know it was so serious with her.

"Ego and Id" is presently maturing and doesn't exist yet in any printed form.[2]

There are all kinds of new things with us, some that one should be happy about, but everything is so mixed with cares and qualms, and one has gotten out of practice with joy.[3] Do you already know about Oliver's engagement?[4] On January 31 he is going to Duisburg in the occupied territory! to assume a position there. A niece of mine, who was in New York, wants to get married on February 4,[5] but it is all so wretched. Also in the finances of the fund, something, which I don't want to say publicly, has changed for the better; but it is not enough by a long shot for the difficulties of these times. You say you find me fresh and indefatigable; I know that I am grouchy and tired.

Varga is at the Russian embassy in Berlin; he wrote to me a few days ago.

At home, everybody is mostly well; the little fellow with Mathilde[6] is magnificent. I hope you and Frau Gisela have nothing to complain about.

I greet you both cordially.

Freud

1. "A Seventeenth-Century Demonological Neurosis" (Freud 1923d).

2. In his *Rundbrief* of January 15, 1923 (Butler Library), Ferenczi had requested a galley proof.

3. Freud does not mention that, shortly before, on January 12, Herbert Silberer had committed suicide.

4. To Henny Fuchs (1892–1971). The wedding took place on April 10, 1923. The couple had a daughter, Eva Mathilde (1924–1944).

5. Rose Beatrice Winternitz (1896–1969), the daughter of Freud's sister Pauline (b. 1864; d. ca. 1942 in the Treblinka concentration camp) and Valentin Winternitz (1859–1900). On February 4 she married the poet Ernst Waldinger, Ph.D. (1896–1970).

6. Sophie's second son, "Heinerle," was living with his aunt Mathilde in Vienna. He died on June 19 of miliary tuberculosis (see letter 933).

918

INTERNATIONALE ZEITSCHRIFT
FÜR ÄRZTL. PSYCHOANALYSE[1]

Sunday, January 28, 1923

Dear Professor,

I can't spare you the sorrowful news about the demise of Frau Dr. Radó Révész. Death occurred despite the sectio caesarea which was performed as a consequence of rapidly progressing hemolysis.[2] Burial probably Tuesday, if not then, Wednesday.[3]

Cordially,
Ferenczi

1. Postcard with sender's address crossed out.
2. Dissolution of the red blood corpuscles.
3. See the brief obituary in *Zeitschrift* 2 (1923): 119.

919

Vienna, February 2, 1923[1]

Dear friend,

The death of a young woman and mother is another loathsome detail of this declining world. I was very sorry to hear about it. I am writing to Radó simultaneously.

Cordially,
Freud

1. Postcard.

920

Budapest, March 14, 1923

Dear Professor,

The main purpose of my letter of today is to give a report about the case of Dr. Feldmann.—After receiving the reply from Rank's and your side, I had him come immediately and presented him with my demand. He was quite dismayed and bewildered—but then he poured forth complaints about the unfairness of the judgment, although he admitted that he did not presume any bad will on my part (at most exaggerated, indeed, unjustified caution). I treated him as if he were a patient suffering from character defects, whom it would be impossible for me to entrust with the treatment of neurotics and allow to retain membership. Finally, he promised to send the document of resignation. Today he came again and wanted to have the whole thing viewed in a much milder light; when he saw my inflexibility, he asked if he wouldn't be allowed to remain a member, he would no longer ask for patients and intended to stay away from meetings. I denied these requests and told him that my main concern was precisely that he should resign from the Association. He had, incidentally,—so I told him—already announced his resignation verbally; this declaration had been acknowledged by me and communicated to you (Herr Professor). Then he requested to make the above request to you personally, which I advised him against. Then he asked at least to be allowed to ask for your opinion in writing. I also forbade him that; but I finally promised that I will ask you. But I told him the answer would quite certainly be in the negative.

Before he left, he made allusions to wanting to remain a psychoanalyst, if only outside the organization, indeed, "if necessity drove him to it," he would make advertisements for himself by writing books. I replied to him that I already knew for a long time that he would like to become the Budapest Stekel.—He then seemed to want to ask for guarantees to the effect that I wouldn't disturb him in this activity; I replied to him that I could not advise him to continue to be a psychoanalyst; he had to change his profession.

So, now I ask you to send me, in a letter addressed to me, *as soon as possible,* in a few lines, your refusal to Dr. Feldmann, so that I can communicate it to Dr. Feldmann by telephone and report his resignation in the next session. In today's Rundbrief I will communicate (without giving any reasons) the word-of-mouth announcement of his resignation.[1]

It would naturally be personally very pleasant for me if I could counteract Dr. Feldmann's Stekelisms [*Stekeliaden*]. But it is difficult to accomplish this with him if I don't apply the most extreme measures (threat to go public), which would be plain impossible considering the circumstances, and even harmful for psychoanalysis (from the standpoint of the confidentiality of the confessional). What do you think *about that?*

My state of health is fluctuating; a slight wave of improvement, for the moment. What do you think about an Easter excursion?

Many kind regards.

Yours,
Ferenczi

1. "Dr. S. Feldmann's *Resignation* from the Association. (The latter has been reported to me only by word of mouth for the time being, and should be kept secret pending written confirmation)" (Ferenczi's *Rundbrief* of March 17, 1923, Butler Library). The problem evidently had to with Feldmann's handling of analytic abstinence (see letter 925).

921

Budapest, March 18, 1923

Dear Professor,

I thank you (or Rank?) for sending in the first sheets of the "Ego and Id," but I would like to call your attention to a small inconsistency in nomenclature. On page four you write (as you already often do) about the fact that "a consciousness of which one knows nothing . . . [is] a good deal *more absurd* than something mental that is unconscious."[1] On page thirteen you write, "despite all voiced contradiction of an *unconscious consciousness* of guilt."[2] I think you would have to ameliorate the judgment "absurd" (with *ucs. knowing*), if you only wanted to express formal reservations about the assumption of unconscious consciousness of guilt. Otherwise you risk having the word you use turned against your [own] term.

I am in complete agreement with the content and await the continuation.

Yours,
Ferenczi

1. Freud 1923b, p. 16, n. 1.
2. Later altered by Freud to "this new discovery, which compels us, in spite of our better critical judgement, to speak of 'an unconscious sense of guilt'" (ibid., p. 27; see letter 923).

922

Vienna, March 19, 1923
IX., Berggasse 19

Dear friend,

I request that you tell Dr. Feldmann that the only thing he can do as penance is to stay completely away from psychoanalysis, and that only under this condition will the secret be kept for the $\psi\alpha$ circles.

Another execution took place more mildly. Dr. Reich admitted his error without hesitation, confirmed that it happened four years ago, before he was a member, and since he is otherwise diligent, eager, and respectable, I absolved him from the youthful prank.[1]—

Glad to hear you are better, I can't dispense with the catarrhs and neuralgias lately; it's supposed to be the modern form of influenzal infection. I am also correspondingly tired.

Where do you want to go now? The world has been divided up into individual cells from which there is hardly any exit, spring is far away, the Adriatic is distant, and Italian or Slovenian-Croatian. You are always welcome with me and Rank in Vienna.

In the last weeks I was pleased about a charming letter and book dedication by Romain Rolland.[2] Otherwise, little is happening. Oli's wedding depends on whether he can find two furnished rooms in Duisberg, where he is now. We were not allowed to go to Berlin for the celebration. Anna is going to Göttingen, to Lou's, for Easter week.

With kind regards to you and Frau Gisela.

Yours,
Freud

1. Wilhelm Reich (1897–1957), one of the most brilliant and controversial figures of early psychoanalysis. After a meteoric career as practitioner, theoretician, teacher, and organizer of analysis, and as an agitator, enlightener, and publisher in the labor movement, he was expelled from both the IPA and the Communist Party and labeled "schizophrenic" by the psychoanalysts and "revisionist" by the Communists. In 1920, as a medical student, he became a member of the Vienna Society; in 1922 he received his doctorate and married Annie Pink. Also in 1922 he became an assistant physician, and in 1928 acting director of the outpatient clinic of the Vienna Society; from 1925 on he was a member of the training institute, and from 1924 to 1930 director of the Technical-Therapeutic Seminar. In 1928–29 he became a member of the Communist Party. In 1930 he moved to Berlin and became a member and training analyst of the Society there; he founded the Imperial German League for Proletarian Sexual Politics ("Sexpol") and the Publishing House for Sexual Politics. After Hitler's seizure of power he went into exile in Scandinavia, and in 1939 he emigrated to the United States. In the 1940s he developed his orgone theory. After being charged with production and sale of "orgone accumulators," he was sentenced to two years in prison. Reich died in prison in 1957. The "youthful prank" could refer to Reich's first female patient ("March 1919," in *Wilhelm Reich*

über Sigmund Freud, place and date of publication unknown [pirated edition]), or it could also refer to Lore Kahn, who had been in analysis with Reich in the winter of 1919–20 (Wilhelm Reich, *Passion of Youth: An Autobiography, 1879–1922* [New York, 1988], p. 162). At the time Kahn was nineteen years old and in training to be a kindergarten teacher. (Information kindly conveyed by Bernd Nitzschke.)

2. See Rolland's letter of February 22, 1923, and Freud's reply of March 4, 1923, in Freud, *Letters*, pp. 341f. "Charming letter and exchange of books with Romain Rolland. One is always astonished that not all people are riffraff" (Freud to Ernst Freud, March 14, 1923, Library of Congress). See Henri and Madeleine Vermorel, *Sigmund Freud et Romain Rolland: correspondance, 1923–1926* (Paris, 1993), pp. 214–228.

923

Vienna, March 22, 1923[1]

Dear friend,

Thanks for your critical remark, which has already had its effect, and request for many others, which will be honored.

Are you coming for Easter?

Cordially,
Freud

1. Postcard.

924

Budapest, March 22, 1923

Dear Professor,

Here I am sending you the terrible manuscript by Varendonck.[1] I read through the first part with the patience of the saints; I only leafed through the second.

This is probably the worst thing that was ever done in psychoanalysis. It is so bad that in places it brings one irresistibly to laughter—most passages aren't even capable of that, but rather repeat the same thing all of *thirty-five times!* in arid boredom, and bring the reader to despair.

After a pretentious introduction, in which Varendonck promises the solution to all of the psychology of aesthetics and symbolism, comes the "material." *Thirty-five* arias and poems, which a "gentleman of his acquaintance" twitters or hums to himself from time to time—along with the "analysis" of the poems. This analysis consists of arranging in sequence the *nearest* preconscious (at the same time tendentiously directed) idea at the place in the text which is in question. Nowhere is there talk of more deeply connecting, layering, evaluating the ideas. The author explains *all the verses and all the content of all the poems* that he cites simply in relation to *a single idea* (marriage complex) of the "one under investigation" (who is doubtless he himself). From time to time he can't restrain himself from putting the best spin on some of his reveries (which, unfortunately, are sufficiently well known from his bad book).

Then comes the theoretical part. Rather shameless theft of all that which you said about the joke, and Rank and I and others about symbolism; the latter simply with reference to Jones's compilation on the symbol,[2] in this regard. Besides this, metapsychology (economy) is almost newly discovered. All that, amid diligent citation of your work, whereby, however, the appearance of the author himself having found something in relation to this remains preserved.

Worthy of recognition is the author's theoretical progress since his book about pcs. thinking.[3] An intimation of the really ucs. seems to be dawning in him.

But it seems incomprehensible why the poor public has to participate in his struggle for recognition;—one must definitely spare those who are way beyond him in depth of knowledge the torment of reading this work.

In French, the work must have spoiled[4] at the outset the effect of the ψα works that haven't been published yet, of which it actually is a plagiarism.

Unfortunately, I was unable to make a better judgment about this work. Perhaps you should have someone else (Fräulein Anna?) criticize it, or perhaps you should leaf through it yourself, so that you can convince yourself of its value or (in my opinion) worthlessness.

Easter trip to Vienna not impossible.

Cordially,
Ferenczi

1. Ferenczi had been asked for his opinion as to whether the Verlag should publish the work (Rank's *Rundbrief* of February 1, 1923, Butler Library); after his devastating judgment, publication did not take place (Rank's *Rundbrief* of April 1, 1923, Butler Library). It was later published in Dutch (*Over aesthetische symboliek: Een psycho-analytisch onderzoek* [Amsterdam, 1923]).
2. "Die Theorie der Symbolik" [The Theory of Symbolism], *Zeitschrift* 5 (1919): 244–273, and 8 (1922): 259–289.
3. See letter 902 and n. 1.
4. Reading uncertain; it could also be "would have to spoil."

925

INTERNATIONALE ZEITSCHRIFT
FÜR ÄRZTL. PSYCHOANALYSE

Budapest, March 28, 1923

Dear Professor,

Despite my longing for Viennese air I am renouncing the Easter trip in favor of works which can't be postponed. I will definitely come for Whitsun.—The expulsion of Dr. Feldmann is complete. Despite the threat, he seems *not* to be willing to adhere to αψ abstinence. His cynical reply was: "What can one do to me; at most, one will accuse me of incorrectness, etc." His attitude at the execution justifies the severity after the fact.

Many kind Easter greetings from

Yours,
Ferenczi

I have only one sheet of the "Ego and Id."

926

INTERNATIONALE ZEITSCHRIFT FÜR
ÄRZTLICHE PSYCHOANALYSE

Budapest, April 15, 1923

Dear Professor,

I have just been reading the second sheet of your Ego-book and hasten to say how gratified I was by the solution to the apparent contradiction in the "unconscious consciousness of guilt." It certainly would never have occurred to me that the "superego" (as a consequence of its ignoble origin from the erotic) can become incapable of consciousness.[1] But as soon as I read it, it became completely self-evident to me. Such recognitions amply reward one for the effort that the attentive reading of your work requires.

Now, a small personal-scientific question: Am I justified in qualifying the *"ego memory systems,"* which I postulate in my paper on tic,[2] as a part of your *ego?* I believe: yes. The ucs. (the latent and the repressed) certainly contains, if I understand you correctly: the *remnants of the memory of things.* But one must also assume similar mnemic traces in the *ego,* and one may presume that they are mostly engraved simultaneously with the objective memory images (similar to double sensation in pain), and there they probably have their own (onto- and phylogenetically acquired) "systems."

Apropos sensation! Would it not be instrumental to retain the, in my opinion, well-acclimated distinction of external perception (sensation) from the internal (feeling)? The overseeability [*Übersichtlichkeit*] of the psychic apparatus, that is to say, its function, would gain something thereby.

The "ignoble" origin of even the most moral representation is already mirrored in the double meaning of the wording in which it[3] is clothed (in the pcs.). In the statement "You should love your parents" the original meaning of the word "love" is resonant. So, no wonder that this (moral) love can be repressed.

Question: Could one not quite generally trace back every character formation to the melancholic mechanism and assume that character traits can always be introjected when one experiences disappointments in this respect with the love object[4]?[5] (Then character qualities would *always* be "*negative* ego-ideal" formations in the superego.)

On page 17 the expression "personal prehistory"[6] should perhaps be replaced by another which would obviate misunderstanding (in the sense of the phylogenetic).

Only one other remark about the sentence on page 7, "*All* perceptions which are received from without . . . are *Cs.* from the start."[7] Don't you think that this view is assailable?

I await the continuation of the book with great interest.

Yours,
Ferenczi

1. Freud 1923b, pp. 26 and 39.
2. "'Ego-memory-system,' to which fell the task of continually registering the subject's own physical or mental processes" ("Psycho-Analytical Observations on Tic," 1921, 232, pp. 155f.; *Schriften* II, 52).
3. Written this way in the original; what is probably meant is "in which the word 'love' is clothed."
4. Cf. "We succeeded in explaining the painful disorder of melancholia by supposing that [in those suffering from it] an object which was lost has been set up again inside the ego—that is, that an object-cathexis has been replaced by an identification . . . Since then we have come to understand that this kind of substitution has a great share in determining the form taken by the ego and that it makes an essential contribution towards building up what is called its 'character' . . . that the character of the ego is a precipitate of abandoned object-cathexes and that it contains the history of those object-choices" (Freud 1923b, pp. 28f.).
5. In the original there is a period instead of a question mark.
6. Freud 1923b, p. 31.
7. Ibid., p. 19.

927

Vienna, April 17, 1923
IX., Berggasse 19

Dear friend,

I vigorously regret that I am going without the advantage of your further remarks. Storfer, seized by blind ambition, has speeded up the printing so much that the thing will already be printed this week. I hardly got a word in myself.—

Now I am in my well-known depression after all the proofreading and swear never again to get onto such slippery ice. It seems to me that the curve has sunk steeply since the "Beyond."[1] It was still rich in thought and nicely written, Group Psychology[2] touches on the banal, and this "Id" is downright unclear, artificially put together, and terrible in its diction. So, I also didn't feel the enlightenment from the second sheet that you praise. Except for the basic idea of the "id" and the aperçu of the origin of morality, actually everything in this book displeases me.

Your remarks take the "id" too seriously; for that reason I don't dare respond to you. Your doubt about whether one can say "all" perceptions from outside are cs. touches on a problem that annoyed me only last night. The passage in question has, by the way, been changed somewhat.

Your inference about identification seems to me to be correct, but too sharp.

I am longing for the summer vacation, am also gradually unlearning cheerfulness.

On the tenth of the month, in Berlin, Oli married the girl who turned him down two years ago. My wife and Martin were at the wedding as a delegation and brought with them very friendly impressions. Unfortunately, the couple has no more than one room (in Duisburg) at their disposal. Much good mood and modesty will be demanded of the young woman.

My little grandson here[3] is the most ingenious child of this age (four years) that I have ever seen. He is also correspondingly thin and sickly, nothing but eyes, hair, and bones.

In your next letter I also hope to hear something personal from you and Frau Gisela.

Cordially,
Freud

1. Freud 1920g.
2. Freud 1921c.
3. "Heinerle."

928

Budapest, May 8, 1923

Dear Professor,

I wouldn't like to wait until Whitsun (when I will be in Vienna and see you), so I ask you to instruct me, if only in a few lines, about the operation that you endured.[1] I fear that you will now have to renounce a main pleasure, namely, smoking, for a rather long time! Please enlighten me with regard to that as well.

Jones added a few lines to today's Rundbrief from England, in which he talks about getting me invited to the Oxford Congress as well.[2] In consideration of your advice to cultivate every connection with England, I didn't out and out refuse, but requested detailed explanation about time, ameliorations of a financial nature, etc.

In the next few days I want to bring to paper a little technical contribution to "activity"[3] and send it in to you and Rank for appraisal. I am curious as to what you will say about it.

I will save the second half of the "Ego and Id" for a few quiet evenings. But things are already humming all around me with "ego," "id," and "superego."

Many kind regards.

Yours,
Ferenczi

1. The first operation on Freud's palate, an excision on the right anterior palatine arch for leukoplakia (the appearance of whitish spots on the mucous membrane of the mouth, often precancerous). On April 7, 1923, Freud had summoned his physician Felix Deutsch. Regarding the consultation, the latter noted: "Professor on April 7, 1923. It is terrible to get old—You will still see it. Regarding the illness: get set to see something that you won't like.—Smoking has rendered me so many services in life that I can only be thankful. It has given me the possibility altogether to work so much. I need a physician for what I have in mind: If the disease is malignant, then I will have to see how one can disappear from this world with decorum. The matter has only one catch. You won't know that I still have a mother; she is 87. It will be difficult to do that to the old woman" (Library of Congress). Evidently out of fear that Freud would commit suicide, Deutsch and the surgeon, Markus Hajek, concealed from Freud the fact that this was a case of carcinoma. See also Jones III, 90f.; Sharon Romm, *The Unwelcome Intruder: Freud's Struggle with Cancer* (New York, 1983); Schur, *Freud*; and Freud to Jones, April 25, 1923, *Freud/Jones*, p. 521.

2. International Congress of Psychology, Oxford, July 27–August 1, 1923. Jones was a member of the Executive Committee of the Congress and had already seen to it that Abraham was invited (Jones's *Rundbrief* of March 16, 1923, Butler Library). See the report on the Congress by Jones in *Zeitschrift* 9 (1923): 540. Also among the speakers were Alfred Adler, Morton Prince, and Pierre Janet.

3. Possibly "On Forced Phantasies: Activity in the Association-Technique" (1924, 265).

929

Vienna, May 10, 1923
IX., Berggasse 19

Dear friend,

Rank can attest to the fact that yesterday I announced the unshakable decision to write to you today, thus, before I had received your inquiry of today. I have had less time than usual these last few days. Eitingon didn't leave until Monday,[1] Ernst until today. Besides that I am still shortening my workday by going to bed early.

What I had was a leukoplakia on the right gum and cheek that grew rather quickly. Hajek explained that he didn't want to wait and see if and when it degenerated, and removed it thoroughly on April 28. I stayed at his clinic for two days, had afterbleeding, etc., canceled work for a whole week. I have been able to speak again for a long time, can swallow and bite almost properly, am again working at full capacity. My wife and Anna have cared for me tenderly. Minna is in the Cottage Sanatorium for a heart cure.

In the next few days I am supposed to get radium for the border of the wound. Smoking is permitted, but limited to a modest number, and contingent upon a tip [mouthpiece] which is shoved in.

Despite the uncertainty of a judgment in one's own case, and the certainty, as a patient, of being deceived by one's physician, I believe that the prognosis for this leukoplakia is not too bad. Naturally, the malady retains its value as a materialization of the general uncertainty that hovers over these years of life.

I am counting on seeing you for Whitsun and greet you and Frau Gisela cordially.

Yours,
Freud

1. Eitingon had come to Vienna on May 4 (Eitingon to Freud, April 27, 1923, Sigmund Freud Copyrights).

930

Budapest, May 29, 1923

Dear Professor,

I was pleased to have seen you in complete work capacity and in a good mood,[1] and share your favorable opinion about the malady, that is to say, its prognosis. Still, I would be very grateful to you if you would be so kind as to have a postcard come my way from time to time with the bulletin—no matter how laconically it may be composed.

The impression that Rank's communications made on me[2] grows with distance. I think you should make certain concesssions to him with regard to the mode of communication. I am convinced that he is quite willing to talk through the individual chapters with you and to leave out the hasty statements, perhaps perpetrated in enthusiasm, or entire chapters.

Enclosed I send you a recently published lead article from the Parisian "Figaro," "L'amnésie du Dr. Freud"[3]—certainly a sign that the ball has started rolling in France as well. *Abel Hermant,* the author, is one of the most gifted belletrists of the last few decades. I recommend to you the reading of his humorous anecdote "Les Transatlantiques";[4] the best parody of the Americans.

I will refer to the few events in the Society in the Rundbrief.

My intention *not* to go to Oxford is predominant for the time being. In the middle of *June* I intend to close up shop in order to go through with the operation. The X-ray examination done yesterday shows *no* retrosternal[5] swelling of the thyroid; so, it probably has only to do with disturbances caused by a lousy goiter by impeding the circulation and irritating the nerves. By stopping work early I do, to be sure, lose two weeks of breadwinning—still, I wouldn't like to shorten my vacation by two weeks, or calculate the weeks of the operation and convalescence in with the vacation.

Many regards to all your dear housemates and to you.

Yours,
Ferenczi

Unfortunately, haven't got a look at the Alexander coin[6] yet!

1. On the occasion of Ferenczi's visit to Vienna at Whitsun.

2. About Rank's *Trauma der Geburt* [The Trauma of Birth] (Vienna, 1924), the manuscript of which Rank had dedicated to Freud on his birthday on May 6. This book and the one jointly written by Rank and Ferenczi, *Entwicklungsziele der Psychoanalyse* [The Development of Psychoanalysis] (Vienna, 1924), were destined to take center stage in the coming scientific and personal disputes within the secret Committee.

3. *Le Figaro,* May 29, 1923.

4. Abel Hermant (1862–1950), *Les Transatlantiques: pièce de théâtre en quatre actes* (Paris, 1897).

5. Behind the breastbone (sternum).

6. Allusion unclear (Sándor = Alexander). Many rulers and popes named Alexander issued coins, especially in classical Greece and in nineteenth-century Russia. There is also a coin with a two-headed eagle, called the "Alexander-Adler" [Alexander-Eagle] (kind communication from R. Scott Carlton).

931

Vienna, June 1, 1923
IX., Berggasse 19

Dear friend,

I must contradict, I am not as satisfied as you assume, either with my condition after the operation or with my prospects. But now it has to do more with you. It seems questionable to me whether your operation is justified enough, and whether one can guarantee its harmlessness. Deutsch, with whom we spoke recently, is making a doubting gesture. For my part, I would certainly not like to have you come to harm on account of an identification with me.

I already made the concessions to Rank that you consider right. I see that one should leave him to his devices and would like best not to influence the work at all anymore. His finding is great indeed, he doesn't grasp it quite yet, and can't put it into proper perspective. Put some pressure on him to see that he certainly gets it done in the summer.

Write to me soon to enlighten and reassure.

Cordially,
Freud

932

Budapest, June 14, 1923

Dear Professor,

The bad news about your dear little grandson's severe illness[1] has deeply saddened us. These are the cases in which one catches oneself still having expected some "providence" or "justice"; one is outraged over the dumb, blind—one would like to say—evil, fate.

I have the news from Lajos Lévy, who seems, by the way, to have given up his trip to Vienna after receiving your letter.

In my affair, in which you are so thoroughly interested, we intend to decide with all necessary caution. These next few days I am still having myself examined by a laryngologist, then (after another X-ray examination) again by the surgeon and Lévy.

This episode disturbed my practice quite severely. In consideration of the possibility of an operation in the second half of June, I had to give notice for June 15 to the patients who are to be let go (among them, Frau D[r.?] Herford,[2] who has improved significantly and become smarter). Now that the decision is being postponed, many hours remain empty for me; naturally, I can no longer accept new patients.

I can't say anything definite yet about my summer plans. I want to spend at least a part of the vacation at the place where Rank is staying.

Rank is highly pleased about the concessions you made to him, and will certainly draw up the formulations quite carefully.—I, too, think that his finding can still achieve undeniable significance. I wrote to him, among other things, that with all recognition of the general importance of the factor of birth trauma, I see the *etiological primacy of the Oedipus complex in the neuroses* as unshaken.

Many kind regards.

Yours,
Ferenczi

1. "Heinele ... is now in a coma ... The doctors say it may last another week and recovery is not desirable, fortunately, not probable ... I bear this loss so badly, I think I have never experienced anything more difficult, perhaps the shock is operating along with my own illness. I do my work by necessity, at bottom, everything is of no value to me" (Freud to Kata and Lajos Lévy, June 11, 1923, Library of Congress).

2. Ethilde B. M. Herford from London, associate member of the British Society after analyses with Flügel (Abraham's *Rundbrief* of October 27, 1920, Butler Library); in analysis with Ferenczi since fall 1922. She was a translator of Freud (1906c, 1907c, 1908d). The question of her suitability as an analyst was discussed frequently in the *Rundbriefen* of the years 1920–1924, in which Jones, especially, expressed skepticism; she was, however, accepted as a full member after her analysis with Ferenczi.

933

Vienna, June 20, 1923[1]

Dear friend,

I am very pleased that your operation has been passed off as superfluous. My dear child died yesterday.

Cordially,
Freud

1. Postcard.

934

INTERNATIONALE ZEITSCHRIFT FÜR
ÄRZTLICHE PSYCHOANALYSE

Budapest, June 26, 1923

Dear Professor,

I hope that you will still get this letter in Vienna.¹ It is probably best for me to keep a strict silence about the profoundly sad case that you communicated to me.

What there is to report about me is that I am well and have decided to make the English trip (to Oxford) after all. Not until after England would I get to Klobenstein, or the place where Rank settles in. I will naturally be present in Wolkenstein, or wherever else the Committee members meet. I will travel to England alone; I will meet my wife in South Tirol.

I would like to know whether you have been informed about the Dick matter² by way of Rank.

Many kind regards.

Yours,
Ferenczi

1. On June 30 Freud and Minna Bernays traveled to Gastein and from there, at the end of July, to Lavarone by way of Annenheim and Bolzano, where Martha and Anna, as well as Mathilde and Robert, joined them (Freud's and Rank's *Rundbrief* of June 30, 1923). Jones met them there on August 1. "The members of the Committee met at Castel Toblino on August 26 and went on to stay at San Cristoforo . . . In the first days of September Martha Freud and her sister went to Meran, Freud and Anna to Rome" (Jones III, 98).
2. See letters 903–905.

935

Budapest, July 15, 1923

Dear Professor,

I hope there is no immediate reason as to why I have had no news from you for so long. In the week before last I was—on the occasion of my fiftieth birthday¹—inundated with congratulations. I honestly admit that a word from you would have outweighed everything else. To be sure, my memory was conspicuous by its absence at your last birthday.

I can allow myself to accept, *only in part* without pangs of conscience, the exceedingly large gift² that you allowed yourself to be carried away with. It is, indeed, a small fortune that I was so immodest as to request. Such a burden will press on me continually! So, you won't think ill of me if I ask you to be allowed to pay back *at least half* with the English pounds that Dr. Eder still owes me. Even so, it is an unbelievably great gift, which is meant to be the equivalent of a library to me. Nowadays, one can't buy books anymore.

I also thank you for your willingness to accede to the somewhat impertinent idea of Radó's for a festschrift;[3] but I promise, despite this grandiose literary accolade, not to rest on my laurels, but to work diligently again.

My wife and I are going first to Klobenstein tomorrow morning. I have given up the trip to Oxford, which would have greatly fragmented my vacation.

I hope you are well in Gastein. I also hope that your iron constitution, which I often regarded with astonishment, will also overcome this bad year.

Many heartfelt greetings.

Your grateful
Ferenczi

1. On July 7.
2. The *Encyclopaedia Britannica*.
3. Issue no. 2 of the *Zeitschrift* for 1923 was dedicated to Ferenczi, with a foreword by Freud (1923i).

936

Bad Gastein, July 18, 1923

Dear friend,

Why didn't I congratulate you on your fiftieth? I don't think it was recompense, but rather, it has to do with my present aversion to life. I have never had a depression before, but this must be one now. I would not have passed up the courtesy toward someone who is more of a stranger.

What you write about sharing the costs of the Encyclopaedia Britannica is, naturally, unacceptable. It was determined that you have to get the work sometime, since you had directly expressed the wish for it, and now you combined the expression of this wish with various admonitions no longer to postpone carrying out the plan.

I would like to urge you not to distract Rank too much;[1] he has important things to write this summer, and, when Sachs comes, keep him away from him [Rank], since he will certainly not provide for his own defense.

I wish you and your dear wife the most efficacious recuperation on the beautiful heights of Klobenstein.

Cordially,
Freud

1. Rank was also spending the holidays in Klobenstein.

937

INTERNATIONALE ZEITSCHRIFT FÜR
ÄRZTLICHE PSYCHOANALYSE

Klobenstein, July 25, 1923
Hotel Post

Dear Professor,

Above all, I beg your pardon for having admonished you. I should have known that you could not be in a mood to participate in a celebration. I thank you again, and this time without reservation, for the great gift, which signifies for me a wish fulfillment that I had given up a long time ago. I must accommodate myself to the fact that you treat lightly the great material difficulty of this question. As you know, I am a curious person, who would like to know all kinds of things, but to whom nothing is more repugnant than aridly looking things up in literature. In the encyclopedia I would now have the learned friend who gives me short and to the point information about everything.

I have in any event—for my part—already taken heed of your admonition not to distract Rank, since I am occupied with writing the Theory of Genitality and the biological speculations.[1] Rank's work has the effect of being a wet nurse in this; I would like—also on account of the historically correct sequence—for my work to appear simultaneously with his, if not before it. Sachs is not much of a disruption.

Right after my arrival, we—actually together, for the first time—looked through the would-be[2] prize work,[3] and find that it does *not* conform to the requirements of the prize topic, and can serve, at most, as a preliminary work for a future compilation.

Klobenstein is beautiful, but the woods are far away and dry. We see Frau Mathilde and Robert daily; yesterday we were in Kematen with them and the Ranks. The individual places in the woods evoke memories in me of conversations that we had with each other here.[4]—Apropos! Will you permit me, in the genitality work (in the biological part), to come back to the assumptions about Lamarckism etc. that we constructed jointly in Pápa and elsewhere?

Many kind regards from your

now really old
Ferenczi

1. Ferenczi 1924, 268.
2. The words "would-be" are in English in the original [Trans.].
3. *Entwicklungsziele der Psychoanalyse: Zur Wechselbeziehung von Theorie und Praxis* [Developmental Goals of Psychoanalysis: On the Interrelationship of Theory and Practice; published in English as *The Development of Psychoanalysis*]. Ferenczi and

Rank (1924, 264) originally wanted to submit it for the prize offered by Freud for the best work on the relationship between theory and technique, but later distanced themselves from it (Freud, 1922d).

4. On their vacation together in 1911.

938

Klobenstein, August 1, 1923[1]

Dear Professor,

We are pleased that you didn't have to go to Vienna,[2] and would have liked to await you in Bolzano, if we hadn't been afraid we would disturb. We will probably move to Lake Garda around the middle of August, so, in your vicinity, and we certainly hope for a pleasant reunion.

Yours,
Ferenczi
Frau Gizella

[In a different handwriting:]
Kind regards to you and yours.

Yours,
Rank and Beata Rank

1. Multicolored art postcard with a woman in costume: "Tirolean Costumes: Leukental <Söll>."
2. "[Hajek] startled Freud by asking him to send a report of his condition every fortnight and to come to see him at the end of July. In the middle of July Freud wrote from Gastein to ask if he really need come to Vienna, whereupon Hajek, after a fortnight's delay, answered that it was not necessary" (Jones III, 92). From Gastein Freud went to Lavarone and from there to Rome with Anna. "My peau de chagrin [skin of distress] (Balzac) has also become short, and it is precisely for that reason that I want to use the last morsels dearly, I want to see Rome once more and give Anna a great joy" (Freud to Alexander Freud, August 11, 1923, Library of Congress).

939

Klobenstein, August 21, 1923

Dear Professor,

I am looking forward to being able to see you again and to speak with you. Brill, about whose comet-like appearance and disappearance you have already been informed,[1] told us you were completely healthy, but one prefers to convince oneself personally.—The day in Lavarone will be a worthy conclusion to a summer of work. I had an American woman along here, to whom I gave hours, wrote the (to you, well-known) Theory of Genitality, and revised with Rank—about five times—the "joint work," about which we would still like to talk to you. I didn't want to burden you in the summer with reading the manuscript of the "Theory of Genitality"; Rank has already read it and will present it to you on request.

I hope that the Committee meeting will conclude peacefully; Eitingon's presence, especially, will contribute much to it. I also hope we will succeed in restoring complete understanding between Rank and Abraham. With Jones the matter is somewhat more difficult, since personal factors also figure in there. But we think it is not yet time to act more energetically against him, although we want to call him to account for certain things.[2]

Rank and I would have liked to come to Lavarone for a few days, but refrained from doing so in order not to arouse the jealousy of the rest of the Committee members.

Urbantschitsch was here recently, expressly for the purpose of talking to me about his sanatorium plans. He claimed that you had decided to work along; under this condition I also agreed in principle [pending getting back to talk with you].[3] Perhaps the sanatorium would be a chance for psychoanalysis; something for Rank's future could also be done there.[4]

My wife, who has been feeling well up to now, but who is at the moment going through the "Klobenstein intestinal catarrh"[5] and is bedridden, sends greetings to you all.

In concordance with that, I am

Yours truly,
Ferenczi

1. On August 16 Brill had paid a surprise visit to Freud in Lavarone (Brill and Freud to Rose Brill, August 16, 1923, Library of Congress) and the day after to Ferenczi and Rank in Klobenstein (Brill to Rose Brill, August 17, 1923, Library of Congress).

2. The meeting of the Committee in San Cristoforo on August 26—in which Freud, who was nearby in Lavarone, did not participate—is said to have been marked by an extremely heated controversy between Rank and Jones. Rank was enraged over an allegedly anti-Semitic remark that Jones had made about him to Brill, and demanded Jones's expulsion from the Committee, which was prevented from happening at Abraham's urging. Cf. letter of Jones to his wife, Katharine: "The chief news is that Freud has a real cancer slowly growing and may last years. He doesn't know it and it is a most deadly secret. Eitingon is here too ... We have spent the whole day thrashing out the Rank-Jones affair. Very painful but I hope our relations will now be better and believe so, but on the other hand expect Ferenczi will hardly speak to me for Brill has just been there and told him I had said Rank was a swindling Jew (stark übertrieben [strongly exaggerated])." August 26, 1923, in Brome, *Jones*, p. 139.

3. Brackets in the original.

4. Urbantschitsch had received an offer from Field Marshal Archduke Friedrich von Österreich to make his estate, Weilburg, in Baden, near Vienna, a psychoanalytic sanatorium. According to Urbantschitsch's questionable version, Freud had agreed to move

there as medical director but renounced this intention after his cancer operation. The plans for the sanatorium fell apart. Rudolph von Urban[tschitsch], *Myself Not Least: A Confessional Autobiography of a Psychoanalyst and Some Explanatory History Cases* (London, 1958), pp. 193–195.

5. An ailment typical at that time on account of the poor quality of the calcium-laden water on the Ritten (kind communication from Inga Hosp).

940

Internationale Zeitschrift für
Ärztliche Psychoanalyse

Budapest,
Sunday, September , 1923[1]

Dear Professor,

Most cordial greetings from me as well on the occasion of your return home from the wonderful city of the Romans. Again and again in the last few weeks I was reminded of the beautiful time when we were able to visit the holy places together[2] (I must admit that I have a kind of religious sensitivity when it comes to the ancient world). I count those days among the most beautiful of my life and gratefully think of the incomparable guide that you were for me.

I plunged head over heels into work. The cases are extremely interesting from a scientific viewpoint, especially since I am occupied with testing the Rankian ideas (in my practice). I find that one can put *more* trust in his points of view than we were inclined to in the first instance, and that major theoretical and technical difficulties can be solved with ease if one decides always to invoke the aftereffects of the birth trauma again and again as an explanation. To be sure, it remains a great and interesting problem to put the unshakable facts of the theory of neuroses in context with it.

But no matter how much, as you see, the work stimulates me intellectually, the less satisfying it is materially, since this time there is no foreigner with me. At the same time, the private burdens and those imposed by the state become heavier and heavier. Political conditions have improved here somewhat,[3] so that we can also begin gradually to appear again in public with psychoanalysis. I had the festschrift issue sent to the Budapest publishers, and it was mentioned by several in an extremely appreciative fashion. So, this issue not only honored me, but also performed a service for the cause in Hungary.

Your wonderful present—the encyclopedia—was already adorning my bookcase upon my arrival. I show it to everyone and am the object of real envy. Binding and fittings are flawless. I already had to look up things several times in it—to be sure, I was in a big hurry to make use of the work.

In a Viennese Hungarian newspaper that knows our Verlag's vice director, there is an excerpt from an interview published in the "Temps" (Paris) that a Frenchman by the name of *Raymond Recouly* is supposed to have had with you. He describes the outward characteristics of your person and home in a more or less anti-Semitic fashion, i.e., he characterizes you as a genuinely rabbinical body and spirit; naturally, he defends the French against the charge that they don't want to recognize foreigners. The interview was published in an August issue of the "Temps."⁴

Please write to me *soon* about how you are, and how your sister-in-law and your other loved ones are.

With kind regards—from my wife as well.

Yours truly,
Ferenczi

1. The day is missing from the date. Balint read the number "3," evidently erroneously, for September 3 was not a Sunday. Since Freud did not return until September 21 (see *Sigmund Freud/Lou Andreas Salomé Letters*, ed. Ernst Pfeiffer [New York, 1966], p. 233, note to p. 126), and a consultation with Pichler took place on September 26, September 23 comes into consideration as the date of the letter.

2. On the vacations they took together in 1910 and 1912.

3. Since 1921 there had been a phase of consolidation under the government of Count István Bethlen. The activities of the extreme right were curtailed, and there was a far-reaching amnesty for former proponents of the Council Republic. In 1924 the government received a credit of 250 million crowns from the League of Nations.

4. *Le Temps*, August 14, 1923.

941

Budapest, October 28, 1923

Dear Professor,

Now that I know you again to be in your abode, I dare to write to you in order finally to give expression to my great joy over the success of the grave intervention that caused us so much worry.¹ I know, to be sure, that you still have great unpleasantness to bear, but I must admit that sympathy that comes into consideration with me is small in comparison with my gratification over the fact that everything that is diseased has been removed and that we are fully justified in hoping for your restoration.—As a genuine "Jewish orderly," I can share with you the fact that I reacted to the news of the operation that was carried out with a severe indisposition, in which I put into operation all the mechanisms at my disposal (intestine, heart, etc.) as never before. The whole thing lasted only a day, and every trace of it was gone in a few days.

I hear from Kata Lévy, who knows it from Fräulein Anna, that you are already restored to the extent that you are reading—whether you are also writing, I don't know, of course. In spite of this, I permit myself a question (the answer to which is not at all urgent), since without its solution I don't understand a passage of your "Ego and Id," which I have to review on instructions from the editorial board.² On page 13 is written the following: "... that in the descriptive sense there are two kinds of unconscious, but in the dynamic sense only one."³—but since you write on page 12 that the latent unconscious is unconscious only descriptively, not in the dynamic sense,⁴ I thought that it is precisely the dynamic way of looking at things that requires setting up the two kinds of ucs., whereas description knows only cs. and ucs.

Another question, which can be answered with a simple "yes" or "no," is whether I am correct in construing the sentence on page 30: "It is as if we were thus supplied with a proof [that] ... the conscious ego ... is first and foremost a body ego"⁵—in such a way that the function of the *conscious* ego is limited mainly to the somatic function of perception and to the motoric (will)-impulses that follow from it, but that all remaining ego functions proceed unconsciously.

This not easy reading is becoming especially interesting to me by virtue of the fact that in several places I think I have found the actual theoretical foundation for several practical-technical suggestions which Rank and I made in our joint work.

It will interest you, and especially Fräulein Anna, to know that I wrote to Frau Lou Andreas-Salomé today; she would like to come to us for a few weeks in order to recuperate from Nordic Prussia.

Let's hope I haven't tired you too much with this letter!

I wish for you from the bottom of my heart the speediest recovery—but in the meantime the perseveration of the wonderful attitude that I admired in you at my last visit.

With regards from my wife and from me—

Yours,
Ferenczi

1. The major operation by Hans Pichler on October 4 and 11, in which the whole upper jaw and palate on the affected side were removed. It was not until the day of this letter, October 28, that Freud was released from the hospital (Jones III, 98). On Professor Hans Pichler (1877–1949), see Romm, *The Unwelcome Intruder*, pp. 11–16.
2. No such review by Ferenczi has been published.
3. The mix-up (see Freud's reply, which follows) was never corrected (Freud 1923b, p. 15).
4. Ibid.
5. Ibid., p. 27.

942

Vienna, October 30, 1923
IX., Berggasse 19[1]

Dear friend!

I assume that you have not had any part in the excesses of the rumor about my good health. I have been free of pain for only two days, and I slept without narcosis for one night. Still very exhausted and incapable of anything. You are right, the severe intervention seems to have succeeded. Now we will have to see what it will accomplish for me.

I am, to be sure, not writing myself, but I am having Anna write for me. Your question about the passage "Ego and Id," page 13, downright frightened me. What is written there is the complete opposite of page 12, and in the sentence on page 13, descriptive and dynamic are simply interchanged—I would like to decline your second question as to how you should interpret the sentence that the conscious ego is above all a body ego. The genetic meaning is certainly clear, and I would not like to touch the indefiniteness further.

Your news that you have invited Lou has made us very happy. But perhaps you didn't know that she is tied to Königsberg for months.

Let's leave it for today with this short note. I greet you and Frau Gisela cordially.

Yours,
Freud

1. The letter was written on a typewriter; only the signature, "Freud," and the underlinings are handwritten.

943

Budapest, December 20, 1923

Dear Professor,

Since I am postponing my intention to go to Vienna until New Year's, and I won't be seeing you again at Christmas, I am pressed to tell you at least in writing how very happy I am about the, albeit difficult, nevertheless so favorable course of your convalescence. I hope that we will be able to talk with each other pleasantly again in the new year about various subjects of mutual interest. Some things are certainly less pleasant, such as, among other things, the signs of disharmony among the members of the Committee. I have also contributed to the discord with my energetic coming out against Jones;[1] still, it was and is my opinion that, at least in the close confines of the Committee, one should be capable of giving one's opinion honestly to one another. I hope that you weren't offended by my method of operation, even if I found it understandable that you were unpleasantly affected by all these things among us. I will spare myself thediscussion of these and other similar matters, as mentioned, until we meet personally—a reassuring statement on your part, however, would be very desirable to me in the meantime.—Less unpleasant are the scientific things that we would have to talk about, inasmuch as personal things are, in general, always more burdensome than matters of fact—at least for me.

I am working at full steam, am now letting three patients go and am taking three new ones in their place, and am happy with the technical and scientific success.

I would like you to ask Fräulein Anna to share with me Lou Salomé's address in Königsberg.

With the best holiday wishes to you and all your dear ones.

Yours truly,
Ferenczi

P. S. Have you read the advance proofs of the "Theory of Genitality"?

1. Whom Ferenczi accused of plagiarism (see letter 586 and n. 1).

944

Budapest, January 20, 1924

Dear Professor,

I am already very eager to hear something about how you are since the resumption of your activity. If it won't cost you much effort, I ask you for a brief bulletin.

Since we didn't see each other anymore after the Committee meeting, I was not in a position to ask you about your personal impression of my lecture.[1] Your facetious remark in which you apostrophized Rank as a "co-conspirator" comes to my mind again and again, however, and I have the—perhaps hypochondriacal—idea that you are not in agreement with everything. That naturally contradicts your frequently expressed assent—and in spite of this, I would like to ask you to reassure, that is to say, enlighten me in this regard.

My practice has increased since the middle of January: I have an American [female] patient and an English [female] colleague in treatment, that is to say, training. The difficulties with language are not as great as I thought.

We intend shortly to come out of our shell and to hold five to six lay lectures in the "physicians' casino." Besides myself, Hollós, Hermann,

Pfeifer, Eisler, perhaps also Róheim will speak. The main purpose is not so much to make propaganda as it is more to get the "latent analysts" to speak, and if appropriate, to recruit new initiates from among them.[2]

The devaluation of the Hungarian crown[3] is making rapid strides; it will soon reach the lowest level of the Austrian. Misery prevails in the middle class; medical practice has almost come to a complete standstill, people have no money for being sick. Will a "carpenter" help us as well?[4]

Kind regards,
Ferenczi

1. "On January 2, 1924, Ferenczi read a paper from the book [Ferenczi and Rank, *The Development of Psycho-Analysis*] before the Vienna Society in Freud's presence" (Jones III, 57. See also Rank's *Rundbrief* of January 4, 1924, Butler Library).

2. "From February 15 on, the Society will give a weekly lecture in the medical club (only for physicians). I will give the introductory lecture, Hermann will talk about "Psychoanalysis and Psychology," Pfeiffer about dreams, Eisler about the theory of sexuality, then I about neuroses, Hollós about psychoses, Róheim about the relationship between the psychology of neurotics and [that] of savages. After a hiatus of more than ten years we will thus appear before the public again (the last time I spoke before a *medical* group was fifteen years ago!)" (Ferenczi's *Rundbrief* of February 3, 1924, Butler Library). The seven-hour course (*Zeitschrift* 10 [1924]: 243) was attended by approximately one hundred persons (letter 995).

3. The Hungarian crown had been introduced in March 1920. After initial successes on the part of the Bethlen government to get inflation in check, it again had to print more money in order to control expenditures. It was only the League of Nations' approval of a credit of 250 million crowns in June 1924 that put an end to inflation for the time being.

4. Meaning unclear. Possibly an allusion to the mayor of Vienna, Jakob Reumann, a skilled woodworker, who carried through far-reaching reforms (see letter 841 and n. 5).

945

Vienna, January 22, 1924
IX., Berggasse 19

Dear friend,

You shall have the report that you ask for. On the whole, I am not doing badly. On the positive side should be entered the fact that my six hours of work do not leave a trace of intellectual or bodily fatigue, but rather that the whole form of life is perceived as a comfortable laziness. The damaged functions are exercised in a very uneven fashion, good and bad days diverge greatly from one another. On the other hand, all sorts of torments—not surprising with half of the face hypesthetic—won't cease, and disturb my comfort. Some advantage will be promised me from improving the prosthesis; up to now I have felt nothing reassuring from the effects of the Steinach operation.¹ My mood is not yet firm, I don't trust the peace and await disaster with every indication.

The paper on masochism² is finished, remains not up to my expectation. I am not completely in agreement with your joint work,³ although there is much in it that I value. I have discussed some of it critically with Rank, but on the whole, I would prefer to hold off so that all of you won't be disturbed in your production. In this fashion I want to make my still being present in old age harmless. Your lecture was very strange; it didn't treat the book you wrote together at all, but rather your own thing, active therapy, as though you wanted to place it in opposition to the Rankian birth trauma. A derailment in the long-abandoned tracks of the brother complex.

I greet you and Frau Gisela cordially. Yours, unchanged by being sick and old,

Freud

1. "On November 17 Freud underwent a Steinach operation . . . ligature of the vas deferens on both sides. This was in the hope that the rejuvenation such an operation promised might delay the return of the cancer" (Jones III, 98–99).
2. "The Economic Problem of Masochism" (Freud 1924c).
3. The Development of Psychoanlysis.

946

Budapest, January 30, 1924

Dear Professor,

Your letter has shaken me considerably. For the first time since our acquaintance, which you soon elevated to friendship, I hear words of dissatisfaction from you. I didn't want to respond in the first affect, therefore I postponed this letter until today.

Since I had no news from Rank which would have informed me of your critical discussions, and since I heard only words of assent from you in Berlin, Lavarone, several times in Vienna, your statement to the effect that you were not in agreement with everything in the joint work caught me completely by surprise. I and, as I know for certain, also Rank were, at the outset in composing the work, striving to avoid everything with which you might not agree, which we succeeded in doing more easily by virtue of the fact that we did not deviate from psychoanalytic ground by a hair's breadth. As a precaution we read to you the first (still rough) draft aloud in Berlin, in order to be sure of your assent (in general). We were glad to see you in agreement and wove the few remarks that you made, whose correctness we saw immediately, into the later conception. You were then so kind as to cheer us up, to involve us with this work in the prize competition that was announced immediately afterwards, which we likewise interpreted as assent, as you were still of the opinion not very long before that the work should be handed in and awarded a prize. Since you also read the galleys for it and gave us valuable suggestions for reordering the chapters and emphasizing more sharply individual points (which we gratefully accepted and turned to good account), we thought we could assume that you had no objections to the content. But we certainly would have also examined most conscientiously and very probably also taken into consideration further reservations on your part, if you had expressed them.

But now we are referred to conjectures, especially I, about which I heard nothing from the critical statements. Permit me to refer to the points which, in my instance—especially after the discussions with the Viennese and with Sachs—come into question as such, against which objections could be made on the part of psychoanalysis.

There is above all the reference to the possibility that at some time psychoanalysis could be amalgamated with suggestion (hypnosis). It goes without saying that we spoke of this possibility only in extremely hypothetical form, not much differently than you, Herr Professor, spoke about it in the Budapest lecture.[1] We also emphasized that this amalgamation would be allowed only for practical (healing) purposes, not for scientific ones. Naturally it was, and is, quite beside the point whether we bring this, in and of itself questionable, prophecy to bear in the work or not; we would gladly have omitted it at your request, had you only expressed a sign of displeasure.

The only thing that we heard from you in the way of objection was, at the time, the fear that we were putting too much emphasis on the factor of experience and too little on remembering. But we were making an effort in the pamphlet to stress more emphatically the view, which corresponded totally to our own conception, that analysis should not dissipate in "experiences." We do not cease to refer to the absolute necessity of *conscious anchoring* [memory][2] as the only prophylactic measure. In fact, we are actually suggesting a more generous utilization of the repetition tendency than before, but that is only a quantitative difference, as it were, about which further experience has to decide. For that reason, I don't believe that your dissatisfaction could pertain to this point.—

The objection to setting a date in every case would be the strongest. Nevertheless, experiences of the last few years have convinced me still more of the correctness of this "activity." I must admit, certainly, that the finer *setting of indication* for this measure is not entirely certain and will be presented only after further experience. Perhaps we should have referred to these still open questions.

The contrast between the more "observing" technique, which collects scientific facts, and the "active" technique could also have been raised (to our disadvantage). But we thought it was time to place, for once, the practical-technical possibilities (which brought us success) in opposition to the all too scientific tendency, which is somewhat remote from practice, which prevails in our circles. We also hope with certainty that scientific experience is also to be had along these lines. What we attempted was only an attempt to use the knowledge already gleaned more energetically in technique, for once.

It is certainly possible that I am defending myself against objections that you don't even raise. But I didn't want to keep silent about my efforts to solve this riddle, so that you see already how unawares your remark has caught me.

I can myself, in part, confirm the remarks that you let drop about my lecture. Brother envy actually did play a part in the conception of the work, but only as *a reaction, as conscious defense against the influence of this complex.* Instead of occupying myself with the theoretical content of the book, I made an effort to emphasize more clearly than was done in the book that the most significant part: the *setting of a date* and the analytic situation, which is *always* to be considered *without exception,* comes from Rank, and not from me. The fact that I unduly emphasized my "activities" on the side was only owing to the fact that I illustrated the book with *my* examples, whereby my technique had to be described. But I concede that the repressed was able to return in the repressing and to be responsible for the impression that you had of the lecture.

Permit me finally to refer to a contradiction that fortunately exists between two sentences in your letter. You speak about the fact that, on the whole, you prefer to withdraw, so that we won't be disturbed in our production and so that you will make your still being present in old age harmless. But in the end you take leave of me as "Freud, unchanged by being sick and old." Allow me to hold to the latter and to ask you, as before, to acknowledge all your objections also in statu nascendi of the works. We can and will not renounce your criticism and your pointers. You should not, after so many years of collaboration under your leadership, not even in such a polite form, leave us to our own devices.

For me, personally, it would be an almost inconceivable idea no longer, as before, to discuss everything significant with you, and to know that the whole production of psychoanalysis, but especially my own, is no longer under your leadership. It can, and could, never be a question of a "disturbance" on your part. Indeed, we can on no account do without your help.

I would like to suggest to you to agree to a meeting of three (you, Rank, and I), still before the Congress, to discuss the wavering scientific questions.

I and my wife are glad from the bottom of our hearts for the good news about your ability to work; we only regret that you also still have worse days.

Your gratefully devoted
Ferenczi

1. "It is very probable, too, that the large-scale application of our therapy will compel us to alloy the pure gold of analysis freely with the copper of direct suggestion, and hypnotic influence, too, might find a place in it again" ("Lines of Advance in Psycho-Analytic Therapy," Freud 1919a, pp. 167f.).
2. Brackets in the original.

947

Vienna, February 4, 1924
IX., Berggasse 19

Dear friend,

I am writing still on the evening of the day when I received your letter because I am sorry that you are in distress and I don't understand you completely. Above all, you must let me know what I actually wrote about your joint work. I don't remember the quoted remark exactly and would not like to appear to myself to be two-faced. The one fact exists that I don't like it as well as at the beginning, before I had gained some distance from it. I would now make a judgment that it has its birth defect, in that it emphasized the "experience," in the manner of a slogan, and overcame its dissolution too little, or not entirely. In the beginning I was probably too corrupted by the correction that you brought to bear on my former skittishness about "acting out [*Agieren*]."¹

But now I wouldn't know how to say what I don't agree with. I have already shared with Rank and Sachs an impression that, on the path that has been broken there, one could come out of analysis, that it promises to be a path for traveling salesmen.² But there is no doubt that it doesn't have to be that way. The warning ought to suffice.

My open criticism was related to your lecture, as you had requested it to be, and objected to the fact that you did not speak to the content of the book, but rather about active therapy, which, by the way, was the general impression. I now think that the lack of clarity of the situation comes from the fact that the opus itself is not honest. Behind it is lodged Rank's "trauma of birth" and your activity, and both go back to the striving to hasten the course of the analyses. But both innovations are hardly talked about in the book.

Now, as regards your effort to remain in harmony with me throughout, I value it highly as an expression of your friendship, but I find the goal neither necessary nor easily attainable. I know that I am hard to approach and that I can't at first get started with foreign thoughts which aren't totally in my backyard. It takes a long while before I have a judgment about them; in the meantime, I have to keep my judgment in suspenso. If you wanted to wait that long every time, then that would be the end of your productivity. So, it won't work that way. It does seem out of the question to me that either you or Rank, in your independent excursions, would ever abandon the ground of analysis. So, why shouldn't you have the right to try and see whether something doesn't go differently than I intended. If you make a mistake in doing so, then you will notice it sometime yourself, or I will take the liberty of telling you so, as soon as I know it for sure myself.

Things are more difficult for me with Rank than with you; he is also personally much more sensitive. At first, his birth trauma made me distrustful. In the first joy of discovery he seemed ready to see the primal motif of neurosis in birth, so that I told him, jokingly: With a finding like that, someone else would make himself independent. Later he moderated himself, his trauma impressed me greatly, I resolved to look out for it in the analyses, and now, after four weeks of fresh work, I have become quite skeptical again. I always talk about it, without it changing anything, or my pupils,[3] analysts themselves, occupy themselves with it and ascertain the lack of effectivenes of this conception. I still don't have a sure judgment about it. The strongest impression that I have is that it is not possible in a short time to penetrate such deep layers and bring about lasting psychic changes. But perhaps I am really already vieux jeu.[4]

I found unpleasant a letter from Eitingon, which arrived today from the Riviera, which says that Abraham is very agitated about the form and content of the Rankian publications (the one you did together included), and that there will be serious discord between him and Rank.[5] Rank does not have the gift for flatteringly convincing presentation, which, e.g., is such a hallmark of your works, and is, unfortunately, uncouth and not very skillful in all literary matters. After the dissension with Jones, that gives bad prospects for collaboration in the Committee. I would have hoped that you, at least, as long as I am here, would keep together. It should not be any other way.

The tripartite talk that you are suggesting would be very nice, but I am too little prepared for it at the moment. It is better if I form an opinion for myself, first. In Berlin they also don't want to believe in the trauma of birth and the possibilities of shortening the treatment in Rank's sense, either.[6]

My health has stood up very well now to a month of work. I have taken in monies once again after half a year, with downright animalistic satisfaction. Physically, I am still suffering in all kinds of places. The most painful is the stricture caused by the scar, which often makes it impossible to stick a cigar between my teeth, and which can only be counteracted mechanically by distention, by means of a clothespin. Speaking and chewing are very irregular, often bad, but are sufficient for treatment and nourishment. But today I tried on for the first time the new and definitive prosthesis, which sits far more securely, and I think it immediately improved my speech very much. I won't get it until a few days from now. So, let's toil on!

I greet you and Gisela cordially and am sure to hear from you soon.

Yours,
Freud

1. See Freud, "Remembering, Repeating, and Working-Through" (1914g).
2. See letter 316 and n. 5.
3. The word "pupils" is written in English in the original [Trans.].
4. French for "old-fashioned," "over the hill."
5. "In the Committee the new books had had the effect of a bomb . . . Abraham . . . is . . . especially angry about the fact that nothing had been previously revealed to the Committee . . . about the content of the new publications. The tension between him and Rank which had been latently present for a long time has now greatly increased." The only way out was for Freud to take a position with regard to the new views (Eitingon to Freud, January 31, 1924, Sigmund Freud Copyrights).
6. Ibid.

948

INTERNATIONAL PSYCHO-ANALYTICAL ASSOCIATION
CENTRAL EXECUTIVE
PRESIDENT: DR. ERNEST JONES   SECRETARY: DR. KARL ABRAHAM
81, Harley Street, London, W. 1.   Bismarckallee 14, Grunewald, Berlin.[1]

Budapest, February 14, 1924

Dear Professor,

First of all, I thank you for such a detailed reply, the smoothness of which may serve as a new sign of your wellness. I thank you likewise for the friendly communications about your health, which gratified me on the whole, although the difficulty caused by the stricture of the scar must signify an unbearable torment. Let us hope that this burdensome after-symptom will soon be eliminated.

Returning to the content of your letter, I will cite the brief sentence from your last letter (at your request) which disconcerted me. You say there that you were "not in agreement with everything." That is all, but that is not little, when one doesn't know what and how much you disagreed with! To this was added the recollection of your facetious remark in the Vienna meeting about my "co-conspiracy" and hollow, unconfirmed rumors from Berlin, which twaddled about your dissatisfaction. All that put together my mood which drove me to confront you with my direct inquiry.

I must admit that, even after your detailed reply, I still don't understand your objections *completely*, as you yourself say in one place that—after you took me to task for a number of things—you yourself don't know what you actually disagree with in the joint work. I conclude from that that you still haven't found the necessary distance for making a judgment, indeed, that the pro and the contra (as in the letter itself) is intermittently put into words. That certainly leaves for me the hope that in the end the favorable impression will win out after all, the one that you often expressed about us and to which you don't hold out anything weighty in opposition in your letter to me.

I would like to return to some of your remarks individually.

1.) The slogan-like use of the factor of experience was, as mentioned, not our intention; immediately after you called our attention to the possibility that our work could be sold by the barrel in this sense (perhaps by Kayserling),[2] we hastened to make the necessary corrections. [Certainly I would like to bring up, in favor of "acting out" or experiencing, the fact that affective analytic experiencing in and of itself already means a kind of "becoming conscious" for the patient and brings along with it a certain protection against a relapse into repression (symptom formation). Naturally, however, this security is significantly increased by connecting with earlier experiencing (or with its "construction").][3]

2.) Your charge that our work was *not honest* can be easily refuted in light of the facts. *"Activity"* is and was, from the very beginning, emphasized as one of the foundations of the work. The "Trauma of Birth," however, *was not able* to be communicated, because this idea did not come to Rank until *after* the second joint revision of the work, as a *consequence* of the work itself, so to speak. *The setting of a date in each case* only gave Rank the opportunity, in the patients' reactions to the setting of the date, to discover the repetition of birth in the analysis. To include this *after the fact* in the *joint* work would have been impermissible and (since Rank alone discovered the idea) also unjust.—In my striving to give illustrations to the work, I did, to be sure, also make references to the "trauma of birth" in Vienna, after the fact, but I couldn't do otherwise, since my cases were *already also* under the influence of the Rankian idea. After all that you will certainly have to admit that not even a trace of a premeditated intention to hide something can be found, either on my part or on Rank's.

3.) We emphasize expressly (in the text) that we were, among other things, also driven by the tendency to hasten the course of the analysis. Naturally, we had, and would have, nothing against a legitimate, somehow productive extension, indeed, if warranted, one which pursued only scientific aims, but we found that very many (also Abraham, among others) are guilty of extensions which bring no scientific return and must only be traced back to a misapprehension of the analytic situation. So, if Abraham, e.g., seems struck, that comes as no surprise to us. We have made an honest effort, in the course of the four- to fivefold revision, to leave out, or at least mitigate, everything of a personal-attacking nature.

Incidentally, I am firmly convinced that Abraham, as a shrewd person, will not hesitate long to test, and perhaps also to accept, what has been suggested by us. But I challenge his right to construe purely matter-of-fact scientific suggestions, made in a moderate tone, as a personal insult.

4.) Only after a fairly long time can, as you yourself say, anything certain be said about the *therapeutic* value of a consideration of the trauma. (It is astonishing that the Berliners were so quick to make a judgment.) But the *theoretical* value remains exalted, beyond any doubt.—I, myself, can no longer dispense with elucidating and tracing back to the trauma of birth, indeed, the material has already forced me to form certain ideas about the relation of this trauma to the traumatic power of the Oedipus complex.

5.) I intended the "staying with you" to be nothing other than what has transpired up to now. Also up to now, my scientifc fantasy has forced me here and there into areas that were remote from you at first; I also occasionally allowed myself to say something, in other words, to influence myself in the direction of work (example: thought transference).

But in the case at hand, the danger of getting onto the "path for traveling salesmen" is not present; you, too, consider the eventuality that Rank and I could slide off analytic ground to be out of the question. But, aside from the personal argument, every word of the joint work speaks *about* and *in favor of* psychoanalysis, so that we, as long as you did not examine our results, were able to have the feeling of working with you.

6.) We can still paste the Committee together. The little personal dissensions would certainly have to cease, and the *amicable* collaboration, which perhaps can't be restored, should make room for one that is *matter of fact*.

Again, many thanks for your clarifications![4]

Yours truly,
Ferenczi

1. Preprinted letterhead with vignette (Oedipus before the Sphinx) midway between the two names (which are here crossed out, as is the line "Central Executive").
2. Count Hermann von Keyserling (1880–1946), German philosopher and cultural psy-

chologist, founder of the "Schule der Weisheit" [School of Wisdom] in Darmstadt. He had just published a book, *Psychoanalyse und Selbstvervollkommnung* [Psychoanalysis and Self-Fulfillment] (Darmstadt, 1923). Keyserling had visited Freud at the end of February 1923 (Rank's *Rundbrief* of March 28, 1923, Butler Library) and visited him for a second time in May 1925 (Freud to Oliver Freud, May 12, 1925, Library of Congress). Cf. letter 980; Groddeck to Freud, December 18, 1924, and Freud to Groddeck, December 21, 1924 (*Freud/Groddeck*, pp. 89, 90); as well as Freud's letter to Keyserling of August 10, 1932 (*Letters*, pp. 415f.).

3. Brackets in the original.

4. On February 15, 1924, Freud intervened in the running debate with a *Rundbrief*, with the conclusion: "I value them [*The Trauma of Birth* and *The Development of Psychoanalysis*] highly, in part accept them, have doubts and hesitations about a good deal of their content, look forward to clarification in the matter from more reflection and experience, and should like to recommend all analysts not to form an opinion about the questions raised too quickly, least of all a negative one" (*Freud/Abraham*, p. 348).

949

Budapest, March 18, 1924

Dear Professor,[1]

Rank shared with me the contents of your last discussion with him (the Wednesday before last). Only for that reason did Abraham's step[2] not have a *more* depressing effect on me, because, behind his cautious politeness I always also recognized the signs of boundless ambition and jealousy. For only these passions could blind him in such a way that he—against all reason—could slander the joint work and "The Trauma of Birth" as garbage publications. He did not summon the courage to appear openly in opposition to us—he also waited—again, extremely cautiously—, until, from certain statements from *your* Rundbrief, he received the—in my opinion, erroneous—impression that you are not in complete agreement with these works, in fact, consider them dangerous.

But with this step he has also evidently sealed the fate of the Committee. Already in S. Cristoforo he behaved rather ambiguously toward Jones and could only be convinced with difficulty that the latter's anti-Semitism is not compatible with membership in the Committee; he also used every opportunity to put Rank in the wrong. And now he has decided upon a mode of operation which makes it impossible for us to work intimately with him.

But I think that with this the question of his presidency is also being reopened, for it is certainly not to be expected of us, precisely in these critical times, to recognize as a leader someone who could misunderstand us so badly and defame us so insidiously. Since only you and Eitingon can be considered "impartial," I am of the opinion that the latter should become president; as founder of the polyclinic, he would have earned this position long ago.

Of course, I am resolved, despite the personal insult from Abraham—if the interests of the cause require it—to maintain personal contact with him and always to return his (now unmasked) politeness with politeness.

Strangely, writing the Rundbriefe had for me the consequence that I—in order not to disturb you with so much correspondence—almost ceased completely my formerly so frequent private and scientific communications to you. The increased personal intercourse that will follow the cessation of the Rundbriefe will offer me the opportunity to seek you out more frequently. Then you will certainly soon be convinced that I have neither personally nor scientifically diverged from your teachings by even a hair's breadth [which you probably wouldn't have believed anyway].[3]

I hope I will again soon hear only good things about the state of your health.

Your grateful and true
Ferenczi

1. Ferenczi simultaneously sent Rank a copy of this letter.
2. Abraham saw "signs of an ominous development concerning vital issues of psychoanalysis" in Ferenczi's and Rank's works (letter of February 21, 1924, *Freud/Abraham*, p. 349); indeed, he recognized "in the *Entwicklungszielen* as well as in the 'Trauma der Geburt' manifestations of a regression in the scientific field, the symptoms of which agree in every small detail with those of Jung's secession from psycho-analysis" (letter of February 26, 1924, ibid., p. 350). The paths taken by Ferenczi and Rank seemd to him "to lead away from psycho-analysis" (letter of March 8, 1924, ibid., p. 354).
3. Brackets in the original.

950

Vienna, March 20, 1924
IX., Berggasse 19

Dear friend,

I know you are eagerly corresponding with Rank, and I have missed your direct letters for a long time already, so I am hastening to reply to today's.

My trust in you and Rank is unqualified. It would be sad if, after one has lived together for fifteen to seventeen years, one could still find oneself deceived. But you are attaching too much importance to the fact that I agree with you in all material particulars, and Rank is terribly uncouth, pits people against him, does not behave with the cheerful superiority which would serve him so well, as the one who is nearest to me in so many respects.

His accomplishments were inestimable; his person would be irreplaceable. Now, when he is preparing to go to America for half a year—certainly no secret to you—, I am concerned that his health might not be up to the exertions that await him there.

And, on the other hand, I am not certain that I will see him again when he returns in the fall.

I don't doubt that the others of the former Committee have consideration and affection for me, and yet it is coming to the point where I am being left in the lurch just after I have become an invalid, with reduced power for work and weakened mood, who rejects every excess burden and no longer feels a match for any further concern. I don't want, with this complaint, to move you to take any step toward maintaining the Committee, which has been given up for lost; I know, gone is gone, lost is lost. I have survived the Committee, which was supposed to become my successor; perhaps I will also survive the International Association. Let us hope that psychoanalysis survives me. But along with everything else it makes for a gloomy twilight of life.

However the both of you stand regarding Abraham's presidency, I can't participate in that. Discuss it among yourselves at the Congress. If the decision is transferred to me, I will maintain the original choice: Abraham–Rank (secretary). The presidency was assured Abraham when they transferred the position of secretary to him. To deny it to him now would be equivalent to a disciplinary action, which I don't believe I am justified in, despite the fact that he is wrong in his hostility toward the both of you. But it doesn't have to depend on me, of course.

Yesterday evening I had a long scientific discussion with Rank and admitted to him that I made regress rather than progress in my estimation of your joint work and his Birth Trauma. (With deference to your Theory of Genitality!) I tested his birth theory in the last theme that I am occupied with (decline of the Oedipus complex),[1] and found too many difficulties and objections, without, naturally, reaching a secure and conclusive opinion. I also find that Rank's inept presentation, which I had already objected to in the first draft, bears much of the blame for misinterpretations and suspicions of the Berliners. But he said he couldn't do it any other way. Now he sees the consequences of that. The enthusiastic-monomaniacal manner in which he presents his innovation is evidently not suited to recruiting friends for it. On top of that, the pieces of evidence are not always carefully chosen or convincing, objections are not discussed, dovetailing with our previous knowledge is downright negligent, there is certainly no lack of hairsplitting, makeshift constructions. Add a little personal ill will, and one can understand that the book is being judged as a for the moment still brazen attempt to push aside our earlier insights in favor of a new and alienating conception. A sober presentation, kept critical, which begins with a demonstration of the new material on which the doctrine is built, would have made it hard for the personal opponents to misunderstand it. On top of that comes the rumor of a new technique, which saves two thirds or three quarters of the treatment time—I admit, I can't imagine myself how that is possible without sacrificing analysis to suggestion—, and one has all kinds of excuses for the behavior of the opponents, even if one can't justify it.

I am sorry that on this occasion your inimical brother complex, which we believed to have been settled, has reawakened. With Rank I see, fortunately, only one similarity to the blessed Jung: being blinded by one's own first experiences, when one begins to practice analysis. Rank is only in the fourth year of analyzing; shortly before his discoveries, Jung had gone over into analytic practice from the psychiatric service. Otherwise, I don't want to compare either the persons or the findings. Jung was a bad guy.

I was as honest with you as possible, without demanding that you keep this letter secret. Do what you want with it. Rank will confirm to you that my little paper about Oedipus, in which I attempt the first critique of the birth trauma, will not be published for the time being, in order not to give the appearance of a rejection on my part. But the manuscript, when finished, also stands at your disposal.

With kind regards to you and Frau Gisela.

Yours,
Freud

1. "Der Untergang des Ödipuskomplexes" [The Dissolution of the Oedipus Complex] (Freud 1924d), later published by Freud without the passages that dealt critically with Rank's theory. (A literal translation of the word "Untergang" in the title is "decline" [Trans.].)

951

Budapest, March 24, 1924

Dear Professor,

I would not like for this day, on which I came into possession of your letter, to pass without my responding to you. Perhaps the swiftness of my reply will come at the expense of mature reflection—but: I was in analysis with you twice—and was also accustomed for years afterward to make known my thoughts to you, without much contemplation, as free associations, so to speak. So I am only returning to the old practice, which was unpleasantly interrupted by the more formal Rundbriefe. Honesty is also naturally better served thereby; and in this respect I would not like to stay back behind your letter.

I will begin with the factual part of my remarks and then add the personal.—

I recall exactly the walk during which *you* shared with me the Rankian discovery (trauma of birth) for the first time. (At the time I still didn't know anything about it, since I had just arrived, and Rank didn't have time until the same evening to communicate the essence of it to me.) You accompanied your narration with the remark: "I don't know if 33 or 66% of it is true, in any case, this is the most significant advance since the discovery of psychoanalysis. Someone else would have made himself independent with this discovery." The matter also impressed me greatly—I believe it was the next day that we had a discussion with you, in which Rank presented his material.—The dream interpretations that he shared with us were not convincing—for me, either. So I departed.—

I must add here that, in the meantime, we—without my having any inkling about the "Trauma of Birth"—continued working on the joint work (Development [of Psychoanalysis]) and were revising it again. The critical and also the positive assertions laid down in the work (especially the *heightened* consideration of the factor of transference ["analytic situation"][1] and of repetition [activity] actually contain the compilation of years of experience of both of us). The work is indebted to *Rank*, especially, for the more courageous (and, as I now believe, unquestionably correct and useful) interpretation in the sense of the "analytic situation," as well as the extension of activity to giving notice *every time*. If the latter took place at the right time and after the requisite examination of the case, etc., then I saw from this measure the *most remarkable* and, for myself, the *most surprising* effect.

After my attention was turned to the "mechanism of birth," which played itself out in the process of detachment, I was unable to turn a deaf ear to the impression that here, actually, a hitherto neglected piece of the unconscious material was making itself known and was demanding interpretation.

Naturally, I found extremely unappealing the idea that the whole ingenious psychoanalytic construction of the neuroses [was supposed to be replaced] by the crude mechanical standpoint that claimed to have the whole etiology of the neuroses be determined one-sidedly by the birth trauma, even after Rank assured me at the outset that such one-sidedness was the last thing on his mind.

On closer inspection, however, I found such a quantity of confirmatory material, and in particular so much that fit my *theory of genitality*, that I could not close myself off to the significance of the factor of the birth trauma. Only by adding in, more correctly: since the more appropriate evaluation of the *traumatic* factor of the womb fixation, which was, incidentally, already emphasized (albeit insufficiently) in the Theory of Genitality, was it possible to test the theory of genitality for its soundness, also practically, so to speak, in the analysis of the neuroses—and the theory passed this test excellently.—In practice the birth trauma (may one call it birth fantasy or real "memory") emerged as one of the most favored hiding places and, certainly, [as] the last and most primitive [fantasy] into which sexuality (genitality) flees from its normal discharge. The *ambivalence* of the neuroses could be studied at its source, and that of castration, for the Oedipus complex was not only not "overcome," but its *necessary* appearance in the neuroses only became properly explicable. Doubtless what is specifically neurotogenic is still the Oedipus conflict; but its traumatic power relates the neurosis which is produced by civilization, originally from the ucs. *identity* of the Oedipus conflict, to the conflict between the longing for the womb and the fear of the womb.

These theoretical insights would retain their value even if they had found no therapeutic confirmation. According to my experience up to now, however, they are also *certainly* useful in this respect as well. These insights, as well as the "activity," which has already been in part *methodologically* attempted on the basis of the theory of genitality, also made it possible for me to shorten the length of the treatment. As you already noted earlier, I reported in Vienna mainly about my own technique. The *more special* technical details that Rank applies could and cannot be known to me, since I have not yet had the opportunity to learn anything specific about them.

But what has already been said sufficed and suffices for me to be convinced 1.) that Rank has, in fact, accomplished something significant for psychoanalysis; 2.) that what is new can be *excellently* assimilated, in fact, now properly consolidated, into the hitherto existing edifice of psychoanalysis; 3.) that Rank, even if, in his joy of discovery, in the beginning he perhaps viewed the motivation for the neuroses more one-sidedly, is already in his book doing justice to most of the possible objections.

In view of these facts I considered and consider it *extremely frivolous* when Abraham and Jones, especially the former, as well as the Berliners who follow him, simply dismiss such a significant work after a relatively *very short* time, some immediately after reading it, and want to have done with it by means of the logical nitpicking of a *Rádo*, etc.

Your position on the matter I find (the promised honesty bids me also to say this) vacillating and contradictory; nevertheless, cautious enough, finally, as I still hope, to leave the way open for a favorable decision. Already the title "Decline of the Oedipus Complex" [perhaps according to

Spengler's book title?²]³ is tinged by affect, however. And yet it is my conviction that no basis for affective reaction exists: nowhere do I see the "decline," only the bio-psychological *foundation* for your immortal discoveries is becoming evident everywhere.—

Now I turn to the personal dissension, which is also burdensome to me. As far as Rank's sensitively irritated mood is known to me, Abraham's presidency is extremely unpalatable to him (as it is to me as well, by the way). I even fear that he could appear publicly in opposition to it, in which case it would be difficult for me to stand anywhere other than by his side. It was for that reason that I asked you to nip this question in the bud in the manner suggested by me (Eitingon).—I assume that you probably considered this before you declared the change in the election for president to be impossible. And still I would like to ask you again to consider the possibility of suggesting a colorless personality (perhaps v. *Emden*); this suggestion in the Committee meeting in Salzburg⁴ would be sufficiently grounded in the quarrel, which is still "sub judice."⁵

But certainly the whole unfortunate discussion (the suggestion of which I, actually, was responsible for!) *should not take place.* You know my belligerent nature and will certainly believe me when I say that I don't suggest this out of fear of a fight. I also declare [if anyone wishes, on my word of honor]⁶ that Rank knows nothing of this suggestion and would certainly speak against it.

The motives for this suggestion are simply: 1.) the fruitlessness of discussions in general; 2.) the still insufficient experience which could serve as a basis for this discussion; 3.) consideration for the undisturbed existence of the Association and for its reputation among those on the outside; 4.) last not least⁷: consideration for your health, which we should guard against upsets.

I will *not* send your letter to Rank; but since we are in active correspondence, and I can't leave you all too long without news, I ask you to reply to me as soon as possible so that I can communicate to him the content (probably also the text) of this, our correspondence—perhaps also already its result.

Should it appear to you to be *absolutely impossible* to say no to Abraham (*who would certainly not be an impartial president!*), then some kind of compensation must be looked after which makes it possible for Rank to stay in the Association. This compensation can only consist in *your* appropriately characterizing Abraham's measures and giving Rank a sign of your trust in unmistakable terms, and in the scientific question, declaring any determination *premature,* but the object worthy of the most serious examination. Naturally, not only would the paper about the "Decline of the Oedipus Complex" have to remain unpublished for a long time, but its existence [would] also [have to remain] unknown. Is the manuscript already finished?

I would have preferred to go to Vienna immediately upon receipt of your letter. But I hope that this letter presents my viewpoint in sufficient detail. I would be pleased if I were successful in improving the situation and contributing something to the mitigation of your concerns.

Yours truly,
Ferenczi

P.S.

1. The rejection of Abraham's presidency would naturally also entail canceling Rank's nomination to secretary, which would also ameliorate the matter in Abraham's eyes.

2. The all too impatient Berlin discussion speakers should be mollified by the publication of your critique in the Zeitschrift.[8]—
over!!

In order to do justice to the urgency of the matter, I will simultaneously write Rank a card in which I will notify him that I received a letter from you, which I answered most urgently, and in which I will request that he speak to you again. Perhaps the matter can be discussed anew in tomorrow's (Wednesday) discussion. Naturally, I have nothing against your showing this letter to Rank.

1. Brackets here and immediately following in the original.

2. *Der Untergang des Abendlandes: Umrisse einer Morphologie der Weltgeschichte* [The Decline of the West: Outlines of a Morphology of World History], 2 vols. (Munich, 1918–1922). Oswald Spengler's (1880–1836) chief work, which greatly influenced the modern view of history. Spengler saw cultures as "organisms" which underlie a process of flowering, maturity, and disintegration.

3. Brackets in the original.

4. The planned meeting of the Committee before the Eighth International Psychoanalytic Congress (April 21–23) in Salzburg, at which Abraham was elected president and Eitingon secretary of the IPA. See Abraham's report to the Congress in *Zeitschrift* 10 (1924): 211–228.

5. According to the Latin (Horace), "sub judice lis est," "the dispute is before the judge," i.e., an unresolved proceeding.

6. Brackets in the original.

7. Written in English in the original.

8. Cf. Hanns Sachs's discussion of Rank's *Trauma der Geburt* (*Zeitschrift* 11 [1925]: 106–113), and Franz Alexander's of *Entwicklungszielen* (ibid., 113–122).

952

Vienna, March 26, 1924
IX., Berggasse 19[1]

Dear friend,

You request a quick reply, Anna is pounding it out today on a new typewriter of her own.

You accuse me of having a position toward the birth trauma that is vacillating and contradictory. You are correct, but only when you neglect the temporal element. The truth is that I liked the thing much better in the beginning than I do now and that, according to your own quotation, I am on the way from the 66% to the 33%.

Let us divide the matter up into the theoretical, practical, and personal. On the first: your partisanship in favor of the Rankian doctrine naturally makes a strong impression on me. But my own, I can't say judgments, but rather intimations, run in a different direction. I have not gotten over the first fear, which you admit to, that our ingenious etiological construction should be cut loose by the crude birth trauma. I tested the doctrine on a special case, on the dissolution of the Oedipus complex, and found it unsatisfactory. Mind you, Rank does conceive the trauma of birth individually and ontogenetically throughout. He endeavors in general to dispense with the phylogenetic where possible. My objections are directed at that. If the trauma of birth works not onto- but phylogenetically, only then does he have the connection to your theory of genitality, which otherwise eludes him, and then we can talk about that. Here, as in other places, it is the fault of Rank's thoroughly inadequate presentation when such misunderstandings can arise. He doesn't say expressly anywhere, I believe, that he wants to put the trauma etiologically in the place of the Oedipus complex, but everybody senses this, and in your letter you come directly to the conclusion that the Oedipus complex owes its dynamic power to the trauma of birth. Hence, the strong contradiction. According to your phylogenetically oriented conception, we would again come back to sexuality. According to Rank's, one would have to require that, first, and before any extensive applications, it be demonstrated statistically that firstborn, difficultly and asphyxically born children, on average, reveal a greater disposition to neurosis, or at least to the production of anxiety in childhood. The observation of children born by cesarean section, hence with brief or weak birth trauma, would also have to be taken into consideration, either positively or negatively. In Rank's position, I would not have published the theory until I had initiated this investigation.

I must return to the thoroughly inept and deficient presentation in Rank's case. One often itches to grasp the matter differently, and indeed, in such a way that the readers also learn what is being offered to them as new, where the connections, the difficulties, the correspondences lie. To that extent I cannot absolve Rank of a certain tragic guilt[2] in the reception of his finding. I maintain, naturally, that he has discovered something important and interesting, but he hasn't worked it up properly.

I believe, incidentally, that you analytically misunderstood the Dissolution of the Oedipus Complex. I didn't mean that the Oedipus complex is succumbing to the Rankian doctrine of birth trauma; my little essay about it would be completely capable of existence even if Rank had not written his book. It treats the fact that the Oedipus complex is normally not simply repressed but demolished, canceled (by means of identification and superego formation), and that its mere repression creates the pathogenic disposition. This difference has been neglected up to now. You may be right that the affect-tinged title indicates an agitation in me that has to do with the birth trauma. But that is an analytic side-meaning, which must not impress itself on any reader. I think the essay will be published omitting the discussion about the birth trauma.

Second: While I hold fast in the theoretical estimation of the at least 33%, from a practical perspective, all valuation fails me. I know, as do you, only very little about the technical modification that Rank bases on his doctrine, and for the time being I can't picture its effects. I have the suspicion that the result is limited to the well-known effect of the setting of a termination date, if this is done at the proper moment and for an appropriate time. The uncertainty in both of these points, the arbitrariness, which can hardly be excluded therein, seem to me to bring not insignificant dangers along with them. But I am naturally prepared to allow myself to be instructed by experience, my own or someone else's, as all my judgments about this are only tentative anyway. I also haven't made them out to be anything else.

Third: Now, the personal. Everything up to now would be merely interesting, a desired spice for our work and material that could occupy us amicably for a long time. The personal is intolerable. I fear that, except with you and with me, it won't be able to be separated from the factual. Here I stand much more on your side. I also find that our Berlin members have not behaved amicably toward Rank, and I would like to seize an opportunity to say so directly, especially to Abraham.[3] But here I also encounter a characteristic of Rank's which would make my partisanship difficult. One will certainly reply to me that Rank is so irritable that there was no prospect at all of turning to him personally instead of to me, and they will cite as evidence the fact that he recently threatened in a Rundbrief that he wouldn't send any more patients to Berlin for training because someone had interrogated one of them in an indiscreet manner about his technique.[4] It is very hard to play the judge when, as is so frequently the case, the injustice is shared by both sides. I would expect it of you, as the one less affected, not to share Rank's bitterness toward Abraham, and not to fortify him with respect to it.

What is to be done now? On April 13 Eitingon intends to come to Vienna in order then to go to Salzburg with us. I think that both of you, as the most discreet ones, should get together to nip in the bud the personal conflicts, which can't be disavowed, and to guard against their worst consequences. You ought not to expect much from me myself. First of all, I don't deny at all that these constant squabbles are enormously repugnant to me and will probably have the consequence that I won't get involved at all, no matter what happens. Second, my state of health since my respiratory infection[5] is so unsatisfactory that I am not even sure I will participate in the Congress. Those who are concerned about me are urging me to use the Easter time for a pure convalescence holiday, perhaps in Abbazia, and if I am not better by then, there is nothing else for me to do. That would then be a simple solution. I could not get involved in the question of the presidency, the discussion in the lap of the former Committee could not take place, and you would by necessity have to settle it all among yourselves. Perhaps it will really happen that way. Your new suggestion to leave off the discussion need not be kept secret from Rank. He has spontaneously made known his inclination to absent himself from such a discussion, which I allowed myself to take amiss.

The compensation that you wish for Rank will be realized in another form. I have the firm intention to step down from the leadership of the Vienna group, since I am too tired in the evening to attend the sessions, and there is no doubt that he will become my successor. I am presently negotiating with him about when this should happen, since I would like him to appear in his new capacity already at the Congress. I don't need to assure you that my personal feelings for you and for Rank are unchanged. I am, to be sure, annoyed by the weaknesses that are coming to the fore in both of you, but that is no reason to forget fifteen years of good offices and collaboration. Only I can't repel the others, who can make similar claims. And a little more or less wrong, if one lets oneself be driven by passions, is no reason to damn people whom one otherwise loves.

I hope that you will come early enough to Vienna to negotiate what is necessary with Eitingon and Rank, and I will let you know in any case when and where I travel, as soon as I know it myself.

With kind regards to you and Frau Gisela.

Yours,
Freud

1. The letter is typewritten; only the signature, "Freud," is handwritten.
2. Cf. letter 221 and n. 13.
3. Cf. Freud's letter to Abraham of March 31: "For to whatever extent your rection to

Ferenczi and Rank may have been justified, quite apart from that, the way you set about things was certainly not friendly . . . I think that it is now up to you to prevent a further deterioration . . . It cannot be your intention because of this anxiety of yours to cause the collapse of the international association and everything that depends on it" (*Freud/Abraham*, p. 355).

4. "Mr. Moxon . . . revealed . . . that he was questioned in Berlin by various colleagues, whose names are also known to me, about the manner of his analysis with me, that is to say, my technique . . . [B]esides that, however, he also believed to have noted clear signs of disapproval of my technique in the reactions of his interviewers . . . After the experience with Mr. Moxon, there is nothing left for me but to come to the obvious conclusion that I should refrain from sending any more of my analysands to Berlin for training" (Rank's *Rundbrief* of January 4, 1924, Butler Library).

5. A "nasal suppuration, which was certainly the manifestation of a grippe" (Freud to Eitingon, March 22, 1924, Sigmund Freud Copyrights), on account of which "for the first time in [his] medical career [Freud] had to stop work over the weekend" (Freud to Abraham, *Freud/Abraham*, March 31, 1934, p. 355) and spent the following weekends at the Semmering.

953

[to Rank][1]

Budapest, March 30, 1924

Dear Otto,

Only now am I in a position to share with you in detail the correspondence with the Professor. Before I wrote to you, I wanted to wait for the Professor's reply, which arrived yesterday.

It is advisable for you to read through the Professor's letter of March 20. My reaction to this letter was essentially as follows:

In consideration of the passage on p. 1, which relates to your health, I originally wanted to withhold this letter from you, and also wrote to the Professor to that effect. In retrospect, however, I decided to do the opposite, and I asked the Professor also to show my letter to you. I also requested that he respond quickly, since I want to come to an understanding with you in these matters, and time is pressing.

In the letter I began with matters of fact; I reminded the Professor of how enthusiastically he had expressed himself to me about your discovery ("greatest advance since the discovery of psychoanalysis, even if only 33 or 66% of it is true"; "someone else would have made himself independent," etc.). I then wrote to him that I actually learned from him (Professor) about your discovery, since up to that time we were only dealing with each other over the joint work. Your (subsequent) communications would—so I wrote further—have made a great impression on me; that was not the case with your material (dreams), about which you lectured to us (on that memorable afternoon at the Professor's).—I then departed, my impression had remained ambivalent, high regard for the new idea on the one hand, but in place of it the fear that the all too one-sidedly emphasized, crass, as it were, idea of trauma could damage the artful edifice of psychoanalysis—very soon my impression changed. On the one hand, you had soon mitigated the all too sharp emphasis on the traumatic factor, on the other hand, the revision of my own material had shown that up to that time we were neglecting an important piece of the ucs. by keeping the birth-traumatic possibilities of interpretation out of consideration. What made the greatest impression on me, however (so I wrote), were the spontaneously appearing mechanisms of birth after the terminations. I also owed technically essential progress and shortening of the treatment to these insights and to termination. But I was and am actually not versed in the details of your technique.

On the basis of all these facts I consider your discovery to be significant progress that deserves recognition. There is no question of an attempt to eliminate psychoanalysis; it is not the "decline" but rather the *basis* of the Oedipus complex that is created thereby: in the dynamic of birth can be found the last (if not the only) source, that is to say, locus of regression of neurosis (neurotic anxiety); the Oedipus complex draws a large part of its dynamic power from the birth-traumatic factor.

The Professor's attitude in this matter has been vacillating and contradictory. His hypothetical fears are unfounded, however. Writing about personal things, I again mentioned my earlier expressed disparaging opinion about the way that Abraham acted. I requested that the Professor reconsider whether, after all is said and done, a neutral personality (van Emden, perhaps) could not become president. I wrote to him that impartiality would be preserved if you, too, renounced the secretariat.

I did, to be sure, leave open a single possibility for a conciliatory resolution of the affair: to wit, if the Professor 1) unambiguously confronted Abraham about his unfair attitude, 2) gives you appropriate compensation for it by making known his certainly not disapproving view of your work and by declaring the discussion premature.—I did formally recommend that the "discussion afternoon" (which was, unfortunately, instituted in Lavarone on my recommendation) be *stricken*. It is unjust to subject your work to half-baked criticisms by people of Radó's ilk, etc.—of course the recommendation would have to come from the Professor. I explained, truthfully, that you knew nothing about this idea of mine. Giving up the open discussions is proffered both in the interest of the reputation of the Association and in consideration of the Professor's health. The reply to this letter was the enclosed (typewritten)[2] communication, which I now ask [you] to read through.

Now I think that the theoretical dispute should cease for the time being: I want to relate only in regard to the objection to the dynamic power of the birth trauma in my response to *birth anxiety* as the source of all (also neurotic) anxiety; to be sure, I will also concede the phylogenetic and the pathogenic efficacy of postpartum (cultural) influences. On the other hand, I will explain quite categorically that I will do everything in my power to see that a politely formal resolution of the personal matters makes the work of the Congress possible. I don't yet know how that can be achieved; I want to confer about it with you and Eitingon in Vienna. Finally, I will write to him how little grounds he has for bitterness,—I will, to be sure, concede that he would have deserved to be spared personal affairs of this kind.

And now it is a question of coming to an agreement as to what we want to do. I find that the Professor is doing everything possible not to spoil the matter with us,—he requests nothing of us but our acceptance of Abraham's presidency. (I forgot to tell you that *I* requested that the Professor postpone his polemic against the "birth trauma" for a long time to come, not to mention it to the Berliners at all. He seems to be in agreement with that.) Abraham will try to justify himself, but will (according to the Professor's promise) be appropriately qualified for his "unfriendliness."

Perhaps the power of the president can be appropriately limited by the creation of an official committee? Incidentally, the president actually has nothing to say; everything depends on the Verlag and the editorial board!

In any case, we must show consideration for the Professor's physical and emotional condition. In the final analysis, he has the right to harbor his scientific reservations until he convinces himself otherwise! He is also prepared for accommodation *in matters of fact*; he will certainly approach the same things from a different side. I place great value on the elimination of the discussion afternoon! Some things will be cleared up by the next Congress, which will take place after one to two years. To see the Berlin "shock troops" withdraw without anything to do would be a very pleasant sight. They can express themselves gradually later in the literature. If nothing else, Jones will be put out of commission for a rather long time.

I think, by the way, that we can only *formally* designate Abraham's attitude as unfair; in merito, he is, after all, permitted to be afraid of a theory. And if he is judged by us on account of his attitude (just like Jones in S. Cristoforo), then a modus vivendi *must* be found with him as president of the Berlin group, if we don't want to break up the Association. But *on no account* would I like to advocate the latter!

I don't yet know the day of my (our) arrival.

I thank Frau Tola for her care. My wife wrote to her in this matter.

Cordially, and in expectation of news *very soon.*

Your Sándor

1. Judith Dupont Archive.
2. This word is written in English in the original [Trans.].

954

Vienna, April 3, 1924
IX., Berggasse 19

Dear friend,

I can only respond to your letter of today[1] [by saying] that my self-preservative drive has won the upper hand. It has been decided that I will not go to Salzburg at Easter, but again to the Kurhaus Semmering, where I am now spending Saturday and Sunday.

The motive of consideration for my person, which you mention, comes pretty late. But I don't want to leave you with the impression that I am avoiding the Congress and my friends on account of the embarrassing affairs that are now floating around; they create for me only a secondary gain from illness. The main thing remains my tormented and weakened condition.

We are thinking of leaving Vienna on the Thursday of Holy Week (17th). I am writing to Eitingon that he has to come to Vienna beforehand if he wants to speak with me.

With kind regards to you and Frau Gisela.

Yours,
Freud

1. The letter has not been found.

955

[Budapest,] April 5, 1924[1]

Dear Professor,

I am *very* sorry that you have decided on abstinence from the Congress, but I think you have, perhaps—with consideration for your health, which suprema lex esto[2] for us all—indeed done the right thing.

I am arriving in Vienna at noon on the 15th (Tuesday), in order to be able to discuss things with you, Rank, and Eitingon already before your vacation trip. I can be reached in Vienna through Max or Rank, and I will also telephone.

Kind regards.

Yours,
Ferenczi

1. Date, without location, at the end of the letter in the original.
2. Latin for "should be the highest law."

956

Budapest, April 9, 1924

Dear Professor,

As you have probably already heard from Rank, in the last Rundbrief I took the first, for now still quite cautious step toward reconnecting the collegial relations among the hitherto existing Committee members.[1] I naturally don't know how the further steps will take shape, but I hope that the "individual discussions" projected in the letter will not exclude the possibility of a joint conference in Salzburg. I am certain that in the end the main interest, that of psychoanalysis, will win out over everything personal and over differences in particulars.

My wife and I are looking forward to being able to see you soon, and greet you cordially.

Yours,
Ferenczi

1. Ferenczi had been of the opinion "that the heads of the most significant Societies definitely have to find a platform that makes it possible, now as before, by means of mutual support, to advance the interests of psychoanalysis, which must especially be taken into account," and that "everything [should be] done that commands the common interest." It remained for "individual discussions to create a modus vivendi" (Ferenczi's *Rundbrief* of April 6, 1924, Butler Library). Shortly thereafter, Rank announced the dissolution of the secret Committee: "The cessation of the Viennese *Rundbrief* in the past few weeks has certainly shown clearly enough that we have ... definitively buried the Committee ... This is my position, as well as Ferenczi's, which the Professor finally also had to endorse ... The Professor conceded to me that the most instrumental thing would be to open the planned Salzburg Committee meeting with the statement that the Committee no longer exists" (Rank's *Rundbrief* of April 10, 1924, Sigmund Freud Copyrights).

957

MAGYARORSZAGI
PSZICHOANALITIKAI EGYESÜLET
(Freud-Társaság)

Budapest, April 26, 1924

Dear Professor,

Although I presume that you have already been apprised in detail by the other side as to the course of the Congress, I still consider it my duty to give you a report.

The general impression was very favorable. Before the discussion afternoon there was still a certain tension in the air—all the Congress participants seemed to have figured on some sort of hostile encounters—but the discussion itself went along in an air of scientific objectivity. The young Berliners occupied themselves mainly with the problem of describing and making explicable the healing process in the technical language of metapsychology.[1] From time to time they also digressed to the problem of activity (furthering repetition, and its later utilization for association [remembering and reconstruction][2]); in principle everyone expressed himself quite sympathetically toward this addition to technique. Occasionally they also got to talking about the theme of the "birth trauma" (as the other Congress lectures also frequently came back to this subject in general). This theme was also discussed with matter-of-fact seriousness and without premature dismissal—so that (especially since the hour was late and the discussion lectures were long) Rank and I were able to limit ourselves to a few factual rectifications. I, specifically, had to repulse somewhat more energetically, however, a hidden accusation by Jones, as if someone wanted to emphasize the phylogenetic and the current *at the expense of the infantile*.

I began the personal exchange of views between the former Committee members by initiating a detailed discussion with Jones and Abraham, into which we later also drew Rank and Sachs.

Abraham tried to justify himself and his attitude by maintaining that his letter *to you* had only the purpose of causing *us* (Rank and me), that is to say, the whole Committee, to handle the questionable and, in his view, dangerous innovations.[3] Jones very soon, Abraham somewhat hesitatingly, gave up the attempt to maintain the Committee in its form up to now, and (after Eitingon also arrived in the meantime) we were able to deal with the suggestion to institute the committee of heads[4] in merito. Although the opinions about the practical usefulness of this instrument remained divided, we decided in the affirmative, and Jones had this suggestion accepted by the conference of heads. At this conference I suggested Abraham's election for president.

Abraham and I did everything possible to approach the mutual personal relations of the old friendship; this also succeeded—actually, much more than with Jones, who, together with his entire group, acted strikingly reserved. Abraham told me he [Jones] didn't forgive my reproach about the hypnosis-annexation.[5]—Altogether, Abraham seemed to put great weight on the fact that you were instructed by me about his honest efforts to restore collegial relations—this was able to take place all the more easily when I was actually able to convince myself of these efforts. Rank, who left after the second day,[6] was nevertheless still able to participate in the most important of these personal and material discussions, and I have the impression that a certain rapprochement—albeit not a very thriving one—can also be noted between him and Abraham.

The Congress lectures were in part very good. That [describes] a lecture by *Glover* (James), the detailed analysis of an oral perversion, and by *Frau*

Dr. Deutsch, who actually took up the history of the origin of female sexuality alluded to in my theory of genitality, but who carried it out in a very nice and highly polished manner. *Dr. Reich's* suggestions also have many points of contact with the theory of genitality; certainly Reich is demonstrating himself to be an originally gifted therapist. *Simmel* was ingenious, as ever, but fanciful, *Landauer*[7] (a very good, honest boy) made a good impression. *Bernfeld* had an effect through his enchanting oratorical talent; *Róheim's* interesting lecture was (in his absence) read in too much of a monotone, and for that reason remained ineffective. Frau *Klein* was good; finally, *v. Emden* insisted upon stuttering forth a detail from a case history which said nothing. *Reik's* mythological lecture was very well done.[8]

In private conversations with the colleagues there was talk of nothing else but your absence; many came only to see you. Eitingon and I tried hard to talk everyone out of organizing a mass visit with you—we don't know with what success.

We have here a brief postlude to the Congress; five Englishmen have announced their visit in Budapest with Róheim for this evening, among them the brothers[9] Glover. Perhaps we will gather for a meeting in their honor.

If I make a judgment about how tired the Vienna and Salzburg negotiations have made *me,* I must admit that you were right in staying away from the Congress. Dr. Lévy just telephoned me about how you recovered at the Semmering; naturally there was no question of "recovery" in Salzburg.

I remain at your disposal with further information on request, but I think I have communicated what is essential in what I have said and greet you most cordially, also in my wife's name.

Yours truly,
Ferenczi

1. On the afternoon of the first day of the Congress, a discussion took place on "The Relationship of Psychoanalytic Theory to Psychoanalytic Technique," with contributions from Hanns Sachs, Sándor Radó, and Franz Alexander. Jones gave an introduction, Ferenczi and Rank a brief rejoinder. See the summary in *Zeitschrift* 10 (1924): 215–217.
2. Brackets in the original.
3. After Abraham had characterized Ferenczi's and Rank's works to Freud as a scientific regression which departed from psychoanalysis (see letter 949 and n. 2), he asked Freud to call a meeting of the Committee in which he would be given "the opportunity to speak [his] mind freely" (Abraham to Freud, February 21, 1924, *Freud/Abraham,* p. 349).
4. See letter 956, n. 1.
5. See letter 586 and n. 1.
6. To go to New York (until October 1924), where Rank opened a flourishing practice and developed a lively lecturing activity (see "Dr. Rank in Amerika," *Zeitschrift* 10

[1924]: 210). He analyzed or supervised many analysts who had previously been in analysis with Freud (Freud to Rank, May 23, 1924, Judith Dupont Archive). On June 3, he was elected an honorary member of the American Psychoanalytic Association.

7. Karl Landauer (1887–1945), psychiatrist from Munich and assistant to Kraepelin there. In 1912 he moved to Vienna, where he received psychiatric-neurologic training with Wagner-Jauregg and was in analysis with Freud. In 1919 he moved to Frankfurt am Main, where in 1926 he, along with Klara Happel, Erich Fromm, Frieda Fromm Reichmann, Heinrich Meng, and others, founded the Frankfurt Psychoanalytic Working Community, from which the Frankfurt Psychoanalytic Institute of the Southwest German Psychoanalytic Working Community (1929–1933) was derived. He was the driving force behind the awarding of the Goethe Prize to Freud. In 1933 he fled, first to Sweden, then to Amsterdam, where, in 1941, he was arrested and deported. Landauer died of starvation in the Bergen-Belsen concentration camp. See Hans-Joachim Rothe, ed., *Karl Landauer: Theorie der Affekte und andere Schriften zur Ich-Organisation* [Karl Landauer: Theory of Affects and Other Writings on Ego Organization] (Frankfurt am Main, 1991).

8. The titles of the lectures mentioned are Siegfried Bernfeld, "Critique of the Previous Application of Psychoanalysis to Pedagogy"; Helene Deutsch, "The Psychology of Woman in Relation to the Functions of Reproduction"; J. E. G. van Emden, "Casuistic Communication"; James Glover, "Notes on an Unusual Form of Perversion"; Melanie Klein, "On the Technique of Early Child Analysis"; Karl Landauer, "Real Value and Pleasure Gain of Psychic Pathological Mechanisms"; Wilhelm Reich, "The Therapeutic Significance of Genital Libido"; Theodor Reik, "The Creation of Woman: Analysis of the Account in Genesis and in Related Themes"; Géza Róheim, "Totemism and Dragon Fight" (read aloud by Hanns Sachs); and Ernst Simmel, "The Psycho-Physical Significance of the Intestinal Organ for Primal Repression." Among the lectures not mentioned by Ferenczi is Abraham's "Contributions of Oral Erotism to Character Formation."

9. This word is written in English in the original.

958

[Budapest, undated][1]

Dear Professor,

I don't know whether it is a "supposed" or a real mistake if I am tormented by the idea that I *didn't* tell you that James Glover traveled with four Englishmen from Vienna to Budapest, was received cordially here, and that we inaugurated an English Society meeting in their honor, in which Róheim lectured in English and I presided in English.[2]

If I did make a mistake, then the mistake was at least good for my being able to reply quickly to the greeting from you which was brought to me today by Urbantschitsch.—What do you and Fräulein Anna think about his new plans?[3]

Kind regards,
Ferenczi

1. Placement here, which can also be confirmed by the format and condition of the stationery, has been made on the basis of the mention of the Englishmen's visit in Budapest (see letter 957) and of Urbantschitsch's "new plans" (see Freud's response to them, letter 960).

2. "April 29, 1924. Dr. G. *Róheim:* 'Dreams and Adaptation in the History of Mankind' (Trauma of Birth and Theory of Genitality, Cosmogeny, Dragon Legends, Culture Heroes, Sacrifices, Origin of Festive Customs).—Dr. S. *Ferenczi* gave a brief, introductory lecture. The meeting was held in English in honor of the members of the *British Psycho-Analytical Society* staying in Budapest" (*Zeitschrift* 10 [1924]: 351).

3. See letter 939, n. 4, and letter 960.

959

Budapest, May 11, 1924

Dear Professor,

Rank handed over to me to look through a part of the works which are located in the editorial portfolio. He told me that issue II is already ready for printing, that is to say, is printed, with the exception of the Congress report, which *Abraham* will send me. In Salzburg I received, further, the (enclosed) papers by two Dutchmen, which *van Emden* gave me as a contribution to the planned Jelgersma issue. Please read through them and have them moved along (to the printer) by *Storfer.* As sole contributions to a Jelgersma issue I find them quite shabby. Still, we could publish them *simultaneously* with the editorial communication of Jelgersma's jubilee. Perhaps we will ask *van Emden* for a brief Jelgersma biography; or do you want to write it yourself?[1]

The most important work of the third issue is "The Dissolution of the Oedipus Complex,"[2] which, unfortunately, I have still not been able to read.

Federn suggested to *Abraham* that we would like to publish the Congress papers in a special issue. Abraham would like to pursue this idea. But since (as Rank told me) we will be strongly advised to take up the Congress material in the next volume, I thought it would be better to stay with what we have been doing up to now, and I replied to Abraham to that effect. In any case, I request your decision.

So much for editorial matters.—

There is not much in the way of personal things to report from here. I would be all the happier to receive good news from you soon.

It will interest you to know that our friend Lajos *Lévy* communicated to me his first psychoanalytic idea that occurred to him, and which I consider very interesting. On the basis of a number of psychiatric observations in morphine addicts, who exhibit the typical disturbances of the sense of reality, he surmises a specific effect of certain toxins on the *ego* (and in connection with that, the *id*), or, as he expresses it, a dissociation from ego and id in intoxications. I encouraged him to describe these cases briefly and to lecture in the Society.³

What impressions did you get after the various reports about the Congress and the near future of psychoanalytic literature? How did *Jones*, in particular, express himself?

Yours truly,
Ferenczi

P.S. I think issue II should also put out an obituary about Stanley *Hall*.⁴

F[erenczi].

1. On the twenty-fifth anniversary of Jelgersma's professorship, the *Zeitschrift* published the following works by Dutch authors: A. J. Westerman Holstijn, "Professor G. Jelgersma und die Leidener psychiatrische Schule" [Professor G. Jelgersma and the Leyden School of Psychiatry] (10 [1924]: 253–257); E. A. D. E. Carp, "Die Rolle der prägenitalen Libidofixierung in der Perversion" [The Role of Pregenital Libido Fixation in Perversion] (ibid., 258–266); J. M. Rombouts, "Über Askese und Macht" [On Asceticism and Power] (ibid., 267–271); H. C. Jelgersma, "Eine eigenartige Sitte auf der Insel Marken in Holland" [A Peculiar Custom on the Island of Marken in Holland] (ibid., 272–275); J. H. van der Hoop, "Über die Projektion und ihre Inhalte" [On Projection and Its Contents] (ibid., 276–288); F. P. Muller, "Über die zwei Arten des Narzissmus" [On the Two Types of Narcissism] (ibid., 289–292); A. Endtz, "Über Träume von Schizophrenen" [On the Dreams of Schizophrenics] (ibid., 292–295); A. J. Westerman Holstijn, "Retentio Urinae" (ibid., 295–300); W. J. J. de Sauvage-Nolting, "Über den Verfolgungswahn beim Weibe" [On Persecution Mania in Women] (ibid., 300–302).
2. Freud 1924d.
3. Lajos Lévy, "Zur Psychologie der Morphiumwirkung" [On the Psychology of the Effect of Morphine], lecture given in the Hungarian Society on May 31, 1924 (*Zeitschrift* 10 [1924]: 434–436).
4. Stanley Hall had died on April 24. Isador Coriat, "G. Stanley Hall †," *Zeitschrift* 10 (1924): 201–203.

960

Vienna, May 13, 1924
IX., Berggasse 19

Dear friend,

Your Congress report, which is worthy of thanks, coincided well with all the other news that got to me—partly oral, partly written. So, the impression was a good one. Credit for the happy outcome does seem to go to Abraham and the Berliners. A few of the latter have even allowed themselves to be moved by their kindness [*gentilezza*] to participate in the Rankian confusion of biological consideration with psychological research.

I read both of the Dutch papers; they are really too poor to characterize as an honorary issue for Jelgersma. I didn't understand from your letter whether these two will remain the only ones. To write an essay about Jelgersma I am missing more than the desire, namely, all the material. That would certainly have to take place from Holland.

I conclude from another remark in your letter that Stanley Hall has died. I didn't know anything about it. Here, the right thing would be to write to Rank that he should get ahold of an obituary in New York that can then go into the 4th issue of the Zeitschrift.

I am in possession in manuscript form of a very nice essay by [Helene] Deutsch (Congress lecture), and an interesting and smoothly written one about tooth symbolism by René Spitz.[1] Let me know in the next letter what and when it is supposed to go to print, or what else I should do with it.

Regarding the separation of the Congress lectures suggested by Abraham, I think as you do, that we cannot diverge from the decision that has been made by Rank.

Yesterday Urbantschitsch was with us and wanted to win Anna over to his new project.[2] She was very distrustful and importuned him sharply that he, so to speak, was appealing to her to vouch for his new character. It turned out today already that he was dishonest on a number of significant points. There are very unfavorable opinions circulating here about his attitude toward psychoanalysis. I would like to ask you to level with us about him *as soon as possible.* I consider him to be a drowning man who is flailing around, and such people are questionable.

Yesterday it was also $\frac{1}{2}$ year since my last operation. Pichler is behaving as if he were fearing no untoward events,[3] he is putting me on leave for three to four weeks, permits me to go far away in the summer, etc. I should, of course, take this as a very favorable sign; what stands in opposition is the fact that the capabilities of my prosthesis for speaking and eating have significantly diminished, without my being able to get him interested in this severe setback in the initial beautiful success. I can't do anything there.

Tomorrow I am expecting Romain Rolland.

Kind regards to you and Gisela.

Yours,
Freud

1. Helene Deutsch, "Psychologie des Weibes in den Funktionen der Fortpflanzung" [Psychology of Woman in the Functions of Procreation], *Zeitschrift* 11 (1925): 40–53. René Spitz's paper was evidently not published.

2. "Urbantschitsch, who is now with us, wants (when he returns home) to set up a psa. consultation center for pedagogic and other things. As co-workers he wants (that is to say, would like) to win over Bernfeld, Aichhorn, and Anna Freud" (Ferenczi to Rank, May 25, 1924, Judith Dupont Archive).

3. The words "untoward events" are written in English in the original.

961

Budapest, May 14, 1924

Dear Professor,

Both of the Dutch papers are, in fact, the only ones that were sent to be edited. We must evidently accommodate ourselves to the fact that we can almost never get serious and more thoroughgoing contributions from the Dutch. According to Rank's arrangements, issue III was meant partly as a Dutch number. Now, in consideration of space, we will have to accept other things for this number—perhaps Dr. Deutsch's *Berlin* lecture about the "conversion symptom."[1]

I ask you also perhaps to send me the papers by Deutsch and René Spitz so that I can take a look at them. The former paper I found to be *very good*, as soon as I heard it in Salzburg—certainly it is a very precise and, in places, ingenious rounding-off of the conception of becoming a woman which was given in my "Theory of Genitality." The main contents of number III will, in any event, remain your work (Dissolution of the Oedipus Complex).—

I will write to v. Emden and Rank, respectively, about Jelgersma's and Stanley Hall's jubilee and obituary.

Now to the case of Urbantschitsch: I would like to say beforehand that, already at the beginning of his analysis, Urbantschitsch got a special promise out of me not to correspond about him with anyone, not even you. Nonetheless, the importance of the matter requires that I omit the otherwise obligatory discretion, but I must naturally ask you as well as Fräulein Anna to make no use of my communications with respect to third persons.

Urbantschitsch is actually in a very bad pecuniary situation; the monetary conditions have for the time being buried his great founding plan. As a substitute for that he hurled himself on the idea of founding the institute that was skillfully projected by him, which—with his adroitness and the patronage of appropriately schooled analysts (in whose selection he already showed himself to be likewise very intelligent)—could have a great future in store for it.

But now he wanted to use the financial crisis of the last few weeks for setting a termination date to his analysis on his own, and thus avoiding the acquisition of his "new character." I prevented that for the time being.

It is evident from his letter to Fräulein Anna that he is judicious and insightful. But what should become of him naturally depends entirely on the further progress and outcome of his analysis;—only then will it be seen how much of his (currently enthusiastic) scientific-serious striving proves to be genuine and how much purely business. If he remains until the end of his treatment, then not only his administrative but also his practical-psychological skill can be placed *very well* into the service of the analytic cause.

I would advise Fräulein Anna [to do] the following: with reference to his admission that his own analysis is unfinished, and, on the other hand, to his affirmation that he does *not* have his eyes on Anna's collaboration on account of the name "Freud," Fräulein Anna should respond to him to the effect that he should ask for the authorization for the time being in his own name—in the process, the prospect of Fräulein Anna's collaboration can be held out to him. (By the way, I can assure that he would actually like to win over Fräulein Anna for the institute on account of her personal qualities.)

Coming back to the theme of the Congress, I admit that the Berliners were very peaceable; but I think that Herr Professor perhaps underestimates the seriousness of the Berliners if you consider them capable of having gone along with Rank's misunderstanding out of "gentilezza." If they did that, then they are just as responsible for this as everyone else who did the same.

Please don't let Dr. Pichler loose until he helps your eating and speaking difficulties!—I set great expectations in Romain Rolland's personality.

Cordially,
Ferenczi

1. Felix Deutsch, "Zur Bildung des Konversionssymptoms" [On the Formation of Conversion Symptoms], *Zeitschrift* 10 (1924): 380–392, based on his lecture at the Seventh International Psychoanalytic Congress in Berlin, September 1922.

962

Budapest, May 25, 1924

Dear Professor,

This time I would like to lay claim to your time in a few more personal matters. First of all, I would like to be informed about your vacation plans and would like to inform you about my own at the same time. Your plans interest me because I—if appropriate, on traveling through on the way to my summer place of residence, but, if appropriate, even sooner, perhaps at Whitsun—would like to chat with you for a few hours, in order to talk through all current matters, and to make possible once again a scientifically and personally significant exchange of thoughts, which eludes me so in my isolation.

I wrote to Frau Oberholzer and asked her to look for an appropriate place for us to stay in Switzerland. I am thinking this time of being away for two and a half months (from the beginning of July to the middle of September), to be sure, I am taking along two pupils (foreigners), so that the vacation won't be a complete one.

The other matter that I want to communicate with you about is an idea that Dr. Bernfeld already talked about in Salzburg. He shared with me candidly the dissatisfaction of the Viennese group with Hitschmann as head of the outpatient department, and offered (in the event that I declare myself prepared to take over the medical direction of the Vienna polyclinic) to carry this through with you and with the Society. As a motive for the plan he indicated the hope that, under my direction, especially the scientific level of the polyclinic would rise, as well as the at the moment completely lacking inspiration to higher achievement of the younger workers.—I naturally gave Dr. Bernfeld no answer, since it is also in principle not easy for me to make a decision in this difficult question; I still owe him an answer today, and would now like to ask you how you (in principle) would stand with regard to this idea, whereby I must note that, even with your assent, changing my place of residence would not be an easy task for me. But if it should really turn out that I (as Dr. Bernfeld says) would render the cause a significant service, then I could *perhaps* decide to do it despite being accustomed to life here. But in order that I don't beat my brains out superfluously, I ask you to tell me whether what Dr. Bernfeld says corresponds to the truth, and what you have to remark, materially and personally, about this idea.

Almost immediately afterwards I recently received an invitation from America, this time to participate in the founding and putting into operation of a psychoanalytic polyclinic, for which money is supposedly available. I am supposed to stay there for two to three years. This eventuality comes into consideration for me only as a financial one, since I would rather do my work on the continent. I responded evasively, and am awaiting Rank's information about America.

Both Dr. Bernfeld and the American woman who wrote to me have entreated me for complete discretion—but I am already used to giving a promise of that kind with the reservatio mentalis of telling you everything, if necessary, in the interests of the cause.—On the other hand, I think I am sufficiently acquainted with his way of thinking and his loyalty to you and to psychoanalysis to know that he can also be in agreement with my turning to you, above all.

The Budapest group is already organized to the extent that my departure at least would not have any dissolution as a consequence. I must also admit that the events of the last six years have cooled off my local patriotism somewhat.

So that you are informed about everything, I will also tell you that the state of my health this year was by a nuance better than in the two previous ones. By I am not very satisfied with it even now.

I learned only by chance about your being honored by the city of Vienna[1] and would like to know some more about it.

Kind regards,
Ferenczi

P.S. For the sake of completeness, I will also share with you the fact that in the previous year I had two foreigners who held my head above water, otherwise I would have been able to keep up with the constantly rising prices only with great difficulty. To be sure, my situation here is assured to the extent that only the inability to work could put me in a state of exigency.

1. The bestowal of the rights of citizenship. "The main play [of my birthday] was the great honor of the city of Vienna. At twelve o'clock on the dot, Professor Tandler and Dr. Friedjung (Social[ist] District Councillor, pupil of mine; born on the same date), representing the mayor in order to inform me that, in consideration of my great service to science, I had been named

Citizen of the City of Vienna.

(It had already been in the newspaper days earlier. It is a kind of honor which is supposed to have a great deal of value placed upon it, but not as much as 'honorary citizen.') I replied that one must always cherish such a distinction on the part of the city fathers, even though it comes so late, whereupon the others [replied] that they were not responsible for the delay, inasmuch as they weren't previously at the helm. You see, the honor proceeds from the Social Democratic Party; the Workers' Newspaper is celebrating me today in a nice little article. A communication from the mayor then let me know that an artistically produced certificate will be handed over to me soon at City Hall.—Oli knows how little ambitious I am, but perhaps Henny doesn't know how much Mama is" (Freud to Oliver and Henny Freud, May 7, 1924, Library of Congress).

963

Vienna, May 28, 1924
IX., Berggasse 19[1]

Dear friend,

First, about the vacation. We are thinking of going away at the end of the first week of July, and are in negotiations with Waldhaus Flims in Graubünden, but haven't concluded a deal yet. This time I am taking along an American patient, who is supposed to pay the costs of the very expensive stay. As you can imagine, this year didn't result in any surplus over what was used. I will be in Vienna for Whitsun, will set Monday aside, and if you only won't forget that I am no longer so accessible and capable of achievement as before, I will be very pleased to discuss all kinds of things with you.

The matter of your moving to Vienna for the sake of the polyclinic here has my complete sympathy and my highest interest. If I were omnipotent, I would move you without further ado by means of a sudden ukase. What Bernfeld told you about Hitschmann is thoroughly correct; the opposition to him is general, and there is no prospect that the institute will ever accomplish anything under his direction. The Society would accept you unanimously as head of the polyclinic, and another result would be connected to that. I think, if you are here, they will elect you, instead of Rank, as my successor, and that would have the two great advantages that you are a physician, and that you have at your disposal a personal authority and a capability of accomplishment that he doesn't.

But now, the difficulties over which I have no power. It is very uncertain as to whether you can get a place to live in Vienna. According to report, a Frau Kraus, the wife of a bank director who has retired with his plunder, has the firm intention to build a house for the polyclinic, and this would have to contain an apartment for the head. But I don't know how this matter, which is, unfortunately, going through Hitschmann's hands, stands. There also is something unpleasant about it, if the polyclinic gets a house at his instigation and he is then chased away himself. I advise you to go for information about this to Bernfeld, who will do everything to shed light on the matter. He has, incidentally, already shared the plan of your appointment with Anna, who is writing this letter. The prospects for a practice are also not outstanding in Vienna. But I don't need to assure you that I would address the foreigners, who still want to come to me, to you to your satisfaction, so that you would be covered in this respect, provided that I am not consigned to the dead, in reality or in public opinion. Your presence in Vienna can also serve the discussion of the matter when you announce yourself to Bernfeld for the holidays.

There is little to say about my rights of citizenship in Vienna, which you ask about. Their application seems essentially to be a ritual: one can make Schabbes² of them.

The state of my health, especially my ability to speak, is still quite wobbly. At the moment, my surgeon is not figuring on recidivism.

With kind regards for you and your dear wife.

Yours,
Freud

1. The letter is typewritten; only the signature, "Freud," is handwritten.
2. Yiddish for "Sabbath" [Trans.].

964

Budapest, June 4, 1924

Dear Professor,

A few difficult analyses force me to work, even during the Whitsun holidays; so this time my visit with you must be canceled. Let us hope you will recover to some extent also in this interim vacation.

I was and am very pleased about the trust that you have in me, and I consider it a high honor that you don't consider me unworthy to take over the direction and education of the Vienna colleagues. On the other hand, I also appreciate your objection that it is unpleasant simply to chase away Hitschmann, who is responsible for the donation. To that should be added, as you correctly say, the difficulty in finding a place to live, which could scare me off as long as it isn't solved somehow. So, the result of our correspondence remains a theoretical one, at least for the time being; I can only think about the practical realization when all these hindrances have been removed.

Since the Vienna problem is not so current, there is nothing holding me back from returning to a plan of Rank's, who wrote to me from America, [asking whether] I would like to come over for a few months, since he is not getting finished with the work over there. (His letter came at almost the same time as your reply to my letter.) A series of colleagues have the intention of having themselves analyzed there by me. I have already agreed in principle, and, in fact, for the fall. Therefore I have to bring the still unfinished analyses to an end in the course of the fall. (No less than four in July!) Should the plan be realized, I will also take my wife along, who will be indispensable to me as a companion (I hope not also as a nurse).

The American plan is a purely financial matter for me. I hope in the process to lay by a sum that will make it possible for me not to work so strenuously, and to get some time for literary activity.

Many kind regards for you and your loved ones.

Yours,
Ferenczi

965

Budapest, June 15, 1924[1]

Dear Professor,

The American trip has become somewhat more doubtful (so I believe), because of the new immigration regulations, even though I still have received no news from Rank about it. The plan's falling through would not be a matter of indifference to me, since I almost sacrificed my summer plans for his sake, and am continuing the work with five patients, who must be terminated, over the summer.

Urbantschitsch is finishing his course of instruction (which was actually a regular analysis of a neurosis) at the end of this month. He has changed much to his advantage, has become more serious, learns diligently, and is, in the process, not untalented analytically. Naturally, he is not completely freed of the tendency toward fanciful innovations, exaggerations, mania for advertising, etc.—so that Fräulein Anna and Bernfeld have to pay attention to his activity, at least for a time. Naturally, he should not know anything about the fact that I have given reports about him; it would be best also to keep silent about this in front of Bernfeld.

Enclosed I am sending you a little paper by Dr. Lévy.[2] It is not uninteresting. Please pass it on to Storfer after you have taken a look at it.

With regard to Abraham's suggestion (choice of type),[3] I am of the opinion that we should not make any decision in principle until Rank's return, that is to say, wait for what he says from America.

I am concluding the work year with not unfavorable (therapeutic) success, and I hope to have time in the summer to write a theoretical and a practical work.

The American plan also brings along with it the disadvantage that I will spend the summer vacation in the vicinity of the city and am giving up the planned Swiss trip.

Kind regards,
Ferenczi

1. In the upper left-hand corner of this sheet there is a dark violet colophon, the letters "vK" entwined inside a circle; Ferenczi has crossed out the colophon.

2. See letter 959 and n. 3.

3. Abraham had "faulted" Ferenczi to the effect that "various papers [in the *Zeitschrift*] were printed in very different typefaces, e.g., in the last issue the first two essays (Freud, Ferenczi) are set in large, in contrast, Nunberg in medium, Hattingberg in very small print. '*This must make an impression on the reader that the quality of the works is supposed to be earmarked*'" (Ferenczi to Rank, May 25, 1924, Judith Dupont Archive).

966

Budapest, June 30, 1924

Dear Professor,

I was very pleased to have seen you before the vacation, but I was especially pleased by the favorable coincidence of being able to experience Lévy's favorable impression already piping hot. Let us hope you will recover very thoroughly on the vacation!

My American plans have been given up for the time being. Rank, who invited me so enthusiastically, wrote uncertainly in a second letter; but since I must prepare my summer plans and the fall campaign, I cabled him for an urgent decision. Instead of that, I received the reply, "situation uncertain."[1] Thereupon I canceled all travel preparations. This episode has severely disrupted my summer and my work.

The American Psychoanalytic Association wrote me that I was elected an honorary member of this association.

On July 1 we are moving into a boardinghouse near the city. Address: Dr. S. F., Budapest I., Rath Georg-Str. No. 5, Sanatorium "Siesta."

Many kind regards.

Yours,
Ferenczi

Over!

I notice a regrettable printing error in the table of contents of the last-received volume of the complete edition.[2] It says there: "An Autobiographical Account of a Case of Obsessional Neurosis" (instead of Paranoia!).[3]

F[erenczi].

1. The reply is written in English in the original.

2. At the beginning of 1923, the Verlag had acquired from Deuticke the rights for a complete edition of Freud's writings (*Gesammelte Schriften von Sigmund Freud*, 12 vols., ed. Anna Freud, Otto Rank, and Adolf Storfer).

3. Freud 1911c.

967

Semmering, Villa Schüler,
July 16, 1924[1]

Dear friend,

I have received the Dutch essay that you intended for me from Storfer, read it, and think it should be printed without corrections. It is in and of itself unnecessary that we are in agreement with all the particulars that we put in the Zeitschrift, and we have no right whatsoever to get involved in a contribution to a festschrift in honor of someone else.

You have here my new address. I inhabit this beautiful villa as the only male creature with seven women (wife, sister-in-law, two daughters, three attendant spirits, if the term is applicable to them), and I occupy myself mostly with writing my contribution for the collection of autobiographical writings in medicine, which is published by a certain Grote. So, once again, a history of psychoanalysis, fourth or fifth infusion.[2]

Despite my gentle surroundings, I am suffering greatly from my nasal suppuration, which disturbs everything for me. Otherwise, I wouldn't have anything to complain about.

I hope you and your wife are enjoying the summer and the relative peace and quiet also near the city. I recently had a conversation with the lady who wants to build the house for the Vienna polyclinic. She seems to be serious. I have arranged with her that the house also contain an official residence for the director of the institute. We were both in agreement about the name of the institute's director. Let us hope it really comes to that.

With kind regards.

Yours,
Freud

1. The letter is typewritten; only the signature, "Freud," is handwritten.
2. Freud 1925d, first published in Louis R. Grote, ed., *Die Medizin der Gegenwart in Selbstdarstellungen* [Contemporary Medicine in Self-Portraits], 8 vols. (Leipzig, 1923–1929), vol. 4 (1925), pp. 1–52.

968

[Budapest, undated][1]

Dear Professor,

I was pleased about the news that you are well lodged at the Semmering. Let us hope that the last (nasal) difficulties will also abate.

We are staying here until August 4 to 5, then we are going to *Alt-Prags*, where Urbantschitsch has arranged quarters for us. I will take along two patients, Sokolnicka and an Englishwoman.

Abraham writes me that he is going home from Switzerland at the beginning of August and also wants to visit you on the way.[2] The news about the Vienna polyclinic has naturally interested me very much. So, the plan of my moving to Vienna still seems to be possible.

I am in complete agreement with the decision about the Dutch article.

We have already ceased having our meetings. The last was a social gathering in the "Stadtwäldchen."

Please greet all four ladies from both of us, and heartfelt greatings from

Yours,
Ferenczi

1. The letter is undoubtedly Ferenczi's reply to Freud's letter of July 16, 1924 (mention of lodging at the Semmering, the nasal suppuration, the Vienna polyclinic, and the Dutch article).

2. After a holiday in Sils-Maria in the Engadin, Abraham visited Freud at the Semmering and returned to Berlin in the middle of August (Abraham to Freud, August 23, 1924, *Freud/Abraham*, p. 366).

969

Budapest, August 3, 1924

Dear Professor,

The strange news that you shared with me about Rank's behavior in America and that you characterized as a sign of his psychoneurosis gives me much to think about.[1] His peculiar attitude in the matter of my invitation to America was not compatible with dispelling these concerns. Nevertheless, I consider it possible that our fears will show themselves to be erroneous, and that with him it is a matter of exaggerations, which find their explanation in the material and other successes which he is raking in there. So, again, a case in which one is "wrecked by success."[2]—Eitingon wrote to me recently and expressed similar concerns, but likewise expresses the hope that the unfavorable impression he made with the American adventure will be eradicated after his return.—I intend to contribute to that with all the power at my disposal.—

My wife and I are going to *Engelberg* (in Switzerland) on Friday. Address there: Hotel Edelweiss. My brother, who lived there, writes very favorable things about the place.—I am taking an Englishwoman along to mitigate the expense. We will stay there about six weeks, then we want to come back via Germany. [We] hope to see Lou Salomé and Groddeck on the way, and perhaps, if we also travel via Berlin, Abraham as well.—

Yesterday Lajos Lévy and Frau Kata were with us; we naturally talked a great deal about the inhabitants of the Villa Schüler.

You might also have received a not uninteresting article by a Frenchman, who has an anatomical explanation of (obviously only a part!) of the cases of frigidity (position of the clitoris in relation to the entrance of the vagina).[3]—I recently read the "Dream Fantasy" of the painter Kubin,[4] to which he also appends his autobiography and case history (dementia praecox). In this case one could plumb the depths of dementia praecox in a similar way as paranoia in the case of Schreber. Do you want to read the book? I can send it to you.

Kind regards,
Ferenczi

I only just now, while reading in the Zeitschrift, fully understood the article about masochism,[5] and I am enthusiastic about it.

1. It is unclear whether Ferenczi had visited Freud at the Semmering, or whether a communication of Freud's is missing.
2. An allusion to Part II of Freud's "Some Character-Types Met with in Psycho-Analytic Work" (1916d).
3. A.-E. Narjani, "Considérations sur les causes anatomiques de frigidité chez la femme" [Considerations about the Anatomic Causes of Female Frigidity], *Bruxelles-Médical*, 27 (April 1924): 768–778. In reality, behind the pseudonym "Narjani" was Princess Marie Bonaparte, who underwent three operations by Professor Halban in Vienna, which reduced the space between clitoris and vagina but did not bring about the desired results. Célia Bertin, *Marie Bonaparte: A Life* (New York, 1982), pp. 140, 141, 170, 180–182. Marie Bonaparte, Princess of Greece (1882–1962), great grandniece of Napoleon, married to Prince George of Greece and Denmark (1869–1957). From 1925 on (with interruptions until 1938), under René Laforgue's mediation, she was in analysis with Freud, whose enthusiatic pupil and friend she became. She was a co-founder (1926) of the Société Psychanalitique de Paris. She dedicated the rest of her life to psychoanalysis, translated several of Freud's works into French, and was the organizer and promoter of French psychoanalysis, against whose development after the Second World War she later turned, unsuccessfully. As an author she is known primarily for her psychobiography of Edgar Allan Poe (Paris, 1933). See, in addition to Bertin, Jean-Pierre Bourgeron, *Marie Bonaparte et la psychanalyse: à travers ses lettres à René Laforgue et les images de son temps* (Geneva, 1993); Roudinesco & Plon, *Dictionnaire*, pp. 136–138; Elisabeth Roudinesco, *Histoire de la psychanalyse en France*, 2 vols. (Paris, 1982, 1986).
4. Alfred Kubin (1877–1959), famous Austrian graphic artist who was also active as a writer. His main literary work is *Die Andere Seite* [The Other Side] (1909).
5. "The Economic Problem of Masochism" (Freud 1924c).

970

[Semmering,] Villa Schüler,
August 6, 1924

Dear friend,

Your letter just arrived, and since it is so intimate, [and] Anna, the mistress of the typewriter, [is] at a picnic with Lampl, I take it upon myself to prepare the reply which is supposed to greet you in Engelberg.

I too am very concerned about Rank. It is hard to make a judgment, since he is so discreet and uncommunicative. Something is happening with him under the influence of the ambitious little woman. His letters to me are rare, brief, and ill-tempered. It will certainly be taken amiss among us that he is also propagating his not yet proven innovation there in America. I already got a letter from Trigant Burrow, who expresses concerns similar to those of the Berliners.[1] Naturally, B. is not the same as Abraham. If he [Rank] is asked how I stand with regard to the birth trauma, he must naturally say: favorably inclined, and I am becoming less and less so the further away I get from the first impression. He is going to pieces, I think, less from success than from not being analyzed. He remains a problem which must be grasped with loving hands when he returns.

To stay with the personal: I gave up Felix Deutsch as my physician, told him so, and since then I have received two long letters from him. The surprising impression from his behavior and utterances is that he has to be counted among the constitutionally *stupid*, a diagnosis to which one does not resort often enough. I have encountered unseemly indiscretions with him;[2] in addition to that, he constantly brags about his intention to deceive me as to the nature of my illness. I have known from the beginning that I have an epithelioma, and had taken him on as a physician under the condition that he tell me the truth every time, so that I may know how I should react. So, I have once again deceived myself in a person; it is too late to profit from that.

I also received the clitoris paper by Narjani. If true, it is very interesting that the type can be characterized anatomically, but it doesn't exhaust the matter and doesn't solve the problem as to why the stimulation of the vaginal zone doesn't release any pleasure. The fact remains that the clitoris has refused to give up its erogenous significance. If the mechanical factor were the only thing, then another position or technique of intercourse would have to eliminate the defect completely.

I very much want to read Kubin's book.

I am living very lazily here, with one hour of treatment a day, but I did have to write something. Grote, in Halle, the publisher of a medical compendium in "self-portraits," left me no peace until I promised him my contribution, which has now already been delivered, something between the

Five Lectures and the "History of the ψα Movement," so, a new infusion over the old tea.

Recently I was met by an urgent request from Albert Cohen[3] in Geneva, who wants to publish a Revue Juive, also to give him a contribution. I had already submitted my name for the editorial committee, and now he very skillfully bribed me with the statement that Einstein and I are the two most outstanding living Jews. What was left for me but to admit to him that I am very flattered and to grant him something harmless? I chose "The Resistances to Ψα."[4] The peace and quiet here is not completely undisturbed. On the 8th, a Swedish pastor Dymling[5] is supposed to come, on the 10th Abraham, and on the 29th of the month Eitingon. Let's hope none stays longer. I feel all obligations to be so pressing. Lajos Lévy will also inspect me here.

During these last four weeks I was in Vienna twice with my physicians or their assistants. Objectively, the state of my health is supposed to be totally satisfactory. In a few days it will be nine months since the last operation, and nowhere has anything suspicious shown up. Neumann,[6] especially, is very optimistic; he is, incidentally, behaving very kindly and talks about you every time. He refused, with great vehemence, to allow himself to be honored in any other way than by the "Complete Edition." So I sent it to him, and he is, supposedly, reading it.

I am less oppressed by the nevertheless undeniable uncertainty of my situation than I am by my present complaints, which are all dominated by the terrible nasal suppuration, and which disturb eating, drinking, and speaking. No one can bring me any relief, all therapeutic interventions only increase the swelling and secretion, but no one claims to find anything suspicious. So it must surely be my old ethmoidal bone or sphenoid bone process, which is now spreading.

But my existence is far removed from comfort. I am also aging rapidly in other respects, only my sleep is still undisturbed, infantilely good.

The Steinach operation of eight and a half months ago has achieved nothing.

I hope that in Switzerland you will get to enjoy some nature.

We are living here thoroughly comfortably, but we don't get a feeling of summer. It is, as it also is elsewhere, mostly gloomy, cold, and rainy.

I greet you and Frau Gisela kindly.

Yours,
Freud

1. On July 4 Burrow had asked Freud whether he was really in agreement with Rank's measure of setting a termination date in therapies, as Rank had claimed at the annual meeting of the American Psychoanalytic Association in Atlantic City. "It is difficult for me to credit it" (*A Search for Man's Sanity: The Selected Letters of Trigant Burrow* [New

York, 1958], p. 77). Freud replied on July 31 that it "was merely a matter of an innovation in technique, which has a right to be attempted . . . I certainly do not want to claim that I expect very much from the recommended change. In general, I maintain my earlier position, but I see no enmity with the new one" (ibid.). Trigant Burrow (1875–1950), American psychiatrist and psychologist, received his M. D. in 1899 from the University of Virginia and his Ph.D. in 1909 from Johns Hopkins; he was a pioneer in social psychiatry and group therapy. An analysand of Jones and Jung, he was a founding member of the American Psychoanalytic Association (1911). Burrow later deviated from psychoanalysis, was expelled from the APA in 1933, and developed a form of group analysis, as well as a "phylobiology," which investigated the inner tension patterns of the organism. Freud, with whom Burrow maintained a correspondence (Library of Congress), had a disapproving attitude toward his innovations from the beginning.

2. "People have told me about utterances from you that are not compatible with the discretion that a patient can expect from his physician, especially when he has opened himself up to him in such a way without restraint. For example, about the dependency of my pains, my longing for Pichler, and the like . . . I don't want to assume that your analyst [Bernfeld; Rank was Deutsch's control analyst] has shown himself to be indiscreet, that would be worse still. My impression is altogether that the analysis did you no good, that it has prejudiced you in your judgment of the organic . . . Think about this for a long time before you reply to me" (Freud to Felix Deutsch, July 22, 1924, Library of Congress). Deutsch defended himself in a long letter of August 10, 1924 (Library of Congress), but he was no longer able to dissuade Freud from his decision.

3. Albert Cohen (1895–1981), a French writer of Jewish-Greek origin.

4. Freud 1925e.

5. The pastor has not been identified.

6. See letters 113, 114, 118, 552, and 686.

971

	Hotel Edelweiss, Engelberg	
Sommer-Saison	Jos. Tschopp-Müller[1]	Winter-Saison
	Engelberg,	
	Schweiz[2]	

August 14, 1924

Dear Professor,

This depiction gives a somewhat imprecise representation of the situation of our hotel; in reality, it is closer to the watering place (open-air health resort). The landscape view of the place is very beautiful; it is situated in the hollow of a high valley, surrounded by snow-capped mountains, today, by coincidence, also covered with new snow that begins about 3 to 400 meters above the place. We had three burning hot days, then rain. There are nice walks here, but (as is usual in Switzerland) no real forest as we know it from the Austrian Alps and the Carpathians. The hotel is very well managed, the food first-class.—I will give three hours here (one to

Sokolnicka and two to an English [female] colleague). Perhaps, in addition to that, I will have the desire to write down and enlarge upon the so-called "activity." In the framework of these discussions I will perhaps attempt also to take a position in the matter of the "birth trauma." My initial enthusiasm over this finding has also given way in me to a cooler judgment and a significant limitation of the *significance in practice [der aktuellen Bedeutsamkeit] for the neuroses.*—My own "Theory of Genitality" has, incidentally, never given up the main significance of the "fifth catastrophe" (Ice Age—father culture) in the etiology of the neuroses, and has only now allowed us to understand the exceptionally high valuation of the genital (organ of womb-regression), as well as the castration anxiety attached to it.—On the other hand, the analyses in fact often also show me an undercurrent behind the castration trauma which permits the "birth" explanation.

Your detailed letter was extraordinarily gratifying to me. Especially because you give me news about the continually favorable, if not undisturbed, state of your health. The departure of Dr. Deutsch is naturally a consequence of the fact that, instead of remaining an internist [which he perhaps should have remained altogether],[3] he played the psychotherapist, for whose handiwork he is not particularly well suited.—He also made similar mistakes in my case, and in so doing overlooked things that should have interested the internist. You are right—a physician must above all be clever.—Incidentally, the state of my health is relatively good, albeit not without nightly disturbances. I can climb 2 to 300 meters at a good pace.

I completely share your view about the way one has to treat Rank; if I still have some influence over him, then I will make use of him along your lines. His wife's influence seems to me rather[4] to be favorable; she endeavors to moderate her husband.

After what you write me about the all too frequent disturbance of your summer rest, I am doubly happy I didn't give in to the temptation to see you on the trip here. But on the way back I think and hope that I will be able to speak with you in Vienna.

Many kind regards from both of us to you and your loved ones.

Yours,
Ferenczi

1. This line has been crossed out with violet ink.
2. Preprinted letterhead with a depiction of the hotel and the area in front of the mountain panorama with the peaks of Engelberg and Titlis, to which Ferenczi refers by means of writing and arrows.
3. Brackets in the original.
4. Reading uncertain. It could also be "however."

972

Semmering, August 27, 1924[1]

Dear friend,

Enclosed [is] a copy of Rank's letter, which I received yesterday.[2] You will see from it how matters stand. I think we have to be prepared for the most unfavorable outcome. You can imagine that for me it means a grave disappointment and an almost unbelievable experience. It is a certain consolation that I really can't ascribe any responsibility to myself for this outcome. You yourself know all the circumstances. I can also claim for myself the right to free choice of judgment and don't have to agree unconditionally to an adherent's innovation, if I am prepared myself to allow everyone his own opinion within the natural limits of the working community.

You will perhaps find my statement too pessimistic, since Rank has not yet officially declared his withdrawal. But it is as good as if it were written in the letter. Certainly, I am also awaiting further developments. But I don't want to be taken by them unprepared. I do hope that I can still rely on you, and for that reason I ask whether, if reality dictates, you will take over the editorship of the journals in Rank's place. I have no one else, and certainly no one who is more dear to me. Anna would support you here as official secretary, and I would help her out, naturally, to the extent that it is possible for me. In suspense, I look forward to your remarks about this assignment and the whole situation. Aside from you, only Eitingon will learn of Rank's letter and my intentions.[3]

I don't know when Rank is coming back. I hope to speak with you in Vienna at the end of September or the beginning of October.

With kind regards to you and your dear wife.

Yours,
Freud

1. The letter is typewritten; only the signature, "Freud," is handwritten.
2. Rank wrote, among other things: "I have the distinct impression that you do not want to or cannot see certain things, for sometimes your objections sound as if you haven't read or heard at all what I actually said . . . Even now you are again talking about the fact that I had shut out the father; that is naturally not and cannot be the case, it would be nonsense. I only attempted to accord him his proper place. In this, you are obviously bringing in the personal relations between you and me, where they don't belong at all. In this connection I was very strangely touched by the fact that it is you, of all people, who reproaches me with the supposition that I would never have had this conception if I had been analyzed. That may well be. The question is only whether that would not have been very regrettable. In any case, I can only consider that fortunate, after everything I have seen in the way of results with analyzed analysts . . . I also don't know to what extent your judgment or prejudice with regard to my conception has been permitted to be influenced by some impertinent screamers. Thus the newest Berlin plans and conspira-

cies strike me . . . as so silly . . . the profound ingnorance of people like Abraham et al. . . . Let's not forget that the psa. movement as such is a fiction. The people who make a movement are not a fiction, and, frankly, I have no regard whatsoever for the people who are now in the act of making movement in psa." (August 9, 1924, Judith Dupont Archive).

3. On the same day Freud composed a draft of a reply to Rank's letter, which he did not send off immediately, however, but sent to Eitingon (August 27, 1924, Sigmund Freud Copyrights). In it he says: "Your letter was . . . very painful to me. I would not have believed that you could write in that way. That there is never an end to surprises. One is never prepared for everything . . . I said at the time that someone *else* would make himself independent with such a finding. I still hold fast to this limitation, otherwise I would have to declare the situation to be hopeless. There are nasty things in your letter. To attribute 'profound ignorance' to Abraham and to declare him to be an 'impertinent [the word "obtrusive" is crossed out] screamer,' that implies a clouding of judgment which is explicable only by means of immeasurable affectivity and is poorly attuned to the mastery of complexes. An evil demon has you saying: the $\psi\alpha$ movement is only a 'fiction' and in the process puts even the enemy's words into your mouth . . . Your bitterly malicious remark, which is based on the existence of the complexes, that you are happy not having been analyzed, otherwise you would not have made your finding, is not justified; you overlook the danger, to which others have already succumbed, of projecting into science as theory what is stirring in oneself, which really doesn't have the value of mastery. That piece of exegesis is very painful to me, but some passages in your letter sound as if you are resolved, after more than fifteen years of intimacy and collaboration, to break off relations with us and with our cause, and in so doing lend credence to the suspicion which made you so indignant in the first place . . . If you are serious about that, what can I do, what can I say to you that you cannot know directly yourself and must have found yourself in these fifteen years. If my being ill had gone further, I would have spared you a certainly not easy decision. Since, as it appears, I have to gear myself up for continuing to live, I am confronted with a situation which only recently I would have dismissed as unthinkable. What is especially painful is the fact that I find the occasion for this loss so inadequate, hardly a consolation that I cannot discover the part that is my own fault. My feelings for you have not been shaken by anything; I can still not give up hope that you will progress to quiet reflection" (Judith Dupont Archive).

973

Villa Schüler
August 29, 1924

Dear friend,

Anna, who typed the last letter to you with the enclosure from Rank, finds that I didn't write to you in a friendly enough manner. I don't share this impression, but I will use it as an occasion to talk things out with you further.

You see, I don't understand Rank at all anymore. Can you contribute anything to my enlightenment?[1] For fifteen years I have known him, tenderly concerned, obliging, discreet, absolutely dependable, just as prepared to accept suggestions as he was uninhibited in working up his own ideas, on my side in all contentious matters, without inner compulsion, so I thought.

And now, where did this change come from? That I first greeted his birth trauma as a great accomplishment and then gradually developed reservations about it is not a sufficient motivation. The fact that I did not give in to his revenge impulse against Abraham, which you, unfortunately, supported at first, should be just as little a motive, after all the privileges whose object he was.

It is also a particularly bad revenge on Abraham when, under the pretense of provocation, he does exactly what one suspected him of doing. The remark in my next-to-last letter, to which he is reacting, to the effect that he probably wouldn't have written the book if he had been analyzed—on account of the danger of projecting one's own complexes into the theory—, was certainly incautious in general and irritated him very much! But am I not permitted to assume that he would tolerate such an admonition on my part? But look how he responds to that: downright venomously. He sees in the analyzed (by me) analysts what good fortune it is that he himself didn't have any analysis. That goes beyond all moderation, just like the unheard-of characterization of Abraham as a profound ignoramus and impertinent screamer.

Now, who is the real Rank, the one I have known for fifteen years, or the one whom Jones has wanted to show me for years?

Aside from this theoretical riddle, I also don't know how the real situation should take shape after his return. If he condescends graciously to maintain his manifold vital functions a while longer, then what comes into consideration is the fact that the distrust against him—in Berlin—has grown considerably. Eitingon has suppressed, not without difficulty, an intention of the Berliners to create a special organ of publication for themselves, since they fear Rank's partisanship and self-aggrandizement in the Zeitschrift. He is already said to have behaved very peculiarly at the Congress. Long before my already mentioned letter to him, my niece Lucy wrote from New York[2] that he was there for a visit and left a bad impression, since he constantly talked about the fact that everything in New York was in disarray, and he had to come to put things in order. Cf. to that the role of redeemer that he assumes in his letter.[3] He was supposed to be working with my nephew Edward in the interest of the Verlag, but he insulted him so much with his impoliteness that there is no intercourse between them.[4] Rank then wrote about it that it seemed to him that he is being regarded as an enemy by my family over there! In that way he makes enemies of everyone, and now he evidently wants to get angry with me.

The next rhyme or reason at hand would be that he has gone "crazy" [*meschugge*], that, under the influence of the analytic welling-up of his material success and my threatening illness, a hitherto latent neurosis has gained mastery over him. What do you think of that? I have composed a long, very considerate reply to his aggressive letter, which I haven't sent to him, however, but sent off to Eitingon for him to pass judgment on, with whom I have already discussed the matter in detail upon his visit. When the draft returns, you will have it. You see, I don't know whether it is good to reply at all, whether every reaction won't have the result of hastening the disintegration and alienation. He will naturally put everything that he learns to his own use, also the fact that I have occupied myself with the possibilities of replacing him—which is, of course, unavoidable. So, be very careful in your communications with him. Nicest thing would be if the attack went away in the same way that it came. One would have to forgive him everything in consideration of his extraordinary services. But I don't place any trust in that hope.

The most uncanny thing in his behavior is the remark about the "Ps A movement," which he declares to be a "fiction" (using the Adlerian vocabulary).[5] Can you imagine that he is prepared to place this fiction further at his disposal? And do you believe that a person in such a frame of mind finds a redeeming new truth or gets into such [a frame of mind] because he has found it? That assumption is difficult for me to make.

I can naturally not be very happy about this first experience after my recovery and the restoration of my will to continue living. In younger years I would have shaken everything off and declared that nothing can be done with people. Today this is remote from me; I am indifferent enough to throw this experience in along with the other, similar ones. But I will be very gratified if my judgment finds support among the few whom I can still trust.

With kind regards,
Freud

1. In the original there is a period instead of a question mark.
2. Leah ("Lucy") Bernays (1886–1980), the daughter of Freud's sister Anna and Martha's brother Eli Bernays.
3. "When the people saw that they work more easily with the modifications indicated by me and achieve better results—both in their own analyses and with their patients—they praised me like a redeemer" (August 9, 1924, Judith Dupont Archive).
4. Rank had given Edward Bernays (Lucy's brother) several possible times for a meeting and added, "Would you kindly phone, and my secretary will make an appointment for you" (Rank to Bernays, May 17, 1924, Judith Dupont Archive). Bernays replied through his secretary: "[Mr. Bernays] does not understand the tenor of Dr. Rank's letter. He certainly has no reason to request an interview with Dr. Rank in the manner suggested" (May 19, 1924, Judith Dupont Archive).

5. A strategy by which the neurotic, according to Adler, denies the uncomfortable reality and in its place sets up an ideal state, "fiction" [*Fassade*], which he desperately defends (with the aid of "securities [*Sicherungen*]") (*The Neurotic Constitution* [Vienna, 1912], passim).

974

Montreux, Hotel Eden,
September 1, 1924

Dear Professor,

Before I go more closely into the details of your last, so significant letter, I want above all to tell you that it goes without saying that I am prepared to perform any service to which psychoanalysis, i.e., you, calls me, and that in the event—which, let us hope, won't transpire—of a break with Rank, I will also assume the editorial tasks. I will return to the personal difficulties and the disadvantages of such a personnel change, but for the moment I would like to occupy myself with the factual parts of the matter, which cannot, to be sure, be entirely separated from the personal.—

You recall, perhaps—I already referred to it in an earlier letter—, that it was you who acquainted me with Rank's particularly ingenious, significant discovery, with expressions of your greatest satisfaction (at the time the expression about the truth content of 66 to 33% also came out). Rank, with whom I was at the time working jointly on the technical essay, had up to then communicated *nothing* to me about his birth theory; he can be very close-mouthed, you know.—The matter captivated me immediately, from a theoretical standpoint; but the practical examples that he brought made no impression, either on you or on me.—But when I began to turn my attention to the mother-role of the analyst, I found the most remarkable confirmations from the most diverse quarters (among the patients). Under the impression of these [confirmations] (which were especially strong among the anxiety hysterics), I amplified my analytic work usually with *these* attempts at interpretation, which, as mentioned, the patients entered into. To be sure, I was far and away not as skilled as Rank in sniffing out the paths of connection between almost every psychic utterance, every symptom of the patient, and the birth trauma, and I always left the question open as to whether there existed an inability on my part or an exaggeration on his part. I continued my analyses in the accustomed way, laid, as I have for some time altogether, great stress—alongside the associative material—on the reactions now known as "activity," which also interested me greatly from a theoretical standpoint, [and I] accepted from Rank the necessity of giving a date of termination, more or less independently of the birth trauma theory itself, which I recognized as effective only in situations which yielded to me unobjectionable and multiply determined material.—My objections seemed to make a certain impression on Rank, and it is not out of the question that, under my influence, he began 1.) to consider the possibility of *too slight* a trauma, 2.) to regain a higher estimation of the significance of the father complex (which he, as he himself writes, never gave up)—to be sure, only as the altered form of expression of a mother anxiety transferred to the father.

I, too, was able in very many cases to make a connection between castration anxiety (father anxiety) and earlier sources of anxiety (mother anxiety), but I didn't know how much of the latter lives on "realistically efficaciously" [*real wirksam*], and how much only as a model, *giving form*, as it were, behind the father complex. I was inclined to allow for both possibilities and to construct a new ranking, so to speak, in whose initial members what is inborn, more correctly: trauma experienced at birth, and on the other end, the later (father) traumata, can be thought of as prominently operative, while in between one could assume an alternating mixture of both trauma factors.—But the more I pushed the mother-factor into the forefront (as Rank also did), the more I was struck by the fact that *the last* difficulties that one must solve before terminating an analysis were again and again the "normal sexual conflicts" (i.e., the resistances that result from the heterosexual Oedipus setting). According to the principle of the locus majoris resistentiae,[1] I then had to think that the actual pathogenic elements do lie in the father complex, whereas the mother complex (mother anxiety) 1.) functions as a form-giving factor in father anxiety, 2.) is pushed to the fore as an *already mastered* form of anxiety also in the unconscious or: up to certain levels of the ucs. in place of what is actually feared (penis envy, father complex). There I also made a theoretical connection with my "Theory of Genitality" by assuming that, after penis formation (after the successful identification with the penis), this organ, which makes possible the reunification with the mother, takes on an uncommon significance which can explain the neurotogenic-traumatic effect of the threat of castration.—To be sure, I found cases again and again in which *this* anxiety (whether only in form or also in essence) struck [me] greatly as originating from the anxiety about the "vagina dentata."

So, as impressed as I was (after the final reading of the Rankian book) by the form-giving significance of birth anxiety for the entire development *of animals*, I was in doubt about whether the *specifically human* development and the formation of neuroses (also a purely human institution) is not caused *specifically* by the latency period, i.e., by the threat of castration, which characterizes this time. (Primal father theory from "Totem and Taboo"; my fantasy about the Ice Age, etc.)

In the meantime I rarely saw Rank. We did, to be sure, correspond a great deal, and I admit I shared his view that his discovery was given too little just estimation from your quarter, and that Abraham and Jones, on the one hand out of ignorance of the matter, on the other out of personal motives, were sowing intrigue with you in this matter. For a time Eitingon also participated in this correspondence; he praised the "Development [of Psychoanalyis]," in particular, as a long-awaited advance, in comparison to the therapeutic ineptness of the Berliners (especially Abraham).—The birth trauma theory did *not* make a good impression on Eitingon.—

In the meantime the news spread in psychoanalytic circles that Rank and I are no longer "kosher" in the psychoanalytic sense (e.g., Frau Oberholzer also expressed herself that way recently to a [female] colleague); Jones's remarks at the Congress, Rank's reserve there, Abraham's remarks to the Berliners, the news of your dissatisfaction, etc. strengthened the colleagues in this view; they placed birth theory, active technique, many even the (certainly innocent) theory of genitality on the list of press productions proscribed by you.—

The book by Rank about the "Analysis of Neuroses in Dreams"[2] was for me again a surprise at the Congress; I didn't know anything about it beforehand. I found the book so unpalatably written that I haven't read it to this day, so I can't express myself about its value.

Then came Rank's enthusiastic invitation (to America)—soon thereafter the refusal that gave me infinitely great difficulties for the summer. This emotional factor has—strangely enough!—further shaken my trust even in the birth theory, i.e., it was only *after* this event that I became fully aware of the doubts that I have just described. There one sees how strongly one can be influenced by personal anti- and sympathies in one's scientific views.—

But it is precisely for that reason that I shouldn't lapse into the other extreme, and must, now as before, support *what is right* in Rank's discovery, and I think we must bring everything to bear to *integrate* his ideas in psychoanalytic knowledge, a work that he himself cannot do unqualifiedly (not everyone has the didactic talent for it). And that is, I think, the path that we must tread: acquiescing to his suggestion for the free expression of opinion, "laying the cards on the table," as he says—naturally under impartial leadership of the discussion. You too must lay out your point of view clearly, and we would have to attempt altogether to settle this matter along the lines of public scientific discussion. Certainly the most important thing in this would be to find out (and to publish) what prepossessed *you* in favor of the matter at first or made you sympathetic to it, and what factors then set you against it, and to what extent—finally, you would also have to say what you also value in the matter at the moment.—

It would not be impossible that in this way Rank's invaluable collaboration for the cause could be saved. For—and now I come to the personal—I feel very imperfectly suited to replace him! The only thing that I could accomplish would be the reading and critical differentiation of the incoming works. Certainly, Fräulein Anna's help would then be indispensable to me (perhaps also *Bernfeld's*, in pursuing the literature).—If, in addition to that, you are also thinking about the Verlag, which has a certainly estimable but incomparably lesser force in Storfer, then you see that three to four people are necessary to represent him alone (incompletely).

What I can on no account approve of is Rank's utterance about the advantages of being unanalyzed. This statement contradicts all of psychoanalysis and would—if it were accepted—degrade psychoanalysis to a kind of poetic divination—. Fantasies are, of course (as the quote from Schiller that Rank found says),[3] necessary; but science will come from it only by means of strict criticism after the fact.—

To return to the personal, I must also refer to the fact that I must work a great deal under the unfavorable material conditions of today, somewhat more than my nevertheless somewhat unstable health makes it appear advisable; but *that* would not scare me away from assuming the burdens of reader and chief editor.

Not last, I must also mention the difficulty of my situation with regard to Rank.—In my last letters to him (he wrote me altogether only those two letters which contradicted each other), I told him that his ill-considered invitation to America put me into great difficulty and made quite a bad mood ensue with regard to him; but that was now over, and I was awaiting—so I wrote—favorable news about his activity in America. I wrote him nothing about my scientific vacillations; I preferred to postpone that until the time of the personal meeting.

This middle position can, naturally, bring[4] me the unpleasant reputation of being a traitor, but it perhaps makes me the appropriate person to salvage the restoration of all of us working together. Naturally, Rank would also have to publish his newest discoveries, which might strengthen him, and put us in a position to make a judgment about them. What I know about his technique *I* can only partially confirm.

But all that is not so essential. The most important thing is that you (perhaps under consideration of what I have written) assure him the possibility of working together, perhaps with reference to what you still consider untenable in his theory.

If he comes home, then that will give us an opportunity to evaluate the situation and do what is necessary. It would be advisable, in any case, for this last correspondence between you and Rank to remain a secret among the few initiates (Eitingon and me). It goes without saying that I will also not let Rank get wind of our arrangement.—

Jones wrote to me recently and, in a somewhat superior fashion, gave me the assurance that "it occurs to no one to mistake me for Rank," etc. I replied to him that Rank's ideas, even if they are exaggerated in their present form, interest me greatly, and that I also consider most of the ideas presented in the "Development [of Psychoanalysis]" to be correct, now as before, even though I concede that the editing and conception should have found a more salutary form.—

I await news from you, that is to say, the reply to this letter, and am prepared to go into particulars that I may have left out.

We moved, as you see, from Engelberg, where we almost froze to death, to Montreux, where it can be beautiful even in dreary weather. I am dragging three analytical hours along with me. Unfortunately!

We are staying here until about September 13, then we want to travel by way of Bern or Basel, [to] Germany, finally to Vienna at the end of September. I begin work in Budapest on October 1. I will certainly stay in Vienna for a few days; I will probably find you already there, but I can naturally also look you up at the Semmering.

Many kind regards to you and to your dear family.

Yours,
Ferenczi

1. Latin for "place of greatest resistance."
2. *Eine Neurosenanalyse in Träumen* [An Analysis of Neuroses in Dreams], published as the third volume of the series "Neue Arbeiten zur ärztlichen Psychoanalyse" [New Works on Medical Psychoanalysis] in the Verlag (1924).
3. Schiller's letter to Gottfried Körner of December 1, 1788 (*Briefwechsel mit Körner*, 1:381–385), read aloud by Rank on March 4, 1908, in the Vienna Society (*Minutes* I, 339) and at the following Congress in Salzburg (Jones II, 42); cited by Freud in *The Interpretation of Dreams* (1900a, pp. 102f.; 1909 Supplement).
4. In the original this word was changed to "bring in" [*einbringen*]. A number of words have been corrected in this sentence. Ferenczi evidently began with "This middle position can naturally [put] me into the unpleasant . . ." and then wished to change it to "This middle position can naturally bring in to me the unpleasant reputation of a traitor."

975

Montreux, September 3, 1924

Dear Professor,

I am writing to you only briefly and in a great hurry, so that you will receive this letter very soon. Your last letter was not only not unfriendly but, on the contrary, of a distinct friendliness and kept especially full of confidence. You can see my reaction from the enclosed letter,[1] which I wrote to Rank already yesterday, when I likewise received from him the copy of his letter that was directed to you. Please send my letter back here after you have read it.

The tone that Rank strikes immediately appeared to me to be extremely repellent. But I intentionally avoided talking about this in my last letter to you, in order not to sharpen the opposition further.

I await your reply and the return of the letter to Rank. In the meantime I will reflect on everything you write and express myself in detail as soon as possible.

With kind regards in old devotion.

Yours truly,
Ferenczi

P.S. I haven't given up hope that Rank can still be kept, with an appropriate attitude on our part. We must at least try everything. Perhaps my letter will also have its effect; naturally, you shouldn't strike such a sharp tone as I.

F[erenczi].

1. The letter has not been found.

976

Semmering, September 4, 1924

Dear friend,

I thank you for your quick reply and the declaration of your preparedness, if necessary, to jump into the breach. I would very much like to spare you the difficult additional effort; Eitingon wants to come to Vienna at the beginning of October to help in ordering things, and you should be there. Naturally it would also be preferable to me if we didn't need to change anything.

If it founders, then I will hardly be to blame for the outcome. I only fear Rank's stiffening in his bitterness, to put it straight-out: his neurosis, which has become manifest.

My behavior is clearly indicated. Since the observations that I was first able to make have shown me nothing new, I will discontinue criticism until Rank has made up for what he still owes us, which is to say in clear presentation what he *believes* and what he, in practice, *does*. Neither of these has happened; I only saw clearly, from a conversation with Reik, who was with me for an hour, how little I know about either.

It is strange that he talks about "laying the cards on the table," for it was he who committed the wrong of carrying over his usual reserve into science. Everything would have stayed on an even keel if at first he had given a comprehensible report about the basis for his discoveries. His "Analysis in Dreams" made the same impression on everyone; it is opaque and unconvincing; actually the book is totally unreadable.

The complaint that I place too little value on his discovery also doesn't sound good. I heard it exactly the same way with Adler. But since you yourself recall my initial inclination toward overestimation, it is also especially unjust. I was so happy that he elevated himself to a thoroughly original achievement in the analytical field that I was prepared for the most amicable prejudice. Naturally, I didn't give up the right thereby to acquire a judgment independent of this position through my own experience. Rank's inclination to reduce everything to intrigues and personal motives is very regrettable.

In your letter you passed over some questionable points in his letter, characterizing Abraham, emphasizing the role of redeemer. The comment about the harm of being analyzed also took you aback.

We must now wait until he is here again. According to reports from Frau Beate, the child is still suffering; she is going with it[1] to Abbazia, he embarks on September 27 and comes first to them, so he won't be in Vienna before the end of October.—

Yesterday Oli's wife in Berlin gave birth to a little daughter, the second granddaughter.[2]

With kind regards to you and Frau Gisela.

Yours,
Freud

1. I.e., the child, Helene.
2. Eva (1924–1944).

977

[Semmering,] September 6, 1924

Dear friend,

I am sitting here despite bad weather in beautiful comfort and complete inactivity, so it is very desirable for me to continue the correspondence with you.

Your draft of a reply to Rank, which I am returning herewith, has a few outstanding spots and shows some omissions. (It would be incorrect to say that he reassured me about your position, for there was no concern.)

What is first-rate is your remark about the impression [he makes], as if *he* couldn't expect to have gotten angry with me, and your request to give an example of how one settles theoretical differences among analysts.

Too weak, in my opinion, [is] your reaction to the advantage of not being analyzed, a regrettable admission of the alienation from analysis which already exists with him.

Quite insufficient [is] your estimation of the grotesque situation that he demands unqualified adherence when he has practiced secretiveness ("lay the cards on the table"!!) and wouldn't tell anyone either what he does in technique or what he derives from it in the way of theory. You could have grabbed him more forcefully in these two weak spots.

My reply, the draft of which went off to Eitingon, was more cautious than yours, more adapted to his attitude toward me. Not without sharp disagreement on a number of points. I originally didn't want to respond at all, but since Eitingon insisted upon it,[1] I decided to send the letter off immediately, in the not ungrounded fear that it would arrive after Rank's departure if it still had to make its way via Montreux and back. Perhaps I was overly cautious; I am sorry that you seem slighted thereby; in compensation I present you with Eitingon's response.

The matter still seems very dismal to me. He is in a discoverer paranoia, overpowered by his production, completely like Adler in his time, but if on the strength of that he makes himself independent, he won't have the same luck, for his theory contradicts the common sense[2] of the laity, who found themselves flattered by Adler's striving for power. Rank's behavior when they questioned his patient Moxon in Berlin about his technique was already very striking and is now falling into a pattern. If he comes to his senses it will naturally be high time to remind him of his extraordinary services and his irreplaceability, and pardon all his aberrations. But I don't dare believe in that; from experience, once the devil is loose, he goes his way to the end. It grieves me greatly that Jones may be right after all.

I will receive him very amicably if he does not already bring with him the announcement of the completed rupture, as if there were no affective factors in play. But there can be no question of a Wallensteinian entreaty ("Max, stay with me");[3] I am fully convinced of the uselessness of such an appeal. Also, the situation is different; our cause can no longer be jeopardized, I am old and less vulnerable. There will be scandal. Stekel will not fail to spread it far and wide, but one also has to accept that. On no account will I copy Zarastro in the Magic Flute, who first sings:

> In these holy halls
> one knows not revenge,
> and if a man falls,
> doing good will lead him to duty;

and then, notwithstanding, sentences Monostatos to be flogged.[4] If we could treat the whole thing as a derailment in the family that has nothing to do with strangers, that would certainly be the best thing.

Theoretically, I don't see clearly in the trauma business, and I don't want to beat my head against the wall before he hasn't [sic] given the information that one can request of him.—

On the 3rd of the month, Oli's wife gave birth to a little daughter at her father's in Berlin, the second granddaughter. There are now seven;[5] none can make me forget the lost Heinele. I still don't know three [of them] at all.

I am well. On the 15th I am dismissing my American and will dedicate myself to correcting the prosthesis through Pichler, who won't return earlier. The summer has deceived us, as it did everyone; now the question is whether fall is preparing to compensate me.

With cordial best wishes to you and Gisela.

Yours,
Freud

1. "He now *deserves* a reply in the double meaning of the word. And yours appears to me to be quite appropriate and the right one" (Eitingon to Freud, September 2, 1924, Sigmund Freud Copyrights).

2. The words "common sense" are written in English in the original [Trans.].

3. Friedrich von Schiller, *Wallensteins Tod* [Wallenstein's Death], III, 18. Wallenstein beseeches Max Piccolomini to support him in his revolt against the emperor after Piccolomini has already decided to stand by his father, Octavio, in the emperor's camp.

4. Mozart and Schikaneder, *The Magic Flute*, act 2. (The last strophe should read: "Love will lead him to duty.")

5. Along with Eva, Martin's children Anton (b. 1921) and Sophie (1924); Ernst's "archangels," Stephan Gabriel (1921), Lucian Michael (1922), and Clemens Raphael (1924); as well as Sophie's son Ernst (1914), Heinele's brother.

978

GRAND HOTEL EDEN, MONTREUX
E. EBERHARD, Prop. (SUISSE)

Eden Hôtel
Montreux, September 9, 1924[1]

Dear Professor,

Since in the meantime you have actually received from my letter to Rank the answer to some earlier questions [addressed] to me, I will omit going into them again and will only reflect on your last letter.

I must, unfortunately, concede that the situation is not a very hopeful one. If Rank has now gone so far that he was able to send you that letter, then he has certainly settled accounts with everything. In spite of this, I don't want to give up hope completely, and I wrote to Frau Beate (to Abbazia, unfortunately, without knowing her more definitive address) that would like to have a meeting with him as soon as possible, perhaps still before his trip to Vienna. The same wish was expressed today by a letter I received from Rank, which insists on the meeting "in my interest." He doesn't know that as far as I am concerned, the die has already been cast, and I don't understand how (—and whether he—) could expect anything different from me.

The most important thing is that he writes to me "from his viewpoint of today" that he wants to lay it out to me in all openness. I will induce him to do this not only before me, but before the whole public, and direct the matter into the normal literary channel.

I also just received a (forwarded, therefore belated) letter from Eitingon, the contents of which confirms only what I also know about his reaction from you. I will reply to him still today and ask him also in future to stay in touch with me.

If Rank shares all his ideas and techniques with us, only then can it be determined (but that also possibly requires time to test it out) how much in his newest experiences is grounded in reality. Be that as it may, his coming out in opposition to you still can't be justified by such a discovery, no matter how great it is, and his state of mind requires a pathological evaluation. But it is precisely his neurotic exaggeratedness that then makes it our duty to examine closely everything that he shares with us as objective, before we pronounce judgment on him. From a human standpoint, his attitude toward you remains almost inexcusable.

We were pleased about the news of the event in Oli's family. Too bad I don't know his address so that I can congratulate him.

Now, to go over to the grotesque—who do you think talked to me here the day before yesterday.—*Stekel*, who is here with some of his adherents. He wanted to hoax me into thinking that you, in a letter to him, had made [your] good treatment *of him* dependent on the fact that *he* (Stekel) treats your adherents better.[2] I told him openly that I didn't believe him.

By the way, he is bragging as always.

Many kind regards from my wife and your

Ferenczi

1. Preprinted letterhead with logo and additional details about the hotel. The words "Eden Hôtel" and the date are written by hand on the right-hand edge of the letter.
2. Freud had written: "My friends and pupils will have it easier to evaluate your publications objectively only when you yourself have adjusted your criticism and polemics to a politer tone" (Freud to Stekel, January 13, 1924, Library of Congress).

979

Semmering, September 13, 1924

Dear friend,

A passage in your letter which arrived today causes me to write to you that Frau Beate didn't go to Abbazia at all. The child is too ill, seems to have glandular fever. Anna visited her during one of our excursions to Vienna; incidentally, she got a cool reception.

The matter with Rank is getting darker and more uncanny. Now it looks as if he wanted from the beginning to establish himself on the basis of a new patent procedure that was kept secret, and requested your participation. I am surprised that you went so far along in this secret humbug! In my innocence I didn't even know that he was concealing so much. I thought the communication that all libido originates from the mother and the setting of a date were all his methods, and thus came to the conclusion that with that one doesn't alter anything essential in the course of the treatment. One can certainly say that such a procedure is also scientifically unheard of. It appears to me now like what was depicted in Victor Hugo's novel Les travailleurs de la mer,[1] where an employee earns a great trust through decades-long correctness, only later to be able to embezzle a large sum. He then gets his deserts in the embrace of a kraken (giant octopus). Another of my presumptions is that he constantly wants to return to America, which can be connected with the invitation to you and the ensuing turndown. I can only imagine that my apparently imminent demise uprooted him so, and that my recovery upset his calculations.

I see I am boiling with rage. I still have difficulty believing that Jones's suspicions should have been right to such an extent. But it is also difficult to conceive of the present indications any other way.

The central point of the situation lies, as you yourself recognize, in his concealments. Certainly it will take time, even if he has inaugurated them, before experience gives one the right to make a judgment. So it is superfluous to beat one's brains out now, inasmuch as he could be right. It simply can't be decided upon at the moment.

If things really are this way, then it is neither very worthy nor very hopeful to want to hold him back. To be sure, I can't imagine how this will take shape when he returns. It is clear that he is figuring on you somehow.

My reaction of today is totally the consequence of my complete disorientation. It will soon be dissipated. But I also didn't want to withhold it from you. In a few weeks, when he is here, I will be in full command of my faculties and very forbearing. Perhaps he will change his plans when he sees that you are not going with him. I don't believe that I will ever again place my trust in him. His present neurosis is probably [a] bad conscience. If he goes away, then you will judge along with all the others how great *my* fault in this is.

—I don't know what expression Stekel had on his face when he reported to you a harmless statement from me (in a letter). He complained that he is being systematically suppressed by the "school," and I replied to him that it was his fault; if, in his statements about it, he struck a more respectful tone, he would also find an impartial consideration. He is eternally in need of making connections, but a rapprochement with him has to remain forever impracticable. He is a partially talented person with intellectual feeblemindedness and Moral insanity.[2]

Today I am letting my American go until October 1. The next week will probably, since Pichler and Neumann are returning, belong to the doctors. I don't know how long we will still be able to stay here; I think we will again be in Vienna on the 27th, so, in two weeks.

Both granddaughters[3] have made us very happy. Oli's address is Duisburg, Thermosbau A. G., Sonnenwall 77; his wife is now with her father, Sanitätsrat Dr. Fuchs, Berlin, Lützowstr. 95.

I don't know whether you still have the intention of visiting the Groddecks and Lou. The latter, so Anna tells me, is supposed to have always been distrustful of Rank. The translation of Everyday Life by Frau Groddeck is supposed to have gone bad. A Herr Landquist has taken over the revision.[4] He was once in Vienna and a guest of the Society, [and] he has now got the authorization for the Interpretation of Dreams.[5] I am thinking of revising this book for the Complete Edition. The *first* edition is supposed to be reprinted in one volume; I intend to have all later additions, put together in new chapters, following as a second part.[6] I have no other plans for the winter in the way of scientific work. Nothing has been heard for a long time about the Hungarian Interpretation of Dreams.

I greet you and Frau G. cordially, and hope that this time has brought you, as it has us here, a few beautiful days here and there.

Yours,
Freud

1. Victor Hugo (1802–1885), *Les Travailleurs de la mer* [The Workers of the Sea] (1866).
2. The words "Moral insanity" (with capital "m") are written in English in the original [Trans.].
3. Sophie, the daughter of Martin and Esti, had been born shortly before Eva, on August 6, 1924.
4. Freud 1901b, translated by Groddeck's second wife, Emmy von Voigt, née Larsson (a Swede), and J. Landquist (Stockholm, 1924).
5. Freud 1900a (Stockholm, 1927).
6. That was in fact done.

980

Baden-Baden,
September 21, 1924

Dear Professor,

The oppressive foehn weather has driven us from Montreux to Basel, from there to here. Here it is very comfortable, and in Groddeck's house, pleasant. The massage, with which one strives to annihilate my (certainly much too ample) fat, is doing me good. Groddeck is very nice; I find he has always been true to psychoanalysis, believes now as before in its applicability in organic suffering—to be sure, mostly in combination with other methods. Kayserling was recently in treatment with him; his analysis seems to confirm your view about him in every point.

I wrote to Lou that she should come here as my guest for a short time; the first refusal already arrived; but I repeated the invitation.

It works out well that your trip home coincides precisely with my itinerary. We plan to arrive in Vienna on the 27th, and I want to resume work on October 1. So I will probably get to discuss with you all the measures that need to be taken in the matter of Rank, without disturbing the peace and quiet of your vacation.—

I, too, fear that Rank has gone too far to be stopped and to be induced to turn around. In any case, we must wait for his arrival and his reaction to Eitingon's and my suggestions for mediation. But even in the very best case, this affair will leave behind inextinguishable traces in all participants, and the old blissful trust will be gone. Perhaps only when he comes out of the self-made atmosphere of overestimation (in America) will he be sobered to some extent and see that, aside from the scientific value of his discovery, the manner in which he wanted to launch his discovery was an impossible one. Perhaps! I say, for in his last letter to me he betrayed an uncommonly high degree of self-aggrandizement, combined with the tendency to undervalue everything else.

Despite the fact that it cannot be pleasant for me to turn my back on my friend and, since recently, my co-worker, I didn't hesitate for a moment to decide along these lines, i.e., to set myself up for this possibility.

You are surprised that I went along with him despite his secret humbug. But only now has the latter gradually become clear to me—on the other hand, I felt that he was right to the extent that he better appreciated the neglected mother relation. Naturally, I am also of the opinion that more time and experience will be necessary for a decision.—All that naturally hardly mitigates the judgment about the way he has acted.

Hoping to see you again soon, I am

Yours,
Ferenczi

981

Vienna, October 7, 1924
IX., Berggasse 19

Dear friend,

Federn was with me, behaved very well, and made a suggestion to me which for the moment eliminates completely the difficulties with Rank. He thinks I shouldn't resign yet, because no successor is available, but request an extended sick leave, as it were, while I accept reelection. I will do that.

I have five hours of work, but a sixth will always be added, either a walk-in or a foreign patient, or both. I can't give up seeing foreigners, for everyone is doing very badly, including Nunberg.[1] Yesterday I was able to send Federn his first patient. Today I will talk to [Helene] Deutsch, tomorrow to Dr. Meng from Stuttgart.[2] My next step will be to call up Frau Kraus, who wants to build the polyclinic, in order to bring light into this matter.

I am naturally also of the opinion that you refrain from any encouragement with Rank; you should only clarify what he intends to do. Jones writes that he has bad reports about him from four or five quarters. "The disparaging remarks about both your person and your work are the most painful though the most comprehensible"[3]—he thinks. Meanwhile, one mustn't forget how unreliable people's talk is. It would, however, fit his letters.

I greet you and Frau G. cordially.

Yours,
Freud

1. See letter 641, n. 2.
2. Heinrich Meng (1887–1972), M.D., analysand of Paul Federn (1921) and Hanns Sachs (1922). He was a member of the Berlin Society (1926), and from 1929 to 1933 he lived in Frankfurt, later, until his death, in Basel (Switzerland), where he was docent for "psychohygiene" at the university. Meng was especially interested in the prophylaxis of neuroses. He was editor, with Federn, of *Das Psychoanalytische Volksbuch* [The Psychoanalytic Chapbook] (Stuttgart, 1926); with Ernst Schneider of the *Zeitschrift für psychoanalytische Pädagogik* (1926ff.); and with Ernst Freud of a selection from the Freud-Pfister correspondence (Frankfurt am Main, 1963). See Tomas Plänkers, "Mit Kupfer legieren: Zur Erinnerung an Heinrich Meng" [To Alloy with Copper: In Memory of Heinrich Meng], *Luzifer-Amor* 6 (1990): 87–130.
3. Letter of September 29, 1924. In English in the original [Trans.]. Jones also writes: "He [Brill] and Oberndorf seem to be the only two who are uninfluenced by Rank's theories. Many other members, including most of those who were with you in Vienna, evidently find them a valuable outlet for their resistances and are having analysis with Rank."

982

Budapest, October 12, 1924

Dear Professor,

I deduce from the fact that Rank has still given no sign of life from himself that he will honor me with no reply whatsoever, so that my planned intervention can't be put into action at all. I won't write to him anymore, on no account will I make the thing easy for him on my part by being insulted. Should he also not write to you (which I do not consider possible), then certainly the time will have come for settling all affairs without asking him. But I still believe that he won't choose this ugly way of taking his leave, and that his indignation is aimed only at me, his former co-worker.

We had the first session yesterday; I gave a lecture,[1] and Hermann handed over to me the manuscript of an entire pamphlet about the psychoanalytic-biographic explanation of the life and scientific activity of *Fechner, Darwin*, and *Bolyai*[2] (a great mathematician).[3] The group seems to be in a mood for work. We congratulated the Würzburgers by telegram.[4]

Lévy told us about a pathologic-anatomic confirmation of the "trauma of birth."

The Congress of Hungarian Psychiatrists, which took place recently, occupied itself much with psychoanalysis;[5] there were nonsensical accusations and nonsensical defenses there. I didn't go, but I enlightened a newspaper writer who interviewed me.

Many kind regards.

Yours,
Ferenczi

1. "Psychoanalyse von Gewohnheiten [Psychoanalysis of Habits], I." The second half followed on December 6 (*Zeitschrift* 11 [1925]: 134). See "Zur Psychoanalyse von Sexualgewohnheiten (mit Beiträgen zur therapeutischen Technik)" [Psycho-Analysis of Sexual Habits] (Ferenczi 1925, 269; ibid., 6–39).
2. János Bolyai (1802–1860), noted Hungarian mathematician.
3. Imre Hermann, "Gustav Theodor Fechner: Eine psychoanalytische Studie über individuelle Bedingtheiten wissenschaftlicher Ideen" [A Psychoanalytic Study on Individual Determinants of Scientific Ideas], published as an article in *Imago* 11 (1925): 371–420, and as a pamphlet by Deuticke (1925) and in the Verlag (1926).
4. Meeting of the German psychoanalysts in Würzburg, October 11–12, 1924.
5. The Eighth Congress of Hungarian Psychiatrists, October 5–7, in Budapest (*Pesti Naplo*, October 7, 1924, p. 6).

983

Vienna, October 12, 1924
IX., Berggasse 19

Dear friend,

I am passing on to you the depressing news that Frau Kraus, who wanted to build the outpatient clinic, has declared in writing that, in view of the generally bad material situation, she is giving up her intention. The assurance that it has only been postponed naturally has no value. With that my last hope that something respectable would become of ΨA in Vienna goes down the drain. I had placed all hopes on your moving here.

No sign of life from Rank, which also has its meaning. I have also [talked about it] with Jekels,[1] in addition to Federn and [Helene] Deutsch. The state of affairs is clear to each, so I don't need to conceal anything.

I get angry when I think about the fact that you had got so deeply involved with him. People naturally often put your names together, and I then explain that you don't know any more about his patent secrets than I do.[2]

Yesterday I received a friendly telegram about the meeting in Würzburg.

A little note about the "mystic writing-pad"[3] as an illustration of my ideas about consciousness is already being edited and is supposed to be published in number I of the next volume.

I greet you and Frau G. cordially.

Yours,
Freud

1. See letter 138, n. 6.
2. Cf. Freud's letter to Eitingon of October 7, 1924: "I received an ... impression of reticence and not complete candor from the conversation with Ferenczi and from his letters since then. I think he had got very deeply involved with him and still doesn't want to say how deeply, although he has distanced himself from him in all essentials" (Sigmund Freud Copyrights).
3. Freud 1925a.

984

Vienna, October 15, 1924
IX., Berggasse 19

Dear friend,

I received a brief letter from Rank from Merano, dated the 10th of the month, in which he sets the date for his return to Vienna for the end of this month, and postpones the reply to my long letter and the discussion of the problems hovering [over us] until then. This for your orientation only. A change in the situation is not in the offing. Your intervention should also not have the meaning of a mediation at all.

Cordially,
Freud

985

Budapest, October 23, 1924

Dear Professor,

My telegram was intended only to leave open the possibility of having a discussion immediately after Rank's arrival (so, before the established date, October 31). After receipt of your reply by telegram,[1] I refrained from informing Eitingon about Rank's telegram, so things stand with the former date . In any event, however, I will come to an understanding with Eitingon.

In the meantime, I also received a letter from Rank, which I sent to Eitingon. In it he hardly talks about scientific differences anymore, but about *personal* (bad) treatment on your part. Obviously projection. I did not respond meritoriously.

Since we will soon see each other personally and can confer about everything orally, I will refrain from discussing the situation, which is on the whole unchanged, in more detail. Abraham seems to suspect something; at least, he wrote me about [his] being concerned about the Viennese relations.

Kind regards,
Ferenczi

1. Neither telegram has been found.

986

Vienna, October 26, 1924
IX., Berggasse 19[1]

Dear friend,

So, Rank was with me today from three to six o'clock, and the result was absolutely surprising, in no way understandable. He said it doesn't occur to him to want to separate from us and analysis; he holds fast to everything he has learned, only he has some things to add to it. He explains his behavior from the feeling that his position in analysis seemed to be jeopardized by the Berlin denunciation,² and that he had to think about assuring himself of a possibility of existence, and for that reason accepted the invitation from America. From this presupposition he claims to have explained everything striking about his behavior. He has the intention, following my suggestion, to give an unambiguous explanation of his point of view at the next session on Wednesday, and he claims that he doesn't understand how all the rumors about him could have formed and doesn't want to admit that his book, his utterances, and his behavior were somehow able to justify this "public opinion." On the technical side, he himself emphasizes the necessity of having facilitation and assistants in his functions, because he thinks that at present one will not put enough trust in him, either as the head of the Verlag or as an editor. So, he is very ready, next Wednesday, to discuss the technical, scientific, and personal element of the affair in detail with the three of us.³

I didn't get the impression of complete honesty in all that. He still owes an answer to some questions and gets disconcerted. As, for instance, at the mention of his insulting statements in the letters, or at the admonition that, already at the time when you went away from me with him, he stated that I will never allow myself to be convinced. I also confronted him with the communication from your last letter, [to the effect that] he is complaining about bad personal treatment on my part. He explains that as a misunderstanding. I didn't spare him at all, and finally sent Anna to give him a going over, who had to confirm to him my own impressions from her perspective. So, on the whole, I don't understand the matter. Perhaps your and Eitingon's presence will contribute further to a clarification. I am still partial to the opinion that he has a neurotically bad conscience that the trains of thought which are connected to the Trauma of Birth frighten him, himself, so that he doesn't dare to make clear to himself the position whose beginning the others surmise with less effort. In any case, an open break has been avoided for now, and the necessary arrangements will be easily carried out. When asked whether he has the intention to return to America, he explained that a move for good was at the moment far from his mind but that a second visit again for a period of a few months is very probable to him. I called his attention to the fact that an editor and head of a publishing house who spends only six months in the upper regions sooner belongs to mythology than to the analytic enterprise.

That is how the matter stands. Now, bring along an open mind, without rancor, and we will see at the end of this week how it develops further.

Cordially,
Freud

1. The letter is typewritten; only the signature, "Freud," is handwritten.
2. See letter 952 and n. 4.

3. "Eitingon and Ferenczi were here on 31 October and 1 November, in order to confer with me and Rank . . . about the necessary changes in the Verlag and *Zeitschrift*. It was decided that Rank will resign from his post as editor of the *Zeitschrift* and director of the Verlag. Together with Sachs, he is to retain his editorship of *Imago*. Storfer has been appointed head of the Verlag . . . The editorial office itself will be moved to Berlin and entrusted to Radó, who will be assisted there by Eitingon and by Ferenczi in Budapest . . . [A]s you see, an open breach has been avoided" (Freud to Jones, November 5, 1924, *Freud/Jones*, p. 559). Freud refrained from transferring the editorship of the *Zeitschrift* to Ferenczi "because I know that he is, as we say here, a 'bungler' [*ein Schlampen*], from whom one ought not to expect proper completion of ongoing work" (Freud to Eitingon, October 13, 1924, Sigmund Freud Copyrights).

987

Budapest, November 16, 1924

Dear Professor,

The railway workers' strike, with which I was able up to now to excuse my not writing, is over, and I must now admit to myself that my tardiness was in large part motivated by the fact that I wanted to withdraw as profoundly and for as long as possible from the embarrassing, I would like to say, disgusting, recollection of the altercation with Rank.[1] Silent doubts about his honesty have also emerged in me earlier from time to time; since his American adventure they became more intrusive, and now I had to convince myself of the fact that the man, whose manifold talents (not least also in the scientific field) made him appear to be the most reliable coworker, wants to fructify his capabilities only for egoistic purposes, and in addition to that, in a dishonest and incorrect manner. Under such conditions there can no longer be any question about personal contact between him and me, and the importance of our common interests makes it my duty, taking the suggestion made by you, to propose the restoration of the Committee and the Committee correspondence. I also simultaneously wrote to Abraham, Jones, Eitingon, and Sachs about this. A copy of the Rundbrief is enclosed with this letter.

As hard as it was for me at the beginning, I see myself forced finally to give up any plan of some kind of understanding between you and Rank, and to assume the from now on necessary viewpoint with respect to him, that he is threatening to become a not unhazardous *opponent*, at least one who ruthlessly pursues his own interests, and to whom the common interests of psychoanalysis count for nothing.

I recently received the news from America that Rank was already traveling to Europe with the plan to set up a psychoanalytic *school* there. I don't know anything about whether he wants with that to found a training institute independent of the Association, or his own school, in the sense of a new psychotherapeutic direction. In any case, every caution is indicated from our side, indeed, there is a question whether it wouldn't be appropriate to declare the independence of his plans from your person and perhaps also from your scientific intentions. We would also have to reconsider, after the experiences with Rank, whether he should remain co-editor of Imago and by virtue of that, retain an official position.

Emil v. Freund (now Tószeghy)[2] will produce the requested piece of writing[3] in a few days; I will send it immediately to Dr. Rosenfeld,[4] and to Eitingon.

I hope you are well. From here there is nothing new to report in the way of facts. In expectation of your written comments.

Yours,
Ferenczi

To Prof. Freud, Dr. Abraham, Dr. Eitingon, Dr. Jones, and Dr. Sachs[5]

Budapest, November 16, 1924

Dear friends:

I cannot deny our friend Ernest the sad satisfaction of having stood closer to the truth than I in judging Rank's personality. After the experiences of the last few months I see myself forced to refrain from any kind of mediation activity between Rank and Herr Professor, indeed, to step in in opposition to certain not unhazardous tendencies on the part of Rank. In order to be able to do this more advantageously, I support the suggestion made by Herr Professor to restore the Committee and the Committee correspondence, and ask the individual members of the former Committee for their response to this.

Kind regards,
Sándor Ferenczi

1. "All more intimate relations with him have come to an end . . . Not only I but also the other two have found it very difficult to regard him as forthright and to give credence to his statements. I am very sorry that you, dear Jones, have been proven right to such an extent" (Freud to Jones, November 5, 1924, *Freud/Jones*, p. 559).

2. Anton von Freund's brother.

3. In the matter of von Freund's estate. It had to do with transferring von Freund's heirs' portion to the Verlag and Eitingon.

4. Otto Rank's brother, a doctor of laws (Eitingon to Freud, December 26, 1924, Sigmund Freud Copyrights).

5. Typewritten enclosure; only the signature, "Sándor Ferenczi," is handwritten [Trans.].

988

Vienna, November 17, 1924
IX., Berggasse 19

Dear friend,

Radó has been here since yesterday, to take over the editorship. He is reliable and eager for work. Rank, from whom we were unable to find out when he is again returning to New York, writes me today that he already has to depart on Friday (!), and wants to take his leave personally.

Enclosed a letter from Brill, who is finally shedding light on Rank's activity in America.[1] I ask you, after you have read it, to send it without delay to Eitingon or Abraham. Eitingon doesn't read English.

Abraham wants to reactivate the Rundbriefe between Berlin-Budapest-London, and says that the main gain will be the renewal of contact with you.[2]

Collection volume I[3] has arrived, as well as the Groddeckian translation of Everyday Life.

Cordially,
Freud

1. The letter, as Freud wrote to Eitingon, had to do with a meeting of the American Association: "One after another of those people [whom Rank had analyzed] . . . stood up and talked, as a result of the stimulation he had received; one [said] that one didn't need to interpret dreams anymore, the other, that one was rid of sexuality altogether, a third, how nice it is that one only has to interrupt the patient and steer him toward the birth trauma" (November 19, 1924, Sigmund Freud Copyrights). Freud replied to Brill on the same day (Library of Congress).

2. "We have lost one of our best members, but he is, after all, only one. During that same time we were threatened by another loss [Ferenczi] from which we were fortunately spared . . . I will shortly take steps to restore the exchange of Rundbriefe . . . I think the most important result of the altercation in Vienna will be that the harmony with Ferenczi will be restored" (Abraham to Freud, November 12, 1924, *Freud/Abraham*, p. 374). The last two sentences of the quoted passage (Library of Congress) are missing from the published version [Trans.].

3. The first volume of Freud's *Collected Papers*, published by Hogarth Press. See Jones to Freud, November 7, 1924, *Freud/Jones*, p. 560.

989

Vienna, November 28, 1924
IX., Berggasse 19

Dear friend,

On the 17th of the month I sent you the splendid letter from Brill, which was supposed to wander to Berlin, but I haven't heard anything from you since. Not from Berlin, either, i.e., on the 18th I received your letter with the stimulus to restore the Committee, about which Jones expressed himself—naturally in the affirmative—a few days ago. Perhaps you were waiting for the results of the correspondence before you replied to me.

In a letter to Eitingon, which you can request from him at any time, I described the course of my farewell conversation with Rank.[1] He then left a week ago today, but, astonishingly, he returned from Paris the day before yesterday, supposedly because it had occurred to him that he hadn't said good-bye to his wife tenderly enough, in reality because he is in a deep depression. He is supposed to travel again in two weeks.

There was a certain George Daudin, he got what he wanted.[2] Brill cabled the day before yesterday: Rank coming what is his actual status with you, give every detail.[3] In my reply I was able to refer to a letter which is, or was, under way since the 18th.

The state of my health is not bad, but is not making any progress, and my ignoble artificial part constantly gives me much too much trouble.

In expectation of news from you and with kind regards for Frau G. and you, I am

Yours,
Freud

1. Letter of November 19, 1924 (Sigmund Freud Copyrights).

2. The spelling "Daudin" is in the original. In *Georges Dandin ou le Mari confondu* (1668) by Molière (1622–1673), Dandin must pay bitterly for the fact that he married a rich woman out of ambition and has to admit: "Vous l'avez voulu, vous l'avez voulu, Georges Dandin . . . vous avez justement ce que vous méritez" [You wanted it, you wanted it, Georges Dandin . . . you have just what you deserve] (1, 7). Freud said farewell to Rank with these words: "You have had an excellent position here. You have actually been generally loved and respected . . . Now you are leaving here as a personality who is actually being avoided. I don't know whether that was necessary for you. But vous l'avez voulu!" (Freud to Eitingon, November 19, 1924, Sigmund Freud Copyrights).

3. The cable is quoted in English [Trans.].

990

Budapest, December 2, 1924

Dear Professor,

Your letter of the 27th of the month crossed mine. Since then I was, to be sure, waiting for the reply of the Committee members, which I have now received.

The matter with Emil v. Tószeghy (formerly Freund) is as follows: After long waiting I finally succeeded in obtaining from him (and Frau Rózsi) the power of attorney with the authorized legalization of signatures required by Dr. Rosenfeld. I sent it immediately to Dr. Rosenfeld, who today sent me the enclosed letter.[1] Since Emil is so difficult to get for a new official function, and since, as he told me orally and in writing, he would like at all cost to dispense with the orphans' agency proceeding for the sale of Tóni's share, it would be good if you or Fräulein Anna would appeal to Dr. Rosenfeld to see that the notary (who is, in fact, very forthcoming) does not require this formality. Unfortunately, I have become so distrustful that I even presume behind this difficulty some dilatory intention or other on the part of the Rank family, without being able to show anything more than subjective reasons for it.—Perhaps you will look up the notary *personally*, already before notifying Rosenfeld, and achieve what is necessary from him (in order to confront Dr. Rosenfeld with a fait accompli).—If all that does *not* work, then I must ask *you* to send the enclosed letter along with the likewise enclosed power of attorney to General Director Emil v. Tószeghy and urgently request from him a settlement of the matter within a specified time limit. He wouldn't deny you that; with me he wouldn't take such trouble. In any case, all this red tape is threatening to delay the matter, perhaps also the general meeting. In any case, I will be in Vienna on December 20, if the general meeting is held; to be sure, neither the transfer of Tóni's share to Eitingon nor his participation in the general meeting would be possible if the matter with Emil and, in that connection, with the notary is not settled beforehand.

Emil v. Tószeghy's address is: Budapest VI., Nagy János utca 43.

I haven't yet received from Eitingon your description of the last discussion with Rank, but I know about him that, as Eitingon expresses himself, it went more miserably than our last discussions.—The return from Paris might indicate the beginning of a neurotic depression.

I am working, as always, eight to nine hours a day, two very severe cases among them.

My group is diligent.

I await your immediate reply and will write to Eitingon at the same time about the unexpected disruption.

Kind regards,
Ferenczi

Over!

I just now found an earlier letter from Dr. Rosenfeld, which I am enclosing. In this one it says that the guardianship settlement *is not necessary* if (as is actually the case) the matter of the inheritance has already been settled.—

Please inform Dr. Rosenfeld that Emil von Tószeghy accepts the price for the share which is to be suggested by you in any case. (Frau Rózsi wants to give this money to the Association.)

1. The letter has not been found.

991

Vienna, December 4, 1924
IX., Berggasse 19

Dear friend,

I had Dr. Rosenfeld come today, after receipt of your letter—he behaved very unsuspicious—and discussed the situation with him. He says one can't get around the approval of the Budapest guardianship authority (his remark in the first letter pertained to the *transactions authority*, which is something else). One can also obtain this from the notary in Budapest, which can, however, require six months, whereas Emil could take care of it in five minutes. He thinks Emil doesn't want any part of the authority, because he didn't indicate Anton's title of possession at the time and now wants to avoid further research. He promised to write to you and to Emil directly, took all the documents in his safekeeping, and hopes to put the matter in order.

At the same time, Eitingon sent me the draft of the declaration that he is supposed to make to the heirs. I showed it to Rosenfeld, who was of the opinion that that is a crooked deal, which one shouldn't make. Certainly, such a document doesn't annul the validity of a notarial record. Its content is, however, incompatible with the power of attorney. I will write to Eitingon to that effect.

You do *not* mention that you sent the Brill letter to Berlin. You will receive my report about Rank's farewell from Eitingon.

Little new from here; on the 15th we will write the first Rundbrief.

Volume II of the Collection has arrived.[1]

Cordially,
Freud

1. See letter 988 and n. 3.

992

Budapest, December 7, 1924

Dear Professor,

Of course I sent off Brill's letter with an accompanying note to Abraham immediately after receipt. At the same time, I wrote to Brill in detail and informed him exactly about my personal and scientific position with regard to Rank. I told him that I most strongly disapproved of his personal behavior in America and also, since his American adventure, toward you; that I was not informed about his technique, and, according to what he (Brill) writes, I also judge his method of treament; in addition to that, I held out the prospect of publishing this position at the next opportunity. Since then Eitingon has already written to me about the impression that the splendid Brillian communications made on him. I have not yet received from him the report about Rank's visit with you.

Our session was yesterday. I lectured on a part of the paper[1] which is known to you. I used the occasion to inform the colleagues about Rank's derailment, but for the time being I only talked about his *scientific* hastiness and about the rumors about his special technique. I found full understanding among everyone.

At Dr. Lévy's invitation Aichhorn is supposed to come to Budapest soon. I had a request made of him to give us a lecture on this occasion.[2]

I was able to speak to Tószeghy by telephone yesterday. He hasn't received Dr. Rosenfeld's letter yet. Tomorrow, after speaking with his lawyer, he is supposed to inform me whether he can settle the matter along Rosenfeld's lines.

In any case, I am coming to Vienna for December 20. In the worst case, as Dr. Rosenfeld writes me, by ceding a part of *our* share to Eitingon, we can put through his inauguration as director and partner.

Kind regards,
Ferenczi

P.S. I also want to send out the first Rundbrief on the 15th. I share Abraham's view that for the time being the Committee should not be extended, but newly consolidated.[3] As the only exception, I would propose Fräulein Anna, who has been initiated as your secretary anyway, and gave us valuable help in the last, difficult negotiations with Rank.

1. See letter 982 and n. 1.
2. Lecture on December 27, 1924, "Die Psychoanalyse in der Fürsorgererziehung (Die ambulatorische Behandlung auf Grund eines Falles)" [Psychoanalysis in Welfare Education (Outpatient Treatment Based on a Case)], *Zeitschrift* 11 (1925): 134. August Aichhorn (1878–1949), pioneer of psychoanalytically oriented work with wayward and delinquent youth. First he was an elementary school teacher, later director of the Vienna Municipal Retreat for Boys (1909). He was an analysand of Paul Federn, a member of the Vienna Society (1922–1949) and its Training Institute, as well as head of the of the Society's Educational Consultation Center (1932). He was a tarok partner of Freud's, and a coeditor of the *Zeitschrift für psychoanalytische Pädagogik* (1932) and the *International Journal of Psycho-Analysis* (1946). During the Second World War, Aichhorn remained active in the Viennese underground, and in 1946 he became head of the Vienna Society, which he reconstituted. His book *Verwahrloste Jugend* [Wayward Youth] (Leipzig, 1925), with a foreword by Freud (1925f), in which he described his experiences in the Institution for Welfare Education, Oberhollabrunn, is considered a classic. See Mühlleitner, *Lexikon*, pp. 20–23; Roudinesco & Plon, *Dictionnaire*, pp. 25f.; Gerhard Steinlecher, "Das Werk August Aichhorns in seiner Bedutung für die Sozialarbeit mit Straffälligen" [The Work of August Aichhorn in Its Significance for Social Work with Delinquents] (dissertation, University of Salzburg, 1986).
3. Abraham's *Rundbrief* of November 26, 1924 (Library of Congress).

993

Budapest, December 13, 1924

Dear Professor,

Emil v. Tószeghy has replied to me and Dr. Rosenfeld in a dilatory manner. Thereupon I wrote by express mail to Dr. Rosenfeld and requested him (pursuant to the modality proposed by him [ceding the share to Eitingon])[1] to call the general meeting for the 20th and to inform me and Eitingon about it immediately by telegram. This communication of mine crossed with Dr. Rosenfeld's letter (which arrived today), in which the latter confirmed the impossibility of the general meeting on November 20.[2]

You know that I am distrustful of Dr. Rosenfeld. I don't consider it out of the question that he will attempt an interminable postponement. At one time he wrote to me that the guardianship settlement is unnecessary, and then he revoked that. Recently he said that the matter can be settled by ceding the shares; now he writes that it is impossible to hold the general meeting!

What can one do?! First *you* would have to question Dr. Rosenfeld about the last-mentioned circumstance. Then, if necessary, prepare the entire matter either directly with the notary, or by bringing in the help of another lawyer.

If the matter would only be postponed until January, then the whole postponement would be nonessential. But the guardianship settlement can last six months, i.e., precisely as long as it takes before Rank gets back.

Tószeghy's point of view can be seen in such a way that he would like at any cost to avoid reviving the bequest matter. His interest actually coincides with ours, so that we can perhaps count on his help. Dr. Lajos Lévy and Béla are engaged in working on him.

Dr. Rosenfeld has not yet replied to my express letter.
In a hurry,

Yours,
Ferenczi

1. Brackets in the original.
2. Evidently an error. What is meant is "December 20."

994

[Rundbrief][1]

Budapest, December 15, 1924

Dear friends,

I want to respond to the suggestions which have come from London and Berlin individually.

I concur with the Berliners and am in favor of corresponding once a month (on the 15th of every month).

Also in regard to the enlargement of the Committee, I do not share the view that we should wait with that. I would definitely like to make an exception in the case of Fräulein Anna, who is de facto Herr Professor's secretary, and who performed inestimable services for us in the last, difficult negotiations with Rank.

I am, now as before, in favor of keeping the Committee secret as an institution, in order to avoid otherwise unavoidable sensitivities; even the Association could take offense at it on constitutional grounds.

We should diligently cultivate the private intercourse with Brill and decide on his acceptance at the next meeting. But in principle I would also have nothing against his being accepted immediately into the Committee.

I don't need to inform Herr Professor and Eitingon, who were witness to my personal and scientific dispute with Rank, about my position with respect to him. For the time being it should suffice to communicate to the remaining members of the Committee that I condemn most harshly Rank's personal attitude, and that I told him this to his face in front of the Professor, Eitingon, and Fräulein Anna Freud. Regarding the "Trauma of Birth," I refer to the one-sidedness of his attempt at explanation, to the inadequate presentation of the connection to previous psychoanalytic knowledge. The ucs. *birth fantasy* deserves our attention, as did earlier the *womb fantasy*; its explanation from the *birth trauma* alone is certainly very premature. I completely reject the manner of Rank's technique, which only became known to me from communications from Anna Freud and Brill. There is no discussion of anything of this kind in our joint book; he also never informed me personally about it. I will specify my position on these questions on the occasion of the publication of my own work on questions of technique. I am coming more and more to the conviction that the birth fantasy plays a role mainly as regression before the Oedipus conflict.[2] Róheim's ethnologic conclusions are very interesting but in part evidently exaggeratedly "traumatic."

I am of the opinion, now as before, that a really unified Committee, which wants to be more than a formal body, is possible only when its members also relate to one another in a human fashion; it goes without saying that they must be united in the pursuit of common aims.

I firmly reject Ernest's claim, as far as it concerns me, that *two* members of the earlier Committee have published works which diverge from psychoanalysis up to now (without laying it out before the Committee).[3] 1) Such a "diverging from psychoanalysis"[4] is not present in any of my works; 2) the joint work with Rank was thought of as a prize work; it was kept secret for that reason. It was, incidentally, presented to the Professor before publication, and his suggestions for revision were accepted. I talked about the "theory of genitality" in statu nascendi with the Professor and almost all the members many years ago.

The Budapest group is lively. We voted in as a regular member Dr. Ladislaus Révész, brother of the deceased Frau Radó-Révész, who, after long analysis and after several of his own analyses under control, gave a very good lecture about a case of migraine.[5] Our provisional member, Frau Vilma Kovács,[6] advanced to regular membership. I have given two lectures to date (parts of one are in the work which is to be published in the first issue of the next volume, which Herr Professor has already read).[7]

Kind regards,
Ferenczi

1. The Rundbrief is typewritten; only the signature, "Ferenczi," is handwritten.
2. Cf. Ferenczi 1925, 269, p. 296; *Schriften* II, 181.
3. "To me it was always clear that our central aim was the safe-guarding of psycho-analytic doctrine that, before publishing anything concerning which there might be any doubt as to its diverging from psycho-analysis, he should first submit such views to a discussion among ourselves; afterwards he would of course be free to publish what he liked ... This condition to which we are all bound ourselves seems a simple and straightforward one, and yet two members of the old Committee have already broken it" (Jones's Rundbrief of November 20, 1924, Sigmund Freud Copyrights).
4. The words in quotation marks are written in English in the original [Trans.].
5. Lecture of November 22, "Analyse eines Falles von *Migraine ophtalmoplégique*" [Analysis of a Case of Ophthalmoplegic Migraine], *Zeitschrift* 11 (1925): 134.
6. Vilma Kovács, neé Prosznitz (1883–1940), central "mother figure" of the Hungarian Society. She was an analysand of Ferenczi's and analyst of Géza Róheim, among others. In 1925 she became head of the Education Committee. She and Ferenczi fostered the "Hungarian School" of training, according to which the training analyst supervised the candidate's first case. Vilma and her second husband, the architect Frigyes Kovács, were promoters of Hungarian psychoanalysis and in 1931 set up the psychoanalytic polyclinic. Her article "Lehranalyse und Kontrollanalyse," (*Zeitschrift* 31 [1935]: 515–524), is considered a classic contribution. She was the mother of the psychoanalyst and ethnologist Alice Bálint, Michael Bálint's first wife. Her niece Judith Dupont is a psychoanalyst in Paris, a translator of Ferenczi and of the present correspondence, the editor of his *Clinical Diary* (1985) and of his correspondence with Groddeck, as well as a member of the committee for the publication of the Freud-Ferenczi correspondence.
7. See letter 982 and n. 1.

995

Vienna, December 21, 1924
IX., Berggasse 19

Dear friend,

You will certainly have received Rank's letter.[1] What do you say about it? It was a satisfaction and a relief to me when he arrived one evening all broken up, in order to—confess, in the process of awakening from a condition that one can summarize hardly any other way than psychiatrically. Since then he has been almost completely free, once again his old self, or better than he was. What he opened up to me was a tragedy, which very easily could have had an equivalent outcome. I don't have the right to give you all the explanations that I have obtained myself. Perhaps he will do that himself one day. Until then, it wouldn't surprise me if a piece of distrust remained in all of you. I, who know everything, have completely overcome it.

We also talked about theory, and he showed himself accessible to all objections. Naturally, self-criticism won't be very easy for him.

He wants to make good, if possible, everything he started in America, where he intends to go after New Year's. That also won't be so easy.

You will agree with me: all tolerance for the sick one and sympathy for the convalescent. I can only repeat, it is a very strange turn of events.

Too bad that the meeting in Vienna, as long as he is here, had to be canceled. But I am happy that in these fifteen years I had not awarded my trust to someone who was unworthy of it, and that I am on the whole really blameless. Kind regards for the Christmas season.

Yours,
Freud

1. In it he writes, among other things: "I have suddenly returned to myself from a condition that I can now recognize as neurotic, and I have not only recognized the immediate cause of the whole crisis in the trauma that was given for me in the Professor's life-threatening illness, but I was also able to understand the manner and mechanism of my reaction to it from my personal childhood and family history—the Oedipus- and brother-complex . . . From analytic conversations with the Professor . . . I glean the hope that I have succeeded in cleansing, for now, the personal relationship, since the Professor has found my elucidations satisfactory and has also forgiven me personally . . . I would be pleased to hear that my elucidations have found the same analytic understanding with you as with the Professor, and that they also afford you the satisfaction which—I hope—can serve as a precondition for the resumption of the working alliance in the not too distant future" (December 20, 1924, Butler Library).

996

Budapest, December 25, 1924

Dear Professor,

I couldn't understand why the correspondence about the general meeting of the Verlag suddenly broke off. Then came your mystical revelation in the Rundbrief, until finally Rank's letter and your note brought the solution to the problem. That was certainly a surprising and—I believe—in every respect favorable turn in this affair, which has been so painful for all of us.

You are right: a trace of distrust has remained in me. But by and large I am reassured by Rank's very honest-sounding letter, and I unhesitatingly replied to him in the old tone of friendship, and I have also already received the very happy response to this reply. But why did he so easily give up the plan to come here? A personal talk with me would have contributed much to clarifying things.

From a practical standpoint we can be very satisfied with the state of affairs; the personal is ironed out in the analytical talk with you, the scientific is relegated to the from now on unobjectionable public discussion. In a hint I prepared Rank for detailed critiques, in which I also intend to participate.

I still don't know how and what the remaining Committee members replied; if you have time, please be so kind as to inform me about that.

I spent the two holidays in complete inactivity in my family circle; on Christmas Eve this extended family (approximately twenty-four persons) gathered at our place. There was a lively exchange of gifts.

Tomorrow Aichhorn will speak in our Society.[1] I also invited a few pedagogues to this session. Aichhorn will also give a public lecture under Frau Kata's patronage.

In my practice, everything is going in the accustomed order; the yield of the work months since the summer has been an interesting series of observations which I won't work up until summer. If I come to Vienna, I'll tell you about them.

When is the general meeting?
Many kind New Year's greetings from us all!

Yours,
Ferenczi

1. See letter 992 and n. 2.

997

[Budapest,] January 7, 1925[1]

Dear Professor!
Most cordial New Year's wishes!

Nothing significant to report from here. I hope you are continuing to do well. Received Rank's Rundbrief.

Budapest, December 16, 1924
To the presidents of the Branch Societies of the I.P.A.

Dear colleague:

I am pleased to be able to inform you that the psychoanalytic movement in Hungary is continually progressing, despite the material difficulties caused by war and peace, which capture a large part of the public interest. The physicians, [who were] formerly almost unanimously in opposition to our efforts, cannot keep from referring again and again to Freud and psychoanalysis as a source of knowledge. They are gradually becoming accustomed to considering the neuroses also from the psychological side and are soliciting my opinion about it more often than before. So, I am in a position also to provide the remaining colleagues with case material; some of them have their own clientele, independent of me.

In the course of the year, several colleagues of the British group graced us with their visit, but we also had some other foreign guests at our gatherings. The number of members, which had been stagnating to a certain extent in recent years, is in the process of increasing; naturally, only those were accepted who were first analyzed and then practically and theoretically trained, for which the means have been appropriately seen to. The scientific accomplishments of the members are very satisfactory; after some years of theoretical work, their interest is turning to more practical-clinical tasks. The interest in psychoanalysis among the educated classes is on the rise. It should serve as an example that a pocket dictionary was published here recently which has included the most important technical terms of psychoanalysis and the names of Freud and several psychoanalysts. In extraordinary events, e.g., criminal cases, the public (and the newspapers) are interested in the opinion of psychoanalysts. Modern Hungarian literature is very much influenced by psychoanalysis in the way that it poses its problems. Under the pressure of public opinion, the official representatives of medicine, the university professors, are, albeit hesitatingly, occupying themselves with psychoanalysis. They are, to be sure, doing so rather ineptly, in the manner of "wild psychoanalysis." The members of the Society are following Professor Freud's example and are avoiding unfruitful public discussions; we want to wait until the interest of the professors expresses itself less ambiguously and with full insight into what they have missed up to now.

The lecture series that we held for the practicing physicians[2] was attended by approximately a hundred colleagues.

I am pleased to be able to confirm the good news about the state of health of Professor Freud, whom I visited frequently in recent times.

With collegial greetings.

Yours truly,
S. Ferenczi

1. The following lines were written by hand at the end of the appended circular letter of December 16, 1924, which—with the exception of the signature, "S. Ferenczi"—is typewritten.
2. See letter 944 and n. 2.

998

[Rundbrief]¹

Budapest, January 17, 1925

Dear friends,

The events in Vienna found me unprepared. My reaction to Rank's letter consisted of an amicable reply, as is appropriate in the case of a ruefully returning "enfant prodigue."² But I don't need to conceal from you the fact that it will still take considerable time before I regain the old unconditional trust with respect to Rank. I thank the Berliners for being so kind as to send their reply to Rank.³ I am refraining from doing the same myself, because my letter contains nothing significant, other than my joy about his conversion. I think Ernest will share our view. I found Rank's response⁴ satisfactory.

I received a detailed letter from Radó, in which he lays out his plan for regulating working relations among the editors. I believe Radó is enthusiastically with the cause, and I hope that he will develop into a good editor, especially if friend Eitingon supervises his activity.

I congratulate Ernest for the brilliant successes that the English group has shown in the way of translation accomplishments. The publication of Herr Professor's works in English will bring in its wake an extraordinary advancement of the psychoanalytic movement. How urgently necessary these publications are I know especially from the analysis of two English colleagues who are presently with me and have up to now had to make do with half an understanding of the German original.

Aichhorn from Vienna recently spoke in our Society; he acquainted us with the principles of the care of youth (especially with the treatment of wayward [youth]). He also gave a well-attended public lecture.

In the next session *Dr. Inman* (one of the Englishmen, an ophthalmologist from Portsmouth) will give us a lecture about the relations between ophthalmology and psychoanalysis.⁵ He came here with autodidactically acquired knowledge and has developed greatly in the course of the four months he has spent here, so that the British group will probably deem him worthy of membership there.

With kind regards,
Ferenczi

Dear Professor,

Dr. Inman is going home next week and would be very happy to be permitted to talk with you on the way through (on the 29th of the month, Thursday). I supported his request and recommend him to you as an extremely respectable, very talented pupil. I also hope to give you satisfaction thereby; it is certainly all too seldom that someone who is really suitable comes to us.[6] Please reply, at least in a postcard!

Cordially,
F[erenczi].

1. This circular letter is typewritten, with the exception of the signature, "Ferenczi." The postscript to Freud is handwritten.
2. French for "prodigal son."
3. In which is written, among other things: "You will make allowances for our slower temperaments when we certainly see in your letter a promising turn of events, but are of the opinion that you should first tread further on the new path in order wholly to belong to us again . . . The neurotic determinedness of your action—of which none of us has had any doubt—in and of itself means nothing in terms of mitigating responsibility . . . As analysts we all know how to appreciate what insight gained with respect to one's own illness and the ability to recognize old family constellations in current conflicts means; they form the prerequisite for the most important piece of the therapy, but they cannot replace the therapy itself. Therefore, we do not fear that you will see it as a misuse of the trust that you have restored to us if we ask you to tell us more about the prehistory of your turnaround . . . From a scientific perspective we assume that, in the near future, when you will be occupied with the revision of your views to date, you intend to publish nothing new" (December 25, 1924, Library of Congress).
4. In it Rank promises, with regard to his forthcoming trip to America: "I will strive, by means of setting things straight, elucidations, setting aside difficulties and resistances in discussions and lectures, to bring people to their senses, but in the process also scientifically clarify my own point of view myself: to take back, qualify, modify premature or uncertain or dangerous things, and to arrange the new, insofar as it should turn out to be tenable, in the context of what has come before . . . My turnaround did not set in until after my departure from Vienna, and I returned from Paris in order to be able to talk things out with the Professor again . . . It was impossible . . . for me to leave the Professor that way—to leave him in the lurch—as I was capable of it the first time in my manic condition, which, as a direct reaction to his illness, was supposed to spare me the grief over the loss . . . The Professor naturally knows the matter in all its details, and I think that that can also suffice completely for you" (January 7, 1925, Butler Library).
5. Lecture of January 24, 1925, "The Application of Psychoanalytic Knowledge in Ophthalmology" (delivered in English). William S. Inman was chief physician of the Division of Ophthalmic Surgery of the hospital in Portsmouth (*Zeitschrift* 11 [1925]: 252f.), later a member of the British Society.
6. "Dr. Inman from Portsmouth looked me up after his analysis with Ferenczi . . . He made an excellent impression on me" (Freud's *Rundbrief* of mid-February 1925, Sigmund Freud Copyrights).

999

Budapest, January 22, 1925

Dear Professor,

Just received your letter from Emil v. Tószeghy. He refuses categorically to effectuate the authorization of the orphans' agency; [he] requests that the power of attorney granted to me be returned, maintains that striking Toni's share in the partnership can best be effected with the help of a death certificate; the family refuses any compensation. "It is impossible," he writes further, "that we" (the Freund family) "will be made partners without our consent." "The general meeting of November 1 cannot have made a decision about the transfer of the share," "a general meeting cannot make a decision about that."

Should a modality for speedy settlement suggested by Dr. Béla Lévy succeed, then he (Emil) will expedite it. A buyout of the heirs, if warranted, is only a formality. The letter is kept very friendly in tone, but he doesn't want to have anything to do with Dr. Rosenfeld, who wrote the unfriendly letter. I want to come to an understanding with Dr. Béla Lévy, and ask you to send or to show this letter of mine to Eitingon, which can at the same time substitute for the reply to his last inquiry. I am very sorry not to be able to be with him simultaneously in Vienna.[1]

How are you and your family? Did you find or write something new recently? What a pity that I am so seldom in a position to talk with you about all kinds of things.

Many kind regards from us all.

Yours,
Ferenczi

1. Eitingon came for the weekend of January 24–25 (Eitingon to Freud, January 7, 1925, Sigmund Freud Copyrights).

1000

Budapest, February 6, 1925

Dear Professor,

Communication with you by letter has become such a need for me that I feel uncomfortable when I go all too long without personal news from you. The Rundbriefe are, first of all, much too infrequent, also to some extent official, and, above all, more matter-of-fact, so that they don't compensate me for the loss of the lines directed to me. In my easterly corner, I also feel scientifically and personally downright lonely. All that presses me no longer to wait until you have the time and the desire to write to me but rather, disrupting the sequence of the correspondence, to burden you anew.

I have been instructed about your personal good health by means of Eitingon's letter and the lines that your wife directed to mine, but I received the most definitive gratifying news from Lajos Lévy and Frau Kata. (N.B.: the latter has recently had a [female] patient [referred by me][1] in treatment and gives me regular reports about the progress of the analysis.)

I can't write anything sad about my own health (with the worst will). Despite poor sleep, I work nine to ten hours a day without disturbance. One should actually be satisfied with an organic illness which, after existing for about ten years, no longer causes disturbances in one's profession.

The actual object of my letter of today is a question which I would like to direct to you. As much as I esteem professional secrecy, I think it should not extend to scientific matters. So, I would like to ask you to give me your impression about Rank's theoretical and practical-technical position before, during, and after his analytical discussion with you. Did you actually get out [of him] what his technical innovation consisted of? I think without this admission you wouldn't have granted him absolution!

I would be especially grateful to you if you could give me, if only briefly, an indication of whether Rank decided to revise his position toward the members of the former Committee, and to me his co-worker. I have had no direct news from him since my last, amicable response to his apology.

It is, among other things, also absolutely necessary that I be informed about all these things for the reason that Frau Rank has appealed to me to be allowed to undergo her own psychoanalysis with me. Please treat this as a discreet matter, i.e., not to tell anyone anything about it (except Fräulein Anna).

I would be pleased to hear a statement about the impression that Dr. Inman made on you. He is an enthusiast, of Dr. Groddeck's type, with much personal charm, but somewhat more respect for exact medicine (he is also an eye surgeon, you know). He has been healing up to now (obviously with much success) with the aid of a skillful mixture of simple transference and analysis. He also became acquainted here with patient investigation of the deeper reasons and an interest in the fine points of $\psi\alpha$ theory. The progress [he made] in the four months that he spent here was very great.

I wrote to Storfer in the matter of the Hungarian translations, but I still haven't received any response to my questions and suggestions.—How is the new director working out?[2]

Did you decide anything with Eitingon about the general meeting? If the date is too far off, and if you don't have anything against it, I will come to Vienna sometime for a Sunday in order to talk things out with you.

Many kind regards,
Ferenczi

1. Brackets in the original.
2. Storfer, in place of Rank.

1001

Vienna, February 9, 1925
IX., Berggasse 19

Dear friend,

You are right; I haven't written to you for a scandalously long time. There were several reasons for that. First and foremost, that I have been spoiled by Anna's help as a secretary with typewriter, and have become unaccustomed to writing by hand. At the same time, this help is not at my disposal every day, and when it happens, as a rule, a mountain of superfluous official correspondence, mostly refusals, thank-you's, information, and the like piles up, so that the intimate is set aside. Furthermore, there comes into consideration a kind of defiance, which wants to prove that things with me aren't the same as before, although everyone strives to assure me of it. I know better. So, e.g., I have not yet at any time in my mature life had four months without any idea, without any kind of stimulus to productivity.

Also real laying claim to things plays a role. My five hours of work have already become six and a half, and in the evening there is always something to correct in the Complete Works, which Storfer is speeding along greatly. He is, by the way, active and competent as director of the Verlag, a head that never rests.

Your news that Beate Rank will take analysis with you (discretion, of course!) has interested and also pleased me very much. Then you will learn everything from her and also understand my behavior against him. It was essentially determined by the consideration that one owes a person in a deep depression. For that reason I did not require such candid admissions, the way they would be necessary for a real catharsis; I also didn't protect myself against extortion concerning his scientific advances, which are now in need of revision. He knows that now the discussion about his theory will get going from Berlin, and he is ready to learn from it. There has been no lack of "hints." I expect only good things, without limitation, from his future position with respect to the Committee members and to you. It is easier to talk than to write about everything that depends on him.

For that reason, your "threat" to come to Vienna next time for a Sunday is thoroughly agreeable to me, and I await notification from you. The general meeting is very far off.

Dr. Inman made a very agreeable impression on me. A good Englishman from a category which exists there more frequently than with us. He left a manuscript for me to read.

I am pleased that you have given up complaining about your health.

I greet you kindly—and pass along a greeting to your dear wife—

Yours,
Freud

1002

Budapest, February 11, 1925

Dear Professor,

I thank you kindly for the detailed letter, which has reassured me in many respects. I was already on the verge of attributing your long silence to some ill humor on your part.

I would be grateful to you if you would drop a kind word Jones's way about *Dr. Inman*. Jones receives people who come from me in a somewhat unfriendly, at least skeptical, manner. Occasionally he makes direct statements [about] why one leaves England if one wants to learn analysis, etc. But Inman *definitely* belongs in the Association.[1]

I handed in my passport for renewal and hope soon to come to Vienna for a Sunday.

Dr. Béla Lévy just telephoned me. I requested from him the urgent settlement of the matter of Toni's heirs. He promised me he would settle everything within two weeks. He will request eight pounds for the sale of the share, but only formally; Emil wants to leave the amount with the corporation. Should such an offer of Emil's get to you, then I ask you to accept it.

I am waiting for Storfer's response to Dick's[2] offers.

Kind regards,
Ferenczi

1. "I hope Jones will find himself persuaded to bind [Inman] closer to the English group" (Freud's *Rundbrief* of mid-February 1925, Sigmund Freud Copyrights).
2. See letter 1005.

1003

[Rundbrief][1]

Budapest, February 19, 1925

Dear friends,

I ask you to excuse the four days' delay.[2] It does, to be sure, (unjustly) put me in a position already now to go into the extremely interesting question of thought transference.[3] As Herr Professor knows, this problem has been occupying me for many years. I have brought together a large number of positive cases and successful experiments that I have done myself, which in part remind one of those of Prof. Murray. It would be high time for us to come to grips with this problem. As is well known, *Myers*[4] has already attempted to explain telepathy with the aid of the unconscious. My own cases are not only of significance as confirmation of the actuality of thought transference, but also as a kind of objective proof of the modes of operation of the ucs. presupposed by psychoanalysis, in particular, of symbolism. I hope to be able to speak with Herr Professor soon about this subject, and I ask him if he would please save for me the issue in question of "Psychical Researches." (I only read a review in the Manchester Guardian.) Too bad that the Harz secret essay cannot be published. Perhaps a somewhat abbreviated communication can be published, or the permission of those concerned can be obtained. I already wanted to begin with a paper about the relationship of psychoanalysis to telepathy in the first volume of the "Zeitschrift." In the meantime, much has been written about it by outsiders;[5] the English and American "Psychical Research" circles have also tried (with little luck up to now) to utilize psychoanalysis for their own purposes.

By moving the Congress to Germany,[6] the number of Hungarian participants could increase substantially. I am also hoping for a lively participation of my group in the scientific deliberations.

The general meeting of the Association occupied itself with, among other things, the question of founding a polyclinic. The decision was made to hold courses for physicians already this year.

Kind regards,
Ferenczi

1. This circular letter is typewritten; only the signature, "Ferenczi," is handwritten.
2. It had been agreed to send out the *Rundbriefe* on the fifteenth of every month.
3. A reaction to Freud's *Rundbrief* of the middle of February: "The strongest literary impression of this month came to me from a report about telepathy experiments with Professor Murray (Proceedings of the Society for Psychical Research, Dec. 24). I confess that the impression of these reports was so strong that I am prepared to give up my opposition to the existence of thought transference . . . I would even be prepared to lend support to the cause of telepathy through psychoanalysis. Eitingon took along the manu-

script of the secret essay from which I derived such analytic confirmations of the telepathic hypothesis at our meeting in the Harz. I would decide today to send this essay into the world and would not shy away from the spectacle that it would unerringly produce. But the barrier of medical discretion looms as an insurmountable hindrance . . . It is precisely the sensation of this publication that makes it obligatory to hold it back; distortions are impermissible, ameliorations won't help. Should fate have the two recipients of the unfulfilled prophecies die before me, then the hindrance would be removed" (Sigmund Freud Copyrights). An abridged version of the essay was published posthumously (Freud 1941d).

4. Frederic William Henry Myers (1843–1901), English writer, co-founder of the Psychical Research Society (1882).

5. This word is written in English in the orignal [Trans.].

6. The Ninth International Psychoanalytic Congress was originally supposed to have taken place in Switzerland (Lucerne or Geneva), but it was moved to Bad Homburg in Germany on account of organizational difficulties.

1004

Vienna, March 3, 1925
IX., Berggasse 19[1]

Dear friend!

As a postscript to your letter, [find] enclosed a letter from Major Daly, who will probably express his willingness to come to Budapest.

Second enclosure [is] the letter from Brill, which finally arrived, about Rank's activity in New York. The presentation is the well-known one of the "Jewish orderly."[2] Aside from that, he confirms what Rank said himself.

The book by the Russian[3] arrived today. By coincidence, I opened it up just at the passage about Hamlet and the Oedipus complex, and I convinced myself that he is a very ordinary ass, with whom it is not worthwhile to keep any further company. At your next visit you can pick up the book again yourself, or request that I send it home to you earlier.

Otherwise, no change in the last two days.

Cordially,
Freud

P.S. Brill's letter is supposed to wander from you to Berlin and London. You also promised to forward the issue of the Journal for Psychical Research to Eitingon soon.

1. The letter is typewritten; only the signature, "Freud," is handwritten.
2. Allusion unclear; see letter 941, however.
3. This person has not been identified.

1005

[Rundbrief]¹

Budapest, March 15, 1925

Dear friends:

The most important event of the last few weeks for me was my visit with Herr Professor and the conversation with Rank. I was anticipating this meeting with great discomfort, but was pleasantly disappointed by the great change which I was able to ascertain in him. In a personal regard, the most striking thing is that no trace has remained of the taciturnity and obvious dishonesty that we had to reproach him with in the last big discussion in November. He has complete insight into the pathological [aspect] of his attitude at the time, as well as his presence on his first visit to America, which he tried to make good to the fullest extent of his powers by means of the second. He expressed the hope that he would succeed in restoring, just as he did the relationship to the Professor, which was clouded by his father complex, also the one to the members of the former Committee; he made a beginning with me—but he seems to put a great value on also establishing personal contact with Berlin and London as soon as possible. From a scientific respect he seems to be holding fast to the basic idea of his thesis (trauma of birth), but he has insight into the methodological errors of his work and anticipates the critique which is to be published with the good intention of allowing himself to be taught. He attempted to justify theoretically his technical modifications, but he seems to have gained insight into their exaggeratedness. He does, to be sure, reduce a portion of the rumors about his technique to a misapprehension of his statements.

I just received the critical work by Sachs about the "Trauma of Birth,"² to which I had only little to add. I wrote these particulars directly to friend Hanns.

It should interest you to know that we made a series of rather successful thought transference experiments in Vienna with Professor and Fräulein Anna.³

Life in the Society here is quite animated. We recently accepted a new member, Dr. Alexander *Loránd* from Kaschau, who has been working here for a year and introduced himself with a lecture on the topic "Birth in Hypnosis." (An analysis of a [female] patient whom he earlier had allowed to give birth in hypnotic anesthesia.)⁴

In April and May we will give a private course for physicians and medical students.⁵

Four to five members intend to participate in the Congress with lectures.

The prospect exists that, with the aid of a monetary settlement, we will get rid of the publisher Dick, who was a great impediment to our freedom of movement in the psychoanalytic literature, and [that we will] be able to entrust the Hungarian literature to the Verlag, first and foremost the Hungarian "Interpretation of Dreams" and the "Lectures."

Today I will return to you in Berlin Abraham's correspondence with Pfister and Stern,[6] which is a new testimonial to the tact and skill of our president.

I had the English "Collected Papers" of Herr Professor come to me, and I can send heartfelt congratulations to the British group for this achievement.

Kind regards,
Ferenczi

1. This circular letter is typewritten; only the signature, "Ferenczi," is handwritten (in pencil).

2. Hanns Sachs, "Rank, O. Das Trauma der Geburt und seine Bedeutung für die Psychoanalyse" [The Trauma of Birth and Its Significance for Psychoanalysis], *Zeitschrift* 11 (1925): 106–113.

3. "Ferenczi was with us for a Sunday. We talked about many things and the three of us did experiments on thought-transference, which came out remarkably well, especially the experiment in which I myself played the medium and then analytically extended the thoughts that came to my mind. The thing is getting more and more under our skin" (Freud's *Rundbrief* of March 15, 1925, Sigmund Freud Copyrights). See also Freud to Eitingon, March 3, 1925 (Sigmund Freud Copyrights).

4. Lecture on March 3, 1925, "Eine Geburt in Hypnose, danach Analyse der Mutter" [A Birth Under Hypnosis, Followed by Analysis fo the Mother], *Zeitschrift* 11 (1925): 253. Sándor Lóránd (1893–1987), a physician at the municipal hospital in Kaschau/Kosice, pursuant to his lecture, was elected to membership in the Hungarian Association. In 1923 he was an analysand of Ferenczi's, and in 1925 he emigrated to New York, where he worked as a training analyst and head of a clinic at Mount Sinai Hospital. In 1947 he became president of the New York Society. He is the author of numerous clinical works and the first short biography of Ferenczi (in Franz Alexander et al., *Psychoanalytic Pioneers* [New York, 1966], pp. 14–35); he was editor of the *Yearbook of Psychoanalysis* (1945ff.).

5. A six-hour introductory course (*Zeitschrift* 11 [1925]: 505).

6. The former probably had to do with moving the Congress from Switzerland to Germany, the latter with whether Caroline Newton (1893–1975), an analysand of Rank's and a member of the Vienna Society who had returned to the United States, could, as a nonphysician, become a full member of the New York Psychoanalytic Society. "In the matter of Newton (A[braham]) I had three letters from Stern, Monroe Meyer (secretary of the NY Ps-A Soc.) and Miss N[ewton] herself. The group takes umbrage at the fact that Miss N, who was admitted as a guest, has begun to practice repeatedly and has sent out letters of introduction. The colleagues in New York are taking a very determined position, they don't want to admit Miss N. any longer . . . They would like an amendment to the by-laws to the effect that persons who are accepted by one group should not have the unqualified right to membership in another" (Abraham's *Rundbrief* of March 15, 1925, Library of Congress). See Mühlleitner, *Lexikon*, pp. 234f.

1006

Budapest, March 16, 1925

Dear Professor,

What would you say if I put together my thought transference experiments of old and new for a Congress lecture and on this occasion attempted to specify the position of psychoanalysis to these events?

Aside from the Rundbrief news there is nothing new to report from here. Rank has still not written to me, but Frau Rank seems to want to maintain contact by letter as well, perhaps also in consideration of her possible analysis.

I now have several foreigners in analysis, so that the material side of existence is assured for the next few months. Major Daly is coming on April 1.

Many kind regards to you and yours.

Ferenczi

1007

Vienna, March 20, 1925
IX., Berggasse 19[1]

Dear friend!

I advise you against it. Don't do it. Your experiences and experiments are certainly no more striking or unobjectionable than what has been set down about it in the literature, to which one has not wanted to grant one's faith up to now. So, the only thing new in your lecture would be the personal factor and the personal effect that would have to proceed from it. With it you are throwing a bomb into the psychoanalytic edifice, which will certainly not fail to explode. But we are in agreement in [our] not wanting to hasten this perhaps unavoidable disturbance in development.

Abraham has announced himself with his wife for Easter. But I will probably ask him not to visit me. I am too tired from the more than six months' work and the incessant treatment with its torments, so that I would like to take a rest over Easter in Vienna, or elsewhere, free from responsibilities. Abraham is an optimist, rather presumptuous in his relations with people, and he evidently cannot see eye to eye with the demands of my condition.[2] You yourself don't need to see the announcement of a worsening of my condition in this communication. I am in a similar position as our poor Austria; I suffer the pains of rehabilitation, about which it has by no means yet been established whether it will succeed. Actually, Pichler has been working on my prosthesis for weeks in order finally to make it more stable and capable of doing what it's supposed to do, but in the meantime it only gives me trouble and is functioning worse than it did months ago.

With many kind regards.

Yours,
Freud

1. The letter is typewritten; only the signature, "Freud," is handwritten.

2. "Your offer pleased me very much at first, subsequently put me somewhat out of sorts, which is, however, not your fault, but mine. I find it very distasteful to turn you down and don't dare accept your visit because it will probably only be a source of disappointment to you" (Freud to Abraham, March 20, 1925, Library of Congress).

1008

INTERNATIONALE ZEITSCHRIFT FÜR
ÄRZTLICHE PSYCHOANALYSE

Budapest, March 30, 1925

Dear Professor,

Naturally I will abstain in deference to your warning, as long as it serves a purpose. I hope to convince the colleagues of the Committee by means of personal experiments. I am pleased about your plan to grant yourself some peace and quiet for Easter.

I am working under strain, now as before. At the moment, the exertion is somewhat more rewarding (increasing number of foreigners).

Let's hope your Dr. Pichler *finally* does something good that lasts!

Dr. Feldmann (our Stekel) has, according to time-honored tradition, published a volume on "Nervous Anxiety."[1]

Our course for physicians begins on April 4. We are holding sixteen lectures in April and May. In the meantime, the activity of the Society is dormant.

Kind regards,
Ferenczi

1. *Az ideges Félelem, és egyéb fejezetek a pszichopatologia köréböl:. A pszichoanalizis alakalmazása az orvosi gyakorlatban* [Nervous Anxiety and Other Chapters from the Realm of Psychopathology: The Application of Psychoanalysis in Medical Practice] (Budapest, 1925). The allusion is to Stekel's *Nervöse Angstzustände und ihre Behandlung* [Nervous Anxiety States and Their Treatment] (Berlin, 1908).

1009

INTERNATIONALE ZEITSCHRIFT FÜR
ÄRZTLICHE PSYCHOANALYSE

Budapest, Easter Sunday, 1925

Dear Professor,

Let us hope that for a time you are—free of all everyday toil and torment—somewhere where it is green. Unfortunately, in consideration of the foreigners, by whom I now allow myself to be devoured for money, I was unable to leave Budapest, and have only the two holidays reserved for myself. Earning money for its own sake is a terribly stupid thing. I always thought that at some time I would give up the business for a rather long time and would live and work for myself, but I am gradually coming to the realization that it is actually the great rest *after* life for which one prepares oneself so. Disturbances in my state of health from time to time actually make this deliberation even more to the point.

Apropos foreigners! A patient from America would like to have one of her (female) acquaintances, who can pay five dollars an hour, come to Europe and be analyzed. I recommended Fräulein Anna; in the event that she agrees (about which I request news soon), I will put the patient into direct contact with Fräulein Anna.

I recently received an editorial letter from Radó, out of whose contents I would only like to speak against the suggestion about renewed alteration of the editorial board. I find it premature for Radó to want to withdraw from being formally assigned to Eitingon and me already after such a short period of activity.[1] It is also better if *the Verlag* remains, now as before, identical, in part, with the editorship. I won't reply to him until I hear your view on the matter.

Chance had it that for some time I have been treating a patient whom Rank analyzed in America, so that I was now able to catch glimpses of his technique. The impression that I received is not very favorable at the moment; I still want to wait before making a judgment, but I hope to be able to report in more detail on my next visit to Vienna. Rank doesn't write to me; I hear from Eitingon that Rank's depression is continuing.

In Alexander's critique of the "Development [of Psychoanalysis]"[2] there is a remark to the effect that in your technical works you did *not* speak out in favor of a technique which works *against* the patients' tendency toward reproduction. But now I have heard this often from you; it is also written somewhere that you designate it as *a triumph* of analysis when one succeeds in getting, instead of reproductions, to hear memories.[3] On the whole I agree with Alexander: the *"active"* therapy must also finally culminate in preconscious binding, only it allows the tendency toward reproduction more play, in fact, it occasionally provokes it.

Let us hope the prosthesis no longer torments you, and bring from the greenery reserve strength for the further work months of the year.

Cordially,
Ferenczi

1. It had been decided, from 1925 on, to cite the names of Eitingon, Ferenczi, and Radó (instead of Ferenczi and Rank, as had been the case up to then) as editors on the title page of the *Zeitschrift*, published by Freud. Freud wrote to Radó on April 5: "As for myself, I am in agreement with your revision regarding the description of the editiorial board on the cover of the Z[eitschrift]. But you must also get Eitingon's and Ferenczi's approval" (Library of Congress)—which Radó evidently did not receive, however.

2. Franz Alexander, "Ferenczi & Rank, Entwicklungsziele der Psychoanalyse," *Zeitschrift* 11 (1925): 113–122. Alexander refers to Freud's description of "transference as . . . a playground in which [the repetition compulsion] is allowed to expand in almost complete freedom," in order to refute Ferenczi's and Rank's assertion that such a repetition had been seen to date as a technical error (p. 116). Franz Alexander (1891–1964), noted analyst of Hungarian extraction, son of the well-known professor of literature Bernát Alexander. As Hanns Sachs's analysand, Alexander was the first graduate of the Berlin training institute, where he then became a training analyst himself. Freud valued Alexander greatly and entrusted him with the analysis of his son Oliver. Alexander emigrated in 1931, first to Boston, then to Chicago, where he founded the influential Chicago Institute for Psychoanalysis. He is known primarily for his works on psychosomatic illnesses and for questions of technique ("corrective emotional experience"), to which, by his own account, he was stimulated by the work of Ferenczi and Rank criticized by him here. After conflicts with the American Association which ensued from this, he founded, along with Roy Grinker and others, the American Academy of Psychoanalysis, which exists to this day. Alexander was the analyst of Lionel Blitzsten, Ives Hendrick, Marianne Kris-Rie, Bertram Lewin, Karl Menninger, Henry Murray, Charles Odier, Leon Saul, William Silverberg, and David Slight, among others. See Roudinesco & Plon, *Dictionnaire*, pp. 26–28.

3. "[The physician] celebrates it as a triumph for the treatment if he can bring it about that something that the patient wishes to discharge in action is disposed of through the work of remembering" (Freud 1914g, p. 153).

1010

Vienna, April 14, 1925
IX., Berggasse 19

Dear friend,

Lajos, who is doctoring with me today, will bring along for you a manuscript by Daly,[1] which I think deserves to be printed on account of a few important ideas. Daly is a simple person, but he sees correctly and is a good chap.

I replied to Radó that I have nothing to object to with regard to the modification, *in the event that* you and Eitingon are in agreement with it. So, the decision should be made between you and Eitingon.

One still can't get started with Rank. He is apathetic, at the same time is also avoiding the explanation of his theory.

I liked Alexander's critique very much. He may have missed a nuance in my postion vis-à-vis reproduction. I also changed it a bit under the influence of experience and your remarks.

Anna will gladly take the American woman, from October 1 on.

I have not left Vienna. My rest was interrupted by numerous visits. You are obviously right in your placing rest in the time after one's demise.

Pichler is coming back tomorrow and should give me a bit of relief.

Cordially,
Freud

1. Nothing by Daly was published in the psychoanalytic journals in 1925 and 1926. Possibly Freud is referring to a work from which ensued *Hindu Mythology and Castration Complex* (in *Imago* 13 [1927]: 145–198, and in the Verlag).

1011

[Rundbrief][1]

Budapest, April 18, 1925

Dear friends,

The main event of the last month is the success of the psychoanalytic course arranged for physicians and medical students, something halfway between popular lectures and an academic course of study. In the meantime, to be sure, the Society sessions are resting, since we are all working so hard that we can't sacrifice more than two evenings a week for the common good.

The Congress will, I hope, be well attended by Hungary; everyone hopes for the presence of Herr Professor and promises not to be a burden to him there in any way. The other group leaders could also instill the same attitude in their members.

I think, dear Karl, that you are handling the case of Groddeck[2] somewhat too rigidly, quite in contrast to your otherwise skillful diplomacy, which is praised by everyone. He is an original, whom one should allow to go his own way in side issues; the main thing is that he is a true adherent, and a respectable person to boot. He does not do pure psychoanalysis, but rather utilizes a not unskilled mixture of various therapeutic measures. It was perhaps not very tactful, even cocky, when he gave an example in public of his own free associations, but with him, cockiness is really only an exaggeration of courage, which he does not lack. He can be influenced by some criticism; threatening him with paragraphs would certainly only make him run wild.

The symposium after the Congress has no supporters in the Hungarian group.³

I maintain my view in the question of thought transference, but for the time being, in concurrence with Herr Professor, I am refraining from publishing my experiences, experiments, and attempts at explanation.

An American woman psychoanalyst, who was also analyzed by Rank in America, is now in analysis with me.⁴ I hope to be able to report in depth about my experiences with this case at the pre-Congress conference. On his second visit, Rank seems to have publicly revoked a great deal.

Kind regards,
Ferenczi

P.S. April 21. In the meantime I received the Berlin and the Vienna letter, but I won't reply to them until the month of May. Typographical errors caused the delay.

P.S. Many thanks for letter and mailing. [I will] reply soon.

F[erenczi].

1. This circular letter is typewritten; only the signature, "Ferenczi," and the second postscript are handwritten.
2. "Groddeck is making himself noticeable here in a particularly disagreeable manner ... In one ... [of his lectures in Berlin] G interrupted himself: he had just heard an automobile horn from the street and just wanted to share his free association to it. After too much idle reporting he then sounded off for much longer than an hour about all the most intimate details of his private life, which had to do with, among other things, his wife, who was present; in so doing he constantly indulged himself in the coarsest expressions. One ought to oppose these carryings-on once and for all" (Abraham's *Rundbrief* of March 15, 1925, Library of Congress). "Landauer, who had just previously visited G[roddeck] in Baden-Baden, was here briefly ... According to [Groddeck's] assertion, he has two friends and two persecutors in the Association. The former are Herr Prof. and Sandor, the latter Abraham and Jones (of all people!). Landauer was of the distinct opinion that G is paranoid—with which, let's hope, he is going too far!" (Abraham's *Rundbrief* of April 13, 1925, Library of Congress).
3. Possibly this relates to an earlier suggestion (Abraham to Freud, February 6, 1925, *Freud/Abraham*, p. 380) to institute a symposium on technical questions at the coming Congress.
4. Possibly the first mention of Elizabeth Severn (see letter 1023 and n. 2).

1012

Budapest, April 27, 1925¹

Dear Professor,

Enclosed the interesting correspondence between Culpin and² the "British Medical Journal,"³ which was copied and sent in for us by Dr. Inman; I think Culpin and Inman are good battle criers. Still, in England, a more respectable tone than the one that we are used to seems to prevail. "Lack of objectivity" there is seemingly an insult that with us corresponds to something like "sonofabitch."

Kind regards,
Ferenczi

P.S. In the affair of the editing of the Zeitschrift I left the final decision to Eitingon, since I wanted by all means to come to a unanimous decision, but I made it evident to him that I consider Radó's request inappropriate. Now I learn from Eitingon that Radó has renounced his intention before he could have become aware of my opinion.

1. Correspondence card.
2. This word is written in English in the original.
3. Dr. Millais Culpin, member of the British Society, author of numerous articles about psychotherapy in medical journals such as *Lancet* and *British Medical Journal*. See Jones III, 127f., and Jones's *Rundbrief* of January 18, 1926 (Sigmund Freud Copyrights).

1013

Vienna, April 28, 1925[1]

Dear friend!

You have certainly also been apprised of the fact that the general meeting will take place on May 6. So, I can count on your being here on that day. Letter and mailing from Inman are very interesting.

Cordially,
Freud

1. Postcard, typewritten; only the signature, "Freud," is handwritten.

1014

Budapest, April 29, 1925[1]

Dear Professor,

The invitation to the general meeting annulled my plan to surprise you on your birthday. But I want to make sure that my coming was already determined beforehand. Arrival on the 5th, in the evening, departure like the last time: (on the 6th) late at night. See you again soon, cheerfully.

Yours,
Ferenczi

1. Postcard.

1015

[Rundbrief]¹

Budapest, May 16, 1925

Dear friends:

I had the pleasure of making an excursion to Vienna with Eitingon on Herr Professor's birthday for the general meeting of the Verlag, and to convince myself of the great progress in his recuperation. Both Eitingon and I determined that, on the two evenings of our being together, the good mood of the prewar (pre-illness) time prevailed, and we were particularly pleased about the Professor's astonishing intellectual freshness and productivity. We expressed the hope that he would appear at the Congress, but we could not get a binding promise. I cannot leave unmentioned the fact that Fräulein Anna is proving more and more to be a full-fledged member of our Committee; I must single out in particular her shrewd objectivity in personal as well as practical questions.

We also participated in a portion of the session of the Vienna Society, and we ascertained that a new and fresh spirit has moved in there, especially through the diligence and liveliness of the young members. Rank related to both of us, this time also to me, in a very reserved manner; he seemed so very dominated by his personal (neurotic) conflicts that, despite much effort, we were unsuccessful in moving him to a discussion about scientific questions.

The question of the membership of Miss Newton, that is to say, permission for her to attend the meetings of the New York Psychoanalytic Society, seems to be kicking up a great deal of dust in America. Brill published an attack in a New York newspaper on the lay analysts, which is considered to be too general and does not make a proper distinction between trained and untrained lay analysts.² This question of lay analyses will certainly be a main topic of our pre-Congress and the official business meeting.

I am just now reading Charcot's works and find that your opinion about him, dear Ernest, is much too harsh.³

Nothing is happening in Budapest (other than the physicians' courses). Next week is the election of the new City Council, on which the political direction of the next six years depends.

Kind regards,
Ferenczi

1. The letter is typewritten; only the signature, "Ferenczi," is handwritten.
2. "In New York a polemic is now playing itself out about the . . . question of lay analysis, and, to be sure, in the newspaper World. Brill has taken the floor there" (Freud to Reik, May 3, 1925, Library of Congress).

3. "I am personally not enthusiastic about the Charcot celebrations [on the occasion of his one hundredth birthday]. We know that Professor's loyalty to his teacher tends to make him over-estimate the part played by Charcot in regard to psycho-analysis ... English neurologists, who were never deceived by Charcot's theatrical performances and metallo-therapy, drew the conclusion that if such a great man as Charcot could so obviously lose his head in the midst of hysterical phenomena it was safer to avoid the subject altogether!" (Jones's *Rundbrief* of April 20, 1925, Sigmund Freud Copyrights).

1016

Budapest,
Whitsunday [May 31,] 1925

Dear Professor,

I am using Whitsunday to take care of my neglected correspondence; above all, I am writing to you not as if I had anything interesting of a personal nature to say to you, but rather to share with you an impression which imposes itself on me as a confirmation of your striking idea about the origin of jealousy from the castration complex.[1]—It already occurred to me before *what disproportionately great sensitivity some husbands evince with respect to their wives' jealous reproaches.* I was formerly inclined to relate this solely to their own consciousness of guilt (fantasies of infidelity), but I think (since your clarifications) that the unconscious surmising of the wife's castration intentions also plays a part in this. I now have the opportunity to observe the sexual life of a married couple being analyzed simultaneously (the man with ejaculatio praecox, the woman with mild jealousy mania). From the moment when the memories of castration threats were verbalized by the man, he became quite wild as soon as his wife expressed only the slightest hint of jealousy, even though he had to adapt himself to it from the beginning of his marriage.

The state of my health is somewhat wobbly, which is not exactly being alleviated by the hard work with the foreigners. Superfluously, I also had to give lectures; two in the last week.[2]

I hope you are continuing to be well!

Kind regards,
Ferenczi

1. Cf. Freud, "Some Neurotic Mechanisms in Jealousy, Paranoia, and Homosexuality" (1922b) and "Some Psychical Consequences of the Anatomical Distinction between the Sexes" (1925j), esp. p. 254).

2. The nature of the lectures has not been determined. Possibly they took place in the framework of the course for physicians.

1017

Budapest, [June][1] 15, 1925[2]

Dear Professor,

It is virtually becoming necessary to decree a special kind of legitimate indiscretion. Dr. Inman shared with me, evidently under the protection of analytic confidentiality, some things about the anti-Jones sentiment prevailing in England. I must, in consideration of their significance, share his communications with you, by relaying Inman's letter to you to read through as well, with the request to be so kind as to send it back along with your response as soon as possible, since Inman is awaiting my reply.

I, for my part, have only little to remark regarding the content, at most perhaps that I have for years actually observed in Jones a number of signs of a less than benevolent acceptance of new interests. Some time ago, he, e.g., wrote that he was pleased to accept Inman, whom you and I recommended, among the members, and now he is putting all kinds of obstacles in his path. Now, I admit that he is a hothead, but certainly one of the most respectable and at the same time most talented colleagues I know. One scares away much too much, I presume, the people who are not *completely* (even in the finest theoretical offshoots) firm in the saddle, and in so doing one harms the movement. You, Herr Professor, should somehow use your influence to ensure that somewhat more freedom of movement is produced.

In any case, I ask you to have your view about Inman's letter and your advice with regard to the attitude that should be taken get to me as soon as possible. I think I have sufficient influence on Inman to prevent him from taking a possibly harmful step. On the other hand, you, since you know the English situation much better, can find a way to determine the, perhaps justified, accusations, that is to say, to eliminate their causes.

In place of the announced Congress lecture, which is supposed to present a contribution to the theory of genitality, I intend to submit a different one with the title: "Some Contraindications to Active Therapy."[3]

With kind regards to you and your loved ones.

Yours,
Ferenczi

The Rundbrief has been omitted for lack of official news.

1. Erroneously written as "July" in the original.
2. The letter is typewritten; only the signature, "Ferenczi," is handwritten.

3. "Contra-Indications to the 'Active' Psycho-Analytical Technique" (Ferenczi 1926, 271).

1018

Vienna, June 18, 1925
IX., Berggasse 19[1]

Dear friend!

It is no news to us that there is a strong movement in England against Jones, and we don't deceive ourselves about the fact that his attitude is far from flawless. But for that reason we must refrain from mixing in with his circle and being all too willing to become partisan against him. Jones is making ample use of the general human right to have flaws, but we know his value too well not to be indulgent toward them. I don't know how I should use my influence there. If I tried, it would probably only have the result of clouding our relations for a long time. In the case of Inman, I can't quite see what one can reproach Jones with. If the Association requires from him that he should introduce himself with a lecture, and in the process appeals to what has been practice for the last two years, then that seems to me to be a faultless procedure. For Inman's part, however, the questions about whether one will accept him after the lecture and whether one will reelect him next year are superfluous sensitivities. He must have the security that he has something or other to offer, he should consider himself protected by your recommendation; and, finally, every candidate for acceptance must risk something, he can't demand any eternally valid guarantees in advance. So the right way seems to me to be to get ahold of him, and not Jones.

If there are really so many persons in England who are only being kept away from the International Association through Jones's personality, then the best means of information would be for them to decide to form a second group. Of course, we ought not to advise that. They have to get to that themselves. It would surely be permitted them without difficulty by the Central Office, provided only that they resolved not to be in competition with the other group, but to work together with it, especially in consideration of the Press. But I repeat, the stimulus for that should not come from us.

Incidentally, I fear that if someone made such an offer to the malcontents, it would soon come to the fore that the resistances against Jones are in reality resistances against analysis, and the formation of the Society would cease. I think it is very difficult from a distance to mix into the relations of a country with such peculiar personal conditions as England. Let us leave the rest to natural development.

I am very much in suspense about your Congress lecture, which unfortunately I won't hear. We are going to the Semmering on the 30th.

The Bryan and Inman enclosures[2] will follow.

With kind regards for you and your wife.

Yours,
Freud

1. The letter is typewritten; only the signature, "Yours, Freud," is handwritten.

2. The enclosures have not been found. C. A. Douglas Bryan, M.D., founding member and secretary of both the London Psycho-Analytical Society (1913) and the British Psycho-Analytical Society; co-director of the Institute of Psychoanalysis, London (1925). He was co-editor of the *International Journal of Psycho-Analysis* and the translator of several German works (e.g., Abraham's) into English.

1019

Budapest, July 27, 1925[1]

Dear Professor,

Our final plan reads: departure from here to Vienna on August 2 (Sunday). Meeting with Storfer and Rank on the same. On the 3rd (Monday), excursion to Semmering. 4th, morning, departure from Vienna to Baden-Baden.

Kind regards until we meet again.

Yours,
Ferenczi

1. Postcard.

1020

Baden-Baden, August 10, 1925

Dear Professor,

I have already spent many beautiful days near you, but seldom one more beautiful than the one of my last visit to the Semmering. The pleasure of seeing you again in good health and in the old good mood, was, if possible, increased still further by the enjoyment that the reading of your two last works[1] gave me. Again and again I am astounded by how later experience shows your earlier determinations in a new light, indeed, makes them logically necessary. One of the works (Gender Differences in Relation to the Castration Complex and the Vicissitudes of the Oedipus Complex) is more memorable to me, but the paper about the $\Psi\alpha$ of the judgmental function (negation) made a deeply convincing impression on me, and I eagerly await the galley proofs of the work in order to read it again and more closely.

Here in Baden-Baden we found the tried-and-true good reception. Unfortunately, the weather had good, even too good, intentions for us; for several days an incredible heat has prevailed here, so that I had to move my analyses to the mornings. In my free hours I chat a lot with Groddeck, who is always his old self; he has his special ways, but he stands unshakably on the ground of psychoanalysis.

I have not yet begun writing the Congress paper, only I have the plan for it almost finished in my head.

Aside from that I want to stimulate a movement at the Congress, which—I believe—should not be insignificant, from the standpoint of both the future of psychoanalysis and that of the Verlag. I want to propose the founding of an "International Society of the Friends of Psychoanalysis," with many urban affiliates, to which membership should not be connected with any special qualification. The purpose of the founding would be: the favorable influencing of the "wild" analysts and interested parties. The influence of the "International Psychoanalytic Association" would have to be assured by the fact that the president and functionaries would have to be delegated by *our* Congress. I would recommend *Pfister* as the first president. The gatherings of the "Friends" would have to be completely separated from *our* Congresses, spatially and temporally, and the tight organization of our Association and the strict censorship of its membership would naturally really have to be maintained. A popular periodical (with many subscribers) and perhaps similar books and pamphlets would lift the Verlag financially. The most important thing in the matter, however, would be the education of the wild ones and the possibility of somehow rounding up and organizing all the interested parties (among them valuable elements) who have no possibility of earning membership in the Association.

Many kind regards from me and my wife to you and your loved ones.

Yours,
Ferenczi

1. "Some Psychical Consequences of the Anatomical Distinction between the Sexes" (Freud 1925j) and "Negation" (Freud 1925h).

1021

Semmering, August 14, 1925

Dear friend,

I am writing to you today on a quiet evening. Anna went to Ischl early in the morning to greet her grandmother a few days before her 90th birthday,[1] and I want to have her and Lou, who in the meantime has arrived in Vienna, brought here tomorrow by car from Vienna. At night there was a railway accident on the line on which she is supposed to travel, so I—as a protection—lost my pince-nez with case as I was bending over in the woods. I would have to go back to the studio once again anyway, for, after an excellent week, there was again a bad one; the beast of a prosthesis is probably not sitting firmly enough.

Actually, the whole time I owed you a letter, which didn't come into being in my comfortable idleness. You see, my nephew Edward Bernays—but now it occurs to me, that is cheating; he was here long before you, and I told you myself about the acceptance of your name into the committee for the supposed American fund.[2] So, the truth will be that I am pressed to write you because you praised both of my last works so, which, as is well known, is felt to be very beneficial in the midst of inner doubt, especially after previously reading some invective. I am naturally referring to the statements in your letter which arrived today.

My idleness here can be compared with the Russian form of government—an absolutism moderated by treacherous assassination—, for I have almost completed a third, larger work here, which will probably appear as an independent pamphlet. Name: Inhibition, Symptom, and Anxiety;[3] character: a little speculative; genesis: in the manner of a newspaper serial in which the author allows himself to be surprised with every installment. The direction didn't come to the fore until the very end, unmasked itself as a criticism of the Rankian theory on the basis of a modified conception of the problem of anxiety. The stuff is so badly written that it will probably have to be rewritten; for a long time there was a question as to whether it shouldn't remain unwritten. But fate has willed otherwise.

Stupid things are happening in matters of film. The company that beguiled Sachs and Abraham has naturally not been able to refrain from proclaiming my "assent" to the world. I remonstrated forcefully with Sachs; today, already, the Neue Freie Presse brought out a disclaimer.[4] In the meantime it came out that Bernfeld is caught up in a similar undertaking with Storfer.[5] I won't stop them, for filmmaking can be avoided as little as—so it seems—bobbed hair, but I myself won't get mine cut, and don't intend to be brought into personal connection with any film.

Your suggestion about the new "Society of Friends" doesn't sound bad. I assume you have already come to an understanding with Pfister and have also assured the tolerance of our authorities. Pfister would certainly be the right head, and a Swiss like, e.g., the valiant Zulliger⁶ would be a suitable editor. Your society would also make sense as a counterweight to the recent tendencies of physicians to monopolize ΨA.—

I, too, very much enjoyed your last visit. I was sorry to note that your dear wife is so hard hit by Elma's fate. Give Groddeck my kind regards. Sympathy is certainly the important thing, and I can tolerate the clever-foolish man very well, despite some dangerous nuances.

Basically, he possibly doesn't belong with us, after all, but:

> Of all the spirits who deny,
> the knave is least burdensome to me.⁷

The last issue of the Journal of Nervous and Mental Disease, August, has an interesting review of a lecture that Jung gave in London in May.⁸ Very pretty to see how, in the twelve years since the separation, he also hasn't taken one step further; he is just as benumbed as Adler. Just as clear what a mean fellow he has remained, for he doesn't shy away from the same distortions of analysis that we could so frequently trace back to lack of knowledge in others. The remainder—to vary Hamlet's last words: the rest is phrases.⁹

The summer up here is very nice now, also never too hot.
May it be very comfortable for the both of you!

Cordially,
Freud

1. On August 18.
2. "In August Freud's nephew, Edward Bernays of New York, visited him and unfolded an ambitious plan of collecting a large fund which would be used to further the opportunities of psychoanalytical training in America and Europe. Freud, who was to be the nominal chairman, chose as European members of the organizing committee Abraham, Eitingon, Ferenczi and Storfer . . . ; the American members were to be A. A. Brill, Edward Bernays and C. P. Oberndorf" (Jones III, 110f.). The plan could not be realized, however. See Freud to Eitingon, August 7, 1925 (Sigmund Freud Copyrights).
3. Freud 1926d.
4. *Geheimnisse einer Seele* [Secrets of a Soul], directed by G. W. Pabst, produced by Neumann. Shooting began in September and lasted twelve weeks. Abraham and Sachs had agreed, much to Freud's displeasure, to work as consultants, and the "film affair" is purported to have cast a shadow over the relationship between Freud and Abraham in the last months before the latter's death. See Karl Fallend and Johannes Reichmayr, eds., *Siegfried Bernfeld oder die Grenzen der Psychoanalyse: Materialien zu Leben und Werk* [Siegfried Bernfeld or the Limits of Psychoanalysis: Material on the Life and Work] (Basel, 1992), and Paul Ries, "Popularise and/or Be Damned: Psychoanalysis and Film at the Crossroads in 1925," *International Journal of Psycho-Analysis* 76 (1995): 759–791.
5. Bernfeld and Storfer were planning a rival film project, with Bernfeld as screenwriter, and in August the Verlag had put out a press release to the effect that the Verlag

itself would be responsible for the production, in order to avoid an erroneous representation or a parody (see Fallend and Reichmayr, Siegfried Bernfeld, p. 137)—a thinly veiled attack on Abraham and Sachs. The project was not realized, in any event.

6. Hans Zulliger (1893–1965), Swiss elementary school teacher. He became interested in psychoanalysis through Ernst Schneider; he was Pfister's analysand and secretary of the Swiss Society. Zulliger was a pioneer of psychoanalytic pedagogy, and a popular author and lecturer. He practiced a form of child analysis which worked with play and as little verbal interpretation as possible. In addition, he developed a projective test for children and participated in working out a test that was analogous to the Rorschach test (Tafeln-Z-Test and Behn-Rorschach-Test).

7. Goethe, *Faust*, 1, prologue in heaven.

8. *Journal of Nervous and Mental Disease* 62, no. 2 (1925): 204–206. The lectures themselves were published under the title "Analytische Psychologie und Erziehung" [Analytical Psychology and Education] in Jung's *Gesammelte Werke* [Collected Works], vol. 7.

9. "The rest is silence" (*Hamlet*, 5, 2). Jung had ended his personal relations with Freud with these words (*Freud/Jung*, January 6, 1913, p. 540).

1022

Baden-Baden, August 15, 1925

Dear Professor,

1) Since we will miss you at the Committee meeting to be held on September 1,[1] at which I will present the recommendation I shared with you (founding the Society of Friends of $\Psi\alpha$), I request your opinion, which I would definitely like to consider.

2) Enclosed a newspaper clipping from the "Times," which shows us (as could be anticipated) that your name cannot be spared from advertisement, as soon as official positions of $\Psi\alpha$ allow themselves to get in with the film industry.[2]

Kind regards,
Ferenczi

1. "I have . . . convened the old Committee members for a Committee meeting in Bad Homburg for Sept. 1, leaving out Rank, naturally. In the next few days I will share this with our youngest member, Anna" (Eitingon to Freud, August 13, 1925, Sigmund Freud Copyrights).

2. The *New York Times* of July 26, 1925, had reported that Freud himself would direct the film, while *The Times* of London (August 4, 1925) had claimed that it would be supervised by Freud (Ries, "Popularise," pp. 765, 771).

1023

Baden-Baden, August, 1925[1]

Dear Professor,

On the occasion of my visit at the Semmering you were so kind as to agree to receive Dr. Severn, an American woman, whom I know as a capable psychologist and who is in analysis with me.[2] I am giving her this letter in order to remind you about it.

With kind regards.

Yours sincerely,
S. Ferenczi

1. No day is given.

2. Elizabeth Severn (1879–1959) was in analysis with Ferenczi from late summer 1924 until shortly before his death. She had no academic degree, but went by the title of doctor. Ferenczi treated her for four to five hours a day (Ferenczi/Groddeck, *Briefwechsel*, p. 83), took her along on vacation, and described her case ("R.N.") in detail in his *Clinical Diary* (1988). She, in particular, was the impetus for his experiment with "mutual analysis." Freud later termed Severn "Ferenczi's evil genius" (Jones III, 407). See Christopher Fortune, "The Case of 'R.N.': Sándor Ferenczi's Radical Experiment in Psychoanalysis," in L. Aron and A. Harris, eds., *The Legacy of Sándor Ferenczi* (Hillsdale, N.J., 1993, and "A Difficult Ending: Ferenczi, 'R.N.,' and the Experiment in Mutual Analysis," in A. Haynal and E. Falzeder, eds., *One Hundred Years of Psychoanalysis: Contributions to the History of Psychoanalysis* (Geneva, 1994).

1024

Budapest, Baden-Baden,
August 23–25

Dear Professor,

Pfister has replied with a refusal; evidently he places more value on his psychoanalytic scribbling [*Schriftstellerei*] than on his aptitude for popular solicitation.—Now, I was deliberating about who should be considered in his place.—First and foremost I am thinking about our *Lou Salomé*, who leaves nothing to be desired in the way of reliability. I think that such a central power would even aid in securing her material future. Please ask her, and show her the letter in which I explain the purpose of the society. Second, the following names would come into consideration: *Aichhorn, Stärcke, Bernfeld, Anna Freud.**—Since time is pressing, I request a reply by telegram. It goes without saying that I consider your suggestion, that is to say, recommendation, as a *purely confidential*, unofficial communication; if warranted, cable me a different name.

*The series is *not* an order of rank!

When I learned from you the title of your third work (still at the Semmering), I told my wife this work could contain the coming to terms with "active therapy," which also concerns itself with the relation of inhibition and symptom (albeit only practically). Now you write to me that a critique of the *Rank*ian theory has come out of it. But since this theory is (in my opinion) only a one-sided and exaggerated application of my "activity," I believe I was basically in the right with my supposition. It would be very kind of you if you would express yourself about this when you get the chance.

My intercourse with Groddeck is very pleasant. He has a refreshing effect. On the other hand, I think I am exerting a moderating influence on his more artistic-intuitive manner of thinking and working, and am facilitating his remaining within the scientific framework.

Healthwise, I am doing very well at his place (as usual). I also learned a few dietetic measures from him which evidently suit me.

I work regularly in the mornings; but unfortunately I am not completely free even in the afternoon, since, along with the ones I brought along, a few that I analyzed earlier have also followed me here.

Just received Eitingon's reply to the "society" project. He is *in favor of* the literary popularization and *against* the "organization of those who know less." With regard to that I persevere on the standpoint that I communicated to you.

After the Congress we are traveling to Genoa, from there to Naples with the Italian ship "Conte Rosso," and we want to find lodgings in Sorrento or Amalfi.

Many kind regards from my wife and

Yours,
Ferenczi

1025

Semmering, August 27, 1925

Dear friend,

You haven't guessed it. My essay contains nothing about active therapy and also concerns itself only with the theoretical side of the Rankian doctrine, which, incidentally, comes off quite well, the relation to anxiety.

I won't reply to your project by telegram. None of the persons named by you is suited for this accomplishment or might feel a desire to do it. You must also first secure the assent of the Committee and the Congress, and perhaps the matter will remain hanging altogether. Who knows if much will then be lost! Things like that don't prosper well with us.

I have taken cognizance of your travel project with the envy that befits it, and wish you both the greatest enjoyment.

It would be interesting to know where the American newspapers get their wealth of fabricated news. I recently offended an American with the suggestion that the Statue of Liberty in New York harbor should be replaced by a monkey holding up a Bible. I.e., I tried; he didn't seem to understand me at all.

Cordially,
Freud

1026

Sorrento, September 11, 1925[1]

Dear Professor,

Wherever I get to, I think of the beautiful trips we took together in Italy. I intend to write about the Congress[2] and other scientific movements as soon as I settle down peacefully somewhere. General impression of the Congress, despite some small disturbing moments, *very favorable*; incidentally, you know everything through Fräulein Anna and Eitingon. Hope to be able to visit you on the way back. My wife greets everyone cordially.

Yours truly,
Ferenczi

1. Multicolored picture postcard: "Sorrento—Panorama da Capodi monte."
2. The Ninth International Psychoanalytic Congress in Bad Homburg, September 3–5, 1925. It opened with Freud's "Some Psychical Consequences of the Anatomical Distinction between the Sexes" (Freud 1925j), read aloud by Anna. Ferenczi spoke about "Contraindications to the Active Psychoanalytic Technique" (1926, 271). Abraham was reelected president of the IPA. In addition, an International Training Commission was constituted to deal with questions of analytic education. See the report of the Congress in *Zeitschrift* 11 (1925): 506–528. The conflict between Abraham/Sachs and Bernfeld/Storfer over their respective film projects was seething behind the scenes.

1027

present address, Sorrento,
September 15, 1925¹

Herrn Univ. Professor Dr. Sigmund Freud
in Vienna.

Pursuant to our oral discussions, I empower you to undertake the revaluation of the capital of the "International Psychoanalytic Publishing House, Inc.," to bring about the acceptance of Fräulein Anna as a new member of the corporation, to increase Dr. Max Eitingon's share, likewise pursuant to the oral discussions, and to represent me at the general meeting.

Sincerely,
Dr. Sándor Ferenczi
Budapest

1. Date and place are at the end in the original.

1028

Sorrento, Hotel Vittoria,
September 16, 1925

Dear Professor,

I am writing on the terrace of my hotel room, before me the Gulf of Naples, the weather splendid, somewhat cool, perhaps, at least in the morning. Difficult to put myself back into the trains of thought that one had in the arduous days of the Congress.—My general impression was, as I already wrote, extremely favorable. The oppressive mood which reigned in Salzburg because of Rank's strange behavior had lifted. The personal intercourse between Rank and the members of the Committee was—if not very intimate, nonetheless not inimical or cool. Rank's personal behavior was normal and friendly. His scientific discussions somewhat roundabout, also difficult for me to understand. Only this much seemed evident, that he now attempted to present the *dogma* of the trauma theory as a *problem*; nevertheless, he holds fast, so it seems, theoretically and technically, to giving notice and to the repetition of the *trauma* in the cure. He¹ had little success, one didn't understand him.² The lectures by *Reik* and *Reich* were good. (The latter [was] somewhat too fine in his differentiation, on the other hand, not clear enough in his conception of the actual- and psychoneuroses.) Of the Americans, *Coriat*³ was especially good; he seems to be the best among the Americans. *Pierce Clark*⁴ was too optimistic; he uses a modification of my "forced fantasies," and with it he claims to cure all kinds of things, even epilepsy. My explanations about the limits of activity seemed to have a calming effect. *Landauer* organized the Congress well, and without making himself noticeable in the process. *Eitingon* was, as always, tactful and kind.[5]

Certain purely material interests—without being referred to as such—were bounced around in the business meetings—not a very nice performance for the Americans, who saw very well that it was a matter of their dollars, and not of scientific interests.[6] *Jones*, especially, was cutting and distrustful. *Abraham* was somewhat self-absorbed (illness narcissism)[7]. His authority seems to have suffered somewhat on account of the film business. But the conflict with Bernfeld went on invisibly behind the scenes.—The social gatherings were animated. One certainly missed[8] your absence from the sessions and the festive meal *very much*. But you had yourself worthily represented by your lecture; I heard it for the second time with even more interest and stimulation, if that is possible.

I withdrew my proposal for the founding of a "Society of Friends of $\Psi\alpha$," since all the members of the Committee were opposed to it. I am sorry. I think if Fräulein Anna had been present at the Committee meeting, I would have prevailed. We missed her very much.

I just read your "Negation"[9] for the second time and find in this essay the answer to many questions which I raised in my earliest works.[10] I think this paper will stimulate me to a small continuation,[11] which I will write down here and send in to you.

Here in Sorrento, I feel—especially since the sirocco has stopped—very well; we are considering traveling from here to Naples around the 24th to the 25th, then to Rome, and finally to Venice, where we will then meet the Groddecks. If you have something to share with me, I will still receive your letter here.

Many kind regards.

Yours,
Ferenczi

I think the Groddecks intend to visit you on their way back via Vienna. In practice, he is extremely successful and clever. In theory, our fine distinctions are too complicated for him; that comes from the fact that he came to psychoanalysis from the organic side, and not from the neuroses.

1. Reading unclear;. it could also be "It."
2. Rank "read his paper at a furious pace so that no one could follow" (Abraham to Freud, *Freud/Abraham*, September 8, 1925, pp. 393–394).
3. Isadore Henry Coriat (1875–1943), M.D., an American psychiatrist from a Jewish-Moroccan family, underwent training in psychiatry under Adolf Meyer. He was a founding member and first secretary of the first group in Boston (1914), founder and first president of the Boston Psychoanalytic Society (1930–1932), and twice president of the Amer-

ican Psycho-Analytical Society (1924–25 and 1936–37). Ferenczi congratulated Coriat on his lecture on stuttering, which he called "epochal." Coriat had visited Freud at the Semmering at the end of August (Freud to Coriat, July 2, 1925; Coriat, Biographical Notes, Ferenczi-Coriat correspondence; all in Archives of the Boston Psychoanalytic Society and Institute; Freud to Coriat, October 26, 1925, Library of Congress).

4. See letter 609 and n. 1.

5. The titles of the lectures are: Rank, "Zur Genese der Genitalität" [On the Genesis of Genitality] (*Zeitschrift* 11 [1925]: 411–428); Reich, "Zur Struktur und Genese der 'hypochondrischen Neurasthenie'" [On the Structure and Genesis of "Hypochondriacal Neurasthenia"]; Coriat, "The Oral-Erotic Components of Stammering" (*International Journal of Psycho-Analysis* 8 [1927]: 56–62); Clark, "The Phantasy Method of Analysing Narcissistic Neuroses" (*Zeitschrift* 12 [1926]: 457–465). Landauer spoke on "Automatismen, Zwangsneurose und Paranoia" [Automatisms, Obsessional Neurosis, and Paranoia], Eitingon about questions of training.

6. "In the business meetings, the main question was the differences arising between the American and Vienna groups" over questions of education (Jones to Freud, *Freud/Jones*, September 19, 1925, p. 580).

7. The first mention of Abraham's illness, which was to lead to his death at Christmas of the same year. After a lecture trip in Holland at the end of May 1925, Abraham had returned with a "feverish bronchitis" (Abraham to Freud, *Freud/Abraham*, June 7, 1925, p. 382), which was attributed to an injury to the pharynx by a fishbone. According to the editors of the Freud-Abraham correspondence, there ensued "septic broncho-pneumonia, lung abscess, and terminal subphrenic abscess. The illness took the typical course of septicaemia, prior to the introduction of antibiotics, with swinging temperatures, remissions, and euphoria. Abraham's previous emphysema had doubtless made him susceptible to such infection" (*Freud/Abraham*, p. 382n.). It is possible, however, that Abraham suffered from an undiagnosed lung cancer.

8. Probably written erroneously instead of "regretted."

9. Freud 1925h.

10. Cf., e.g., "Belief, Disbelief, and Conviction" (Ferenczi 1913, 109) and "Stages in the Development of the Sense of Reality" (Ferenczi 1913, 111).

11. "The Problem of the Acceptance of Unpleasant Ideas—Advances in Knowledge of the Sense of Reality" (Ferenczi 1926, 275).

1029

Sorrento, September 22, 1925

Dear Professor,

Here is the manuscript about which I spoke. I don't know whether you want to accept it at all, and if so: for "Imago" or "Zeitschrift." In any case, I would be happy to hear your opinion.—Unfortunately, I must ask for a written statement, since the detour by way of Vienna could no longer be included in our travel plans, so that we want to travel from Rome via Venice immediately to Budapest. We arrive in Budapest on October 3 or 4.

Last week we made a splendid but constantly life-threatening trip by car to Paestum, by way of Amalfi and Salerno. The impression of the temple columns is just as splendid as that of the ones at Girgentino. Yesterday we visited Capri for the second time and were happy about the unadulterated southern magnificence of the place and the region. For eight and a half lire they gave us 0.3 liters of excellent wine, a basket full of ripe grapes, and two cups of good coffee.

Up to now, no missing trains because of black coffee!

Many kind regards from my wife and

Yours,
Ferenczi

1030

Budapest, October 5, 1925[1]

Dear Professor,

I report that, after an absence of two months, we came home yesterday unscathed (only my wallet with 6,000 lire was literally robbed from me in Naples). After Naples came four Rome- and two Venice-days, both splendidly beautiful. At each stop along the way came reminiscences of the trips with you.—

I await from you, when you get the chance, a statement about the paper on "Advances in Knowledge of the Sense of Reality," which, I hope, has arrived on time.

Many kind regards!

Yours,
Ferenczi

1. Postcard.

1031

Vienna, October 18, 1925
IX., Berggasse 19

Dear friend,

You haven't replied to me yet about what I should do with your last manuscript, whether I should send it back to you or hand it over to the editors.

Yesterday I read with particular enjoyment Alexander's "Uncritical Remarks about the Theory of Genitality."[1] The boy is certainly something extraordinarily good. I haven't read such a fine paper in a long time; it is a credit to him, and I affirm with satisfaction that here is someone who knows how to appreciate your beautiful work. Incidentally, it was news to me that he took up your suggestions already before Rank.

A book by Fritz Mohr (Coblenz), "Psychophysical Treatment Methods,"[2] although therapeutically oriented, makes a great deal out of ΨA, naturally not without a few derailments. I raised vehement objection to some things by letter, e.g., the fact that he contrasts your active therapy with my technique.

On the whole, I am well, but I'm not getting any further with the disturbances of my prosthesis, and I actually speak much more poorly than last year. An intercurrent periostitis of the lower jaw (on the other side) has revealed by means of X-ray an undeveloped tooth sticking in the jaw. Pichler thinks it has to go, and so a tedious operation and approximately a week of painful healing is before me at some time or other. You know the statement: Whatever you don't have coming to you is Rebach.[3]

I now have a very interesting patient, a princess from Greece, née Bonaparte, great-granddaughter of Napoleon's brother Lucien, a really bright, mature woman with a good critical sense, who, partly out of interest in the cause, partly because of her own neurotic remnants, has found her way here by way of Laforgue.[4] She is not an aristocrat at all, but a real person, and the work with her is going excellently. She is a friend of the old LeBon,[5] knows and has a very good opinion of Bergson, and can talk about very interesting things. Such people are most suited for my intention of being bothered only minimally. But there are evidently not many of that type.

I greet you and Frau G. cordially.

Yours,
Freud

1. Franz Alexander, "Einige unkritische Gedanken zu Ferenczi's Genitaltheorie" [Some Uncritical Remarks about Ferenczi's Theory of Genitality"], *Zeitschrift* 11 (1925): 444–465.

2. Friedrich Justinus Mohr (1874–?), *Psychophysische Behandlungsmethoden* (Leipzig, 1925).

3. See letter 253 and n. 1.

4. On Marie Bonaparte, see letter 969 and n. 3. René Laforgue (1894–1962), French psychiatrist and psychoanalyst, a central but controversial figure in French psychoanalysis. He was an analysand of Eugenia Sokolnicka (1923), herself an analyst of many influential French psychoanalysts; he was co-founder of the Societé Psychanalytique de Paris (1926). During the occupation by the Nazis, he attempted to create an "Aryanized" psychotherapeutic group after the model of the Göring Institute in Germany; yet he also hid Jews and helped, for instance, Freud's son Oliver and his wife to flee. See Elisabeth Roudinesco, *La Bataille de cent ans: histoire de la psychanalyse en France* [The Battle of a Hundred Years: History of Psychoanalysis in France], 2 vols. (Paris, 1982, 1986), and Roudinesco, *Dictionnaire*, pp. 603–606.

5. Gustave Le Bon (1841–1931), French social psychologist. His main work, *Psy-*

chologie des foules [Psychology of the Masses] (1895), which made him the founder of mass psychology, was taken by Freud as the point of departure for *Group Psychology and the Analysis of the Ego* (Freud 1921c).

1032

Budapest, October 18, 1925

Dear Professor,

I am pleased, in any event, about the kind words that you let drop about my paper, and I ask you to send the manuscript back to me. I want to read through it once more and then make a decision about publication.

Meanwhile, I feel—by virtue of the long absence and the paucity of epistolary news on the part of the Committee members—isolated from the movement to a certain extent. I learned only by chance of Abraham's renewed illness and don't know how things are with him. I would be very grateful to Fräulein Anna if she would be so kind as to inform me—not only about this, but also about events in general. There would also be room for such communications *alongside* the Committee letters; it was, in fact, Fräulein Anna who made the correct observation in Homburg that there are things that cannot be verbalized in front of all the members of the Committee.

Our first session concerned itself with business matters and with the report about the Congress.[1]

Kindest regards from my wife and from your

Ferenczi

P.S. I can't convey your response to Daly's gift,[2] since he returned to India a long time ago, and I don't know his current address.

1. Meeting of October 10, 1925. "1) *General meeting*. It was decided always to begin the fiscal year of the Association with fall. The previous board was reelected.—2) Dr. *Ferenczi* and Dr. *Hollós*: Report on the Ninth International Psychoanalytic Congress" (*Zeitschrift* 12 [1926]: 124).
2. Reference unclear; cf., however, letter 1050.

1033

Budapest, October 25, 1925

Dear Professor,

Alexander's concoction impressed me as well. I find that his intellectual manner has some similarity to mine, which makes him so especially receptive to suggestions on my part. On the other hand, he is an original thinker who in part guesses by himself the conclusions that I had *inwardly* already drawn, and also continues the trains of thought independently of me. He wasn't able to avoid a few factual errors, but I (as editor) don't want to influence the criticism.—

I will procure Dr. Mohr's book. I will probably also have to raise my objection to the attempted opposition of psychoanalysis and "activity."

The discovery of the wisdom tooth that got stuck and the necessity of an albeit harmless intervention is a troublesome complication; it would also be virtually high time for the prosthesis difficulties to stop. I recently heard about a jaw surgeon respected here, who, after operations of that kind, waits a year before he puts in the prosthesis; he claims that the mucous membrane should be toughened up and hardened first. To be sure, the long period of being without a prosthesis would hardly have been a lesser, for you quite unbearable, evil.

I am pleased that you have to bother yourself less with your patients; my clientele has also become more bearable in this respect. Something should be said about suppressed rage and its consequences in a long-planned work about the hygiene of the psychoanalyst.[1]

My hours are filled from the beginning of the season on, so that I can give away the current practice completely. The interest of the physicians is beginning to turn toward psychoanalysis; probably in consequence of its growing popularity in Germany.

N.B.: In Alexander's paper I am called "old master" in one passage;[2] a kind gesture, but one which is not to be misunderstood! Something similar comes to me by way of public opinion (of physicians). Until recently I was the "disciple" [*Jünger*], the "youthful go-getter," etc.—all of a sudden I am becoming—the old master; in both instances I am "cast aside," for reasons of insufficient or advanced age. In the meantime, the age of *maturity* disappears, i.e., it is not recognized as such; so that all of a sudden one feels transplanted from youth to old age.

A more intimate correspondence is developing—quite spontaneously—between Eitingon, your Anna, and me; a kind of "internal Committee"!

Kind regards from my wife, who always thanks you for your greetings.

Yours,
Ferenczi

My manuscript has not yet arrived.

1. An important theme in Ferenczi's *Clinical Diary* (1988), and a hidden reference to his analysis of Elizabeth Severn.
2. "*Ferenczi*—an old master of research on hysteria" (Alexander, "Einige unkritische Gedanken," p. 448).

1034

[Rundbrief][1]

Budapest, October 25, 1925

Dear friends,

Jones's diligence has gradually encouraged all the members of the Committee to follow his praiseworthy example, as it now also has me.

Locally, there is not much to report: the sessions have begun, the election of new members (more correctly: reelection) was carried out, there was a report about the Congress, and I repeated my Congress lecture [about which evil tongues say that it was a disorderly retreat,[2] in contrast to Rank's orderly one].[3] Dr. Feldmann, who was expelled by us, has now sold himself to Stekel and has founded a branch society here of his "Independent Psycho-Analytic Association."[4] We must now unfold somewhat more propaganda to the public here, and have already been deliberating about the modalities. (Open lectures, publications, etc.)

On to the *international* questions: first and foremost we should report about the general joy that Abraham's recovery also produced in us. We ask him to spare himself as much as possible and also to report further about himself in his communications.

I share completely Herr Professor's view[5]: by limiting training to the few who subject themselves to the *full* strict course of instruction, we are practically driving the majority of those who seek instruction (among them valuable elements) to charlatans like Stekel. We would have to concern ourselves with the possibility of a less complete course of instruction. Almost every week I am contacted by physicians, professors, etc. who run away scared when one tells them the strict stipulations.

Many kind regards!

Ferenczi

1. This circular letter is typewritten; only the signature, "Ferenczi," and a few corrections are handwritten.

2. An allusion to the limitations of the active technique propagated by him, which were addressed in his lecture.

3. Brackets in the original.

4. Vereinigung unabhängiger ärztlicher Analytiker (Association of Independent Medical Analysts). The Association later also published a journal, *Lélekkutatàs* [Investigation of the Psyche] (1929–1932).

5. Freud strove "to moderate certain strictures in the training institute which are now supposed to be established. As is well known, I am an advocate of lay analysis and would like in a liberal manner to make analytic training accessible to all persons who strive for it, even if they cannot subject themselves to the strict requirements of the complete course of instruction" (*Rundbrief*, October 20, 1925, Sigmund Freud Copyrights).

1035

[Rundbrief][1]

Budapest, November 28, 1925

Dear friends,

Groddeck and his wife were in Budapest in the second and third week of November, and they laid claim to every free hour. Hence, the new delay. Groddeck, whose intimations about a possible extension of psychoanalysis to the organic sphere are gradually attracting more attention, is an intuitive spirit who is averse to purely natural-scientific research in the time-honored sense. I believe that his intercourse with me is suited to mitigate his, in a certain sense, also beneficial one-sidedness. He gave a lecture in our society[2] and a public one before an audience of 2 to 300. In both one had to recognize his merits, profit much from him, and both times one could determine the line of demarcation at which he overstepped the bounds of, in our opinion, still legitimate theoretical conclusions. The discussion among our members was very lively. The medical members had to recognize in part the correctness of his main charge, that the organic-minded all too frequently neglect the personality of the patient, although almost all rejected certain exaggerations. Groddeck seemed to be more accessible to our arguments. I, personally, learned something from Groddeck, especially the art of occasionally forgetting the medicine that I have been taught. Naturally, however, I consider it unavoidably necessary occasionally also to remember what one has learned. Only from this combination can something useful for the "psychoanalysis of the organic" be expected.

In the question of the lay analysts, I am, now as ever, of the opinion that one has to deal with them with the greatest strictness in regard to granting *membership*, but if they comply with all the requirements, they must be accepted without qualification. I refer once again to my plan brought forth in the meeting of the Homburg Committee to found, alongside the *academic plan of instruction*, the pursuit of which signifies membership, a kind of *middle school*, which would serve the undeniable interests of the laity, and from which, if warranted, a few, by careful selection, could be admitted to the "academic" career.

Kind regards!

Ferenczi

1. This circular letter is typewritten; only the signature, "Ferenczi," and a few corrections are handwritten.

2. Lecture of November 14, 1925, "Psychoanalytische Therapie innerer Krankheiten" [Psychoanalytic Therapy of Internal Diseases], *Zeitschrift* 12 (1926): 124.

1036

Budapest, November 28,[1] 1925

Dear Professor,

It was a great and pleasant surprise to me to hear that the intervention, the imminence of which I was aware of, has already been surmounted. May we hope that the painful sensations in your mouth are eliminated thereby? That is certainly the main thing—I did already see repeatedly how very much your mood was influenced by the presence of those disturbing tensions and pains. I admired your self-mastery in being able to accomplish so much and of such significance despite this difficulty.

Unfortunately, I know nothing at all, so to speak, about your newest works; not even the pamphlet[2] you wrote in the summer is known to me, let alone its contents. Would it be possible to get a superfluous copy?

I have reports from America, very reliable ones, which I don't want to keep from you, and which you, *if you want to*, could also share with Fräulein Anna and Eitingon. Brill was with Jones in England during the month of October. Having returned home, he gave strong speeches in the New York Society against lay analysis and the Europeans who don't turn away lay practitioners. He even threatened to break with you (H[err]. Professor), if things continue this way. He also cited Jones, about whom he claims that he (Jones) also wants to get rid of the lay analysts.

Now that the matter of the Freund (Toni) heirs has been settled, there is nothing standing in the way of finally regulating the Verlag matter.

I must communicate the following about the Hungarian translations: As you know, Storfer has taken over from me *all* of your Hungarian translations which have been circulating here to date; he is also in possession of the Hungarian translation of the "Interpretation of Dreams" and the "Lectures." Thus, the Hungarian book trade has been *completely denuded* of psychoanalytic literature; in the face of this, Storfer is making no move in the Verlag to have the works printed there, which signifies a severe disadvantage for psychoanalysis in Hungary. He should give up the beautiful, but (as we know from experience) dangerous, plan for the Hungarian complete works and, instead of that, *quickly* publish, that is to say, reprint *what is available*. The Hungarian translation of "Jokes" is also lying there finished and is waiting for publication.

What I had to say about Groddeck is talked about in the Rundbrief. He is, personally, as always, a respectable and loyal adherent of analysis—I would like to say—admirer of your person. What was your impression?

If you have time, I ask for news about how you are. Or would Fräulein Anna be so kind as to please me again with a letter?

Many kind regards from me and my wife to you and your loved ones.

Ferenczi

1. The second digit of the date has been corrected several times; it could also be a "9." Balint read "23"; but since Ferenczi refers to his circular letter dated November 28, this cannot be the case. Comparison of pen and ink suggests it is not out of the question that the letter was written on the same day as the previous circular letter (letter 1035).

2. *Inhibitions, Symptoms, and Anxiety* (Freud 1926d).

1037

Vienna, December 1, 1925
IX., Berggasse 19

Dear friend,

Just received your letter, which I am answering immediately, because few have so much right to information about me as you. This is the way it went: In the night of the 18th to 19th of November, a severe periostitic inflammation set in (from the retarded tooth of the lower jaw on the side that was not operated on) in the course of a fresh infection from a cold, which even now disrupts my speech. The operation was done the next morning, very elegant, minimally arduous, trephination of the jaw, extraction of the tooth, which showed suppuration of the root. But the consequences of the operation have not been overcome to date. The pain didn't stop until yesterday, a piece of the mucous membrane has died off, and a little piece of bone lies free, which has yet to be knocked loose. The defect is not yet covered, recovery will certainly take weeks, and until then I can't chew and have to nourish myself with fluids. That doesn't have a good influence on my general condition, so that the pathological event which was meant as an episode has become downright significant after all. I feel the inhibition very distinctly, since it has not been possible for me to take up the revision of the essay "Inhibitions, Symptoms, and Anxiety" for printing, as I should. I had suspended my practice for a week. Now I am working again, not entirely without exertion.

Certainly more serious is what is being reported about Abraham's condition. Renewed fever, repeated attacks of pain, preparedness for an operation, stay in a sanatorium, now, again a hiatus in the fever, but complete diagnostic helplessness. I fear it will have a bad end before one learns what it is about.

Brill's threat will not cause me to change my position on lay analysis. I won't hold on to the Americans.

Groddeck was here just at my worst time. I saw him only once for an hour. Personally, I like him very much, but scientifically, he is probably not usable; he overtaxed himself with the ψ influence on the organic and [with] the It, and he is not the right man for working out an idea.

Storfer's hesitation in the matter of the Hungarian translations can easily be explained by the present inconsolable material situation of the Verlag, with whose restoration Eitingon will concern himself, although there is only one way out, put more money in, which, however, isn't there. The edition of the Complete Works was—as I prophesied—a nonsensical enterprise. I think little more than 100 copies were disposed of (printing 3,000!).

I greet you and Frau G. cordially.

Yours,
Freud

1038

Vienna, December 10,[1] 1925
IX., Berggasse 19

Dear friend,

As Anna told you on the telephone, the last report from Berlin was that it is going better today "as if by a miracle." They tell me that with lung abscesses one shouldn't despair so quickly. I always had the inclination to take Abraham's illness seriously and am even now prepared for the lethal outcome. When it comes to pass, I should go to Berlin and on this painful occasion get to know some of my grandchildren. But I don't believe I will do it. My speech has been quite miserable since the last cold infection; I don't want to show myself to anybody in this state, and the unremitting complaints and paresthesias rob me of all ability to achieve, except for listening for a few hours to what my people are saying, whereby I, myself, say as little as possible about it. If you want to go to Berlin, then I would like to speak with you on the way back. We are the nearest ones to be concerned about what will happen with the Society, especially since Eitingon is in Sicily and will hardly be able to divest himself of his fetters in order to get to his post.

We may not, as long as he lives, portray what we have lost in him. But it is hard, especially for me. A test of what looks out at you when you live a long time. Whereby everything again empties out into conciliation.

I greet you and Frau G. cordially, and this time I would like to be wrong.

Yours truly,
Freud

1. The date is not clearly legible; it could also be "16."

1039

[Rundbrief][1]

Budapest, December 19, 1925

Dear friends:

The past month was filled with worry about the health of our Karl. The very last reports sound less pessimistic and give us hope for his recovery.

(I am sending these lines from the Berliners only to Sachs and Eitingon.) Compared with this concern, all particulars which may have otherwise occurred seem much too insignificant. So, I will mention only the fact that on January 9, Dr. Wilhelm Reich from Vienna is giving a lecture as guest of our Society here about disturbances of the orgasm.[2]

Kind regards,
Ferenczi

1. The letter is typewritten; only the signature, "Ferenczi," is handwritten.
2. "Die psychischen Störungen des Orgasmus" [The Psychic Disturbances of the Orgasm]; see letter 1045.

1040

Budapest, December 20, 1925

Dear Professor,

Yesterday brought me no news from Berlin; I would like to garner the justification for some hope from that. Should it come to the end which is so feared by us, then it goes without saying that I will fulfill all the painful duties which are coming to me. You, dear Herr Professor, should, as long as your condition does not improve, *on no account* risk the torment of such a journey.

I will definitely see you over Christmas, since I have arranged an editorial meeting with Radó in Vienna. My wife will accompany me.

In consideration of your holiday peace and quiet, which should be disturbed as little as possible, I don't want to disturb you any more than is absolutely necessary; so I ask you, without any obligation on your part, to be apprised of the fact that I am checking into the Hotel Regina on the afternoon of the 24th. It would certainly be a great pleasure for me if I could at least greet Fräulein Anna at our discussions, and I ask you to leave word for me at the hotel. If you want to receive me, dear Herr Professor, then I ask Fräulein Anna to inform me of the time. I intend to return to Budapest on Sunday (the 27th).

Kind regards,
Ferenczi

1041

Vienna, December 25, 1925
IX., Berggasse 19

Dear friend,

I enclose here the draft of the obituary for Abraham,[1] for your appraisal.

If you want to speak with me tomorrow morning, I ask you to come at ten o'clock. Dr. Stefan Zweig[2] has already been scheduled for ten thirty, and I have things to do from eleven to one. I am free again at three thirty.

Cordially,
Freud

1. Freud 1926b. Abraham had died on the same day.
2. Stefan Zweig (1881–1942), the famous Austrian writer. See his book *Die Heilung durch den Geist: Mesmer, Mary Baker Eddy, Freud* (1931) [in English, *Mental Healers: Franz Anton Mesmer, Mary Baker Eddy, Sigmund Freud* (New York: Viking, 1932)] and his correspondence with Freud, *Briefwechsel mit Hermann Bahr, Sigmund Freud, Rainer Maria Rilke und Arthur Schnitzler* (Frankfurt am Main: S. Fischer, 1987).

1042

Berlin, December 28[, 1925][1]

funeral service dignified frau abraham composed her brother assures to care completely for future offered help refused with much thanks tomorrow conferences with eitingon my trip home thursday greetings = ferenczi

1. Telegram.

1043

Hotel Hessler
Berlin-Charlottenburg
Kantstr. 165–166
Am Bahnhof Zoologischer Garten
Fernsprecher Amt Steinpl.
7080–7089[1]
Berlin, Wednesday
[December 30, 1925,] A.M.

Dear Professor,

I want to try to summarize events briefly.

I already reported on the course of the burial by telegram; also about the financial situation of the Abraham family. My statements in this regard have been confirmed in the meantime; Abraham's brother-in-law promised to care for the family in such a way that *nothing* in their lifestyle will have to change. (He is well-to-do and unmarried.) Frau Abraham did, to be sure, express the wish to seize any opportunity for work, that is to say, accept a position which suits her.—

Eitingon arrived fresh and eager for action.[2] Before his arrival there were all sorts of partisan stirrings here of the dei minorum gentium[3] (Böhm,[4] Liebermann[5]). At my urging he himself publicly announced his candidacy,[6] whereupon all those voices grew silent.—With regard to the presidency,[7] I did careful research as to what he would say to my candidacy, but I found that he would interpret that as a denigration of his person, as incompetence for the presidency, etc., whereupon I immediately made a motion simply to take over the agendas of the leader until the next Congress without any mandate.[8] I had to tell him, to be sure, that long absences are incompatible with all these positions. He thereupon informed me that his wife had made the "heroic" decision to subordinate her private wishes etc. to Max's work plans. [That] she had behaved *extremely* rationally these last few days. We all seem—so Max believes—to underestimate his wife in this regard.—The conference of the foreign guests (Emden, Ophuijsen, Jones, I) and Sachs went—according to Eitingon's avowed declarations—quite smoothly; everyone is in complete agreement with the solution. Before Eitingon's arrival there were also voices which spoke in favor of a different solution (my possibly moving, among others).—There also seems to be a certain interest among the Berliners in favor of the latter. Alexander spontaneously turned to me in this regard; Simmel also spoke to me about it. But it seems that youth first wants to try to show what it can do without help from outside.

Finally, I also talked with Eitingon about the Verlag; he is also full of activity with regard to it.—Thus, for the moment he is unifying all the important posts in his person: International, Berlin, Verlag, and Polyclinic, and he seems to have a desire to dedicate himself entirely to these great tasks.

I am leaving today (Wednesday) by way of Prague, arrive in Budapest Thursday morning. Am very tired.

See you again perhaps at Easter—and with many greetings.

Yours,
Ferenczi

1. Preprinted letterhead with a line of commercial advertisements along the left edge.
2. From Taormina, where he had accompanied his wife for her convalescence.
3. Latin for "gods of the lesser peoples" (Cicero, *Tusculan Disputations* 1.13.29), i.e., "smaller deities," that is to say, rather insignificant persons, according to the differentiation of the Roman aristocratic tribes into *patres maiorum gentium* and *patres minorum gentium*.
4. Felix Böhm (1881–1958), a member of the IPA since 1913. From 1920 to 1926 he was an associate at the Berlin Institute, and in 1931 he became secretary of the German Psy-

choanalytic Association. Böhm was a decisive participant in the "Aryanization" of psychoanalysis under the Nazi regime.

5. Hans Liebermann (1883–1931), an early analysand of Abraham's. See the obituary by Eitingon in *Zeitschrift* 17 (1931): 296–297.

6. As head of the Berlin Society in place of Abraham. Ernst Simmel subsequently took over this function, however.

7. Of the IPA, likewise in place of Abraham.

8. As in the original. What Ferenczi evidently meant was that Eitingon would take over the agendas of the leader.

1044

Vienna, January 3, 1926
IX., Berggasse 19[1]

Dear friend!

I thank you for your telegraphic and written report. The matter has, to be sure, turned out differently than we had imagined, but we had not counted on the possibility that Eitingon would tear himself so energetically from his isolation and take over these serious duties. We have a telegram from him[2] [to the effect] that he is coming to Vienna on Wednesday evening. On the same evening we are holding a mourning session, to which I will also come. I am in favor of having the second issue of the Zeitschrift totally or in large part dedicated to honoring Abraham (bibliography, picture, etc.). The first issue will contain only my brief obituary notice.[3]

The questions about your moving to Berlin and the definitive presidency have not been finally solved. Further developments should determine that.

Not much new to report about us. The vacation is over today.

With kind regards to you and your wife.

Yours,
Freud

With kind regards.

Yours,
Anna

1. The letter is typewritten; only the signature, "Freud," and the greeting from Anna Freud are handwritten.
2. Telegram of January 2, 1926 (Sigmund Freud Copyrights).
3. The obituary (Freud 1926b) appeared in the first issue of 1926; the second issue was dedicated to Abraham's memory, with his picture and the following contributions: Karl Abraham, "Psychoanalytische Bemerkungen zu Coué's Verfahren der Selbstmeisterung" [Psychoanalytic Remarks about Coué's Procedure of Self-Mastery] (131–154; 1926, 115); Ernest Jones, "Karl Abraham, 1877–1925" (155–183); "Verzeichnis der Wissenschaftlichen Veröffentlichungen von Dr. Karl Abraham" [Index of the Scientific Publications of

Karl Abraham] (184–191); as well as eulogies by Max Eitingon, Hanns Sachs, Sándor Radó, Theodor Reik, and Mosche Wulff (195–218).

1045

Budapest, January 14, 1926

Dear Professor,

I still owe you an accounting of your $200. I paid $13 for the wreath; so there remain $187, which I would gladly send to you if I only knew the bank where you have your account. Please send me this address.

I would like to find out about the result of your discussions with Eitingon;[1] if you have no time or mood for that, perhaps Fräulein Anna will be so kind as to share some things with me.—I have had no direct news from Berlin since my departure, although everything has concentrated there for the time being. It is very reassuring to me to know that the direction of the various organizations remains in Eitingon's hands.

Anticipating the Rundbrief, I will share with you the fact that Dr. Reich was our guest last Saturday and gave a well-composed lecture, the contents of which interested us.[2] Such guest lectures stand the test very well, and enliven the scientific enterprise, which otherwise gets monotonous.— Fräulein Anna is expected as the next guest (in the spring).[3]

Do you hear anything from the Abraham family? I received only a few heartfelt lines of thanks from the widow.

You should in the meantime have found out through Eitingon about the film presentation, to which we (to our displeasure) were witnesses.[4] I fear that the Societies will have to protest against the manner of presentation of $\psi\alpha$. therapy; what is particularly annoying is that, despite firm promises, Abraham's rank as president of the IPA, and Sachs's as "training analyst of the Berlin Polyclinic," is being loudly publicized. Sachs is hiding more and more in the cloak of Abraham, who can't defend himself. I am often reminded of your opinion that Sachs actually doesn't belong on the Committee.

Kind regards,
Ferenczi

1. During Eitingon's visit in the first week of January, among other things, the question of Ferenczi's move to Berlin and the future of the secret Committee were discussed (Eitingon to Freud, January 22, 1926, Sigmund Freud Copyrights).
2. See letter 1039 and n. 2.
3. Anna Freud did not give a lecture.
4. A preview of the film *Geheimnisse der Seele* in Berlin, probably on December 29 or 30, 1925. Present were, among others, Eitingon, Ferenczi, Jones, and possibly Sachs; see

Paul Ries, "Popularise and/or be Damned: Psychoanalysis and Film at the Crossroads in 1925," *International Journal of Psycho-Analysis* 76 (1995): 759–791).

1046

Vienna, January 18, 1926
IX., Berggasse 19

Dear friend,

Your letter reminds me that I haven't written to you since the 3rd of the month. Reason: still during Eitingon's presence I got the flu, had a fever for several days, lay in bed, and since then I haven't gotten much better. Cough, lassitude, and the swellings in my nose persist.

Eitingon requested my intervention in the Berlin group to the effect that they should not insist on his being the head. I did as he wished; main argument, that one couldn't require it of him if he thinks he isn't the right one for it. He has instituted a presidium made up of Simmel (head), Radó, and Horney,[1] about the provisional character of which he is not deceived. But he wants them to try it, and is figuring on the fact that your election as president will happen by itself in time if you come to Berlin. He laid it out to me in the way that I am repeating it to you. He himself wants to remain in Berlin until the end of January, and then only go back to Taormina over February. He was very fresh, energetic, and motivated by the most serious of intentions. His sick wife is said to have pulled herself together on this occasion, to leave him a free hand.

The titles of the film authors were stricken at the second performance, in consequence of Eitingon's protest. I don't consider an official protest expedient; the misuse can't be maintained in the long run, and doesn't seem to be bad this time, notwithstanding how unpleasant the matter is to us.

In figuring the dollars, you haven't taken into consideration the fact that you also traveled on my behalf and that we want to share the expense equally. The delivery of the remainder can wait until you come back to Vienna.

I have heard about annoying things that are being planned for my birthday, and will be grateful to every friend who makes an effort to spare me them. Ceremonies are detestable to me, especially one such as that. When I only think about the nonsensical and dishonest wishes for "a long life," I get a powerful wish to avoid that date. I don't know yet how I will get off the hook in the upcoming case. I thought of going away, but that is so extremely uncomfortable for me, and perhaps impossible, on account of the children who don't live in Vienna.

During my sick days I read several intimate publications about Anatole

France, which indicate a not very transparent picture of his person. Have you also followed these things?

Kind regards,
Freud

1. Karen Horney, née Danilesen (1885–1952), M.D., lived in Berlin from 1909. The analysand of Abraham and Sachs, she was the first woman teacher at the Berlin Institute. In 1932 she emigrated to the United States, first to Chicago to Franz Alexander, then to New York, where she became a member of the Society there (1935). In 1941 she was forbidden to teach at the New York Institute, whereupon she left the Society and, with Erich Fromm, Clara Thompson, and others, founded the *Association for the Advancement of Psychoanalysis*. She was a very successful author, who, with her contributions to the psychology of women and the psychology of culture, exerted great influence but also unleashed strong controversy. See Susan Quinn, *A Mind of Her Own: The Life of Karen Horney* (New York, 1987); Roudinesco & Plon, *Dictionnaire*, pp. 460–462.

1047

Budapest, January 24, 1926

Dear Professor,

It was extremely painful for me to hear that you weren't feeling well recently, and even had to take to your bed. But I confidently hope that since then not only the illness, but also the conditions that followed it, along with the bad mood, are things of the past.

I don't know about any "annoying" things that are being planned for your birthday. If you understand by that the plan for a festive gathering in Vienna, and if this is so repugnant to you, then I will gladly do what I can to prevent it. I will take the first steps to do so at the same time as I send off this letter. Nothing would be more nonsensical than to mar your birthday with honors which are disagreeable to you. I am firmly convinced that I will succeed in suppressing these well-intended but obviously inappropriate manifestations, so that you can at least look forward to this day without particular cares.

I agree completely, after the fact, with the solution of the Berlin presidency, which was arrived at by Eitingon and approved by you. It cannot be determined for the time being whether this solution is definitive or provisional. It is possible that the young Berliners, in marshaling all their powers, which have also proved themselves to date, will be capable of maintaining the viability of the Berlin center. The election of persons is, in any event, a fortunate one.

Of the Anatole France books I have read only "Anatole France en pantouffles,"[1] the content of which surprised me greatly. The amorality which characterizes his Abbé Coignard and the amicably benevolent skepticism of Professor Bergeret seem to have been only diminutions of a bitter cynicism, which he withheld from us in his writings.

Kind regards!

Yours,
Ferenczi

1. Jean-Jacques Brousson, *Anatole France en pantoufles* [Anatole France in Slippers] (Paris, 1924).

1048

Vienna, January 26, 1926
IX., Berggasse 19

Dear friend,

It is true, even the consequences of the flu are eventually over, and I am again the way I was.

You have, with unjustified urgency and neglect of our agreement, sent me a packet of dollars, the receipt of which I must confirm—without any other concession.

Your letter of today expresses your willingness, deserving of thanks, to ease as much as possible the travails of the ceremony which lies ahead. I have since allowed myself to be convinced by my family that I can do nothing better than to take up the yoke with clenched teeth. Traveling is too burdensome for me, long absence is costly, especially hated formalities (on the part of the university, the city, etc.) are certainly not to be feared. To the earlier considerations comes a new one, that a general meeting of the corporation is supposed to take place around the same time. So, I will stay, and count on the forbearance of all those who call themselves friends. On the occasion of the discussion of the Abraham volume of the Zeitschrift, I learned from Storfer that one volume each of both of our periodicals[1] is supposed to be dedicated to me. I find that unobjectionable, if it happens in a dignified way, i.e., the introductory statement is limited to a minimum, so that one avoids the tactlessness of having oneself, as the publisher, celebrated in one's own organ; the scientific contributions on such occasions customarily show clearly the disadvantageous influence of provocation, but they retain their affective value as signs of eagerness.

The Abraham volume should, according to my suggestion, appear as soon as possible, that is, before mine, and doesn't need to contain anything other than the reports on the funeral orations in the groups which were given precedence as official by Jones. I will write about this to Radó, who had other intentions. "La séance continue"²—the eternally uniformly set clock of duty³—must be maintained on happy and sad occasions.

Kind regards to you and your dear wife.

Yours,
Freud

P.S. We have sent our housewife to Baden (Herzogshof), so that she has it more comfortable as long as she has to suffer from her herpes.⁴

—Two thick volumes of Psicanalisi from Morselli in Genoa.⁵ Manure and rubbish!

1. *Zeitschrift* and *Imago*.
2. See letter 832 and n. 3.
3. See letter 833 and n. 1.
4. "Martha is suffering of a nasty, obstinate eczema on her body and has been sent to Baden, half an hour far from Vienna, where we can easily pay her visits" (Freud to Sam Freud, February 1, 1926, Sigmund Freud Copyrights). Written in English [Trans.].
5. Enrico Agostino Morselli (1852–1929), *La Psicoanalisi Studii ed appunti critici*, vol. 1, *La Dottrina*, vol. 2, *La Pratica* (Turin, 1926). At Freud's request, Edoardo Weiss wrote a critical commentary (*Zeitschrift* 12 [1926]: 561–568). See *Freud/Weiss*, pp. 51–55.

1049

[Rundbrief]¹

Budapest, January 31, 1926

Dear friends:

The reason for the delay this time: indisposition, which got better in the meantime.

The Berlin solution seems to me to be the only right one at this time. I am convinced that Simmel, a talented man, will grow in every respect in the consciousness of his important position. In his productive fantasy he does, to be sure, incline in a direction which is opposite to Abraham's; but Radó's critical talent will be a good counterweight.

We should, as Ernest correctly thinks, reserve the possible enlargement of the Committee for a later time.

Kolnai has resigned from the association. He bases it on the fact that he will publish a doctoral dissertation in Vienna which is critical of some of the main views of psychoanalysis.² (I think he is writing a new ethics.) It's a good thing that we are rid of him.

Kind regards!
Ferenczi

February 1926

Dear Professor,

Received your letter with thanks. After a renewed conversation with Eitingon and Federn I return to the question of the birthday celebration. For the time being I waved them off.

My health is also somewhat shaky, now as before.

Cordially,
Ferenczi

1. The circular letter is typewritten; only the signature, "Ferenczi," and the postscript to Freud are handwritten.
2. Probably *Der ethische Wert und die Wirklichkeit* [Ethical Values and Reality] (Freiburg, 1927). On Kolnai, see letter 840 and n. 2.

1050

Budapest, February 21, 1926[1]

Dear friends:

The activity of our Society is the only thing I have to report about in my Rundbriefen. The next-to-last session brought the lecture of a Dr. (of Laws) Dukes, who treated the criminologic applicability of psychoanalytic doctrine (in connection with Reik's book).[2] In yesterday's session, several members brought casuistic material. A colleague who was analyzed in Berlin by Sachs, then here by me (Dr. Bálint),[3] a learned bio- and physiologist, delivered a paper about, among other things, a case of coronary disturbance with extrasystole, in which the absence of the pulse was demonstrably connected with suppressed erotic (clitoral) impulses and was able to be influenced by analysis.[4] [The supposition] that many coronary disturbances, and related aggravations, can be interpreted as "conversion hysterical" is gaining more and more probability.

The training commission began its activity by admitting some (medical) petitioners to training analysis.

Kind regards,
Ferenczi

February 26.

Dear Professor,

There was a delay in sending you the Rundbrief, and so your letter of today with Daly's money shipment preceded it. The latter is forced by his obscure descent (on the mother's side) to outdo his noble father—hence, the tendency to surpass you and me. But it is precisely his ucs. that makes him clear-sighted for certain connections of the castration complex, so that his work,[5] at least from the perspective of content, should be of some interest. His predilection for alcohol is connected with his homosexuality; he masters both rather well; his wife is also (aside from [being] the Australian colonial type) not *so* bad as she appeared to him earlier. His work certainly won't lack exaggerations.

What do you say about the strange coincidence that, just now, when you are concerned about heart ailments, from the many cases that were being presented by us, I happened to cite the theme of coronary disturbances. What was said there is plainly already an answer to what you have heard. I am firmly convinced that—even if nicotine plays a part in the matter—something psychic can be decisive in the so-called myocardites and stenocardias. As vehemently as I pleaded in favor of intervention in the solution of your jaw malady, I believe just as decidedly that the heart can and should be not only medicinally but also psychically supported. Perhaps this is the occasion on which I can say to you that I find it actually tragic that you, who endowed the world with psychoanalysis, find it so difficult to be—indeed, are not at all—in a position to entrust yourself to anyone.— If your heart ailments continue, and if the medications and diet don't help, then I will come to you for a few months and place myself at your disposal as an analyst—naturally: if you don't throw me out.
Best regards to all.

Yours,
Ferenczi

1. The circular letter is typewritten; only the signature, "Ferenczi," and the postscript to Freud of February 26 are handwritten.

2. Lecture of February 6, 1926, "Eine neue Strafrechtstheorie (Referat und Kritik der Theorie von Th. Reik)" [A New Theory of Criminal Law: Review and Critique of the Theory of Th. Reik], *Zeitschrift* 12 (1926): 225.

3. Michael Balint (Mihaly Bálint)(1896–1970). In 1919 he became interested in psychoanalysis through Alice Székely-Kovács, the woman who later became his wife; she had attended Ferenczi's lectures that year. Both were in analysis with Sachs in Berlin; after their return in 1924, Balint was in analysis with Ferenczi for an additional two years. In 1926 he became a member and, in 1931, vice president of the Hungarian Society and a member of its Training Committee, and in 1935 he became director of the Budapest Psychoanalytic Institute. In 1938 he emigrated to Manchester, in 1945 he moved to London, and from 1968 until his death he was president of the British Society. Balint was an important representative of the so-called Middle Group and can be considered an important propagator of the ideas of Ferenczi, of whose literary estate he became the administrator. "Balint takes up things there where I got stuck" (Ferenczi, note of September 26, 1932, in Judith Dupont, "The Notion of Trauma According to Ferenczi: Progress or Regression in Psychoanalytic Theory?" in André Haynal and Ernst Falzeder, eds., *One Hundred Years of Psychoanalysis* [Geneva, 1994], p. 212). He is known especially for his works on the doctor-patient relationship, his introduction of "Balint groups," and for his writing on early object relations ("the basic fault"). The present edition represents the completion

of one of the projects begun by Balint. See André Haynal, *Controversies in Psychoanalytic Method: From Freud and Ferenczi to Michael Balint* (New York, 1989); Ernst Falzeder, *Die "Sprachverwirrung" und die "Grundstörung": Die Untersuchungen S. Ferenczis und M. Balints über Entstehung und Auswirken früher Objektbeziehungen* [The "Confusion of Tongues" and the "Basic Fault": The Investigations of S. Ferenczi and M. Balint on the the Origin and Working Out of Early Object Relations] (Salzburg, 1986).

4. On February 20, 1926, Balint gave three casuistic contributions: "*a)* Eine agorophobische Kranke mit Extrasystole. *b)* Analytische Deutung von Magensymptomen. *c)* Baldigste Identifizierung mit dem Verstorbenen nach dem Todesfall" [An Agoraphobic Woman Patient with Extrasystole;. Analytic Interpretation of Stomach Symptoms; Identification with the Deceased Immediately after Death] (*Zeitschrift* 12 [1926]: 225).

5. "Hindu-Mythologie und Kastrationskomplex," *Imago* 13 (1927): 145–198.

1051

Vienna, February 24, 1926
IX., Berggasse 19

Dear friend,

This Indian letter with valuable enclosure arrived here today, intended for you. Let's hope the poor boy didn't flip under the influence of alcohol and a bad woman.

Inhibitions, Anxiety, and Symptoms[1] will be sent off to you today by the Verlag.

My health has suffered a new disturbance today through stupid attacks on the street along the lines of stenocardia. The internist, Ludwig Braun, wants to treat me for myocardia and make me lie down and rest for two weeks;[2] this time I am more optimistic, diagnose an intolerance to smoking, and continue to resist—successfully, up to now. I really have heart ailments for a long time after every de-nicotinized cigar, and—a bad sign—abstinence is not at all difficult for me. State of health otherwise undisturbed.[3]

Kind regards to you and Frau G.

Yours,
Freud

1. The title is given this way in the original.
2. See letter 817, n. 3.
3. On the same day, Freud reported in detail to Lajos Lévy: "On the 17th of the month I went on the street after lunch, noticed with astonishment, but without anxiety, that I was struck by an attack of pain, which, beginning in the left hand, engulfed shoulder and thorax, involved the left leg somewhat, and was relieved through burping. So, clearly of stenocardic nature. I crept home slowly. Friday, February 19, the same experience. At my

wife's urging, I went out again and visited the internist Dr. Braun, who lives nearby, during his office hours. He gave me a thorough going-over, was of the opinion that it was nothing immediately dangerous, probably a small clot in a blood vessel of second rank, but caution, two weeks' complete rest, preferably at the Cottage Sanatorium, prescribed diuretics (blood pressure 165) . . . I have no desire whatsoever for therapia magna, can only interrupt work in case of absolute necessity" (Library of Congress).

1052

Vienna, February 27, 1926
IX., Berggasse 19

Dear friend,

Many thanks for your touching suggestion. But you know, my main anxiety is the one about a useless existence; how should I make friends with one that is harmful for my loved ones!

I am, incidentally, not doing badly; no attack since February 19, only mild pains; objectively, the finding is not supposed to be great at all—i.e., if one is finding out the right thing.

There may indeed be a psychic root, but let's not forget, dying also has its psychic root, and it remains quite doubtful whether it can be mastered through analysis, and finally, whether at seventy years of age one doesn't have a good right to rest of any kind.

I am making a beginning of it in this first week of March; I am granting leave to three cases, so I am treating only three hours a day, and I want to indulge myself in everything good otherwise, only no sanatorium, in which one would have to bolster up one's being sick out of boredom and helplessness.

Levy has written to me very rationally, is in complete agreement with Braun; I am staying in communication with him.

If you want to move to Vienna, my analysis need not be the motive. I will hand over to you in patients whatever comes to me.

Cordially,
Freud

1053

Budapest, March 1, 1926

Dear Professor,

[I] was very pleased by the news about the improvement in the state of your health. Dr. Lévy, who is visiting you these days, was likewise able to reassure me.—One can and may naturally not be forced into analysis, but please keep in mind that, as soon as your disinclination (should I say resistance?) has been halfway overcome, I can come to Vienna immediately. I can simply bring my American patients to Vienna and divide up the few local ones. My intention of coming has nothing to do with plans to move; I was thinking of a stay of a few months.—

Enclosed I am sending you the letter I just received from Wittels,[1] whereby I am possibly injuring the discretion I owe him. But I can't reply without having learned your opinion about the society mentioned by him, about the appropriateness of my appearing in that circle, about the eventual possibility of avoiding having this celebration. Federn, too, won't let go, even though Eitingon and I already decidedly advised against it; Federn is likewise figuring on my coming. It would be unjust to turn down Federn and accept Wittels's invitation.

I am sorry to have to bother you so often with this matter.

Please reply—with good news about how you are.

Yours,
Ferenczi

1. The letter has not been found. On behalf of the Vienna Society for Medical Psychology, Wittels had invited Ferenczi to give a celebratory lecture on the occasion of Freud's birthday. Shortly beforehand, Wittels had sought readmittance to the Vienna Society, and Freud had "intervened very energetically on his behalf, for a strong intellectual potency and excellent writing abilities are recognizable in that man. Despite some reservations regarding his person, I see an advantage in his joining" (Freud's *Rundbrief* of November 15, 1925, Sigmund Freud Copyrights).

1054

Vienna, March 3, 1926
IX., Berggasse 19

Dear friend,

Regret very much that so many difficulties are cropping up now out of our relationship. Everything must be paid and atoned for, that is my newest insight, even when no civil guilt is present. In the case of Wittels, I can easily give you information, but advise with difficulty. Wittels himself is, despite his faults, a respectable and serious person; the society has good intentions and will perhaps have an effect on reducing the gulf between analysis and medicine. The friendly attitude already proceeds from the offer to let you speak alone.

I don't know if it serves a purpose to avoid every reaction—perhaps the opposite. Only two things stand firm: that it would be preferable *to me personally* if no one cared about the date, and that I am not up to the task of being harassed [*angestrudelt*] into psychic irritation and then having to defend myself in the prescribed modesty. What happens without my presence can be judged purely objectively, from the standpoint of serving a purpose. I am enclosing Wittels's letter.

Unfortunately, I can't accept your congratulatory message on my getting better. Levy, who had a council with Braun at my place, will give you a report. Both were not satisfied with my willingness to reduce the work at home by half. They insisted on a sanatorium stay of several weeks for the purpose of therapy against a heart ailment (evidently considered myocarditic). Levy, who I hoped would be on my side, was pulling on the same strand as the very serious Braun. So, there remains nothing left for me but to give in. Martha is going to the Cottage Sanatorium today to inquire about accommodation; if it is possible, I am supposed to go out there already this week. I am allowed to have my three more difficult patients come out for treatment; that protects me from deathly boredom and also covers the costs of the stay.

I can naturally not know whether that is only an episode, about which one will no longer speak, or the beginning of the end, and then how long the way from this beginning to this end will be. Futile to think about that once one is experiencing it.

I respond to your repeated cordial offer to take me into analysis on account of a supposed ψ factor with the argument that one would also not think of such a therapy with any other septuagenarian with toxic etiology and anatomical findings. It cannot be presumed that I would have more advantage from such an attempt.

Anna and Martin were laid low by the flu yesterday.

Cordially,
Freud

1055

Vienna, March 4, 1926
IX., Berggasse 19

Dear friend,

I was repeatedly disturbed yesterday while I was writing to you, and thus I fear I aroused a false impression, as if I wanted to promote your appearance as toastmaster. Nothing is further from my mind; I presume that you will write the welcoming essay in the Zeitschrift[1] and [I] know of myself: If they had forced me to write *three*, instead of the one commemorative article for your 50th birthday, then I would finally have become aggressive against you. But I wouldn't like to experience that from you, so don't leave the piece of emotional hygiene out of consideration for its own sake.

Don't make yourself responsible for everything that people set up.

I am going to the sanatorium tomorrow morning, am dissatisfied with myself and what is outside myself.

Cordially,
Freud

1. "Zum 70. Geburtstage Sigmund Freuds: Eine Begrüssung" [To Sigmund Freud on His Seventieth Birthday: A Greeting," *Zeitschrift* 12 (1926): 235–240 (Ferenczi 1926, 273).

1056

Budapest, March 28, 1926

Dear Professor,

I ask you to tell me quite honestly if it would be convenient for you if I came to Vienna for the Easter days (Sunday and Monday). You can and will, naturally—in the event that I am permitted to come at all—dispose of your time *completely* independently of my being there; I, on the contrary, have nothing to do in Vienna except possibly to chat with you for one to two hours.—Since time is pressing, I ask Fräulein Anna to let me know by telegram (perhaps also about whether and which hotel is worth recommending in the vicinity of the sanatorium).

Cordially,
Ferenczi

1057

[Rundbrief][1]

Budapest, April 18, 1926

Dear friends:

An Easter visit to the Professor convinced me that the stay in the sanatorium did him a lot of good. Our conversations took place in the aura of the Professor's newest work, which is occupying us all so animatedly; I took it upon myself to review it for the Zeitschrift.[2]

In the Hungarian group there was a not uninteresting discussion with a guest who is interested in the cause, but analytically almost ignorant, a gynecologist, who requested enlightenment and leadership from us for himself and his professional colleagues.³ It is becoming more and more clearly evident that care must somehow be taken for the practical education of colleagues who are not professional analysts. The practice is gradually *forcing* all physicians to consider their cases also from our points of view, and it would be unjust to require of them that they should turn to an analyst because of every somehow psychically complicated case. The analytically oriented general practitioner could take care of some things himself,⁴ just as our guest, despite many theoretical misunderstandings and practical naïvetes, has also achieved very much in some cases by means of analytic research.

Many kind regards.

Ferenczi

Dear Professor,

I hear from Eitingon that Rank has *moved* to Paris; is he leaving Vienna altogether? What else do you know about him?

Nothing new here!

Regards,
F[erenczi].

1. The circular letter is typewritten; only the signature, "Ferenczi," and the postscript to Freud are handwritten.

2. Ferenczi did not subsequently review Freud's *Inhibitions, Symptoms, and Anxiety*, but he did write the foreword to the English edition (Ferenczi 1927, 280a).

3. Meeting of April 10, 1926: "Dr. B. *Totis* (as a guest); Das Seelenleben der Frau und die Frauenkrankheiten" [The Mental Life of Women and the Illnesses of Women] (*Zeitschrift* 12 [1926]: 986). Béla Totis, gynecologist, socialist, produced a number of works about themes which were considered taboo at the time, such as, for example, contraception.

4. A preformulation of the goal of Balint groups.

1058

Vienna, April 23, 1926
IX., Berggasse 19

Dear friend,

Yes, Rank is gone from Vienna, first to Paris, but that is probably only a stop on the way to America. The motives may be manifold; the fact that he can't find a proper place to live here certainly plays a part; also the need to conceal difficulties with his wife, the outcome of which can't be foreseen. The main thing, however, is that he has now carried out in a so to speak sober, cold way what he originally wanted to achieve in the stormy attack of illness: loosing himself from me and from all of us. What is unambiguous are the two facts, that he didn't want to give up anything of the theory in which his neurosis had precipitated itself, and that he also didn't take the smallest step to approach the Society here.

I don't belong to those who demand that one has to manacle and sell oneself for eternity out of "gratitude." He received much as a gift and accomplished much in return, so we're even! But on his farewell visit I didn't see any occasion for the expression of extreme tenderness; I was honest and hard. But we can make the sign of the cross over him.[1] Abraham was right.

I am not doing badly, and I greet you cordially.

Yours,
Freud

1. "Yesterday Rank was with me—for the definitive farewell . . . On the whole, again: Requiescat! Peace will probably not come for a long time" (Freud to Eitingon, April 13, 1926, Sigmund Freud Copyrights). The allusion is to the common Latin tombstone inscription "Requiescat in pace" (R.i.p.), "May he rest in peace" (Vulgate).

1059

Vienna, May 20, 1926
IX., Berggasse 19[1]

Esteemed colleague!

A substantial sum of money was given to me for my seventieth birthday by the acting head of our International Association as a

"Psychoanalytic Jubilee Fund."

I have allocated the larger part of it to the International Psychoanalytic Verlag and the smaller to the Vienna outpatient clinic,[2] and in so doing I hope to be faithful to the intentions of the donors. I know that, as a Committee member, you have taken special pains to bring this collection into being, and I thank you cordially for doing so.

Sincerely yours,
Freud

1. The letter is typewritten; only the signature, "Freud," is handwritten.
2. On Freud's birthday, "eight or ten of his pupils assembled in Freud's drawing room and presented him with a sum of 30,000 marks ($4,200.00) collected from the members of the Association. He gave four-fifths of it to the *Verlag* and one-fifth to the Vienna Clinic" (Jones III, 124). This circular letter also went to Burrow, Laforgue, Oberholzer, and Rickman, among others (all in Library of Congress).

1060

Budapest, May 30, 1926

Dear Professor,

Almost four weeks have passed since the memorable May 6, without my having sought you out with my lines.[1] To be sure, I had a "swelled head" in the meantime. The personal and practical factors and motives undulated back and forth, and the result was—as usual—at first, absolute paralysis, from which actually only the publication of Rank's book[2] roused me. So, for the moment, I would like to talk about it.

I haven't read the book yet, only leafed through it. But the whole presentation, the manner of its publication (with Deuticke),[3] keeping this plan a secret, Rank's departure immediately before having it published, etc., make the most unedifying impression on me from the outset. I will naturally be able to form a *definitive* opinion about the value or worthlessness of the contents only after reading the book, but the little that I have seen of it suffices to make it appear as though my suspicion that Rank wants to replace psychoanalysis with a special method, which we should from now on call *birth therapy*, is justified. You recall that I shared with the Committee my intention to subject the Rankian theory to a critique. This has been made easy for me by the publication of the book. As soon as I have finished the review of your last book, I intend to write the critique of Rank.[4] I have the feeling that you have given the Rankian ideas their full due in your book, so that I can now concern myself without reservation with the weaknesses of his technique. My working relationship with Rank, which was very intimate for a time ("Development [of Psychoanalysis]"), also forces me, by the way, once again publicly to make clear my position with regard to his ideas and measures. I am happy that through this—in full recognition of his good qualities and also of some of his ideas—I can finally free myself from him, since his character traits also downright force me to tear up coram publico [in public view] the all too brotherly commonality that we manifested publicly for a time.

Unexpectedly (but not inexplicably), my problem with moving has been complicated by the reemergence of personal difficulties. You recall, perhaps, that from time to time, lastly in Vienna at Easter, I came to talk about my old "heart ailments"; I mean the organic and psychic disturbances in equilibrium in my inner and outer household. Through this, the question became: Budapest? Vienna? or America?—from a purely matter-of-fact to an in part difficult personal matter.—My wife, who, incidentally, offered from the first instant to follow me wherever [I go], is also suffering inwardly, I think, not a little when she thinks about leaving her home forever. She is *very* tied to her family and would have little substitute for it in Vienna. The difficulties in finding living quarters in Vienna also require serious consideration, and the eventual selection of a suitable home would certainly be a matter requiring mature reflection and discussion.—I hear the favorable news about your state of health, I even hear[5] that you are again working five hours, so, gratifyingly, there is no question about my urgently having to take over your practice.—The last news about the Vienna group reports nothing of imminent urgency or a wish for me to come (*Deutsch* [Felix][6] was here yesterday and gave a lecture).[7]—Taking all this into consideration, it seems to me that the most instrumental thing would be to carry out the *America plan* first (perhaps reduced to a somewhat shorter time), to consolidate my already existing personal relationships in America, and to assure the future. But this would simultaneously be a time of weaning for me and my wife, in consequence of which the move to Vienna, which could be decided upon later, if events warrant, would be made easier for us both.

I write all this on the presumption that I can obtain your agreement with the motivation presented, and that I am correctly oriented with regard to the practical conditions. If it should be different, and especially if you consider the fight which is to be taken up with Rank to be so serious that my remaining here is *definitely* required, then I won't go. Of course, there is nothing preventing me from taking my part in this fight also from America.

I find it untimely, and, fortunately, improper, to conduct the foreign applications directed at you to me; I even certainly hope that your physical capacity for accomplishment will be completely restored. In the meantime, I can consolidate my practice, which has begun to develop from modest beginnings.

I certainly don't need to tell you what the cause of psychoanalysis means to me, and *am prepared,* if and when circumstances urgently demand it, *joyously* to fulfill the duties assigned to me. So, consider what has been brought up in this letter to be the quite honest representation of my inner and outer relations, but not as a final decision on my part. I ask you and Fräulein Anna (who, incidentally, also promised me) to be so kind as to express yourselves again.

Next week we are having a public *Freud celebration* here (in the old Parliament building). I and Róheim will be the speakers.[8]

Kind regards,
Ferenczi

1. On the occasion of Freud's birthday; the remaining Committee members had come to Vienna, and they held a meeting on May 7.
2. *Die Technik der Psychoanalyse,* 1, *Die Analytische Situation* [*The Technique of Psychoanalysis,* vol. 1, *The Analytic Situation*] (Leipzig, 1926).
3. Therefore, not in the Verlag.

4. "Review of Rank, O.: 'Technique of Psycho-Analysis'" (Ferenczi 1927, 277).

5. Reading uncertain; "even hear" could also be "hear say."

6. Brackets in the original.

7. Lecture of May 29, 1926, "Psychoanalytische Gesichtspunkte bei angina pectoris" [Psychoanalytic Views of Angina Pectoris], *Zeitschrift* 12 (1926): 586.

8. "On June 5, the Society sponsored a public festive meeting in honor of Prof. *Freud* in the meeting hall of the old Parliament building, in which approximately 500 guests participated. Dr. *Ferenczi* gave a lecture on the medical-natural scientific accomplishments of psychoanalysis. Dr. *Róheim* praised its significance for the humanities and social sciences. The lectures were received by the public with great enthusiasm" (ibid., 586f.).

1061

Vienna, June 6, 1926
IX., Berggasse 19

Dear friend,

I had a specific reason for postponing the reply to your last letter; about that later. Today I received your official telegram about the festive gathering[1] and ask you to convey my most heartfelt thanks to the Society.

It is no surprise to me that you won't decide so easily to move to Vienna. There also exists no necessity that would be tantamount to being summoned to service for the cause; you remain master of your decisions. If they lead you to America, then I can only hope that this journey will not signify the disappointment that some predict. I don't think it necessarily has to be that way. To be sure, one would have an easier time there with Rank's character traits.

With that, we have arrived at the theme of Rank. His demon is egging him on to a course where there is no stopping and no turning back. His whole behavior is evidently calculated to cut the tablecloth between us and him, and he must succeed. I, too, have not yet thoroughly studied his book (Anna has it), but I have read enough of it to have an opinion. Everything is much worse than I had imagined. The worst thing that people said about his technique is confirmed here. Its main character is crafty perspicacity without critique, an unusable work attitude. He combines the worst errors of those who have fallen away from us; like Stekel, he acknowledges boundless arbitrariness in the interpretation of dreams, like Adler, he sees, of all analytic reactions, only one, the struggle for the undisturbed possession of the mother object; Adler, the striving to be superior to authority (of the father). Both occur naturally; they don't need to be discovered.

One thing strikes me personally, an insinuation, which, [while] not clearly articulated, is in and of itself not at all nice. He interprets the wolf-dream of my Russian (at age four) from the analytic situation twenty years later!² If that isn't an attempt at self-parody, then it can have only one purpose. One is given to understand that I was taken in by the patient and misperceived a recent product of transference as a report out of the past. (The fact that, instead of transference he always puts "analytic situation" is characteristic in and of itself!) Now that is just as frivolous as it is, I would like to say: fresh. According to my distinct recollection, one doesn't have the slightest right to doubt the dating of this dream. If it was dreamed up by the patient during the treatment and is supposed to have been deceitfully transposed into childhood, then the next step is to conceive of all the childhood material which is produced, and which explains the dream, as invented ad hoc. Did Rank make this clear to himself, and how did he withdraw from the obligation to share his doubt with me and to ask me what I think about the possibility of such a deception?

I wrote to the patient that he should again carefully share with me everything he can say about this dream. The reply is still forthcoming. This was the reason for the intended postponement in my reply to your letter. I am also not certain about [getting] the information about my matter, but I will naturally share with you everything I find out from the Russian.

The inadequacy of Rank's assumption can also be demonstrated earlier. You know the strip on the wall with the six photos, which is supposed to have produced the five—six—or seven wolves on the tree. Well, those are the pictures of the Committee, which was instituted after Munich in 1913. Two of them are dated, yours from 1913, Abraham's 1914. There were never seven, for Eitingon wasn't added until after Toni's death, and Toni's picture, which I didn't get until very late, as Anna confirms with certainty, never hung on this wall. There were always only five pictures from 1913–14, also a long time afterward. I dismissed the Russian on July 14, 1914, so he can have seen the five pictures for about a year, never six or seven. But he had told me the wolf-dream, as it says in the case history, "very early," I think in the first of the four years, of which 1913/4 was the last. But how did this wall with the pictures look before this date? It could only have had two or three pictures, of Rank, Jones, and you, for I know that your picture of today is a substitute, as is the undated one of Jones. I didn't have an earlier one of Abraham, Sachs came late, Eitingon was not yet a member at the time. So what remains of the source for the five to seven wolves?³ The fact that two to three pictures hung on one wall opposite the patient, above the Leçon du M. Charcot,⁴ which has now been moved up high. Further, the strange fact that some trees can be seen from the window of the room, chestnut, not nut trees. Incidentally, the wall there is full of the images of the hated sibling rivals, and despite the typical analytic situation, it hasn't provoked any new dream of the sort in the last twelve years.

I am very much in agreement with your writing the critique of the Rankian book, and I ask you then to carry out the refutation of Rank's insinuation before the public.⁵ I will then place at your disposal the evidentiary material that is still outstanding. It doesn't need to become a dramatic struggle against Rank. A silent rejection from all sides will probably follow your critique. Too bad, but such is life.⁶

This letter has gotten long enough. I am again well, am still tormented by my prosthesis. We want to go to the Semmering on the 27th of the month.

With kind regards to you and Gisela,

Yours,
Freud

1. The telegram has not been found.
2. Rank postulated a specific type of dream, the "dream of the family tree" (*Technik der Psychoanalyse*, 1, *Die Analytische Situation*, p. 134), which, to be sure, is clothed in historic material, but is determined by the current analytic situation. Rank cites as an example the dream of the Wolf-Man (Freud 1918b, pp. 29–47). The wolves in the dream are the photographs of Freud's pupils, which hung in Freud's consultation room. "Thus, when he opens his eyes, he catches sight of these six or seven wolves (analysts)" (p. 153).
3. In the original there is a period instead of a question mark.
4. Depicted in Ernst Freud et al., eds., *Sigmund Freud: His Life in Pictures and Words* (New York, 1978), pp. 114f.
5. "The data . . . , which Prof. *Freud* now puts at my disposal, are downright annihilating for Rank's assumption"; "our trust in the author's judgment [is] most severely shaken" (Ferenczi 1927, 277; *Bausteine* II, 127, 128).
6. The last three words are written in English in the original [Trans.].

1062

Vienna, June 8, 1926
IX., Berggasse 19

Dear friend,

I don't want to leave you for long in uncertainty about the Rankian insinuation. The patient (Dr. Pankejeff) writes to me¹: "Ad point 1 and 2: I believe I am quite certain that I dreamed the wolf-dream in the way I related it to you then. (I didn't write to him about the possibility that it was a dream which had been made up later; he doesn't even suspect it.) There is no occasion for me to doubt the correctness of this recollection. On the contrary, the brevity and clarity of this dream always seemed to be what is characteristic of it. Also, as far as I know, the memory of this childhood dream never underwent a change (that is what I was concerned with). After it, I was afraid of similar dreams and, as a countermeasure before going to sleep, I was accustomed to holding before my eyes those things that I was afraid of, this dream as well. The wolf-dream always seemed to me to stand in the middle point of my childhood dreams, already because the wolf dominated my childhood fantasy. To be sure, when I then later saw a real wolf in a menagerie, I was very disappointed and didn't recognize the wolf of my childhood in him. The wolves sitting in the tree were also actually not wolves but white spitzes, with pointed ears and bushy tails. To point 3: I related the wolf-dream to you at the beginning of the treatment, and, in fact, to the best of my recollection, after one or two months after its commencement. [So, in 1911, that is important.]² The solution then came, as you write quite correctly, only after the treatment."

He then adds some associative material to the dream, which actually strengthens the interpretation of a love scene.

Is that sufficient for you to make a secure judgment about Rank's method of working?

Cordially,
Freud

1. Letter of June 6, 1926 (Library of Congress).
2. Brackets in the original. These, and the remarks enclosed in parentheses within the quoted passage, are evidently Freud's [Trans.].

1063

INTERNATIONALE ZEITSCHRIFT FÜR PSYCHOANALYSE
Herausgegeben von Prof. Dr. Sigm. Freud
Redigiert von Dr. M. Eitingon, Dr. S. Ferenczi und Dr. Sándor Radó¹

Budapest, June 17, 1926²

Dear Professor,

I acknowledge receipt, with thanks, of your last and next-to-last letter; the latter contains, among other things, your approval of my trip to America. The disappointment that some prophesy cannot occur, since I am going without any great expectations. What I want is solely to make certain connections which will ensure future clientele, at least for a few years. According to all expectations, I should achieve this quite modest goal; my appointment calendar in New York is already overbooked, so that I can make a certain choice.—I have also already written to Brill, who replied to me amicably but with the remark that he is "pleased that I am also giving lectures and am not only coming on account of the patients." It didn't occur to him that I could also instruct the members of the group.

Rank's insolence reaches its peak in the analysis of the wolf-dream. My wife and I moved recently into the Villa Montana, Budapest I., Mártonhegyi ut 45. I am gradually decreasing the number of my hours so that I can get into the critique of Rankian technique. My pen will be downright pointed. The Russian's reply comes just at the right time, and will suffice completely to make *this* point clear.

I am sending enclosed the quite interesting work of an *English* [female] pupil, who was in analysis with me for more than two years and is going home at the end of July. I think the paper is quite suitable for the Zeitschrift. I ask you to be so kind as to read through it and let me know your opinion. The paper is not *purely* psychoanalytic, but much more honest and scientific than the analytic articles about epilepsy that have been published to date. *Dr. Franklin* already made the observations in London, before her analysis, and was honored with a prize for them. The psychoanalytic commentaries are already the result of her analysis here.[3]

We are in good hands in the villa where we live. I do my analyses in another villa ten minutes away, for the time being, unfortunately, still eight hours a day.

I hope you are all well; the weather was terrible here; today is the first beautiful day.

In expectation of news from you.

Yours,
Ferenczi

1. Preprinted letterhead. On the left upper half of the sheet there is, in addition, a column with detailed information on how to submit written material to the *Zeitschrift*, along with address information.

2. Erroneously written as "1927" in the original.

3. "Die bedingten Reflexe bei Epilepsie und der Wiederholungszwang" [The Conditioned Reflexes in Epilepsy and the Repetition Compulsion], *Imago* 14 (1928): 364–376. On Dr. Marjory Franklin, later a member of the British Society, see letter 1070.

1064

[Semmering,] Villa Schüler,
June 19, 1926

Dear friend,

It is now easy for me to reply quickly; I am here without anything at all to do, while Anna has taken along all her American children.[1]

That damned America! So you will go, you're still not saying when. Will I still see you beforehand? In any case, I will give you the address of Ruth

Mack-Blumgart,[2] who left Vienna today and will probably stay over there until October 1. She hopes to be able to be of use to you. You know that she has become an excellent analyst and is very close to us all. [Her] address is:

> Hotel Ansonia
> 73th[3] Street and Broadway
> New York

Your pupil's paper is certainly clever and honest, but it has little to do with us. The conditioned reflex is somewhat removed from analysis. Tell me what you intend to do with the work. I won't oppose accepting it in the Zeitschrift. Perhaps it would fit better in Jones's journal, where one would save having to translate it. I will keep the manuscript in the meantime.

It would be very beautiful here if it weren't so cold and didn't rain so vehemently. This time I don't take to the altitude particularly well; perhaps only the first few days.

Greetings to you and Frau G.

Cordially,
Freud

1. The children of Anna Freud's friend and later companion through life, Dorothy Burlingham: Bob, Katrina, Mabbie, and Michael, all in analysis with Anna Freud. "The villa next to us is occupied by the mother of Anna's American children, who has brought along a Ford, and since, in practice with children, the reserve which otherwise sets in between patient and analyst is impractical, there is a pleasant neighborliness" (Freud to Jeanne Lampl de Groot, July 25, 1926, Library of Congress). Dorothy Burlingham, née Tiffany (1891–1979), left her husband, Robert, in New York and went to Vienna. She was an analysand of Reik and of Freud (1927–1939), with whose family she soon lived in "symbiosis" (Freud, in Roudinesco & Plon, *Dictionnaire*, p. 157) in the same house on the Berggasse. In 1932 she became an associate, and in 1934 a full member of the Vienna Society. She was initiator of the project-oriented experimental school in Hietzing, where Erik Erikson and Peter Blos taught (see Peter Heller, *The Burlingham-Rosenfeld School, Vienna, 1927–1933: A Documentation* [forthcoming]). From 1938 to 1940 she lived in the United States, then from April 1940 on with Anna Freud in London. She was a training and control analyst in the British Society. In 1949 she founded, with Anna Freud, the Hampstead Child Therapy Course. She published especially on the psychology of the blind. See Michael J. Burlingham, *The Last Tiffany: A Biography of Dorothy Tiffany Burlingham* (New York, 1989); Mühlleitner, *Lexikon*, pp. 55–57; Young-Bruehl, *Anna Freud*, passim.

2. Ruth Mack (1897–1946), in her first marriage to Dr. Herman Blumgart, whose brother Leonard (see letter 1088 and n. 7) had been in analysis with Freud. In 1922 she went to Vienna and began an analysis with Freud. "Ruth and [her later husband] Mark Brunswick completed an analysis with Freud at the same time, as did Mark's brother David. Ruth Brunswick's analysis lasted, with interruptions, from 1922 to 1938" (Mühlleitner, *Lexikon*, p. 214). In 1928 she married Mark Brunswick; Freud and Oscar Rie were witnesses at the wedding. The Brunswicks were in similarly close contact with the

Freuds as were the Burlinghams. Ruth was a member of both the Vienna (1930–1938) and the New York Society (1929ff.), and, despite her addiction to morphine, a prominent analyst of, among others, the "Wolf-Man," Robert Fliess, Muriel Gardiner, Karl Menninger, and Max Schur and his wife. In 1938 she re-emigrated to the United States. Her papers on preoedipal development have found particular recognition. See Mühlleitner, *Lexikon*, pp. 214f.; Paul Roazen, "Freud's Patients: First-Person Accounts," in Toby Gelfand and John Kerr, eds., *Freud and the History of Psychoanalysis* (Hillsdale, N.J., 1992), pp. 289–306; Roazen, *How Freud Worked* (Northvale, N.J., 1995), pp. 61–88; Roudinesco & Plon, *Dictionnaire*, pp. 635f.

3. Written this way in the original. Cf. the preprinted hotel letterhead in letter 1084.

1065

Budapest, I. Martonhegyi ut 45.
Villa Montana
Sunday, June 20
[postmark: 926 Jun 21][1]

Dear Professor,

About to read through Rank's break[2] with a critical eye, I came upon something right at the beginning, about which it does not seem superfluous to determine its factuality. Rank likes to talk about the fact that he is "in the comfortable position" of being able to refer to your words; among other things, he calls it a "Freudian technique" when one *has to terminate obsessional neurotics*; I know nothing about any such Freudian technique, so I ask you to indicate to me what he is alluding to. In the end, is it only a matter of your establishing a *compulsion to analyze* on the part of some patients?

The passage in question is on page eighteen of Rank's book.—

Have you perhaps had time to look at Dr. Franklin's paper on epilepsy? With kind regards to all.

Yours,
Ferenczi

1. Letter with perforated flap; the address is on the reverse, and that is why the postmark has been preserved.

2. In the original, the "r" in this word [*Bruch*] has been underlined four times, and an exclamation point has been set over the letters. What is evidently intended is to call attention to a slip of the pen involving the German *Bruch* (break) and *Buch* (book) [Trans.].

1066

[Semmering,] Villa Schüler,
June 24, 1926

Dear friend,

You will have received in the meantime my reply which is due you. Rank's statements on pages 16–18[1] are perhaps not the right point of departure for the critique. Even though he also distorts things here. He is completely under the impression of the "Infantile Neurosis,"[2] in which he also sinned with the childhood dream. But I never set up a rule that one has to terminate every treatment of an obsessional neurosis by setting a date, but in this case I found the indication for the rule (one work year earlier) in the fact that the patient was *well*, wasn't accomplishing anything more, and evidently didn't want to give up the protection of the transference against independence.

When Rank finds himself in the "comfortable position," he isn't referring to a communication from me, but rather to his own interpretation of the termination of the treatment as "rebirth," about which I am not at all convinced.

I am not at all well in these—beautiful—days.

Cordially,
Freud

1. The second number is not clearly legible; the last digit could be an "8" which has been written over a "9" or a "9" which has been written over an "8."
2. The analysis of the "Wolf-Man," published under the title "From the History of an Infantile Neurosis" (Freud 1918b), to the termination of which Freud had applied the method of giving notice.

1067

Budapest, July 4, 1926
Mártonhegyi ut 45

Dear Professor,

My Rundbrief was omitted this time for lack of important news; instead of that, I wrote private letters to the Committee members.—I was saddened by the last news from you, since you were reporting about feeling bad. Please, reassure me about this as soon as possible.—We had miserable weather here until two days ago; floods, scare stories about the crops, etc.—The financial situation of the population is desolate; suicides with this as a motive are accumulating. I am sometimes ashamed that I am not doing badly, personally—thanks to the foreign encouragement. Yesterday, I cabled to America the program for several introductory lectures to be given there.[1]

1. The Freudian Conception of the Unconscious.
2. Freud's Metapsychology; the Repression.
3. The Instincts (the "It").
4. Development of the Sex-Instinct.
5. Development of the Ego.
6. The Psychoneurosis.
7. The Psychosis.
8. Dreams and Psychopathology of Everyday-Life.
9. Psychotherapy. (Suggestion. Analysis.)
10. Transference, Resistance, Repetition. Activity (pro and con).
11. Sublimation and Character.
12. Application of Psychoanalysis on Science, Art, Mythology, Education, Sociology, Anthropology. Biological consequences.[2]

A nice program! I hope to be able to prepare for it in the course of the summer vacation.—In the meantime, I am working with the gradual diminution in the number of my hours (seven, at the moment).—Dr. Franklin (the English physician) is leaving me at the end of this month after two and a half years of analysis. An intelligent, scholarly virgo; difficult character analysis, significantly improved. I ask you to be so kind as to keep the epilepsy paper for the Zeitschrift; Dr. Franklin will take care of the translation here; I will send it directly to Radó. Along with Miss Potter,[3] whom I see now and again, Dr. Franklin also requests the honor of being received by you on *July 28*. Like Inman, she, too, sees herein the last consecration before entry into the work in London.

How are Fräulein Anna and your wife doing at the Semmering—I hope they are all well. Is Fräulein Minna there?

My wife thanks you for the greetings you sent her.

In expectation of news from you.

Yours,
Ferenczi

P.S. Perhaps I will also give an enlightening lecture about the schismatics.

On the way through to Germany (Lou Salomé, Groddeck) and America, we will stay at the Semmering for at least two days. Perhaps somewhat longer, if it's nice.

F[erenczi].

1. At the New School for Social Research in New York, which had invited Ferenczi to give a series of lectures.
2. The list is written in English in the original [Trans.].

3. A Miss Grace Potter, who a year later made a contribution of $5,000 (see letter 1096).

1068

[Semmering,] Villa Schüler,
July 6, 1926

Dear friend,

Received your letter just as Storfer was here with me, who brought the unpleasant news that the authenticity of the Diary[1] cannot be maintained. Not Hug, but the author, seems to have set things straight, out of understandable motives, albeit obviously with the use of notes and recollections. It doesn't lose its value to us completely in the process; she was certainly quite a stranger to analysis, but we have been exposed as being gullible. Storfer will naturally continue the investigations impartially.

Nothing special is going on with me. My heart ailments have, to be sure, started up again to a slight extent—Braun was here yesterday for a friendly visit and didn't ascertain anything objectively—but the prostheses torment me disgustingly, so that I can also hardly speak, and at the same time I don't know why; they fit well, and Pichler has given me to understand, after I already went to him twice from here, that he doesn't have anything to improve on. He finds a general swelling, which he attributes to the last X-rays, but their effect should be long gone. In any case, these ailments rob me of all good mood and every desire to see anyone. I don't say a superfluous word. But if you request it, I will receive Frau Dr. Franklin on the 28th.

To fill up my free time, which I can't use enjoyably—I don't have any patients now; the Princess won't be coming until the 11th of the month—I am writing a pamphlet about the question of lay analysis,[2] shallow stuff with a few nasty remarks, which, because I am in such a bad mood, come out bitter. The thing will be finished when you—not known when—come here. You have made yourself a great program for America. Just don't let yourself be run into the ground there. You know the American exploitation, the Taylor system.[3]

I would like to know, finally, when you are departing and when you want to take your leave here. You shouldn't go so far away without saying good-bye.

Our weather is miserable, as everywhere; this morning we clearly felt an earthquake.

I greet you both cordially.

Yours,
Freud

P.S. Eitingon was here on the 28th and 29th. The Interpretation of Dreams has been published in French.[4]

1. See letter 828 and n. 5.
2. *The Question of Lay Analysis: Conversations with an Impartial Person* (Freud 1926e), "provoked by the charge of quackery against Dr. Reik, who has given our newspapers much material" (Freud to Jeanne Lampl de Groot, July 25, 1926, Library of Congress).
3. A system of "scientific management," going back to Frederick W. Taylor (1856–1915), which is predicated on breaking down work procedures into individual motion sequences for the purpose of rationalization.
4. The first French edition of Freud 1900a, translated by J. Meyerson, published by Alcan (1926).

1069

[Rundbrief][1]

Budapest, July 25, 1926

Dear friends:

The Viennese newspaper attacks on Reik and psychoanalysis have also caused a stir in Budapest. I was interviewed by a newspaper on the question of lay analysis and gave rather vehement explanations.

The Budapest group held its farewell session yesterday. The colleagues agreed on a comprehensive work program for next year. They will institute lectures and seminars (for advanced students).[2]

I will end my work on August 15, go visit the Professor at the Semmering on the 22nd, then make some visits in Germany (Munich, Baden-Baden), and go to New York with my wife on September 22 on board the *Andania* (Cunard). A few colleagues and pedagogues are already signed up for training analyses. I am also taking along two American patients from here, so that I am already fully booked. I will give eighteen lectures, for which the program has already been set, in the "New School for Social Research."

Cordially,
Ferenczi

1. The circular letter is typewritten; only the signature, "Ferenczi," is handwritten.
2. "In the course of the next winter, the Hungarian Ps. A. Society ... will institute systematic courses for introduction to psychoanalysis. In the months November–December: Dr. I. *Hermann*, Psychoanalytic Psychology; Dr. M. *Bálint*, Psychoanalytic Drive Theory; Dr. G. *Róheim*, Ethnology (twelve hours each). In the months January–February there will follow courses of clinical content, given by Dr. M. J. *Eisler*, Dr. St. *Hollós*, Dr. S. *Pfeifer*" (*Zeitschrift* 12 [1926]: 587).

1070

Budapest, July 25, 1926

Dear Professor,

Our travel program seems to be established. We are leaving from here for Vienna around August 22 and should arrive at the Semmering on the same day or a day later. Since I will be taking leave of you for such a long time, I would like to take this opportunity to spend some time near you, and—if you have a desire—to chat with you—to talk through personal and scientific things. So, we will probably stay at the Semmering for about a week, but we want *on no account* to disrupt your normal time schedule and lifestyle, especially not with meals with you. We would be very grateful to you if Fräulein Anna would be so kind as to reserve for us a good room with convenient bath facilities in the Südbahnhotel or somewhere else in your vicinity. August 22 can be given as the date of our arrival; in case of a change, we will send a telegram to the hotel. I am very much looking forward to being together.

For local news, see the Rundbrief.

Kind regards,
Ferenczi

P.S. I couldn't very well talk Dr. Franklin out of visiting you. She is a somewhat peculiar person with very much knowledge and sharp logic. The analysis was able to ameliorate some of her character traits. She carried out three analyses under my direction. She is the niece of the former Viceroy of Palestine (Herbert Samuel)[1] and the late English minister, Montagu.[2] Her father [is] a rich banker in London. She was in analysis for two and a half years. Naturally, you are *not* supposed to have learned all these data from me, that is to say, don't mention them in the event that she doesn't tell you about them herself.—

1. Herbert Louis Viscount Samuel (1870–1963), liberal British politician and philosopher, one of the first Jewish cabinet members (minister of the interior, 1916, 1931–32). First British High Commissioner in Palestine (1920–1925).
2. Edwin Samuel Montagu (1879–1924), liberal British politician, state secretary for India (1917–1922), one of those responsible for the Government of India Act (1919).

1071

Semmering, July 29, 1926

Dear friend,

Your announcement that you want to visit me for a few days before your trip to America is exactly what I had expected. You are, after all, going away for a long time, and all future is uncertain. You are naturally not surprised to hear that you can't have as much of me as in [my] healthy days. I am, to be sure, working for only two hours a day (3:30 to 5:30), but I also have less and less endurance otherwise, speaking is unpleasant for me, the eternal struggle with the prosthesis makes me tired, and the certainty that things won't get better with it has a disgruntling effect. To the extent that I am still able to, I am happy in the anticipation of being able to discuss with you everthing that is important to us. We will reserve a room for you in the hotel when the time comes. You will certainly still share with us the exact date.

Your patient, Dr. Franklin, was with me today; I was still affected by yesterday's trip to Vienna, and I didn't quite know what to say to her. She is also not a mistress of small talk.

The booklet on lay analysis is already in press. You will still be able to read it here, in proof, or even in the final printed version. I don't have any other work plans.

My family is well here, the weather is very unsatisfactory. It is annoying to freeze at the height of the summer.

With kind regards to you and your dear wife.

Yours,
Freud

1072

Budapest, August 3, 1926

Dear Professor,

I am writing this time only to share with you a small discovery. In a patient who accomplished the feat of forgetting an entire day of his life (and in the process experienced all kinds of things, but mostly "forbidden" ones on that day), who thus produced one of the otherwise so famous instances of splitting of the personality, I found out that this symptom was an indirect (and unconscious) communication in my direction, to wit, that he had consciously concealed from me or misrepresented to me a whole lot of things. I am convinced that all other instances of this kind can be explained in a similar way—they are an admission of mendacity, that is to say, the fact that, in various situations in their lives or in relation to various groups of people, these people expose only *parts* of their total character and conceal a large part of their behavior. The cause lies, naturally, in the infantile lie in sexual matters—at the same time, an imitation of the mendacity of adults.

Many thanks for your last letter!

Yours,
Ferenczi

1073

Budapest, August 18, 1926[1]

Dear Professor,
In order to head off any misunderstanding, I am writing again that we will arrive at the Semmering on Sunday, the 22nd, in the evening. On no account will we make our—that is to say, my—first visit before Monday morning. I will telephone first from the Südbahnhotel, where Fräulein Anna probably had a room reserved for us.

I am very much looking forward to seeing you again.

Yours,
Ferenczi

P.S. In Vienna, I hope to be able to have a discussion with Storfer between two trains.

1. Postcard. Date and location appear at the end in the original.

1074

[Postmark: Munich,]
August 30, 1926[1]

The memory of the beautiful days with you will probably be the most beautiful that we take with us to America. Again, many thanks for everything!—For two days we have been living comfortably here as a threesome, with Frau Lou.

S. and G. Ferenczi

This greeting naturally also goes for Fräulein Minna, Fräulein Anna, and Mrs. Burlingham.

[In Lou Andreas-Salomé's handwriting:]
Dear Professor,
How warmly and heartfelt I think of you all.

Yours,
Lou

1. Picture postcard: "Munich: Marienplatz, Kaufingerstrasse, cathedral and city hall."

1075

S. Ferenczi M.D.

Budapest,
vii., Nagydiófa-u. 3.[1]

Baden-Baden,
Sanatorium Groddeck,
September 7, 1926

Dear Professor,

Up to now, our trip has gone according to plan. The only change in our time schedule was the decision to shorten the stay in Munich by two days and to take Lou along with us to Baden-Baden for three days. She will probably share her impressions with you herself, so that I can confine myself to reporting about her that I found her again somewhat aged, but in every other respect unchanged, as the true adherent of our movement and as a reliable friend. Too bad that her life in Göttingen is so lonely and without diversion. Perhaps one could ask Eitingon to invite her to Berlin once again. Being together with us has visibly done her good.

After her departure I quickly took care of the painful duty of finishing the Rank matter.[2] In order not to lose any time, I sent the manuscript, about six to seven printed pages long, to Berlin to Eitingon with the request to send a copy to you (and, if Eitingon finds it necessary, also to Jones). I asked him to have this done by the editorial staff, since there is no typewriter at my disposal here. I believe I accomplished the task well; the tone is matter-of-fact, but it comes out stern, which I don't regret at all. I hope you will still be in a position to get your opinion about the critique to me in Europe. We are staying here until September 17, i.e., we are going to Paris on the 18th. The Paris address is not yet certain, but we will be reachable in any event in Cherbourg (on board the "Andania," Cunard Line, [sailing on the 23rd of September]).[3] The New York address is, *for now:* 129 East 10th Street, c/o Miss Ruth Gates. In all probability we will live in the Hotel St. Andrew (Broadway and 72nd Street). The hotel is situated in the vicinity of Central Park and Riverside Ride,[4] so climatically favorable.

We are feeling very well at the Groddecks', as usual. Groddeck doesn't philosophize with me, and remains a physician and friend, as ever. Dr. and Frau Groddeck are also treating my wife's somewhat sore ankles.

Even though it is certain, the trip to America appears to me to be downright dreamlike and improbable; strangely, it doesn't arouse me in either a good or a bad sense. I haven't looked at the lecture notes yet.

I often think about the beautiful days at the Semmering, not just on account of the beauty of the place, but only because I was permitted to see you in such a good mood and so throughly refreshed. After the Alps, the hilly country of the Black Forest also seems much too tame.—

Please give our regards to all your loved ones, who positively vied with one another in being friendly to us. I will write to you once or twice more.

Yours,
Ferenczi

My wife greets you all cordially.

1. Preprinted letterhead, the right side of which has been crossed out.
2. See letter 1060 and n. 4.
3. Brackets in the original; the closing bracket is missing. The words enclosed in brackets are written in English in the original [Trans.].
4. Given this way in the original.

1076

Baden-Baden, September 9, 1926

Dear Professor,

Just read through "Lay Analysis." I thank you for the pleasure that this reading brought me. Unequaled in objectivity and clarity. Some of what you teach wasn't totally evident to me until now. Even the stupidest Austrian judge won't be able to shun *completely* the impression of the book. But will our colleagues also learn from it?

It would be good to look after translating it into English very soon. Perhaps I will find a suitable translator and publisher in America—if you are in favor of this in principle.[1]

The James Glover catastrophe[2] has affected me *very greatly*; I had the impression that it had to do with something tragic, not accidental. What do you know about the case?[3]—I considered him—intellectually—the best, certainly the most talented in England.

Groddeck will have his 60th birthday on October 13. Perhaps you would write him a few lines, which would make him happy.[4] He is true to us and to our cause, even if he also goes his own way.

The course about child analyses that Fräulein Anna gave me was very instructive. I would like to remind you of your promise to publish these experiences soon.[5]

N.B.: To the best of my knowledge it is not "Chi tocca muore," but rather *muori*.[6] But I could be mistaken.

Many kind regards,
Ferenczi

1. An English edition was published by Brentano in 1927, translated by A. Paul Maerker-Branden, with an introduction by Ferenczi (Ferenczi 1927, 280b).
2. Glover "had been quite wrongfully convicted of being drunk while driving a car a month ago, his real condition certainly being one of insulin intoxication . . . He then

went to Spain where he got an attack of acidosis. They found it impossible to regulate his sugar metabolism and he died in less than two days" (Jones's *Rundbrief* of September 16, 1926).

3. In the original there is an exclamation point instead of a question mark.

4. Freud initiated an official statement of congratulation on behalf of the Vienna Society (October 11, 1926; see *Freud/Groddeck*, pp. 94f.) and sent him a personal telegram (see letter 1083 and n. 3).

5. See letter 1083 and n. 5.

6. "On the main roads of Italy the pylons that carry high-tension cables bear the brief and impressive inscription: '*Chi tocca, muore* [He who touches will die]' . . . The corresponding German notices exhibit an unnecessary and offensive verbosity: '*Das Berühren der Leitungsdrähte ist, weil lebensgefährlich, strengstens verboten* [Touching the transmission wires is, since it is dangerous to life, most strictly prohibited]'" (Freud 1926e, pp. 236f.).

1077

Semmering, September 13, 1926

Dear friend,

No, it is certainly: muore.

The journalist and poet George Sylvester Viereck[1] (Macfadden's Building), whom I like very much, has applied for the translation in America. (He is an illegitimate Hohenzollern.) I have transferred it to him. If you come to an understanding with him, you will get to know an interesting person.

Many thanks for the hint about Groddeck's 60th birthday. Will think about it.

I don't know anything about Glover, other than what Jones has communicated: coma diabeticum, nothing about the background.

I am now maintaining a very amicable correspondence with Havelock Ellis, who sent me a book by the American Isaac Goldberg, which deals with his person.[2]

The last few weeks here were very nice and actually enjoyable, despite prosthesis. I am sending away both of my patients on the 15th. If weather permits, we intend to stay until the last day of the month.

I greet you, your dear wife, and the Groddecks cordially.

Yours,
Freud

1. George Sylvester Viereck (1884–1962), American journalist, writer, and editor, born in Munich. His translation of the *Lay Analysis* did not come about (see letter 1076, n. 1). See Viereck's representation of Freud in *Glimpses of the Great* (London, 1930). The Freud-Viereck correspondence is available in the Library of Congress.

2. Isaac Goldberg (1887–1938), *Havelock Ellis: A Biographical and Critical Survey*,

with a Supplementary Chapter on Mrs. Edith Ellis (London, 1926). See Freud's letter to Ellis of the day before in *Letters,* pp. 370f.

1078

Baden-Baden,
September 17, 1926

Dear Professor,

A few lines yet, before our departure for Paris.

A short time before his death, Glover was stopped by a policeman in a (supposedly) drunken state, because he was jeopardizing public safety with his car. The court sentenced him to pay a fine for "drunkenness." The affair was there in all the newspapers for people to read.—I can't say what the connection was between this incident and his sudden death—or even if there is a connection.

I just received the news from an American [female] student that Brill succeeded in seeing to it "that the bill before the New York State legislature to prevent non-medical analysis *is passed.*"[1] A lawyer claims that it will take about another two years before this decision is in force.—The publication by your *Viereck* and an appropriate propaganda are therefore very urgent.

I request the address of your relative in New York—our final address is: Hotel St. Andrew, Broadway and 72nd Street.

Kind regards from us both![2]

Ferenczi

Enclosed, the first example of the American advertisements![3]

    1. Quoted in English in the original [Trans.].

    2. Ferenczi's stay in the United States had a significant influence on the develpment of American psychoanalysis. For most of the time he stayed in New York, where, in addition to the lectures at the New School, he spoke at the following associations: the New York Psychiatric Society, the National Research Council, the Child Study Association of America, the New York Society for Clinical Psychiatry, the Greenwich Psychiatric Round Table Society, Columbia University, and last but not least, the Hungarian Medical Society in New York. Besides that, he gave lectures at the Medical Society in Philadelphia and the Psychoanalytic Association in Washington, D.C. He made contact with all the leading psychiatrists on the East Coast. In addition, he carried on a lively practice eight hours a day. The fact that he conducted training analyses with non-physicians and even encouraged them to organize led to strong tensions with the official representatives of American psychoanalysis.

    3. The advertisements have not been found.

1079

Semmering, September 19, 1926

Dear friend,

Before you entrust yourself to the sea in order to call on the land of the dollar barbarians, accept a cordial farewell greeting—for yourself and your dear wife—from me as a commitment to give me news about yourself often enough.

I received your Rank critique, find it decisive enough, somewhat flatter on the point about the analysis of the wolf-dream than it would have turned out with me. In this I am certainly laden with affect, of which you were able to sense only a reflection. I didn't recommend any changes. He will have enough as it is.

I haven't heard anything further from G. S. Viereck.

Yesterday Federn brought over to me the "Psychoanalytic Chapbook," published by him and Meng.[1] Meng and Alexander seem to be our best hope for the future.

Eitingon wants to visit us on the 25th of the month; we will decide the future of Imago, probably in favor of keeping it.

The weather is magically beautiful, everyone well. We are thinking with regret about the departure on the 30th of the month.

Now, in the spirit of the omnipotence of thoughts,[2] a forceful "good luck" for journey and return!

Yours,
Freud

1. Paul Federn and Heinrich Meng, eds., *Das psychoanalytische Volksbuch* (Stuttgart, 1926).
2. "Animism, Magic, and the Omnipotence of Thoughts," the third essay of *Totem and Taboo* (Freud 1912–13a).

1080

Dr. S. Ferenczi,
Broadway and 72. Street
(Hotel St. Andrew)
New York City[1]
September 23, 1926

Dear Professor,

I met Rank yesterday in the ocean line office. We had a discussion which lasted about an hour. He seems to be less optimistic. I did not leave him in doubt about the unbridgeable scientific difference between him and us.

Kind regards,
Ferenczi

1. Picture postcard: "Grand Hotel du Périgord, 2, rue de Grammont—Paris (2e arr.) R. C.: Seine 244-443."

1081

New York Address: Hotel St. Andrews, Corner Broadway and 72nd Street— N.Y. West[1]

ON BOARD THE
CUNARD
R.M.S. ANDANIA[2]

September 27, 1926

Dear Professor,

Our ship is also stopping in Halifax—I would never have thought that I would ever learn anything about this city other than that there are ice skates by that name—, and that is the occasion to write you a letter somewhat earlier than I thought.

Your letter made me and my wife very happy—the latter is especially grateful for Frau Professor's kind message, and will reply to it from New York as soon as possible.

Here, on board the—not very big, but tidy and quietly running ship, I am reminded every step of the way of our Argonaut journey back then.[3] [That is the way I will also refer to it in my first lecture, with an allusion to how little gold there was in the fleece[4] for us at the time.][5] Wonderful images emerge for me—the sunny days on board, the interesting conversations with you, the expectation of something unknown—, along with that, also reminiscences of deeply sad moments (which I kept secret at the time), in which I had to struggle with my—infantile—jealousy (on account of Jung). What all has not taken place since that time. How many have been exalted in the meantime, and how many, by their own fault—humbled.[6] It is thus a joy to sense that this long—long time has passed for both of us without anything seriously disturbing having ever come up in our personal and scientific relations. So, one can say, after all, that it will remain so between us. Naturally, at the same time I must also think about the great illness that you went through in the meantime, and rejoice in its fortunate, albeit not always pleasant, outcome.

Now, back to the present. The stay in Baden-Baden was, as always, a good convalescence for me. Even behind Groddeck's strange-sounding, occasionally confusing talks about illness, his "It," etc., I could see things which may still have a future ahead of them. Only, his intuition would need to have an appropriate logical and scientific sorting out. Perhaps I will get a chance to accomplish a part of this work.—Paris was beautiful, as always. In the Café de la Paix we repeated the good lunch (hors d'oeuvre) that we once enjoyed there. The French have not yet sobered up from their "gloire." Everything revolves around the victory at the Marne.[7] We felt little of the mood of peace and the League of Nations.—I spent almost the whole time in Paris with Dr. Inman from London, who called on me there.—He, too, is somewhat Groddeckish, but without philosophical ambitions.

Between Paris and Cherbourg I was overcome by a very severe colic—perhaps a last, desperate attempt to stop me from continuing this adventure. Since this failed, I feel completely well.—(Not so my wife, who, after suffering from seasickness for three days, is only now beginning to recover.)

On the discussion with Rank in Paris, I have to add as a postscript that he—evidently to ward off competition from me—will likewise give lectures at the (Old) School for Social Research. Mine are supposed to be given at the *New* School for Social Research.—Further, he made the suggestion to me that we should go together, "at least in the question of lay analysis." I told him that, in this question, my point of view coincides entirely with yours. He spoke a few times about the fact that, in the end, he had nothing to fear; he is, after all, analyzing physicians and pupils, so he is not a healing zealot. It is more interesting for him altogether to do such educational work. I replied to him that I, on the contrary, have learned, and hope to learn, something only from the analysis of severe neuroses. This statement of his brilliantly confirms your explanation of the origin of his technique from the circumstance that he has almost never analyzed serious cases of neurosis.—This confining himself to teaching is, incidentally, possibly a symptom of disillusionment: perhaps he wants to disparage his competence in the neuroses himself. By the way, his acting modest is perhaps not so above board—he did also tell me that he was just now working on two new books, among them, a "genetic psychology."[8]—"So that we don't offer the Americans the theatrics of a dogfight"—he opined further—"I shouldn't attack his book in the New York group." I naturally did *not* promise him that.

You may be right about the "flatness," characterized as such by you, of my critique of the wolf-dream-palin[9]-analysis. Not unintentionally did I leave everything affective out of the critique; the purely factual objections, I thought, then have an effect that is all the more weighty. In any case, I *completely share* your views about the inappropriateness, indeed, the impudence of his method of operation, so that I will give you a *free hand* in changing the text as you see fit.

In Cherbourg I also found a kind letter from Dr. Frankwood Williams, the American with whom we spoke at the Semmering.[10] I sent him from Baden-Baden a brief communication for his journal "Mental Hygiene" (about the significance of Freud for the mental hygiene movement).[11] He will have it translated and published immediately.—Incidentally, Dr. Williams was meanwhile in Switzerland with Rank for two weeks. (I can report on the side that Rank is putting his child up in Switzerland, while Frau Rank is supposed to live in Paris.)

Another—friendly and enthusiastic—letter was also there, from H. Sweetse,[12] the American patient of *Reik's*, who has got it into his head somehow to arouse the interest of the Rockefeller Foundation for psychoanalysis—with my help. I will try, but I don't believe in it much.

Regards,
Ferenczi and

greet just as cordially Frau Professor, Fräulein Minna, and Anna from us both.—

1. Written by hand above the preprinted letterhead.
2. Preprinted logo with a representation of the ship.
3. The trip to America in 1909, taken together with Jung.
4. The reference is to Jason and the Argonauts, those heroes of Greek mythology who set sail on the ship *Argo* to fetch the Golden Fleece, which was in the possession of King Aetes of Colchis, on the Black Sea, a quest in which they were ultimately successful after undergoing many adventures.
5. Brackets in the original.
6. "But he that is greatest among you shall be your servant. And whosoever shall exalt himself shall be abased; and he that shall humble himself shall be exalted" (Matthew 23:11–12; Luke 14:11, 18:14).
7. The Allied victory at the battle of the Marne on September 1914, which effectively destroyed the German Schlieffen Plan (the encirclement of Paris).
8. *Grundzüge einer genetischen Psychologie—Auf Grund der Psychoanalyse der Ichstruktur* [Basic Characteristics of a Genetic Psychology—on the Basis of the Psychoanalysis of the Structure of the Ego], 2 parts, Vienna, 1927–28, perhaps Rank's most significant work, which prefigures many aspects of so-called object relations theory.
9. Greek for "renewed, repeated" analysis.
10. Frankwood Earl Williams (1883–1936), from New York, received his M.D. from the University of Michigan in 1912. He was a socialist and a central figure in the American mental hygiene movement. From 1917 he was the editor of *Mental Hygiene* and from 1922 to 1931 medical director of the National Committee for Mental Hygiene. He was a faculty member of the New School for Social Research, co-editor of the *Psychoanalytic Quarterly*, and a member of the board of directors of the New York Psychoanalytic Institute. He was an analysand both of Ferenczi's and of Rank's, whose views he increasingly espoused. See Johannes C. Pols, "Managing the Mind: The Culture of American Mental

Hygiene, 1910–1950" (Ph.D. diss., University of Pennsyvania, 1997). When Ferenczi visited Freud at the Semmering before his departure, they had "occasion to enlighten Dr. Frankwood Williams—an influential person from New York, who was analyzed by Rank and was one of his hopes—about Rank's distortion of analysis" (Freud to Jones, *Freud/Jones*, August 30, 1926, p. 604).

11. "Freud's Importance for the Mental Hygiene Movement" (Ferenczi 1926, 274), published in *Mental Hygiene* 10 (1926): 673–676.

12. Evidently Arthur Sweetser (1888–1968), writer and journalist, M.A. Harvard, 1912, a friend of Dorothy Burlingham's. During the war, Sweetser was a war correspondent, after 1918 was with the League of Nations, and was a co-founder of an English school in Geneva. He was the father of Harold and Adelaide, both analysands of Anna Freud's. A year later Sweetser gave Freud a contribution of $5,000 (Freud to Eitingon, July 15 and July 29, 1927, Sigmund Freud Copyrights). See Burlingham, *The Last Tiffany*.

1082

Hotel St. Andrew
(Broadway and 72nd St.)
New York, October 10, 1926

Dear Professor,

Finally, a Sunday afternoon, when I have some free time to write.

So—to continue my last letter—, our ship held up well up to the last day; the weather was very favorable, especially on the last days of the trip. But I became quite unwell on a somewhat stormy evening—strangely enough, not sick to my stomach, but I again had intestinal ailments—, certainly an example of the fact that with these things it is also a matter of phenomena of regression; my intestinal tract was always not very capable of resistance.

Last Saturday, on October 2, at ten in the evening, we were already anchored at the quarantine island; but they didn't let us get any farther, and it wasn't until Sunday, on the morning of the 3rd, that we were permitted to tread the soil of America. On the pier I was greeted by the hurly-burly, already well known to me, of hanging around for hours on account of passport and customs inspection. But to greet us specially, there also appeared Herr Dr. Johnson,[1] the director of the "New School for Social Research," where I am lecturing, as well as a small group of former patients and pupils. A lady from this group procured an apartment for us and helped me fill my hours. In the afternoon we took a brief tour. Not far from our hotel begins Riverside Drive, which you probably still recall (along the Hudson River), which we drove along; then we went straight across Central Park toward the east[2]—finally up part of Broadway, home.—The impression of the city was imposing, but not attractive in the slightest; *everything* that could be called friendly or kind is missing. The difference from Paris, where we last spent four days, made the contrast with Europe more clearly palpable. My relationship to the city itself has also not improved much since. On the first day and during the first night, the street noise disturbed me uncommonly; I already thought about having to move out immediately. Strangely, I accommodated myself quickly, and the noise doesn't disturb my work anymore.

Things went relatively better for me here with regard to my relationship with people. Some of the patients are giving me interesting material for observation. Among the pupils, I can single out for you Dr. Kempf[3] as the most interesting, and the person who is perhaps most significant for the future in America.

In the mornings I work from eight to one, in the afternoons from three to six, so, altogether eight hours a day. On Saturday, only in the morning. Instead of that, I have a lecture every Tuesday evening, and every Wednesday a seminar with the group of lay analysts. Most of the evenings have been filled up to now with invitations pro and contra, partly also the lunchtime. An invitation to lunch[4] is now here a practical and time-saving way of taking care of business.—

The first lecture, which caused me considerable worry on account of my very defective English, went quite well. Brill was entrusted by the director of the school with opening the course—and he did it in a friendly manner and one which was flattering to me. There were approximately 300 people in the audience, of both sexes, among them many physicians, very many university auditors, and countless laymen. Each one pays twenty dollars for the course, and since I get 2,000, the school earns 4,000 with this business. That pleases me, because otherwise the deficit from the deposit paid on the part of an enthusiastic [female] student would have been taken off my honorarium.

I first talked about the first trip with you, about Stanley Hall, James, and Putnam. Then I started right away with the metapsychology. This time, you see, I am systematic with regard to the historical presentation, which is familiar to me and which I also followed. It is interesting that the last advances in your constructions already make possible such a treatment of the material.—The audience seems soon to have adapted to the broken English which I proffered them—they were very benevolent and seemed eager to learn. The next lecture will give me fewer difficulties after this good beginning.

I didn't share the date of my arrival with Brill, to whom I reported my coming two to three weeks ago, but who didn't react to my last letter, although he learned of my arrival through Dr. Johnson and announced himself by telephone right on the first day; still on the same evening, he came to see me in my hotel, also invited me to a dinner at his place in the meantime, and, on the occasion of my being here, is organizing a second evening, at which all the more important (?) members of the Association are supposed to be present.

He is friendly, as always, but he grumbles about the statements from you, which come to him from all sides, about the unfitness of all Americans (including him). I attempted to inform him gently that the Americans are, in fact, in need of instruction, whereupon he informed me that he is quite willing to found an institute with the money (I believe 30,000 dollars) which is already at his disposal, and to invite a European faculty to it. He seems to be much less accessible in the question of lay analysis, although he is by far not so aggressive in this question as, e.g., Oberndorf[5] and Stern.[6] The latter, strangely, lodged a grievance with Brill and complained that I had not informed the Association of my coming and only made contact with the "New School." They acted as though they were insulted; in reality, they all knew for a long time that I was coming and didn't contact me. I am curious as to how that evening at Brill's will go.— In the first lecture I declared myself with all candor in favor of lay analysis. Dr. Jelliffe,[7] who was present, shook his head at the mention. I spoke in considerable detail about your last book.—

In the meantime, some kind of "law" for the State of New York regarding further impediments to physicians from Europe and other states from setting up shop seems to have been accepted. The lay analysts (they call themselves "non-medical analysts"[8] here) can only work as practitioners of "Psycho-Analytical Education"; the medical society (American Medical Association) forbids its members any contact with "quacks." Hence, supposedly, the resistance of the New York group to lay analysis. I am curious as to whether anything can be done there, and if so, what. Unfortunately, I have every reason to believe that our friend Jones, who is in lively contact, personally and by letter, with Brill, will further widen the rift between New York and us. In any case, even the so thoroughly trained Mrs. Powers,[9] even though she is a medical doctor and graduated from the Vienna training institute, is having difficulties in being accepted into the Association because her old California diploma won't be accepted by the authorities in Albany without a reexamination. For that reason she also can't be accepted now as a member of the New York Psychoanalytic Society! I will try to intervene in her interest.

I am animating the little non-medical[10] group to organize itself.

Dr. Frankwood Williams, with whom we conferred at the Semmering, was—although he is evidently very intimate with Rank (whom I haven't seen here)—also very courteous to me. Already this month he is publishing the article that I wrote at his request (The Significance of Freud for Mental Hygiene). It could be (in part) due to his urging that a joint meeting of the Mental Hygiene Society and the New York Neurological Society is being planned, at which I am supposed to give a lecture. In addition to that, Brill is expecting a lecture from me (in the New York group), Coriat is inviting me to Boston, and Dr. Craven[11] to Washington. I will postpone these latter excursions until after New Year's.

Immediately after my arrival I contacted, in writing and by telephone, the lawyer of the Burlingham family. In the meantime, he has prepared everything for the planned consultation—but now, *Herr Burlingham* Senior[12] wants to confer with the doctors *beforehand*, so that my visit with Dr. Burlingham[13] will suffer a probably not too long postponement. As soon as I am in a position to do so, I will write to Mrs. Burlingham about the result, but in the meantime I ask Fräulein Anna to inform her of the facts of the case. According to the wording of Herr Cravath's[14] letter, incidentally, Herr Burlingham Senior is *quite prepared,* in fact, *pleased* about my visit to his son.

I will next make a visit to Eitingon's family and to your relatives; to the latter when Frau Heller-Bernays (Judith) arrives.[15]

In order that this letter is finally sent off, I will refrain from completeness and will fill you in on everything else that happens or has happened in brief communications.

Please present this letter also to Fräulein Anna and Eitingon.
With kindest regards to you all from my wife and from me!

Yours,
Ferenczi

1. Alvin Saunders Johnson (1874–1971), renowned economist and political scientist. He received his Ph.D. from Columbia in 1902 and was a professor at various renowned universities: Columbia, Cornell, and Stanford, among others. He was editor of *The New Republic* and, from 1923, director of the *New School for Social Research.*
2. This word is written in English in the original [Trans.].
3. Edward J. Kempf (1885–1971), M.D., a member of the American Psychoanalytic Society, in analysis with Ferenczi (Ferenczi's *Rundbrief* of December 13, 1926, British Psycho-Analytical Society). He is the author of *Psychopathology* (St. Louis, 1920).
4. The words "lunchtime" and "lunch" are written in English in the original [Trans.].
5. Clarence P. Oberndorf (1882–1954), an American psychiatrist and psychoanalyst, received his M.D. in 1906. Together with Brill, he was founder of the New York Psychoanalytic Society (1911) and twice president of the American Psychoanalytic Association; he was a determined opponent of lay analysis and an analysand of Freud's, though the latter had little respect for him.
6. See letter 860, n. 5.
7. See letter 882 and n. 6.
8. This term enclosed in quotation marks, as well as the one immediately following, are written in English in the original [Trans.].
9. Lillian Delger Powers. As Freud's analysand and supervisee of Helene Deutsch, Hermann Nunberg, and Wilhelm Reich, she was trained in Vienna from 1924 to 1926.

She underwent further control analysis with Ferenczi in America from 1926 to 1927 (accounting notation of Freud's, June 1925, Library of Congress; Powers to Bertram Lewin, March 5, 1934, Library of Congress). She is entered in the subsequent membership list as a member of the New York Society (*Zeitschrift* 16 [1930]: 556).

10. The term is written in English in the original [Trans.].

11. Evidently Philip Graven, a member of the Washington-Baltimore Society, in whose house Ferenczi lived during his subsequent stay in Washington. See Douglas Noble and Donald L. Burnham, *History of the Washington Psychoanalytic Society and the Washington Psychoanalytic Institute* (Washington, D.C., 1969), p. 15.

12. Charles Culp Burlingham (1858–1959), renowned New York lawyer and public figure.

13. Robert Burlingham, Dorothy's husband, a surgeon, who was hospitalized several times for a manic-depressive illness. His father supported him and tried to estrange his grandchildren from Dorothy's influence and that of psychoanalysis. For that reason he and his father went to Vienna in August 1929, but were unsuccessful. Robert consulted Ferenczi, but did not go into analysis with him. He later became Amsden's analysand (see below).

14. Reading uncertain; the letter between the two "a"s has been written over; it could also be an "f" or a "p." Probably Paul Drennan Cravath (1861–1940), LL.D., a respected New York lawyer (Cravath, Henderson & de Gusdorff).

15. See letter 97 and n. 3.

1083

Vienna, October 23, 1926
IX., Berggasse 19

Dear friend,

Received both of your letters, the one from the ship and the first from the city. Very pleased that you are letting us experience jointly everything that happens to you there. Let us hope that America doesn't change anything in this inclination of yours as you go along.

Don't expect any recompense from me. Little is happening with us, and I have little to relate. Jones writes that the clinic is open[1] and already has much to do. In Berlin they have decided to move the birthday greeting for Groddeck to the top of no. 4 of the Zeitschrift.[2] I told him by telegram that my Ego and my Id congratulate his It, and hope that it may please its inscrutable decree to allow him a long happy lease of life, whereupon he replied cordially, but quite humorlessly.[3] In order not to lose complete contact with the Viennese, I have decided to invite the (extended) leadership for one evening a month, which found much applause.[4] I, myself, have sometimes more, sometimes less catarrh (at present more), along with the corresponding disruptions, and am otherwise playing with my five people. There is no lack of new problems, but I am not very eager to find solutions, and, above all, terribly uneager to work, which, in bourgeois life, one calls lazy. I am resting, so to speak, on my laurels.

Anna is working enthusiastically, is pleased about the successes with her children, and is preparing her course for November.⁵ I think she is going forward. Mrs. Burlingham is still picking us up in the morning for an excursion by auto, on which poor Wolf⁶ can then run free. She has been apprised of your good news. Your letter is going off to Eitingon tomorrow.

You probably already know by way of Lajos Lévy that I have received 10,000 Swiss francs from Emil Freund for the fund—it is supposed to be kept secret out of patriotic motives.

In matters of lay analysis you can go right ahead and move the emphasis away from medical matters and onto the necessity for proper training, and thus abandon all laypeople who don't fulfill this condition. It's not too much of a shame about Powers, who naturally formally has all rights; she is of a stupidity which is rare even in women and even in physicians, far in excess of the human mean.

You don't write about what your wife says about America. Greet her cordially for me, and don't forget that everything from you is now more interesting than usual.

Cordially,
Freud

1. The opening of the psychoanalytic clinic in London on September 28, 1926, made possible through a contribution of an ex-patient, Pryns Hopkins (Jones III, 128). "The staff is madeup [sic] of a Director, myself, Assistant Director, Dr. Edward Glover, nine Physicians, Dr. Bryan, Cole, Eder, Herford, Inman, Payne, Rickman, Riggall, and Stoddart, with five Clinical Assistants" (Jones's *Rundbrief* of October 16, 1926, Sigmund Freud Copyrights).
2. The contribution (Ernst Simmel, "Georg Groddeck zum sechzigsten Geburtstag" [Georg Groddeck on his Sixtieth Birthday]) was placed at the end of the volume (*Zeitschrift* 12 [1926]: 591–595).
3. See Freud's telegram of October 13, 1926, and Groddeck's reply of October 17 in *Freud/Groddeck*, p. 95.
4. "Besides the members of the Board, the older and somehow significant members were invited, and a certain fraction of those who came in most recently. The first such evening took place on Friday, November 12, and lasted over four hours" (Freud's *Rundbrief* of November 23, 1926, Sigmund Freud Copyrights).
5. A course on the technique of child analysis at the training institute of the Vienna Society. "These lectures have hitherto found much approval and were attended by forty to fifty people" (Freud's *Rundbrief* of November 23, 1926, Sigmund Freud Copyrights). Published under the title *Einführung in die Technik der Kinderanalyse* [Introduction to the Technique of Child Analysis] (Vienna, 1927).
6. Anna Freud's German shepherd.

1084

Hotel St. Andrew
Broadway at 72nd Street
New York[1]
November 30, 1926

Dear Professor,

This is only a brief precursor to a letter that I have been writing to you in spirit *for weeks*. I fear that you have already entrusted emissaries with the task of investigating whether I am still alive. Yes! and how! I am following your advice, "Don't let yourself be sucked dry by the Americans," *where possible*, and in spite of this, I have been in a state of breathless, intense activity for weeks. It will abate somewhat in two weeks.

So, for now, only this much, that my program will be carried to its conclusion seemingly successfully, that I am gaining a good insight into the ψα situation here, am fighting on three fronts (Rank, Brill, public opinion),[2] and that the cause, as well as I, personally, should get some use out of my being here. If my health continues to hold up, it will have been an interesting episode—pleasure I can't call it.

In addition to the weekly lecture and the lay seminar, this week I am giving a special lecture in the Society for Research on Children—and next week one on "the ψα explanantion of Gulliver fantasies" as an opening lecture in the New York Psychiatric Society.[3] (Actually also a reckoning up with Rank before the circle of scientific physicians.)

Burlingham case is stuck for the moment. I seem to have succeeded in talking him out of receiving me—but Dr. Salmon[4]—a devoted friend of the Tiffany family—tells me that *in a few weeks* I should have the opportunity to see him. Meanwhile, reassure Mrs. Dorothy, whom I greet cordially, as well as all your dear ones! Everywhere here, people are asking about Anna Freud. I see her here, already in spirit, repeating your lectures.

My English is terrible, but the cause that I represent seems to be stronger than all aesthetic reservations. The lecture is always oversubscribed. I let my initial nervousness drop and do what I can. So—details soon—only now in a hurry.—

Yours,
Ferenczi

1. Preprinted letterhead with logo.
2. The last two words are written in English in the original [Trans.].
3. "Gulliver Phantasies" (Ferenczi 1927, 280); lecture given at the annual meeting of the New York Society for Clinical Psychiatry on December 9, 1926.
4. Probably Thomas William Salmon (1876–1927), M.D. Albany Medical College, 1899; he was medical director of the National Committee for Mental Hygiene from 1912

to 1921 and a professor of psychiatry at Columbia University. See Ferenczi's *Rundbrief* of December 13, 1926: "Dr. Salmon . . . with whom I had long conversations, uses psychoanalysis in his psychological practice with a great deal of understanding. He told me that he would rather give up everything he learned about medicine than what he learned from Freud" (British Psycho-Analytical Society).

1085

Vienna, December 13, 1926
IX., Berggasse 19

Dear friend,

Really, I had already determined the day on which I intended to cable you, when your dear wife's letter[1] came, from which it could be inferred with certainty that you are still living and are working very hard. I now thank you for the "pre-letter" of November 30, which finally arrived, and declare myself completely satisfied with more frequent such pre-letters, for the "full letters" could be too long in coming. In the meantime, a Rundbrief from us[2] will have reached you, which contains everything of general interest that is worth communicating.

So, I have little to add in the way of a postscript. Now as before—if you want to hear from me—I leave the burden to others, you among them, unfortunately also Anna, and will continue my inactivity, which is hardly interrupted by four hours of work. Excuse [is], that the catarrhs annoy and disturb me too much; otherwise, I am well. On Christmas Day, we—wife and I—intend finally to go to Berlin to see the big and the small children. It can't be postponed anymore. Ernst is supposed to go to Jerusalem in the spring to build Dr. Weizmann[3] a villa, Oli finally has his own place to live; I know only one of my four grandsons, and he was a year old at the time.

All other interests fade in the face of this adventurous intention. Besides, not much is happening in old Europe, and I have had so little occasion to write to you that I don't know what I have already and what I haven't yet told you. E.g., that on October 25 I called upon Tagore[4] about his request; that last week, another Indian, Dos Gupta, a philosopher from Calcutta,[5] was with me—my quota of Indians has now been filled for quite a long time—, that a psychiatrist from Rio de Janeiro[6] brought over to me his textbook on psychiatry, in which ΨA fills a large chapter—I don't allow in anyone at all but exotics; Americans have already been scared off and don't show up anymore. Meng was a very pleasant visitor; the man is very agreeable, a hard worker, and he achieves extraordinary things in the way of sensible propaganda by means of books for the general public, and periodicals. He also wants to undertake the preparation of the Congress, which is supposed to take place in the fall, probably in Stuttgart.

Frankwood Williams has requested by letter my authorization for the translation of Lay Analysis. I had to reply to him that I had already given it to G. S. Viereck, whom he is supposed to contact. Since then I haven't heard anything from him, also nothing from Viereck. Adler is also supposed to be in America now;[7] the Americans will be all ears when they hear from him that one has to cover one's back, otherwise one gets into the feminine line, which is held in such low repute.[8] But perhaps he will discover there that the striving for power is also very widespread in the New World. The lucky fellow has only theories that are constantly being confirmed.

Mrs. Burlingham is staying very close to us; she insists on taking me and Wolf for a drive every morning; for that we have adorned the Ford with a bronze figure of a witch and an internal clock.

I am intentionally writing nothing about America.

Cordially,
Freud

1. The letter has not been found.
2. Of November 23, 1926 (Sigmund Freud Copyrights).
3. Chaim Weizmann (1874–1952), Jewish scholar and statesman, former professor of biochemistry at Manchester. He was the founder of the Democratic-Zionist coalition (1902), a substantive participant in the coming into being of the Balfour Declaration. From 1920 to 1931 and 1935 to 1946, he was president of the World Zionist Organization. After Israel's independence, he became its first president.
4. Rabindranath Tagore (1861–1941), Indian poet, painter, educator, and philosopher. He was a representative of India's intellectual clash with the West in the first half of the twentieth century. He received the Nobel Prize for Literature in 1913 (see also Jones III, 128).
5. According to the kind suggestion from Sonu Shamdasani, this could refer to Surendranath Dasgupta (1885–1952), the famous Indian philosopher, author of, among other things, *A History of Indian Philosophy* and *Yoga as Philosophy and Religion* (both London, 1924). C. G. Jung met him in 1938 in Calcutta and induced him to come to Zurich and lecture to the Psychological Club. See S. Shamdasani, ed., *C. G. Jung: The Psychology of Kundalini Yoga* (Princeton, 1996), pp. xxi–xxii.
6. This person has not been identified. He is, however, evidently not José Pirés Porto-Carrero, as Jones (III, 129) claims, from whom Freud did not receive a letter until 1928 (Freud's *Rundbrief* of January 24, 1928, British Psycho-Analytical Society).
7. On his first lecture tour in America, in which he gave more than thirty lectures "in New York, Boston, Providence, Chicago, Philadelphia, Cincinnati, Milwaukee, in California and in Indiana. He spoke at universities, among other places, at Harvard under the aegis of Morton Prince, to physicians, religious communities, educators, in hospitals and schools, to parents and teachers." Bernhard Handlbauer, *Die Entstehungsgeschichte der Individualpsychologie Alfred Adlers* [The History of the Development of Alfred Adler's Individual Psychology] (Vienna, 1984), p. 356.
8. Freud's sarcasm has to do both with Adler's theories of "masculine protest" and the "securities" to the "lines of retreat" (*Rückzugslinien*) to the feminine role and with the role, little esteemed by him, which women assumed in America.

1086

Hotel St. Andrew
Broadway at 72nd Street
New York
December 13th, 1926[1]

Dear Professor:

I have not much to add to the general account given in the Rundbrief.[2] Knowing the intimate relationship between Brill and Jones, I, of course, mitigated my observations about the New York members.

Dr. Feigenbaum[3] seems to be the only member who is enthusiastic about the work and is more than just a member of the Analytical Trade Union. He attends the seminar which I give to the lay analysts.

In my lecture to the Child Study Association, I mentioned Anna Freud's pioneer work in the Grenzgebiet of Psycho-Analysis and Child Education.

We spent a weekend with your sister, Mrs. Bernays,[4] in New Rochelle. She is in excellent health. Her house and estate are exceedingly beautiful. Mr. and Mrs. Heller were there, too. Mr. Edward couldn't come but I met him at one of my lectures and we will soon have a talk about financial questions. I am afraid that he didn't like my English very much at the New School lectures, but the general benevolence of my audience prevents me from being discouraged.

I have not yet called on the relatives of my friend Eitingon but I will do it after Christmas.

Yesterday Mrs. Heller's sister came up to speak to us in a restaurant on Fifth Ave. opposite her antiquity shop. We hope to see more of her.

Radó asked me to send him a report of my work and observations in America. I entitle Max to use out of the Rundbrief as much as seems suitable to him for this purpose.

I hope soon to see Viereck and have a talk with him about the English translation of the "Lay Analysis."

I am very, very glad about the excellent news you give of your state of health and, seeing your renewed activity in the Society, I am glad not to have accepted your urgent invitation to move to Vienna.

Please send this letter to Eitingon, too, with my very best wishes for them.

With all our best wishes for the New Year to you and all your family, I am

In old friendship,

Ferenczi

1. The letter is typewritten; only the signature, "Ferenczi," is handwritten. The entire text, with the exception of the word "Grenzgebiet" [border region] and the final phrase, "In old friendship," is written in English in the original [Trans.].

2. *Rundbrief* of the same day (British Psycho-Analytical Society).

3. Dorian Feigenbaum (1887–1937), a member of the American Psychoanalytic Association and the New York Psychoanalytic Society; he later became co-editor of the *Psychoanalytic Quarterly*.

4. Freud's relatives in New York were his sister Anna Bernays (1858–1955) and her five children: Judith ("Ditha") Heller (1885–1977); Leah ("Lucy") Wiener (1886–1980); Edward Louis (1891–1995), married to Doris Fleischmann (1891/2–1980); Hella (1893–1970); and Martha Randolph (1894–1979).

1087

Vienna, January 2, 1927
IX., Berggasse 19

Dear friend,

Cheers to the New Year! May everything that is hopeful for you remain good, and all that is adverse disintegrate. Since this world has room for all possibilities, good wishes can also be realized for once.

I returned this morning with my wife from Berlin, where I had gone on December 25.[1] Was up to everything, but fitted with bad prostheses. The, let us hope, better, new one had not been finished.

Naturally, I kept my distance from all professional matters; I saw only Eitingon, who almost counts as family, and Simmel obligated me for a consultation, on the day of the departure, no less. As a deterrent, I demanded 1,000 marks; it was agreed to, but not paid. Now, had I been "stood up," and the eagerness came from that? I also saw Frau Abraham, hardly recognized her, her fate has changed her so.

Otherwise, I devoted my time to my big and small children, four of each kind, and had nothing but pleasant impressions of them. Both couples are doing well, and the children, the three archangels and little Evchen, are charming, by all accounts.[2]

Yes, I also chatted away two hours with Einstein; he came to Ernst's with his wife in order to see me. He is cheerful, confident, and kind, understands as much about psychology as I do about physics, and so we had a very good conversation.

Eitingon already showed me your Rundbrief; I will send in to him the addendum that I found here. I find the group's behavior toward you revolting. I find all your news very interesting.

René Spitz assures me in a picture postcard from Victoria Nyanza that psychoanalysis is now also being debated about in central Africa. You probably know that Frau Kempf[3] has requested analysis with me, but only for three months. I wrote and told her no. But she cabled that she will come on March 1.

I will write more next time, only wanted to acknowledge your letter; for today I greet you and Frau G. cordially.

Yours,
Freud

1. Freud's first trip since his major operation. He visited his grandchildren and underwent "a very painful treatment with Pichler" which was supposed to "dull the sensitivity to the new muzzle" (Freud to Eitingon, January 8, 1927, Sigmund Freud Copyrights).
2. The couples Henny and Oliver, as well as Lux and Ernst, with whom Freud stayed. For the children, see letter 976 and n. 2, as well as letter 977 and n. 5.
3. See letter 1082 and n. 3.

1088

[Rundbrief][1]
INTERNATIONALE ZEITSCHRIFT FÜR PSYCHOANALYSE
Herausgegeben von Prof. Dr. Sigm. Freud
Redigiert von Dr. M. Eitingon, Dr. S. Ferenczi und Dr. Sándor Radó

New York, January 9, 1927

Dear friends,

I thank you for the Rundbriefe and continue my report. Of the psychologists in America, Dr. Watson, the behaviorist,[2] is probably the most active. In the "New School for Social Research," where I am also lecturing, he gave a series of lectures about his doctrine, which essentially consists of the application of Pavlov's experiments on conditioned reflexes on human "behavior" in general. In completely failing to realize the complicatedness of "behavior"[3] (that is probably the best translation of the word behaviourism[4]), and without the slightest sense for the historical, in complete denial of the significance of heredity on top of that, he thinks he has theoretically solved the whole problem of the psychic with the aid of the simplest experiments which he performed on animals, newborns, and children. Indeed, he considers himself called upon, also in a prophylactic regard, to be able to replace all psychology, naturally also psychoanalysis. In reality, in his behavioristic experiments he unconsciously—or in misperceiving the sources of his knowledge—utilizes the knowledge that he gained from analytic sources. After ending his course of instruction, he organized a discussion in the school, to which he invited Adolf Meyer (Johns Hopkins University),[5] William A. White (Washington),[6] Dr. Edward Kempf (New York), Jelliffe, and Blumgart.[7] Meyer's lecture, which I read in manuscript, is the most confused; it is full of controlled wrath against psychoanalysis, which he doesn't dare to attack openly, but casts doubt upon with allusions like "financial exploitation," "theoretical formalism," "sexual drilling," etc. At the same time, he can't offer anything positive himself, that is to say: what he offers is undigested psychoanalysis + resistances. In contrast to Bleuler, who alternatingly expresses himself for one *year* pro, then contra psychoanalysis, Meyer contradicts himself in every other *sentence*. Result: unscientific confusion.

White is more insightful; his resistance shows itself in "eclecticism." Freud, Jung, Adler—he sees everything on the same plane. (He told me he has to remain *objective.*)

Kempf, a very talented man with many original ideas, approaches psychoanalysis from the physiological side. His theory about the way the autonomic nervous system works, about its connection with the cerebrospinal mechanisms, which are standardized and regulated by the psyche, deserves attention.

Jelliffe and Blumgart were, I think, not energetic and skillful enough in their defense, even though both are reliable psychoanalysts. Jelliffe is too occupied with his own theories about paleopsychology, but he was, on the whole, the best representative of psychoanalysis in the discussion. Blumgart is nice, but not very talented.

Watson finally didn't shy away from challenging me to a duel, either. He gave a lecture in an elegant ladies' club ("Cosmopolitan Club"), had me invited to dinner by the president, and personally apostrophized me in his lecture. In the lecture he called everything which is called "psychology," "psyche," "conscious," "unconscious";[8] unscientific, mystical; the only thing scientific is behaviour and what can be derived from it. He explains the most complicated psychic processes in the most simplistic way as "conditioned reflexes," etc.

Although unprepared, I had to counter him. It was not difficult to show him the nonsensicalness of his denial of psychic reality (although I doubt whether that would have done him any good). I conceded that the form of exactness that natural science demands is not at the disposal of psychoanalysis. We can't measure the psychic. *Freud's* metapsychology is a temporary expedient until the esteemed psychologists and behaviorists complete their work. But one can't wait that long, and making use of introspectively gained facts brings not only a deeper understanding but also help, which one doesn't get from the scientific quarter. I would—I said—perhaps send white rats and rabbits, but not people, to Watson for treatment.—The audience seemed as though they were redeemed, and they were happy about the fact that one perhaps doesn't have to give up one's soul after all.[9]

Within the psychoanalytic movement itself, the semiannual meeting of the "American Psycho-Analytical Association" on the second day of Christmas was the main event of the last few weeks. About forty to fifty members from the whole country appeared; among them six to seven New Yorkers. The provincials made a not unfavorable impression on me from a scientific perspective. *White* in Washington lets his people, among other things, also freely do analytic research; in the St. Elizabeth Asylum there, they have enough opportunities (6,000 patients). *Dr. Reeds*[10] (Cincinnati) spoke with much understanding. *Trigant Burrow*[11] pleaded in favor of his "group analysis"—I had to speak energetically in opposition to this technique. *Kempf* spoke, not uninterestingly, about analogies between animal and human behavior (especially in relation to jealousy, hate, fear, shame).—Jelliffe's son-in-law Stragnell[12] seems to be the joker of the Association, otherwise nothing outstanding.[13] Finally, I gave a lecture "on the newer problems of psychoanalysis"[14] (ego and id, dissolution of the Oedipus complex, "trauma of birth," etc., vehemently letting loose against Rank in the latter part). The auditorium seemed to have been in need of instruction; they obviously thanked me very honestly for it. To be sure, two colleagues asked me about the lecture: "Please, what actually is the superego?"[15] (Just as in the well-known joke about the American medical student after the course on ophthalmology: "It was very interesting, only there is one thing I don't know: is the iris situated in front of, or behind, the pupil?")

Rank is said to have suddenly fallen ill and unexpectedly gone to Europe. The newest reports about him are worse than everything that we already know about him. He is supposed to have bragged about being able to cure homosexuality, which Freud declared incurable, in six weeks. Dr. W. A. *White* in one of his lectures announced a work by Rank in which he (Rank) attacks the most fundamental theoretical tenets of Freudian psychoanalysis. The paper is supposed to be published in the January issue of the Psycho-Analytic Review.[16]—

Adler is also here, is making very many advertisements, is giving lectures in four to five places, among others, also in my "New School." What I have heard about the contents is *extremely* simple.

The American Psycho-Analytic Association also wanted to pass a formidable resolution against lay analysis. I only succeeded, with a great deal of difficulty, in getting them to postpone passing the resolution until they had read Freud's "Lay Analysis."[17]—The New Yorkers (Stern, Oberndorf, Meyer,[18] Lehrman,[19] Kardiner,[20] Frink) were all very aggressive in their opposition to the laymen. (Frink now seems, N.B., to be recovered and to want to continue his work in New York.)—*Pierce Clark*[21] is active, but agitating one-sidedly in favor of a new technique ("forced fantasies" in psychoses). I haven't seen his institution yet.

I had a discussion with Professor's nephew *Edward Bernays*. We want to make an attempt to collect some money for the purposes of the Verlag and the Institute. The success is doubtful, to be sure. I am continuing my lectures in the New School and am working the whole day; I am already somewhat tired of America. I longingly await European news.

Kindest regards!
Ferenczi

1. The letter is a carbon copy, which is written in a different hand (probably Gizella Ferenczi's) up to "otherwise nothing outstanding" (in the seventh paragraph; see n. 13). The remainder, likewise a carbon copy, is written in Ferenczi's hand.

2. John Broadus Watson (1878–1958), the renowned American psychologist. From 1908 to 1920 he was a professor in Baltimore. He was the main founder of behaviorism, which rejects self-observation and confines itself to the examination of stimulus and reaction. In so doing, it bases itself on Pavlov's doctrine of conditioned reflex. Ivan Petrovitch Pavlov (1849–1936), Russian physiologist. From 1895 to 1924 he was a professor in Leningrad; in 1904 he received the Nobel Prize for Medicine for his work on the physiology of digestion. According to Pavlov, conditioned reflexes and their conditioning are the principle of all "mental" activity; psychology can thus be linked to a physiology of conditioning. Although both theories were untenable in their original form, they had an immense influence on the development of psychology in the twentieth century.

3. Ferenczi uses the word *Gehaben*, which is probably best translated as "affected behavior" [Trans.].

4. This word is written in English in the original [Trans.]

5. Adolf Meyer (1866–1950), born in Switzerland, possibly the most influential American psychiatrist of the first half of the twentieth century. After emigrating to the United States (1892) and holding responsible positions at Worcester, Ward's Island, and Cornell University Medical College, from 1910 to 1941 he was a professor at Johns Hopkins University and director of its Henry Phipps Psychiatric Clinic (1914). Meyer underscored the significance of psychological and social factors in the origin of mental illnesses, which he viewed as a result of a disturbance of the total personality rather than as a result of brain pathology.

6. William Alanson White (1870–1937), a key figure in American psychiatry and psychoanalysis, a noted editor (see also letter 882 and n. 6). White was director of St. Elizabeth's Hospital in Washington, D.C., for over thirty years. He preferred to distance himself from the "pope in Vienna," but was open to Ferenczi and to Rank, whose analysand he was. See Arcangelo R. T. D'Amore, ed., *William Alanson White: The Washington Years, 1903–1937* (Washington, D.C., 1976); W. A. White, *Forty Years of Psychiatry* (New York, 1933), and *The Autobiography of a Purpose* (New York, 1938).

7. Leonard Blumgart (1880–1951), psychiatrist, received his M.D. from Columbia University College of Physicians and Surgeons in 1903. He was an analysand of Freud's.

8. The last two words, as well as "behaviour" and "conditioned reflexes" below, are written in English in the original [Trans.].

9. Ferenczi depicted this dispute in his Madrid lecture the next year (*Bausteine* III, 424).

10. Spelling in original [Trans.]. Dr. Ralph Reed, psychiatrist and psychoanalyst from Cincinnati, member of the American Association.

11. See letter 970 and n. 1.

12. Gregory Stragnell (1888–1963), a neuropsychiatrist, received his M.D. from Columbia in 1913. He was editor of *Medical Record* and co-editor of the *Journal of Nervous*

and Mental Diseases. He was a member of the Washington Psychoanalytic Association and the American Psychoanalytic Association.

13. The remainder of the letter, continuing from here without paragraph indentation, is written in Ferenczi's hand.

14. "Present-Day Problems in Psycho-Analysis" (Ferenczi 1927, 278).

15. "Superego" is capitalized in the original [Trans.].

16. "Psychoanalytic Problems," *Psychoanalytic Review* 14 (1927): 1–19.

17. In May a resolution against "lay analysis" was drafted (Jones to Freud, July 18, 1927, *Freud/Jones,* p. 622, n. 3).

18. Munroe A. Meyer (1892–1939) received his M.D. from Cornell University Medical College in 1916. He was a member of the New York Psychoanalytic Society and an analysand of Freud's (1919).

19. Philip R. Lehrman (1895–1958), professor of clinical psychiatry and neurology at Columbia University. He was a member of the New York Society and an analysand of Freud's. Today he is also known for his amateur filming of Freud.

20. Abram Kardiner (1891–1981), American anthropologist and psychoanalyst, received his M.D. in 1917. He was an analysand of Horace Frink's and Freud's (see *My Analysis with Freud: Reminiscences* [New York, 1977]). He followed Sándor Radó to the Psychoanalytic Institute at Columbia University, which was finally recognized by the American Association. In 1949 he took over the directorship of a psychiatric clinic and, from 1955 on, a professorhip in psychiatry at Emory University in Atlanta. Kardiner represented a culturist approach to psychoanalysis.

21. See letter 609, n. 1.

1089

Vienna, January 26, 1927
IX., Berggasse 19

Dear friend,

Thank you for your detailed reports, with the pertinent judgments about persons and conditions strewn in. Your letter is certainly already quite American, in the lack of details about your own state of well-being and other trivialities. There is no doubt that you will exert a very beneficial effect; palpable results probably can't be achieved at all. We are now eager to know when you will come again. Anna has suggested to Eitingon that the +++ question of lay analysis should not be negotiated at the Congress, but at a special meeting beforehand, to which each of the groups that can be reached will send three representatives. Eitingon will write more to you about it. This discussion cannot take place without your being there.

Eitingon was here on his regular inspection trip; he left—unfortunately with a fever—yesterday. He was as reassuring as ever; affairs are in good hands with him. Not that everything is that good otherwise. Lay analysis is also making people everywhere rebellious. Stekel has, incidentally, written an essay in the Neue Freie Presse about this question, of which an elementary analysis can ascertain, in addition to the twenty-five percent meanness which is to be expected, at least fifty percent feeblemindedness. Such things are read and make an impression. But nobody can make a decision to write a polemic against him.

What you write about Rank sounds very strange. One would very much like to know more. To proceed in rank, Adler must have an excellent impresario. Before me is also an interview that he gave about Mussolini (The World, Dec. 26, '26). Perhaps you haven't read it and don't yet know how Fascism can be explained. I will tell you: from Mussolini's infantile inferiority and his striving to compensate for it. Now, it is dead certain that Adler would have given the same explanation if Mussolini had introduced, e.g., a homosexual social order in Italy, according to which normal coitus is punished by imprisonment, or a Trappist regime, in which talking is forbidden as unpatriotic. The only phenomenon to which he hasn't yet applied his famous theory is Socialism, because he, himself, belongs to it—indeed, perhaps [he hasn't applied it to] his own theory as well—, and hence there is the noteworthy result that, of all human things, these two—Socialism and Adlerism—are the only unexplained phenomena. But [they are] stupidities!

I can't take Frau Kempf; today I cabled her my agreement that she should go to you. Why didn't she do it right away, when her husband is with you[?] You are certainly too indulgent of his pollution of analysis by segment physiology. Your duel with Watson must have been fun. The entire impoverishment of the American mentality has become manifest in pragmatism and behaviorism.

Greetings to you and Frau G.

Cordially,
Freud

1090

R[und].-Br[ief].[1]

H. St Andrew, Brway at 72nd St.
New York, February 26, 1927

Dear friends,

After a long pause I can continue my report.

I have finished the lectures in the "New School for Social Research"; the participation of the auditors hardly abated right up to the end. I think I gave them a conception of what psychoanalysis is. Yesterday, the director of the school, Dr. Alvin Johnson, and approximately 100 auditors organized a dinner for me in the Hotel Pennsylvania. Of the medical psychoanalysts, Glück[2] and Blumgart were present. The latter presided. Dr. James

Harvey Robinson,³ Dr. Frankwood Williams, and Dr. Johnson functioned as principal speakers. The former, next to John Dewey⁴ the best-known and most recognized intellectual authority in this country (a historian), tried in his talk to clarify the historical significance of psychoanalysis. According to his presentation, Freud and psychoanalysis deserve the credit, by discovering the child in man, by sloughing off the shamefulness in sexual questions, by explaining many expressions of mentality hitherto considered nonsensical, by standardizing biological and psychological knowledge (etc.)⁵ for having ushered in a new era in the history of man and the history of science.—Alongside fine remarks and sage summaries, the talk contained some bias, which betrayed the speaker's predilection for premature monistic-materialistic explanations. Thus, he said, among other things, that there is no more room in modern teachings about man for mystical concepts like instinct, unconscious. He also diminished rather strongly the significance of the cs. Now and again he spoke about Jung and Kempf as commendable psychoanalysts. Reflecting on this talk, I singled out the speaker's sense of historical perspectives, but I had to set some of his statements straight; strangely, this time I had to defend consciousness as a psychic factor and remind people of the fact that, in the final analysis, the knowledge of the unconscious mechanism is also indebted to the function of the cs.—Dr. Frankwood Williams talked about Freud's epochal significance for psychiatry and "Mental Hygiene," an institution whose director he is. (He is an influential personality here.) Johnson and Blumgart concerned themselves with my person. The evening was actually a celebration in honor of psychoanalysis.

A few days before, I gave a lecture in the "Greenwich Psychiatric Round Table" Society—a group of psychiatric social workers⁶ (about 100), who held their gatherings in a building dedicated to general purposes (Greenwich House). On special request I had to talk about the Professor's *personality*, a new and stimulating task for me.

Unexpectedly, a few *personal* invitations to dinners degenerated into lectures about psychoanalytic subjects. I think I already shared [with you] the fact that a partner in the Morgan banking house (more precisely: his wife) gave a dinner in my honor; after dinner they asked me to talk about psychoanalysis. Since then, this was repeated several times; I thought of myself as Andersen's "Improvisator."⁷

Unfortunately, up to now that hasn't done the psychoanalytic institutions in America any good financially; the successes remained of a purely intellectual nature, although Edward Bernays, Professor's nephew, is also interested in our affairs. One of the richest Jews in New York, Sam Lewisohn⁸ (pronounced: Luisen), the owner of the big private gallery here, from whom I expect help, has proved to be only theoretically interested.

Lately, new invitations for lectures have been accumulating with me. At the suggestion of Professor Salmon (a psychiatrist),⁹ I will next give a lecture to fourth-year auditors at Columbia University. (The invitation came from the Dean of the University.) The psychological and the neurological *faculty* of this university (professors) each requested a special lecture of me, I also agreed to a lecture for a group of psychiatrists of the older school (chair: Sanger-Brown)[10] and will also accept an invitation of the (very conservative) official Medical Society of Philadelphia. I am planning to stay here until the middle of May, then plug in a two-week travel period, in order to accept invitations to Washington (St. Elizabeth Hospital), <perhaps>: Baltimore and (probably) Chicago. I almost forgot a lecture in the Hungarian Physicians' Society here.

In the meantime, I am working, as usual, on my analyses (eight), with the exception of Saturday afternoon and Sunday; I am spending this time mostly with acquaintances in the area; but traveling back and forth is also tiring.

For June 2, I booked a cabin for myself and my wife on the new ship of the Hamburg-America Line, the "New York." We are planning to travel to London via Southampton; our friend Dr. Rickman wants to tap from me there a—thank God, last—lecture for the Medical Psychological Association. After a week's stay in England, we want to go to Baden-Baden, in order to rest there for a rather long time. Further plans before the trip home are still incomplete. I will write to Eitingon about the pre-Congress and my participation in it.

Another short report about the apostates.

Jung's name is very well known. His best-known representative is Frau Dr. Hinkel.[11] I once met her socially, but gave up the discussion with her; she speaks a language which is strange to me, full of "group ucs" and other mysticism.

Adler's American journey was—scientifically—a failure. Intellectuals and scientists found his teachings very banal and primitive. He is popular in certain pedagogical circles, and he also received a friendly reception in Boston (Harvard). He spoke, so I hear, with great emphasis, demagogically, as it were, found the neuroses uncommonly simple, and promised to cure even the most serious cases in one to two hours. His manager[12] made great advertisements and had him give a lecture over the radio.

Rank has adherents in certain Jewish circles and with certain psychiatrists. A few severe cases of neurosis have reported to me uncured after the birth analysis, but I also hear about successes (I believe, mostly in healthy people or in easy cases). I have frequently spoken publicly about his teachings and thoroughly destroyed the idea that he has Professor's consent. He is now in Paris with ten Americans, who are being exchanged about every three months.

The new technique of Trigant Burrow (group analysis) could also soon put him among the apostates.

Dr. Watson, who interrupted his university career on account of private (family) matters, is now a partner in an advertising company, to which he gives psychological (behavioristic) suggestions. He is well liked in society. One hopes [to see] the "demise" of psychoanalysis from him.

I spoke with Brill by telephone once or twice since my last letter; he was friendly, as always, but we haven't had a meeting since Christmas, perhaps partly also through a fault of mine. From March 1 on I want to limit the seminar for lay analysts to one evening in two weeks, and instead of that begin a seminar for members of the New York group. Approximately twenty have applied (one evening a week), among others, also Brill, who canceled afterward, however. At the same time, Kardiner is beginning a seminar for physicians.—In general, something is stirring in psychoanalytic circles; Brill is beginning to spur on his people to work.—At the end of May the second semiannual congress of the American Psycho-Analytic Society is taking place (in Cincinnati, simultaneously with the general American Congress of Psychiatrists).—I conditionally agreed to come and to give a lecture.

A journalist made me an offer to say something about psychoanalysis into a newly invented *cinema talking machine*. I would agree to that only if they gave enough money to set up a polyclinic in Budapest.

At Edward Bernays's we once met the leader of the Zionist movement, Dr. Weizmann. A clever man, agreeable, hasn't a clue about psychoanalysis, and reveals himself in his stories as one who identifies (ucs) with *Joshua* (the prophet). He comes to America every winter in order to collect the budget for the next year in Palestine.—If only we were so popular!

Thanks and greetings to all the Committee members from

Ferenczi

Postscript (March 5) 1927

The case of Hug-Hellmuth[13] is regrettable. The public presentation of the facts [is] the only correct procedure. I never liked her personally, and I also found her book about the sexual life of the child[14] to be one-sidedly sexually interested, with little sense for the significance of the powers of defense. God knows if she didn't also falsify things there.

Too bad Jones is against the meeting before the Congress.[15] We could also hold a Committee meeting without Americans (as before). To be sure, I wouldn't be able to participate in it before the middle of June.

Yesterday was the first (medical) seminar; there were approximately twenty present; absent were Brill, Oberndorf, Kardiner, Gaston Mayer,[16] Stern, Ames.[17]

F[erenczi].

1. This letter is a carbon copy written on the front and back of thin yellow carbon copy paper.

2. Bernard Glueck (1884–1972), an American psychiatrist of Polish descent, received his M.D. from Georgetown University in 1909 and then studied in Munich and Berlin. He was director of the psychiatric clinic at Sing-Sing (1915–1918) and director of the Department of Mental Hygiene at the New School for Social Work. He was a member of the American Psychoanalytic Association. With John E. Lind, he was the translator of Adler's *Der Nervöse Charakter* [in English, *The Neurotic Constitution*] (1917); he is known for his works on forensic psychiatry.

3. James Harvey Robinson (1863–1936), renowned American historian and authority in European history, received his Ph.D. from the University of Freiburg and his LL.D. from the University of Utah. He was a professor of history at Columbia University (1895–1919) and co-founder of the New School for Social Research (1919). Robinson is one of the founders of "New History," an interdisciplinary approach to historical research which takes the position that research should first and foremost serve the present and the understanding of it, a controversial but extremely influential point of view.

4. John Dewey (1859–1952), one of the most significant American philosophers, received his Ph.D. from Johns Hopkins University in 1884 and his LL.D. from the University of Wisconsin in 1904; professor of philosophy at Columbia University from 1904. Co-founder and most influential representative of pragmatism, he was a pioneer of "functional psychology" and a representative of the progressive movement in American education.

5. Reading uncertain; the letters have been written over. It could also read "ucs."

6. "Social workers" is written in English in the original [Trans.].

7. *The Improvisator* (1835), a partially autobiographical novel by Hans Christian Andersen (1805–1875), the famous Danish author and writer of fairy tales.

8. Sam Adolph Lewisohn (1884–1951), received his LL.B. from Columbia University in 1907. Of the firm Adolph Lewisohn & Sons, investment bankers, he was a board member or director of a myriad of firms and organizations, as well as vice president of the Museum of Modern Art.

9. See letter 1084 and n. 4.

10. Possibly Sanger Monroe Brown (1852–1928). He received his M.D. from New York University in 1880 and was a professor at the medical school of the University of Chicago. From the vivisection of apes, he proved that the center of vision is localized in the occipital lobe.

11. Spelling in the original [Trans.]. Beatrice M. Hinkle (1874–1953) received her M.D. from Cooper Medical College (Stanford University) and was the first woman public health official (City Physician, San Francisco, 1899–1905). After moving to New York, she opened the first psychotherapeutic clinic in America at Cornell Medical College (1908). She was a productive author and the translator of Jung's *Wandlungen und Symbole der Libido* [in English, *The Psychology of the Unconscious*].

12. Written in English in the original [Trans.].

13. The exposure of *A Young Girl's Diary* (Vienna, 1919), edited by Hug-Hellmuth, as a probable forgery led to a recall of the book from public sale. See letter 828 and n. 5.

14. *Aus dem Seelenleben des Kindes: Eine Psychoanalytische Studie* [From the Mental Life of the Child: A Psychoanalytic Study] (Leipzig, 1913).

15. Jones's *Rundbrief* of February 16, 1927 (Sigmund Freud Copyrights).

16. This person has not been identified.

17. Thaddeus H. Ames (1885–1863), an American neurologist, received his M.D. from the University of Michigan Medical School, Ann Arbor, in 1907. He was interested in re-

ligion and pastoral theology and was president of the New York Psychoanalytic Society in 1921. He worked on war neuroses, malingering, and pastoral psychiatry. Dudley Shoenfeld, "Thaddeus Hoyt Ames, 1885–1963, *Psychoanalytic Quarterly* 22 (1963): 573.

1091

Hotel St. Andrew
Broadway at 72nd Street
New York
March 6, 1927

Dear Professor,

I thank you kindly for the detailed news. I am very pleased about its favorable content.

You ask how I am. Now—at the moment I feel *very* exhausted—but I keep my tiredness a secret. Only my wife suffers under my growing displeasure and impatience. The state of my bodily health is variable. I long for absolute rest. *Strong* overwork is evidently partly responsible for my mood of dissatisfaction, which the great outward successes that I reported also can't mollify. Please tell only Fräulein Anna about this perhaps only transitory feeling of tiredness, no one else. (The material result will be approximately double that which I normally save in Budapest.)

Brill seems to be very annoyed about my being here. But I guard against giving him grounds for being personally insulted. His behavior is, to be sure, downright unfriendly.

In expectation of news from you.

Yours,
Ferenczi

P.S. Enclosed a lecture written in English.[1] If you accept it for the Zeitschrift, then Radó will have to have it translated. Then the English original can be sent on to London (Jones).

1. "Gulliver Phantasies" (Ferenczi 1927, 280), published in German in the *Zeitschrift* and in English in the *Journal*.

1092

Vienna, March 25, 1927
IX., Berggasse 19

Dear friend,

What work, what accomplishment! It is astonishing and admirable. And, unfortunately, only for Americans, who don't know how to appreciate anything and who never form a lasting impression. And [you] only saved twice as much as you would have been able to in Budapest; I'm especially sorry for that.

Permit me to complete your travel program after you return; I am counting on a long visit at the Semmering, where we have again rented a place. I gladly grant you your friend Groddeck, but lately he has been doing all too much trickery and nonsense, the "It" has gone to his head.

From Rank one can learn that it is indeed the most profitable thing in the world to be a scoundrel. A villain, not on your life, that could bring one punishment; but scoundrelness [*Lumperei*] is not dangerous. His wife visited me and indicates that she is seeing her way through the situation without being happy in it. She said: If one has undertaken to be a horse, etc.

Anna was in Berlin for two days to give a lecture,[1] and was well liked, according to the general view. She is working really well, but fanatical, like all women, and she makes herself much too tired.

The question of lay analysis will continue very much to disquiet the analytic circles and won't find a solution at the Congress. I remain firm in my conviction.

If you want personal news from me that you don't need to tell the savages over there about, then listen. My new prosthesis, although not ideal, is certainly a great improvement and makes my existence much easier. My desire for production finally seems to be extinguished, but the five analyses are going easily for me; I am pleased about the many things that are being confirmed and the individual things that can be recognized as being new. I am becoming more and more secure in technique, and I recognize the wrong paths more clearly. My doctors—for Lajos is also blowing this horn—demand that I again go to the sanatorium for a few weeks in order to undergo heart therapy, but since they are at the same time assuring me that this is happening in the absence of an immediate cause, and only for prophylactic purposes, I won't do it. One should only let the noble organ, my dearest hope for the future, alone. Gifts are no longer being accepted until my 80th birthday. I find a good justification for my continued existence in earning money, for the family can use much. Martin is faced with losing his job.[2] How will one find another one in Vienna, and he can't go to America. My mother is approaching her 92nd in undiminished freshness.

I have directed your lectures to the editors without postponement.[3]

I greet you and your wife cordially. If you knew how happy we are with your news, you would take up letter writing as one of your recreations.

Yours,
Freud

1. "Zur Technik der Kinderanalyse" [On the Technique of Child Analysis], delivered in the German Psychoanalytic Society (*Zeitschrift* 13 [1927]: 367).

2. "I found employment in one of the newly founded banks . . . None of them could last long; and thus I changed my employers a number of times . . . Finally, I succeeded in making a living by writing articles on economic subjects for newspapers." Martin Freud, *Glory Reflected: Sigmund Freud—Man and Father* (London, 1957), p. 199.

3. Freud had sent "Gulliver Phantasies" and "Present-Day Problems in Psychoanalysis" (1927, 278) to Radó (Freud to Radó, March 22, 1927, Library of Congress).

1093

New York,
April 8, 1927. Saturday.

Dear Professor,

My wife has gone off to Los Angeles to visit her sister (five days' train ride); so I have been alone here since Tuesday, which considerably increases the feeling of emptiness.

I intend to sketch further in the Rundbrief the work that I have accomplished since. Today I would like to speak with you, Eitingon, and Fräulein Anna alone, in order to share with you, after the fact, certain impressions that I received and have been holding back.

My intention with regard to Brill was peaceful. I wanted to move him to give up his attitude of insulted innocence; but since the first day of our meeting here I became doubtful about the success of my efforts. He does, to be sure, place the stress on lay analysis—in reality it is his fatally wounded vanity that makes him so obstinate. He cannot forgive you in your statements to the effect that there is *no* well-trained analyst in America. The business with Frink[1] has also not been forgotten, and is being bandied about against you; there is also no lack of allusions to the Rank case.—My being here is also extremely burdensome to him. The idea that someone from Europe comes over to teach the people is in and of itself an affront; he believes himself to be in possession of a monopoly, which he has well deserved through his pioneer work. In the end, one wouldn't hold that against him, if, in order to safeguard his ambition and financial interests, he had not also impeded the progress of others. Unfortunately, I have the impression that he is sooner being strengthened in his attitude by the moral support of his former rival (Jones). Jones, with regard to England, seems to aspire to similar rights of autocracy as Brill does in America; both see themselves threatened by Berlin, Vienna, Budapest.—Dr. Brill's more intimate circle of adherents consists of Stern, Oberndorf, Kardiner, and Gaston Mayer—recently—risum teneatis![2]—also Frink. Of all these, Gaston Mayer seems to be the only one (besides Frink) with a good educational background. In the seminar that I direct, which numbers about twenty, with the exception of Jelliffe and Kempf, no original worker has shown up up to now; Glück is well informed theoretically, but is for the most part interested in mental hygiene and social work.—Many physicians in positions of leadership told me it is regrettable that I didn't come ten years earlier; the way in which Ψα was presented to them has scared them away. Of course, one must also take into account the abatement of resistance in the last ten years.

Brill and Oberndorf have, so to speak, blown up the "foundation"[3] planned by your nephew; they did it by wanting *first and foremost* to collect [money] for national American purposes (institute, etc.); in other words: for now, nothing for the Verlag and nothing for Europe. At the same time, they brag about the fact that they have already raised $50,000 for these American purposes. Incidentally, I almost never see them; Brill withdrew after one or two formal invitations at the beginning. He will certainly justify a reason to be insulted by me.—The fact that, despite this attitude on the part of the more intimate colleagues, I find so much interest here is a sign that the people were downright hungry for enlightenment.

Last week I got right up close to dollar fortune. The dollar millionaire McCormick family, in which several cases of praecox have occurred, has a member (a man),[4] who, according to Professor Meyer's directions (previously also Kraepelin's), is being treated on an estate in Santa Barbara (Calif.), similar to the way Ludwig II of Bavaria was back then (twice daily musical bands, daily cinema performances ad personam, etc.). This [has been going on] for twenty years. They seem to have got tired of the thing and are consulting all psychiatrists in order. In a discussion lasting two and a half hours, the question was also put to me whether I want to make the ψα attempt (the possibility of which I posed as an *experiment*). I declined, and recommended Dr. Kempf, who was thereupon consulted once again. In my zeal to be conscientious, I also replied hesitatingly to the question of whether I have to visit the patient in order to make a diagnosis, and in so doing misplayed the pleasure trip to California. Dr. Glück—who, strangely, already knew of my impending mission—asked me to recommend him "in the interest of the cause of psychoanalysis."—But I couldn't do that; Dr. Kempf is, after all, the only one here who can demonstrate successes with psychotics.

Herr and Frau Liebmann, the parents of your patient,[5] have already called on me twice to have me explain certain sentences from your letters. I did it to the best of my knowledge and strove to reconcile them, above all, with the long duration of the treatment.

Viereck will soon publish the interview with you (from the Semmering);[6] at this moment he is traveling to Europe and will look you up.

I was very pleased about the news about the *finally* successful improvement in your prosthesis, but the motive for your increased analytic activity (Martin) is very regrettable!

I received Fräulein Anna's book with thanks, and am especially grateful for the kind dedication. Pierce Clark wishes that I write a foreword to it.—It will not be difficult for me also to give public expression to my pleasure over the book.⁷

P.S. It has become April 14 in the meantime, and, since there is nothing special to report, I will take my leave.

Cordially,
Ferenczi

Brill didn't go to Germany, but to Italy. We were certainly hoping to be able to have a longer stay at the Semmering, before or after Innsbruck.⁸

1. See letter 860, n. 4.
2. Latin for "Would you keep from laughing" (Horace, *Ars Poetica*, verse 5: "Risum teneatis, amici?") [Would you keep from laughing, friends?].
3. See letter 1021 and n. 2. The word "foundation" is in English in the original [Trans.].
4. Stanley McCormick, brother-in-law of Edith Rockefeller McCormick (see letter 373, n. 2), "who was diagnosed as schizophrenic, and for whom a series of well-known American and European psychiatrists were consulted over some forty years." William McGuire, "Firm Affinities: Jung's relations with Britain and the United States," *Journal of Analytical Psychology* 40 (1995): 309. Edith's husband, Harold Fowler, had not been Jung's patient in 1910, as is erroneously stated in the *Freud/Jung Correspondence* and in letter 121, n. 2; this was rather Medill McCormick (kind communication from William McGuire; see his essay "The Wrong McCormicks," ibid., 99).
5. Carl Liebman, an adolescent psychotic. His case plays a major role in the unpublished portion of the Freud-Pfister correspondence (Library of Congress). See David Lynn, "Freud's Analysis of A.B., a Psychotic Man, 1925–1930," *Journal of the American Academy of Psychoanalysis* 21 (1993): 63–78; Ernst Falzeder, "Whose Freud Is It? Some Reflections on Editing Freud's Correspondence," *International Forum of Psychoanalysis* 5 (1996): 77–86.
6. See letter 1077 and n. 1.
7. The book was published in English in 1928 (*Introduction to the Technique of Child Analysis*) in the translation by Pierce Clark, without Ferenczi's foreword.
8. The city which, after lengthy discussion, was agreed on to be the site of the Tenth International Psychoanalytic Congress (September 1–3, 1927).

1094

[Rundbrief]¹

New York, May 1, 1927

Dear friends,

Unfortunately, I can't find the copy of my last Rundbrief, so that in this—probably concluding—report, I will perhaps repeat some things that I have already said.—The lecture that I gave to the students of the *psychiat-*

ric clinic of Columbia University seems to have had an enlightening effect. Dr. Salmon, the professor, was appreciative; unfortunately, his goodwill is limited to flirting with Ψα; "Can't we be good relatives, do we absolutely have to be brothers?" he asked me. I replied to him that in science such diffuse relationships don't count; one is either a brother or an enemy. One does not allow oneself to get into compromises.—Another lecture, which a very closed circle of leading psychiatrists invited me to give, was interesting. Professor Adolf Meyer from Baltimore was the main discussant. But since I anticipated his arguments, which were to be expected, his remarks granted agreement halfway, rather reluctantly. An excursion to Philadelphia (at the invitation of the Academy of Medicine there) was very successful; a large circle of physicians, up to now scared away and disdainful, behaved amicably and full of understanding. Perhaps I already said that I turned down the invitation of Dr. H. Adler (Chicago)[2] to come there; his program was to present to me difficult cases of "problem children";[3] naturally, it contradicts the spirit of Ψα to want to produce quick "lightning diagnoses" and "lightning treatments." I still have left two lectures for the neurological faculty (professors) of Columbia University and a few lectures in Washington in the very strongly analytically colored Psychopath. Association (president, W. A. White). The seminar evening with my lay pupils and (separately) with approximately twenty medical psychoanalysts are continuing; next Thursday is the last (tenth) evening. I was able to give some enlightenment. Dr. Glück is well informed, theoretically; practically, not yet so very.

Jelliffe is erudite, but one-sidedly biologically oriented. Kempf, very talented, but inclined toward isolation, with his own terminology, etc. He has come *somewhat* closer to us. Otherwise, much disorientation among the members. Brill, Stern, Kardiner, Gaston, Mayer,[4] Oberndorf stayed away from the seminar.—I recently attended a meeting of the New York group. I find that Frink, the smartest one among the members, shows signs of great skepticism since his recovery from a deep depression.—In the administrative meeting they are said to have discussed how one could restrain the psychoanalytic physicians coming from Europe from subjecting themselves to the American licensing regulations (examination). Union interests are certainly the motive.—The "Ps.A. Foundation,"[5] planned at one time by the Professor and his nephew (Edward Bernays), cannot function, because Brill wants to apply the money to be raised (when the time comes) *first and foremost* to American ends. Since the Committee is first and foremost supposed to help the needy European institutions, I can't collaborate with him.—Brill has, so I hear, gone to Europe; he keeps his distance from me personally.

In March I had a period of tiredness, which has now been overcome, so that I can accept the kind invitation of the London colleagues after all, and will give a lecture in the British Psychological Society. I sail away from here on June 2, and will stay in London for about a week; then I will rest up in Baden-Baden (arrival in Baden-Baden on about June 20).

My wife has gone to visit her sister in California and will return on May 10–15.

Many kind regards,
Sándor Ferenczi

1. The letter is written in pencil on the front and back of yellow carbon copy paper.
2. Herman Morris Adler (1876–1935?), an American psychiatrist, received his M.D. from Columbia in 1901. He was an assistant professor of psychiatry at Harvard Medical School from 1912 to 1917. In 1916 he moved to Chicago, where he undertook studies in epidemiology and psychosocial welfare. He was a professor of criminology at the University of Illinois (1919–28) and of psychiatry at the University of California (from 1930).
3. The words in quotation marks are in English in the original [Trans.].
4. There is a comma between "Gaston" and "Mayer" in the original.
5. The words in quotation marks are written in English in the original.

1095

N.Y., May 21, 1927

Dear Professor,

This time only brief communications.—I was in Washington for three days, gave a lecture on sexual and genital theories in the United Ps.An. and Ps.Pathol. Association. Then *four* long lectures for active psychoanalysts on technical questions. Dr. W. A. White was very forthcoming; he is a reliable friend of psychoanalysis and is influencing his staff of physicians along these lines.[1] They inundated me with attentiveness, to which the more intimate New York colleagues had not accustomed me.

Now, only one more week here, then we embark (on June 2) and travel on board the Hamburg-America Liner "New York" to Southampton; from there, Rickmann[2] takes us in his car to Portsmouth, where I will visit Inman; then comes the stay in London (The Goring Hotel, Grosvenor Gardens, Belgravia, London S.W. 1). From there we intend to travel to Paris and would like to use the opportunity to get to know your Princess—only you would have to be so kind as to pave the way for this encounter—naturally, only if you consider it to be advisable and feasible.

Many kind regards to you all.

Yours,
Ferenczi and Frau G.

Please send the reply to London.—

P.S. At the congress of the American Medical Association in Washington, a morning was devoted to the theme: "Psychic Effects in Organic Illnesses."—Your name was *not* mentioned.

1. White, an analysand of Rank's, had been urged by Harry Stack Sullivan (1892–1949) to invite Ferenczi to Washington. E. James Lieberman, *Acts of Will: The Life and Work of Otto Rank* (New York, 1985), p. 268.

2. Spelling in the original.

1096

Vienna, June 9, 1927
IX., Berggasse 19

Dear friend,

I greet you cordially on European soil after all your American efforts. I know that you still don't grant yourself peace and quiet.

It would be absurd to write a recommendation to the Princess for you. She knows your name and will be very pleased to make your acquaintance as well. So, I will give you the address,

St. Cloud, 7 Ave. du Mt. Valerien, and will let her know that she may expect a visit from you.

We are going to the Semmering on the 16th of the month. This time I am very glad that there is an end to it here, and would only not like to have to go into the city too often. I will probably not have any patients up there until September, "live my money," as the Germans say.

You have given too little indication about the dating of your further intentions.

I received $5,000 for our institutions from Miss G. Potter.[1] It was urgently necessary; naturally it won't go far.

Be careful with Jones and don't neglect to have a thorough talk with Eitingon before the Congress. The fate of the Association lies in the hands of both of you.

With warmest wishes for you and Frau Gisela,

Yours,
Freud

1. Freud used this donation from an "old Jew," which Ms. Potter delivered, primarily for the Verlag, which was in need, and for the training institute (Freud to Eitingon, June 7, 1927, Sigmund Freud Copyrights).

1097

INTERNATIONALE ZEITSCHRIFT FÜR PSYCHOANALYSE
Herausgegeben von Prof. Dr. Sigm. Freud
Redigiert von Dr. M. Eitingon, Dr. S. Ferenczi und Dr. Sándor Radó

Baden-Baden, June 30, 1927
Werderstrasse 14.

Dear Professor,

Many thanks for your welcome-greeting, which I received in London. I feel much better on European soil—indeed, I would say that I think back on the whole American adventure as if on a dream. It was perhaps only a flight out of the world of reality. The fact that it was, nevertheless, something real is proved by the sum of money that I have saved up and that increased somewhat toward the end; it amounts, not to double, but to three times what I saved annually during the last few years in Budapest. I hope that the possession of this, albeit modest, fortune will make it possible for me to give fewer hours and to dedicate somewhat more time to science. To do both evidently requires a capacity for accomplishment which we admired in you but sought in vain to imitate.

Now I will share with you the last chapter of my Argonaut journey. In New York, I worked almost up to the last hour. I am not dissatisfied with the result of my work. I seem to have shaken the movement, at least temporarily, out of a state of indolence. Even the New York group, which usually has so little interest in the common cause, seems to have thought better of it: they want to hold meetings more frequently than only once a month; they talk about courses, about founding an institute, etc. To be sure, I don't know to what extent they will hold to it if no one is breathing down their necks. The bigwigs: Brill, Oberndorf, Stern, Kardiner, Monroe Meyer, consistently kept their distance from me. Brill and Oberndorf even excused themselves from the little farewell party that my wife and I gave at the hotel. Jelliffe and approximately twenty other New Yorkers honestly wanted to learn; but it was difficult to get anything across to them in ten seminar evenings, except perhaps the fact that they still have a lot to learn. In eight months I got so far with Kempf that he conducts himself *personally* (both in his family and in the profession) less inhibitedly and more socially. There was insufficient time to win him over to us scientifically (theoretically) as well. In the end I was able to give his wife only about twelve hours, with resounding success. Perhaps she will come to Europe in order to continue.—Dr. Asch,[1] a tough nut, allowed himself to be softened up *to a certain extent*. He got married before my departure.—You don't know the other patients and pupils.—

Your nephew Edward and his wife were the kindest and most helpful among our new acquaintances, right up to the end. With Edward, helping has become downright instinctual.—We met them and your brother Alexander again in Paris; he will have told you about the fun evening at Rouzier (in the excellent French restaurant). Your niece, Frau Wiener,[2] also sent us a sign of her attentiveness just before our departure.

To return to Brill once more: he seems to have been insulted to death by your statements about the incompetence of the Americans and about my unsolicited coming and my statements about lay analysis. "I am fed up" [*Ich bin satt*], was his statement about this. The last expression of his wrath is the circular letter which the New York group is sending to all the other groups and [which] welcomes the colleagues who come to America only under certain conditions.—I am convinced, now as before, that he and Jones were together in Italy, even though this was denied by Jones (on direct questioning).

I must also say a few more words about Pierce Clark. In contrast to his great personal civility toward me, he seems to be uncommonly egoistic in practical matters, even ruthless; a few smaller and larger inaccuracies and errors in his statements urge caution; he himself can *not* translate from German to English; he leaves the work to a not very adept secretary. I don't know how the matter of the translation of "Child Analysis" was arranged, and I would very much like to be informed about this by Fräulein Anna.

Viereck and his Sancho Panza (Branden)[3] are, to be sure, two typical journalists, but easy to handle and compliant.

In the last few days before my departure (where one could accuse me less of chasing after patients) I expressed myself to some interviewers. You may have read the (in part displaced) traces of them in newspaper clippings. But I could not and would not go into battle with Adler's grandiose press campaign. On the whole, he has thoroughly disgraced himself with the simplicity and pigheadedness of his statements.

In Southampton we were received by Dr. Rickmann,[4] an interesting oddity. He drove us in his car across southern England to London, where we didn't arrive until the next evening. On the way he showed us churches, castles, typical English landscapes. We have become fond of England and London; it was my first visit to this country. Rickman[5] was extraordinarily friendly with me.

We spent twelve days in London; almost the entire time was devoted to invitations, lectures, conversations with individuals. Jones strove to heap every conceivable personal honor (in contrast to the American reception) upon me. (Meeting of the British group, with the request to lecture something to them; several large dinners, even a garden party[6] in Jones's nice house*.) Naturally, my former pupils Inman, Eder, Cole,[7] used the occasion to testify to their friendship. The actual conversation with Jones took

---

*The other lecture was in the British Psychological Society, of which you are an honorary member.

place in his country house in Elstead. I was mindful of your warning "Be careful." Actually, I found Jones's statements lacking in full and complete honesty. In lay analysis (the main topic of our conversation), he claims already to have found and shown the golden mean between the extremes (you and Brill); I also didn't succeed in moving him to admissions that go beyond his suggestions that were published in the "Journal." It seems to me that that can sooner be effected by Eitingon; in this question I identify (as Jones says) too much with you, Herr Professor.—

[That brings me to the association that I would be *very* pleased if Eitingon, to whom I ask you to send this letter, could decide to pay me a short visit in Baden-Baden.[8] I was and am too exhausted to look him up now. A detailed discussion with him of all current matters would be extremely important. It is very beautiful here; one to two days' stay would not be unpleasant for Max. If that is completely impossible, then we would have to choose a different place for a meeting. I will write about my plans with regard to the visit to the Semmering at the end of the letter.][9]

The second observation that I made in London, which surprises me, was determining the prominent influence that Frau Melanie Klein has on Jones and almost the entire group. Jones is adopting not only Frau Klein's method, but also all her more personal relations to the Berlin group, etc.— Aside from the scientific value of her work, I find in this a point directed toward Vienna. Jones wanted to press me to take sides in this question as well; but I refused, and said that that was a scientific and not a partisan matter; one has to wait and see what develops.—

The last day in London, on which we were supposed to visit the House of Commons, was disrupted by the fact that my wife left her purse with money and all her keys in a taxicab. This impediment was also overcome with the help of a kindly English locksmith. Here, in Baden-Baden, we then received the news from the London police that the purse had been turned in by the driver![10]

The trip across the English Channel was smooth, Paris received us in old beauty. We spent four days there, did some shopping, visited Sainte Chapelle, spent a Bohemian evening on Montmartre with new American friends (the lawyer *Uterhart*[11] and his family. Mr. U. is an extremely intelligent, almost European man; he reads everything that calls itself analysis, and is critical, and not as superficial as his countrymen).

In Paris I got to know Laforgue somewhat better. He is a pleasant and reliable man, so it seems. The impression that Rank's birth theory made on him is softening. N.B. Rank is living like a king in Paris; he resides in a villa in the Bois de Boulogne, has a maître d'hotel and a chef de cuisine.— (Jones tells me he is doing good business in the stock market with the aid of American patients; otherwise, I also wouldn't be able to account for this degree of luxury.) Naturally, he also has a car and a chauffeur. To be sure, he has made himself look somewhat ridiculous by sending out his calling card with the telegram address "Ottoranks."¹² That kind of thing is viewed as highly inappropriate in Paris.—The Princess was, unfortunately, not in Paris.—

Another, I believe, extremely important communication. Dr. Seligman,¹³ Professor of Economics at Columbia University, suggested to me on the boat trip to work out a plan for the collaboration of psychoanalysis in the "Encyclopedia of the Social Sciences,"¹⁴ which is to be edited by him. He is expecting (perhaps from me) a *for the time being comprehensive* work on the social relations of psychoanalysis; in addition to that he requests our collaboration on the work itself and wants to put sufficient space at our disposal. Naturally, he requests your collaboration above all; but he is also thinking about the collaboration of a group of psychoanalysts that you and I might suggest to him. I am enclosing the plan of his work, and request your thoughts about it and that you return the memorandum.

Here in Baden-Baden I was greeted by splendid weather and the house of Groddeck, already so familiar to me (which sends you best regards). I am resting here after the stresses and strains of the last year, which my health has, to be sure, stood up to, but lately only with difficulty. I am living first and foremost only for the care of my body; but I will slowly pull myself together for intellectual work.—

After the Congress I am planning to go to the Semmering for about two weeks, and to spend another two weeks in Vienna before I go home. On *July 15* some patients from America are coming here, and some others on the 20th. In August and September I want to work five hours a day.—

We were happy to hear such good news from your brother about your being well—and we are looking forward to being able to convince ourselves of that personally in the not too distant future.

With kind regards to all your dear ones—and to the Eitingons, from both of us.

Yours,
Ferenczi

P. S. Your clever nephew, Edward, when he heard about the existence of a princess among the psychoanalysts (more correctly, his likewise very intelligent wife¹⁵), proposed immediately to accept this lady of high repute among the members of the leaders of the American "Foundation" committee. He is expecting a great impression on the Americans and financial success from it. I am very much in favor of it, but I would naturally first like to hear Professor's opinion. I was, unfortunately, unable to make the Princess's acquaintance; she was absent.¹⁶

1. Joseph J. Asch (1880–1935), M.D., urologist, chief of the clinic at Lenox Hill Hospital, co-founder of the New York Society; in 1922 he was an analysand of Freud's (Freud to

Jones, December 9, 1921, *Freud/Jones*, p. 446). At the beginning of 1924, Asch had invited Abraham to go to New York; Abraham refused, after Freud had characterized Asch as a "pathological fool." "His analysis with me was the saddest thing that could be imagined, without any trace of insight, either analytic or general (common sense)" (Freud to Abraham, May 4, 1924, Library of Congress). The words in parentheses at the end of the quotation are in English in the original [Trans.]. See "In Memoriam Joseph Jefferson Asch," *Psychoanalytic Quarterly* 4 (1935): 630.

2. Leah Bernays, married name Wiener; see letter 1086, n. 4.
3. This person has not been identified.
4. Spelling in the original.
5. Spelling in the original.
6. The words "garden party" are written in English in the original [Trans.].
7. See letter 909 and n. 2.
8. The meeting, which Eitingon considered "not at all so urgent" (letter to Freud, July 4, 1927, Sigmund Freud Copyrights), did not come about.
9. Brackets in the original.
10. This word is written in English in the original [Trans.].
11. Henry Ayres Uterhart (1875–1946), prominent New York attorney, M.A., LL.B., 1896.
12. Reading uncertain. The last letter could also be an "o."
13. Edwin Robert Anderson Seligman (1861–1939), prominent American economist, received his Ph.D. in 1885 and his LL.D. in 1904 from Columbia University. He was McVickar Professor at Columbia University from 1904 to 1931; president of the American Economic Association, the National Tax Association, and the American Association of University Professors.
14. Edited by Edwin Seligman, associate editor Alvin Johnson (15 vols. [New York, 1930–1935]). An informed but critical entry about psychoanalysis was finally written by Horace M. Kallen of the New School for Social Research, the one on psychiatry by Harry Stack Sullivan.
15. Doris, née Fleischmann (1891/2–1980).
16. This postscript is written on a separate sheet, which has been placed in the Balint folder under 1930, attached to a longer postscript to Ferenczi's letter of January 17 (see letter 1179, n. 7). To be sure, there would have been enough space on the last page for an additional postscript. In terms of content, however, the text better fits the present context (Ferenczi did, after all, make the Princess's acquaintance in the same summer; cf. letter 1109). Handwriting and ink give no clear indication, but do not speak against placing it here.

1098

Semmering, July 2, 1927

Dear friend,

Your letter was welcome, it is going to Eitingon today. I hadn't heard anything from you in three weeks and was worrying superfluously. I haven't seen my brother after Paris since June 16, up here. What he has told you about my glowing condition doesn't seem to me to be very justified, unfortunately. I also send kind regards to the Groddecks, but his [Noah's] Ark fantasies¹ are becoming less and less palatable to me. (Between us.) Rank is developing his talent as a confidence man. Will he have overcome his conflicts thereby? Very possibly. His wife could bring about a breakdown, but she has now become subservient to him and accepts his bribes.

[I am] very much in agreement with your intentions to spend two weeks each on the Semmering and in Vienna. In September I also have several work hours, to be sure, but there will be enough time left for us, and I wouldn't be able to endure constant company.

The main thing now seems to me to be that you recuperate thoroughly from the toils of your adventure. I would hope that your program for July and August doesn't disturb you in this. I find it very good that you are participating extensively in Prof. Seligman's work. From my point of view it would be meaningless for me to make a promise or take on a responsibility, but I hope to discuss everything with you.

Now, kind regards to you and Frau G., and warm wishes that you might like Europe again!

Yours,
Freud

N.B. The prospectus will soon be returned.

1. *Die Arche* [The Ark], a bi-weekly newsletter, published privately by Groddeck, "in which Groddeck and his patients and friends could publish everything that seemed of value to them ... At the end of 1927 [it had to] cease publication ... , because the printer could no longer tolerate the revelations of its content ... There had been attempts already since 1925 to prevent the publication of the 'Arche' with the help of the police." Herbert Will, *Georg Groddeck: Die Geburt der Psychosomatik* [Georg Groddeck: The Birth of Psychosomatics] (Munich, 1987), p. 77.

1099

Semmering, July 5, 1927

Dear friend,

Also received your second letter¹ and forwarded it to Eitingon. Don't forget to speak with him in timely fashion before the Congress, even if it should require sacrifices. There is much to consider, with regard to Jones and America, that can be handled only by word of mouth. I presume that Jones will put difficulties in the way of your presidency. Eitingon doesn't want to be president, and I absolutely don't want Jones to.²

Your suggestion for the three kinds of groups that the Association should recognize seems to be the most expedient one for overcoming the existing differences of opinion. It is only a matter of winning the others over to this solution.

Cordially, to you and G.

Yours,
Freud

1. A letter of Ferenczi's is evidently missing.
2. Cf. Jones's letter to Freud of July 18, 1927: "I urged Eitingon to accept the Presidency at the Congress and hope you approve of this. He is universally acceptable, whereas—especially at present—Ferenczi might not bring the harmony we need" (*Freud/Jones*, p. 622).

1100

Baden-Baden, July 13, 1927

Dear Professor,

Again I have visited a European capital. It is not uninteresting to allow the images and impressions of cities to pass before one in such rapid succession. Only then does one see how much truth lies in the banal general judgments in the hackneyed expressions of homey London, coquettish Paris, and awkward Berlin.—But this time I didn't go in order to get aesthetic impressions. I hurried over there because the recommendation I received from Eitingon about lay analysis[1] brought me "out of the house." I found such a crass difference between our (your and my own) opinion in this question, on the one hand, and Eitingon's suggestions on the other, that I felt incapable of assuming, or even running for the presidency sanctioning such a program (with a majority in the advisory council around my neck that is hostile to lay analysis, on top of that). Friend Eitingon was somewhat surprised by my coming, but I told him that our conference before his meeting with Jones would be unavoidable, indeed, it would have been much, much better if it had taken place *before* his recommendations were sent to Jones (before asking us!).

Friend Eitingon is an absolute friend of physicians, with a decided guild mentality. As a favor to you, he decided in the end to demand the recognition, in principle, of lay analysis (by the Americans). In compensation, he fed them (the Americans), in the introductory commentaries, with theoretical, and in the second paragraph of the resolution, with extremely important practical concessions. I tried to mitigate his recommendation in the enclosed text,[2] which I handed over to Eitingon for his consideration. In the beginning I insisted on this text and said that, in the event that my modifications remain unconsidered, I would prefer to begin the cheerful opposition to Eitingon and the new president. After lengthy discussions, in which Alexander and Radó (along with Simmel and Frau Dr. Horney) also took part in the evening, we agreed (I with a heavy heart) on a *different* modification of Eitingon's resolution. I consented to require the analysts to *share* the names of non-indigenous training candidates of a teaching group of the country in question. But the foreign country should not make a judgment itself in the event of differences between the analyst and the "non-indigenous" person, but rather present them to the *International Training Commission*. I did *not* urge the constitution of the lay group in New York. Perhaps we will come to some decision or other after hearing Brill's reaction to the recommendations.—

The usual program of my Berlin stay was also very full. I visited Simmel's really beautiful (in addition, decorated by your Ernst) psychoanalytic sanatorium,[3] for which I prophesy a brilliant future; I made the acquaintance of Radó's newest family, had a lengthy discussion with Alexander, and spent several hours and meals with my brother, and one with Frau Eitingon.

In case I really become president (and Eitingon does *not* want to)—then these visits in London, Paris, and Berlin would not be superfluous, but aside from that, also very instructive.

Jones writes to me today that he received a letter from you [showing you] in a good mood.[4] I hope it will persist, now as before.

Kind regards to you all, also from my wife.

I want to write soon to Fräulein Anna, in particular, about a literary matter.—Dr. Amsden[5] wrote to me about his visit to the Semmering, but nothing about the results of his discussions.

Yours,
Ferenczi

1. Eitingon essentially aligned himself with the English conception, to restrict training to medical candidates, with few exceptions (cf. letters of Eitingon to Freud, June 27 and July 2, 1927, Sigmund Freud Copyrights).

2. The text is missing.

3. The psychoanalytic sanatorium Schloss Tegel, opened by Simmel, for the interior design of which Ernst Freud was responsible. Freud later stayed there several times when he visited Professor Schröder in Berlin on account of his prosthesis. It had to be closed in 1931 for lack of money.

4. Freud to Jones, July 6, 1927 (*Freud/Jones*, pp. 620f.).

5. Dr. George S. Amsden (1870–1966), a member of the New York group. He had followed Ferenczi to Europe and went into analysis with him.

1101

Semmering, July 16, 1927

Dear friend,

I had already received a report from Eitingon about your visit, from which it was apparent that he was no more satisfied with you than you were with him.[1] I am, of course, totally on your side in the question, but I have turned my interest away from it and am not even reading through the resolutions carefully. I have done my utmost, accomplished little, and can do no more.

To minimize the difference between you and Eitingon, I only want to say that you are probably deceiving yourself as to the extent of what can be accomplished at the Congress. Eitingon is proceeding as a practical diplomat and is trying—perhaps only as a favor to me—to get as much through as possible. But it would be very regrettable if you made victory in the lay question a condition for accepting the presidency. The practice will take a different shape than the prescription, and in a position of leadership you can exert a great influence along our lines.

This summer is actually catastrophic, as if a great comet were in the heavens. We now hear about uproar in Vienna,[2] are almost cut off, and without knowing for sure what is going on there and what will come of it. It is a foul thing.

A little too much sickliness here.
Kind regards.

Yours,
Freud

1. Letter of July 12, 1927 (Sigmund Freud Copyrights).
2. The burning down of the Palace of Justice of July 15, 1927, in which the conflicts that were coming increasingly to resemble civil war culminated.

1102

Baden-Baden, July 28, 1927[1]

Dear Professor,

I thank you for your letter of July 16, and would be grateful for some lines in which I could learn your impressions after Eitingon's personal reports. In principle, I understand completely that it would not be right to postulate an unconditional quid pro quo between the presidency and victory in the lay question. In the event that the presidency is offered to me (about which I would like to learn more), I will strive to take into account the constitutional rights of the majority (without relinquishing my own ideas and tendencies).

Your letter was written in the mood of the threatening Viennese catastrophe; in the meantime, everything has quieted down there—indeed, perhaps this event will have shown the whole world the untenability of the Austrian situation and signified the beginning of a new epoch.

Dr. Amsden is speaking enthusiastically about the Burlingham children and is also grateful to you for the friendly reception.

Kind regards,
Ferenczi

1. This line was written under the crossed-out letterhead of the Hotel St. Andrew, New York (see letter 1084).

1103

Semmering, August 2, 1927

Dear friend,

I found Eitingon unchanged in his decision to hand over the presidency to you, if it can be put through, but this time he is also prepared to take it on himself, if there is too strong opposition to you. It has not become clear to me whether he means Jones or the Americans. In any case, you should work with him without restraint. I find *you* more reserved than you were before America. Damned country!

You have become acquainted with the parents of my patient Liebman. They are now in Germany, and I have advised them to look you up once more. When you come, have a look at my last letter to Frau Liebman. The highly intelligent boy is developing his paranoia more and more clearly, and I am harboring reservations about bearing the responsibility for him longer. I have struggled with him a great deal; it seemed to have a good chance for a while.

I greet you and Frau G.

Cordially,
Freud

P.S. Give my kind regards to the Groddecks as well. He should cease the agitation in the Ark for my Nobel Prize. It doesn't suit me.

1104

INTERNATIONALE ZEITSCHRIFT FÜR PSYCHOANALYSE
Herausgegeben von Prof. Dr. Sigm. Freud
Redigiert von Dr. M. Eitingon, Dr. S. Ferenczi und Dr. Sándor Radó

Baden-Baden, August 5, 1927

Dear Professor,

The sentence in your last letter, that you find me more reserved since America, is quite incomprehensible to me, and as far as I can judge, undeserved. On the contrary! My American experiences have, where possible, increased even more my interest in the cause of psychoanalysis (which I consider essentially to be a purely European cause). It is important for me to know from what symptoms you have drawn this conclusion! With regard to you, I don't feel the slightest reason to be more reserved; the only difference that exists between me and Eitingon is on the question of lay analysis, in which you and I do agree.

I passed on to Groddeck your admonition in the Nobel Prize question.— I am working here with five patients (five hours)). Dr. Amsden is a respectable person—naturally, quite unsuspecting.—I am sorry that the Liebman case doesn't have better prospects; but if I were in your position I wouldn't give up the struggle. Should the Liebmans come here, I would advise them to persist further, naturally, less hopefully. Is it true that you are preparing a work on fetishism?[1]

Received Fräulein Anna's letter with thanks; I am waiting for the critique of the manuscript I sent in.[2]

I send many kind regards and request a reply.

Yours truly,
Ferenczi

1. "Fetishism" (Freud 1927e).
2. Possibly "The Adaptation of the Family to the Child" (Ferenczi 1928, 281), a lecture given in London in June.

1105

Semmering, August 8, 1927

Dear friend,

I am glad as hell that you contradict me so vehemently. I probably wanted to hear only that, or I am not happy after all that I haven't seen you yet, months after your return from Dollaria.

Incidentally, I confess to a six-page-long essay about fetishism, which is designated for the Zeitschrift I, 1928. A strange circumstance compels me still to hold back the manuscript. As is well known, Stekel wrote a fat book on the subject;[1] I can't get myself to read it, but I must know whether by chance my solution is being touched on by him. So, I wrote to Wittels for information and must await his reply.[2] I can imagine that somebody can't go into a room in his house because someone else has done his business on the threshold.

And further, I am also writing an essay on humor, for the Almanac.[3] Let's hope it comes together. Of course, everything is more arduous than formerly, in the good times. No wonder I am eternally ill and in torment. The last few weeks were taken up by what I hope was a spastic intestinal disturbance, which is just today beginning to put on a good face. Otherwise, however, this summer is splendidly beautiful, the Semmering radiates in its entire, so charming, magnificence.

The Liebmans will probably not come to you. They have requested [me] by letter to have more patience with the boy, and since they don't seem to be deceiving themselves about the diagnosis, I gave in.

Have you already received the new French Revue?[4] If not, ask me for it in a card. I received about a dozen copies. Unfortunately, Secretary Pichon[5] has rendered them a very doubtful service in the editorial. Laforgue did not bear in mind that he, Pichon, has become Janet's brother-in-law. The Princess is very angry about this mishap. You will get to know her thoroughly up here in September.

I greet you and Frau G. cordially.

Yours,
Freud

1. *Der Fetischismus, dargestellt für Ärzte und Kriminologen* [Fetishism, Presented for Physicians and Criminologists] (Berlin, 1923).
2. Freud to Wittels, July 31, 1927 (Library of Congress).
3. "Humour" (Freud 1927d), first published in the *Almanach für das Jahr 1928* (Vienna, 1927). The *Almanach* printed popular psychoanalytic writings.
4. The *Revue Française de Psychanalyse*, which exists to this day, whose first issue was published on June 25, 1927.
5. Edouard Pichon (1890–1940), French pediatrician, hospital physician, monarchist, and member of the anti-Semitic, chauvinistic Action Française; he was an analysand of Sokolnicka's. Pichon wanted to "Frankify" psychoanalysis.

1106

Baden-Baden, August 19, 1927

Dear Professor,

I know that Dr. Laforgue (who called on me here and spent a few pleasant days by auto with us in what is now French Alsace) is coming to the

Semmering after the Congress.* Possibly you, despite the planned flight from being overrun, will also have to receive others. Well, so that you don't have too many around your neck, I will leave it to you to decide whether you prefer to have my visit with you (which I have been looking forward to for so long) in the first or the last half of the month of September. Please, *telegraph* me your wish, since I am not completely independent; I must also dispense with the time of my five pupils (five hours).

Besides the visit of Laforgue (who makes a very favorable impression on me), I am expecting for next Sunday the announced visit of the "Southwest Germans" (Landauer, Happel, perhaps Meng, Herr and Frau Dr. Fromm-Reichmann).[1] Together with me and Groddeck, it will be quite a respectable number. Frau Dr. Fromm-Reichmann is coming over to me once a week from Heidelberg. She is an astute, analytically extremely talented person.

In the question of the presidency, I will follow your advice, however it may sound. I request a word about it.

Kind regards,
Ferenczi

My wife, as always, thanks you for the greetings and returns them cordially.

*He wants to stay there for about two weeks.

1. Frieda Fromm-Reichmann (1889–1957), psychiatrist and psychoanalyst of German-Jewish descent. She was an analysand of Wilhelm Wittenberg, Hanns Sachs, and, evidently, also Ferenczi. She later worked closely with Groddeck and acted as a scientific hostess in his sanatorium. In 1933 she emigrated to America, where she headed the famous Chestnut Lodge clinic and played a pioneering role in the psychoanalytic treatment of psychoses. She dedicated her chief work, *Principles of Intensive Psychotherapy* (Chicago, 1950), to her teachers Sigmund Freud, Kurt Goldstein, Georg Groddeck, and Harry Stack Sullivan. Erich Fromm (1900–1980), probably one of the most brilliant and influential psychoanalysts, came from a German-Jewish family. He began with the study of law, but quickly changed to sociology, psychology, and philosophy. He was an analysand of Hanns Sachs, Theodor Reik, Karl Landauer, and his future wife, Frieda. He was a co-founder of the South German Institute for Psychoanalysis (1929) and a coworker in the investigations of the Frankfurt Institute for Social Research. From 1934 on, Fromm lived in New York and worked at the Institute for Social Research at Columbia University, where he became acquainted with Harry Stack Sullivan, who strongly influenced him. In 1941 Fromm, along with Clara Thompson and Karen Horney—of whom Fromm was a close friend and whose daughter Marianne he analyzed—left the New York Psychoanalytic Association and founded their own institute, the Association for the Advancement of Psychoanalysis, but in 1943, along with Thompson and Sullivan, Fromm left it. Along with the latter two and his now former wife, Frieda, he founded the New York branch of the Washington School of Psychiatry (from 1946 on the William Alanson White Institute of Psychiatry and Psychoanalysis), which had been brought into being by

Sullivan. In 1949 he moved to Mexico City, in 1974 to Ticino. He was founder, along with Igor Caruso, Gerhard Chrzanowski, and others, of the International Federation of Psychoanalytic Societies. Imbued with and fascinated by the Talmud, Marx, Freud, Spinoza, Christian mysticism, Zen Buddhism, philosophy, religion, socialism, sociology, and psychoanalysis, Fromm attempted a synthesis of diverse trends, especially of the Bible, Marx, and Freud. He developed what he called Humanistic Psychology, which was strongly oriented toward social and cultural but also ethical factors and attempted to postulate a human ethic, not a priori, but out of the realities of the *conditio humana.* Erich Fromm, *Gesamtausgabe,* ed. Rainer Funk, 10 vols. (Munich, 1988); Rainer Funk, *Erich Fromm* (Reinbek, 1983).

1107

Semmering, August 22, 1927

Dear friend,

I telegraphed you that I prefer the *first* half of September for your visit.[1] Naturally, your reasons remain the deciding factor; I will also be happy with your visit in the second half. But my reasons are as follows: We had a very beautiful summer, an early and raw fall is being predicted, which would be quite unsatisfying for you up here. Very many visitors have been announced for September after the Congress, but also two or three patients. The visitors can't expect that I will dedicate myself to them[2] all day long. Your presence will more likely defend me against these demands, but we will still find time for talking things out. I am finally beginning to become the enemy of every postponement; one is, after all, never quite sure.

Nothing has changed in matters of the presidency. Eitingon has very skillfully set things up in the new statutes so that both of the last ex-presidents should become council members, so that with you as president, our intentions will be realized. Only in case of strong opposition against you would I like you to support the election of Eitingon, in order to exclude that of Jones. The situation is clouded by distrust of Jones.[3]

I greet you and Frau G. cordially; Anna will tell you everything that you want to know about us.

Yours,
Freud

P.S. Anna will read aloud a little contribution from me about humor at the Congress.

1. The telegram has not been found.
2. "To you" in the original.
3. Freud wrote to Eitingon on August 26, 1927: "I thought you already knew that, from the bottom of my heart, I would like to see *you* in this position [president of the IPA], only the intensity of Ferenczi's wish in conjunction with your oft-expressed disinclination have inclined me to the other solution" (Sigmund Freud Copyrights). The Tenth In-

ternational Psychoanalytic Congress took place in Innsbruck, September 1–3, 1927. Ferenczi spoke on "The Termination of the Analysis" ("The Problem of Termination of the Analysis"; Ferenczi 1928, 282); Anna Freud read aloud her father's piece about humor (Freud 1927d). Eitingon was elected president. The Congress was marked by tensions between Anna Freud and Melanie Klein, as well as by the question of lay analysis and of requirements for membership. Since they couldn't reach agreement on the disputed points, the Training Commission was charged with working out a draft proposal for the next Congress, which also fell through.

1108

INTERNATIONALE PSYCHOANALYTISCHE VEREINIGUNG
INTERNATIONAL PSYCHO-ANALYTICAL ASSOCIATION[1]

Budapest, October 2, 1927

Dear Professor,

I wouldn't like to let the correspondence with you rest all too long. The main purpose of my letter of today is to thank you for the pleasant and—I would almost like to say, uplifting—hours that I was permitted to spend in your company. I felt as though I had been put back in the good old times in which the two of us talked through the still virgin problems of psychoanalysis and in between negotiated with the chances of gathering mushrooms. The mood at the Semmering was certainly first and foremost due to the restoration of your health—but perhaps also to the conviction that neither the time nor the many storms that are howling around us can ever change anything in the solidity of our personal and scientific bond.

I feel very well here in Budapest. I found everything the way it was. The members of the group were diligent in my absence, in fact, their activity increased. I want to further this tendency, and I hope in not too long a time find a house and home for an outpatient clinic and a training institute. I know that you don't care much for us Hungarians—but there is something like injustice in extending antipathy toward the country and its rulers also toward those who struggle under such difficult conditions. I think that somewhat more trust and encouragement on your part would significantly strengthen us in this struggle—but you seem entirely or in large part to have given up on this country—and this pessimism is enough to paralyze our energy.

Yesterday was the first orientation session, in which we discussed only administrative questions (publication of Hungarian writings, plans for founding an outpatient clinic). Dr. Hermann is a great help to me as secretary.

Kindest regards to your loved ones and to you yourself.

Yours,
Ferenczi

1. Preprinted letterhead, which contains, in addition, the names and signatures of the president, the Advisory Council members, the central secretary, and the treasurer.

1109

Vienna, October 23, 1927
IX., Berggasse 19

Dear friend,

Between the lines of your last letter, which I haven't answered for so long, partly out of laziness, partly out of the discomfort that very frequent visits to Pichler have produced, can be read the news, which is important to us all, that you are determined to remain in Budapest. What else could be meant by the reproach that I have a low opinion of the trusty Budapest group? Certainly only the fact that a secret wish of mine wanted to rob it of its irreplaceable leader. I don't deny this wish, but I will gladly exclude the group from the antipathy that I have developed since the Horthy period against a Hungary cleansed of Jews. And if you remain in her possession, we will all joyously recognize her significance.

In the meantime you have seen for yourself the energy devil of a Princess and have received the galleys[1] (advance proofs) of my new pamphlet[2] for more comfortable reading. It already strikes me now as childish, I basically think differently, consider this work analytically frail and insufficient as a confession. It may be good for giving the Verlag a little business.

The Rundbriefe are beginning again;[3] we are awaiting yours. I will take part in the correspondence only indirectly, through Anna.

I can't say that the analytic work interests me very much now. I would like best not to do anything, as [I did] for a few weeks at the Semmering. I used a few unkind words with Brill and Jones by letter; let us hope it does both of them good.[4]

Anna is developing analytically very well and independently. One may question with concern whether her virginal attitude will always be compatible with the often offensive reality of the other analysts.

My wife wanted to go to Berlin with Mathilde; the latter turned her down on account of her wavering state of health, and since Minna is unwell at the same time, she postponed the trip, but certainly not for long.

I greet you and your dear wife cordially, and I hope to hear from you regularly and to be able to give you news myself.

Yours,
Freud

1. This word has been crossed out in the original.
2. *The Future of an Illusion* (Freud 1927c), published in November.

3. "After the Innsbruck Congress we changed the structure of the Committee by converting it into a group, no longer private, of the officials of the International Association. They were Eitingon, the President; Ferenczi and myself, Vice-Presidents; Anna Freud, Secretary and van Ophuijsen, Treasurer. Sachs . . . dropped out" (Jones III, 135).

4. Freud reproached Jones for his vacillating position regarding a possible secession of the New York group, and because of his support for Melanie Klein and the "regular campaign" (letter of September 23, 1927, *Freud/Jones*, p. 624) that he was organizing in London against Anna's conception of child analysis: "Two points remain inexcusable: the reproach, which is not customary among us and offends against all good practice, that she [Anna] was not analyzed sufficiently—put forward by you publicly and in private—and Mrs. Klein's remark that she believed Anna is avoiding the Oedipus complex on principle" (letter of October 9, 1927, ibid., p. 633). He criticized Brill on account of his "purely negative attitude" toward lay analysis and Brill's assumption that he, Freud, wanted "to force the New Yorkers out of the International. That is a magnificent piece of projection . . . but if it is necessary for us to deal with this possibility, we must ask ourselves what we will lose thereby. The answer is: nothing . . . And now the most personal matters of all! I know very well what profit you have gained by introducing analysis in America. But it did you no harm, and it aroused the expectation that you will gain further profit instead of putting yourself to rest after you have become a rich man. You know my dissatisfaction began when I heard how many patients you see in a day and that you give treatments of thirty-five minutes in order to be able to see so many patients" (letter of September 20, 1927, Library of Congress).

1110

Vienna, October 25, 1927
IX., Berggasse 19

Dear friend,

I received today the American translation of Lay Analysis and Autobiographical Study and must thank you in a few words for the beautiful introduction[1] that you wrote for it.[2] It honors you yourself no less than me. Since 1909 we have covered a nice piece of trail with each other, always hand in hand, and it won't be any different for the short stretch that still remains to be trod.

Cordially,
Freud

1. This word is written in English in the original [Trans.].
2. See letter 1076, n. 1.

1111

Dr. S. Ferenczi
vii., Nagydiofa-Utca 3.[1]

Budapest, November 13, 1927

Dear Professor,

You will certainly already have thought that my long silence is no coincidence. Well, since the cause has already—I think—for the most part been removed, I can write to you again. The nocturnal disturbances of my well-being have "afflicted" me again since my return home, so that during the day (despite significant diminution of my work hours) I only just acceded to the demands of unavoidable activity, but lacked any desire or strength for other work or correspondence. I made an exception with regard to Society matters, which I took up out of a feeling of duty.—I evidently bear *bodily* inactivity badly; this insight then also helped me toward rational therapy, which brought considerable success for the time being. Calisthenics and breathing exercises brought better nights—along with that, also improvement in my energy and desire for work. I will let the final decision about my plan for the future depend on, among other things, whether this improvement continues.

To get back to your latest news, I thank you especially for the kind words that you wrote to me on the occasion of the publication of the "Introduction" to the American Lay Analysis. I don't recall anymore the wording of that introduction; but I think I know it to the extent that it cannot have contained anything other than what I have been thinking and preaching for twenty years: the thanks that we owe you for the light that you brought to the darkness of knowledge about man. Now it occurs to me that you give the year 1909 as the beginning of our collaboration. That is an error—it began in 1907.[2] I hope that the other statement, that our future path is a short one from now on, will also prove to be false.

As I like to have my patients tell me the bad things that they think about me, I would like to know, unadorned, everything that Brill and Jones said about themselves in their correspondence with you. Could you send me these letters (about which Eitingon also made mention), so that I can have a look at them?

The day before yesterday, I presented to the Hungarian circle the "Gulliver Phantasies,"[3] which are being published in the Zeitschrift. I was able to supplement the essay in two points. 1.) The *massiveness* of dwarfs in dreams, hallucinations, etc. can be explained by the fact that the *fear of being broken into pieces* is concealed by "individualization" of the fragments (of the body). The cut-off thumb or penis becomes a "little man." A young psychiatrist who was present was able to confirm that with the case of a schizophrenic who relates again and again how he is always reborn through the sprouting of such pieces. 2.) The "feeling of strangeness," the alienation of the world of perception, showed itself in a case *clearly* to be the last piece of a castration fantasy in which the entire ego identifies with the (cut-off, dead) penis.—Thus, the penis becomes a "little man"—as if the ego, when the member is cut off, would rather stay with the cut-off member than with the remainder of the body, which has been cut up.—I am convinced that this can be confirmed from many quarters.

My wife always thanks you for your greetings. Elma is now in Italy for a visit.

Kind regards,
Ferenczi

The renegade of our group, Feldmann, writes (skillfully played up) books in the manner of Stekel (he is his representative here). Since we have learned his secret analytically, our hands are tied, and we have to let him continue. He is becoming more and more popular here.

1. Preprinted letterhead.
2. Ferenczi is mistaken here: it began in 1908. In 1907, to be sure, Ferenczi was introduced to psychoanalysis by C. G. Jung.
3. See letter 1091, n. 1.

1112

Vienna, December 18, 1927
IX., Berggasse 19[1]

Dear friend,
What does your silence mean? I hope you are not ill. Send news still before Christmas.

Yours,
Freud

1. Correspondence card with preprinted letterhead.

1113

Dr. S. Ferenczi
vii., Nagydiofa-Utca 3.

Budapest, December 20, 1927

Dear Professor,
In fact, the consistently bad nights that have been going on for a long time have made me morose. I did [not] want to bother you, or anyone else,

with my burdensome "illness reports." It still has to do with something not very palpable: a breathing disturbance, which always appears at night and which consists of a kind of tiring of the activity of expiration. I awaken with a severe headache, or also half frozen;—a swallow of warm coffee suffices to restore me—but for the next day I am functional to the extent that I can take care of my hours only with considerable attentiveness. I try all kinds of internal and external palliative remedies—usually one or the other helps me. I don't want to start up with the internists; friend Lévy has the sure talent to make one hypochondriacal.—At the moment I am reasonably all right again.—

With all that, psychoanalysis, also therapeutically, gives me more and more satisfaction. One evidently has to get as old as I to gain the proper familiarity and the technique which is free of excesses, and still capable of alteration. I am sometimes sorry that I waste my hard-earned knowledge on foreigners who pay well, instead of handing it over to younger colleagues.

Nothing special is going on in the family. The mood is dominated by the usual Christmas preparations.

Apropos Christmas! I wanted to come to you, but this time I decided to get complete rest; I am staying in this country—and, verily, am feeding myself![1] I await—I hope, favorable!—news from you, Fräulein Anna, and the rest of the members of the family. N.B.: You, too, owe me another reply!

Many cordial holiday wishes.

Yours truly,
Ferenczi

P.S. (actually belongs to the Rundbrief!): Rumors are circulating in American, but also in English analytic circles, according to which I had "a very good time with all those ladies"[2] in America, and am also keeping an American mistress at the moment.

1. See letter 818 and n. 1.
2. The words in quotation marks are written in English in the original [Trans.].

1114

Dr. S. Ferenczi
vii., Nagydiofa-Utca 3.

Budapest, January 1, 1928

Dear Professor,

Cheers to the New Year!

A somewhat better night and an afternoon nap on top of that on the Sunday *and* holiday of today permits me to see the world and the future in a somewhat friendlier light. I am making use of this moment to offer you New Year's wishes, and I wish ya good healt' an' a vera, vera, long life![1]— myself, among other things, that you remain well disposed to me, now as before.

I naturally greet all the members of your family and also wish them all the best—already in order that you be more satisfied—but also in addition to that.—

Enclosed I send a little paper.[2] I also for the time being put off replying in the affirmative to the enclosed invitation of the Berlin "Medizinische Welt."[3] But perhaps it is not inappropriate to give the general practitioners a look into our witches' kitchen for once. I would also gladly put these pages at the disposal of the Revue Psychanalytique.[4]

I request your kind opinion about the paper altogether, and then about whether it belongs in the Zeitschrift, the Medizinische Welt, or both.

Cordially
Ferenczi

1. The preceding phrase is written in dialect in the original, perhaps as a reflection of Ferenczi's jovial mood. [Trans.].
2. "The Elasticity of Psycho-Analytical Technique" (Ferenczi 1928, 283).
3. The invitation has not been found.
4. *Revue Française de Psychanalyse,* in which the paper was later published (2 [1928]: 228–238).

1115

Vienna, January 4, 1928
IX., Berggasse 19

Dear friend,

Yesterday's mail brought two rare pieces: a report from S. Paulo (Brazil) that a ψα group has been formed there, which will apply for acceptance to the International,[1] and your letter, to whose New Year's wishes I cordially respond, as [I did] twenty years ago. We are both certainly conscious of the impotence of our thoughts and the value of our basic attitude. Your enclosed paper—here reinclosed—testifies to that superior maturity that you have acquired in the last few years and in which no one approaches you. The title[2] is excellent and deserved to be applied to more. For my recommendations on technique which I gave back then were essentially negative. I considered the most important thing to emphasize what one should not do, to demonstrate the temptations that work against analysis. Almost everything that is positive that one should do I left to "tact," which has been introduced by you. But what I achieved in so doing was that the obedient ones didn't take notice of the elasticity of these dissuasions and subjected themselves to them as if they were taboos. That had to be revised at some time, without, of course, revoking the obligations.

I still have to raise an objection to your paper, which obviously doesn't belong in any journal but our own, to the effect that it is not three times as long and doesn't divide into [parts] I, II, III. There is no doubt that you still have many similar things to say, which would be very beneficial to hear. As true as what you say about "tact" is, this admission seems to me to be all the more questionable in this form. All those who have no tact will see in this a justification of arbitrariness, i.e., of the subjective factor, i.e., of the influence of one's own unrestrained complexes. What we undertake in reality is a weighing out, which remains mostly preconscious, of the various reactions that we expect from our interventions, in the process of which it is first and foremost a matter of the quantitative assessment of the dynamic factors in the situation. Rules for these measurements can naturally not be made; the analyst's experience and normality will have to be the decisive factors. But one should thus divest "tact" of its mystical character for beginners.

It would be a beautiful piece of propaganda if you wrote articles for a German medical newspaper. But they couldn't be elementary enough, and one customarily finds that either very interesting or very boring. (Letter enclosed.)

Nothing new with us. The old mother [was] very wobbly for a while, but recovered valiantly.

With kind wishes for you and your dear wife, also for your nights in all of 1928.

Yours,
Freud

1. Sociedade Brasileira de Psicanálise, the first Latin-American psychoanalytic society, founded on October 24, 1927, by Francisco Franco da Rocha (1864–1933), president, and Durval Marcondes (1899–1981), secretary. The other board members were Raul Briquet and Lourenco Filho. The *Revista Brasileira de Psicanálise* (1928) was also founded shortly thereafter (*Zeitschrift* 15 (1929): 142).

2. The passage from here to the end of the following paragraph (with the exception of the latter's first two sentences, and not quite literally) was quoted by Ferenczi in his paper as "criticism [from an anonymous] colleague" (Ferenczi 1928, 283, p. 99; Schriften II, 248f.).

1116

ANNA FREUD
Wien Ix., Berggasse 19[1]

Vienna, January 11, 1928

Dear Doctor!

I just received a letter from Eitingon and one from Jones, in which both write about the meeting of the Committee planned for Easter. You have probably also just received letters about it.

I would be very much in favor of the meeting, for I think it is more than necessary if the Congress[2] is to go anywhere near peacefully, but I have no intention of traveling as far as Paris,[3] and I hope you don't either. Paris for two days is so far and expensive for the both of us that one can really hardly expect it of us. Rather, I find that Jones could impose more distance upon himself because this time he won't have a long trip to the location of the Congress. Do you think that with [our] forces united, we can draw the Westerners somewhat closer to the East?

I haven't wished you well for the New Year yet, but I am doing it now after the fact, and hope that it is still valid.

Yours,
Anna

1. Preprinted letterhead. The letter is typewritten; only the signature, "Anna," is handwritten.
2. There had been plans for a Congress in Oxford, which was, however, postponed until the following year.
3. Jones writes that he "had arranged a meeting of the Committee in Paris at the end of February. The fatal illness of my daughter prevented me from going, and Ferenczi found the distance too great, so the meeting was confined to Anna Freud and Eitingon" (Jones III, 139). This seems improbable, because Eitingon wrote to Freud on March 1, "I am pleased . . . that Anna is in Paris" (Sigmund Freud Copyrights). Such a meeting actually did take place a year later.

1117

Dr. S. Ferenczi
vii., Nagydiofa-Utca 3.

Budapest, January 15, 1928[1]

Dear Professor,

The personal Rundbrief[2] (directed to me), as well as the one sent afterward, have arrived in a timely fashion. Many thanks for both. Yesterday, in the Society meeting, I lectured on the "Elasticity of Technique." You yourself figured in as the first of the discussants; you see, presupposing your assent after the fact, I read aloud the sentences from your letter which pertain to the paper. As a reply to your comments, I endeavored (and it didn't cost me much effort to do so) to prove that there is essentially no difference between your conception and mine. I know that you occasionally told me that I strive all too much to produce complete identity between your views and mine. But I believe that this time I am in the right. "Tact," as I view it, does not intend to be a concession to the arbitrariness of the subjective factor, still less [does it intend] to favor "the influence of one's own unrestrained complexes." On the contrary, I demand the strictest control of the latter. I only think that one should put oneself first and foremost into the patient's position, one must "empathize" [einfühlen], but I am completely of your opinion regarding the topography of this psychic process. The empathy of the analyst must not take place in the unconscious, but [must take place] in the preconscious. The analyst's properly being analyzed is the same thing that you call "normality." If this condition is present, then one can correctly weigh out the various reactions (and, in fact, one's own, as well as the patient's) and make the pertinent decision. In conclusion, I also agreed with the assertion that, despite all precautions, a misuse can occur, even with these technical recommendations. I prophesied directly (after the sadistic "active") the possibility of a "masochistic" period of analysis, of which I warned our members.

Now, I request your express consent for me to append the pertinent sentences in your letter, along with my reply, to the publication.

I gave another small contribution to the metapsychology of character analyses, which I likewise want to add to the text.[3]

The energetic tone of your letter against the Americans did me good.[4] My response to Ophuijsen was kept somewhat too "tactful," with conscious intention. It may serve you as a private communication that another member of the lay group as well, a pupil of Dr. Pierce Clark, whom the group, on my advice, accepted only as an associate member, is evidently being publicly accused of various really defamatory things. In order to get rid of him, the lay group decided upon its temporary dissolution.

The few (six to seven) intact members, mostly trained by me, will, however, continue their meetings and are waiting for a favorable time to constitute themselves. So, to that extent, the methodical persecution has had a result. (N.B. such a cleanup among the medical analysts would probably have had at least as great a success.) Incidentally, I also consider it an advantage that, through the dissolution, the president to date, Miss Potter,[5] who is certainly not a match for this role scientifically, officially disappears from the picture. She is a nice person, though anything but a representative analyst.

Your good wishes for me have not come true for the time being; my night's rest is still being disturbed, which makes me morose and uneager for work during the day.*

Did you speak to Róheim in the meantime; what is your opinion about his plans?[6]

We are extraordinarily looking forward to your Anna's February lecture.[7]
With kind regards.

Your old,
Ferenczi

*P.S. This has improved in the meantime!

1. The letter is typewritten; only the signature, "Ferenczi," and the postscript, are handwritten.

2. *Rundbrief* of January 11, 1928 (British Psycho-Analytical Society).

3. See *Schriften* II, 249f.

4. Van Ophuijsen had protested vehemently against the Vienna Society's admitting an American "lay" candidate, even though it had "been warned." "The Vienna Institute, in my opinion, thus bears full responsibility for the difficulties which the American colleagues are experiencing and for the harm which psychoanalysis in the U.S. is incurring and will incur on account of the certified pupil" (*Rundbrief* of December 30, 1927). In his reply Freud again criticized the American attitude toward lay analysis: "The training institute which has seized the opportunity to change an unschooled layman into one who is halfway educated has done something good that would otherwise not have occurred" (*Rundbrief* of January 11, 1928, both in British Psycho-Analytical Society).

5. See letter 1096 and n. 1.

6. An expedition, which was in fact undertaken, to the Pacific islands and to Australia, which was made possible through the support of Marie Bonaparte and pursued the aim of refuting the anthropologist Bronislaw Malinowski's (1884–1942) critique of the Oedipus complex. See Jones III, 139.

7. Lecture of February 25, 1928, "Zum Thema Kinderanalyse" [On the Topic of Child Analysis], *Zeitschrift* 14 (1928): 429.

1118

Dr. S. Ferenczi
vii., Nagydiofa-Utca 3.

Budapest, February 8, 1928[1]

Dear Professor,

I am sorry that my last stay in Vienna was disrupted by the presence of the Swiss woman.[2] I was thereby deprived of the so rare opportunity of being able to chat with you about all kinds of personal and nonpersonal things, which I so seldom have the opportunity to do. I took it upon myself, in future, not to let myself be deterred from my first impulse to visit you by any other considerations.

There are rumors of a summons of Róheim to Berlin (probably to the training institute). If the emigration to Berlin continues in this manner, I will one day pack my bags and move there myself. What do you think about the reception I will get there?

Next Tuesday I begin the series of public lectures, which haven't been delivered that way since the outbreak of the war.[3] I will review the result in the Rundbrief.

Jones wrote to me in a private letter that he requests that I show him, before publication, the text of my planned critique,[4] which I incautiously happened to mention. He would consider this, so he says, a great kindness on my part. I only replied that the text is not at all fixed yet, but I find that such censorship is an unjustified request.

We are very much looking forward to your Anna's visit.

Kind regards,
Ferenczi

1. The letter is typewritten; only the signature, "Ferenczi," and a correction are handwritten.
2. Mira Oberholzer, who had come to Vienna to defend the action of her husband, who, on January 7, after resigning his presidency of the Swiss Society, had withdrawn from it along with other members and had founded the Swiss Medical Society for Psychoanalysis. The IPA turned down the application for affiliation; Philipp Sarasin (1888–1968) assumed the leadership of the old Swiss group, whose president he was to be for thirty-two years (*Zeitschrift* 15 [1929]: 140). Eitingon, who had likewise been present at Mrs. Oberholzer's visit, reported: "We all found . . . that all of the otherwise clever woman's pleas made Oberholzer's attitude seem again and again to be what has been rather clear to all of us, namely, that of a quite intractable neurotic" (*Rundbrief* of February 16, 1928, British Psycho-Analytical Society).
3. In the spring of 1928 Ferenczi gave six lectures on psychoanalysis to over 1,200 listeners in the Great Hall of the Academy of Music (*Zeitschrift* 14 [1928]: 252).
4. The critique has not been identified; probably the "critique of the Englishmen" mentioned in letter 1124. In any case, Ferenczi did not publish any critique of the kind.

1119

Vienna, February 27, 1928
IX., Berggasse 19

Dear friend,

Anna has returned from Budapest elevated, gratified, lavished with gifts, and [is] already on the way to Paris. I thank you, your dear wife, and the whole Society most warmly for the cordial and honorable reception that you accorded her.

The one of your reports that pleased me the most was the fact that you are finally experiencing a revival of interest in analysis in your Hungary, and are nourishing it by means of your excellent lectures. It will soon be exactly ten years since our Congress and everything that was connected with it.

So little is happening here—the house is so quiet—, that I may close the short letter with a cordial greeting.

Yours,
Freud

1120

Budapest, March 25, 1928

Dear Professor,

I am pleased to announce to you my trip to Vienna, which will take place on the week-end[1] of this week. Unfortunately, I am not free Friday evening (lecture[2] and communal supper), but I hope to be able to spend a few hours with you after your hours on Saturday, and above all, Sunday morning.—

My wife will accompany me this time.

Kind regards and until we meet again!

Yours,
Ferenczi

1. This word is written in English in the original [Trans.].

2. The lecture has not been identified; possibly, however, the lecture on "Psychoanalyse und Kriminologie" [Psychoanalysis and Criminology] (Ferenczi 1928, 283a) in the Verein für angewandte Psychopathologie in Vienna, the date of which is (erroneously?) given in *Bausteine* III, p. 399, as April 30, 1928. It seems improbable that Ferenczi would have written to Freud on April 29, 1928 (letter 1124), without mentioning a trip to Vienna on the following day. See also Anna Freud's *Rundbrief* of April 30, 1928: "There is nothing worth communicating" (British Psycho-Analytical Society). But on April 1, 1928, Freud reported to Eitingon, "Ferenczi gave a nice lecture here on Friday" (Sigmund

Freud Copyrights)—a lecture that is not mentioned in the minutes of the Vienna Society and evidently took place under different auspices.

1121

Budapest, April 11[, 1928]¹

arriving saturday evening hotel regina greetings = ferenczi

1. Telegram.

1122

INTERNATIONALE PSYCHOANALYTISCHE VEREINIGUNG
INTERNATIONAL PSYCHO-ANALYTICAL ASSOCIATION

Budapest, April 14, 1928

Dear Professor,

The talk about the organic conditions which threaten to make me prematurely senile has obviously shaken me up. On the one hand, I decided to try it again with Lajos Lévy. He advised controlling intestinal function by means of magnesia and belladonna, but is decidedly *opposed to* Karlsbad and Marienbad. Up to now, a moderate improvement can be noted through the medication—but I have to wait and see how long it persists.—A second source of the disturbance is of a neurotic nature and is composed of current and infantile things.

The subjective ailments abate immediately when I can sleep properly, so that I am occasionally my old (i.e., young) self again, grasping things quickly, full of ideas, etc. So, everything doesn't seem to be lost yet. (N.B.: the ideas are connected to ego psychology; they are very useful to me in my cases. Perhaps something will come out of them sometime!)

This evening I am going to Lovrana (Hotel Excelsior) for a week with my wife (for a belated Easter vacation). We will be home again next Monday.

Perhaps I will use the (let's hope, not all too windy) time on the Adriatic to bring to paper thoughts that are hovering around me but are for the moment too unclear to be shared.

I was pleased to see you again in good health. Let us hope it stays that way until you are again at your Semmering—and there I am sure of the matter.

Kindest regards to everyone.

Yours,
Ferenczi

1123

Vienna, April 22, 1928
IX., Berggasse 19

Dear friend,

Now you are probably home again. I was very pleased to hear that you indulged yourself in the little excursion. I didn't doubt that you could still be young, still have ideas, and will share all kinds of important things with us.

Don't write to me again about my health. I am clearly in a decline. If I owned more, I would give up working.

Perhaps you will smile about the contrast when I ask you not to forget to send back the two issues of the English journal, if you have finished with them. But one continues one's small interests by force of habit.

The inner development of Ψα everywhere runs counter to my intentions, away from lay analysis to the purely medical specialty, which I sense to be ominous for the future of analysis. Actually, I am *only* sure about you that you share my point of view without reservation.

Cordially,
Freud

1124

INTERNATIONALE PSYCHOANALYTISCHE VEREINIGUNG
INTERNATIONAL PSYCHO-ANALYTICAL ASSOCIATION

Budapest, April 29, 1928[1]

Dear Professor,

It was a pleasure to find your kind letter here upon my return from the Adriatic. I was particularly pleased to see the fact of my unshakable maintenance of the necessity of lay analysis being recognized. That also brings me to making a confession to you that I sought the presidency mainly because I found our friend Eitingon, notwithstanding all his other assets, too lukewarm in this connection. To be sure, my politics would have been less compromise-prone than his; in place of that, a small crowd would have grouped around me, which, unconcerned by other interests, would do pure psychoanalysis.

The week in Lovrana was instrumental as an intellectual rest period, although we both got a terrible attack of cold and coughing, with which we are still laboring; in the end, one was glad to find the accustomed Budapest spring climate again.

Yesterday we had a session with the Viennese guest lecturer, Dr. Reich.[2]

He told us about his technical scheme; I recognized his endeavor to enlist the aid of character analysis as legitimate, but I criticized his hasty and one-sided emphasis on the ego resistances. I had the impression that he has taken our arguments to heart, at least in part.

You touched on a debt of honor when you mentioned the two issues of the Journal. I don't want to send back the volumes without having written down my critique of the Englishmen beforehand.

With kindest regards and best wishes.

Yours truly,
Ferenczi

1. The letter is typewritten; only the signature, "Ferenczi," is handwritten.
2. Lecture on "Handhabung der Übertragung" [Management of the Transference]; see the brief review in *Zeitschrift* 14 (1928): 57.

1125

Vienna, May 13, 1928
IX., Berggasse 19

Dear friend,

I see it would be unfriendly not to thank you and your Society for the birthday greetings,[1] even though I had requested that no notice be taken of the date up to the 75th time. But I am so free as to extend this wish to the 80th.

My main reaction on the festive occasion was my astonishment that I have become so old. I haven't noticed any difference in the 73rd year in relation to the earlier ones. The prosthesis makes a fool of me and torments me just as before. And in the face of that—so wretchedly can interests dry up—everything else retreats.

Today Anna is—a weekend excursion—in Berlin, in order to argue around with Bernfeld, who has got things to the point where they want to terminate the analytic training of pedagogues. Bernfeld is abetting the reactionary cause as a proper nihilist, Anna is fighting honestly for lay and pedagogic analysis. You will have read with satisfaction how liberally our Indian friends have expressed themselves about lay analysis.[2] You are right, Eitingon's heart isn't in it; he finds it necessary to assume a friendly attitude out of consideration for Anna and me. He was here for a few days as usual, and I made use of his presence to paint him a picture of a bleak future for psychoanalysis if it doesn't know how to create a place for itself outside of medicine.

The Verlag now has a nice place in the stock exchange building, is being generously led by Storfer, and would actually only need one thing, or one person, namely Anton v. Freund. If only he hadn't died on us! We would have been able to do without others so much more easily. Let's not think about it too much!

Kind regards to you and Frau G.

Yours,
Freud

1. The birthday greetings have not been found.
2. Reference unclear.

1126

INTERNATIONALE PSYCHOANALYTISCHE VEREINIGUNG
INTERNATIONAL PSYCHO-ANALYTICAL ASSOCIATION

Budapest, May 31, 1928

Dear Professor,

Frau Ilona v. Kosztolányi,[1] a close acquaintance, to whom I am indebted for the case of the *"Little Rooster-Man,"*[2] which is so interesting to both of us, requests the honor of being received by you, if only for a moment. She wants to decorate one of your works with your autograph.

In support of her request, I am

Yours truly,
S. Ferenczi

Frau v. Kosztolányi can visit you both in Vienna and at the Semmering.

1. Ilona Harmos (1885–1967), married to the poet Dezsö Kosztolányi since 1913. She was an actress, a writer, and Strindberg's Hungarian translator. She was the editor of a biography of her husband.
2. Ferenczi 1913, 114.

1127

Semmering, June 19, 1928

Dear friend,

I quickly read through the paper by Zilboorg[1] and think, as you do, that it is worthy of publication. It should be handed over to the editors as soon as possible.

We have been here since Saturday, I, probably not for long. That is news that I ask be kept strictly secret.

Pichler's attempts this year to get me a usable prosthesis turned out so badly that I have finally decided to break [with him].[2] On the 24th, Professor Schröder[3] from Berlin is coming to Vienna to examine me, and if he promises me something I can hardly do otherwise than go to Berlin to him. That may then cost a large part, or all, of the summer. But I have no choice and must assume the uncertainty of the result and the certainty of the great expense.

Dr. Burlingham[4] is a charming person, satisfied with everything here, and seems to be feeling very well.

I greet you and Frau Gisela cordially.

Yours,
Freud

P.S. You will, naturally, be hearing more from me soon.

1. "Schizophrenien nach Entbindungen" [Postpartum Schizophrenias], *Zeitschrift* 15 (1929): 67–81. Gregory Zilboorg (1890–1959), a Ukrainian, studied medicine in St. Petersburg. In 1919 he emigrated to the United States, where he received his M.D. from Columbia in 1926. He was an analysand of Franz Alexander and president and chairman of the Education Committee of the New York Society. He was a prolific author, especially about psychoses. He was at the center of a scandal when, in addition to the fee for analysis, he charged a patient $5,000 as a "business fee." Susan Quinn, *A Mind of Her Own: The Life of Karen Horney* (New York, 1987), pp. 342f.

2. "This was not easy for me, as it basically means turning away from a man to whom I already owe four years' prolongation of my life. But I could not continue" (Freud to Jones, July 1, 1928, *Freud/Jones*, p. 648).

3. Hermann Schröder, jaw surgeon, director of the Institute of Dental Medicine of the University of Berlin.

4. Robert Burlingham was visiting in Austria with George W. Wickersham, former U.S. attorney general, a friend of his father's. Michael Burlingham, *The Last Tiffany* (New York, 1989), pp. 197f.

1128

Semmering, July 11, 1928

Dear friend,

The presence of Dr. Burlingham in the house next door promises us a visit from you over a weekend. He still wants to visit you and Amsden in Budapest, and this letter of mine is hurrying in advance of him.

After the breakup of the analysis with Reik, I have begun to concern myself with Dorothy Burlingham, in consideration of the new situation created by the arrival of her husband. I am beginning to get my bearings with her, but I don't know if I will set something up in these two months. The situation between both of them is difficult, [and] can be the source of bad developments. As long as Anna and I stand in between, probably nothing will happen. Dr. Amsden should make some provisions for September, when we will both be in Berlin.

Things are not going badly at present, but the two of them are also not getting any further with each other. From her I have the impression that she doesn't like him, doesn't want him in the house with her, and probably never really did like him. Reik seems to have greatly overestimated her dependency on him. He is, in fact, not the right man for her, and never was, from a physical respect. He is a charming, tender person, but not smart enough to reconcile himself with his very complicated situation. His character is incoherent, his behavior contradictory. He wants to talk himself into thinking that she loves him, but sees what speaks against it, then he forgets that he is actually a kind of Rip van Winkle,[1] and can't put back the requirements that he naturally must have. It can't be discerned what was wrong with him. His present condition doesn't fit a typical cyclothymia at all. If Dr. Amsden thinks he can easily fall ill again, then caution is very much indicated.

I greet you kindly and await you.

Yours,
Freud

1. According to a German legend and short story by Washington Irving (1783–1859), a man, married to a shrew, goes hunting in the mountains and meets a group of bizarre little men. He takes a drink and thereupon goes to sleep for twenty years. When he awakens, his wife is dead, and he can lead a carefree life.

1129

Semmering, July 13, 1928

Dear friend,

Enclosed [is] the letter[1] from a man who belongs to the uncomfortable category of those who never come to grips with the father imago, and for that reason eternally run after it, but in order to bark at it, the way dogs do with an automobile. I am happy to be able to refuse him; try him out yourself, if you have time. If not, direct him, perhaps, to Berlin.

In expectation of your weekend, cordially,

Yours,
Freud

1. The letter has not been found.

1130

Budapest, July 20/21, 1928[1]

am without passport can't come for time being please telegraph in case amsden's coming unpostponable - ferenczi

1. Telegram. It appears from the code numbers on the form that the telegram was put in at 10:30 P.M. on the twentieth and registered at 7:28 A.M. on the twenty-first.

1131

Budapest, July 23, 1928[1]

passport in order request report when coming desired = ferenczi =

1. Telegram. It is not in the folder of the Austrian National Library but was later found by Judith Dupont in Ferenczi's papers.

1132

Budapest, August 7, 1928

Dear Professor,

Today I was able to convey the contents of your last letter to Dr. Amsden. As you know, he has been in Vienna in the meantime, where he was lured by a false alarm report about Dr. Mackenzie's[1] condition. He shares your view that the situation at the Semmering is untenable, only he considers it advisable (and not dangerous, considering Dr. Burlingham's previous conditions) that the breaking away from the Semmering not be carried out all too quickly. In any event, he plans to go to Vienna again next Saturday to prepare things; he will also go there a second time, if warranted. He has not yet finalized the details of his plan; perhaps he will succeed in getting Dr. Burlingham to America *with* Mackenzie; apart from that, he is having Dr. Burlingham come to Budapest. But all that is uncertain. In any case, he is planning [to have] an honest talk with Dr. Burlingham and is counting on its having a corresponding effect on him.

The few hours that I was permitted to spend in your circle also had an invigorating effect on my intellectual and moral powers.

I hope, along with you, for the favorable effect of the arts of the Berlin miracle man.

Kind regards,
Ferenczi

Dr. Amsden spoke to me about an American (from Albany), who would like to be analyzed by you, if possible. I encouraged him to ask you directly. If you can't take him, I will take him. But—as mentioned—he prefers *you* in any case.

1. The doctor has not been identified.

1133

Budapest,
August 16, 1927 [1928][1]

Dear Professor,

The psychoanalysis of a case with mild manic-depressive cycles gave (and gives) me the opportunity to recall your ideas about "psychological time."[2] It became evident to me that the manic (in whom anxiety has been totally shut off) becomes, so to speak, "simultaneous" in his entire associative activity; his ability to communicate only limps along with difficulty behind the impressions that storm over him. In the anxiety-free manic phase he sometimes suddenly becomes "enlightened." He really resembles the bird which can be in two (or many) places at the same time.[3]

In contrast to this, in times of anxiety, he is, like every melancholic, especially ponderous in thinking—he is persecuted by a single thought, which he cannot mitigate in a compromising fashion by comparison with others, etc.

I was thinking that I should share this triviality with you, especially since I hope that you will perhaps be occasioned by it to occupy yourself further with your extremely significant idea.—

I can imagine how calming an effect Dr. Burlingham's departure has had on both of the villas at the Semmering. Dr. Amsden behaved, as usual, very skillfully and tactfully.

I am still working six hours a day—next week (on the 23rd) Rickmann,[4] whom you sent to me, will be added to this. I am always pleased to be recommended by you.

With kind regards from all of us.

Yours,
Ferenczi

What do you think about the size of Rickmann's hourly fee?[5] [I] request in this regard a brief but mailed reply, which I would like to get before his arrival.

Thanks.

F[erenczi].

1. This letter was in the folder for 1927. Balint noted by hand under the place designation, "Error: correct, Baden-Baden." However, the content of the letter (Dr. Burlingham's departure from the Semmering; a postscript which could relate to that of the previous letter) suggests that the place is given correctly but that the date was written incorrectly. An examination of the stationery and ink favors placing the letter here.
2. The ideas were evidently communicated by word of mouth.
3. An allusion to a passage in Balzac in which a miser pretends to be dumb in order to

collect his thoughts, then all at once stammers, "I'm n-not a l-little b-b-bird, I c-c-an't be in t-two p-p-laces at once." Honoré de Balzac, *Eugénie Grandet*, trans. Sylvia Raphael (New York: Oxford University Press, 1990), p. 98.
    4. Spelling in the original.
    5. There is a period instead of a question mark in the original.

1134

Semmering, August 17, 1928

Dear friend,

I will entertain you anew about the Burlingham affair. It is not easy to say how you come into this. In addition, it means a disturbance in your analysis with Amsden. But I can't do otherwise, in all sympathy with the damage for which you are blameless. I have no direct access to Dr. Amsden. Amsden is certainly a nice man, and the fact that he is acceptable for analysis at such an advanced age says a great deal in his favor. But he is an American, i.e., somewhere very simplistically constructed in areas where we expect complications, and for that reason incomprehensible to us.

Last week Amsden had the intention, in a conversation in Vienna, to operate on Dr. Burlingham to remove his illusions with regard to the future with Dorothy and then to send him back to the Semmering as a harmless man of honor. I prevented this with my urgent letters to Amsden; I forced Amsden to accompany him here and, after the enlightenment, to take him with him to Budapest. In our conversation, Amsden seemed to agree with my conception, just as he also followed it up in his actions. But it only seemed that way, for on his departure from here, he told Dorothy he had never had such a difficult task to solve, and he didn't know whether he had done the right thing.

These statements are quite strange in and of themselves, but they also show that he gave in to me without believing me. So, why did he give in to me? Perhaps because he didn't want to take the responsibility for possible disaster. Actually, he considered the patient harmless and my caution exaggerated. But one should be amazed at that, for he has participated in his [Burlingham's] case history and must know what kind of violence he is capable of.

Now Dr. Burlingham doesn't let a day go by without talking to his wife on the telephone, so that he has actually not been disposed of. He says the strangest things on the telephone, constantly contradicting himself, sometimes accusations, sometimes tendernesses—the poor woman gets no rest, and is afraid of his turning up again here with us. But there is an advantage in all this. One learns what is actually going on in him, and how Amsden treats him. First, that Amsden is very much mistaken if he considers his authority to be on firm ground. Burlingham has stated that he has no desire to stay with Amsden and to be "bread and butter"[1] to him, i.e., to let himself be exploited by him. Thereupon he asked Dorothy to send him money, which Amsden should not find out anything about. It is very possible that he is capable of pulling the wool over Amsden's eyes, to bolt from Amsden, and to use this money just for that purpose. The last thing that makes us uneasy took place yesterday. Burlingham found out that I wrote letters to you that have to do with him, and he inquired very excitedly and distrustfully whether Dorothy knew about this, which she had to deny. How else should he have learned about it other than through communication with Amsden, and what sense does it make for Amsden to tell him about these secret events? I imagine that Amsden is acting under the influence of his analysis and wants to have a curative influence on his patient by means of such enlightenments. Amsden seems now to be behaving like internists who become acquainted with analysis and thereby forfeit the certainty of judgment in organic things. He forgets, if he wants to treat Burlingham analytically, that the latter has no ego with which one can work, that he is a very disturbed personality, devoid of inhibition, incapable of accepting instruction, of gaining insight into his illness, in short, a psychotic, for whom analysis does not come into consideration, who can only be treated according to the old psychiatric practice.

If Dr. Amsden can't see Burlingham that way despite his experiences, then we are probably faced here with one of the American primitivenesses of which I spoke. Amsden doesn't want, as he once said here, to forfeit his prestige with the Burlingham family, i.e., not lose the patient, and this postulate brings along with it the blindness toward Burlingham's psychotic state.

Why do I bother you with all this? Because I have no prospect of convincing Dr. Amsden directly of the fact that, with his trust in Burlingham, with his enlightenments and his allowing things to continue in this fashion, he is going down a false, perhaps dangerous path. I leave it up to you how much you want to share with him, but he should certainly not be spared instruction about the difference in the treatment of neurosis and psychosis, and enlightenment about the relation of the patient to his person.

From a practical viewpoint, all kinds of things would have to be required. The ideal measure would be to keep the patient in a sanatorium in Budapest until Amsden takes him along to America. He probably won't want to do that. He should at the very least decide to keep a stricter watch over Burlingham, should put an end to the upsetting telephone conversations by prohibition, *certainly not* let him come here *alone* for Bob's birthday on the 29th of the month, either not at all, or accompany him himself, and limit as much as possible the unavoidable intercourse until the trip home.

Thoroughly natural conclusions from a different, more cautious psychiatric conception of the case. Dorothy also requires some consideration; she now speaks more freely about her earlier experiences with her husband and makes no secret of the fact that she is afraid of him.

We want to leave on the 30th of the month, the day after the intended visit for Bob's birthday.

I very much beg your pardon, and thank you for your help, if you can give it to us.

Cordially,
Freud

1. In English in the original [Trans.].

1135

August 18, 1928[1]

dr b. acquired amsdens correspondence on his own amsden quite reliable is taking proper measures letter tomorrow = ferenczi

1. Telegram. It is not in the folder of the Austrian National Library but was later found by Judith Dupont in Ferenczi's papers.

1136

Budapest,
August 19, 1920 [1928][1]

Dear Professor,

As I already informed you by telegram, the fact of Dr. Burlingham's being unproductively informed can*not* be explained by Dr. Amsden's inattentiveness or indiscretion, nor by his false scientific or therapeutic attitude, but by the slyly-skillfully instituted violation of the confidentiality of the mails by Dr. Burlingham.

Dr. Amsden soon discovered this and reproached the patient for it.

Your letter of today had some effect, to the extent that Dr. Amsden (who is accessible to all my <and your> arguments) will accelerate his plan to take upon himself the surveillance of Dr. Burlingham. He also plans, I think, to keep Dr. Burlingham from traveling to the Semmering for Bob's birthday party.

I think Dr. Amsden will also write to you personally.

It goes without saying that I am also prepared for any further mediation.

Yours,
Ferenczi

1. The letter has been placed under 1920 in the Balint folder (as well as in the Austrian National Library in Vienna). But according to its content, it doubtless belongs here; thus, "1920" must be a misprint on Ferenczi's part for "1928."

1137

Semmering, August 21, 1928

Dear friend,

I thank you for all the pains that you have taken—and will continue to take—in the Burlingham matter. Despite your warm partisanship in favor of Dr. Amsden, I cannot praise his actions. They seem to me to be weak, sentimental, incautious, and still founded on false assumptions. Thus, he has now requested of Dorothy that she should put together a list of her husband's transgressions, which he will reproach him with. As if that could have any other effect on the insightless patient than to incite him even more against the woman!

The last incident of searching through his correspondence should finally convince him of the patient's complete unreliability. It should be quite out of the question for him to come here for Bob's birthday. I don't trust Burlingham an inch. Dr. Amsden will be responsible for everything that may happen, from which one doesn't gain anything, of course.—

Formally, the information that we, Anna and I, will leave for Berlin on Thursday, the 30th of the month.[1]

Kind regards,
Freud

1. Their visit lasted until the end of October or the beginning of November. Cf. Freud's account to his brother: "A graphologist would have to see from my handwriting that I have already lost several teeth. Perhaps also that the absolute certainty of being in the best hands with Schröder is doing me a lot of good. I can still talk and am treating every day [Freud was continuing two analyses] . . . We are being maintained like grand princes or like newborn babies, according to Anna. The sanatorium, made invisible by a number of trees, is silently at our feet. Dr. Simmel, the chief physician, has handed over to us the first floor of the physicians' villa. Only three pictures of me are hanging on the walls, but I don't need to look at them . . . Since Schr. has the ambition of carrying out the treatment 'without professional interruption,' I can easily absorb all the costs of the enterprise" (Freud to Alexander Freud, September 4, 1928, Library of Congress). In addition to Ferenczi, Freud was also visited by Marie Bonaparte in Tegel (Jones III, 142).

1138

Tegel, September 20, 1928[1]

Dear Doctor!

I am not answering your letter until today because in the meantime I had sent it to the sister-in-law of Yvette Guilbert (the mother of my friend Eva Rosenfeld in Vienna),[2] in order to request the necessary recommendation from her. I have just learned that she has taken care of everything, has written one letter to Yvette Guilbert and one to Paris, to Mrs. Rogers. So, everything is in order.[3]

I am very much looking forward to your visit here, there will be much to talk about; just now, new difficulties are emerging again with the Americans. I don't see how a row will be avoidable at the next Congress. In any case, I haven't forgotten what kind of a role you played for me after the last Congress.

Papa is now at the height of his treatment and is under a great strain from it. But the unheard-of good care and nourishment that he has here makes up for a great deal. When you come, we will already know something about the results; now one can't say anything at all yet, there are all kinds of provisional arrangements.

Many kind regards and auf Wiedersehen!

Yours,
Anna

1. The letter was written by hand by Anna Freud. In the blank space on the page, below the signature, are written, in pencil and in a different handwriting (Ferenczi's), various partly illegible headings, signs, and mathematical calculations in a discernible order, for instance: "Hermann—superego?—homos heteros—identification—love—ego, not superego—ego-ideal remains—Eisler—sublimation symptom."
2. Yvette Guilbert (1867–1944), renowned French songstress, much admired by Freud. She was married to the Viennese biologist Max Schiller. Her niece Eva Rosenfeld (1892–1977) had been a close friend of Anna Freud's since about 1924. She was co-initiator of the Experimental School in Hietzing, a (gratis) analysand of Freud's (1929–1931), and a co-worker in Simmel's sanatorium in Tegel. Her relationship and analysis with Melanie Klein (1938–1941) further cooled the already somewhat tense relations with the Freuds. See Peter Heller, ed., *Anna Freud's Letters to Eva Rosenfeld* (Madison, Conn., 1992).
3. The background of this incident could not be elucidated.

1139

[Rundbrief][1]

Budapest, February 29,[2] 1928

Dear friends:

On the morning of September 30, I initiate my this year's vacation, which has become strongly autumnal. Since the Berlin meeting was canceled in consideration of Herr Professor's being occupied elsewhere, we are traveling, as per our original plans, to Madrid, then to Seville and Granada. Letters can reach me through the address: Hotel Florida, Madrid, Calle di Carmen. I would be pleased to receive a sign of life occasionally.

Kind regards,
S. Ferenczi

P.S. In Budapest, our secretary, Dr. Hermann, will represent me in my absence.
Many thanks for Fräulein Anna's letter.

1. The letter is typewritten; only the signature, "S. Ferenczi," a few corrections, and the last sentence of the postscript are handwritten.
2. An error; September 29 is the correct date.

1140

Toledo, October 6, 1928[1]

Dear Professor,

The sly painter Del Greco[2] naturally sought out for himself as an atelier, of all places, the wonderfully situated house of Samuel Lévy, the builder of the beautiful synagogue which was then changed into a Catholic church.—In Madrid I met a colleague, Dr. Sacristan (José Maria), the director of an insane asylum. He is (as are the majority of the younger ones, in general) half a cathartic and already half a Jungian. Perhaps I will meet your translator, Ballesteros,[3] in Madrid tomorrow. I hope to give you news from Seville (Hotel Madrid).

Ferenczi

1. Picture postcard (probably from a series): "6. Toledo.—Casa del Greco."
2. Ferenczi's spelling [Trans.]. El Greco ("The Greek"), actually Doménikos Theotokópoulos (ca. 1541–1614), the renowned Spanish painter of Greek origin, lived in Toledo from about 1577.
3. Luis Lopez Ballesteros y de Torres, who had introduced himself to Freud with a translation of Nietzsche (Freud to Oberholzer, November 10, 1921, Library of Congress). He was the translator of the complete works of Freud in Spanish (17 vols., Biblioteca Nueva, 1922ff.).

1141

Berlin-Tegel, October 12, 1928[1]

Dear friend,

Out of envious participation, I don't want to deny my former travel companion, who now permits himself on his own recognizance to fulfill my unsatisfied travel wishes, a cordial greeting. Even I am approaching marked improvement, which I hope to bring home this month, still.

Many kind regards also to Frau G. and also from my loyal Antigone[2]-Anna.

Yours,
Fr[eud].

1. Postcard sent to Madrid, forwarded to the Hotel Alhambra, Granada.
2. The elder of Oedipus' and Jocasta's two daughters, faithful companion of her blind father.

1142

Granada, October 17, 1928[1]

Dear Professor!

Many thanks for your card!—In Madrid I finally succeeded in speaking with Herr Ballesteros y de Torres. An extremely nice young professor of philology, enthusiastically fired up about $\Psi\alpha$, on top of that, a lawyer. He didn't allow me any peace until I gave him a promise on the way back to give a lecture to a select circle of intellectuals (Sociedad de Cultura).[2] I will talk about "the training of the psychoanalyst" and focus in on the analyst's being analyzed.[3] Kind regards to everyone.

Yours,
Ferenczi

1. Picture postcard: "Sevilla. Catedral Tumba de Colón."
2. As in the original; the correct name is Socieded de Conferencias (cf. letter 1145).
3. "Einführung in die psychoanalytische Technik und Charakteranalyse" [Introduction to Psychoanalytic Techique and Character Analysis], given October 27, 1928, in the Residencia de Estudiantes, Sociedad de Cursos y Conferencias in Madrid. On the following day, the newspaper *ABC* published a notice about it, which was reprinted in German in *Zeitschrift* 15 (1929): 133. The lecture was published posthumously in *Bausteine* III (422–431) under the title "Über den Lehrgang des Psychoanalytikers" [On the Psychoanalyst's Course of Study].

1143

Madrid, October 28, 1928[1]

Dear Professor,

Now we head for home. Our friend Ballesteros did everything to promote my lecture of yesterday in Madrid. I will tell you everything by word of mouth. I hope you are already quite well.

Greetings from Dr. Ferenczi and wife

[In a different handwriting][2]

Since I have not yet been granted the pleasure of knowing the father of psychoanalysis personally, I was very fortunate to honor him in the person of one of his most loyal and more sage adherents. Dr. Ferenczi, with his forceful, youthful spirit, has instilled in me the courage to continue, or perhaps better said, to begin, the fight for psychoanalysis here.

Luis Lopez Ballesteros

1. Picture postcard (from a series): "118. Madrid—Salón del Prado."
2. L. L. Ballesteros's handwriting also extends across the entire picture side.

1144

Nice, November 31, 1928[1]

Dear Professor,

We had to decide (in consideration of digestive disturbances which were caused by the "Spanish" cuisine) to take the shortest way to Budapest via Venice, without touching Vienna. I hope to be able to visit you soon; in the meantime I will write about my Spanish experiences from Budapest.

Kindest regards,
Ferenczi

1. Picture postcard: "Bords de Mer à Antibes." The date must be either October 31 or November 1; the card is postmarked November 1.

1145

INTERNATIONALE PSYCHOANALYTISCHE VEREINIGUNG
INTERNATIONAL PSYCHO-ANALYTICAL ASSOCIATION

Budapest, November 14, 1928[1]

Dear Professor,

I have always said that you are leading the way [*vorangehen*], but now I must say that you are flying ahead [*vorausfliegen*]![2] I am very eager to get at least a few words about your impressions, although your son-in-law already informed us about a few things the day before yesterday. I found his communications about the results which were achieved in Berlin very gratifying. We all hope that the success will be a lasting one and a new era of your well-being will be inaugurated.

Now a few things about ourselves and our experiences in Spain. Despite the fact that in Granada, just where we wanted to rest up—probably in consequence of the water or the unfamiliar cuisine—, we were constantly tormented by intestinal catarrhs, and because of this, I, in particular, missed the hoped-for recuperation during the vacation, the total impression of our stay has been an extraordinarily interesting one. You must positively somehow, perhaps by airplane, also get to know this country, which abounds with historical and artistic treasures, with its remarkable population. We saw only a few cities and landscapes. First Madrid, then Seville, and finally, Granada. On the way back from Madrid, I was already awaited by our friend Ballesteros, whom I already had to promise earlier to give a psychoanalytic lecture in the Sociedad de Conferencias. Ballesteros arranged everything; I had nothing to do but read the paper, which had been translated into French by Ballesteros. That Sociedad is an interesting group of people; a tightly closed society of high nobility and university professors. The Duchess of Alba is the president; she and a lot of other Marquesas and Contessas were present. Although Ballesteros has contributed so much to the enlightenment of his country about psychoanalysis, through his translations, I considered it very necessary to choose the following theme: "Apprentissage de la psycho-analyse"; with that I accomplished the task of showing the audience that analysis can be learned only in our institutes, but not in Spain. As a bonus, I said something about the possibility of an analytic therapy of character.

In Barcelona I met Dr. Sarró, whom you perhaps know, and a few university neurologists, who are less knowledgeable, but more conceited, than the Madriders. Madrid is still the proper Castilian, Barcelona a kind of American industrial city. Naturally, the psychologists here are a bunch of psychotechnicians. Ballesteros, I think, deserves our complete trust; he understands very much, although, to his chagrin, he is unable to go through an analysis for external reasons. He is right when he says about himself that he is less fit to be the leader of the psychoanalytic movement than to be the secretary to that leader. I encouraged Sarró to move to Madrid, which is hard to do, however, since he—a typical Catalan—has his relatives in Barcelona.

Here in Budapest we are gradually recovering, I too, although I immediately began with eight hours.

In expectation of news from you and Fräulein Anna.

Yours truly,
Ferenczi

Ballesteros would be extremely pleased if you dropped him a line occasionally.

1. The letter is typewritten; only the signature, "Ferenczi," a few corrections, and the postscript are handwritten.
2. Probably an allusion to a pleasure trip of Freud's by plane.

1146

Vienna, November 17, 1928
IX., Berggasse 19

Dear friend,

Robert[1] has reported, with his accustomed pessimism, that you both returned from beautiful Spain sick and miserable. So I was very pleased that you corrected this horror message in your letter. I hope you will soon feel restored and will then soon really seize an opportunity to give me a verbal picture of your impressions of the trip.

Just today I received volume XII of the Spanish edition from Ballesteros.

I am living naturally better and more independently than before with an approximately seventy percent improvement in my prosthesis. Psychological laws, unfortunately, demand that I feel the remaining thirty percent all too markedly.

Today Pötzl gave his inaugural speech as the successor to Wagner-Jauregg. As is well known, he is our member, but he exhausted himself, as Anna tells us, in devotion to his teacher and predecessor, so that he has only a few cool references to analysis left.

In rearranging my library, I found, to my horror, that vol. VIII, 1 and 3,[2] of the International Journal are still at your place. If you send me these two issues, in order to disprove my distrust, I can have the volume bound.

With kind regards to you and Frau G.

Yours,
Freud

1. Burlingham.
2. Reading uncertain; the number could also be "2."

1147

Internationale Psychoanalytische Vereinigung
International Psycho-Analytical Association

Budapest, December 5, 1928[1]

Dear Professor!

Finally, you get possession of your English issues; I am sending them with today's mail. In one of the issues you will find a strange baroque statue of our prophet Moses in photographic reproduction. I believe the statue represents a moment in which Moses (perhaps indignant over the behavior of the Jews) puts on his sandals to climb Mount Zion. In Toledo we saw, likewise in a Catholic church, a much more grotesque Moses statue as an object of veneration.

I am occupied almost exclusively with the not very numerous cases, and am feeling more and more secure in my technique. Am also uncommonly satisfied with my therapeutic and characterological results. Healthwise, somewhat better, but still not completely well.

Many kind regards.

Yours,
Ferenczi

Many thanks to Anna for her communications.

1. The letter is typewritten; only the signature, "Ferenczi," is handwritten.

1148

Internationale Psychoanalytische Vereinigung
International Psycho-Analytical Association

Budapest, January 2, 1929[1]

Dear Professor,

Instead of the usual New Year's letter I am making do this time with a congratulatory telegram.[2] I don't have much to add to it. We are all happy along with you about the unexpectedly favorable outcome of the Berlin prosthesis correction. Everyone who saw you, lastly, Dr. Lehrmann, were saying miraculous things about the improvement in the subjective and objective state of your health and spirit.

I can't produce anything comparable, but I also don't have all too much to complain about lately. I am, to be sure, limiting my activity to the seven to eight hours of work with pupils and patients. Otherwise, I rest; now and then I think about the things that happen to me in the sessions, and thus come to quite respectable conclusions. Unfortunately, I can decide only with difficulty to put these ideas on paper.

Dr. Lehrmann writes to me that Eitingon is coming to Vienna in the course of this month;³ he suggests that this be used as an occasion for an intercontinental conference. Max himself, from whom I just received a letter, makes no mention of his travel plan. In the event it seems desirable to you, I will gladly come to take part in this conference. To be sure, I would perhaps prefer a meeting of the kind that once took place so often without any external pretext. On the other hand, I see that the public interest sometimes also requires sacrifice.

Yesterday I received the first issue of a periodical published by Kronfeld (I think it is called "Advances in Neurology and Psychiatry").⁴ Kronfeld himself wrote the second essay. In it he tries to demonstrate, among other things, that the new psychoanalytic generation does not agree with you in regard to the basics of the methods, since we, but especially I and Anna Freud, concede that psychoanalysis should be supplemented by educational measures. Ask Anna if she isn't of the opinion that we—perhaps in a joint protest—should set the erroneous construction of our communications straight?⁵ It is certainly one thing to concede that in certain cases (perhaps with children, the mentally ill, savages) psychoanalysis is not to be used in its original purity, but it is something else to say (as Kronfeld expects it of us) that there is no longer any such thing as pure psychoanalysis. What Fräulein Anna does is, in fact, only the application of psychoanalysis to child rearing. But it is also quite erroneous if Kronfeld thinks that my so-called activity is a purely instructional measure; he neglects the triviality that I consider all those measures only an aid to analytic work, but never an end in themselves.

With many kind regards.

Your old,
Ferenczi

1. The letter is typewritten; only the signature, "Ferenczi," is handwritten.

2. The telegram has not been found.

3. Eitingon came on the weekend of January 25–27, 1929 (Eitingon to Freud, January 6, 1929; Freud to Eitingon, January 27, 1929; both Sigmund Freud Copyrights).

4. *Fortschritte der Neurologie und Psychiatrie und ihrer Grenzgebiete* [Advances in Neurology and Psychiatry and Their Allied Fields] (1929ff.), edited by Arthur Kronfeld (1886–1941), *Privatdozent* in psychiatry in Berlin.

5. No publication along these lines has been found.

1149

Vienna, January 3, 1929
IX., Berggasse 19

Dear friend,

I cordially return your New Year's greeting and accept your promise to come to Vienna this month. I will have even less to do in the second half than I have now. Eitingon also wants to visit us around this time. As soon as I know his exact date, I will inform you of it so that you can meet or avoid him as you wish. He will certainly be happy to see you, for he asks about you in every letter.

The new year has already brought me a kind of grippe with excessive runny nose, so that I am not very well despite the better prosthesis. But that doesn't matter much to me, since I already have to consider any kind of being as a gift. Senectus ipse morbus.[1]

I think that there is also little else happening, or I am interested in fewer things. I am probably doing that in order not to have to—get angry so often and so intensely. I don't even write anymore myself.[2] Occasionally people send me manuscripts, which I then read and criticize. But I don't want to preempt in this letter what we can chat about later.

With kind regards for you and your dear wife.

Yours,
Freud

1. Latin for "old age is itself a disease." Origin unknown.
2. In the years 1928 and 1929 Freud wrote only a congratulatory address for Ernest Jones's fiftieth birthday (Freud 1929a).

1150

Vienna, January 4, 1929
IX., Berggasse 19

Dear friend,

The first letter was lying ready to be sent off when the mail brought yours in the morning. So I opened it in order to enclose my reply.

I have, of course, expressed myself in detail about the question of your visit. You had better not believe miracles that you hear about me. Lehrman is a good boy, but an enthusiast. I like your idea about refuting Kronfeld. Anna will be very much in agreement if you also express yourself in her name. These convulsive efforts to point out contradictions where none exist are but poorly disguised expressions of the deep enmity of just such hangers-on as Kronfeld, who is, incidentally, enjoying a very bad reputation.

Cordially,
Freud

1151

Internationale Psychoanalytische Vereinigung
International Psycho-Analytical Association
Association Psychanalytique Internationale

Budapest, January 10, 1929[1]

Dear Professor!

Many thanks for both letters, which arrived simultaneously. I hope that in the meantime your catarrh has disappeared without a trace, so that you can enjoy the general improvement in your condition undisturbed. I myself am evidently suffering from the great cold which prevails here; as always under such conditions, my nocturnal rest disturbances proliferate. Naturally, that way my capacity for accomplishment becomes limited to taking care of the analytic hours, with the progress of which I have been extremely satisfied lately. I seem to have penetrated to a kind of technique which allows one to work calmly and successfully; at the same time, a number of theoretical connections become clearer without any strain. Perhaps I will write something about this for the next Congress.[2]

I was surprised by the news of your Dostoevsky essay,[3] which I was, unfortunately, unable to procure.

I admire the forbearance with which you are able to read manuscripts. I no longer even read attacks which are directed against me personally.

I received a letter from Ophuijsen, in which he, significantly, forgets that we have been corresponding with [the familiar form] Du up to now. The tone of the letter is otherwise friendly.

My trip to Vienna depends partly on your news with regard to Eitingon, partly on the state of my health.

Many kind regards.

Yours,
Ferenczi

1. The letter is typewritten; only the signature, "Ferenczi," is handwritten.
2. See letter 1167, n. 3.
3. "Dostoevsky and Parricide" (Freud 1928b [1927]), first published in René Fülöp-Miller and Fritz Eckstein, eds., *Die Urgestalt der Brüder Karamasoff* [The Primal Form of the Brothers Karamazov] (Munich, 1928).

1152

January 25, 10:58 A.M.[1]

Arriving Saturday noon hotel regina departure Sunday afternoon greetings = ferenczi

1. This and the following telegram, which evidently belong together, are not in the folder of the Austrian National Library, but were subsequently found by Judith Dupont in Ferenczi's papers. The telegrams are on forms which were printed in 1925 and were used until 1930; according to their content, the earliest possible dating would be 1928 or 1929, but the fact that [in 1929] January 26–27 fell on a weekend seems to speak in favor of placing them here.

1153

January 25, 7:30 P.M.

= not arriving until Saturday evening = ferenczi

1154

Vienna, February 7, 1929
IX., Berggasse 19

Dear friend,

The pension animal who will come to you, Mr. William Blumenthal, was just with me to get a recommendation to you. But he was afraid that I will draw something from my prejudices toward him which will turn you against him, and therefore he wanted—in all politeness—to prescribe what should be written in the recommendation: I refused and said that he should only turn to you on his own; incidentally, you are not the kind of man who makes judgments about patients from others.

So, he will appear before you on the 20th of the month. You might know him from the Semmering, and from occasional remarks from me; our last conversation about him and today's letter, naturally, did not take place.

He doesn't know what a favorable situation he is getting into. The contempt that I showed for him on account of his conceited asininity can make him more pliable toward someone else, and in you, I know, he will encounter fearless therapeutic ambition. But I don't want to refrain from warning you about his dishonesty, artistry in dissimulation, and his arrogance. He may be quite well behaved for a while; he seems to be very much intimidated. It seems impossible to me to awaken in him a spark of warm feeling for another.

I greet you and Frau G. cordially.

Yours,
Freud

P.S. I have a summons in Berlin for March 11.[1]

1. Freud was again staying in Tegel; he returned to Vienna on March 23 (Freud to Lehrman, March 21, 1929, Library of Congress).

1155

[undated, location unknown][1]

Dear Professor,

I telephoned you immediately after receiving the Rundbrief, before I had studied closely Eitingon's letter and the appended correspondence. My first impression was that one has to undertake something radical in order to get free rein, e.g., resigning from the Association (under your leadership) and founding a new, small society consisting of reliable adherents (without Ophuijsen, Brill—also without Jones, if it comes to that). Reading through the letters more closely showed me that you consider the matter more coolly than I, perhaps rightly so, and don't by a long shot ascribe the same significance that I do to the secessions, which are accumulating.[2] For that reason I will postpone the visit with you that I announced by telephone to a time when a scientific discussion, independent of such unpleasant business matters, will become necessary. Let us hope, very soon!

Eitingon's question regarding the Washington group is easy to answer. The Washingtonians, whose acceptance we proposed, are justifiably upset by the refusal.[3] Jones brought this about, evidently because he was not requested to support the acceptance. Could *you* not write a few friendly lines to *William A. White?*

Kind regards!

Ferenczi

1. The original of this letter is missing; it is also not in the Austrian National Library in Vienna. There is only a typewritten transcript in the Balint folder. The page contains the following handwritten statement: "undated, probably first half of 1929 (B[alin]t)." The Freud-Eitingon correspondence shows that this letter was probably written between December 29, 1928, and March 3, 1929 (we are grateful to Gerhard Wittenberger for research on the dating).

2. This pertains to the conflict over lay analysis, to which no end was in sight, which then was the subject of a discussion in April (see n. 1 of the following letter). Ophuijsen, Brill, and Jones were opposed to lay analysis. The earliest *Rundbrief* from the year 1929 which has been found is the one of May 29.

3. This, too, had to do with the question of lay analysis, which many members of the

Washington Society opposed. In 1932 the APA was reorganized with three branch societies: New York, Chicago, and Washington-Baltimore. This arrangement was accepted by the Wiesbaden Congress of the IPA in the same year, and the Washington-Baltimore Society was formally accepted into the IPA.

1156

Budapest, February 11, 1929

Dear Professor,

1.) I anticipate with interest the patient announced by you.—

2.) In order to deprive Jones of any possibility of "personal discrimination," I am now also *in favor of* the *Paris* trip and will write to Eitingon to that effect.[1]

3.) I am receiving reports from America as a result of which Wittels has gained the sympathy of the New York group by virtue of statements *in opposition to* lay analysis. He lets himself be referred to everywhere as your "right hand."—

Even Schilder[2] is said to be behaving overcautiously, indeed, occasionally ambivalently, which contributes to the increase in his popularity. It would be good if Wittels's *real* significance were somehow made public.—

The trip home from Vienna was adventurous; I didn't arrive in Budapest until four o'clock in the morning, instead of half past nine—but the train was well heated.—I am very pleased that you are well.

Cordially,
Ferenczi

1. The meeting around April 6, 1929, in Paris about questions of lay analysis and the IPA; present were Eitingon, Ferenczi, Anna Freud, Jones, and Ophuijsen.
2. Paul Schilder (1886–1940), M.D. and Ph. D., noted Viennese philosopher, neurologist, and psychiatrist. He was a co-worker of Wagner-Jauregg from 1918 to 1928 and became a professor in 1925. He was a member of the Vienna Society from 1919 to 1932 and in 1929 became the head of the division for the treatment of psychoses in its outpatient clinic. From 1929 on he made several visits to the United States, and in 1932 he finally emigrated to New York and became a member of the Society there. In 1930 he became clinical director of the psychiatric division of Bellevue Hospital and research professor of psychiatry at New York University College of Medicine. In 1935 he founded the New York Society of Psychology. Along with his well-known works on the bodily schema, he concerned himself with, among other things, the relation of psychoanalysis and psychiatry, hypnosis, group therapy, and the treatment of psychotic children. See Mühlleitner, *Lexikon*, pp. 286–288. Schilder was always careful to maintain his independence with re-

gard to the psychoanalytic movement. In 1935 his status as training analyst was withdrawn; his question to Freud whether the latter considered him justified in doing further training analyses was clearly negated by Freud: "You refused your own analysis, place little value in what can be acquired in this manner, and carry out analyses yourself which you declare to be terminated after a few months" (November 26, 1935, Library of Congress).

1157

Budapest, February 17, 1929

Dear Professor,

I received the news from Max that he and Fräulein Anna have decided on the Paris trip. I replied to Max that I will naturally come along—but at the same time I called his attention to the fact that Jones's actions in this matter are also a symptom of his other intentions. He pursues the politics of threats and brutality. If we show ourselves [to be] weak (as in the case of the matter of the trip), he will push through completely all his plans (which are, in the final analysis, purely personal-ambitious). The problem of lay analysis is for him only an excuse to unite the Anglo-Saxon world under his scepter—I mean financially, as well!

Many thanks for the information about your raccoon. He hasn't shown up yet.

With kind regards, and in the hope that the railroad will be so kind as to advance this letter.

Yours,
Ferenczi

1158

Budapest, February 17, 1929

Dear Professor,

With yesterday's mail I had sent, by the treasurer of our group (Pfeifer), the equivalent of 1500 Hungarian pengös as the amount that our educational commission can relinquish to the Verlag from its fund, which amounts to approximately 4,000 P. Please dispose of it as you see fit.[1]

Another mailing will get to you in the next few days.—Please don't be frightened by it. It is the Hungarian translation of the "Theory of Genitality," which I had published under the title: "Catastrophes in the History of the Development of Genitality."[2]

The nearer the date of the Paris trip approaches, the angrier I get about the fact that we have to bend to Jones's inconsiderate rigidity. Do you think that my refusal will significantly disrupt the aims of the meeting?

Kind regards,
Ferenczi

1. By means of a drive for donations, especially through a generous contribution from Marie Bonaparte, the Verlag was saved from bankruptcy (see Jones III, 144).
2. Ferenczi 1924, 268, published by Pantheon-kiadás, Budapest.

1159

Vienna, March 5, 1929
IX., Berggasse 19

Dear friend,

I think I can anticipate Eitingon's warm thanks here for your group's expenditure on behalf of the Verlag. The amount, as well as the spirit, are equally deserving of recognition.

Be tolerant of Jones. He demands this subordination to his wishes in consideration of his 50th birthday (January 1 of this year) and the misfortune in his family,[1] certainly childish, but hardly to be rebuffed! Giving in on this point doesn't mean that one has to acquiesce to him in all other matters. Your staying away would spoil a great deal, for the greatest tension within the former Committee does, after all, exist between you and him.

Some time ago I brought myself to compose an introductory article for the issue of the Zeitschrift which has been dedicated to him.[2] It was not very easy.

On Sunday, the 10th of the month, I will go to Berlin with Anna for the long-anticipated adjustment of the prosthesis. Stay: one to two weeks; residence: Sanatorium Tegel.

With kind regards for you and Frau G.

Yours,
Freud

1. The death of his daughter Gwenith (b. 1920) of broncho-pneumonia in February 1928; to that was added his wife's falling ill from a lung infection at year's end 1928–29, and his own falling ill from neuralgia or rheumatism, intensified by two attacks of influenza—all this without Jones's interrupting his work. "The past months since Christmas have been among the hardest in my life" (Jones to Freud, *Freud/Jones*, May 28, 1929, p. 659).
2. Freud 1929a, in no. 2/3 of the *Zeitschrift* (15 [1929]: 147f.).

1160

INTERNATIONALE PSYCHOANALYTISCHE VEREINIGUNG
INTERNATIONAL PSYCHO-ANALYTICAL ASSOCIATION
ASSOCIATION PSYCHANALYTIQUE INTERNATIONALE

Budapest, April 25, 1929[1]

Dear Professor,

Through your reliable reporter, I mean Fräulein Anna, you have been so precisely informed about all the elements of our downright unpleasant negotiations in Paris that I felt freed of the duty also to report to you about my impressions. The only pleasant thing about the affair was the harmonious collaboration of representatives of the three central groups, but I was especially pleased by the firmness and inflexibility that became manifest in your instructions to us. I truly felt in my element in defending your point of view; on the other hand, I must admit that the clever and perhaps not even ineffectual manner in which you allowed us to talk about a possible separation[2] was far more appropriate than the somewhat more severe remarks that I would have made otherwise.

You have probably also received news from Jones and Eitingon in the meantime; I didn't have the impression from the former that he would gladly let it come to a rupture.

The state of my health is passable, but I have no inner need for literary work at the moment, although the interesting material of my experiences should urge me to it.

Have you already decided about your summer plans? It would be nice if I could call on you at your summer residence around the beginning of July, from when I will probably be working somewhere in Switzerland.

Your Herr Blumenthal looked me up once about a week ago; he came a second time after a short hiatus caused by feverish indisposition; I think that these temporary skirmishes before the decision for treatment, if warranted, might claim several weeks more.

In between times, I am dealing with agents who are offering to sell me villas. But perhaps I will make do with a residence somewhere out in the open.

With kind regards to you all.

Yours truly,
Ferenczi

1. The letter is typewritten; only the signature, "Ferenczi," and a correction are handwritten.

2. Freud had introduced into the discussion the possibility of a "peaceful split" from the proponents of purely medical analysis (Freud to Eitingon, March 27, 1929, Sigmund Freud Copyrights).

1161

Vienna, April 27, 1929
IX., Berggasse 19

Dear friend,

Wife and daughter went to Berchtesgaden yesterday to look for a place to stay. (You recall perhaps a Herr Gulyas,[1] who visited us there.) With our complicated needs, the choice won't be easy for us this year.

Brill (according to Lehrman's communication) is supposed to be coming to the Congress; he is, nonetheless, a reconciling factor. Eitingon now seems to see the situation in a more unfavorable light than immediately after Paris. He wrote me that my suggestion for an amicable separation—with the retention of some commonalities—seems unfeasible to him.[2] I fear we will be happy if we only get that much through.

The Paris group is also sticking with us, on account of the Princess. But the danger is that in the event of a vote, the people will take positions as individuals, and not along the lines of their group. The last mask of resistance to analysis, the medical-professional one, is the most dangerous for the future.

I, too, am experiencing a good time physically, and am getting along better with my prosthesis. But production has no prospects at all with me.

Let's hope I can soon give you a beautiful travel destination for your visit in July. We let ourselves be scared away from Switzerland by the sirocco warnings from all sides.

I greet you and your dear wife cordially.

Yours,
Freud

1. See letter 1163.
2. Freud to Eitingon, April 10, 1929, Sigmund Freud Copyrights.

1162

Dr. Ferenczi
Budapest.
May 9, 1929[1]

Dear Professor,

Eitingon's letter, which I received recently, is somewhat more optimistic than yours. He hopes that the Congress will go peacefully. The number of the Hungarian visitors to the Congress is diminishing from day to day. If it had been a matter of our being able to help with our votes, almost all of us would have come. I think the Congress will be sparsely attended. I had half a mind to stay away myself, but I know that would be impermissible.

Let's hope you already have your summer residence. We are still in correspondence with Swiss hotels. The most probable thing is that we will be somewhere in the Engadin at the end of June.

My favorite theme, analytic therapy, is developing in an extremely interesting manner. Some of it will come already before the Congress.

With kindest regards to you all.

Yours,
Ferenczi

1. The letter (including letterhead) is typewritten; only the signature, "Ferenczi," is handwritten.

1163

Vienna, May 11, 1929
IX., Berggasse 19

Dear friend,

A passage in your letter of today leaves me to presume that one of my letters did not arrive at your place. So I will repeat the news that we have rented the Schneewinkel estate in Berchtesgaden [from Dr. Gulyas][1] on the road to Königssee, which we want to move into after June 15.

Your little essay in the new "ΨA Movement"[2] reminded me of the fact that you are the first and, up to now, the only one who can explain why the male wants to perform coitus. Not a small riddle!

You are naturally not permitted to stay away from the Congress. You know that Jones wants to visit me in June, wherever I am. When he does, he will get to hear a few choice words [from me].

How does my flown-away patient Blumenthal taste to you? Just don't let yourself be taken in by him. He feigns intelligence and is a dyed-in-the-wool ass, worse, in every respect, than he at first appears.

With kind regards to you and Frau G.

Yours,
Freud

1. Brackets in the original.
2. "Männlich und Weiblich: Psychoanalytische Betrachtungen über die 'Genitaltheorie' sowie über sekundäre und tertiäre Gechlechtsunterschiede" [Male and Female: Psychoanalytic Considerations on the "Theory of Genitality" as well as on Secondary and Tertiary Sexual Differences] (Ferenczi 1929, 286), first published in the newly founded journal *Psychoanalytische Bewegung* (1 [1929]: 41–50).

1164

Dr. S. Ferenczi
Budapest
June 7, 1929[1]

Dear Professor,

By chance, in Budapest I recently met the doctor who is treating you, Károlyi,[2] who informed me about the lessening of your subjective complaints. This same happy piece of news was recently brought to me by your pupil, Dr. McCord,[3] who didn't deprive himself of also making my acquaintance after Laforgue, Jung, and Freud.

I assume that you will move to Berchtesgaden on the 15th, according to plan. I am considering going to St. Moritz at the end of June with a small crowd of patients and spending the larger part of the summer there. I will postpone my actual vacation (without patients) until October and not begin again in Budapest until the beginning of November. On the trip to St. Moritz, we (my wife and I) want to get off in Salzburg and spend a day with you. In the hours in which you are busy I hope to converse with Fräulein Anna and your family circle, again enjoy the region which is so familiar to me, with the beautiful memories.

I decided to report on my technical experiences of the last few years in the form of a lecture at the Congress.

With kind regards to you all.

Yours,
Ferenczi

1. The letter (including letterhead) is typewritten; only the signature, "Ferenczi," is handwritten.
2. An assistant of Schröder's (Jones III, 144).
3. Clinton Preston McCord (1881–1953), M.D., from Albany, New York. At Jelliffe's urging, from May to September 1929 he was an analysand of Freud's (and also accompanied Freud to Bavaria). He was a member of the New York Society and founder of the Psychoanalytically-Oriented Study Group in Albany. He wrote to Jelliffe about his meeting with Ferenczi: "I had several days in Budapest and had a delightful evening at an old Hungarian restaurant with Dr. and Mrs. Ferenczi with excellent Hungarian wine to flourish the experience" (letter of June 24, 1929). (Kind communication from Anne-Louise S. Silver.)

1165

Vienna, June 10, 1929[1]
IX., Berggasse 19

Dear friend,

Do I need to assure you that both of you will be welcome to all of us, whenever you come?

I am already quite impatient to end this work period. The prosthesis treatment that your countryman Károlyi is performing on me also makes me fidgety (people say: nervous). He is doubtless very bright and skillful, but up to now we are having little success, and I am not yet certain whether I won't have to make the great sacrifice of a trip to Berlin.

I replied to Ophuijsen myself by responding to his Rundbrief, and, in fact, in an unambiguous fashion.[2] Now I can be curious about Jones's visit.

I greet you cordially.

Yours,
Freud

1. This letter was found in the folder for 1919; since the "2" in the date "1929" is so small, it can also be read as a "1." The content (mention of the Ferenczis' planned visit in Salzburg, as well as the treatment of the prosthesis by Károlyi) shows, however, that this letter represents Freud's (otherwise missing) reply to Ferenczi's letter of June 7, 1929 (letter 1164).

2. "If you don't want to destroy the IPA, you had better be careful. The first one who would resign from the IPA in the event that you should give in to the Americans in the question of lay analysis would be I, the author of 'The Question of Lay Analysis'" (Freud to Ophuijsen, May 26, 1929, in Peter Heller, ed., *Anna Freud's Letters to Eva Rosenfeld* [Madison, Conn.: 1983], p. 135).

1166

Budapest, June 19, 1929

Dear Professor,

We (my wife and I) are arriving in Salzburg (probably Hotel Europa) on the 29th, Saturday, at seven in the evening, and want to call on you Sunday. Departure from Salzburg Sunday evening, seven o'clock. Let's hope Jones doesn't come right on the same day! Request a report.—

See you soon.

Yours,
Ferenczi

1167

Professor Freud
Schneewinkel
Berchtesgaden
Germany

London, July 26, 1929[1]

at last everything hopeful[2]

ferenczi[3]

1. Telegram. It is not in the folder of the Austrian National Library, but was later found by Judith Dupont in Ferenczi's papers.
2. The text of the telegram is written in English in the original [Trans.].
3. On the next day the Eleventh International Psychoanalytic Congress began under the direction of Eitingon (running until July 31, 1929). Ferenczi spoke on "Fortschritte der analytischen Technik" [Advances in Analytic Technique] (1929, 287a; revised as "Relaxationsprinzip und Neokatharsis" [The Principle of Relaxation and Neocatharsis] [1930, 291]) and gave an introductory paper to a discussion on "Termination of the Analysis." In the meeting of the International Training Commission, a new committee on clarification of the question of lay analysis was instituted, of which Marie Bonaparte, Brill, Helene Deutsch, Eitingon, Ferenczi, Anna Freud, Jelliffe, Jones, van Ophuijsen, Sachs, and Sarasin were members. Eitingon was reelected president of both the IPA and the International Training Commission by acclamation. See Anna Freud's detailed report of the Congress in *Zeitschrift* 15 (1929): 509–542.

1168

Baden-Baden, September 9, 1929
Werdestrasse 14

Dear Professor,

Now it is necessary to report about a very, very long period of time.

The pleasant visit with you was followed by two months' stay in St. Moritz. Being inundated with work made it impossible for me, with the exception of a few days, to enjoy the region and its incomparable beauties; it was positively the torments of Tantalus. In between came the Congress in Oxford—which went uneventfully, to be sure—but was, on the whole, extremely unpleasant and arduous, and which friend Jones strove, where possible, to make even more disagreeble for us (or only for me?). All that seemed not to have done my body and my mood any good—I also thought that the constant high altitude (St. Moritz is situated above 1,800 meters) makes me uncomfortable—, and so I decided to go to the Groddecks' again, in whose friendly house I usually recuperated well. So I packed up my belongings (seven patients),[1] and came here on August 27. I am actually already noticing the improvement and am hoping for further recovery.

In the meantime I am working intensively on my cases and am satisfied with the progress in insight (as well as in the therapeutic results). In October (my actual vacation) I will perhaps write down some things, above all the Congress lecture, a copy of which I will send you without delay. It is still quite uncertain where I will spend October.—

My wife continues to be well and asks me to convey her greetings to you all.

I would be very grateful if you or your Anna had time to report to me about more important events in the movement.

What are your plans? How is your health?

Kind regards,
Ferenczi

1. A play on words involving the number seven *(Sieben)* and *Siebensachen*, the German word for "belongings" [Trans.].

1169

Berchtesgaden,
September 12, 1929

Dear friend,

Schneewinkel has remained beautiful up to the end; the stay was disrupted only by visitors[1] and prosthesis, and the loss of our dear Lun[2] cast a shadow on it. Now I am going with Anna to Berlin-Tegel on Saturday evening.

In the Association, a reduction of tension seems to have set in after the Congress; I haven't heard anything more. But I wish both of you a nice October, and soon.

Cordially,
Freud

1. Among the visitors were Marie Bonaparte and her daughter Eugénie, Max and Ernst Halberstadt, and the de Forests with daughter Judy (see letter 1186, n. 1). In Schneewinkel, Freud wrote *Civilization and Its Discontents* (1930a). The house, which Freud loved so much, was later bought by Hermann Göring.

2. Freud's chow Lun (or Lün), a gift from Dorothy Burlingham, was supposed to have been brought from Vienna to Berchtesgaden by Eva Rosenfeld, but she got loose at the Salzburg train station and was found several days later, run over on the tracks.

1170
Dr. S. Ferenczi
vii., Nagydiofa-Utca 3.

Budapest, November 6, 1929

Dear Professor,

It is high time that I call myself and you—where possible—to account about the probable causes of the extreme sparseness and apparent flimsiness of my correspondence.

I think it has essentially to do with a temporary calling upon of even highly significant libidinal relations for the purpose of some kind of inner process.

Two thoughts [*Einfälle*] may illuminate the nature of these things. My relationship to the psychoanalytic *movement* (and politics) seems to be less intensive (especially since the relative calm in the question of lay analysis); in place of this, interest is turning again to purely scientific problems. A product of this change was the Oxford lecture, which was, however, only an indication of the individual observations made in generalities. (These are developing and deepening—I believe—constantly.)

The other (purely personal) thought is the evidently shocking impression that your statement, which was made in passing, to the effect that my appearance was an indication of *premature senility*, made on me. My life drive evidently reacted to that with defiance and contradiction; it threw itself zealously upon unsolved problems of psychoanalysis and in this way wants to display its youthfulness. But it is not completely out of the question that this is a case not only of such reaction formation, but also of the reexperiencing of long-repressed intellectual and other strivings, which could also contain and produce something really valuable.

A certain anxiety (which ought to be well known to you—you did call it to my attention) about coming into conflict with you even in questions of the finest detail is contributing to my taciturnity; I want to wait and see about the growth of certain ideas before I divulge them; I am struggling with doubts and am impaired by the idea that my communications must be firmly fixed in order to make an impression, and not, perhaps, to be dismissed lightly.

In the meantime I feel (physically) not significantly better; my sleep is being disturbed by the well-known symptoms; but my daily work is (despite seven-eight-nine hours) of undiminished, often enthusiastic interest. I am learning more every day.

I hope that this letter signifies the overcoming of a deadlock and that our cordial personal and scientific relations haven't lost anything in the way of their long-standing warmth.

With really cordial greetings.

Your "old"
Ferenczi

1171

November 21[1]

according to cable new york group decided to admit laymen[2] regards = ferenczi

1. Telegram without year. It is not in the folder of the Austrian National Library, but was later found by Judith Dupont in Ferenczi's papers. Its placement here could not be confirmed with certainty. November 21, 1930, could also be a possibility.

2. "Brill moved a resolution in The Society altering the rule about the admission of lay members. This was carried by a considerable majority" (Jones's *Rundbrief* of December 18, 1929, Sigmund Freud Copyrights).

1172

Vienna, December 13, 1929
IX., Berggasse 19

Dear friend,

This November I again heard my dear Yvette—you know we get along with each other very well—singing again with her incomparable intonation:

> J'ai dit tout ça? C'est possible,
> mais—je ne m'en souviens pas.[1]

I am supposed to have said that you are looking prematurely senile? Really, I don't remember. To you yourself? Or to someone else who reported it to you? And to whom? At most, I could have said that you look older than I did at your time of life. But as always—if it had the result of having rekindled your activity and even had the further result of [having rekindled] your desire for correspondence with me, then I am glad if I said it.

For you have doubtless outwardly distanced yourself from me in the last few years. Inwardly, I hope, not so far that a step toward the creation of a new oppositional analysis might be expected from you, my paladin and secret Grand Vizier.² What I thought to myself, instead of such calumny, was that you were holding it against me—or us—that we didn't give you the position that was due you of being the head of the IPA, which, in fact, did not occur in consideration of the nasty politics, the danger of increased enmity from Jones and of the disintegration of the Association.

But you yourself will tell what it is with you. One task of correspondence by letter is certainly to give news about yourself. You have only heard about me through Rickman, who on his visit treated me somewhat too much as a grandfather. Well, as a matter of public interest I only have to communcate the fact that the new piece of writing³ will appear immediately after New Year's, and that I am bored with the eighth edition of the Interpretation of Dreams.⁴ Privately, the matter stands that I have to employ the largest part of my activity for the maintenance of that piece of health that I need for the firmly set daily work. A true mosaic of measures, by which my recalcitrant organs are supposed to be forced into its service. Finally, my heart has also been added, with extra systoles, arrhythmias, attacks of fibrillation. My wise personal physician, Prof. Braun, says, to be sure, that all that has no serious significance. He should know. Is he already beginning to swindle me? One can't, after all, defend against one's own fate; perhaps the deception of physicians is also part of that.

Incidentally, I am mostly in a good mood, not so tense as you, since I have less work and fewer expectations before me than you.

I greet you and Frau G. cordially.

Yours,
Freud

1. French for "I said all that? Possible, but I don't remember it anymore."
2. The Grand Vizier was the highest official in the Ottoman Empire, who, subordinate only to the Sultan, directed affairs of state. He wore the Sultan's ring as a symbol of his power.
3. *Civilization and Its Discontents* (Freud 1930a).
4. Eighth revised edition, published by Deuticke in 1930.

1173

DR. S. FERENCZI
vii., Nagydiofa-Utca 3.

Budapest, December 25, 1929

Dear Professor,

I admit that my intention to reply to you has to struggle with resistances. Being accustomed for a long time to being alone and settling everything in myself has the consequence that the machinery creaks to a certain extent when one tries once again to communicate with someone.—It could be that—perhaps for purely personal reasons, or for ones that are complex-determined, possibly to spare you, etc.—I have suppressed something for which I didn't think I could expect any agreement or any proper understanding on your part; it could also be that my misgivings in this regard were in part exaggerated.—Be that as it may, now that the ice is broken, I want to share with you the essentials of what I know about myself.

The reference to my premature aging was, as I can determine from reviewing the facts once again (by asking my wife, whom I informed at the time), not literally so, and did not take place at one single time in the manner that I wrote to you; it has to do with the summation of several statements of yours about me which are separated in time. At one time, such a remark about my appearance, certainly dictated by sympathy, was in the final analysis a facetious reply to *my* remark that I am so gray. "You are white, I am gray," is the way it went at the time. But it would be pointless to specify, with paranoid precision, what was said, or even meant; suffice it to say that I—evidently also pressed by my own anxious images about growing old before I had an opportunity to fulfill my tasks—took your statements to heart.—I don't know of *any* occasion on which I learned anything unfavorable about myself from your mouth by means of anyone else.

The repeated renunciation of the dignity of [being] president did, as you correctly surmise, hurt me; it also seemed to me that the last rejection in Paris—especially after Brill's visit in Berchtesgaden—was also no longer politically motivated: everything seemed to be in order with America (Brill); I considered sparing Jones to be superfluous, in fact, disadvantageous in many respects. I am sorry, but in Jones I can see only an unscrupulous, not innocuous man, who also does not disdain the weapons of slander, with whom one should deal more strictly; the British group should sooner be freed from his tyranny, which suppresses every free impulse that doesn't suit him.

But as honestly as I acknowledge as painful my, evidently final, being cast aside, I can tell you frankly that I have overcome this pain, to the extent that such overcoming exists at all (you believe in it!). Just as after every overcoming (renunciation of a university career, renunciation of the direction of the Berlin Institute, etc.), I now also feel to a certain extent freed from superfluous cares, and my interest turned to much more important things; my actual disposition is, after all, that of an investigator, and, freed of all personal ambitions, I immersed myself with redoubled curiosity in the study of my cases. I strove to do things naively, so to speak, without looking at any theoretically preconceived, at least any all too rigid, opinion, and my experiences accumulated in a specific direction, to which my Oxford lecture alluded.

Summarized most succinctly, I can share with you approximately the following:

1.) In *all* cases in which I penetrated deeply enough, I found the traumatic-hysterical basis for the illness.

2.) Where I and the patient succeeded in this, the therapeutic effect was much more significant. In many cases I had to call in already "cured" patients for follow-up treatment.

3.) The critical view that gradually formed in me in the process was that psychoanalysis engages much too one-sidedly in obsessional neurosis and character analysis, i.e., ego psychology, neglecting the organic-hysterical basis for the analysis; the cause lies in the overestimation of fantasy—and the underestimation of traumatic reality in pathogenesis.

I don't know if you can term that an "oppositional direction." I don't think that it is justified. It is only a matter of a tendency, based on experience, to even out a one-sidedness, to the deveopment of which no field of knowledge is immune.

I, too, can confirm almost everything that modern ego psychology has brought about; these studies have uncommonly facilitated and advanced the understanding of pathological processes; but I do not place these investigations, which I myself take up in every case, so very much in the center of theoretical and technical interest.

4.) The newly acquired (although they do essentially sooner hark back to old things) experiences naturally also have an effect on details of technique. Certain all too harsh measures must be relaxed, without completely losing sight of the didactic secondary intention.—

I am pleased about your unclouded moral power in being able to dedicate yourself to your patients and your work even in times of bodily difficulties.

I, too, have no greater satisfaction than work, for which I am and remain unalterably grateful to you.

Many kind regards to you, Fräulein Anna, Frau Professor, and Fräulein Minna on the occasion of the change of year.

Yours,
Ferenczi

1174

INTERNATIONALE PSYCHOANALYTISCHE VEREINIGUNG
INTERNATIONAL PSYCHO-ANALYTICAL ASSOCIATION
ASSOCIATION PSYCHANALYTIQUE INTERNATIONALE

Budapest, December 30, 1929

Dear Professor,

You certainly recall the tiresome Dr. Feldmann, whom we allowed to resign from the Association on account of criminal actions admitted to in the course of analysis.—Well, the rascal is getting more and more impudent, since he knows that I am bound by medical discretion. In addition to that, he is proliferating a huge amount of printed matter, embellished with Stekel and Adler, which he hands out as psychoanalysis. I permitted myself to protest against this in your, as well as in my, name by reclaiming the right of the purely Freudian analysts to call themselves psychoanalysts (just like the British Medical Association). I gladly, as I declared, buy into the reproach of orthodoxy; *Feldmannism,* on the other hand, wants both advantages: that of the cheap revolutionary laurels, but also that of the mimicry of orthodoxy. The declaration will appear in a medical periodical; let's hope you are in agreement with it.[1]

I hope you had pleasant vacation days; Eitingon was with you, I hear.

I have been plagued recently by morning headaches, from which I slowly recover in the course of the morning.

I had a discussion with Aichhorn, whose special talent I admired. Nevertheless, I called his attention to a certain bias in his psychoanalytic conception of youthful boasting, etc. He acknowledged my statement with a willingness, indeed, gratitude which is rare in authors. He is a very nice person.

Many kind regards.

Yours,
Ferenczi

1. "A 'psychoanalysis' név illetételen használata" [On the Illicit Use of the Term "Psychoanalysis"] (Ferenczi 1930, 289; *Gyogyászat,* no. 1 [1930]). Feldmann responded with an ad hominem polemic, which centers on Ferenczi's "renowned brother complex," which he, Feldmann, could nonetheless cure (*Gyogyászat,* no 2 [1930]). The same volume also contains Ferenczi's concluding rebuttal (p. 290).

1175

Vienna, December 31, 1929
IX., Berggasse 19

Dear friend,

You have certainly done the right thing in the matter with Dr. Feldmann, but that seems to me to be of little importance. It is a matter of more urgency to me to rectify an opinion to which you gave expression in your previous letter.

You consider yourself to have been finally cast aside since the election in Oxford. You are really mistaken. As far as we, Eitingon, Anna, and I, have any influence on the election, the intention continues to exist to confer the presidency on you. It only failed to occur this time in order not to immediately revive the arduously exorcised enmity of Jones, after we achieved success against him.

If I assume that he is similarly exercised against you as, according to what is attested to in the letter, you are against him, then caution seems to me not to be superfluous. In the meantime, you might think more calmly until the next election. Meanwhile, he has also, as you know, committed himself in the question of lay analysis.[1]

Anna thinks it is unmistakable that you are isolating yourself from us, and would like, as a countermeasure, to come to Budapest sometime and provoke your visit to Vienna in response. What do you think about that?

Science next time; today only kind regards for 1930 for you and Frau Gisela.

Yours,
Freud

I ought not to spare you a "Discontent."

1. In his letter to Jones after the Oxford Congress, Freud had spoken of the fact "that the New Yorkers reached a clear rapprochement with our standpoint" (*Freud/Jones*, August 4, 1929, p. 661) and was of the opinion that Jones and Brill certainly deserved the credit for it.

1176

INTERNATIONALE PSYCHOANALYTISCHE VEREINIGUNG
INTERNATIONAL PSYCHO-ANALYTICAL ASSOCIATION
ASSOCIATION PSYCHANALYTIQUE INTERNATIONALE

Budapest, January 5, 1930

Dear Professor,

The editor of one of the better Hungarian daily newspapers (Pesti Napló),[1] who is not inimicably disposed toward psychoanalysis and has already been of some service to us, called me up yesterday and asked me if he, too, like the "Neue Freie Presse," might publish a few pages of your new book in Hungarian translation, naturally with reference to the source. I promised him to get your permission, if possible; so, I request your kind reply. I will monitor the correctness of the translation.

The Feldmannian attack on my part has already been published, and I eagerly await its repercussions.

Many thanks for both books, which I treasure as the most beautiful New Year's gifts. I read Anna's book[2] with unalloyed joy; it combines all the advantages of her style: superiority, intelligence, moderation, intellect, and humanity. Her maturity is really admirable. I am pleased that she wants to visit us, and am waiting in suspense for further information about her travel plan. Would she like to give a public lecture?—Or should we be satisfied with a lecture in the Society? May I put her up as my guest in a good hotel, or does she want to stay with Kata?

N.B.: I was always aware of the friendliness on your, Anna's, and Eitingon's part; the "final elimination" of my presidency had more to do with the fact that *my* interests were diverted from the politics of science in the meantime.

If you have time, please don't forget, Herr Professor, to return to the scientific questions that I raised. I then hope, on the occasion of my reply, also to be able to return to the impressions that I owe to Professor's book (Civilization and Its Discontents).

Many kind New Year's greetings to you and all your dear ones.

Ferenczi

1. Possibly either Lajos Hatvany (see letter 685 and n. 4), the founder of *Pesti Naplo*, or its chief editor at the time, Sándor Mester (1875–1958).

2. *Einführung in die Psychoanalyse für Pädagogen: Vier Vorträge* [Introduction to Psychoanalysis for Teachers: Four Lectures] (Stuttgart, 1930).

1177

Vienna, January 11, 1930
IX., Berggasse 19

Dear friend,

My annoyance has dissipated. This reaction becomes less and less frequent in me with the motivation: it's no longer worth it. My conception of the state of affairs between us has remained the same; your letter also does not reveal any knowledge of the signs which support [it]. You are of such an honest nature that you always communicate in parapraxes what you want to conceal.

Here are the two grossest ones from your letter of January 5. I had suggested an exchange to you. Anna was supposed to come to Budapest sometime, and in exchange for that, you were supposed to pay us—or me—a visit. In your reply, you eagerly seize upon the first part of the suggestion; you don't say a word about the second one, which is the more important one to me. (Naturally, I can't repeat the wish now; forced kindnesses are, as is well known, worthless.) Then, further down in the letter, it says: "I then hope, on the occasion of my reply, also to be able to return to the impressions that I owe to *Professor's*[1] book (Civilization) . . ." That sounds, naturally, as though you are writing not to me but perhaps to Anna, and reveals an alienation, the extent of which would probably surprise you yourself.

In earlier letters you passed over some jocular and tender things that I wrote, and surrendered to an "objectivity" which is "new," at least in our relations. I understand that the analysts' behavior toward you from New York on up to Jones's low gestures at the Congress must have embittered you. If I didn't expressly support you with respect to the latter, then that happened only because I have no interest in stirring up discord, but rather [wish] to neglect it. What I don't understand in you is why this mood of yours had to be directed against me, in whose esteem you haven't gone down for an instant. If I resort to the use of signs, then I can be of the opinion that something from the practice is taking part in this. Thus, e.g., I complained facetiously that Rickman, now your patient, had treated me as though I were his grandfather, rationally, with ill-concealed disdain, because in his analysis I didn't find out the truth, which was, of course, only to be found in the continuation of the analysis. Or, as little regard as I have for the person of Blumenthal, whom I chased away out of boredom, I still had expected that you would write to me one day that Blumenthal came, he is so and so; or: that he didn't come. Very possible that you are doing analysis better with both, or with all, your patients than I am, but I also don't have anything against that. I am saturated with analysis as therapy, "fed up,"[2] and who, then, shouldn't do it better than you?

So, you see, if you can illuminate something, there is no lack of problems. I would also like to recommend something less personal to you. You know that Vienna—Budapest—Berlin form the nucleus of the IPA, which was, in the event of a different behavior on the part of Brill, prepared to peel itself away from his periphery. But while Vienna and Berlin entertain the most frequent personal relations, you are letting Budapest sink into isolation, from which we all bear a loss. In so doing, you are also making your election to the presidency at the next Congress more difficult for us.

I know that Anna has written to you and will continue to write to you. She is certainly the intermediary most apt to be able to solve this little, quite superfluous disturbance.

Kind regards,
Freud

1. This word has been underlined with a wavy line.
2. Written in English in the original [Trans.].

1178

Internationale Psychoanalytische Vereinigung
International Psycho-Analytical Association
Association Psychanalytique Internationale

Budapest, January 1930[1]

Dear Professor,

I understand that my letter left you *unsatisfied,* since I perhaps didn't concern myself in sufficient detail with the problems to be dealt with. But I hope that this feeling will disappear when our correspondence once again gets into its old track. But I am pained by the fact that you have to *be annoyed* on my account, and even allow *doubts* about me to emerge in yourself—in the former case, because I would like to spare you unpleasant feelings, but in the latter, especially because this word casts a shadow, as it were, upon the hitherto unclouded relationship between you and me. Naturally, herein only unadorned honesty and openness on the part of both of us can help. I promise you to respond openly to all your questions or reservations.—

Feldmann has, as was to be expected, responded impudently, and does not intend to renounce his right to be called a psychoanalyst. I protested against this again, but did *not* follow in the personal realm, into which he seemed to entice me, and in my reply, I only said as much as: "Feldmann has the nerve to drag the matter into the personal realm; he knows very well what reservations keep me from making my opinion of him public." I couldn't go any further without injuring analytic-medical discretion. I think his provocation was aimed at tearing down the whole psychoanalytic movement along with him, Herostratically,[2] as it were.

Returning to your letter, I must still express the supposition that my statement about the abatement of my interest in the politics of science produced doubts in[3] you. And yet I meant very simply thereby that I (what I also heard from Eitingon, by the way) am less suited for carrying on business that requires diplomacy than I am for research. I hope for your reply soon and am, in old admiration and love,

Yours,
Ferenczi

Special thanks for the kind words that you sent along with your book.

1. No day is given.
2. After Herostratos, who set fire to the Temple of Artemis in Ephesus in order to make a name for himself.
3. This word has been corrected several times. It could also read "with."

1179

Dr. S. Ferenczi
vii., Nagydiofa-Utca 3.

Budapest, January 17, 1930

Dear friend,

You see, I am beginning again with a parapraxis! I just read your letter through once again, sat down, in order to write to you, and, look there: instead of the "Professor," I suddenly see the friend on the paper, in black and white. That immediately changed the whole, rather depressing, mood in which I found myself since the receipt of your letter, and I decided to let the parapraxis stand simply as a sign of my real feelings.

Now, in the relationship between you and me, it is (at least in me) a matter of the most diverse conflicts of feeling and attitude. First you were my revered teacher and unattainable model, for whom I harbored the, as you well know, not completely unalloyed feelings of an apprentice. Then you became my analyst, but the unfavorable conditions did not permit carrying out my analysis to completion. I was especially sorry that you did not comprehend and bring to abreaction in the analysis the partly only[1] transferred, negative feelings and fantasies. As is well known, no analysand can do that without help, [not] even I, with my years of experience with others. For that, a very laborious self-analysis was necessary, which I carried out quite methodically afterwards. Naturally, this was also connected to the fact that I exchanged my somewhat boyish attitude for the insight that I should not rely so *completely* on your goodwill, i.e., that I should not overestimate my significance for you. Little events on our trips together for their part also allowed a certain inhibition to arise in me, especially the strictness with which you punished my obstinate behavior in the matter of the Schreber book.[2] I still ask myself, even now: Would not leniency and consideration on the part of the bearer of authority have been more correct? On the other hand, I understand that you wanted to travel with a healthy person and not with a neurotic. But do you believe that there are people without character difficulties?

I followed the train of my associations when I began with old reproaches, as it were. Now, self-reproaches and confessions may follow. A, certainly exaggerated, consideration for your health kept me for a long time from communicating certain reservations which I began to harbor in relation to the one-sidedness in the development of psychoanalysis. For years I have been carrying around in me the ideas which finally became voiced in the Oxford lecture. That was decidedly wrong! Instead of an honest talking things out, sulking restraint—that was certainly infantile, perhaps also simply stupid, of me. I didn't seem to have valued your ability to take criticism as highly as it deserves.

I do not, e.g., share your view that the process of healing is an unimportant procedure, or one that should be neglected, which one ought to neglect only because it doesn't appear to us to be so interesting. I, too, often felt "fed up" with it, but I overcame this impulse and can report to you with joy that precisely here a whole series of questions is apparently moved into a different, sharper light, perhaps even the problem of repression!

You are doubtless correct in [your assertion] that I have withdrawn somewhat from the common field of work since New York and Paris; disgruntlement about the behavior of Brill and Jones, and the, what you call, "neglect" of our dispute were the causes.

The simplest thing would be to break off this letter and to inform you that: I am coming next Saturday, etc.—unfortunately, I must wait a few more weeks, because a difficult case is tying me to Budapest.[3] Let us hope that you trust me to the extent that you won't consider that an excuse.

I have been continuing Blumenthal's and Rickmann's analysis again since November. I have been cultivating the greatest indulgence with regard to the latter—the result up to now has been that he has also been slowly assimilating a vast amount of what he learned from you. He still hasn't learned anything from me, and yet he is beginning spontaneously to give up his compulsive ceremonials. I don't consider the case to be hopeless.

Let this letter be regarded as the beginning of the, let us hope, again lively correspondence. I will treat problems which are still to be discussed in the next letter.

With thanks for your kindness and your tendernesses!

Yours,
Ferenczi

P.S. The importance of the matters of the Association has never eluded me, despite the momentary concentration on the purely scientific. I appreciate the results that the Berlin Institute has to show, which can serve as a model for us all. To be sure, there hovers before me an enlargement of the plan of organization through the creation of several new forms of instruction.

1.) Membership in the *master school* (guild) (academy) would have as a prerequisite a personal analysis, albeit one requiring years, which, however, encompasses the knowledge and mastery of the total personality, i.e., that which I call "termination of the analysis."

2.) *The analytic faculty* (training of practicing analysts) should remain now as before, about the way the Berlin Institute is.

3.) The great medical and pedagogic public demands *more and more vehemently* shorter special courses (requiring about three to four months), in which they want nonetheless also to learn something personal, and not just hear lectures. (Corresponding roughly to the postgraduate[4] courses of instruction at the university.) By brusquely turning down these people who are eager to learn, we are enlarging the group of Stekel and Adler pupils and are losing almost all contact with the professional circles, especially in the provinces. The physicians of Hungary who trained with Schilder and Stekel and with a pupil of Stekel's are already organizing independently of us.—[5]

4.) The work of enlightenment (Univ. Extension) also belongs on the agendas of the Association and ought not to be relinquished totally to the Adlerians. (Founding of a society, "Friends of Psychoanalysis," under the aegis of the groups.)

So much about my *positive* relation to the movement, for which I have fought tirelessly (and am still fighting! I was just debating very energetically before the public in favor of a special position for our analysis and hope to have enlightened the medical circles).—In the group itself I maintained the "Middle European spirit" and the spirit of belonging together with Berlin and Vienna; in these respects I have nothing on the debit account. The fact of the infrequency of personal meetings and the halt in the correspondence remains. To be sure, personal feeling factors which have been referred to also played a role, and the impression that Eitingon and you take care of Association matters much better and more advantageously; I admit that I am not worth much as an administrator[6] and don't always let the unavoidable diplomacy reign in the treatment of the groups and group leaders. It remains for you to judge whether, with regard to that, other factors aren't present which speak in favor of my presidency.

I certainly hope that this open talking things out signifies the end of the "sulking" on my part, and there is suddenly a reawakening of feelings of thanks for the many signs of your friendliness. This kindness should be doubly credited to you, since you had to struggle with so many and burdensome bodily ailments.

Excuse the perhaps in part somewhat bitter tone of my letter—it was, after all, intended to be "free association," and not only self-criticism.

I await your reply.

Yours,
F[erenczi][7]

1. Reading uncertain. It could also be "in me."
2. See letter 168, n. 1.
3. Very probably Elizabeth Severn.
4. This word is in English in the original [Trans.].
5. The year 1929 saw the founding of the Vereinigung unabhängiger Ärzte [Association of Independent Physicians], to which Imre Décsi, Sándor Feldmann, Pál Gartner, Richard Hajnal, Lajos Ornstein, Konstantina Pollák, Samu Rapaport, Károly Szalay, and Ernö Szinetár, among others, belonged. It published the quarterly *Lélekkutatás* [Psychological Research].
6. This word is in English in the original [Trans.].
7. The postscript ends in the middle of the sheet; the remainder of the page under the signature is blank. In the Balint folder, appended to it, was another loose page with an additional, undated postscript, which was, however, for contextual reasons placed under the year 1927 (cf. letter 1097, n. 16).

1180

Vienna, January 20, 1930
IX., Berggasse 19

Dear friend! (without parapraxis)

Your good letter strengthens my confidence that the ill feeling between us will not be of long duration. So little trace of annoyance has remained with me that I myself was amused by some passages of your confession, after I had gotten over the initial reaction that something like that is possible at all between us. E.g., when you reproach me for having neglected the foreseeable negative reactions in your analysis. Whereby you fail to consider that this analysis goes back fifteen years, and that at the time we were by no means so sure that these reactions could be expected in every case. At least, I wasn't. You yourself [should] consider how long this analysis would have had to last until the inimical impulses in our excellent relationship had succeeded in getting through.

No, I sooner have the impression that you—probably as a result of the presumed slighting in the presidential election—reactivated the remnants of your earlier neurosis and for that reason also became so sensitive toward the rudeness of the "brothers," after you had previously so brilliantly corrected your brother complex as the leader of the Budapest group. But actually, we are both too old for such youthful pranks—I hope your youthfulness will not take umbrage anew at this equivalency. In reality, we should be content with determining that the theoretical differences between us also don't go any further than is unavoidable with two different workers when they don't have a constant exchange of thoughts and along with that mutual influencing!

On another side, I will gladly admit to you that my patience with neurotics runs out in analysis, and that in life I am inclined to intolerance toward them. Especially earlier—so, fifteen years ago—I lived in the hope that one could rely on a kind of letting the not directly addressed abnormal reactions be swept along. Certainly, in so doing, I behaved like that less potent man who told his young wife after the first coitus of the wedding night: So, now you have become acquainted with that; everything else is also only always the same.

I ascertain that, in connecting with our analysis, you have pressed me back into the role of the analyst, which I would otherwise not have reassumed vis-à-vis the tried-and-true friend. Certainly I would have liked to have seen and spoken with you again, but not in order to recoup what was perhaps missed at the time. I would gladly have left it to your self-analysis to take care of that. You have renewed my curiosity about your lecture in Oxford; I know it only from the brief note in the report of the Congress.

For today, then, only kind regards from your old

Freud

1181

Budapest, January 30, 1930[1]

Dear Professor,

The cause of my long silence is this time motivated purely by externals—I want to send you the Oxford lecture in fair copy simultaneously with the letter, and I can get it back only in a few days.

In the meantime, I greet you most cordially,

Yours,
Ferenczi

1. Correspondence card.

1182

Dr. S. Ferenczi
vii., Nagydiofa-Utca 3.

Budapest, February 14, 1930

Dear Professor,

I know you too well to fear that my long silence will be falsely construed; you will understand that the reply to your letter has required such a long reaction time. It was no small thing for me to see in black and white that an "ill feeling" could arise between us.—After the fact, I can tell you that my first reaction, which I didn't want to express by letter, was one of defiance. Now that this has been overcome, I can reply to you without affect that it is, in my view, not a matter of the reactivation of my earlier neurosis, but rather the fact that I could finally tell you that a certain inhibition on my part has constantly existed; I must rather designate the ability to tell you about it as progress, as the beginning of a freer, more uninhibited intercourse between us, thus, the end of a "subneurotic" epoch.

The inhibition of which I speak here has certainly contributed much to the fact that I was unable to give wholly free expression not only to my personal feelings, but also to certain scientific views. These are now beginning to consolidate, and my Oxford lecture, which I enclose in fair copy, is the beginning of this process.

In addition to this, my self-analysis led me to the insight that the childish sensitivity toward your facetious allusion to my getting old was actually the expression of a deep inner unease about my bodily ailments. My nightly rest disturbances (respiratory disturbance and spells of headache) have been returning almost uninterruptedly for more than a year and make me fear premature aging. Also at this moment I am writing early, at five o'clock in the morning, frightened by the symptoms that I have often related to you (which, incidentally, usually increase during the cold months, especially in February). This hypochondriacal, but in part also justified, anxiety may, incidentally, also be one of the reasons that urge and have urged me to publish ideas that have been held back.

I can also, I would like to say, with satisfaction, report to you that what pressed the pen into my hand today was not only pangs of conscience, but also the inability to bear the idea that my communications to you could do lasting harm to our amicable relationship. I just reread your last letter; I found much understanding and goodwill in it. I would only like to contradict you on one point: analytically open talking things out on no account means, in my view, that I am pressing you back into the role of the analyst and in so doing am relinquishing that of the tried-and-true friend. My, I think, not unjustified hope extends to the point where an also analytically free talking things out can be possible, even between old friends. I must admit that I would no longer feel good in the one-sided role of the analysand. Do you consider such mutual openness impossible?

It will interest you to learn (or have you also heard it from somewhere else?) that my writing inhibition with regard to you extended to writing letters in general. E.g., Jones's letter, which was full of one-sidedly erudite claims and hypocritical declarations of love, certainly made it very difficult for me to respond to his peace offer.

Here in Budapest the Feldmann affair brought about unpleasant excitement. I could no longer tolerate his swindling publications, which made him popular, and publicly gave a clear hint as to his personal honesty. The consequence was that his position within his closer circle was somewhat shaken—he, on the other hand, tried, with various weapons (among them also by means of dangerous threats by his wife) to extort from me some little Band-Aid or other for his wounds; up to now in vain. But I must admit that this whole thing had an effect on me that I can only describe with the French word "écoeurant."[1] Would it not have been better to keep the man with us and to correct him? It is, after all, impossible to abandon the material against him that has been gained analytically!

Many kind regards.

Ferenczi

February 15. [1930][2]
Postscript

Dear Professor,

I wanted to save my impressions (about "Civilization and Its Discontents") for my planned visit to Vienna, but already now I must at least express my feelings of admiration about the clarity and lucidity of the presentation. The content is essentially unassailable and contains very much that is unexpectedly new and beneficial. I would only like to suggest something on one point (evidently from the "traumatic" standpoint): Instead of accepting the view of Melanie Klein (page 111),[3] would it not be more correct to hold fast to the individually acquired (i.e., traumatic) nature, that is to say, origin, of conscience and of the neurosis, and to maintain that the all too strict conscience (that is to say, inclination to self-destruction) is the result of a *relatively too strict*[4] treatment—i.e., too strict in relation to the individually varied strong need for love. The latter could, to be sure, be innate.—

Now, another postscript:

The semiofficial Association, "League for the Protection of Children,"[5] which is partly subsidized by the government, has asked me to organize a psychoanalytic consultancy for children and parents with them. The blemish in this invitation is that the Adlerians[6] may also set up office hours there. I accepted in spite of this, and entrusted Dr. Margit Dubovitz with the direction of the office.

Again, kind regards!

Ferenczi

1. Disgusting, revolting.

2. This postscript (without indication of year) is written on a separate sheet; the letter ends at the bottom of the preceding page.

3. "Experience shows ... that the severity of the super-ego which a child develops in no way corresponds to the severity of treatment which he has himself met with. [Footnote:] As has rightly been emphasized by Melanie Klein and by other English writers" (Freud 1930a, p. 130).

4. Underlined three times in the original.

5. Országos Gyermekvédö Liga [National League for the Protection of Children], founded in 1906 by Count Lipot Edelsheim-Gyulai and Sándor Karsai. The League built, among other things, homes for mothers and children, orphanages, and outpatient departments, and organized convalescent holidays. Its organ was *A Gyermekvédelem Lapja* [Journal for the Protection of Children].

6. The Hungarian Association for Individual Psychology, founded in 1927 by István Máday. Máday (1879–1959) was a professor at the University of Debrecen (1925). He was interested in animal psychology, developmental psychology, pedagogy, and family therapy (see also letter 230, n. 2). Among the members were Olivér Brachfeld, István Kulcsár (a friend of Béla Bartok and Attila Jozsef), Béla Székely, and Ernö Kahána.

1183

Vienna, February 25, 1930
IX., Berggasse 19[1]

Dear friend,

I didn't misunderstand your postponement; I knew you were preparing something. My postponement isn't revenge either; I am correcting [proofs of] the Interpretation of Dreams and am otherwise lazy. Very much in agreement with the content of your lecture, except for a few general points of view, which can better be talked than written about, but which I will do, if the opportunity for the former gets postponed too long.

Kind regards,
Freud

1. Correspondence card with preprinted letterhead.

1184

INTERNATIONALE PSYCHOANALYTISCHE VEREINIGUNG
INTERNATIONAL PSYCHO-ANALYTICAL ASSOCIATION
ASSOCIATION PSYCHANALYTIQUE INTERNATIONALE

Budapest, March 23, 1930

Dear Professor,

I am making use of the better mood into which I was brought by a night which I almost slept through entirely in order to write to you once again. The most important thing that I have to say to you is a question for you; our correspondence of the last few months was actually a discussion of *my* personal and practical relations—in the meantime, my interest in how you are came too briefly—at least in the letters. Now I would like to ask you, in your next missive, which, let's hope, will be soon, to express yourself in somewhat more detail about the state of your health, about your plans for the summer, your work program. To be sure, your Anna's imminent visit will also bring news about you.—We are all looking forward to seeing and hearing her again; the news of her coming spread in the city, and I am being approached from all sides for permission to attend the session; but I permitted admittance only to really analytic guests, in conformity with Fräulein Anna's intention.[1]

A few days ago a club of young people requested me to appear with them as a guest; they wanted to direct questions at me. Instead of that, I turned the spear around and interviewed them about whether the psychoanalytic way of thinking changed their views, and to what extent. (They were young, well-educated people, almost all with postsecondary education.) The highest-quality and most insightful explanations were given to me by a very young woman, who was present as a guest; otherwise, there were many nonsensical, exaggeratedly sexual-liberal, and exaggeratedly reactionary responses. The Adlerian superficialities are very popular here as well.

With kind regards to you and your dear ones.

Yours,
Ferenczi

1. Lecture of March 26, 1930, "Beispiele zur Technik der Kinderanalyse: Eine Schilderung der Arbeit des Wiener Seminars für Technik der Kinderanalyse" [Examples of the Technique of Child Analysis: A Depiction of the Work of the Vienna Seminar for Technique of Child Analysis] (*Zeitschrift* 16 [1930]: 593f.).

1185

Vienna, March 30, 1930
IX., Berggasse 19

Dear friend,

I can't refrain from thanking you kindly for the reception that you prepared for Anna, and the honor which you bestowed upon her. Her development seems so gratifying to me that every reverberation also does me very much good.

You now know everything about me, and I also [know] much about you. The best was for me to hear that I have the prospect of seeing you before my trip to Berlin. It has now been confirmed that we will make a pilgrimage to Berlin on April 23 (so, right after Easter).[1] My wife, in consequence of Schröder's request, went yesterday alone, and intends to be back in about two weeks.

Kind regards in the meantime to you and your dear wife.

Yours,
Freud

1. Ferenczi visited Freud on the weekend of April 12–13. It was not until May 4 that Freud and Anna finally traveled to Berlin, accompanied by their former analysands Dorothy Burlingham and, in that connection, Judy de Forest (see letter 1186 and n. 1) and Mabbie Burlingham. From April 22 to May 3, Freud had to undergo a diet treatment in the Cottage Sanatorium on account of colic (see letter 1186; *Diary*, pp. 65–69; Michael Burlingham, *The Last Tiffany* [New York, 1989], p. 211; Peter Heller, ed., *Anna Freud's Letters to Eva Rosenfeld* [Madison, Conn., 1992], pp. 134f.).

1186

Dr. S. Ferenczi
vii., Nagydiofa-Utca 3.

Budapest, April 30, 1930

Dear Professor,

This letter would downright like to be a work of condensation: thanks for the friendly reception that you prepared for me, congratulations on the occasion of the anniversary that we are celebrating with you today (i.e., on May 6), and most heartfelt joy that I was permitted to see you so fresh and healthy at my last visit.

Unfortunately, I heard that in the meantime you had to withdraw for a few days to the Cottage Sanatorium on account of a transitory indisposition, but the news that you didn't have to postpone the Berlin trip reassured me completely about the innocuousness of the incident.—

Very often I think of the friendly and pleasant mood during the hours which I experienced the Sunday before last in your study, which is so familiar to me. I left with the conviction that my fear that my somewhat too independent manner of working and thinking could bring me into such painful conflict with you was exaggerated to a high degree. So, I will continue my work with heightened courage and hope assuredly that these little detours can never divert me from the main road on which I have been strolling at your side for almost twenty-five years now.

Enclosed a letter that a Hungarian patient sent to your daughter. She is an evidently incurable paranoia. She has a little son, whom I would have liked to remove from her proximity—for that reason I spoke about Fräulein Anna and Zulliger.

The decision in the matter of Izette and Judith[1] was, in any event, the right one.

Kind regards and repeated congratulations.

Yours,
Ferenczi

Not until after your return from Berlin can I have handed over to you an Egyptian Osiris figure that I came up with here (supposedly a Hungarian discovery from Roman times). My wife, who succeeded in finding this piece, sends hearty congratulations.

1. Izette Taber de Forest, an American psychotherapist, Ferenczi's analysand, and her daughter Judy, a pupil at the Hietzing School, in analysis with Anna Freud and living in the Burlingham household (the Burlinghams were relatives). Izette later wrote an enthusiastic book about Ferenczi, *The Leaven of Love: A Development of the Psychoanalytic Theory and Technique of Sándor Ferenczi* (New York, 1954), and supported her friend Erich Fromm in his effort to stand in opposition to Jones's assertion of Ferenczi's alleged mental illness. Her relationship to the Freuds and Dorothy Burlingham was not free of tensions. So, for example, she was criticized for her "unnatural" appearance (made up and fashionably dressed), and she received a share of the blame for her daughter's neurosis. See Peter Heller, ed., *Anna Freud's Letters to Eva Rosenfeld* (Madison, Conn., 1992).

1187

Tegel, May 7, 1930

Dear friend,

This in the way of a report: Heart and intestinal ailments made it necessary for me to flee to the Cottage Sanatorium on April 22. The turnabout began with the painful recognition that a cigar which was smoked on April 25 had to be the last for a rather long time. I was able to go to Berlin on May 4, almost recovered. I am doing quite well here, but it was a piece of autotomy, the way the fox does it when he bites off a leg in the snare. I also don't feel very happy, rather distinctly depersonalized.

Schröder wants to make a new prosthesis for me, that means I won't see Vienna in May, and probably not until late in June. In the meantime, this Tegel is an ideal place to stay if one is treated the way we are.

Your Osiris was just brought over to me, for which I thank you very much. There is half of him, but [he is a piece] of good work; he will soon find company here.

Kind regards,
Freud

1188

Budapest, May 25, 1930

Dear Professor,

It will interest you to hear that I decided to buy a house in a somewhat better area on the slope of the right bank of the Danube (in Buda) in order to move into a residence with a garden, which suits me better. On this occasion I am pressed to express the hope that at some time or other you will give us the pleasure of spending a few days in our city.

I still remember how, on your first visit to Budapest, you showed me a villa (it was the villa of the surgeon, Professor Herczel) and said: "In ten to twelve years you will also have a villa and an automobile, like Privy Councillor Herczel."

The automobile is not yet here, but your prophecy has come true—except for the time (twenty-two years).

The purchase of the house also signifies to a certain extent what you called the "idyllic solution" to my problems, but that on no account means limiting intercourse with the outside world.

Kind regards to you and Fräulein Anna.

Yours,
Ferenczi

1189

Tegel, May 28, 1930

Dear friend,

Hearty congratulations for the long-anticipated, finally attained, villa! So, I didn't deceive myself. If I didn't estimate the time period correctly, it was only a consequence of not having taken the war into account. My prophetic gift is, like that of all prophets, very one-sided; while we recognize one element of the future, another eludes us.

The temptation to inspect your new address is naturally very great. I can't yet predict whether I will remain mobile enough. It would become even more pressing if it should turn out, through excavations in your garden, that the place had been taken up already earlier by a Roman villa, whose owner had even spent time in Egypt and had brought back some mementos from there.

The new dignity of being mistress of a castle will suit Frau G. very well. Well, when will you move into the idyll? We think we will stay another three weeks in Tegel.

Kindest regards,
Freud

1190

Budapest, June 29, 1930

Dear Professor,

I am infinitely sorry to hear that you have to stay in Berlin so long beyond the time that was anticipated. I presumed for a long time that this doesn't happen without much pain and trouble; I also greatly regretted the fact that you have to spend the most beautiful time of the summer with dentists. Let's hope your imprisonment doesn't last much longer and that soon you will be able to breathe the mountain air, which is so indispensable to you.

We are already packing; the new house, almost spic-and-span, awaits us. The move will take place on July 3 or 4. The new address will read:

I. Lisznyai utca 11.

But the worries of a house owner are already beginning: the second large residence meanwhile stands empty for August (that does, to be sure, increase the intimacy of accommodation).

In the meantime, I am working diligently: seven-eight-nine hours a day; the finer mechanism of "psychic trauma" and its relation to psychosis is also shaping up into a very impressive picture, at least for me. Perhaps I will make something of it during the October vacation. (We want to stay in Budapest all summer.)

Many kind regards and best wishes.

Yours,
Ferenczi

1191

Tegel, July 5, 1930

Dear friend,

Received your call for help.¹ All sympathy, but it is purely a business problem. If Storfer had money or considered the Hungarian editions to be a secure business, he would have published the books a long time ago. If you think you can arrange more without the Verlag, he will certainly be prepared to give you back the rights that were acquired. It has to be decided between you and Storfer.

I am making use of this occasion to ask something of you in a different, certainly no less important, matter. You know that Eitingon dosen't want to keep the presidency beyond the next Congress. You also know that we all knew that it is due you, and that we postponed your election only for diplomatic reasons. The danger existed that the IPA would disintegrate over the question of lay analysis; it was to be feared that your justifiably inflexible position, meeting head-on with Jones's enmity, which was especially dedicated to you, would make this undesired outcome unavoidable. Eitingon placed himself at [our] disposal, in the person of a cooler and more disinterested mediator. Now the danger has been exorcised, so it seems, at least. Eitingon is resigning, and you should step forward as a matter of course. Eitingon says he already asked you whether you are prepared to accept, but you haven't replied yet. If you turn it down because the old wish has fermented in the interim, only Jones is left as the new president. And you know, I hope, without my issuing any further declarations, to which side my preference inclines. Perhaps I should withhold my most personal argument, but I will venture it anyway. If I hold on beyond September 31, it is really long enough. But if I last longer, then I wouldn't want anyone other than you to give the epitaph for me.

I hope you enjoy the new weeks in your own home, and most especially for Frau Gisela [I hope for] the proper dignity of a housewife. We are counting the days until the departure; there are not many more of them. Then:

> Rebenburg, *Grundlsee*,
> Salzkammergut.²

Cordially,
Freud

1. The "call for help" itself has not been found, but its content can be inferred from a *Rundbrief* of Ferenczi's of November 30, 1930 (letter 1201). Ferenczi wanted to reclaim the rights to the Hungarian Freud editions from the Verlag; the attempt failed, however, for lack of funds.

2. Freud arrived there on July 28. This would be Freud's last vacation outside the immediate environs of Vienna.

1192

Budapest, July 20, 1930
I Lisznyai utca 11

Dear Professor,

Somewhat more prematurely than you, Herr Professor, but I, too, am occupying myself greatly with the problem of death, naturally, likewise in connection with my own fate and its chances for the future. A part of my bodily self-love seems to have sublimated itself into scientific interest, and this subjective factor has sensitized me, I believe, to psychic and other processes in our neurotics, which are playing themselves out in moments of real or supposed lethal danger. That was certainly the way in which I came to freshen up the apparently antiquated (at least temporarily cast-aside) trauma theory. For the moment I am satisfied with the insights, and also with the therapeutic results that I am getting on this path, so that I consider it useful to continue with my work method in this regard. Our last meeting in the Schneewinkel convinced me that my fear that you wouldn't approve of the reactionary tendency in me was very exaggerated. The analysis of this exaggerated fearfulness goes, as you know, far back into the infantile. Both of us (you as my analyst, and I as the one who has been analyzed) are also clear about the fact that my relationship to you and to the colleagues in the Association is in many respects rooted in father and brother bonds. But for the moment I have the feeling that my, perhaps also here subjectively colored, investigations can also lay claim to a certain objective value. I think to myself that with me it is a matter of a relatively belated flaring up of productivity, and I give in to this at times very lively urge to produce, without relinquishing control.

The only seemingly neurotic symptom in my relations with the world around me is the writing inhibition, which is, to be sure, rather marked. The only things that I write are notes, which I cursorily put on paper, about my observations and ideas;[1] but I very much neglect my correspondence. I admire your constant preparedness to respond punctually to letters!

By chance, my last letter to Eitingon crossed with yours, which made me particularly happy, since from it you can gather the spontaneity of my decision in the question of the presidency. But now I can add that your expression of trust in me does me a lot of good; it strengthens me in my intention to participate in the common work, not only as an individual researcher, but also in collaboration with those of like mind, i.e., through the Association. I consider literally true what I wrote to Eitingon about my suitability for the presidency. I am thinking of a collaboration with him which goes beyond my association up to now in the advisory council.

I, too, see that we have to seek understanding with Jones, despite his unreliability in so many things. On the other hand, I can't help viewing what is despotic and hateful in his character and his way of acting as harmful for analysis; here, too, Eitingon's friendly mediation will be indispensable.

I am infinitely sorry that you, Herr Professor, have to spend so much time, and on top of that under painful circumstances, in Berlin instead of in the Alps. Since you didn't say exactly when you are leaving Berlin, I am still sending this letter to the Tegel Sanatorium.

The move is over. I inhabit the ground floor premises of a pretty villa (the second floor is empty—the cares of a homeowner!). The purchase, the setting things in order, and the unavoidable new acquisitions have devoured quite a large part of my assets; the regular expenditures will also increase in the new household, so that I have to work very diligently in order to bring in only[2] enough to meet expenses. But I'm not worried about that for the time being, and what comes later will somehow get straightened out.—The nicest thing about the villa is the fact that, for being situated in a capital city, it has a very spacious garden with much grass and some big old trees. Unfortunately, the quiet is often disrupted by gramophone and radio loudspeakers in the neighborhood, but my study is hermetically sealed.

For now, we have guests daily who want to see the new home.

Kind regards to you and to all your dear ones.

Ferenczi

1. See the posthumously published "Notes and Fragments" (Ferenczi, Posthumous, 308).
2. Reading uncertain. This could also be "to me."

1193

Grundlsee, August 1, 1930
Rebenburg

Dear friend,

We have been back from Berlin for a week, here for four days. The place is marvelously beautiful, the house roomy and comfortable, despite some crazinesses, the view across the lake enchanting. It rains too often and too much; that's the way it is here, we have missed the most beautiful time of the summer.

My prosthesis promises to get better; in some respects it is a distinct advance.

The day before yesterday I received official news of [my] being awarded the Goethe Prize of the city of Frankfurt. Incidentally, in a very charming, very understanding letter from the secretary, Dr. Paquet, who must be somebody himself.¹ Through its relation to Goethe, the prize has something more worthy than many others. I ought to be pleased with it. It amounts to 10,000 marks, approximately the cost of the stay in Berlin. The festive awarding of the prize is supposed to take place in Frankfurt on August 28, Goethe's birthday, in the presence of the one who is being honored, who in return for that is supposed to deliver a speech about his relationship to Goethe. I can naturally not come. Anna will represent me and read aloud what I bring together about Goethe's relationship to analysis and its right also to take him up as its subject.²

With kind regards to you and Frau Gisela in the new house, and [with] the question as to whether you are still going on a trip this year.

Yours,
Freud

1. The Goethe Prize of the city of Frankfurt was commissioned in 1927 and was supposed to honor persons "whose creative impact is worthy of an honor dedicated to Goethe's memory." Stefan George, Albert Schweitzer, and Leopold Ziegler had received the prize before Freud. Alfons Paquet (1881–1944), secretary of the committee since 1928, was the author of numerous travel books, stories, and essays. He was personal physician to Heinrich Meng, by way of whom the contact with Freud was made. The decision on awarding the prize (by a vote of 7 to 5 in favor) was preceded by vehement discussions in which Paquet and the physician and writer Alfred Döblin (1878–1957) (an analysand of Ernst Simmel's), in particular, came out in favor of, and representatives of Goethe institutions in opposition to, Freud. Julius Petersen (1878–1949) of the Goethe Society and Hans Wahl (1885–1949) from the Goethe Museum refused altogether to participate in the awarding of the prize. See Tomas Plänkers, "Die Verleihung des Frankfurter Goethe-Preises an Sigmund Freud 1930: Aus den Sitzungsprotokollen des Goethe-Preis-Kuratoriums" [The Awarding of the Frankfurt Goethe Prize to Sigmund Freud, 1930: From the Minutes of the Meetings of the Goethe Prize Committee], in Plänkers et al., eds., *Psychoanalyse in Frankfurt am Main* (Tübingen, 1996), pp. 254–331.

2. "Address Delivered in the Goethe House at Frankfurt" (Freud 1930e), read there by Anna Freud on August 28, 1930.

1194

an unforgettable example of motherly wisdom and love¹

Cordially yours Ferenczi²

1. Undated, handwritten telegram. It is not in the folder of the Austrian National Library, but was later found by Judith Dupont in Ferenczi's papers.

2. Condolence telegram on the occasion of Freud's mother's death on September 12 at the age of ninety-five.

1195

Grundlsee, September 16, 1930

Dear friend,

Above all, many thanks for your beautiful words on my mother's death. It had a strange effect on me, this great event. No pain, no mourning, which can probably be explained by the secondary circumstances, the advanced age, the sympathy with her helplessness at the end. At the same time a feeling of liberation, of being set free, that I also think I understand. I was not permitted to die as long as she was alive, and now I may. Somehow, in deeper layers, the values of life will have been markedly changed.

I was not at the funeral. Anna also represented me there. Today she went on a Swiss-Italian tour with her friend Dorothy, for which I must only wish her better weather.

The gruesome newspaper reports about my health will also have reached you. I find them very interesting as proof of the difficulty in thrusting upon the public and people in general what they don't like. They are, you see, the reaction to the Goethe Prize, and may warn us about the deception which resistance toward analysis has left behind in a practically palpable way. The same character of reaction is also demonstrated by Bumke's[1] speech, which I know only from a note in the Neue Freie Presse, as well as by the increased activity in the Adlerian band of apes, where they are now publishing about the meaning of life (!) and [about] homosexuality.[2] In short, the Goethe Prize will cost us dearly.

The new views about the traumatic fragmentation of mental life that you indicated seem to me to be very ingenious and have something of the great characteristic of the Theory of Genitality. I only think that one can hardly speak of trauma in the extraordinary synthetic activity of the ego without treating the reactive scar formation along with it. The latter, of course, also produces what we see; we must make the traumas accessible.

I am pleased that you are working. I am not amounting to anything, what with the congratulations for the prize, the condolences for my own fatal illness and now for my mother's death, and with the discomforts of my continuing abstinence from smoking.

Cordially,
Freud

---

1. Oswald C. E. Bumke (1877–1950), psychiatrist in Munich, discoverer of the sign named after him of the absence of the psychoreflexes of the pupils in schizophrenia.

2. Alfred Adler, *Das Problem der Homosexualität: Erotisches Training und erotischer Rückzug* [The Problem of Homosexuality: Erotic Training and Erotic Retreat] (Leipzig, 1930). Adler's essay "Der Sinn des Lebens" [The Meaning of Life] was not published until

1931 (*Internationale Zeitschrift für Individualpsychologie* 9:161–171); his book of the same name was published in 1933 (Vienna).

1196′

Budapest, September 21, 1930[1]

Dear Professor—

The signs of increased resistance since the Goethe Prize are undeniable; but the fact can't be removed from the world and signifies progress.

I was pleased to hear that you find my new views "very ingenious"; I would have been much more pleased if you had declared them to be correct, probable, or even only plausible. The comparison with the "theory of genitality" is perhaps only a superficial one. The "theory of genitality" was the product of pure speculation at a time when, far removed from any practice, I totally gave way to contemplation (military service). The newer views, only fleetingly alluded to, originate from the practice itself, were brought to the surface by it, extended and modified daily; they proved to be not only theoretically but also practically valuable, that is to say, usable.

It goes without saying that you are completely right when you place the never resting tendency to unification in mental life alongside the trauma. I can not only confirm that in principle, but also plaster with examples the various modes of the tendency to heal. Only I find that the expression "scar formation," as far as my experience goes, does not characterize mastery of trauma by means of pathological reaction quite accurately, inasmuch as the mental pathological products are not so rigid and incapable of regeneration as are the scars of bodily tissues.

At the beginning of October we are going to Baden-Baden, then to Paris, so that my wife also has something of a vacation. A severe case has to go along.[2] You see, relaxation therapy is not always very comfortable for the doctor.

Could you tell me if our Madrid friend with the long name[3] has a special reason for not answering my letters?

Many kind regards.

Yours,
Ferenczi

P.S. October 1,[4] 1930

I waited before sending off this letter until I knew for sure that you were in Vienna. We are leaving today.

F[erenczi].

1. The letter is typewritten; only the signature, "Ferenczi," a few corrections, and the postscript are handwritten.
2. Again this refers to Elizabeth Severn.
3. Luis Lopez Ballesteros y de Torres.
4. Corrected from "September 30."

1197

Baden-Baden, Werderstrasse 14,
October 11, 1930[1]

Dear Professor,

I am finally getting a rest after a hard year of work—although I had to take along a [female] patient![2] I always recover quickly here. My wife also feels well, I think. Beneficial boredom characterizes the stay; the body is kept thoroughly busy.

Cordially,
Ferenczi

The Groddecks send regards!

1. Picture postcard: "Baden-Baden, new castle—terrace."
2. It was possibly around this time that the photograph of the Ferenczis depicted in the Ferenczi-Groddeck correspondence (p. 52) was taken. The unidentified third person in the photograph is Elizabeth Severn (kind communication from Christopher Fortune).

1198

Vienna, October 13, 1930
IX., Berggasse 19

Dear friend,

I am pleased to hear that you are again permitted to get a comfortable rest with the Groddecks in Baden-Baden. My impression of your last years of work was that you are tormenting yourself too much, anyway, while you can't fall back on the excuse, which is valid for me, that you must because you have to take care of countless people. But the intensive work does give you great satisfaction right now.

I cordially return Groddeck's greetings. I now have somewhat more to do with doctors and treatments than is absolutely necessary. Lately it has been the stomach that causes inconveniences. There is something unsatisfying in living essentially for one's health.

My work is limited to four hours. No wonder people don't force their way to me when rumor so strongly exaggerates the state of my health. The French American, Provot,¹ who was with Laforgue for so long, and whom you also know well, is also with me now, probably not for very long.

Granting you and your dear wife the beautiful fall convalescence.

Cordially,
Freud

1. A Monsieur Provot (or Prouvot), who was alternately in analysis with Freud and with Laforgue, is frequently mentioned in their correspondence ("La Correspondance entre Freud et Laforgue, 1923–1937," *Nouvelle Revue de Psychanalyse* 15 [1977]: 288, 306f. 312; kind communication from Jean-Pierre Bourgeron).

1199

Vienna, November 5, 1930
IX., Berggasse 19

Dear friend,

On October 14, on Pichler's wish, I had a little follow-up operation done on my scar.¹ The wound still causes me problems now. The histological examination showed nothing suspicious. On October 17 I suddenly fell ill with a fever, which turned into a little broncho-pneumonia. I was in bed for about ten days, and since then I have resumed my work to a modest extent, but I don't feel very strong and am not very much in agreement with the task of living for my health.

Externally, it seems to be a quiet time. Storfer confirms that since the Goethe Prize there has been a considerable increase in resistance on the part of his customers. Political unrest² and economic misery certainly have the right to draw people's attention first and foremost to themselves.

I hope you are both well.

Cordially,
Freud

1. Two days earlier Freud had written to Eitingon: "I also don't know anything more specific about Ferenczi. It is possible that he hasn't heard anything at all about my illness. Despite all our efforts he is going deeper and deeper into isolation. Some date or other has been missed by him" (Sigmund Freud Copyrights).

2. The situation was characterized by increasingly sharp clashes between the political factions and their paramilitary organizations. In the forthcoming National Council elections on November 9, the Nazis did not, to be sure, gain a mandate, but they were able to triple their share of the vote. The Christian Socialists lost the relative majority to the Social Democrats, but they formed a governing coalition under Otto Ender.

1200

Dr. S. Ferenczi
Budapest, I. Lisznyai U. 11.
Telefon: 573-87[1]

Budapest, November 23, 1930[2]

Dear Professor,

This time I will dictate, instead of writing. The trip to Vienna did me good. I was pleased to see that the things on which I am working are, in the final analysis, not so revolutionary at all; you know how averse I am to having a difference of opinion with you, even in questions of detail.

I hope you are well, now as before; my impression of your state of health was excellent.

Please hand over the enclosed communications to the addressees.

Yours,
Ferenczi

1. Preprinted letterhead.
2. The letter is typewritten; only a few corrections and the signature, "Ferenczi," are handwritten.

1201

Dr. S. Ferenczi
Budapest, I. Lisznyai U. 11.
Telefon: 573-87

Budapest, November 30, 1930[1]

Rundbrief

Dear friends,

I greet with joy Ophuijsen's initiative to reassume the Rundbrief communication among the members of the advisory council. Brill's giving way in the question of American lay analysis has doubtless removed this problem from the order of the day for the time being and in so doing created the cool, unpolitical atmosphere in which one can again treat, without affect and with greater prospect for success, scientific problems and such of the psychoanalytic movement. It is certainly desirable that we members of the advisory council also remain in touch and exchange thoughts during the time between Congresses.

In Hungary the antirevolutionary and Catholic reaction is at the height of its power and hinders, wherever possible, any kind of official activity.

Thus, e.g., the authorities are delaying granting the license to open the psychoanalytic polyclinic. But in truth, I must add that the authorities are less responsible for this delay than are the authorities' experts, the university professors, who are hostile to psychoanalysis. We will probably have to withdraw our application for the time being.

But that doesn't hinder the training institute in its fruitful activity. Recently, about four thoroughly trained analysts were advanced to membership.[2] Another five will complete their training in the not too distant future. A technical seminar treats practical-analytic questions in an intimate exchange of thoughts. Every semester three to four theoretical workshops are held, which are eagerly attended and are in part also accessible to outsiders. In two child outpatient clinics, parents and children are being helped with advice and in part with analytic treatment.

The meetings have been held twice a week lately, little that is new, just like in the other groups of Europe. We seem to be in a period of working through.

I, personally, am still holding back with certain results of my newer investigations, but I hope to come forward with them in the not too distant future, if my being overburdened with practical work allows me the time to do so.

The depressed financial situation in Hungary forces the younger colleagues to do analyses often for low fees that are unseemly. Still, the average income of the better-known colleagues is perhaps somewhat higher than that of the rest of the practicing physicians, who are doing quite miserably.

In the hope of soon receiving reports from all groups, and in that connection, members of the advisory council, I remain, with collegial regards,

Ferenczi

December 7, 1930

Postscript. As a supplement to the above, I would like to communicate that the theoretical interest, here as well as elsewhere, is turning to questions of child analysis. At my behest, an evening was recently dedicated to the critical discussion about communications relating to this from the English group.[3] On the invitation of the group, Anna Freud will give three lectures in the Budapest group in the course of this semester.[4] In general, the observations from our group in many instances supported the Viennese views,[5] without denying in principle the significance of the courage with which Melanie Klein has attacked these problems. Perhaps the discussions here are being influenced to some extent by my newer investigations on traumatogenesis.

[written on a separate sheet]
Dr. S. Ferenczi
Budapest, I. Lisznyai U. 11.
Telefon: 573-87

Budapest, November 30, 1930

To Herr Professor Freud and Dr. Max Eitingon, as well as Fräulein Anna Freud as members of the Advisory Council of the International Psychoanalytic Verlag.

With the request [that you] consider the following lines for the time being as private and discreet communication, I can't help turning to you for urgent help, that is to say, a remedy, in a matter that pertains to the Hungarian Freud editions.

Numerous external and internal difficulties, not least a lack of money and the weariness of the publishers, has delayed for years the publication of Hungarian Freud translations which have been finished for a long time. A number of shorter works: the Three Essays, the paper "On Dreams," and Freud's Five American Lectures have been sold out for a long time; two other works by Freud, "Everyday Life" and "Group Psychology,"[6] were in the hands of an inept publisher. Then Storfer's suggestion to have all of Freud's works published by the Verlag came to us like a deliverance. The work was set in motion, the manuscripts bought by the Verlag, even printing was begun. But printing was suddenly stopped as a result of the Verlag's financial difficulties, and more years passed, so that, e.g., the Interpretation of Dreams, the manuscript of which originates from the prewar times, still hasn't been published.

When I complained about this about five months ago, Storfer declared himself prepared to give us back the rights and manuscripts at cost. Unfortunately, we didn't have the money necessary to take them over. But recently, the possibility opened up to get the largest Hungarian book publisher (Athenäum) interested in our cause, so I turned to Storfer with the request to give an accounting of the cost price. Instead of [his] response to it, I received from him the enclosed, in places unnecessarily sarcastic, but in merito hostilely disdainful letter,[7] which I ask you to read.

And here is the place to indicate that Storfer has strong conscious and unconscious motives to hate Hungary, his own fatherland, which he can't stand and which also didn't treat him very amicably. I must relate his dichotomous behavior in this matter in part to this hatred.

But it is extremely unjust that the Hungarian psychoanalytic movement also has to suffer from it. So I have to request the council members, especially friend Eitingon, to insist that the desired data be communicated to me, and, in the event that an agreement can be realized with Athenäum, the right be given to conclude the sale. I must again indicate that, during the hiatus of more than ten years, the Hungarian book market was flooded with the works of a pupil of Stekel's, which are, so to speak, the only source from which the Hungarian reader can glean psychoanalytic knowledge today.

Unfortunately, I must add that the negotiations with Athenäum have not been concluded by a long shot, so that here, too, it is only a matter of a possibility, and not of something that has been firmly established.

But if the Verlag could assure us of a certain and not all too distant deadline for completing the printing and distribution, then we would naturally have nothing against leaving the books with the Verlag.

So I ask Eitingon to take this matter into his own hands and to settle it as soon as possible, with the objectivity that is his wont.

Kind regards,
Ferenczi

1. The entire letter is typewritten; the signature, "Ferenczi," is in each case written over by hand with an "F."
2. According to the Society's reports in the *Zeitschrift*, Fanny K. Hann and Gyula Szüts had been accepted on March 26, 1930; Lilian K. Rotter followed on December 13, 1930; Klára G. Lázár and Endre Almásy on March 13, 1931 (16 [1930]: 540; 17 [1931]: 300).
3. Alice Bálint, "Referat und Kritik der kinderanalytischen Arbeiten von Melanie Klein" [Review and Critique of the Child-Analytic Papers of Melanie Klein] (November 7, 1930; *Zeitschrift* 17 [1931]: 300).
4. Only one lecture has been found, that of February 13, 1930, "Eingehende Beschreibung der Analyse eines Kindes mit Pavor nocturnus" [Detailed Description of the Analysis of a Child with Pavor Nocturnus], in which Anna Freud described the case of Peter Heller (see Heller, *Eine Kinderanalyse bei Anna Freud, 1929–1932* [Würzburg, 1983]).
5. In the original, "prospects."
6. Respectively, Freud 1905d, 1901a, 1910a, 1901b, and 1921c.
7. The letter has not been found.

1202

Dr. S. Ferenczi
Budapest, I. Lisznyai U. 11.
Telefon: 573-87

Budapest, February 20, 1931[1]

Dear Professor,

I am sending you the enclosed letter from Dr. Amsden[2] in the hope that you can be of help with your advice in the matter which is provoked by it and which is not unimportant for psychoanalysis. If I were not overtired and overburdened with cases which can't be postponed, I would not hesitate to accept the invitation to Philadelphia myself. I felt much more at home on the only evening that I spent there in the circle of academic notables, as well as during the lecture, than in the hurly-burly of New York. Since I myself do not come into question, I turned to Dr. Radó, to whom I indicated that he come to an agreement with Dr. Eitingon in this matter. His response, evidently in consideration of the journals, turned out negative.[3] I think Dr. Nunberg would be the next best person in line. Now, my request extends so far as to have a decision on the part of Nunberg get to me *as quickly as possible,* perhaps through Anna's mediation, so that I can reply to Amsden, who has since been pressing again by telegram. I am writing this to you, and not to Nunberg directly, since I didn't want to take this step without your assent. I consider our friend Federn to be less of a good teacher and representative. In the event that Nunberg doesn't want to, I will ask Amsden to turn to Eitingon for further suggestions.

Nothing special is happening in and around me, except for the therapeutic and theoretical experiments, which I am continuing with undiminished energy and, for the time being, without halting.

From the latest news from Vienna, your sister-in-law's letter, I know that you must still be in torment with your prosthesis.[4] I hope this difficulty has been removed in the meantime.

Unfortunately, I still have to report that, at Lajos Lévy's urging, I allowed myself to be seduced into giving an orienting lecture before a larger circle of physicians (Monday, February 23). I promise neither myself nor them much good from it.

We are awaiting the promised visit from Anna or your [female] pupil![5]
With many kind regards.

Yours,
Ferenczi

1. The letter is typewritten; only the penciled signature, "Ferenczi," and a few corrections are handwritten.
2. The letter has not been found.
3. Radó was the editor of *Zeitschrift* and *Imago.* He was actually already preparing to emigrate to New York, on the basis of an invitation from Brill.
4. Freud's condition since his last operation in October of the previous year had not improved, "and in February another suspicious spot showed itself which was dealt with by electro-coagulation. This healed badly, however . . . Moreover . . . another suspicious place developed . . . that on April 24 . . . was excised. Examination of it revealed that it was removed 'at the twelfth hour'" (Jones III, 156f.).
5. On April 11, 1931, Jenny Wälder from Vienna spoke on the "Analyse eines Falles von Pavor nocturnus (Mit besonderen Hinweisen auf die angewandte Behandlungstechnik)" [Analysis of a Case of Pavor Nocturnus (with Special Reference to Applied Technique of Treatment)] (*Zeitschrift* 17 [1931]: 433). Jenny Wälder, née Pollak (1898–1989), M.D., 1925, an analysand of Hans Jokl. In 1926 she began training to be a child analyst in Vienna; in 1928 she became an associate and in 1930 a full member of the Soci-

ety, and in 1936 she became a training analyst. In 1930 she married the psychoanalyst Robert Wälder. She emigrated to Boston in 1938, was divorced from her husband, and married Duncan Hall. In 1943 she moved to Bethesda, Maryland, and was active in the Baltimore-Washington, Philadelphia, Michigan, and Miami groups. See Mühlleitner, *Lexikon*, pp. 351f.

1203

Vienna, February 22, 1931
IX., Berggasse 19

Dear friend,

This evening, as soon as Anna returns, I will authorize you to get in touch with Nunberg. But I think I can predict that he will refuse. He is expecting his wife (Margarethe Rie) to deliver any day now, in anxious suspense, after last year's pregnancy ended so badly, and he won't want to leave mother and child so soon. Besides that, he is being made full use of in Vienna, mostly occupied with foreigners, and is suffering from chronic gall bladder ailments, which demand that he look after himself.[1]

Radó has, as far as I know, been requested by Brill for the institute which is to be opened in New York, and it is said that he will accept this offer.

In the next letter I will enclose Amsden's; I am still saving it for Anna.

The wound from my last operation hasn't healed yet. All these interventions were passed off to me as unavoidable, but then as unnecessary. Their consequences are filling up the next weeks with misery.

I greet you and Frau G. cordially.

Yours,
Freud

1. Nunberg subsequently accepted an invitation in September 1931 for training at the University of Pennsylvania, where he remained until August 1932 (Mühlleitner, *Lexikon*, p. 237).

1204

Vienna, February 23, 1931
IX., Berggasse 19

Dear friend,

Anna just talked to Nunberg. To our surprise, he didn't refuse a limine,[1] but stated that he couldn't take a position with regard to the offer as long as it was so indefinite and uncertain. He would like to hear more about it.

I do hold fast to the conviction that Nunberg doesn't seriously come into consideration. Since you wish suggestions, we both thought about the following possibilities: First and foremost [we thought] of Helene Deutsch, who would certainly like to go and has the stuff for the performance which will be expected of her. Second, of Ophuijsen, who would also pick it up. Naturally, neither will be notified by the both of us.

There is still another way. As far as we know, Alexander is having a hard time in Chicago. It may be straightened out through the influence of President Hutchins,[2] but at the moment it doesn't seem out of the question that he will leave the matter in the lurch without even lasting the one year. If that happens, then it would be very appropriate to offer him the position that Amsden has his sights on. But I ask you to treat the information about Alexander as strictly *confidential on all fronts.*

Kind regards,
Freud

1. Latin for "outright" ("from the threshold").
2. Robert Maynard Hutchins, president (since 1929) of the University of Chicago.

1205

Dr. S. Ferenczi
Budapest, I. Lisznyai U. 11.
Telefon: 573-87

Budapest, March 22, 1931[1]

Dear Professor,

I know only too well that it is mainly my fault if I am so little oriented with regard to the more intimate processes of the movement. Radó's reserve, for instance, goes so far that, even after the recommendation to Philadelphia, he didn't communicate anything about his upcoming trip to New York; I learned about it only through your communications. As president in spe [in hope] I would at least like to orient myself about events after the fact. Do you think that this effort might be expected of our dear secretary,[2] who should also read this letter?

The last news about your prosthesis difficulties sounds less bad, which especially pleased me. I also heard that you want to spend the summer in the vicinity of the city, as do I. Let's hope you will find, as you hitherto always have, some charming and peaceful corner or other, where you can bring to paper this year's opuscule, which we are all already waiting for.

Looking back over the past year, one is astonished by the amount of glorification, criticism, and senseless twaddle that you have had to allow to go out about you. Here with us, the various renegade groups are the loudest; yet it seems to me that the respectable restraint that we learned from you is visibly increasing the reputation of the Hungarian group, albeit in slow tempo. Quoad me [as for me]: my efforts in a number of practically and theoretically important problems are continuing. Unfortunately, that means, given the intensity of my manner of work, ten hours of analytic work daily; there is then hardly any strength left for writing things out. On April 15 we will probably travel to the Adriatic (Ragusa) for ten days. On the trip along the Dalmatian coast I can probably get a look at the island of Arbe, among whose enchanted castles we spent some very beautiful days.³

Perhaps you will find time to write again occasionally!

Kind regards,
Ferenczi

1. The letter is typewritten; only the signature, "Ferenczi," and a few corrections are handwritten.
2. Anna, chief secretary of the IPA.
3. Easter 1912; cf. letters 288ff.

1206

Dr. S. Ferenczi
Budapest, I. Lisznyai U. 11.
Telefon: 573-87

Budapest, May 31, 1931¹

Dear Professor,

Instead of directly communicating what is new with us, I am taking the liberty of sending in a piece of a copy of a letter to Eitingon. With the opening of the polyclinic,² our training institute is really only now becoming an institution for training. Naturally, with us things are also going in the direction of vanity, not without sensitivity and injury. The older members of the group, even though they don't partcipate much themselves any longer, look askance at the young ones' industriousness. Strangely, Lajos Lévy and Kata are also not very friendly with the younger ones; our secretary³ handed in his resignation, but I hope to appease him.—Isn't it strange that again and again only private protection of a just cause can help [achieve] victory? Every medical forum that was asked was rude and disdainful. The authorities had to accommodate the professors to a certain degree, and thus, it says in the permit: "Since psychoanalysis is not an independent science but a part of general psychology and neuropathology, the Association must express this in the title of the polyclinic by having it call itself simply a clinical agency for nervous and emotional illnesses in which, among other things, psychoanalysis is practiced." Thus, the name of the polyclinic will be something like: "Clinical Agency of the Hungarian Psychoanalytic Society for Nervous and Emotional Illnesses."

Please thank your Anna in my name for her kind letter.

We are all happy to hear that your condition is improving all the time. I am infinitely sorry not to have seen or talked with you on the way back.[4]

Much luck and good weather for your move on June 1.[5] Thus both of us will spend our summer, for a while at least, near the city, I, to be sure, also the winter.

Also in hopes of further favorable news, I am your old

Ferenczi

[Enclosure 1]

Dr. S. Ferenczi
Budapest, I. Lisznyai U. 11.
Telefon: 573-87

From a Letter to Eitingon *(Copy)*[6]

May 31, 1931

"Here at home things are going along very lively in the Society. The young people, mostly women physicians,[7] are eager for work; the laymen and laywomen[8] are occupying themselves mostly with the analysis of children. A young [female] colleague became a psychoanalyst for a workers' organization (child protection). Another child protection society, in which Frau Dr. Dubovitz was keeping hours, dissolved, unfortunately (financial difficulties). In place of this I can this time officially give you the unexpectedly pleasant information that, thanks to the efforts of Dr. Bálint, Frau Kovács, and one of her patients, despite vehement opposition from the State Health Council, permission to establish the polyclinic was finally granted us by the Ministry of Public Welfare. We have, totally from our own means, rented a five-room apartment and will set it up in a few weeks, so that I will already be able to report to the Congress the beginning of the therapeutic and instructional activity there.

As you see, we are completely dependent on the help of the members, while Berlin, Vienna, and London have munificent helpers.

I had a talk with Storfer in Vienna. Unfortunately, it seems to me that he succeeded in letting you and the Professor get the wrong impression that we don't want to give anything to the Verlag for literary purposes which are of benefit to the public. In reality, conditions are such that we have to use for the polyclinic everything that we can give out. Also, most of the colleagues are doing *very* badly. In spite of this, Storfer demands that in the foreseeable future we can count on the publication of the Hungarian Lectures only if we pay an additional 1600 Pengös,* even though an earlier agreement exists with regard to this and some other Hungarian editions. The manuscript of the 'Interpretation of Dreams' has been waiting for *fif-*

*and later even more—with every individual book!

teen years to be published, while the Hungarian market is being flooded with psychoanalytic junk literature. Those are the true conditions, and I ask you and the Professor to take them into consideration.⁹

I am sending you enclosed the title and the few introductory sentences of my Congress lecture."

[Enclosure 2]

Dr. S. Ferenczi
Budapest, I. Lisznyai U. 11.
Telefon: 573-87
Congress Lecture of Dr. Ferenczi.¹⁰
*Preliminary Communications.*¹¹

1. Does the dream have a second function?

Supported by experiences with deep relaxation during the analyses, whereby traumatic experiences tend to repetition, as well as by the analysis of dreams in general, one arrives at the supposition that sleep state and dream seek to unburden the psychic system also by reexperiencing traumatic day's and life's residues, thus revealing something about the nature of traumatic-neurotic dream processes.

2. A possible extension of our metapsychological world of ideas.

Freud's metapsychological constructions are the result of analytic experiences with neurotics (repression). By the same right one could also take seriously as psychic reality the mechanisms, which are of a different nature and rather universal, behind the productions of psychotics and those who have been traumatically shocked, in fact, utilize them for psychic *knowledge. (Examples: fragmentation and atomization of the personality; sequestration.)

*structure-

1. The letter is typewritten; only the signature, "Ferenczi," and a correction (both in pencil) are handwritten.

2. "After much fighting with the officials, the Society was allowed to set up a polyclinic under the name 'General Ambulatorium for Nervous and Mental Patients.' The polyclinic already assumed its activity in premises which are well adapted and equipped for analytic purposes (I. 12 Mészáros St.). The Society requested Dr. *Ferenczi* to direct the polyclinic. Dr. M. *Balint* became his representative. In attendance beside them at the polyclinic are Dr. Hermann, Dr. Hollós, Dr. Pfeifer, and Dr. Révesz. Dr. Almásy, who is dedicating the greatest part of his activity to the Institute, is acting in the capacity of assistant" (*Zeitschrift* 17 [1931]: 434). The official opening took place on December 18, 1931 (ibid., 18 [1932]: 141).

3. Imre Hermann; he continued to be entered in the membership list as secretary.

4. On his birthday on May 6, Freud had "seen Ferenczi for only two minutes, otherwise received no visitors" (Freud to Eitingon, May 7, 1931, Sigmund Freud Copyrights).
   5. On June 5 the Freuds rented a house in Pötzleinsdorf, in Vienna's eighteenth district.
   6. This copy is typewritten; only the insert and a few corrections (in a different hand) are handwritten.
   7. E.g., Fanny Hann, Lily Hajdu, Klára Lázár, and Lilian Rotter.
   8. E.g., Alice Bálint, Vilma Kovács, Margit Dubowitz, Kata Lévy, Edit Gyömröi, and Géza Dukes.
   9. In his reply of June 6, 1931 (kindly placed at our disposal by Michael Schröter), Eitingon was of the opinion that Ferenczi ought not to envy the Berliners and Viennese for their financial condition; he took Storfer under his wing and, for his part, asked Ferenczi to be considerate of the precarious condition of the Verlag, which had for a long time been unable to produce any more books without financial contributions from their authors.
   10. These introductory sentences are typewritten; only the addition and a few corrections are handwritten (both in a different hand).
   11. No Congress took place in 1931. The thoughts sketched out here were further adumbrated in the posthumously published manuscript "Zur Revision der Traumdeutung" [On the Revision of the Interpretation of Dreams] of March 26, 1931 (*Bausteine* IV, 242–248). They can also be viewed as the first indications of Ferenczi's paper "Confusion of Tongues between Adults and the Child" (1933, 294), which he presented at the next Congress (September 1932, Wiesbaden), though, to be sure, leaving out the thoughts about the "second function" of the dream.

1207

[Vienna,] XVIII
Khevenhüllerstr[asse] 6¹

Dear friend,

It was also a great disappointment for me that you had to break off your second stay in Vienna so quickly.² How one shouldn't postpone anything! Everything is so uncertain.

Thanks for your many interesting reports, not least for the excerpts from your Congress lecture. The so-called second function of dreams is certainly its first (mastery, see Beyond the Pleasure Principle)!³ Your second piece is of that characteristic which is so inestimable to me, which I respect so very much, like your theory of genitality.

I think I am slowly coming up to strength here. Our place of residence in Pötzleinsdorf is ideally beautiful and pleasant. Dogs and humans feel very well here. One forgets that one is actually living in the eighteenth district of a large city. I am giving all five hours, am wrestling with the last remnants of what I owe in replies, and have not yet got to my actual work. My good dentist comes out daily, so finally and in the end I am carrying on the existence of a great gentleman and a rich man.

With kind regards to you and Frau G.

Yours,
Freud

1. The letter bears no date. It was found in the Balint folder for 1932, but probably belongs here according to its context. The color of the stationery also suggests 1931.
2. See letter 1206, n. 4.
3. The dreams in traumatic neuroses and "the dreams during psycho-analysis which bring to memory the psychical traumas of childhood . . . arise . . . in obedience to the compulsion to repeat . . . Thus it would seem that the function of dreams, which consists in setting aside any motives that might interrupt sleep, by fulfilling the wishes of the disturbing impulses, is not their *original* function. It would not be possible for them to perform that function until the whole of mental life had accepted the dominance of the pleasure principle" (Freud 1920g, pp. 32f.).

1208

Dr. S. Ferenczi
Budapest, I. Lisznyai U. 11.
Telefon: 573-87

Budapest, June 14, 1931[1]

Dear Professor,

Of course I know only too well that the function of the dream which was emphasized by me is the same one that you described and explained in "Beyond the Pleasure Principle" as being characteristic of the dreams of traumatics. But my experiences press me to emphasize this point of view more strongly than is the case in your "Interpretation of Dreams." In other words: I would like to generalize somewhat the point of view of mastery of trauma in sleep and dream.

Enclosed a letter from Eitingon[2] and the copy of my reply to it.

I am very pleased that you feel so well in Pötzleinsdorf. Too bad you didn't already begin earlier to be a great gentleman and a rich man. We, too, are staying in the country and are feeding ourselves properly,[3] up to the Congress. My vacation begins on October 1, not known yet where.

Give our regards to all the members of the family in and around the Khevenhüllerstrasse.

Yours,
Ferenczi

[Enclosure]

Dr. S. Ferenczi
Budapest, I. Lisznyai U. 11.
Telefon: 573-87

Budapest, June 14, 1931[4]

Dear Max:

Thanks for the congratulation.

On the matter of the polyclinic: Nothing is further from my mind than to *envy* Berlin and Vienna. I don't begrudge either group the progress that it has demonstrated; I also know that the economic conditions there are also very bad and lay claim to the members' capacity for accomplishment; I only wanted to give one to understand that we are worse off by a degree because we are totally left to our own devices.

And this is the reason why we can't come up with anything in the way of literary contributions; the polyclinic gobbles up everything at our disposal. Frau Kovács and I are at present paying the entire rent; the remaining members are mostly too poor to be able to give anything worth mentioning.

We also know all too well what difficulties the Verlag has to struggle with, and at your request we have contributed out of the polyclinic's fund an insignificant, but considering our state, nice, amount for purposes of the Verlag. Of course it doesn't occur to us to demand great material sacrifices from the Verlag. On the contrary: my last proposal was that we, or a publishing house here, reimburse the Verlag for all cash outlays, but in exchange for that be granted the rights to the Hungarian translations; but this suggestion was rejected, even though it wouldn't cost the Verlag a penny, aside from the release of payment for the translation rights.

I, personally, didn't hesitate, naturally, to make available the entire cost of production for the German edition of my essays.

Unfortunately, I can't even promise that even in that event (that is, if we get the Verlag's agreement) we can conclude the deal with the publisher here; but without this agreement in principle, we can't take one step, and we have to sit back while years, even decades go by without our being able to publish the Hungarian translation of the "Lectures" and the "Interpretation of Dreams," which are finished in manuscript.

I leave it to you to decide whether this explanation of the facts deserves consideration or not.

As a member of the central executive, I naturally give my approval to lengthen the Congress, but I would like to ask you in this eventuality also to make room for Frau Dr. Bálint's lecture.[5]

The title of my Congress lecture should be, word for word:

"1. SLEEP RELAXATION AND TRAUMATIC REPRODUCTION TENDENCY."
"2. ON EXTENDING OUR METAPSYCHOLOGICAL WORLD OF IDEAS." (PRELIMINARY COMMUNICATIONS.)

I would like it to be expressly stated in the program that both contributions are "preliminary communications."

Kind regards,

1. The letter is typewritten; only a few corrections and the signature, "Ferenczi," are handwritten.
2. See letter 1206, n. 9.
3. See letter 818 and n. 1.
4. This carbon copy of a letter to Max Eitingon is also typewritten; only a few corrections are handwritten.
5. Alice Bálint spoke at the Wiesbaden Congress on "Versagung und Gewährung in der Erziehung" [Renouncing and Giving in Child Rearing] (*Zeitschrift* 19 [1933]: 253).

1209

ANNA FREUD
Wien, Ix., Berggasse 19.[1]

Vienna, July 29, 1931

Dear Doctor!

So, the Congress has finally been canceled. I have already received news several times from Eitingon. He, you, and I were in favor of it, Jones and Ophuijsen were opposed to it. But this majority was sufficient for Eitingon, although that will probably create difficulties later on. Eitingon also exchanged telegrams with Brill and the French group, and both showed much understanding for the situation. Even if the German exit tax should still be lifted, monetary conditions are too uncertain, and all circumstances speak in opposition to a Congress altogether. I, personally, am also glad, by the way. Now one can at least afford the luxury of being tired.

Things are going very well with us, and we are having a very peaceful summer.

When does your vacation begin?

Very cordially,
Anna

1. Preprinted letterhead. The letter is typewritten; only the signature, "Anna," is handwritten.

1210
Dr. S. Ferenczi
Budapest, I. Lisznyai U. 11.
Telefon: 573-87

Budapest, September 15, 1931

Dear Professor,

You are probably thinking how hard it is to connect again after such a long hiatus. But you have encountered so much that is human in the course of your life that you can also understand and excuse such conditions of being drawn back upon oneself.

Enough of that: I was and still am immersed in a very difficult inner and outer, certainly also scientific, "work of purification," which has not produced any final results as yet—and one can't come forward with anything that is half finished. The scientific is still grouping around technique, the working over of which, however, allows some theoretical things to appear in a somewhat altered light. In my usual fashion, I do not shy away from coming to conclusions, to the extent that this is at all possible—often up to a limit where I lead myself "ad absurdum"; but that doesn't discourage me. I try to move forward in other, often precisely opposite ways, and I still have the hope of finding the right path at one time or another.

That all sounds very mystical—please don't be frightened by it. As far as I can judge myself, I am not (or only rarely) overstepping the bounds of normality. To be sure, I often make mistakes, but I am not rigid in my prejudices.

Healthwise, I have been doing somewhat better very recently. Will that also become connected with the psychic? I don't know for sure.

For the time being I am making do with these intimations and am utilizing this occasion to inquire about your health. Your Anna recently reassured me about it.

In October we are going to Italy, without patients, for once.

We were thinking about you and Frau Professor on your wedding anniversary.

Kind regards to everyone.

Yours,
Ferenczi

1211

Vienna, September 18, 1931
IX., Berggasse 19

Dear friend,

Finally, a sign of life and love from you! After how long! The last time you were in Vienna we hardly saw each other. I was very miserable at the time, to be sure, but today I am significantly better.

There is no doubt that with this interruption of contact you are distancing yourself from me more and more. I say, and hope not: alienating. I accept it as fate—like so many other things; I know that I am not personally to blame for it; in recent times I also preferred no one else to you.

It is with regret that I term it an expression of inner dissatisfaction that you are trying to press forward in all kinds of directions which to me seem to lead to no desirable end. But I have—you, yourself, bear witness to this—always respected your independence and am prepared to wait until you yourself take steps to turn around. With you it could be a new, third puberty, after the completion of which you will probably have reached maturity. But I definitely have to deal with the next, for me, perhaps last, president of the IPA.

With cordial wishes for your October trip and warm thanks to your dear wife.

Yours,
Freud

1212

Capri, Hotel Quisisana,
October 10, 1931

Dear Professor,

I composed the reply to your last letter in Budapest more than two weeks ago, but I thought it was preferable to let myself be influenced beforehand by the mild air of Italy and the beautiful memories that are connected with this country.

For the first time in years I am on vacation again without patients; body and spirit were already passionately longing for bountiful peace and quiet. Now, Capri offers everything one can expect from the Italian landscape (sun, sea, and people). We feel extremely well here. Let's hope you will once again be capable of traveling; then you mustn't refrain from having a longer stay here.

For a few days (we were in Rome and Naples earlier) all problems of science and the movement faded away from me. Only today I awoke to consciousness of my duties.

Now I want to cite a few sentences from my letter that was composed in Budapest:

"I definitely won't deny that subjective factors often significantly influence the manner and content of production with me. In the past this has occasionally led to exaggerations. Finally, I have succeeded, I think, in realizing where and how I went too far. On the other hand, even these excursions into uncertainty also always were of significant use to me.—I must presuppose something similar from your diagnosis of 'third puberty.' Let us assume that the diagnosis is correct: the value of what is created in this condition should for the moment be judged objectively. I, too, can also refer to a quotation from Schiller (which I heard from you),[1] according to which emboldening interest can also be brought to what is unaccustomed, even if it looks in part to be erroneous or fantastic.—My newer insights are only in the process of being formed; it would be very desirable to me if you could write something special about the points that seem to lead to 'no desirable end.'—Do you consider it out of the question that, after the maturity that is expected by you, i.e., after the turnaround, I will be able to produce something that is practically or even theoretically useful?

["]I am above all an empiricist (which may appear strange to you, when you think of the wealth of theoretical bold ventures). The ideas are always connected with the variations of the treatment of patients and find either rejection or confirmation in them. I am also careful enough in publication; perhaps all too much—so that I may appear to many as lost.

["]On the question of the presidency: perhaps it would redound to the advantage of the cause if, in your statements, you didn't feel tied down by the consideration of having to 'deal' with the president. Isn't Eitingon supposed to be reelected?"

I thank you cordially for the friendly and kind words of your letter. We will be staying here for about another two weeks.

Yours,
Ferenczi

Many kind regards to your dear family.

1. The quotation from Schiller's correspondence with Körner, found by Rank (see letter 974 and n. 3).

1213

Vienna, October 19, 1931
IX., Berggasse 19

Dear friend,

Only a few lines to congratulate you on the extended stay in Capri. I myself was there for only two days with my brother. In exchange for that, we lived for weeks in heavenly Sorrento.[1] Once again, I envy you—but you seem to have earned this enjoyment with difficulty. Who knows how much good it will do you to be withdrawn for a time from the problematics of your patients.

I hope you didn't take my remark about having to deal with the next president of the IPA tragically.

Cordially, for you and your dear wife.

Yours,
Freud

1. In 1902. See Jones II, 21–23.

1214

Grand Hotel Quisisana
Capri[1]
October 22, 1931[2]

Dear Professor,

We have already packed everything up—hence the letter written in pencil—I only want to thank you for your last lines and at the same time inform you that we will spend approximately the time between October 27 and 30 in Vienna. I hope to be able to see you and await news in the Hotel Regina as to when I will disturb you the least.—My wife wants to have her bad knees looked at in Vienna (the radiologist Robinson supposedly understands these things).

I certainly hope to be able to discuss all matters in detail with Fräulein Anna.

See you again soon, this time undisturbed, let us hope!

Yours,
Ferenczi

1. Preprinted letterhead with the logo, "UNITI The Sign of Hospitality," and a list of other hotel locations.
2. The letter is written in pencil.

1215

Dr. S. Ferenczi
Budapest, I. Lisznyai U. 11.
Telefon: 573-87

Budapest, December 5, 1931

Dear Professor,

Don't think that the days I spent in Vienna left me uninfluenced. The long silence on my part is only an expression of the significance of our conversations; such a far-reaching and first-time examination of the differences in our views, or at least the technique that we comply with needs time to be settled. We are of one mind in principle as well as in the manner of acting; no less than you do I want to circumvent unnecessary and avoidable dangers; it is only a matter of a difference in the pace of what is *unavoidably* to be communicated and in the conception of the duty of science to communicate everything, even what is risky (if it is true), in the hope that from truth, ultimately only good can sprout. So, above all, the investigation should be predicated on whether the things that I have observed are true and whether their interpretation by me is correct. In that respect I will also make an effort to exercise the strictest objectivity possible—especially after objections from such a significant quarter. The time is still too short to be able to make any final statements about this work of revision. But honesty obliges me to say that, *up to now,* I don't feel called upon to change *anything essential.*—On no account does that mean defiant wanting to hold fast to what is my own (although I, like others, surely, am not completely free of such tendencies); in any case, I will endeavor to keep such purely personal motives (being insulted, infantile rebellion, etc.) in check.—It is still possible that some of what I am now experiencing in the analyses also has objective validity.

I hope that you continue to be well. I was very pleased about your state of well-being during my stay in Vienna.

Kind regards,
Ferenczi

1216

Vienna, December 13, 1931
IX., Berggasse 19[1]

Dear friend,

As always, I was pleased with your letter, less with its content. If you were unable to decide on any change in your position up to now, then it is certainly very improbable that you will do it later. But that is essentially your affair; my opinion that you have not embarked upon any fruitful path is a private matter that doesn't need to disturb you.

On the other hand, I see that the difference between us comes to a head in the smallest thing, a detail in technique, which certainly deserves to be discussed. You have made no secret of the fact that you kiss your patients and let them kiss you; I had also heard the same thing from my patients (via Clara Thompson).[2] Now, two paths are diverging for you, if you want to give a detailed report about technique and results. Either you share this, or you keep it quiet. The latter, as you may well think, is dishonorable. What one does in the way of technique one must also represent publicly. Besides, both paths would soon merge. Even if you don't say so yourself, it will become known, just as I knew about it before you told me.

Now, I am certainly not one to condemn such little erotic gratifications out of prudishness or consideration for bourgeois convention. I also know that in the times of the Nibelungenlied a kiss was only a harmless greeting, which was bestowed on every guest. I am further of the opinion that analysis is also possible in Soviet Russia, where complete sexual freedom is sanctioned by the state. But that doesn't change the fact that we are not living in Russia and that with us a kiss is an indication of unmistakable erotic intimacy. Up to now in technique we have held fast to the proposition that erotic gratifications should be denied the patient. You also know that in instances where ample gratifications are not to be had, lesser caresses assume their role very well, in love affairs, on the stage, etc.

Now, picture to yourself what will be the consequence of making your technique public. There is no revolutionary who is not knocked out of the field by a still more radical one. So-and-so many independent thinkers in technique will say to themselves: Why stop with a kiss? Certainly, one will achieve still more if one adds "pawing," which, after all, doesn't make any babies. And then bolder ones will come along who will take the further step of peeping and showing, and soon we will have accepted into the technique of psychoanalysis the whole repertoire of demiviergerie and petting parties,[3] with the result being a great increase in interest in analysis on the part of analysts and those who are being analyzed. The new ally will, however, easily lay too much claim to this interest for himself, the younger of our colleagues will be hard put, in the relational connections that they have made, to stop at the point where they had originally intended, and Godfather[4] Ferenczi, looking at the busy scenery that he has created, will possibly say to himself: Perhaps I should have stopped in my technique of maternal tenderness *before* the kiss.

Little is accomplished with essays "about the dangers of neocatharsis."[5] One should obviously not get into the danger at all. I have intentionally refrained from speaking about the increase in all the calumnious resistances against analysis through the kissing technique, although it seems to me to be wanton to provoke them.

I don't believe at all that I have said anything to you in this warning that you don't know yourself. But since you like to play the tender mother role with others, then perhaps [you will do so] with yourself. And then you should hear the warning from the brutal fatherly side[6] that—to the best of my recollection—the inclination toward sexual games [*Spielerei*] with patients was not alien to you in pre-analytic times, so that one could put the new technique into context with the old misdemeanor. Hence I spoke in an earlier letter about a new puberty in you, a Johannis impulse,[7] and now you have forced me to be unambiguously clear.

I don't expect to make an impression on you. The basis for that is missing in your relationship to me. The need for defiant self-assertion seems to me to be more powerful in you than you recognize. But at least I have done my part; I have acted true to my father role. Now carry on.

Kind regards,
Freud

1. This letter is cited by Jones (III, 163-165) in the original English edition with a significant misreading: instead of "Godfather" (*Pate*; see n. 4) it reads "God the father" (p. 164); the error was corrected in the German edition (p. 198).

2. The material in parentheses is missing in Jones's version. This incident, about which he is still subjected to reproaches today for a "kissing technique" (in Freud's words), is described by Ferenczi in his *Clinical Diary:* "See the case of Dm. [Clara Thompson], a lady who, 'complying' with my passivity, had allowed herself to take more and more liberties, and occasionally even kissed me. Since this behavior met with no resistances, since it was treated as something permissible in analysis and at most commented on theoretically, she remarked quite casually in the company of other patients, who were undergoing analysis elsewhere: 'I am allowed to kiss Papa Ferenczi, as often as I like.' I first reacted to the unpleasantness that ensued with the complete impassivity with which I was conducting this analysis. But then the patient began to make herself ridiculous, ostentatiously as it were, in her sexual conduct (for example, at social gatherings, while dancing) . . . Simultaneously it became evident that here again was a case of repetition of the father-child situation. As a child, Dm. had been grossly abused sexually by her father, who was out of control; later, obviously because of the father's bad conscience and social anxiety, he reviled her, so to speak. The daughter had to take revenge on her father indirectly, by failing in her own life" (pp. 2f.). Clara Mabel Thompson (1893-1958), American analyst, can be viewed as the most influential pupil of and successor to Ferenczi in North America, by virtue of her general orientation and especially her works on countertransference and the personality of the analyst. At the urging of Harry Stack Sullivan, she was in analysis with Ferenczi in the summers of 1928 and 1929, and then continuously from 1931 until the latter's death. Along with Fromm and Sullivan, she founded the William A. White Institute in New York and the Washington School of Psychiatry.

3. This term is written in English in the original [Trans.].
4. This word is written in English in the original [Trans.].

5. An allusion to Ferenczi's at first enthusiastic approbation and then significant curtailment of the "active technique" ("Contra-Indications to the 'Active' Psycho-Analytical Technique," 1926, 271).
6. From here to the end of the sentence is missing in Jones.
7. An expression derived from botany (lammas shoot), describing late romantic stirrings in a person [Trans.].

1217

Dr. S. Ferenczi
Budapest, I. Lisznyai U. 11.
Telefon: 573–87

Budapest, December 27, 1931

Dear Professor,

You are already used to my being able to respond only after a long reaction time; but this time you will also find it understandable; perhaps it is happening for the first time that factors of not being in agreement are mixing into our relationship in general. Well, now that I have allowed the affective current to run its course, I believe I am in a position to reply to you in a reassuring sense.

You will probably recall that it was I who declared it to be necessary also to communicate matters of technique, so long as one applies them methodically; you were more in favor of being sparing with communications about technique. Now *you* think it would be dishonorable to keep silent, and I must counter that by saying that the *pace* of publication should be relegated to the tact and insight of the author.

But that is not the most important thing that I would like to talk about. I consider your fear that I will turn into another Stekel unfounded. "Youthful sins," misdemeanors, when they have been overcome and analytically worked through, can even make one wiser and more careful than people who did not go through such storms. My extremely ascetic "active therapy" was surely a precautionary measure against tendencies of this kind; for that reason, in their exaggerations they took on an obsessional character. When I gained insight into this, I relaxed the stiffness of the prohibitions and avoidances to which I condemned myself (and others). Now, I believe I am capable of creating a mild, passionless atmosphere, which is suited to incubate also what has hitherto been concealed.—But since I fear the dangers just as much as you do, I must and will, now as before, keep in mind the warnings that you reproach me with, and strive to criticize myself harshly. So, I would be remiss if I wanted to bury the productive layer that is beginning to uncover itself before me.

Since I overcame the sorrow about the tone of our correspondence, I can't help expressing the hope that the amicable personal and scientific harmony between us will not be disrupted by these developments, or: that it will soon be restored.

With cordial New Year's wishes.

Yours,
Ferenczi

1218
Dr. S. Ferenczi
Budapest, I. Lisznyai U. 11.
Telefon: 573-87

Budapest, January 21, 1932[1]

Dear Professor,

Dr. Reich's circular[2] seems to indicate a dull fermentation in our Socialist youth. For myself, I consider your intervention not only justified but absolutely necessary to establish our political nonpartisanship. I would be very grateful to you or Anna if I could learn something more specific about these events. Don't you consider it necessary that others besides yourself also express themselves in this question? I am quite willing to express my opinion, alone or in concert with the Central Committee in the event you consider it necessary or useful.

Today I wrote to Eitingon and cast my vote *in opposition to* holding the Congress in the coming spring. The times are not right for it! Instead of that, I suggested the Central Committee should meet in March or April, perhaps in Lugano as a central location. [I] would naturally be willing to come to Vienna instead; naturally, I hope that Fräulein Anna also learns of this intention.

Since our last correspondence, a kind of emotional calm has set in with me, which—I hope—will have a favorable effect on the solution of the scientific-technical problems with which I am occupied.

Nothing significantly new in the family; my wife's foot difficulties are wavering in both directions. She has been feeling better for some days.

The polyclinic is flourishing; we are positively overrun and are striving to master the difficulties that are arising in this manner.

Kind regards,
Ferenczi

1. The letter is typewritten; only the signature, "Ferenczi," and a few corrections are handwritten.
2. Reference unclear; see, however, the following letter and n. 1.

1219

Vienna, January 24, 1932
IX., Berggasse 19

Dear friend,

With Reich, two affairs are presently merging. I have nothing to do with his circular letter; I only learned about it yesterday. On the other hand, the other matter is hovering directly between me and him. I received in proof an article by him to read, which culminated in the nonsense that what one considers the death instinct is the activity of the capitalist system. I thereupon let him know that I would not allow it to be printed without appending an explanation by the editor which calls attention to the marching route of Bolshevism to which it is bound, and to his party affiliation. He went along with it, but others, Eitingon, Jekels, Bernfeld, objected, and a remark by the latter, to the effect that we should not get a jump on the Soviets with a declaration of war, changed my mind, so that for the time being I have had his (Reich's) article and my note set aside. But that is no solution, and I would like to see the leadership of our Association (Eitingon and Jones, with you) be able to work out such a solution and suggest it to the editor.[1]

You are, unfortunately, correct about the Congress difficulties. Our members will certainly not receive the monetary means from the National Bank for a trip to Switzerland. It is very regrettable, almost equivalent to a paralysis of the life of the Association. The new election should also not be postponed any longer. You certainly did the right thing in taking up the negotiations over it in the committee, and I welcome altogether the fact that you are emerging from your isolation, which you have maintained for too long.

We rented the same house in Pötzleinsdorf for the summer as last year; we want to move in already at the end of May. Something to look forward to in these gloomy times. Anna has a bad week with the flu behind her; we hope to put her in the Semmering cure house for just as long.

Big changes have taken place in the Verlag. We are making a last attempt to keep it going. Martin is the director, in place of Storfer, who will remain the editor until the end of April.[2] Great monetary sacrifices have become necessary, but without the Verlag we would be impotent.

We had hoped that the new therapy has brought your dear wife lasting relief?

Cordially,
Freud

P.S. In Imago I you will find a new fire essay by me.[3]

1. This has to do with Reich's "Der masochistische Charakter: Eine sexualökonomische Widerlegung des Todestriebes und des Wiederholungszwanges" [The Masochistic Character: A Sexual-Economic Refutation of the Death Instinct and the Repetition Compulsion] (*Zeitschrift* 18 [1932]: 303–351). Freud was "appalled at Reich's . . . attempt to misuse the Zeitschrift for Bolshevistic propaganda" (Freud to Eitingon, January 9, 1932, Sigmund Freud Copyrights), and wanted first to provide the essay with a disclaimer, and later not to have it published at all (Freud to Bernfeld, January 18, 1932, Library of Congress). He finally decided to have it published with a detailed rebuttal by Bernfeld ("Die Kommunistische Diskussion um die Psychoanalyse und Reichs 'Widerlegung der Todestriebhypothese'" [The Communist Discussion about Psychoanlysis and Reich's "Refutuation of the Death Instinct Hypothesis"] (*Zeitschrift* 18 [1932]: 352–385). "It remains out of the question that I open up room for expression in our Zeitschrift to Reich without a defense reaction [*Abwehrreaktion*]" (Freud to Bernfeld). Reich was later given room for a brief countercritique (*Zeitschrift* 18 [1932]: 386f.).

2. In a circular letter at the end of January, Storfer announced his resignation as director of the Verlag and the appointment of Martin Freud as managing director (Library of Congress).

3. "The Acquisition and Control of Fire" (Freud 1932a).

1220

[to Max Eitingon]

[Budapest,] January 26, 1932[1]

Dear Max,

Aside from who is in the right in the Reich affair (I, myself, am totally on Professor's side), I consider it absolutely necessary, in view of the sensation that this matter has already caused, that the leadership of the Association (you, I, and Jones) gives some kind of an official explanation in the Korrespondenzblatt, which winds up this affair, finally, and in good form. Without this explanation, refraining from publication would appear to be a retreat out of fear; but such an appearance could leave behind a lasting bad impression. But in order not to stir up unnecessarily those who feel injured, I consider a purely academic explanation, without naming names and the subject, appropriate, something like the following:

"On the occasion of a concrete instance, the leadership of the Association decided to request that the publisher of our official journals see to it that authors who want to publish an article of a distinctly partisan or religious-political cast acknowledge their affiliation with a party of a non-scientific character. Naturally, this does not change anything in the fact that, in the journals, now as before, the most diverse views can be expressed. Signed: Eitingon, president, Ferenczi, Jones, vice-presidents."

This publication naturally belongs in the appropriate column of the

Korrespondenzblatt. For the time being I am only making this proposal to you and the Professor; in the event that we come to an agreement, I ask you to procure Jones's assent.
With kind regards.

Yours,

January 26, 1932[2]

Dear Professor!
I am sending the above letter to Eitingon by the same mail.
Many thanks for the detailed letter.

Yours,
Ferenczi

1. This is a carbon copy of a typewritten letter.
2. This postscript is typewritten; only the date and the signature, "Ferenczi," are handwritten (in pencil).

1221

Dr. S. Ferenczi
Budapest, I. Lisznyai U. 11.
Telefon: 573-87

Budapest, April 21, 1932

Dear Professor,
Your Rundbrief to the presidents of the branch societies[1] made a very deep impression on me, which I hope also to arouse very soon in the other members of the Association. For now I have had discussions only with Lajos and Kata Lévy, then with Frau Kovács, as the only ones who come into consideration with regard to financial help. Strangely, I found more understanding for the seriousness of the situation and the necessity to help to the best of one's ability with Lajos than with Kata; but even Lajos seems to want to help much more with financial advice than with a hearty grab for his wallet. Enclosed, a plan for restructuring composed by him,[2] the practical feasibility of which I must leave to you to be the judge of. Frau Kovács is, as always, quite willing to do what is possible and to take part in the work of redevelopment; to be sure, she is already giving so much for the maintenance of the polyclinic (like me, about 1400 pengö per year) that she would only be able to pay the sum that is apportioned to it in installments. So, I am the only one here who would come into significant consideration as a donor. The remaining members are poor, i.e., they earn approx-

imately what they need. It goes without saying that the majority will still assert themselves in favor of raising the membership contribution by the amount of the contribution to the Verlag.—

Before we express ourselves about the payment which is to be made, we would, however, like to be in the position to give out information about the size of the amount that the Verlag needs, in the first place, urgently, in the second, as annual aid; at least voices have already been raised in this regard; the people want to know what the finances of the institution they are supposed to help look like.

In principle, they are generally in agreement, as far as I can judge the matter, about the necessity of maintaining both journals, even with greater sacrifices. It goes without saying that we all feel obligated to you and would be happy if it would somehow be possible for you to take possession of your author's fees.

My restructuring plan would preferably be that forty members of the International Association were to nullify this debt, above all, with the payment of 500 dollars each.

Almost everything that you say in your detailed letter finds general agreement, except for your judgment about the value of the works in the discipline which were published by the Verlag in the last ten years, insofar as they were not reprints or new editions of your works. Besides that, two or three valuable books come into consideration, and since the Freud works would also be in demand even without the Verlag, that raises the question of whether the sparse valuable productions of others justify the maintenance of a publishing house. As already mentioned, the necessity of maintaining both of the journals goes without saying for us all. Everything you say about the internationality of the German journals is recognized by us Hungarians as correct; let's hope the English, Americans, and French, etc., do the same. It would be very pleasant for me if you and our new director, taking what has been said into consideration, could give us a hint as to the size of the immediate and long-range amount that is expected and also reassure us with regard to the doubts which prevail here, before I present the restructuring plan to the plenum of the Hungarian group. (I have the nonbinding assent of Frau Kovács that she may contribute approximately 500 dollars in installments.)

I will utilize this opportunity to ask Martin about approximately how large the sum is which is still needed to publish the Hungarian Interpretation of Dreams. On this point we are hoping for more accommodation than was to be expected from Storfer, who was hostile to Hungarians. (Nice case of ambivalence. He wanted to make a great Hungarian edition and bought Hungarian rights, but showed absolute resistance in getting it done, and yet the financial situation was not worse than today, when two volumes will be published anyway.)

I have been receiving ongoing reports from various quarters about the state of your health, about the recent little complication[3] and its favorable course. With me, bodily and intellectual tiredness is increasing to a certain extent; a small interruption of work (for about ten days in Abbazia or Venice) is being planned for the beginning of May. In the meantime, my scientific interest is fluctuating—albeit not always at high tide—around the old problems, occasionally also about quite a few new ones. I hope that a God exists, for only he alone can know when and whether anything will come of them.

We were sorry that Frau Dr. Sterba[4] had to cancel her visit; but we are still counting on Fräulein Anna's promise.[5]

With many kind regards.

Your old,
Ferenczi

1. A report on the bad state of the Verlag, and an appeal for financial support, sent to the presidents of the individual branch societies.
2. The plan has not been found.
3. The recent removal, on March 7, of a suspicious spot (Jones III, 483).
4. Editha Sterba, née von Radanowicz-Hartmann (1895–1986), Rank's secretary at the Verlag, in 1925 associate and in 1930 full member of the Vienna Society. In 1926 she married the Viennese analyst Richard Sterba (1898–1989). In 1928 she became head of the psychoanalytic educational consulting center and engaged in collaboration with August Aichhorn. In 1938 the Sterbas emigrated, first to Switzerland, then to the United States; after residing in New York and Chicago, they settled in Detroit, where Edith Sterba developed a lively activity in projects and research in the psychosocial sphere, in addition to her private practice. See Mühlleitner, *Lexikon*, pp. 328–330.
5. Anna Freud did not give any lectures in the Hungarian Society in 1932.

1222

Vienna, April 24, 1932
IX., Berggasse 19

Dear friend,

Among the wished-for effects of the Rundbrief I am also counting on having received news from you, for, with all the undemandingness that I have acquired over the years, I still can't conceal the fact that your interest has failed me noticeably lately.[1]

Well, I am pleased about having shaken up our members to participate in the fate of the Verlag. I won't bother about the details of giving aid for a while. The groups should confer, make suggestions, and direct them to the president in Berlin. Martin, whom we have alone to thank for the fact that we have avoided an ignominious bankruptcy, is prepared to give any desired information. I will also present Lajos's plan to him. I have only to remark that the—probably unfulfillable—task of procuring my outstanding fees should not be among the concerns of the IPA.

I don't share your opinion about the worthlessness of the greater part of the psychoanalytic literature, although I do share to a large extent your critical views. Without such ruminations, returning in countless combinations, mixtures, contaminations, an assimilation of the material would not be able to occur. I also don't believe that we will be able to provide for our nourishment with concentrated nutrient pills. The worst of these contaminations, in which the purity would be choked off, were, after all, supposed to have been kept away by the selection made by the Verlag.

You, too, will have heard in how sad a way the Eitingon firm has broken down, so that the members of the family are completely impoverished.[2] Our friend has fallen ill with a paresis of the left arm,[3] certainly under the effect of this material catastrophe. He is improving, but the incident casts a dim light on his brain circulation. I hope you will find in yourself the willingness to sacrifice the comforts of your isolation to date to the duties of a leader of the movement.

With kind regards to you and Frau Gisela.

Yours,
Freud

1. Even before receiving Ferenczi's last letter, Freud had written to Eitingon on April 18, 1932: "Isn't Ferenczi a cross to bear? Again no news from him for months. He is insulted because one isn't delighted by the fact that he is playing mother and child with his [female] pupils" (Sigmund Freud Copyrights).
2. See Jones III, 165.
3. On account of a cerebral thrombosis.

1223

Dr. S. Ferenczi
Budapest, I. Lisznyai U. 11.
Telefon: 573-87

Budapest, May 1, 1932[1]

Dear Professor,

The quiet reproach that issues forth from your letter is well deserved. To be quite honest, I was prepared for worse; in any event, I reproached myself much more energetically. But since you yourself mention the only excuse that I can give for my negligence, it is easier for me to talk about it. In the last few years I have, in fact, been very, perhaps all too immersed in the work of understanding my cases. Whatever the favoring motive of such isolation may be, it is not altogether anything bad or reprehensible; everyone probably has to go through such periods, which, with me, to be sure, turned up somewhat late, or, as you once wrote, as a belated puberty crisis. More deeply penetrating self-analysis showed me, to be sure, that since my earliest childhood I have had the tendency to get into situations which I could master only with an exceptionally large exertion of strength. I never allowed myself a real psychic vacation. Now I seem to want to rest up after a kind of superperformance lasting half a lifetime; by rest, I understand here immersing myself in a kind of scientific "Poetry and Truth,"[2] from which at some time or other, sometimes I think: definitely, something not worthless will come. I don't believe that one can deliberately change such an attitude, and so my feeling of responsibility commands me to ask you if you want to have a president whose interest is in part manacled in this way? If so, then I will do my utmost to fulfill the tasks that are before me. But should you be of the opinion that much more is demanded of this activity in today's hard times than I can offer, then I will renounce the role of leader without the slightest bitterness. Indeed, I am quite willing to be of assistance to you in the selection of the person who is suited. A special personal difficulty is my relative ineptitude in economic questions, where assuring the activity of the Verlag in the future will foreseeably demand the energetic involvement, perhaps even the collaboration, of the president in the business of the Verlag. What you report to me about Martin's activity, however, certainly mitigates this special concern.

I was sorry that the circumstances presented here also had a delaying effect on the personal correspondence; to be sure, I sometimes had the pleasure of hearing favorable things about you through the visits of Budapesters in Vienna and Viennese in Budapest. Unfortunately, the news about Eitingon sounds less favorable, so that prolonging his presidency certainly doesn't come into question; what all still confronts us!

With many kind regards also to all your dear ones.

Yours truly,
Ferenczi

P.S. Of course,—in the event that the Association reflects on me—I am counting on the assistance of your Anna, who would have to be at my side as secretary (or president's representative)!

1. The letter is typewritten; only the signature, "Ferenczi," is handwritten.
2. A reference to Goethe's autobiography, *Dichtung und Wahrheit*.

1224

Budapest, May 5, 1932

Dear Professor,

To be sure, I have commissioned my wife, who is going to Vienna for two days on account of her knees, to bring you personally my birthday congratulations, but I also want to remain true to the old way of doing things by also commemorating this day by letter and wishing you all the good imaginable.

Yours,
Ferenczi

1225

Vienna, May 5, 1932
IX., Berggasse 19

Dear friend,

I talked with your wife for a while on my birthday, and reexperienced with satisfaction the phenomenon that is familiar to me. Being together with her after such long interruptions, we are immediately able to be intimate and to exchange intimacies. Age has changed nothing in her special charm.

I was unable to reply earlier to your letter of May 1; it also didn't press me, because I was so certain of the decision.—

I am sorry that you are so easily able to renounce the presidency; I would like to insist on it for you. In the last few years you have without a doubt gone back into the isolation which you had so brilliantly overcome as a leader and teacher in Budapest; the presidency should have the effect on you of a drastic measure, to move you again to convivial participation and to the acceptance of the role of leader to which you are entitled. If you assert your disinclination or slight suitability for practical measures to be a hindrance, then don't forget that willing assistance is at your disposal in both of the vice presidents and in Anna as secretary. According to a sensible recommendation of Eitingon's a third vice [president's] position is supposed to be created for Brill at the Congress.[1] But you should leave the island of dreams which you inhabit with your fantasy children and mix in with the struggle of men.

Enticed by the advantages of concentration, and dissatisfied with Fenichel,[2] I have decided to transfer the editorship of the journals to Vienna. Federn and Hartmann[3] will take over the International [Zeitschrift], Kris[4] and Waelder,[5] Imago. It will naturally take several months before this change has been carried out.

Kind regards,
Freud

1. This is in fact what happened.
2. "Fenichel . . . is fundamentally repugnant to me; I also don't credit him with any special suitability for editing Imago" (Freud to Eitingon, February 12, 1932, Sigmund Freud Copyrights). Freud's displeasure had primarily to do with Fenichel's Marxist orientation. Otto Fenichel (1897-1946), Viennese physician and analyst, was engaged in the "left wing" of the Youth Movement and was interested in sexual research and enlightenment. He was in analysis with Federn and a member of the Vienna Society (1920). In 1922 Fenichel moved to Berlin and continued his analysis with Radó. In the early 1930s Fenichel stood very close to Reich's views, although they distanced themselves from each other very soon thereafter. In 1933 Fenichel emigrated to Norway and began a secret correspondence by circular letter with left-leaning analysts (see *Otto Fenichel: 119 Rundbriefe [1934–1945]*, vol. 1, *Europa [1934–1938]*, ed. Johannes Reichmayr and Elke Mühlleitner; vol. 2, *Amerika [1938–1945]*, ed. Elke Mühlleitner and Johannes Reichmayr. In 1935 he went to Prague, then in 1938 to Los Angeles. Fenichel is considered to have been an extremely astute person and an "encyclopedist of psychoanalysis" (*The Psychoanalytic Theory of the Neuroses* [New York, 1945]). See Gabriele Gschwendtner, "Psychoanalyse, Institutionalisierung, Dissidententum, untersucht anhand der Biographie und Theorieproduktion von Otto Fenichel" [Psychoanalysis, Institutionalization, Dissidence, Investigated in the Light of the Biography and Theory Production of Otto Fenichel] (dissertation, Salzburg, 1991); Russell Jacoby, *Repression of Psychoanalysis: Otto Fenichel and the Political Freudians* (New York, 1983); Mühlleitner, *Lexikon*, pp. 93–95.
3. Heinz Hartmann (1894–1970), son of Ludo Moritz Hartmann, a professor of history at the University of Vienna, and his wife, Margarete, the daughter of the gynecologist Rudolf Chrobak. He was an assistant physician with Wagner-Jauregg until 1934 and Radó's analysand; in 1925 he was an associate, in 1927 a full member, and in 1933 on the board of the Vienna Society, and he underwent a second analysis with Freud. He was a co-editor of the *Zeitschrift* with Federn and Radó, and he founded the journal *Psychoanalytic Study of the Child* with Anna Freud and Ernst Kris in 1945. In 1938 he emigrated to France, in 1939 to Switzerland, and in 1941 to New York. From 1952 to 1954 he was president of the Association there, from 1953 to 1959 president of the IPA, and from 1959 on its honorary president. Hartmann is considered the most outstanding representative of psychoanalytic "ego psychology" and one of the most significant psychoanalysts of all time. For a long while he dominated the New York scene and, in part, North American psychoanalysis. Hartmann, *Ich-Psychologie und Anpassungsproblem* [Ego Psychology and the Problem of Adaptation] (1939; rpt. Stuttgart, 1970); *Ich-Psychologie: Studien zur psychoanalytischen Theorie* [Ego Psychology: Studies in Psychoanalytic Theory] (New York, 1964). See also Mühlleitner, *Lexikon*, pp. 131–133.
4. Ernst Kris (1900–1957), Viennese art historian, curator of the Kunsthistorisches Museum in Vienna. He was in analysis with Helene Deutsch (1924–1927) and Anna Freud. In 1927 he married Marianne Rie (the daughter of Freud's friend Oscar Rie); in 1928 he was an associate and in 1933 a full member of the Vienna Society. In 1938 he emigrated to England, then in 1940 to New York, where he became a training analyst and a

professor at the New School for Social Research. Along with Hartmann and Rudolph Löwenstein, Kris ranks among the central figures of ego psychology. With Anna Freud and Marie Bonaparte he published the first, abridged version of Freud's letters to Fliess and wrote a comprehensive introduction to it (*Origins of Psycho-Analysis* [London, 1950]).

5. Robert Wälder (Waelder) (1900–1967), Viennese physicist and analyst. His first analysis was with Hans Jokl; later he underwent training analyses with Hermann Nunberg and Anna Freud. In 1924 he became a member of the Vienna Society, in 1934 secretary and member of the Training Committee. In 1938 he emigrated to the United States, first to Boston, then, in 1943, to Philadelphia. From 1953 to 1955 he was president of the newly founded Institute of the Philadelphia Association for Psychoanalysis. In 1963 he became professor of psychoanalysis at Jefferson Medical College. Wälder was unusually well educated and extraordinarily well read; he was conservative politically. A volume of his collected writings was published in English (Samuel Guttmann, ed., *Psychoanalysis: Observation, Theory, Application: Selected Papers of Robert Waelder* [New York, 1976]).

1226

Dr. S. Ferenczi
Budapest, I. Lisznyai U. 11.
Telefon: 573-87

Budapest, May 19, 1932[1]

Dear Professor,

I must honestly admit that, by speaking about my present activity in expressions like "dream-life," "daydreams," "puberty crisis," this does not signifiy in me total insight into illness, and that in reality I have the feeling that out of the relative confusion something useful will develop and has already developed. So, I can't conceive of the presidency as a drastic measure against an illness which I don't actually recognize as such. So, I don't think I am doing useless work if I continue my present manner of working for a time. If you believe that this can be brought into harmony with the expectations which one has for the president of an association, and if, as you assure me, I can count on the active assistance of Anna and the two vice presidents, I will consider it an honor also to stand for once as president of the society on the founding of which I collaborated and in the activity of which I actively participated for a long time.

I consider Eitingon's idea to elect Brill as the third vice president to be excellent.

The list of members that Eduardo Weiss[2] presented to us seems to me to be too immature for founding a society in Rome. Colleague Weiss has to work diligently until the next Congress to get a more presentable group. So, I cast a negative vote. The day after tomorrow I am traveling with my wife to Venice (Hotel Danieli) for about ten days. We will probably move from there to the Lido; I hope to be able to bathe in the ocean. Then I will work for the whole summer, until the Congress, on Lisznyai-utca, and then I am thinking, assuming I am alive, to go to France, a country whose inhabitants I don't particularly love, but whose atmosphere always attracted me. Actually, I only know Paris, and also not very much of it.

You will certainly already be in your Tusculum when you receive this letter; I hope you will also feel very well again there.

With kind regards.

Yours,
Ferenczi

1. The letter is typewritten; only the closing, "Yours, Ferenczi," is handwritten.
2. Edoardo Weiss (1889–1970), from Trieste, a pioneer of psychoanalysis in Italy. He studied medicine in Vienna and was an auditor of Freud's at the university (1909–1913). He was an analysand of Paul Federn, to whom he remained attached for the rest of his life. He became a member of the Vienna Society in 1913. After the First World War he became a physician at the psychiatric hospital in Trieste (1919–1928), and he was active as an analyst in private practice. He moved to Rome in 1931; there, in 1932, he reorganized the Società Psicoanalytica Italiana, which was recognized by the IPA in 1935, and he founded the *Rivista Italiana di Psicoanalisi.* In 1939 Weiss emigrated to Topeka, Kansas, to the Menninger Clinic, then moved to Chicago in 1940. From 1959 to 1961 he was guest professor at Marquette University in Milwaukee. He himself published his (abridged) correspondence with Freud (*Sigmund Freud as a Consultant* [New York, 1970]). See Weiss, *Elementi di Psicoanalisi* (Milan, 1931); Arnaldo Novelletto et al., *L'Italia nella psicoanalysis / Italy in Psychoanalysis* (Rome: Istituto della Enciclopedia Italiana, 1989); Mühlleitner, *Lexikon,* pp. 359–361.

1227

Venice, Café Florián,
May 22, 1932[1]

Dear Professor,

P.S. to the last letter. It will interest you to know that in our group lively debates are going on about the female castration complex and penis envy.[2] I must admit that in my practice these don't play the great role that one had expected theoretically. What has been your experience?

Venice is lovely, as always.

Yours,
Ferenczi

I am staying [in the] Hotel Danieli.

1. Picture postcard: "Venezia—Piazzetta S. Marco e Palazzo Ducale dal mare."
2. See the lectures by Lillian Rotter, "Eine Phase der weiblichen Libidoentwicklung" [A Phase of Female Libido Development] (April 22, 1932); Alice Bálint, "Referat über die psychoanalytischen Arbeiten von Frau Dr. Horney" [Review of the Psychoanalytic Works of Frau Dr. Horney] (May 6, 1932); and Fanny Hann-Kende, "Daten zur Entwicklungslehre der weiblichen Sexualität" [Data on the Developmental Theory of Female Sexuality] (May 20, 1932), before the Hungarian Society (*Zeitschrift* 18 [1932]: 560).

1228

Vienna,
XVIII Khevenhüllerstrasse 6
[postmark: June 2, 1932][1]

Italian Zweig[2] arrived, reads very well. I found myself again very interesting, although not altogether similar.
Many thanks.

Yours,
Freud

1. Postcard. (The entire text is written in Latin characters.)
2. "A friend of mine was recently in Venice, saw the Italian translation of 'Mental Healers' in a bookstore there, and made a present of it to me" (Freud to Stefan Zweig, June 2, 1932, in Zweig, *Über Sigmund Freud: Porträt, Briefwechsel, Gedenkworte* [Frankfurt, 1989], p. 161). The reference is to Zweig's *Die Heilung durch den Geist: Mesmer, Mary Baker Eddy, Freud* (in English, *Mental Healers: Franz Anton Mesmer, Mary Baker Eddy, Sigmund Freud* [New York, 1932]).

1229

Dr. S. Ferenczi
Budapest, I. Lisznyai U. 11.
Telefon: 573-87

Budapest, June 11, 1932[1]

Dear Professor,

Enclosed I am sending you two letters, one was directed to me by Prof. Brouwer[2] (Amsterdam); I am enclosing the copy of my reply along with it.

The other letter comes from Prof. Laquer,[3] the Amsterdam pharmacologist; I was asked to convey this letter to you.

The story of this whole affair is essentially that Dr. Révész,[4] who was Associate Professor of Pharmacology at the University of Budapest, was chased away from his teaching post after the revolutions, probably mostly because of his Jewish religion, about the same way I was. He moved to Holland, became a Privatdozent in Amsterdam, and would now have the chance to become a professor there, if the Budapesters and the Dutch anti-Semites hadn't organized a hate campaign against him.

To be sure, Révész has concerned himself only quite superficially with psychoanalysis, whereas Dr. Rünke,[5] his competitor, even though I don't know anything about his activity, is still a member of the Dutch Branch Society.

It is interesting that now in Holland being affiliated with psychoanalysis carries such great weight in decisions about professorship. Tempora mutantur![6]

In the last session of our group, Eitingon's suggestion regarding restructuring of the Verlag was accepted. To be sure, the three most well-to-do members have to come up with more than two thirds, since the remaining members can't afford more. I hope the Americans will follow the English example.

The beautiful days in Venice were a real and very necessary recuperation. Since then, the work has been going much more smoothly. I must also gradually begin writing the Congress paper. If my wife has to go to Vienna again, I hope to be able to accompany her and to talk to you again.

Kind regards,
Ferenczi

1. The letter is typewritten; only the signature, "Ferenczi," is handwritten.

2. Bernardus Brouwer (1881–1949), a professor of neurology at the University of Amsterdam from 1923 on.

3. Ernst Laqueur (1880–1947), a professor of pharmacology at the University of Amsterdam from 1923 on. Along with K. G. David, he discovered the male sex hormone testosterone. He was a co-founder of the Amsterdam pharmacologic-therapeutic laboratory.

4. On Géza Révész, see letter 81 and n. 3. In 1922 Révész went to Groningen and actually was appointed professor of pychology at the University of Amsterdam until 1949.

5. Henricus Cornelius Rümke (1893–1967), Dutch psychiatrist. From 1928 to 1933 he was a professor at the University of Amsterdam, from 1933 to 1963 a professor at the University of Utrecht. He had a critical but positive attitude toward psychoanalysis. (We are grateful to Jaap Bos for information about the persons involved and the situation in the Netherlands.)

6. "Tempora mutantur, nos et mutamur in illis" (The times are changing, and we along with them), words ascribed to the Holy Roman Emperor Lothair I (795–855).

1230

Vienna, June 13, 1932
X., Berggasse 19

Dear friend,

I am returning to you enclosed those enclosures in your letter that were directed to you. I admired your reply to Brouwer as a model of benevolent diplomacy. I expressed my opposition to Laquer in a reserved manner, which I had a right to do. Suddenly someone remembers that he was always a good friend, which we hadn't noticed.

Your promise to come along if your wife travels to Vienna again made me very happy, for in consequence of the gaps in our correspondence there are a number of things about which I don't know whether I shared them with you or not. It is precisely those things that are fresh that already frequently elude my memory. Such is the case in the matter of changing the editorship in the journals. Federn and Hartmann are the new editors for the International, Kris and Waelder for Imago. The motives were economizing, the advantages of concentration in the Verlag, and Fenichel's siding with Reich's Bolshevism, and other lapses of tact. If your name is omitted in all this, you probably won't take it amiss; Eitingon wishes, to be sure, that his remains. I think a person should be called an editor only if he does the work.

[I report] further that I am again writing on "Extended Introductory Lectures," which are supposed to make some of the results of the intervening fifteen years generally accessible. There will be eight or ten new lectures; the last, "Weltanschauung," is finished; I am just now working on the first "Revision of the Theory of Dreams." It is naturally not going as easily as fifteen years ago, and ruminating is also not the most pleasant business.[1]

We have been out here in Pötzleinsdorf for four weeks, a wonderfully beautiful time, and if one were healthier, a great pleasure (XVIII Khevenhüllerstr. 6).

Kind regards,
Freud

1. *New Introductory Lectures on Psycho-Analysis* (Freud 1933a). Freud told Eitingon that he wrote them "for the Verlag" (letter of May 20, 1932, Sigmund Freud Copyrights).

1231

Dr. S. Ferenczi
Budapest, I. Lisznyai U. 11.
Telefon: 573-87

Budapest, June 14, 1932[1]

Dear Professor,

I, too, am of the opinion that neither Eitingon nor myself figure by right to be editors of the Zeitschrift, and I hope only good things from the enthusiasm of the new editors. The news about a continuation of the "Lectures" is very interesting. I think that this task and along with it the revision of the advances in the last fifiteen years will soon also fascinate you.

What have you heard about the members' participation in the Congress? Are the Americans coming, and how many?

In the certain hope that I will be coming to Vienna in the course of the summer, I am

Yours,
Ferenczi

1. The letter is typewritten; only the signature, "Ferenczi," is handwritten.

1232

Dr. S. Ferenczi
Budapest, I. Lisznyai U. 11.
Telefon: 573-87

Budapest, August 11, 1932[1]

Dear Professor,

The material for my Congress lecture is more or less in order, but conditions in Germany are such that I am postponing putting it together from day to day, especially since other problems have also been occupying me in the meantime. Even if the Congress comes about, it will be only a kind of rump parliament. One way or another we will have to call upon everything to lift the somewhat sinking mood.

I am very much in agreement with the suggestion made by Eitingon (Brill third vice president). In reality, I know from experience that the Americans are still sabotaging lay analysis, but it seems that we will have to be satisfied with this formal peace treaty for the time being; with us it looks more or less the same as in the League of Nations.[2]

Dr. Lévy heard the best news from Dr. Braun about the state of your health. We are all happy about it.

Kind regards,
Ferenczi

1. The letter is typewritten; only the signature, "Ferenczi," and a correction are handwritten.
2. The name is written in English in the original [Trans.].

1233

Dr. S. Ferenczi
Budapest, I. Lisznyai U. 11.
Telefon: 573-87

Budapest, August 21, 1932[1]

Dear Professor,

After long, anguished hesitation, I have decided to renounce my candidacy for the presidency. The motives about which I have already reported to you have since been joined by the circumstance that, in the course of the exertion to structure my analyses more deeply and more effectively, I have gotten into decidedly critical and self-critical waters, which seem to necessitate in some respects not only extensions but also corrections of our practical and, in part, also our theoretical views. Now, I have the feeling that such an intellectual constitution is on no account commensurate with the dignity of a president whose main concern should be conserving and consolidating what already exists, and my inner feeling tells me that it would not even be honest to occupy this position.

I am sorry that I have come to this decision so late, at the eleventh hour, so to speak; but I had to fight through a difficult inner struggle, and that perhaps excuses the delay.

Kind regards,
Ferenczi

1. Freud sent this letter to Eitingon with the following remarks: "I don't doubt that he [Ferenczi] also notified you, but read, nevertheless. One will hardly be mistaken in assuming that he will go the way of Rank . . . What a pity! If I had only experienced one case of theoretical diversion without previous personal motivation! With Fer[enczi]., I am totally innocent, for once. The bad reception in America, in Berlin, when he was supposed to move after Abraham's death, the postponement of his election to the last Congress, were decisive. Well, then!" (August 24, 1932, Sigmund Freud Copyrights).

1234

Vienna, August 24, 1932
IX., Berggasse 19

Dear friend,

I regretted your refusal in the interests of all who are involved. Your argument doesn't make much sense to me. As long as the technical and theoretical changes that have recommended themselves to you are not earth-shaking enough to necessitate your founding a new variety of analysis, you don't need to avoid the presidency in the old formation. But, far be it from me to try to influence [you]. You have to know best yourself what is going on in you.

Kind regards,
Freud

1235

Budapest, August 28, 1932[1]

thanks for letter arrive vienna noon september 2 departure wiesbaden 11 night will visit you and opportunity to talk through regards = ferenczi

1. Telegram, undated. It is not in the folder of the Austrian National Library, but was later found by Judith Dupont in Ferenczi's papers.

1236

Budapest, August 29, 1932

Dear Professor,

I can tell you with certainty that the things that I have to communicate are, *according to the way I feel,* not "earth-shaking"; I feel free of the tendency to found a new school; I will first turn to the colleagues of the "old formation" with my suggestions for discussion and hope to be understood by them—I am naturally figuring on counter-suggestions, which I am resolved to accord the respect they deserve.

I only thought that even *that* degree of critical spirit to which I am alluding is more appropriate for a simple member than a president—and, in particular, I though that you, especially, don't want to have such a president.

I want to visit you in Vienna on my trip to Wiesbaden—I am sorry that I can't come earlier.[1]

I thank you very much for your kind letter.

Yours,
Ferenczi

1. Ferenczi's visit with Freud before the Congress was a dramatic and defining moment in their relationship. Earlier, Eitingon had already learned by way of Radó about Ferenczi's Congress lecture and had asked him "not to give it before he has discussed his new views in detail with us . . . [I]n any case, Ferenczi is very ill" (letter of August 30, 1932, Sigmund Freud Copyrights). Freud telegraphed Eitingon about the meeting in Vienna: "Ferenczi lecture read aloud[.] Harmless stupid otherwise inaccessible" (September 2, 1932, Sigmund Freud Copyrights). Ferenczi gave his version to Izette de Forest,

who placed it at the disposal of Erich Fromm for his Freud biography: "When I visited the Professor . . . I told him of my latest technical ideas . . . The Professor listened to my exposition with increasing impatience and finally warned me that I was treading on dangerous ground and was departing fundamentally from the traditional customs and techniques of psychoanalysis. Such yielding to the patient's longings and desires—no matter how genuine—would increase his dependence on the analyst. Such dependence can only be destroyed by the emotional withdrawal of the analyst . . . This warning ended the interview. I held out my hand in affectionate adieu. The Professor turned his back on me and walked out of the room." Erich Fromm, *Sigmund Freud's Mission* (New York, 1959), pp. 63–65.

The Twelfth International Psychoanalytic Congress took place in Wiesbaden from September 4 to 7 under Eitingon's direction. The Training Commission decided on educational guidelines which did not in principle exclude lay candidates from training, but left the concrete procedure up to the local organizations. Eitingon was reelected president of the ITC. The Japanese group and the Chicago and Washington-Baltimore Branch Societies were accepted into the IPA. Ernest Jones was elected president of the IPA, in place of Eitingon; Brill was elected third vice president; van Ophuijsen and Anna Freud were confirmed in their functions. Freud had advised Ferenczi against giving his lecture; Brill, Eitingon, and van Ophuijsen found it "a scandal" and wanted to forbid it altogether. According to Jones, it was only through his intervention that Ferenczi was able to give it after all (III, 173). The lecture, "The Passions of Adults and Their Influence on the Sexual and Character Development of Children" ("Confusion of Tongues between Adults and the Child," Ferenczi 1933, 294), opened the scientific portion and made "no special impression" (Eitingon to Freud, September 4, 1932, Sigmund Freud Copyrights). Ferenczi already knew that he was suffering from pernicious anemia.

1237

Hotel Majestic
Bagnères-de-Luchon
Haute-Garonne[1]
Luchon, September 27, 1932

Dear Professor,

You can measure by the length of the reaction time the depth of the shock with which our conversation in Vienna before the Congress came to me. Unfortunately, such things are always connected to bodily ailments in me, so that my trip to the south of France by way of Baden-Baden was and is, actually, a "voyage de lit-à-lit."[2] We have also decided to go home as soon as possible and to arrive in Budapest already on the 1st rather than the 8th of October, this time without stopping in Vienna.

Strangely, it was (at least in my cs.) less the substance of the scientific differences that affected me in so painful a fashion than two seemingly externally symptomatic facts: bringing in a third person (as a witness or help), on top of that one about whom we know—with every recognition of his "bon sens"[3]—that he doesn't deserve to be a judge between us, either from a practical or a theoretical standpoint.[4]

The second bad surprise was your desire that I abstain from publication; even today I can't acknowledge that I would harm myself or the cause with my communications. I still hope you will drop this idea.

You certainly know just as well as I do what a loss it means for both of us that my visit with you could transpire in such a way. You can be assured that I remember all the beautiful earlier visits, even though I also have to concede that more courage and more open talk on my part about practical and theoretical things would have been advantageous to me. But, unfortunately, there is usually a lack of such courage in those who are younger and weaker.

I intend only to pursue peace and quiet until around October 10; one never finds that in a foreign country. I also hope soon to get straightened out regarding my health.

With friendly greetings from us both.

Yours truly,
Ferenczi

A special greeting to Fräulein Anna.

1. Preprinted letterhead.
2. French for "trip from bed to bed."
3. French for, roughly, "common sense."
4. Brill had happened upon them during the conversation (Freud to Eitingon, September 20, 1932, Sigmund Freud Copyrights).

1238

Vienna, October 2, 1932
IX., Berggasse 19

Dear friend,

Your letter contains a reproach which will be hard to maintain. There was never any consideration of ascribing to Brill the role of a judge; he didn't even begin to play it. Remember, he wasn't there when you came in. You said, without a word of greeting: I will read my Congress lecture aloud to you. Brill only came in the midst of things and had to recoup the first half, which he had missed. I had put up with his presence, not so that he should make a judgment, but because you had talked with him about the same thing a few days before and in so doing had told him more than you did me. I also knew from him that you don't credit me with more insight than a little boy. [Just as Rank did, back then.]¹ We had a common interest in having your lecture on the opening of the Congress, at which you were supposed to have been elected president, not produce a sensation. I saw that that would not be the case, and he really didn't disturb.

The request that you shouldn't publish for another year was predominantly in your interest. I didn't want to give up hope that in your continuing work you would still recognize yourself the technical impropriety of your procedure and the limited correctness of your results. You seemed to agree with me, but I naturally relieve you of your promise and, of necessity, forgo any influence, which I don't possess anyway. I don't any longer believe that you will rectify yourself, the way I rectified myself a generation earlier.

In the next sentence of your letter you accuse yourself, to be sure, and in that I can only say you are right. For three[2] years you have been systematically turning away from me, probably developed a personal hostility that goes further than it could express itself. Each of those who were once near to me and then fell away was able to find more to reproach me with than you, of all people. [No, Rank, just as little.][3] The traumatic effect dissipates in me, I am prepared, and used to it. Objectively, I think I would be in a position to point out to you the theoretical error in your construction, but for what? I am convinced you would not be accessible to any doubts. So there is nothing left for me but to wish you the best, which would be very different from what is going on at present.

Yours,
Freud

1. Brackets in the original.
2. Reading uncertain; it could be "two," or perhaps another number.
3. Brackets in the original.

1239

Budapest, December 14, 1932

Dear Professor,

Many thanks for kindly sending the "New Introductory Lectures,"[1] which I have begun to read with great interest.

At the same time I thank you for your and Fräulein Anna's inquiry about the state of my health, about which I have favorable things to report.—The anemia and its consequences have disappeared for the time being, the signs of fatigue, etc., are over, number and shape of the cellular blood components is normal again.

Unfortunately, I hear that you had great ailments recently; I confidently hope that these, like the previous ones, will soon be overcome.

With best regards to you and to the members of your family.

Yours sincerely,
Ferenczi

1. Freud 1933a.

1240

Dr. S. Ferenczi
Budapest, I. Lisznyai U. 11.
Telefon: 573–87

Budapest, January 10, 1933

Dear Professor,

The occasion of the change of year is only the external opportunity to assure you that I am and remain always conscious of the many years of being on good terms between us and of gratitude for your interest and kindness.

With best regards to you and your dear ones, also on the part of my wife.

Yours sincerely,
Ferenczi

1241

Vienna, January 11, 1933
IX., Berggasse 19[1]

Dear friend,

I thank you and your dear wife cordially for the New Year's greeting, which arrived today. Not necessary to say that we all completely return your good wishes. You write about our being on good terms, which has lasted for many years. I think it was more than that, rather an intimate community of life, feeling, and interest. When I have to conjure this up from memory today, then what remains to me as consolation is only the certainty that I have contributed especially little to this change. Some psychological misfortune or other has brought it about in you. Nonetheless, we are happy about the restoration of your health, a precious piece of the more beautiful past.

Always yours,
Freuds

1. This letter is also in Jones III, 177.

1242

Anna Freud
Wien, IX., Berggasse 19.

Vienna, March 2, 1933

Dear Doctor!

I was lying around with a small grippe just as I received your letter. It couldn't compare with the serious grippes of other Viennese, but I did have a diminished capacity for work for a while, and [was] very tired in addition to that, so I didn't reply right away. If it's all right with you, I would also like to postpone the trip to Budapest for that reason, but still not give it up. If you also accept me later, between Easter and the summer vacation, I will come then.

It will always be difficult with two lectures, because I do have to use the second evening for travel again. I couldn't very well miss a day of patients here.

How are things with you, and how are you? Everything is going well with us, we are beginning again to look for our spring and summer residence in Vienna.

With kind regards to your wife and to you.

Yours,
Anna

1243

INTERNATIONAL PSYCHOANALYTICAL ASSOCIATION
INTERNATIONALE PSYCHOANALYTISCHE VEREINIGUNG
ASSOCIATION PSYCHANALYTIQUE INTERNATIONALE[1]

Budapest, March 29, 1933

Dear Professor,

Two current factors are pressing me today finally to interrupt my childish sulking and to resume contact with you as if nothing had happened. That does not intend to, nor should it, mean that I am not willing to talk through together, at the next opportunity, the chronically accumulated motives of the exaggerated mode of reaction bet[ween][2] us. But first, I would only like to get into the current motives of my being pressed.—Perhaps you heard from Dr. Lévy that, in the last few weeks, I experienced a relapse in the symptoms of my illness (anemia perniciosa)—but this time less in the worsening of the condition of my blood than in a kind of nervous breakdown, from which I am only slowly recovering. The other, and last, motive was the letter from our friend Ophuijsen about the situation in Berlin, about Eitingon's attitude—which is similar to mine—and the measures which should be taken in such exigency. As little as I value Dr. Ophuijsen's mental acuity in general, I must admit that this time his sense of the reality made a keen impression on me, and in fact my pessimistic impression also extended to the situation in Vienna and, finally, also to that in Budapest.

Short and sweet: I advise you to make use of the time of the not yet immediately dangerously threatening situation and, with a few patients and your daughter Anna, to go to a more secure country, perhaps England. Dr.

Lévy finds my advice to be much too pessimistic; perhaps he connects it with my generally depressed (pathological) mood.

I, myself, am harboring the idea, in the event that the political danger gets closer to Budapest, of, at the proper time, going to Switzerland, where some patients who are still capable of paying will accompany me.

What also comes into play along with the idea of using England as a place to stay is the thought that there are excellent dentists and surgeons there.

Please take my warning seriously, and don't treat it more or less the way Eitingon did with Dr. Ophuijsen's warning.

With kind regards.

Your grateful,
Ferenczi

The publication of the correspondence with Einstein[3] will make the enemies snort with rage, but will otherwise help psychoanalysis in the civilized countries.

P.S. Take notice of my writing and the errors in penmanship.[4]

F[erenczi].

1. Preprinted letterhead. Appended to it are also the names and addresses of the president, the three vice presidents, the central secretary, and the treasurer.
2. A piece of the letter paper has been torn off here.
3. "Why War?"; a correspondence between Freud and Albert Einstein, in three languages, edited by the International Institute for Intellectual Cooperation in the League of Nations (Paris, 1932); Freud's part (1932b). The pamphlet was banned in Germany.
4. In this letter Ferenczi's handwriting, in contrast to his former bold lines, is noticeably distorted; many letters are truncated or written over one another—on the whole, a shocking picture. The "errors in penmanship" mentioned by Ferenczi do not go beyond normal errors made in haste, however.

1244

Vienna, April 2, 1933
IX., Berggasse 19[1]

Dear friend,

I heard with great regret that your convalescence, which had set in so nicely, recently underwent a disruption, but for that reason I greet all the more joyfully the fact that, according to every testimonial, you are again fully on the upswing. I ask you, let all the hard work rest for now; your handwriting really shows how tired you still are. The discussions between us about your technical and theoretical innovations can wait, and will only profit from lying fallow. It is more important to me for you to regain your health.

Now, as concerns the current motive for your writing, the motive of flight, I will gladly inform you that I am not considering leaving Vienna. I am not mobile enough, too dependent on treatment, little alleviations and comforts, also don't like to leave my property in the lurch, but I would probably also remain if I were intact and youthfully fresh. An emotional attitude naturally lies at the base of this decision, but there is also no lack of rationalizations. It is not certain that the Hitler regime will also overpower Austria; it is, of course, possible, but everyone believes that it will not reach the height of brutality here that it has in Germany. There is certainly no personal danger for me, and if you assume life in oppression to be amply uncomfortable for us Jews, then don't forget how little contentment life promises refugees in a foreign country, be it Switzerland or England. Flight, I think, would be justified only in the case of lethal danger, and incidentally, if they kill you, it's one kind of death like any other.

Ernstl arrived from Berlin just a few hours ago, after arduous experiences in Dresden and at the border. He is a German, can't go back anymore now; from now on, no German Jew will be let out anymore. Simmel, I heard, escaped to Zurich. I hope you will remain unmolested in Budapest and will soon give me good news about how you are. With kind regards to you and Frau Gisela.

Yours,
Freud

1. This letter is also in Jones III, 177f.

1245

DR. S. FERENCZI
Budapest, I. Lisznyai U. 11.
Telefon: 573-87

Budapest, April 9, 1933[1]

Dear Professor,

Your kind and understanding letter made a deep and beneficial impression on me. My view about immediately necessary measures, which I presented to you, has been significantly ameliorated, and even though I am, perhaps, under the influence of still existing physical debility, much more inclined to panic than you, I have to admit that I have complete understanding for your attitude with regard to the current tasks. The state of my health has improved significantly—not least by following your and Dr. Lévy's advice (cessation of all work for the time being). My strength is increasing, the condition of my blood consistently normal. The only upsetting thing in the last two weeks was the double-sided cataract operation in Budapest of my sister-in-law, who usually lives in Rome, and that, too, is now successfully over. I don't know at the moment how long the cessation of work will last, at least several more weeks. The, I would like to say, feverish, concern with psychoanalytic problems has also abated, so that I am very amenable to the idea of postponing talking these problems out. Many thanks for your kind sympathy, and be assured that I am grateful for any news about events in your family.

Everything is quiet here in Budapest; who would have thought, ten to fifteen years ago, that my fatherland would be a relatively calm place on the European continent.

Your correspondence with Einstein is kept dignified and moderate.

With kind regards to you all, also on the part of my wife,

Yours truly,
Ferenczi

1. The letter is typewritten; only the signature, "Ferenczi," and a correction are handwritten.

1246

F.G.[1]

[Budapest, May 4, 1933]

Dear Professor,

Only a few short lines to indicate to you that the date of your birthday is still in our memory. Let us hope that the year to come won't bring the same ugly events as the past.

I am pretty much on an even keel; my symptoms are unchanged. I exert myself in giving credence to the optimistic statements of my doctors.

Yours,
S. and G. Ferenczi

[On the reverse, in Gizella Ferenczi's handwriting]

May 4, 1933

Dear Professor—from the few lines that Sándor wrote in bed, you can see that he is still not the one he was. I don't know what I can believe and hope! Lévy is hoping for improvement soon, and I want to *believe him*. My heart is very heavy at the moment. Dear Professor, I wish you all the best for your birthday!

Kind regards to your family.

Yours truly,
Fr[au]. G.

1. Correspondence card with these preprinted initials (Ferenczi,Gizella).

The following two telegrams, undated, are not in the folder of the Austrian National Library, but were later found by Judith Dupont in Ferenczi's papers. Placing the first in 1912 and the second in 1914 seems most probable.

Addendum 1 [unnumbered]

Munich, July 5

= am in Vienna this evening will telephone you but don't be disturbed = ferenzi [sic]

Addendum 2 [unnumbered]

Budapest, April 26

quite in agreement ferenczi

Works by Freud and Ferenczi Cited in the Text

Sigmund Freud

1900a	*The Interpretation of Dreams.* S.E. 4–5.
1901a	*On Dreams.* S.E. 5:633–686.
1901b	*The Psychopathology of Everyday Life.* S.E. 6.
1905c	*Jokes and Their Relation to the Unconscious.* S.E. 8.
1905d	*Three Essays on the Theory of Sexuality.* S.E. 7:135–243.
1906c	"Psycho-Analysis and the Establishment of the Facts in Legal Proceedings." S.E. 9:103–114.
1907c	"The Sexual Enlightenment of Children." S.E. 9:131–139.
1908d	"'Civilized' Sexual Morality and Modern Nervous Illness." S.E. 9:181–204
1910a [1909]	"Five Lectures on Psycho-Analysis." S.E. 11:7–55.
1911c [1910]	"Psycho-Analytic Notes on an Autobiographical Account of a Case of Paranoia (Dementia Paranoides)." S.E. 12:9–79.
1912–13a	*Totem and Taboo.* S.E. 13:1–161.
1914d	"On the History of the Psycho-Analytic Movement." S.E. 14:7–66.
1914g	"Recollecting, Repeating, and Working Through (Further Recommendations on the Technique of Psycho-Analysis, II)." S.E. 12:147–156.
1916d	"Some Character-Types Met with in Psycho-Analytic Work." S.E. 14:311–333.
1916–17a	*Introductory Lectures on Psycho-Analysis.* S.E. 15–16.
1918b [1914]	"From the History of an Infantile Neurosis." S.E. 17:7–122.
1919a	"Lines of Advance in Psycho-Analytic Therapy." S.E. 17:159–168.
1919c	"A Note on Psycho-Analytic Publications and Prizes." S.E. 17:267–269.
1920c	"Dr. Anton von Freund†." *Zeitschrift* 6 (1920): 95f.
1920g	*Beyond the Pleasure Principle.* S.E. 18:7–64.

1921b	"Introduction" to Julien Varendonck, *The Psychology of Daydreams*, London, 1921, pp. 9f.
1921c	*Group Psychology and the Analysis of the Ego. S.E.* 18:69–143.
1921d	"A Note on Psycho-Analytic Publication and Prizes." *S.E.* 17: 269–270.
1922b	"Some Neurotic Mechanisms in Jealousy, Paranoia, and Homosexuality." *S.E.* 18:223–232.
1922d	"Prize Offer." *S.E.* 17:170 [in 1919c].
1922f	"Some Remarks on the Unconscious." *S.E.* 19:3–4 [in 1923b].
1923b	*The Ego and the Id. S.E.* 19:12–59.
1923d [1922]	"A Seventeenth-Century Demonological Neurosis." *S.E.* 19:72–105.
1923i	"Dr. Sándor Ferenczi (on His Fiftieth Birthday)." *S.E.* 19: 267–269.
1924c	"The Economic Problem of Masochism." *S.E.* 19:159–170.
1924d	"The Dissolution of the Oedipus Complex." *S.E.* 19:173–179.
1925a [1924]	"A Note upon the 'Mystic Writing-Pad.'" *S.E.* 19:227–232.
1925e [1924]	"The Resistances to Psycho-Analysis." *S.E.* 19:213–224.
1925f	"Preface to Aichhorn's *Wayward Youth.*" *S.E.* 19:273–275.
1925h	"Negation." *S.E.* 19:235–239.
1925j	"Some Psychical Consequences of the Anatomical Distinction between the Sexes." *S.E.* 19:248–258.
1926b	"Karl Abraham." *S.E.* 20:277–278.
1926d [1925]	*Inhibitions, Symptoms, and Anxiety. S.E.* 20: 87–172.
1926e	*The Question of Lay Analysis. S.E.* 20:183–250.
1927c	*The Future of an Illusion. S.E.* 21:5–56.
1927d	"Humour." *S.E.* 21:161–166.
1927e	"Fetishism." *S.E.* 21:152–157.
1928b [1927]	"Dostoevsky and Parricide." *S.E.* 21:177–194.
1929a	"Dr. Ernest Jones (On His Fiftieth Birthday)." *S.E.* 21:249–250.
1930a	*Civilization and Its Discontents. S.E.* 21:64–145.
1930e	"Address Delivered at the Goethe House at Frankfurt." *S.E.* 21:208–212.
1932a	"The Acquisition and Control of Fire." *S.E.* 22:187–193.
1932b [1931]	"Preface to Hermann Nunberg's *General Theory of the Neuroses on a Psycho-Analytic Basis. S.E.* 21:258.
1933a [1932]	*New Introductory Lectures on Psycho-Analysis. S.E.* 22:5–182.
1933c	"Sándor Ferenczi." *S.E.* 22:227–229.
1941d [1921]	"Psycho-Analysis and Telepathy." *S.E.* 18:177–193.

Sándor Ferenczi

1913, 109	"Belief, Disbelief, and Conviction." *F.C.* 437–450.
1913, 111	"Stages in the Development of the Sense of Reality." *C.* 213–239.
1913, 114	"A Little Chanticleer." *C.* 240–252.

1917, 195	"Disease- or Patho-Neuroses." *F.C.* 78.
1919, 210	"Technical Difficulties in the Analysis of a Case of Hysteria." *F.C.* 189.
1921, 232	"Psycho-Analytical Observations on Tic." *F.C.* 142–174.
1921, 233	"The Symbolism of the Bridge." *F.C.* 352–356.
1921, 234	"The Further Development of an Active Therapy in Psycho-Analysis." *F.C.* 198–217.
1921, 236	"General Theory of the Neuroses." *International Journal of Psycho-Analysis* 1 (1920): 294–315.
1921, 238	Review of G. Groddeck, *Der Seelensucher. Imago* 7(1921): 356–359; *Fin.* 344–345.
1922, 239	(with S. Hollós) *Psycho-Analysis and the Psychic Disorder of General Paresis.* New York and Washington: Nervous and Mental Disease Publishing Co., 1925; *Fin.* 351–370.
1922, 240	*Populare Vorträge über Psychoanalyse.* Leipzig: Internationaler Psychoanalytischer Verlag, 1922.
1922, 242	"Bridge Symbolism and the Don Juan Legend." *F.C.* 356–258.
1922, 246	"Versuch einer Genitaltheorie." Report given at the 7th International Psychoanalytic Congress, Berlin, 1922; *International Journal of Psycho-Analysis* 4 (1923): 359–360.
1924, 264	(with O. Rank) *The Development of Psycho-Analysis.* Madison, Conn.: International Universities Press, 1986.
1924, 265	"On Forced Phantasies." *F.C.* 68–77.
1924, 268	*Thalassa: A Theory of Genitality. Psychoanalytic Quarterly* 2 (1934): 361–403; 3 (1934): 1–29, 200–222.
1925, 269	"Psycho-Analysis of Sexual Habits." *F.C.* 259–297.
1926, 271	"Contra-Indications to the Active Psycho-Analytical Technique" *F.C.* 217–230.
1926, 273	"To Sigmund Freud on His Seventieth Birthday." *International Journal of Psycho-Analysis* 7(1926): 297–302.
1926, 274	"Freud's Importance for the Mental Hygiene Movement." *Fin.* 18–21.
1926, 275	"The Problem of the Acceptance of Unpleasant Ideas—Advances in Knowledge of the Sense of Reality." *F.C.* 366–379.
1927, 277	Review of O. Rank, "Technique of Psycho-Analysis." *International Journal of Psycho-Analysis* 8 (1927): 93–100.
1927, 278	"Present-Day Problems in Psycho-Analysis." *Fin.* 29–40.
1927, 280	"Gulliver Phantasies." *Fin.* 41–60.
1927, 280a	Foreword to Freud's *Inhibitions, Symptoms, and Anxiety.* Stamford, Conn.: The Psycho-Analytic Institute, 1927.
1927, 280b	Foreword to Freud's *The Question of Lay Analysis.* New York: Brentano, 1927.
1928, 281	"The Adaptation of the Family to the Child." *Fin.* 61–76.
1928, 283	"The Elasticity of Psycho-Analytical Technique." *Fin.* 87–101.
1928, 283a	"Psychoanalyse und Kriminologie." *Bausteine* III, 399–421.
1929, 287a	"Fortschritte der analytischen Technik." *Zeitschrift* 15 (1929): 515.
1930, 289	"A 'psychoanalysis' név illetéktelen használata" [On the Pro-

	hibited Use of the Term "Psychoanalysis"], *Gyógyászat*, no. 1 (1930).
1930, 290	"'Viszonválasz' Dr. Feldmann válaszárá" [Reply to Dr. Feldmann's Response] *Gyógyászat*, no. 2 (1930).
1930, 291	"The Principle of Relaxation and Neocatharsis." *Fin.* 108–125.
1933, 294	"Confusion of Tongues between Adults and the Child." *Fin.* 156–167.
Posthumous, 301	"Mathematics." *Fin.* 183–196.
Posthumous, 308	"Notes and Fragments." *Fin.* 216–279.

Index

Note: Numbers refer to correspondence numbers.

Abraham, Hedwig, 1087
Abraham, Karl, 851n2, 860, 895, 909, 1018n2, 1021; dispute with Rank, 864, 939, 947, 948, 949, 951, 952, 960, 973, 976, 985, 1058; as secretary of the IPA, 911n1, 950; friction in the Secret Committee and, 912, 913, 916, 939n2, 948, 974; Ferenczi and, 949, 965, 968, 969; as president of IPA, 950, 951, 953, 957, 1026, 1045; Freud and, 952, 953, 968n2, 970, 1007, 1021n4, 1038, 1061; at International Psychoanalytic Congresses, 957, 959, 960, 1028; Verlag and, 959; Berlin Psychoanalytic Society and, 974; as member of Secret Committee, 992; Groddeck and, 1011, 1011n2; involvement in film making, 1021, 1026n2, 1045; funding for training analysis and, 1021n2; illness and death, 1028n7, 1032, 1034, 1037, 1038, 1039, 1041, 1042, 1043, 1045, 1048, 1233n1. *See also* Secret Committee: disputes within
"Acquisition and Control of Fire, The" (Freud), 1219n3
Acting out, 947, 948
Activity (active therapy), 907, 1024, 1025, 1067, 1117, 1148; Ferenczi's theory of, 836, 846n3, 847, 909, 917, 928, 945, 946, 951, 971, 974, 1031, 1033, 1216n5, 1217; Freud on, 947; preconscious and, 1009; Rankian theory and, 1024, 1025; limitations of, 1034n2, 1216n5; associative, 1133

"Adaptation of the Family to the Child, The" (Ferenczi), 1104n2
Adler, Alfred, 913, 928n2, 973, 976, 977, 1021, 1085, 1088, 1090, 1097, 1195; politics of, 1089; dissent and factions within IPA and, 1174, 1182, 1184
Adler, Herman Morris, 1094n2
Adolescent psychoses, 1093n5
"Advances in Analytic Technique" (Ferenczi), 1167n3
"Advances in Knowledge of the Sense of Reality" (Ferenczi), 1030
Aesthetics, 924
Aichhorn, August, 960, 992, 996, 998, 1024, 1174
Alexander, Bernát, 1009n2, 1010
Alexander, Franz, 837n11, 951n8, 957n1, 1009, 1031, 1033, 1043, 1046n1, 1079, 1100, 1127n1, 1204
Almanach für das Jahr 1928, 1105n3
Almásy, Endre, 1201n2, 1206
Ambivalence, 840, 951
American Academy of Psychoanalysis, 1009n2
American Congress of Psychiatrists, 1090
American Medical Association, 1082, 1095
American Psychoanalytic Association, 836n5, 860n5, 957n6, 970n1, 988n1, 1009n2, 1028, 1088, 1090, 1155n3, 1231; Ferenczi and, 965, 1082; opposition to lay analysis, 1155n3, 1156, 1232
Ames, Thaddeus H., 1090

Amsden, George S., 1082n13, 1100, 1102, 1104, 1128, 1132, 1133, 1202; analysis of Burlingham, 1134, 1136, 1137; recommendation to Philadelphia and, 1202, 1205
Analysis of Neuroses in Dreams, An (Rank), 974, 976
Analytical Trade Union, 1086
Analytic situation, 951, 1061
Analytic therapy, 1162
Andreas-Salomé, Lou, 879, 888, 892, 895, 941, 942, 943, 969, 980; Anna Freud and, 892n3, 908n8, 922, 943, 979, 1021; Rank and, 979; Society of Friends of Psychoanalysis and, 1024; Ferenczi family and, 1074, 1075
"Animism, Magic, and the Omnipotence of Thoughts" (Freud), 1079n2
Anxiety, 952, 953, 1021, 1025, 1133; castration, 971, 974; hysteria, 974; nervous, 1008
Arche, Die (newsletter), 1098n1, 1103
Asch, Joseph J., 1097
Association for the Advancement of Psychoanalysis (New York), 1046n1
Association of Independent Medical Analysts, 1034n4
Association of Independent Physicians (Hungary), 1179n3
Athenäum (publishing house), 1201
"Attempt at a Theory of Genitality" (Ferenczi), 907n1, 911n1
Australian Totemism: A Psycho-Analytic Study in Anthropology (Róheim), 836n6
Autobiographical Study (Freud), 1110
Autonomous nervous system, 1088

Bálint, Alice, 837n11, 994n6, 1201n3, 1206n7, 1208, 1227n2
Bálint, Michael, 837n11, 1050, 1057n4, 1069n2, 1206
Ballesteros y de Torres, Luis Lopez, 1140n3, 1142, 1143, 1145, 1146, 1197n3
Basic Characteristics of a Genetic Psychology (Rank), 1081
Behaviorism, 1088, 1089, 1090
Bergson, Henri, 1031
Berlin Institute, 1046n1, 1173, 1179
Berlin Polyclinic, 837, 1043, 1045, 1208
Berlin Psychoanalytic Society, 864n3, 947, 950, 951, 953, 957, 960, 961, 970, 1043, 1097, 1177, 1206, 1243; outpatient/polyclinic, 837n11, 848n5; Rank and, 952, 986; Ferenczi and, 974, 1046, 1047; correspondence among members, 994; training institute, 1009n2, 1118; Eitingon and, 1041
Bernays, Anna, 1086n4
Bernays, Doris (née Fleischmann), 1086n4, 1097n15
Bernays, Edward Louis, 197, 859n7, 973n4, 1021, 1086n4, 1088, 1090, 1094
Bernays, Eli, 841, 973n2
Bernays, Hella, 1086n4
Bernays, Judith ("Ditha") (married name Heller-Bernays), 899, 1082, 1086n4
Bernays, Leah ("Lucy") (married name Wiener), 973, 1086n4, 1097
Bernays, Martha Randolph, 1086n4
Bernays, Minna, 837, 846, 848, 929, 934n1, 1109
Bernfeld, Siegfried, 830, 837n11, 878n1, 909, 957, 960n2, 962, 963, 965, 970n2, 974; involvement in film making, 1021, 1026n2; Society of Friends of Psychoanalysis and, 1024; at Ninth International Psychoanalytic Congress, 1028; Anna Freud and, 1125; current politics and, 1219
Bernfeld, Suzanne, 837n11
Bethlen, István, 940n3, 944n3
Beyond the Pleasure Principle (Freud), 845, 848, 850, 866, 870, 879, 908, 927, 1207, 1208
Bijur, Angelika, 860n4, 908n6
Birth/birth trauma, 929n2, 932, 940, 945, 947, 948, 951, 953, 957, 982, 994; Freud's critique of, 950, 952; affected by cesarian section, 952; Ferenczi's theory of, 971, 974, 1088, 1192; fantasy, 994; under hypnosis, 1005; therapy technique (Rank), 1028, 1060, 1061, 1062
"Birth in Hypnosis" (Loránd), 1005
Bleuler, Eugen, 1088
Blumenthal, William, 1154, 1160, 1177, 1179
Blumgart, Herman, 1064n2
Blumgart, Leonard, 1064n2, 1088, 1090
Body ego, 941, 942

Böhm, Felix, 837n11, 1043n4
Bolshevism, 848n6, 1219, 1230
Bolyai, János, 982n2
Bonaparte, Eugénie, 1168
Bonaparte, Marie, Princess of Greece, 970, 1031, 1068, 1095, 1096, 1097, 1117n6, 1137n1, 1161, 1225n4; donations to the Verlag, 1158n1; Freud and, 1168; as member of International Training Commission, 1168
Boston Psychoanalytic Society, 878n1, 1028n3
Brachfeld, Olivér, 1182n6
Braun, Ludwig, 1051, 1054, 1068, 1172, 1232
Brill, Abraham Arden, 836, 837, 908n7, 939, 988, 992, 1004, 1090, 1177, 1237n4, 1238; differences and reconciliation with Freud, 837n5, 866n5; Ferenczi and, 866, 1063, 1082, 1084, 1090, 1091, 1093, 1094, 1097, 1173; Freud and, 882, 939n1, 1036, 1037, 1082, 1097, 1109, 1111; Jones and, 882, 1036, 1082, 1086, 1097; Rank and, 981n3; Eitingon and, 992; Secret Committee and, 994; lay analysis and, 1015, 1036, 1037, 1082, 1097, 1109n4, 1155, 1171, 1201; funding for training analysis and, 1021n2; politics of, 1078; New School for Social Research and, 1082; Eleventh International Psychoanalytic Congress and, 1161; separation of medical analysis from psychoanalysis in IPA and, 1161; as member of International Training Commission, 1167n3; division between American and European groups and, 1175, 1201, 1232; IPA and, 1177; New York Psychoanalytic Institute and, 1203; at Twelfth International Psychoanalytic Congress, 1209; as vice president of IPA, 1225, 1226, 1232, 1236n1
Briquet, Raul, 1115n1
British Medical Association, 1174
British Medical Journal, 1012
British Psychoanalytical Society, 845n2, 909n1, 958, 997, 998, 1002n1, 1005, 1017, 1018, 1018n2, 1050n3, 1097, 1173, 1201, 1206
British Psychological Society, 1094

Brother: complex, 945, 946, 950, 995n1, 1174n1, 1180; bonding, 1192
Brouwer, Bernardus, 1229, 1230
Brown, Sanger Monroe, 1090n10
Brunswick, Mark, 1064n2
Bryan, C./A. Douglas, 1018
Budapest group of the Hungarian Psychoanalytic Society, 866, 878, 893, 962, 994, 1008, 1039, 1060n8, 1061, 1069, 1176, 1177, 1180, 1243; polyclinic, 851n3, 1090, 1201, 1206, 1208, 1218; Freud and, 1108; training institute, 1108, 1206; Anna Freud and, 1119, 1184; dissent within, 1205; child analysis in, 1206; lay analysis and, 1206. *See also* Hungarian Psychoanalytic Association/Society
Budapest Psychoanalytic Institute, 1050n3
Bumke, Oswald C. E., 1195
Burlingham, Charles Culp, 1082n12
Burlingham, Dorothy, 1064, 1074, 1081n12, 1084, 1085, 1128, 1134, 1137, 1169n2; Anna Freud and, 1064n1, 1082, 1083, 1128, 1185n1, 1195
Burlingham, Mabbie, 1185n1
Burlingham, Michael, 1185n1
Burlingham, Robert, 1082, 1084, 1127, 1128, 1132, 1133, 1146; as analysand of Amsden, 1134, 1136, 1137
Burrow, Trigant, 970, 1088, 1090

Castration, 951, 1016; anxiety/complex, 971, 974, 1016, 1050, 1227; fantasy, 1111; female, 1227
Catatonia, 854
Catharsis, 1001
Cerebral pathoneuroses, 851
Character, 893; formation and traits, 847, 926, 961; analysis, 1117, 1124, 1142n3, 1145
Charcot, J. M., 1015, 1061
Chicago Institute for Psychoanalysis, 1009n2
Child analysis, 1021n6, 1125, 1201, 1202n5, 1206. *See also* Freud, Anna
Civilization and Its Discontents (Freud), 1168n1, 1172, 1176, 1177; Ferenczi on, 1182
Clark, Pierce, 1028, 1088, 1093, 1097, 1117

Clinical Diary (Ferenczi), 994n6, 1023n2, 1216n2
Cohen, Albert, 970
Coitus, 1089
Cole, Estelle Maude, 909, 1097
Collected Papers (Freud), 988n3, 991, 1005
Columbia University, 1090, 1094
Compulsion, 897, 1179
Conditioned reflex, 1064, 1088
"Confusion of Tongues between Adults and the Child" (Ferenczi), 1206n11, 1236n1
Conscience, 1182
Consciousness, 983
Control analysis, 1082n9
Conversion symptom, 961, 1050
Coriat, Isadore Henry, 1028, 1082
Cravath, Paul Drennan, 1082n14
Culpin, Millais, 1013

Daly, Claude D., 837n2, 1004, 1006, 1010, 1032, 1050
Dasgupta, Surendranath, 1085n5
David, K. G., 1229n3
Death instinct, 1219
Décsi, Imre, 1179n5
De Forest, Izette Taber, 1186n1, 1236n1
De Forest, Judy, 1168n1, 1185n1, 1186n1
Dementia praecox, 969, 1093
Demole, Victor, 848
Detachment, 951
Deuticke, Franz, 903, 909, 910, 982, 1060, 1172n4
Deutsch, Felix, 878, 879, 880, 928, 931, 970, 971, 1060
Deutsch, Helene, 830n5, 909, 957, 960, 961, 981, 983, 1082n9, 1204, 1225n4; as member of International Training Commission, 1167n3
Development of Psychoanalysis, The (Ferenczi and Rank), 929n2, 937n3, 939, 941, 944n1, 945, 946, 948, 950, 951, 1060; critiques of (Freud, Eitingon), 945, 946, 947, 950, 974, 1009
Dewey, John, 1090
Dick, Manó, 893, 894, 903, 905, 909, 910, 934, 1002, 1005
"Dissolution of the Oedipus Complex, The" (Freud), 950n1, 951, 952, 959, 961
Döblin, Alfred, 1193n1
"Dostoevsky and Parricide" (Freud), 1151
Dream: interpretation, 951, 1061; function, 1206, 1207n3, 1208
Dubowitz, Margit, 834, 855, 859, 866, 1182, 1206
Dukes, Géza, 893, 894, 1050, 1206n8
Dupont, Judith, 994n6

"Economic Problem of Masochism, The" (Freud), 945
Eder, David, 845n2, 935, 1097
Ego, 840, 928, 1067, 1195; character traits and, 847; psychology, 864, 1122, 1173, 1225n3; memory systems, 926; body, 941, 942; effect of toxins on, 959; Ferenczi on, 1088; castration fantasy and, 1111; resistance, 1124
Ego and the Id, The (Freud), 908n5, 911n1, 917, 921, 926, 928, 941, 942
Eighth Congress of Hungarian Psychiatrists, 982n5
Eighth International Psychoanalytic Congress (1924, Salzburg), 951n4, 952, 953, 956, 957, 959, 974; Freud declines to attend, 954, 955, 960
Einstein, Albert, 970, 1087, 1243, 1245
Eisler, Joszef Mihály, 836, 837, 846, 866, 944, 1069n2
Eitingon, Max, 832, 833, 870, 891n4, 929, 939, 952, 957, 1015, 1061, 1075; Freud and, 829, 848n7, 970, 973, 977, 1003n3, 1053, 1061, 1087, 1125; founds Berlin polyclinic, 837, 1043; Verlag activities, 844, 845, 848, 986n3, 998, 1009, 1027, 1037, 1043, 1045, 1201, 1206n9, 1230; Secret Committee and, 913, 949, 986; as secretary of the IPA, 951n4; Ferenczi and, 969, 1033, 1097, 1101, 1148, 1243; Berlin Psychoanalytic Society and, 973; Freund endowment and, 987, 990, 991, 993, 999; Brill and, 992; as editor of *Zeitschrift*, 1009n1, 1010, 1013, 1044, 1045, 1086, 1230, 1231; funding for training analysis and, 1021n2; Society of Friends of Psychoanalysis and, 1024; at International Psychoanalytic Congresses, 1026, 1028, 1090, 1099, 1162, 1209, 1236n1; Anna Freud and, 1033, 1089; as president of the IPA, 1043, 1099, 1100, 1101, 1102, 1103, 1107n3, 1124, 1167n3, 1179, 1191, 1192, 1212, 1219, 1220, 1223; eulogy for Abraham, 1044n3; as proposed head

of Berlin Psychoanalytic Society, 1046; protests film *Secrets of a Soul,* 1046; *Imago* and, 1079, 1230; lay analysis and, 1100, 1102, 1103, 1157; separation of medical analysis from psychoanalysis in IPA and, 1161; as president of the Eleventh International Psychoanalytic Congress, 1167n3; proposed collaboration with Ferenczi, 1192; publication of Freud's books and, 1201; Amsden and, 1202; current politics and, 1219; health, 1222, 1223; as president of the ITC, 1236n1. *See also* Secret Committee: disputes within

Eitingon, Mirra, 1043, 1046, 1100
Ejaculatio praecox, 1016
"Elasticity of Psycho-Analytical Technique, The" (Ferenczi), 1114n2, 1117
Elasticity of technique, 1115, 1117
Electrotherapy, 853n4
Elements of Psychoanalysis (Ferenczi), 880, 882
Eleventh International Psychoanalytic Congress (1929, Oxford), 1116, 1138, 1151, 1167n3, 1180; proposed separation of medical analysis from psychoanalysis at, 1161, 1162; Ferenczi's lectures and attendance at, 1162, 1164, 1167n3, 1168, 1170, 1173, 1179, 1180, 1181, 1182, 1233
Ellis, Edith, 1077n2
Ellis, Havelock, 1077
Empathy, 1117
Ender, Otto, 1199n2
Epilepsy, 1028, 1063, 1065, 1067
Erotic impulse, 1050
Everyday Life (Freud). *See* Psychopathology of Everyday Life, The (Freud)

Fantasy, 1016, 1173, 1179; forced, 1028, 1088
Father: ideal of becoming, 840; culture, 971, 972n2; complex, 974, 1005, 1129; bonding, 1192; role of analysts, 1216
Federn, Ernest, 959, 981, 983, 1049, 1053, 1202, 1226n2; *Zeitschrift* and, 1225, 1230
Federn, Paul, 992n2, 1079
Feigenbaum, Dorian, 1086

Feldmann, Sándor, 916, 920, 922, 925, 1008, 1034, 1111, 1174, 1175; Ferenczi and, 1176, 1178, 1182; as member of the Association of Independent Physicians, 1179
Fenichel, Otto, 1225, 1230
Ferenczi, Gizella (sister) (married name Fleiszner), 830, 836, 846, 847, 859n5, 885
Ferenczi, Henrik, 859n5
Ferenczi, Ilona, 859n5
Ferenczi, Jozsef, 859n5
Ferenczi, Károly, 859n5
Ferenczi, Lajos, 859n5
Ferenczi, Miksa, 859n5
Ferenczi, Rosa (née Eibenschütz), 847n8
Ferenczi, Sarolta, 842
Ferenczi, Vilma, 859n5
Ferenczi, Zsigmond, 859n5
Ferenczi, Zsofia, 859n5
Fetishism, 1104, 1105
"Fetishism" (Freud), 1104n1
Filho, Lourenco, 1115n1
Five Lectures on Psycho-Analysis (Freud), 882, 908n10, 970, 1201
Fleiszner, Zsigmond, 885n1
Fliess, Robert, 1064n2, 1225n4
Flournoy, Henri, 861
France, Anatole, 1046, 1047
Franco da Rocha, Francisco, 1115n1
Frankfurt Psychoanalytic Working Community, 957n7
Franklin, Marjory, 1063, 1065, 1067, 1068, 1070, 1071
Free association, 1179
Freud, Alexander, 1097, 1098
Freud, Amalie (mother), 857, 908, 928, 1115, 1194n2, 1195
Freud, Anna (daughter), 833, 837, 844, 845n2, 887, 899, 902, 908, 938n2, 941, 952, 960, 963, 965, 970, 979, 1028, 1084; travels, 848, 852n2, 860, 867, 934n1; Lou Andreas-Salomé and, 892n3, 908n8, 922, 943, 979, 1021; membership in Vienna Society, 907; Ferenczi and, 961, 974, 1033, 1040, 1100, 1116, 1148, 1150, 1184, 1185; Verlag and, 971, 1027; Rank and, 992; as secretary to Freud, 994, 1001, 1085, 1141, 1160; thought transference experiments, 1005; as analyst, 1009, 1010, 1225n4; in Secret Committee,

Freud, Anna (daughter) *(continued)*
1015, 1022n1, 1032, 1116; Society of Friends of Psychoanalysis and, 1024; at Ninth International Psychoanalytic Congress, 1026; Eitingon and, 1033, 1089; Dorothy Burlingham and, 1064n1, 1082, 1083, 1128, 1185n1, 1195; child analysis practice, writings and lectures, 1076, 1083, 1086, 1092, 1109n4, 1117n7, 1125, 1148, 1184n1, 1201, 1201n4, 1221n5; lay analysis and, 1089, 1225n5; Melanie Klein and, 1107n3; at Tenth International Psychoanalytic Congress (1927, Innsbruck), 1107n3; correspondence with Ferenczi, 1116, 1138, 1139, 1242; Budapest group of the Hungarian Psychoanalytic Society and, 1119; Eva Rosenfeld and, 1138n2; as member of International Training Commission, 1167n3; accepts Goethe Prize for Freud, 1193; as secretary of the IPA, 1205, 1223, 1225, 1226, 1236n1; at Twelfth International Psychoanalytic Congress, 1209; *Psychoanalytic Study of the Child* journal and, 1225n3; publication of Freud's correspondence, 1225n4

Freud, Anna (sister), 841n2, 973n2
Freud, Anton Walter, 857n1, 868, 977n5
Freud, Clemens Raphael, 841n1, 977n5, 1087n2
Freud, Emil, 842
Freud, Ernst (grandson), 977n5, 1087, 1244
Freud, Ernst (son), 832, 833, 837, 841, 844, 847, 848, 867n4, 981n2, 1085, 1087n2, 1100
Freud, Esti, 979n3
Freud, Eva Mathilde, 917n4, 976n2, 977n5, 979, 1087
Freud, Henny (née Fuchs), 917n4, 962n1, 1087n2
Freud, Lucian Michael, 841n1, 977n5, 1087n2
Freud, Lucie ("Lux") (née Brasch), 841, 844, 848, 1087n2
Freud, Martha (née Bernays), 830, 833, 841n2, 863, 880, 973n2, 1048n4, 1109, 1185; travels, 934n1; Freud's illnesses and, 1054

Freud, Martin, 837, 857, 862, 977n5, 1092, 1093; as director of the Verlag, 1219, 1221, 1222, 1223
Freud, Mathilde (married name Hollitscher), 832, 833, 837, 908, 934n1, 1109
Freud, Oliver (Oli), 832, 833, 837, 862, 870, 908, 962n1, 1031n4, 1085; engagement and marriage, 917, 922, 927; birth of daughter Eva, 976, 977, 978; in analysis with Alexander, 1009n2
Freud, Pauline, 917n5
Freud, Regina (Rosa) (married name Graf), 882n3, 910
Freud, Sophie (married name Halberstadt), 831, 837, 977, 979n3
Freud, Stephan Gabriel (Stephen), 841n1, 977n5, 1087n2
"Freud's Metapsychology" (Ferenczi), 896n1
Freund, Antal von, 836n12
Freund, Anton (Toni) von, 831, 833, 836, 844, 863, 868n1, 893, 1125; endowment/Anton von Freund Foundation, 829, 830, 837, 841, 842, 899, 906, 987n3, 990, 991, 993, 999, 1002, 1036, 1083
Freund, Emil von (later Tószeghy), 830, 834, 838, 987, 990, 991, 992, 993, 999, 1002
Freund, Erzsébet, 836n12
Freund, Regina von (married name Vidor), 836n11
Freund, Rózsi von, 834, 836, 842, 847, 863, 866, 893, 990
Freund, Vera von, 830, 836
Friends of Psychoanalysis. *See* Society of Friends of Psychoanalysis
Frigidity (clitoris position), 969, 970
Frink, Horace Westlake, 860, 860n4, 866, 908, 913, 1088, 1093, 1094
Fromm, Erich, 837n11, 957n7, 1046n1, 1106n1, 1186n1, 1216n2, 1236n1
Fromm-Reichmann, Frieda, 957n7, 1106
"From the History of an Infantile Neurosis" (Freud), 1066
From the Mental Life of the Child (Hug-Hellmuth), 1090n14
Frost, Walter, 842

Functional psychoses, 851
"Further Development of an Active Therapy in Psycho-Analysis, The" (Ferenczi), 836n4, 852n2
Future of an Illusion, The (Freud), 1109n2

Gardiner, Muriel, 1064n2
Gartner, Pál, 1179n5
Genitality theory (Ferenczi), 907, 911n1, 937, 950, 951, 952, 957, 971, 994, 1017, 1196, 1207; favorable criticism of, 1030. See also *Thalassa: A Theory of Genitality* (Ferenczi)
Glimpses of the Great (Viereck), 1077n1
Glover, Edward, 837n11, 845n2, 909, 957, 1083n1
Glover, James, 837n11, 909, 957, 958, 1076, 1077, 1078
Glueck, Bernard, 1090n2, 1093, 1094
Goethe Prize, 957n7, 1193, 1195, 1196
Goldberg, Isaac, 1077
Goldstein, Kurt, 1106n1
Göring, Hermann, 1168n1
Göring Institute, 1031n4
Graf, Cäcilie ("Maus"), 882, 910
Graf, Heinrich, 882n3
Graven, Philip, 1082n11
Grinker, Roy, 1009n2
Groddeck, Georg, 867, 878, 893, 899, 969, 1011n2, 1021, 1106, 1168; Ferenczi and, 888, 911, 1020, 1024, 1028, 1035, 1075, 1081, 1097, 1198; sanatorium, 902, 1106n1; Freud and, 908, 1036, 1037, 1076, 1077, 1092; organic animism concept, 909; translations of Freud by, 979, 988; healing methods, 980; correspondence with Ferenczi, 994n6, 1197n2; Abraham and, 1011; Vienna Psychological Society and, 1076; Berlin Psychoanalytic Society and, 1083
Grote, Louis R., 967, 970
Group analysis, 1088, 1090
Group Psychology, 840, 853, 860, 862, 864, 876, 927
Group Psychology and the Analysis of the Ego (Freud), 840n3, 848n7, 852, 1031n5, 1201
Guilbert, Yvette, 1138, 1172
Guilt, 921, 926, 1016

"Gulliver Phantasies" (Ferenczi), 1084, 1091n1, 1092n2, 1111
Gyömröi, Edit, 1206n8

Hahn, Fanny K., 1201n2
Hajdu, Lily, 1206n7
Hajnal, Richard, 1179n5
Halberstadt, Ernst, 837n13, 868, 882, 1169n1
Halberstadt, Heinz Rudolf (Heinerle), 837n13, 917n6, 927, 931, 932, 977
Halberstadt, Max, 832, 833, 848n7, 862, 1169n1
Halberstadt, Rudolph, 832
Hall, Duncan, 1202n5
Hall, Stanley, 959, 960, 961, 1082
Hampstead Child Therapy Course, 1064n1
Hann, Fanny K. (married name Hann-Kende), 1201n2, 1206n7, 1227n2
Happel, Klara, 957n7, 1106
Harmos, Ilona, 1126n1
Hartmann, Heinz, 4, 1225n3, 1230
Hatvany, Lajos, 1176n1
Heller, Peter, 1201n4
Herford, Ethilde B. M., 932
Hermann, Imre, 840, 944, 982, 1069n2, 1108, 1139, 1206n3
Hermant, Abel, 929
Hinkle, Beatrice M., 1090
Hitler, Adolf, 922n1, 1244
Hitschmann, Eduard, 909, 962, 963, 964
Hollitscher, Mathilde, 837n11
Hollitscher, Robert, 832, 833, 837, 934n1
Hollós, Istvan, 836, 851, 861, 944, 1069n2, 1206
Homosexuality, 1050, 1088, 1195; female, 830, 847, 865; jealousy and, 864
Hopkins, Pryns, 1083n1
Horney, Karen, 837n11, 1046, 1100, 1106n1
Horney, Marianne, 1106n1
Hug-Hellmuth, Hermine, 1090
Humanistic Psychology, 1106n1
Humor, 1105, 1107
Hungarian Association for Individual Psychology, 1182n6
Hungarian Psychoanalytic Association/Society, 836n4, 840, 872, 920, 994n6, 997, 1005, 1011, 1035, 1069n2, 1201,

Hungarian Psychoanalytic Association/ Society *(continued)*
  1205, 1221; Education Committee, 994n6; Training Committee, 1050n3; outpatient clinic/polyclinic, 1108, 1201, 1206; birthday greetings to Freud, 1124. *See also* Budapest group of the Hungarian Psychoanalytic Society
Hutchins, Robert Maynard, 1204n2
Hypnagogic hallucination, 878
Hypnosis. *See* Suggestion (hypnosis)
Hypochondria, 859, 1180, 1182; of Freud, 870; of Ferenczi, 871, 879, 893, 897, 1113
Hysteria, 1033n2, 1050

Id, 927, 928, 959, 1067, 1088
Identity, unconscious, 951
Imago, 986, 1029, 1079, 1221, 1225; Freud published in, 1219; political articles in, 1220; changing editorship, 1230
Indian Psycho-Analytical Society, 837n2
Indulgence, 847, 1179
Infantile neurosis, 1066
Inhibition, 1024
Inhibitions, Symptoms, and Anxiety (Freud), 1021, 1036n2, 1037, 1051, 1057n2
Inman, William S., 998, 1000, 1001, 1002, 1012, 1017, 1018, 1067, 1081, 1095, 1097
Instinct, 1090
Institute of Psychoanalysis, London, 1018n2
International Congress of Psychology, Oxford (1923), 928, 930, 934, 935
International Federation of Psychoanalytic Societies, 1106n1
International Journal of Psycho-Analysis, 852n2
International Psychoanalytic Association (IPA), 852n2, 987, 1002, 1020, 1043, 1059, 1096, 1115, 1177; Jones as vice president and president of, 852n2, 862n2, 911n1, 1099, 1107, 1191, 1219, 1220, 1236n1; Abraham as president and secretary of, 911n1, 950, 951, 953, 957, 1026, 1045; Freud and, 950, 1107; polyclinic (General Ambulatorium for Nervous and Mental Patients), 1003, 1043, 1205n2; Eitingon as president of, 1043, 1099, 1100, 1101, 1102, 1103, 1107n3, 1124, 1167n3, 1179, 1191, 1192, 1212, 1219, 1220, 1223; Ferenczi and, 1043, 1172, 1192; Ferenczi as candidate for presidency (1925), 1043, 1044, 1124, 1191, 1192, 1205, 1223, 1225, 1226; restructuring of, 1109n4, 1179, 1221; dissent and factions within, 1156n1, 1165n2, 1172, 1174, 1179, 1191; proposed separation of medical analysts from, 1160n2, 1161, 1206; Ferenczi fails to secure presidency (1929), 1172, 1173, 1175, 1176, 1178, 1179, 1180; New York Psychoanalytic Society and, 1175n1; analytic faculty, 1179; master school, 1179; University Extension, 1179; Ferenczi as vice president of, 1211, 1212, 1213, 1220; Central Committee, 1218; financial circumstance, 1221; Brill as vice president of, 1225, 1226, 1232, 1236n1; Ferenczi renounces candidacy for presidency (1932), 1233, 1234, 1236. *See also* Secret Committee
International Psychoanalytic Congress (scheduled for 1931), 1208, 1209, 1218
International Training Commission (ITC), 1026n2, 1100, 1167n3, 1236n1
Interpretation of Dreams, The (Freud), 842, 974n3, 979, 1172, 1183, 1201, 1206, 1208; translations of, 903, 905, 909, 1005, 1036, 1068, 1208, 1221
Intoxication, 959, 1076, 1078
Introduction to Psychoanalysis for Teachers: Four Lectures (A. Freud), 1176n2
"Introduction to Psychoanalytic Technique and Character Analysis" (Ferenczi), 1142n3
Introduction to the Technique of Child Analysis (A. Freud), 1083n5, 1093, 1097

Janet, Pierre, 928n2, 1105
Jankelevitch, Serge, 861, 862
Jaspers, Karl, 848
Jealousy, 864, 1016, 1081
Jekels, Ludwig, 983, 1219
Jelgersma, Gerbrandus, 959, 960, 961

Jelliffe, Smith Ely, 882, 1082, 1088, 1093, 1094, 1097, 1167n3
Johnson, Alvin Saunders, 1082, 1090
Jokes, 924
Jokes and Their Relation to the Unconscious (Freud), 837, 893, 1036
Jokl, Hans, 1202n5, 1225n5
Jones, Ernest, 837, 860, 862, 953, 1015, 1043; Loë Kann and, 837n10; lay analysis and, 844n5, 1036, 1097, 1155, 1157; Ferenczi and, 849, 913, 916, 939n2, 943, 998, 1017, 1097, 1118, 1156, 1159, 1168, 1173, 1180, 1186n1, 1191; as president of the IPA, 852n2, 862n2, 911n1, 1099, 1107, 1191, 1219, 1220, 1236n1; Verlag activities, 867, 917; reviews of Freud's works, 879; Brill and, 882, 1036, 1082, 1086, 1097; Secret Committee and, 912, 913, 916, 943, 974, 989, 994, 998, 1034, 1049; as analysand of Ferenczi, 913n1; Freud and, 917, 1061, 1107, 1109, 1109n4, 1111, 1149n2; work on symbolism, 924; dispute with Rank, 939n2, 951, 973, 974, 977, 979, 987n1, 1093; at Eighth International Psychoanalytic Congress, 957, 959, 974; patient referrals from Ferenczi, 1001; Groddeck and, 1011n2; negative reception in England, 1017, 1018; at Ninth International Psychoanalytic Congress, 1028; *Zeitschrift* and *Imago* activities, 1048, 1064; International Psychoanalytic Association (IPA) and, 1099, 1100; Melanie Klein and, 1109n4; issue of *Zeitschrift* dedicated to, 1159; personal life, 1159n1; as member of International Training Commission, 1167n3; at Eleventh International Psychoanalytic Congress, 1168, 1177; dissent in the IPA and, 1175, 1192; division between American and European groups and, 1175; at Twelfth International Psychoanalytic Congress, 1209. *See also* Secret Committee: disputes within
Jones, Herbert, 837n9
Jones, Katharine, 939n2
Journal of Nervous and Mental Disease, 1021
Jung, Carl Gustav, 843, 882n6, 950, 1021, 1081, 1085n5, 1088, 1090, 1164; symbolism concept, 864; secession from psychoanalysis, 949n2; Ferenczi and, 1111n2

Kaháná, Ernö, 1182n6
Kahn, Lore, 922n1
Kallen, Horace M., 1097n14
Kann, Loë, 837
Kapp, Wolfgang/Kapp Putsch, 837n8
Kardiner, Abram, 1088, 1090, 1093, 1094, 1097
Karpinska, Luise von, 847
Kempf, Edward J., 1082, 1088, 1090, 1093, 1094, 1097
Kempner, Salomea, 848
Keynes, John Maynard, 908n8
Keyserling, Hermann von, 948
Klein, Melanie, 11, 837n2, 891n4, 957, 1097, 1138n2, 1182, 1201; controversy with Freud, 845n2, 909n1; Anna Freud and, 1107n3; Jones and, 1109n4
Kola, Richard, 853, 854, 855
Kolnai, Aurel, 840, 849, 854, 1049
Königsberger, David Paul, 850n1, 870
Körner, Gottfried, 974n3, 1212n1
Korrespondenzblatt, 916n1
Kosztolányi, Dezsö, 1126n1
Kováca, Frigyes, 994n6
Kovács, Vilma, 994, 1206, 1208, 1221
Kris, Ernst, 4, 1225n3, 1230
Kronfeld, Arthur, 1148, 1150
Kubin, Alfred, 969, 970
Kulcsár, István, 1182n6

Laforgue, René, 969n3, 1031, 1097, 1105, 1106, 1164, 1198
Lamarck, Chevalier de, 937
Lampl, Hans, 837n11
Landauer, Karl, 957, 1011, 1028, 1106, 1106n1
Landquist, J., 979n4
Laqueur, Ernst, 1229, 1230
Lay analysis, 944, 1015, 1036, 1068, 1089, 1101, 1117, 1125, 1156, 1157, 1175, 1191; qualification for, 1035; Ferenczi and, 1069, 1081, 1082, 1086, 1090, 1100, 1102, 1103, 1124, 1170; Freud and, 1071, 1083, 1092, 1100, 1123; Rank and, 1081; APA and, 1082, 1088, 1097, 1232; nonmedical, 1082;

Lay analysis (continued)
opposition to, 1088, 1097, 1107n3, 1109n4, 1155n2, 1232; Secret Committee and, 1097; Eitingon and, 1103; accepted by the New York Psychoanalytic Society, 1171
Lay Analysis. See *Question of Lay Analysis, The* (Freud)
Lázár, Klára G., 1201n2, 1206n7
League of Nations, 940n3, 944n3, 1081, 1232, 1243n3
Le Bon, Gustave, 1031
Lectures (Freud), 844, 1005, 1208
Lehrman, Philip R., 1088, 1148, 1150, 1161
Lévy, Béla, 829, 834, 837, 894, 993, 999, 1002
Lévy, Kata, 831, 832, 841, 910, 941, 996, 1000, 1176, 1206; as analysand of Ferenczi, 866; IPA and, 1221
Lévy, Lajos, 829, 830, 848n7, 850, 910, 1000; IPA and, 842, 993, 1083, 1221, 1222; as Ferenczi's doctor, 856, 857, 1113, 1122, 1202, 1243, 1245, 1246; observations on ego and id, 959, 965; as Freud's doctor, 966, 970, 1052, 1053, 1054, 1092, 1232; in Budapest group of the Hungarian Psychoanalytic Society, 1206
Lévy, Samuel, 1140
Lewisohn, Sam, 1090
Libido: autoerotic compensation for, 859; of Ferenczi, 878, 897; origin in mother, 979
Liebermann, Hans, 864n3, 1043
Liebman, Carl and family, 1093n5, 1103, 1104, 1105
Ligha, Országos Gyermekvédö, 1182n5
Lind, John E., 1090n2
"Little Rooster Man" (Ferenczi), 1126
London Psychoanalytic Clinic, 1083
London Psycho-Analytic Society, 1018n2
Loránd, Alexander (Sándor), 1005
Love object, 926
Low, Barbara, 837n11, 845, 846
Löwenstein, Rudolph, 837n11, 1225n4

MacCurdy, John Thompson, 836, 837
Mack-Brunswick (Blumgart), Ruth, 1064
Máday, István, 1182n6

"Male and Female: Psychoanalytic Considerations on the 'Theory of Genitality'" (Ferenczi), 1163
Malinowski, Bronislaw, 1117n6
Manic-depression, 860n4, 1133
Marcinowski, Johannes Jaroslaw, 879, 888
Marcondes, Durval, 1115n1
Marriage complex, 924
Marxism, 840n2
Masculine protest theory (Adler), 1085n8
Masochism, 945, 969, 1117
Mass psychology, 1031n5
Masturbation, 847, 865
"Mathematics" (Ferenczi), 859
Mayer, Gaston, 1090, 1093, 1094
McCord, Clinton Preston, 1164
McCormick, Edith Rockefeller, 1093n4
McCormick, Stanley, 1093
Medical psychoanalysis, 872n2
Medical Psychological Association, 1090
Medical Society. See Physician's Society of the Interior Ministry
Melancholia, 926n4, 1133
Memory, 926, 946, 951, 957, 1009, 1009n3, 1072
Meng, Heinrich, 837n11, 957n7, 981, 1079, 1085, 1106, 1193n1
Menninger, Karl, 1064n2
Mental Hygiene journal, 1081
Mental hygiene movement, 1081, 1093
Mental Hygiene Society, 1082, 1090
Mester, Sándor, 1176n1
Metapsychology, 896, 924, 957, 1067, 1081, 1082, 1088, 1117, 1206, 1208
Meyer, Adolf, 1028n3, 1088, 1094
Meyer, Munroe A., 1005n6, 1088n18, 1093, 1097
Middle Group, 837n2, 1050n3
Migraine, 994
Mohr, Friedrich Justinus, 1031, 1033
Montagu, Edwin Samuel, 1070, 1070n2
Morality, 927
Morselli, Enrico Agostino, 1048n5
Mother: anxiety, 974; role of the analyst, 974, 1216; object, 1061
Müller-Braunschweig, Karl, 837n11
Müller-Ebsen, Josine, 837n11
Munro, Hector, 844, 846
Murray, Jessie, 844n5, 1003
Musicality, 893

Mussolini, Benito, 1089
Mutual analysis, 1023n2
Myers, Frederic William Henry, 1003

Nacht, Sacha, 837n11
Narcissism, 851
Narjani. *See* Bonaparte, Marie, Princess of Greece
National League for the Protection of Children, 1182n5
Nazi party, 1199n2
"Negation" (Freud), 1028
Neocatharsis, 1216
Neue Freie Presse, 1021, 1089, 1176, 1195
Neumann, Joseph, 970, 979, 1021n4
Neurotic Constitution, The (Adler), 913n1
New Introductory Lectures on Psycho-Analysis (Freud), 1230n1, 1231, 1239
New School for Social Research, 1067n1, 1069, 1078n2, 1081n10, 1082, 1086, 1097n14; Ferenczi at, 1088, 1090. *See also* School for Social Research
Newton, Caroline, 1005n6, 1015
New York Neurological Society, 1082
New York Psychiatric Society, 1078n2, 1084
New York Psychoanalytic Society, 860n4, 1005n6, 1015, 1036, 1046n1, 1082, 1084, 1090, 1097, 1109n4, 1156, 1203; opposition to lay analysis, 1165n2
New York Society for Clinical Psychiatry, 1078n2, 1084n3
New York Society of Psychology, 1156n2
Ninth International Psychoanalytic Congress (Bad Homburg, Germany), 1003, 1011, 1015, 1017, 1032; Freud declines to attend, 1018; Society of Friends of Psychoanalysis and, 1025; Ferenczi at, 1026, 1028
Nirvana principle, 845n3
Nobel Prize, 1103, 1104
Nunberg, Hermann, 981, 1082n9, 1202, 1203, 1204, 1225n5
Nyanza, Victoria, 1087

Oberholzer, Emil, 1118n2
Oberholzer, Mira, 962, 974, 1118n2
Oberndorf, Clarence P., 981n3, 1021n2, 1082, 1088, 1090, 1093, 1094, 1097

Object relations theory, 1050n3, 1081n8
Obsessional neuroses, 836, 1065, 1173, 1217; infantile, 847
Occult, 882
Oedipus Complex, 932, 950, 951, 952, 953, 974, 994, 995n1, 1004, 1088, 1109n4, 1117n6; Ferenczi on, 948; birth trauma and, 953, 994
"On Australian Totemism" (Freud), 872n2
On Dreams (Freud), 1201
"On the History of the Psycho-Analytic Movement" (Freud), 843n3, 970
On the Revision of the Interpretation of Dreams (Ferenczi), 1206n11
"On the Technique of Child Analysis" (A. Freud), 1092n1
Ophuijsen, Johan H. W. van, 846, 849, 1043, 1117, 1151, 1204; opposition to lay analysis, 1155, 1165; as member of International Training Commission, 1167n3; *Rundbrief* communications, 1201; at Twelfth International Psychoanalytic Congress, 1209; in IPA, 1236n1; Ferenczi and, 1243
Organic animism concept, 909
Orgasm, 1039
Origins of Psychoanalysis (Kris, ed.), 1225n4
Ornstein, Lajos, 1179n5
Oxford Congress. *See* Eleventh International Psychoanalytic Congress (1929, Oxford); International Congress of Psychology, Oxford (1923)

Paleopsychology, 1088
Pálos, Elma, 830, 831, 836, 837, 847, 855, 868, 873, 878, 907, 909, 911, 1021
Pálos, Géza, 847n7
Paquet, Alfons, 1193n1
Paralysis, 897
Paranoia, 847, 848, 853, 969, 977, 1103
Partós, Zoltán, 837
Paternal hypnosis, 840
Pathoneuroses, 896n1
Pavlov, Ivan Petrovitch, 1088
Payne, Sylvia, 837n11
Pedagogic analysis. *See* Child analysis
Penis envy, 847, 974, 1227
Petersen, Julius, 1193n1

Pfeifer, Sigmund, 893, 944, 1069n2, 1158, 1206
Pfister, Oskar, 1020, 1021, 1024
Philadelphia Association for Psychoanalysis, 1225n5
Physician's Society of the Interior Ministry (Budapest Medical Society), 846, 848n6
Pichler, Hans, 941n1, 960, 961, 970n2, 979, 1007, 1008, 1010, 1031, 1068, 1087n1, 1109, 1199; Freud's break with, 1127
Pichon, Edouard, 1105
Pirquet, Clemens, 841
Poe, Edgar Allan, 969n3
Pollák, Konstantina, 1179n5
Popular Lectures on Psychoanalysis (Ferenczi), 866n2, 899
Potter, Grace, 1067, 1096, 1117
Pötzl, Otto, 1146
Powers, Lillian Delger, 1082, 1083
Pragmatism, 1089
Preconscious, 902n1, 924, 1009, 1117
Preoedipal development, 1064n2
"Present-Day Problems in Psycho-Analysis" (Ferenczi), 1088n14, 1092n3
Prince, Morton, 928n2
Principles of Intensive Psychotherapy (Fromm-Reichmann), 1106n1
"Problem of Termination of the Analysis, The" (Ferenczi), 1107n3
Psyche, 1088
Psychical research, 1003
Psychical Research Society, 1003n4
Psychic reality, 1088, 1206, 1210
Psycho-Analysis: A Brief Account of the Freudian Theory (Low), 845n2
"Psychoanalysis and Criminology" (Ferenczi), 1120n2
"Psycho-Analysis and Telepathy" (Freud), 882n5, 889n2
"Psycho-Analytical Observations on Tic" (Ferenczi), 846n3
"Psychoanalytic Chapbook" (Federn and Meng, eds.), 981n2, 1079
Psychoanalytic Pioneers (Loránd), 1005n4
Psycho-Analytic Review, 1088
Psychoanalytic Study of the Child (journal), 1225n3
Psychoanalytische Bewegung (journal), 1163n2
Psychological time, 1133
Psychology, 1173
Psychology of Day-Dreams, The (Varendonck), 902n1
Psychology of the Masses (Le Bon), 1031n5
Psychopathology of Everyday Life, The (Freud), 844, 893, 979, 988n3, 1201
Psychoses, 851, 1067, 1088, 1134, 1190
Psychosomatic medicine, 878n1

Question of Lay Analysis, The (Freud), 1068n2, 1071, 1076, 1085, 1086, 1088, 1110, 1165; Ferenczi's introduction to, 1111

Radó, Sándor, 3, 837n11, 854, 855, 916n2, 919, 935, 951, 1011n2, 1044n3, 1203, 1205, 1225n2; criticism of Rank's work, 953; at Eighth International Psychoanalytic Congress, 957n1; Verlag activities, 986n3, 988, 998, 1009, 1040; as editor of *Zeitschrift* and *Imago*, 1009n1, 1013, 1048, 1086, 1091, 1202; in Berlin Psychoanalytic Society, 1046, 1049; lay analysis and, 1100
Radó-Révész, Erzsébet, 916, 917, 918, 994
Rank, Beate, 976, 978, 979, 1000, 1001, 1006, 1058, 1092
Rank, Helene, 976n1
Rank, Otto, 837, 847, 861, 867, 876, 1011, 1034, 1233n1; Ferenczi and, 838, 849, 871, 880, 909, 910, 911, 912, 922, 929, 936, 939, 940, 950, 951, 952, 953, 971, 971n2, 974, 975, 978, 979, 982, 983, 987, 994, 996, 998, 1084; Verlag and journals publishing activities, 844, 853, 855, 912, 917, 959, 961, 965, 972, 973, 974, 986, 986n3, 987, 1000, 1009; at Sixth International Psychoanalytic Congress, 849; at Sixth International Psychoanalytic Congress (1920), 861; dispute with Abraham, 864, 939, 947, 948, 949, 951, 952, 960, 973, 976, 985, 1058; Sokolnicka as analysand of, 865; involvement in the *Zeitschrift*, 873; at Seventh International Psychoanalytic Congress (1922), 889, 909; Freud and, 891, 931, 944, 947, 949, 950, 952, 953, 970, 972, 973, 975, 977, 978, 985, 992, 995, 996, 1058, 1061; Secret

Committee and, 912, 913, 916, 939, 956n1, 1000, 1028; symbolism theory, 924; dispute with Jones, 939n2, 951, 973, 974, 977, 979, 987n1, 1093; birth trauma theory, 945, 947, 948, 950, 951, 952, 953, 970, 974, 986, 994, 1005, 1097; collaboration with Ferenczi, 945, 946, 948, 982, 994, 1060; at Eighth International Psychoanalytic Congress, 957, 973; in America, 957n6, 960, 962, 964, 965, 966, 969, 973, 974, 986, 988, 989, 992, 995, 998n4, 1004, 1005, 1058, 1097; as successor to Freud, 963; on termination of analysis, 970n1, 1066; personal life/mental state, 973, 986, 998n4, 1005, 1009, 1081; break with Freud and Ferenczi, 974, 981, 986, 987, 989n2, 990, 1005, 1060, 1061, 1065, 1080, 1081, 1092, 1093, 1238; Anna Freud and, 986, 992; as Freud's analysand, 1000; at Ninth International Psychoanalytic Congress, 1028n2; in Paris, 1057, 1090, 1097; Ferenczi's critique of, 1060n4, 1061, 1063, 1075, 1079; object relations theory, 1081n8; distortion of analysis, 1081n10; offers cure for homosexuality, 1088. *See also Development of Psychoanalysis, The* (Ferenczi and Rank); Secret Committee: disputes within

Rapaport, Samu, 1179n5
Reality, 959, 973n5, 1030, 1173. *See also* Psychic reality
Recouly, Raymond, 940
Reed, Ralph, 1088
Regression, 971, 1082
Reich, Wilhelm, 922, 957, 1028, 1039, 1045, 1082n9, 1124; politics of, 1218, 1219, 1220, 1225n2, 1230
Reik, Theodore, 844, 876, 891, 957, 976, 1028, 1050, 1069, 1081, 1106n1; eulogy for Abraham, 1044n3; Freud and, 1128
Relaxation therapy (Ferenczi), 1167n3, 1173, 1196, 1206, 1208
Remarks on the Theory and Practice of Dream Interpretation (Freud), 908
Remembering. *See* Memory
Repetition, 946, 1067, 1206
Repression, 926, 946, 948, 1179, 1206
Reproduction, 1009

Resistance, 1067
"Resistance to Psychoanalysis, The" (Freud), 970
Reumann, Jakob, 841n5
Révész, Ladislaus, 994, 1206, 1229
Revista Brasileira de Psicanálise journal, 1115n1
Revue Française de Psychanalyse, 1105n4, 1114
Rickman, John, 837n2, 913, 1090, 1095, 1097, 1133, 1172, 1177, 1179
Rie, Margarethe, 1203
Rie, Marianne, 1225n4
Rie, Oscar, 909, 1064n2, 1225n4
Robinson, James Harvey, 1090, 1214
Rockefeller Foundation, 1081
Róheim, Géza, 836, 872, 895n2, 944, 957, 958, 994, 1060, 1069n2, 1117n6
Rolland, Romain, 922, 960, 961
Rosenfeld, Paul, 987, 990, 991, 992, 993, 999
Rosenfeld, Eva, 1138, 1169n2
Rothschild, Lionel Walter, 853
Rotter, Lilian K., 1201n2, 1206n7, 1227n2
Rümke, Henricus Cornelius, 1229n5
Rundbriefe (circular letters among members of the Secret Committee), 853n1, 909, 913, 951, 988, 1000, 1109; by Ferenczi, 853n1, 916, 920, 949, 987, 997, 998, 1003, 1005, 1011, 1015, 1035, 1049, 1050, 1057, 1084n4, 1087, 1088, 1093, 1094, 1118, 1201, 1221; by Freud, 913, 948n4, 1003n3, 1085; by Jones, 932; by Ophuijsen, 1165

Sachs, Hanns, 830n5, 837, 845n2, 848, 895n2, 909, 946, 981n2, 1009n2, 1043, 1106n1; training analyses, 837n11, 1045; Secret Committee and, 916, 1045, 1109n3; Rank and, 936, 951n8; Freud and, 947, 1021, 1045, 1061; at Eighth International Psychoanalytic Congress, 957; as editor of *Imago*, 986n3; on birth trauma, 1005; involvement in film making, 1021, 1026n2, 1045; eulogy for Abraham, 1044n3; as member of International Training Commission, 1167n3
Sacristan, José Maria, 1140
Sadism, 1117

Salmon, Thomas William, 1084, 1090, 1094
Samuel, Herbert Louis, 1070
Sanctis, Sante de, 842
San Francisco Psychoanalytic Society, 830n5
Sarasin, Philipp, 1118n2, 1167
Schilder, Paul, 1156, 1179
Schiller, Friedrich von, 974
Schiller, Max, 1138n2, 1212
Schizophrenia, 1093n4, 1111, 1195n1
Schloss Tegel sanatorium, 1100n3
Schmideberg, Melitta, 891n4, 909n1
Schmideberg, Walter, 891, 901
Schneider, Ernst, 981n2
School for Social Research, 1081. *See also* New School for Social Research
Schreber, Daniel Paul, 969, 1179
Schröder, Hermann, 1127, 1137n1, 1185, 1187
Schur, Max, 878n1, 1064n2
Secret Committee of the IPA (Administrative Committee after 1927), 860n3, 911n1, 912, 1045, 1109n3, 1116; disputes within, 912, 913, 916, 929n2, 939n2, 943, 947, 948, 952, 956, 972n2, 974, 977, 980, 986, 987, 994, 1159; Freud and, 950, 957n3, 1060n1; Eighth International Psychoanalytic Congress and, 951n4; dissolution and restoration of, 956n1, 987, 989, 992; Society of Friends of Psychoanalysis and, 1022, 1025, 1028; prior to Tenth International Psychoanalytic Congress, 1090; funding to European institutions, 1094; becomes Administrative Committee of the IPA, 1109n3. See also *Rundbriefe*
Secrets of a Soul (Geheimnisse einer Seele) (film), 1021n4, 1045n4
Seelensucher, Der (Groddeck), 867n4
"Self, The" (Freud), 872n2
Self-analysis by Ferenczi, 1179, 1182, 1223
Seligman, Edwin Robert Anderson, 1097, 1098
Sensation, 926
Seventh International Psychoanalytic Congress (1922, Berlin), 860, 899n4, 902, 907, 911n1; Freud at, 908, 911n1; Ferenczi at, 911n1

Severn, Elizabeth, 1011n4, 1023, 1179n3, 1196n2, 1197n2
Sharpe, Ella Freeman, 837n11
"Significance of Freud for Mental Hygiene, The" (Ferenczi), 1082
Silberer, Herbert, 917n3
Simmel, Ernst, 837n11, 957, 1043, 1083n2, 1087, 1100, 1193n1, 1244; in Berlin Psychoanalytic Society, 1046, 1049; psychoanalytic sanatorium, 1100, 1137n1, 1138n2
Sixth International Psychoanalytic Congress (1920): circular letters among members *(Rundbriefe)*, 849, 850, 851, 853n1, 855, 860, 863, 867, 892; Ferenczi at, 836n4, 852n2
Sleep state, 1206
Social Democratic Party (Austria), 5, 841nn3, 962n1
Sociedad de Conferencias (Madrid), 1142n2, 1145
Sociedade Brasileira de Psicanálise (Brazil), 1115n1
Società Psicoanalytica Italiana, 1226n2
Société Psychoanalitique de Paris, 969n3
Society for Research on Children, 1084, 1086
Society of Friends of Psychoanalysis, 1020, 1021, 1022, 1024, 1025, 1028, 1179
Sokolnicka, Eugenia, 833, 834, 836, 847, 848, 851, 860n4, 861, 862, 971, 1031, 1105n5; as analysand of Ferenczi's, 864, 865, 866, 968
"Some Neurotic Mechanisms in Jealousy, Paranoia, and Homosexuality" (Freud), 862n1, 889n2, 908, 1016n1
"Some Psychical Consequences of the Anatomical Distinction between the Sexes" (Freud), 1016, 1020
Soviet Russia, 1216, 1219
Spengler, Oswald, 951
Spitz, René, 960, 961, 1087
Splitting (fragmentation), 1072, 1111, 1195, 1206
"Stages in the Development of the Sense of Reality" (Ferenczi), 845n3
Stagnell, Gregory, 1088
Stärcke, August, 867, 868, 872n2, 1024
Stekel, Wilhelm, 882n6, 888n2, 911, 920, 977, 978, 1008, 1034, 1105, 1217; break

with Freud and Ferenczi, 1061, 1089, 1111; dissent within IPA and, 1174, 1179
Sterba, Editha, 1221
Stern, Adolph, 860, 1005n6, 1082, 1088, 1090, 1093, 1097
Storfer, Adolph Josef, 927, 959, 967, 974, 1000, 1021n2, 1068, 1199; publication and translation of Freud's complete works, 1001, 1036, 1037, 1201, 1206, 1221; involvement in film making, 1021, 1026n2; Verlag and journals publishing activities, 1048, 1125, 1191, 1206, 1219; Ferenczi and, 1073, 1201
Strachey, Alix, 837n11
Strachey, Lytton, 908n8
Stuttering, 897, 1028n3
Sublimation, 1067
Subordination, 840
Suggestion (hypnosis), 840, 946, 950, 957, 1033, 1067
Suicide, 847, 861, 865, 878, 1066
Sullivan, Harry Stack, 1095n1, 1097n14, 1106n1, 1216n2
Superego, 926, 928, 1088, 1182n3
"Supplements to the Theory of Dreams" (Freud), 852n2
Sweetser, Arthur, 1081n12
Swiss Medical Society for Psychoanalysis, 1118n2
Swiss Psychoanalytic Society, 867n4, 909n1, 1118n2
Symbolism, 864, 873, 924, 1003
"Symbolism of the Bridge, The" (Ferenczi), 873n2
Symptom, 1024
Szaly, Károly, 1179n5
Székely, Béla, 1182n6
Székely-Kovács, Alice, 1050n3
Szinetár, Ernö, 1179n5
Szüts, Gyula, 1201n2

Tact, 1115, 1117
Tagore, Rabindranath, 1085
Tandler, Julius, 841
Taylor, Frederick W./Taylor system, 1068
"Technical Difficulties in the Analysis of a Case of Hysteria" (Ferenczi), 847n2
Technique of Psychoanalysis, The (Rank), 1060nn2,4, 1075

Telepathy, 1003
Tenth International Psychoanalytic Congress (1927, Innsbruck), 1085, 1089, 1093, 1093n5, 1099, 1101, 1107n3; Ferenczi and, 1090, 1099, 1100, 1101; Training Commission, 1107n3
Termination of analysis (setting of a date or time), 946, 948, 951, 952, 953, 961, 970n1, 974, 979, 994, 1017, 1065, 1066, 1107n3; Ferenczi's theory of, 1167n3, 1179
"Termination of the Analysis, The" (Ferenczi), 1107n3
Thalassa: A Theory of Genitality (Ferenczi), 830n7, 937, 939, 943, 950, 961, 1158, 1195
Theory of Genitality. See Thalassa: A Theory of Genitality (Ferenczi)
Theory of Sexuality (Freud). See Three Essays on the Theory of Sexuality (Freud)
Thompson, Clara Mabel, 1046n1, 1106n1, 1216n2
Thought transference, 1003, 1005, 1006, 1011
Three Essays on the Theory of Sexuality (Freud), 837, 844, 1201
Tic, 846, 851, 853, 854, 855, 926
Tószeghy, Emil. See Freund, Emil von (later Tószeghy)
Totem and Taboo (Freud), 974, 1079n2
Totemism, 836
Totis, Béla, 1057n3
Training analysis, 837n11, 899, 952, 952n4, 965, 1005n4, 1015, 1021n2, 1034, 1050, 1117, 1179, 1225n5, 1236n1; Ferenczi and, 944, 1069, 1078n2, 1142, 1145, 1201; Hungarian School of, 994n6; of non-physicians, 1078n2, 1125; Rank and, 1081; Freud and, 1156n2
Training Committee, 909n1, 1225n5
Training institutes, 830n5, 987, 992n2, 1083n5, 1096n1, 1108, 1118, 1201, 1206
Transference, 951, 1000, 1009n2, 1061, 1067, 1124n2
Trauma, 1028, 1173, 1182, 1190, 1192, 1195, 1196, 1206, 1207, 1208. See also Birth/birth trauma

Trauma of Birth, The (Rank), 929n2, 932, 948, 949
"Trauma of Birth and Its Significance for Psychoanalysis, The" (Sachs), 1005
Traumatogenesis, 1201
Troubridge, Ernest Charles Thomas, 864
Twelfth International Psychoanalytic Congress (1932, Wiesbaden), 1155n3, 1206n11, 1208, 1231, 1236n1; Ferenczi at, 1206n11, 1226, 1229, 1232, 1233n1, 1236n1, 1238

Unconscious, 926, 951, 1003, 1067, 1090; Freud on, 941, 942
"Unconscious Pregnancy Fantasy under the Picture of a Traumatic Hysteria, An" (Eisler), 837n7
United Psychoanalysis and Psychopathological Association, 1095
Urbantschitsch, Rudolf von, 939, 958, 960, 961, 965, 968
Uterhart, Henry Ayers, 1097

Van Emden, Jan E. G., 951, 953, 957, 959, 961, 1043
Varendonck, Juliaan, 902, 924
Varga, Jenö, 833, 840, 841, 842, 844, 917
Vásárhelyi (unidentified patient of Ferenczi's), 838
Verlag (Internationaler Psychoanalytischer Verlag) (publishing house), 829, 830, 836, 853, 855, 953, 974, 1015, 1043; funding/financial circumstances, 837, 868, 876, 891, 892, 899, 913, 1020, 1027, 1036, 1037, 1059, 1088, 1093, 1096n1, 1219; pending sale of, 853, 854; Ferenczi published by, 866, 897n2, 1206; Freud published by, 893, 894, 966n2, 970, 979, 1051, 1109, 1191n1, 1201, 1206, 1208, 1221; Storfer as president of, 986n3, 1125, 1219; changing editorship, 1009, 1219; Ferenczi and, 1020, 1223; Society of Friends of Psychoanalysis and, 1020; on film making activities, 1021n5; funding/financial circumstances, 1158, 1159, 1191n1, 1201, 1206n9, 1208, 1221, 1222; Advisory Council, 1192, 1201; restructuring of, 1229
Vienna Psychoanalytic Society, 836n5, 854, 891, 922n1, 944n1, 1005n6, 1015, 1038, 1053n1, 1060, 1097, 1177, 1201, 1206, 1243; Training Institute, 830n5, 992n2, 1083n5, 1096n1; outpatient polyclinic, 855n1, 962, 963, 967, 968, 1059, 1156n2, 1208; Freud and, 952, 1059, 1083, 1086; Rank and, 952; Ferenczi and, 962, 963, 964, 967, 968; Training Committee, 1225n5
Viereck, George Sylvester, 1076, 1078, 1079, 1085, 1086, 1093, 1097
Voigt, Emmy von, 979n4

Wagner-Jauregg, Julius, 853n4, 957n7, 1146, 1156n2, 1225n3
Wahl, Hans, 1193n1
Wälder, Jenny (née Pollak), 1202n5
Wälder, Robert, 1202n5, 1225, 1230
Waldinger, Ernst, 917n5
War neuroses, 853, 1090n17
Washington School of Psychiatry, 1216n2
Washington Society, 1155n3
Watson, John Broadus, 1088, 1089, 1090
Weiss, Eduardo, 1226
Weizmann, Chaim, 1085, 1090
Western Committee, 917
White, William Alanson, 882n6, 1088, 1094, 1095, 1155. *See also* William A. White Institute
Wickersham, George W., 1127n4
Wild psychoanalysis, 997, 1020
William A. White Institute (New York), 1216n2
Williams, Frankwood Earl, 1081, 1082, 1085, 1090
Winternitz, Rose Beatrice, 917n5
Winternitz, Valentin, 917n5
Wittels, Fritz, 1053, 1054, 1105, 1156
Wittenberg, Wilhelm, 1106n1
Wolf-dream, 1061, 1062, 1063, 1079, 1081
Wolf-Man, 1064n2, 1066
Womb fantasy, 951, 994
Wulff, Mosche, 1044n3
Wyss, Walter Heinrich von, 848

X-rays, 1068

Young Girl's Diary, A (Hug-Hellmuth), 1090n13
Youth care, 998

Zeitschrift, 912, 960, 986n3, 1029, 1083, 1219n1, 1221; on Sixth International

Psychoanalytic Congress, 852n2; Ferenczi published in, 873, 897, 1003, 1091, 1105, 1111; Freud published in, 908, 951, 1067; Rank and, 913; issue dedicated to Ferenczi, 935n3, 940; Freud and, 967; changing editorship, 1012, 1225, 1230, 1231; obituary and memorial issue for Abraham, 1043n5, 1044, 1048; issue dedicated to Freud, 1048; Freud's 70th birthday greeting in, 1055; Ferenczi and, 1063; Anna Freud published in, 1117; issue dedicated to Jones, 1159; political articles in, 1220

Zilboorg, Gregory, 1127

Zulliger, Hans, 1021, 1186

Zweig, Stefan, 1041, 1228